REFERENCE

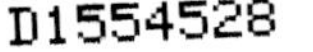
D1554528

Donated by
Loretta Berry

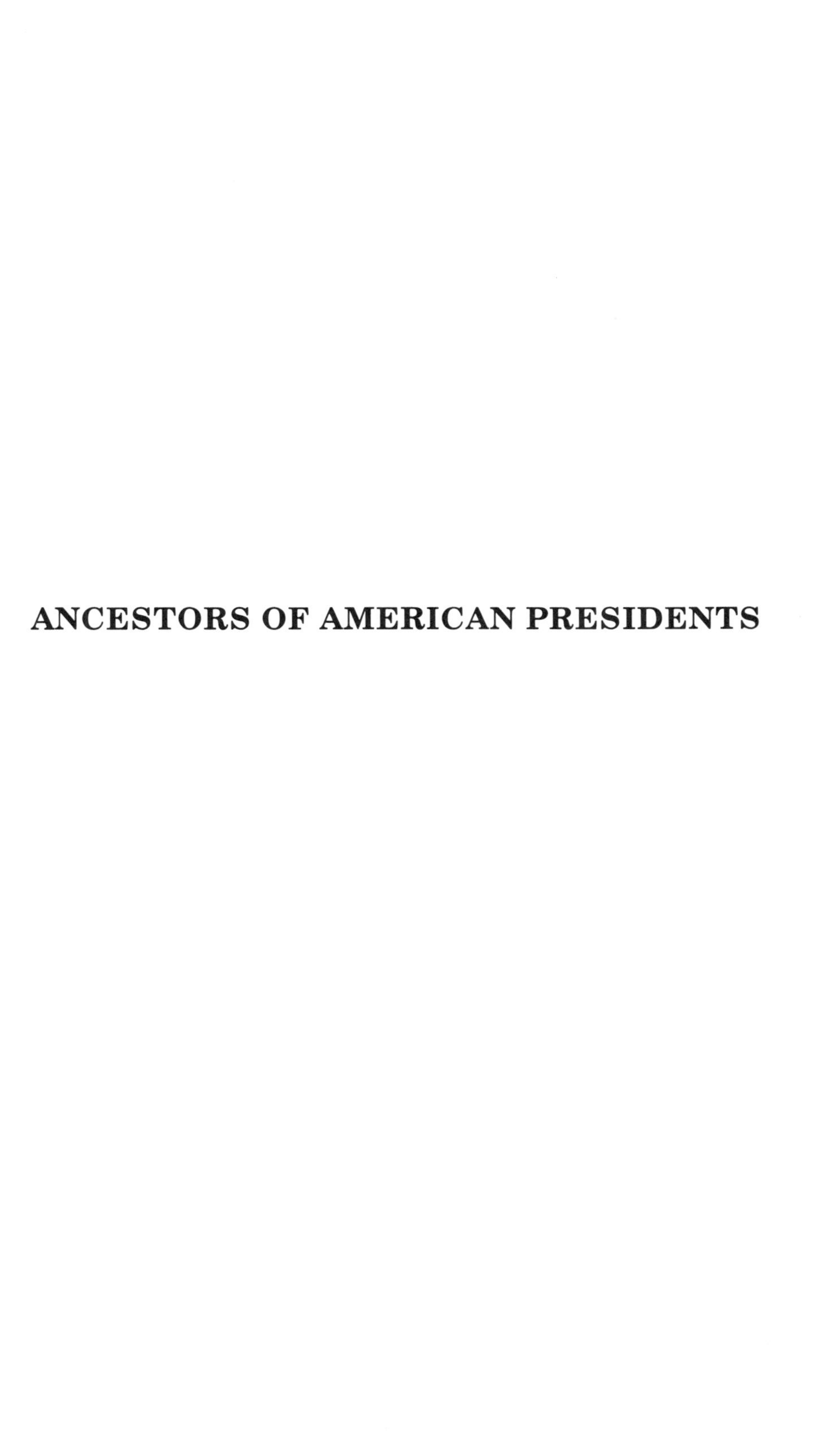

ANCESTORS OF AMERICAN PRESIDENTS

ANCESTORS OF AMERICAN PRESIDENTS

compiled by

Gary Boyd Roberts

with charts drawn by

Julie Helen Otto

Preliminary Edition, Revised

Published in cooperation with the
New England Historic Genealogical Society,
Boston, Massachusetts

by

Carl Boyer, 3rd

Santa Clarita, California

1989

LIBRARY OF CONGRESS CATALOG CARD NUMBER: 89-83321

ISBN 0-936124-15-6

Carl Boyer, 3rd
P. O. Box 333
Santa Clarita, California 91322-0333

TABLE OF CONTENTS

To the memory of
my four grandparents

John Christopher Roberts (1878-1951)

Mary Louise Fry Roberts (1881-1963)

George Wesley Boyd (1880-1952)

Fannie Kate Root Boyd (1888-1964)

My father's father, a Langdon descendant, may have shared ancestors with President Nixon.

My father's mother, a Howland and Twining descendant, shared ancestors with Presidents F. D. Roosevelt, Nixon, Ford and Bush.

My mother's father, a Hull, Spooner, Ligon/Lygon and Worsham descendant, shared ancestors with Presidents Ford and Bush and may have shared sixteenth-century English ancestors, via Virginia immigrant Anthony Savage, with Presidents Madison and Taylor.

My mother's mother, a Royce, Lathrop, Hale, Stebbing, Stanley, Hough, Alcock and Whiting descendant, shared ancestors with Presidents Fillmore, Grant, Hayes, Cleveland, Coolidge, F. D. Roosevelt and Bush.

Introduction

I

In the past dozen years, since the 1976 Bicentennial, Americans have rediscovered genealogy -- the tracing of ancestors and plotting of specific kinships. During this period I have been variously associated, as a member, reference librarian, and director of research, special projects, or publications, with the New England Historic Genealogical Society (henceforth NEHGS) in Boston, the oldest and most distinguished genealogical institution in the nation. As a working scholar and author, as the colleague of many other scholars, authors, librarians, and genealogical enthusiasts, and as, since 1981 or so, the recipient of occasional media attention, I have been lucky enough to be able to "nudge" American genealogy toward a few specific subject areas and projects. Among the most important of these topics, both for its intrinsic interest and as a delineator of major patterns in American genealogical evolution, has been presidential ancestry. As with other genealogical subjects, a first task was to call attention to the superb work of many recent predecessors, in this case primarily a group of scholars who contributed presidential ancestor lists (minus dates or places, or sometimes with years and states only) or full ancestor tables, to **The American Genealogist** (henceforth TAG) before 1977 -- notably Clarence Almon Torrey (the Adamses and Taft), TAG editor George Englert McCracken (Van Buren, Grant, and later Hayes), Washington scholar George Sydney Horace Lee Washington, and Nixon scholar Raymond Martin Bell. A second initial task was to correct the rather poorly researched patrilineal descents and often erroneous royal lines published in the first edition of **Burke's Presidential Families of the United States of America** (1976), and a third task was to stimulate more such TAG ancestor tables, so that a comprehensive work detailing the full known ancestry for more than six generations, of all American presidents to date, could be begun.

The first two of these tasks were more or less completed with the publication of my "American Presidential Ancestry: A Bibliography" in TAG 54(1978):211-20, 55(1979):46-52 (with addenda in vols. 56[1980]:28-30, 57[1981]:87-89, 59[1983]:2-5, and 61[1985-86]:171-79), and of Appendix C (which I undertook with David G. Williamson), "Ancestral Tables of the Presidents" (for six generations in all lines, with years of birth and death but no places), to the second edition of **Burke's Presidential Families of the United States of America** (1981) (the omitted Woodrow Wilson chart appeared in reviews in TAG and The New England Historical and Genealogical Register, henceforth NEHGR). TAG presidential articles continued also -- volume 53(1977) included a Coolidge ancestor table by Robert Charles Anderson, my listing of Kennedy's known forebears, and an initial Ford article by Mr. Anderson, myself, and my frequent colleague, William Addams Reitwiesner of Washington, D.C.; and volumes 55(1979), 56(1980), and 63(1988) included Pierce, Hayes and Fillmore ancestor tables by Edward F. Holden, G.E. McCracken, and myself respectively. The TAG bibliographies and the six-generation ancestral charts also highlighted the work of various earlier or often non-TAG scholars, notably George Harrison Sanford King (Monroe and Truman), Charles Penrose Keith (the Harrisons), Eben Putnam (Cleveland), Howard K. Beale (T. Roosevelt), W.E. Norman (Wilson), Hulda Hoover McLean (Hoover, her uncle), Alvin Paige Johnson (F. D. Roosevelt) and Mrs. Rebeckah Baines Johnson (L. B. Johnson, her son). Kenneth H. Thomas, Jr., combed Georgia sources, corresponded extensively, and wrote twice on Carter's ancestry in **Georgia Life** (winter 1976 and spring 1980 issues), Michael Pollock, Nancy Gubb Frederick, D.G. Williamson, W.A. Reitwiesner and I all undertook research on Reagan's ancestry, and I reported some results of initial Bush research in the February 1989 issue of the **NEHGS NEXUS**.

Thus has the scholarly stage been set for this preliminary edition of **Ancestors of American Presidents**. I had originally planned to publish such a work, to have been titled "Presidential Pedigrees," with the Institute of Family Research in Salt Lake City. After the institute's dissolution in the early 1980s, however, I concentrated on article publication, the NEHGR reprint program undertaken by Genealogical Publishing Company of Baltimore, **American Ancestors and Cousins of The Princess of Wales** (1984, co-authored with W.A. Reitwiesner), development and publications at NEHGS, and as regards presidential genealogy, updating the ongoing TAG bibliography and "nudging" various research efforts. Thus I was delighted when, after the fourth bibliographical addendum appeared in TAG, Carl Boyer, 3rd of Santa Clarita indicated an interest in publishing a collection of presidential ancestor tables, bibliographies, and royal descent and kinship charts. I set the timetable for a preliminary edition, to be published on the occasion of, and to honor, the 200th anniversary of Washington's first inaugural address, and thus the institution of the presidency itself, April 30, 1989. NEHGS and its director, Ralph J. Crandall, generously allowed me time to prepare this work, my colleague Carl Boyer spent hundreds of hours computer-inputting my handprinted tables and bibliographies, Julie Helen Otto of NEHGS on her own time lettered the handwritten charts herein, the Associated Press graciously mentioned this forthcoming book in its November 1988 coverage of the Bush-Quayle-Lincoln and other Bush presidential and notable kinships, and People magazine did so likewise in an article on the Bush family in its issue of January 30, 1989.

It is important, however, to emphasize the preliminary nature of this edition. The ancestor tables and bibliographies have not been reviewed by my many genealogical colleagues with presidential interests, although in the late 1970s and early 1980s Raymond Martin Bell not only shared with me his ongoing Nixon research, a Lincoln ancestor table, and Eisenhower articles as he found them, but also at my request examined and subsequently published his findings on the Scots-Irish, western Pennsylvania and/or New Jersey ancestry of both Benjamin Harrison and Harding. I particularly look forward to the response this preliminary edition elicits from Mr. Bell, and from Andrew and L.B. Johnson scholar Hugh Buckner Johnston, from Ford scholar Joseph L. Druse (who has other presidential interests also), Roosevelt scholars Timothy Field Beard and Henry Bainbridge Hoff, and TAG editor David L. Greene among colleagues not already mentioned. I have also myself noted numerous presidential forebears about whom further research, even perhaps in printed sources, might uncover more information, and I hope to undertake much of that research, or suggest it to others, over the next two years and before a "first" edition of this compendium is published. Also desirable, especially for recent presidents, since I have generally been able to visit only New England archival depositories, is further research in primary sources -- especially vital records, wills, deeds, and court records (Nancy Gubb Frederick combed such Illinois material for Reagan but much similar work might be undertaken for others, often in several states). Thus the book in hand is definitely a work in progress and I wish to invite corrections and I hope fairly extensive additions for future versions.

Carefully abstracted and referenced herein are most, if not perhaps absolutely all, of pertinent printed sources known to me covering the full traceable ancestry of all forty individual U.S. presidents, April 1789-April 1989 -- for seven generations for those born in the 18th century, eight generations for those born in the 19th century, and nine generations for those born in the 20th century. Also included are charts showing all kinships among presidents through American or 16th or 17th (for Washington to Coolidge, F. D. Roosevelt, and Bush, 15th) century English ancestors -- a total of over one hundred kinships linking between two and five of twenty-six presidents; the best royal descent, through each immigrant ancestor who bore one, for nineteen presidents and at least one wife of eight others; Edith Wilson's descent from Pocahontas, and Bush's double kinship to Pocahontas's Bolling descendants; the Mayflower descents or connections of nine U.S. presidents (proved descents for seven, connections for two); and kinships between eleven U. S. presidents, and six first ladies, to either Queen Elizabeth the Queen Mother or The Princess of Wales and Princes William and Henry. Preparing and proofing this much text required the full two years between Carl Boyer's proposal and publication. Another year of research and scholarly review might have been desirable -- thus a "preliminary" edition only. Ten years is enough incubation for any project, however, and 200th anniversaries and the interest they stimulate occur only once. Now, unfortunately after the deaths of G.E. McCracken, G.S.H.L. Washington, and G.H.S. King but still during the lifetime of many of the major presidential genealogical scholars whose work I synthesize herein, is a one-volume, affordable, computer-generated (and thus easily corrected) summary of much of my life's scholarly work, much of the best work of many genealogical predecessors and colleagues, and many of the patterns that make American genealogy fascinating. I hope this volume pinpoints many genealogical problems of more than ordinary interest which require further study, that it encourages young genealogists especially to tackle them, and that this volume is considered a fitting tribute by the genealogical community to our forty presidents to date and to the nation at large. For its compiler and publisher at least, this book's preparation was an act of both genealogical scholarship and private patriotism.

II

Having treated the history of this project, and emphasized its "preliminary" quality, we may now move to the more interesting topics of presidential ancestry as a reflection of American genealogical evolution; the ethnic, national-origin, or regional associations of presidents and their near ancestors; the various social groups, sometimes regional or national elites, to which these forty individuals belonged; the unknown, unexplored, or problematic areas in the immediate ancestry of our forty presidents to date; and the seemingly undemocratic but not-to-genealogists surprising matter of presidential royal descents. As regards ethnic, national-origin or regional affiliations we may note firstly that the entire ancestry of Jackson, Polk, Buchanan, Andrew Johnson, McKinley, Wilson, Kennedy, and Reagan -- eight in all -- was almost certainly Scottish, Scots-Irish, Irish, or post-1840 English artisan. Eight more -- the two Adamses from Massachusetts; Fillmore from upstate New York; Pierce from New Hampshire; Hayes, Garfield and Taft, all natives of Ohio; and

Coolidge, from Vermont -- were almost exclusively of New England (and usually Great Migration) English-derived Yankee descent. Ten presidents may be considered southern: Washington, Jefferson, Madison, William Henry Harrison, Tyler and Taylor (the "Virginia dynasty" somewhat extended), of largely Tidewater English-derived planter ancestry, although Taylor also had Allerton and Brewster Mayflower lines; Monroe, of Scots and Welsh-derived Tidewater planter background; and Truman, Lyndon Johnson and Carter, of modern southern pioneer background, with multi-ethnic colonial origins (including lesser English-derived planters, Scots-Irish, German, French Huguenot and for Carter even Delaware, New Jersey and Rhode Island descents). Van Buren's ancestry was exclusively New York Dutch; Eisenhower's, except for his possibly Scots-Irish Hannah and likely Boone descent, was exclusively Pennsylvania German or Swiss; and Nixon's is largely Quaker -- California, midwestern, mid-Atlantic, and Yankee. These last three may be grouped together as "sectish."

In addition to these twenty-nine there are also, I think, three distinct groups of national-origin or regional mixtures. Arthur (half Scots-Irish and half Yankee), Cleveland (three-eighths Yankee, five-sixteenths Irish, one-fourth Pennsylvania or Maryland German, and one-sixteenth Channel Island), and F.D. Roosevelt (three-fourths Yankee, one-fourth Dutch and a few other strands) were all New York-associated presidents the bulk of whose traceable ancestry is derived from New England. Lincoln, Grant, Harding and Bush all bear early New England surnames, but have mothers, grandmothers, and even great-grandmothers of migrating pioneer, especially New Jersey, Pennsylvania and Upper South or border state ancestry or origin, as does the half Scots-Irish and Pennsylvania-derived Benjamin Harrison, also of one-fourth Virginia Tidewater and one-fourth Long Island and Yankee ancestry. Bush is also the first president whose traceable ancestry is almost evenly divided between New England Yankees, mid-Atlantic residents (including New York Dutch, Quakers and Germans) and widely dispersed but probably mostly Virginia-derived Southerners (in Missouri, Kentucky, Tennessee and Georgia). The third group of presidents of mixed ethnic or regional ancestry consists of Theodore Roosevelt, who, bearing a Dutch name, was of approximately one-fourth New York Dutch, one-fourth Pennsylvania Scots-Irish or Quaker, and half Georgia Scots-Highland or Charleston planter ancestry; Hoover, who, bearing a German name, was of Pennsylvania German, Pennsylvania Quaker, New England Yankee, and a few other derivations; and Ford, who, bearing an adopted name, is of mostly unknown paternal ancestry but through his mother at least one-eighth Scots-Canadian (Reagan is one-fourth) and almost one-fourth New England Yankee.

As regards the major social groups, often regional or national elites, to which our forty presidents have belonged, Washington, Jefferson, Madison, Monroe, W.H. Harrison, Tyler and Taylor were all Virginia Tidewater planters, or the sons or grandsons of such men. The two Adamses and Pierce, whose colonial ancestors were a mixture of both notables and ordinary New England farmers, can be said to represent, as regards social standing and regional and ancestral background if not always party or ideology, the New England Federalist mercantile elite and its intellectual offspring responsible for Unitarianism, the abolitionist movement, the "flowering of New England," and much early feminism and other reform. The more "democratic" pioneer-derived presidents who succeeded these "aristocratic" groups, then seemed for two decades to alternate in office with them, and finally overwhelmed them completely, may themselves be divided into the Scots-Irish Tennessee (Jackson, Polk), Pennsylvania (Buchanan) and North Carolina (Andrew Johnson) contingent; the first New Yorkers (Van Buren, descended from non-patroon Dutch, and Fillmore, an upstate Yankee); and the midwestern or upstate-New York Yankee-derived pioneer mixtures (Lincoln, Grant, and Arthur) or "pure Yankees" (Hayes and Garfield). By the 1880s, however, patriciates had also formed even among midwestern, upstate New York Yankee or Virginia planter-derived border state "pioneers," and to this new ruling elite, often associated with big business, newer industrial cities, or "good government" reform belonged Cleveland, Benjamin Harrison, and Taft, from Buffalo, Indianapolis, and Cincinnati respectively. The last Scots-Irish presidents, McKinley and Wilson, both also had patriciate connections -- McKinley through his sponsorship by Mark Hanna, and Wilson as president of Princeton. The two Roosevelts and Bush represent the eastern inner-city Social Register "establishment," Theodore Roosevelt more or less at its moment of solidification into a national upper class, F.D. Roosevelt at the beginning of its decline (both Roosevelts were Harvard graduates with genealogical connections to Astors, Livingstons, and/or many of the "400") and Bush (a Livingston descendant and thus a distant Astor cousin), as perhaps its swan song. Our new president, a Yale graduate and the son of a Connecticut senator (with kinsmen among Boston Brahmins and immediate forebears associated with Rochester, New York, and Columbus, Ohio) by a St. Louisan born in Kennebunkport, Maine, was nonetheless a Texas oilman and congressman whose major political support still lies outside the northeast. Harding (from Ohio, bearing a New England surname), Coolidge (a Vermont Yankee of mostly ordinary farmer immediate background), Hoover (of

Pennsylvania and Yankee stock, from Iowa), and Ford (from Michigan, although born in Nebraska, at least one-fourth Yankee) may be considered the last "pioneer"-derived presidents, often, but not always, associated with rural, small-town, or small-city interests and values.

Five of the nine U.S. chief executives since World War II have been either descendants of non-conformist sects and largely non-regionally affiliated (Eisenhower and Nixon), or associated with the modern re-emergent South, especially its newly risen cities and national suburban culture (Truman, from Independence, Mo. and Kansas City; Johnson, from Stonewall and Austin, Texas; and Carter, from Plains and Atlanta, Georgia). A third type of ancestry, post-1840 immigrant "ethnic" -- often Catholic, working-class in its first few American generations, and either Irish, Italian, Scandinavian, non-colonial German, Greek, Slavic, Jewish, Hispanic, Oriental, or Canadian -- has been represented thus far by Kennedy, a Boston Irish Catholic, and Reagan, a mid-westerner half Catholic Irish and one-fourth Scots-Canadian, whose adult life has been associated largely with Hollywood and California. Among recent first ladies, vice presidents, or presidential or vice presidential candidates such ethnic ancestry is also a major component. Mrs. Eisenhower and vice presidents Humphrey and Mondale are all half or more Scandinavian; Mrs. Kennedy and Mrs. Nixon are half Irish, and the latter half German as well; Vice President Agnew and Governor Dukakis are of Greek, and Senator Goldwater of patrilineal Jewish descent; and among vice presidential candidates Senator Muskie, Congresswoman Ferraro and Senator Bentsen are Polish, Italian, and half Danish respectively.

Much, then, of American social history is reflected in the ancestry of our forty presidents to date. As a partial summary of these movements I wish to comment briefly on perhaps a major, although unplanned, result -- kinship among the American people overall and between our presidents and the populace generally. Although I readily admit that the figures below are only guesses, I think it likely that of the roughly 250 million living Americans (U.S. residents), as many as 100 million may well have considerable New England ancestry; 100 million or more may have colonial mid-Atlantic or southern ancestry (with certainly a hefty overlap -- say 25% -- between these New England and mid-Atlantic or southern-derived groups, especially in the midwest, border states and far west); and a third 100 million, with again a 25% possible overlap with the preceding groups (especially in the northeast and northern midwest), are of 19th or 20th century "ethnic" ancestry. Americans of "ethnic" ancestry descend from millions of 19th or early 20th century (and for Hispanic and Asian Americans often quite recent) immigrants, and are usually related, via these forebears, to only a few, a few hundred, or for the progeny of mid 19th century groups like the Irish, perhaps a few thousand other living Americans. Many Americans of mid-Atlantic or southern ancestry are descended from thousands of 18th century Scots-Irish or German immigrants and through these forebears are related probably to only a few hundred thousand or a few million other living Americans. Descendants of 17th century New York Dutch, Pennsylvania Quakers, or Virginia planters might perhaps expect tens of millions of living American cousins. Descendants, finally, of between fifty and two hundred of the 10,000-25,000 (bachelors, wives, and children included) Pilgrim and Great Migration immigrants to New England, 1620-50, may be related to almost all of the perhaps 100 million living Americans with considerable New England ancestry -- a group I have labelled the "New England family." "Considerable New England ancestry" can be derived though only a single revolutionary soldier or 1750-1850 New England "pioneer" ancestor who moved west, and this massively extended New England family of perhaps 100 million Americans is the largest group of probably genealogically related individuals in the country, mostly eighth to twelfth cousins.

Twenty-one of the forty U.S. presidents to date -- the two Adamses, Taylor, Fillmore, Pierce, Lincoln, Grant, Hayes, Garfield, Arthur, Cleveland, Benjamin Harrison, Taft, Harding, Coolidge, Hoover, F.D. Roosevelt, Nixon, Ford, Carter and Bush -- had some New England ancestry, and only Taylor (an Allerton and Brewster **Mayflower** descendant), Lincoln (of only Lincoln, English Gilman, Lyford, Jones, Whitman and Holmes descent) and Carter (only an Almy and Cornell descendant) had less than "considerable" such ancestry. Probably anyone, in short, with between twenty and fifty 1620-50 New England ancestors will have five to ten presidents among his distant kinsmen, and very likely anyone with fifty to two hundred such forebears will have over ten presidents among his American cousins. Of the one hundred-plus immigrants or their English parents or grandparents, etc. identified in this volume as ancestors of two or more presidents (and perhaps over a million living Americans each) over 85% are New Englanders, and through only these forebears F.D. Roosevelt, Bush, Taft, Ford, Coolidge and Fillmore are distant kinsmen of ten or more other presidents. Nixon, J.Q. Adams, Hayes, Cleveland, Benjamin Harrison, Grant, Hoover, Pierce and Harding are kinsmen of five, six, seven, eight or nine other presidents. In addition, Washington, Jefferson, Madison, the two Harrisons, Tyler and Taylor were descended collectively from a sizable number of Jamestown founders and both pre- and post-1660 Tidewater planters (Truman, L.B. Johnson, and Carter together add a few other such lines, and Bush adds even more); and Van Buren, the two Roosevelts,Harding, Ford and Bush collectively descend from a fair number of early New York Dutch settlers. Sixteen of the remaining one hundred-plus kinships between presidents treated herein are through these 17th century Virginia planters and Dutch New Yorkers, and probably most Americans with considerable Tidewater Virginia or New York Dutch ancestry have a fair chance, say one in two, of a presidential kinship thereby. Also worth noting, despite the lack of any known presidential kinships to date so derived, is the Pennsylvania Quaker ancestry of Lincoln, Theodore Roosevelt, Hoover, Nixon, and Bush. Collectively this Quaker presidential heritage is also sizable, and Americans with many late 17th century Pennsylvania Quakers in their ancestry may also have perhaps as much of a one-in-four or one-in-five chance of a presidential kinsman thereby. Although many thousands of Americans, probably even a few million, descend from 18th century Scots-Irish and German presidential forebears (presidents with such German ancestors include probably Cleveland and certainly Hoover, Truman, Eisenhower, L.B. Johnson, and Bush), Scots-Irish and German immigrants were so many in number and so late in arrival that probably anyone with considerable such ancestry has only a slight chance of presidential kinsmen thereby.

One final thought is in order: as the first 20th century president whose known ancestry is almost evenly divided, three ways, between New England, the mid-Atlantic region, and the South, and with descents from over fifty 17th century New England immigrants, several known New York Dutch, Pennsylvania Quaker and Maryland families, and various early 17th century Virginians, George Bush may well be also the first U.S. President who is a likely kinsman of perhaps half of the Americans whose government he heads.

III

Before moving to the various formats used in this book I wish to comment on the subjects of unknown and royal presidential ancestry, sometimes seen as "mirror-images" of each other -- our "most obscure" or simply most genealogically difficult, and our "most distinguished" or simply "most ancient" or easiest-to-trace forebears. In these matters also, presidential ancestors, a few generations back, look like anyone else's and can be studied only in the standard genealogical sources -- written monographs or books and archival documents such as vital records, wills and deeds. The immediate ancestry, for say five or six generations, of most presidents has indeed been well studied, and one may expect to find more readily available about it than about one's own such background or that of a friend. But even in these first few generations scholars have found the same blocks that genealogists always find -- many forgotten, lost or untraceable 19th century immigrant origins, 1750-1850 pioneers, 18th century Scots-Irish, German and other European immigrants, and 17th century English or Dutch origins. And beyond the immediate five or six generations, the patrilineal descent, and sometimes the patrilineal descent of a president's mother, presidential forebears are no better studied genealogically than any colonial families -- in part, no doubt, because until now there has been no synthesis of our knowledge about them to date. Unexplored or problematical areas in the ancestry of twenty-six of our forty presidents, through four generations, are listed below. The extent of this unknown ancestry may at first seem surprising.

1. Washington - identification and ancestry of his maternal grandmother, Mary ---, very likely Mrs. Mary Bennett Johnson, wife of Col. Joseph Ball
2. Jefferson - origins of three great-grandfathers fathers (Thomas Jefferson, Peter Field, and Charles Rogers)
3. Madison - parentage of a great-grandmother, Mrs. Isabella Todd Madison
4. Monroe - ancestry, beyond parents, of his mother (Elizabeth Jones), paternal grandmother (Christian Tyler), and patrilineal great-grandparents (William Monroe & Margaret Bowcock)
5. Jackson - entire Scots-Irish ancestry (only his his parents, paternal grandfather, patrilineal great-grandfather and the maiden surname of his maternal grandmother are known)
6. W.H. Harrison - origin of William Churchill, his matrilineal great-grandfather
7. Tyler - origins of two great-grandparents, Dr. Louis Contesse and his wife, Mary Morris; wife of Ellyson Armistead, his mother's paternal grandfather
8. Polk - origins of four great-grandparents (Mrs. Margaret Taylor Polk, Samuel Wilson, John Knox, and Thomas Gillespie), identification and origins of Mrs. Naomi (--) Gillespie, Polk's matrilineal great-grandmother
9. Taylor - ancestry of his maternal grandmother, Mrs. Sarah Bayly Pannill Strother, and of a great-grandmother, Mrs. Susannah Dabney Strother
10. Pierce - identification and ancestry of his matrilineal great-grandmother, Mary ---, wife of Stephen Harris

11. Buchanan - entire Scots-Irish ancestry beyond his paternal grandfather (and a possible patrilineal descent from Thomas Buchanan of Carbeth, whose wife and cousin, Janet Buchanan, was of royal descent) and maternal grandparents, and beyond his father's maternal grandparents
12. Lincoln - the entire ancestry of his mother (Nancy Hanks) and paternal grandmother (Bathsheba Herring[?])
13. A. Johnson - entire ancestry beyond his parents, maternal grandfather, and mother's paternal grandparents
14. Grant - identification and ancestry of his paternal grandmother, Mrs. Rachel Kelley Grant; origins of two great-grandparents (Samuel Weir and his wife Mary ---)
15. Hayes - paternity of his maternal grandfather, Roger Birchard (alias Cornwall)
16. Garfield - ancestry of his paternal grandmother (Asenath Hill) and patrilineal great-grandmother (Sarah Bryant)
17. Arthur - entire Scots-Irish paternal ancestry beyond paternal grandparents and patrilineal great-grandparents
18. Cleveland - entire ancestry of his maternal grandparents
19. McKinley - entire ancestry of his mother, beyond her parents and maternal grandparents; origins of his father's maternal grandparents, Andrew Rose and Hannah Chapman
20. Wilson - entire Scots-Irish and Scots ancestry beyond his paternal grandparents and three of his mother's grandparents (all except John Woodrow, whose patrilineal ancestry is known)
21. Harding - ancestry of his maternal grandfather (Isaac Haines Dickerson) and of three great-grandparents (Joshua Crawford and Sophia Stevens, his wife; and Mrs. Deborah Watters Van Kirk)
22. Coolidge - origins of John Moor, his mother's paternal grandfather
23. Eisenhower - origins of his mother's paternal grandmother, Mrs. Mary Anne Hannah Stover
24. Kennedy - entire Irish ancestry beyond great, great-great or great-great-great-grandparents
25. Ford - entire paternal ancestry (only his paternal grandparents and patrilineal great-grandparents are known); origins of his mother's paternal grandmother, Mrs. Sally Miller Gardner
26. Reagan - origins of three great-grandparents (Patrick Cusick and Sarah Higgins, his wife, and John Wilson); entire Irish, Scottish and English ancestry beyond great- or great-great-grandparents

Royal descent, perhaps the polar opposite of unknown ancestry, is certainly borne by 17 presidents -- Washington, Jefferson, Madison, J.Q. Adams, the two Harrisons, Pierce, Hayes, Cleveland, the two Roosevelts, Taft, Coolidge, Hoover, Nixon, Ford, and Bush; probably by an eighteenth (Taylor); and possibly, although much further research is required, by a nineteenth (Buchanan). F.D. Roosevelt had at least nine immigrant ancestors of royal descent, Bush has seven, Coolidge had four, Washington and Jefferson three, Pierce and Ford two (Ford possibly three), Madison, Benjamin Harrison, Hayes and Theodore Roosevelt certainly one and possibly two each, and J.Q. Adams, W.H. Harrison, Cleveland, Taft, Hoover and Nixon one apiece. Also of note are the royal descents of first ladies married to eight other presidents - through one immigrant ancestor of Abigail Adams, two immigrant ancestors of Julia Grant, two of Lucretia Garfield, one of Ellen Arthur, three (possibly four) of Ellen Wilson, five of Edith Wilson, one (possibly two) of Bess Truman, one (not fully proved) of Mamie Eisenhower, and one (possibly two) of Nancy Reagan. Fully charted and referenced herein, these presidential royal descents are often from Edward III (d. 1377), Edward I (d. 1307), Henry II (d. 1189), or Henry I (d. 1135), Kings of England, from Henry I (d. 1060), Hugh Capet (d. 996) or Louis IV (d. 954), Kings of France, or from medieval kings of Scotland (both the French and Scots kings had many descendants who married English nobles).

One can find discussions of the phenomenon of royal descent in Sir A.R. Wagner's **English Genealogy**, in D.L. Jacobus's **Genealogy as Pastime and Profession** and A.J. Camp's **Everyone Has Roots**, in J.I. Coddington's fine chapter on "Noble and Royal Genealogy" in volume one of **Genealogical Research: Methods and Sources**, and in my own life's work, "The Mowbray Connection," 23 vols., a manuscript at NEHGS, the New York Public Library, and the Society of Genealogists in London, and about which see **The Connecticut Nutmegger** 10(1977-78):3-12, 187-98, 393-400, **The Detroit Society for Genealogical Research Magazine** 41(1977-78):141, 42(1978-79):191, and **Genealogical Journal** 12(1983-84):70, 13(1984-85):66. In general, however, a very large number of middle-class Americans, perhaps most with extensive colonial ancestry, have royal descents because about 300-350 colonial immigrants who left sizable American progeny belonged to the English gentry -- or in some cases its Scots, Welsh, Anglo-Irish, or even some continental equivalents. These often younger sons of London merchants or aldermen, of gentlemen or knights in the various English counties, and sometimes even of baronets or peers, often became colonial governors or officials, town founders, leading ministers, manorial lords (on

Long Island and along the Hudson), wealthy Quaker merchants (in Rhode Island and Philadelphia especially), and major Tidewater planters (mostly in Maryland, Virginia, and South Carolina). Some of these royally descended immigrants, sometimes armigerous and often called "Mr." in the colonies, led quieter lives or were town, county, or colony officers, or merchants or planters on a lesser scale, and most had large colonial progenies, so that after four or five generations many descendants could no longer be labelled an elite. This dispersal, coupled with the English mobility that produced their own royal descents -- daughters and younger sons of kings marrying nobles, daughters and younger sons of nobles marrying "gentry" (landowning "gentlemen") and scions of the gentry seeking their fortune in trade or the colonies, or leading congregations in Puritan reform -- has spread descent from medieval kings to much of modern America.

For its own intrinsic interest, to show some further ramifications of the phenomena of royal descent and presidential royal descent in particular, and as both another indicator of massive Anglo-American kinship and a hint of possible continental extension, I have also charted for this volume the presidential descendants of John of Gaunt and of Sancha de Ayala, and the presidential cousins, via Virginia, New England, or New Jersey, of Queen Elizabeth the Queen Mother and The Princess of Wales. Via John of Gaunt, Duke of Lancaster (d. 1399, a son of Edward III, King of England) and his daughter Joan Beaufort, Countess of Westmoreland, both Washington and Jefferson were eleventh cousins once removed, twice over, of King George III. Through Sancha de Ayala, d. 1418, Spanish wife of Sir Walter Blount, ancestress of a dozen or more colonial immigrants, and sister of a great-great-grandfather of Ferdinand II, King of Aragon (and V, King of Castile, often called the first king of united Spain, husband of the celebrated Queen Isabella of Castile) seven - and possibly eight - presidents are descended from fourth cousins of the king who sponsored Columbus's discovery of America. Among these eight, moreover, are Washington and Benjamin Harrison, fourth cousins eight and ten times removed respectively of King Ferdinand, who were presidents in 1792 and 1892, the 300th and 400th anniversaries of the discovery of the New World, and Bush, a fourth cousin fifteen times removed of King Ferdinand, who will be president during 1992, the 500th anniversary of Columbus's first voyage. The Virginia ancestry shared by Washington and Queen Elizabeth the Queen Mother, who are second cousins six times removed, is covered in the NEHGS **NEXUS** 4(1987):24-28. The New England-derived kinships between The Princess of Wales and her sons and presidents John and J.Q. Adams, Fillmore, Hayes, Cleveland, Taft, Coolidge and F.D. Roosevelt, plus first ladies Frances Cleveland, Edith Roosevelt, Ellen Wilson, Grace Coolidge, Bess Truman, and Nancy Reagan, all charted herein, are also covered in my and W.A. Reitwiesner's **American Ancestors and Cousins of The Princess of Wales**; so too is the Princess's very likely kinship, via the Claytons of New Jersey, to Nixon.

IV

Having now treated the history of this project, emphasized its preliminary quality, and discussed at some length various patterns in presidential ancestry that reflect American social history generally, we turn at the conclusion of these remarks to some explanation of format. The bulk of this volume consists of thirty-eight presidential ancestor tables (the Adamses and Harrisons are treated together), thirty-eight bibliographies of sources used to compile the ancestor tables, and charts outlining kinships between presidents and the best royal descent of each presidential immigrant forebear with such ancestry. The kinship and descent charts follow standard genealogical form, but with all spouses not ancestral to presidents generally omitted, no places, and dates in years (often just death years), and only for kings, presidents, and most ancestors of two or more presidents. The bibliographies include many abbreviations, all listed, and families treated in periodicals, multi-ancestor works, and genealogies of other families are named in parentheses after the citation. I have also listed compilers of major TAG ancestor tables in parentheses after these citations, and at the end of each bibliography I have listed any and all immigrant ancestors of royal descent (RD), ancestors who were passengers on the **Mayflower** (MD), ancestors shared by The Princess of Wales and her sons (PW), and other presidential kinsmen (PK), with common ancestral families again given in parentheses. Also noted are any descents from the men or women executed for witchcraft in Salem, Massachusetts, in 1692, or from their siblings.

The ancestor tables herein cover, as already noted, the full known ancestry for seven generations of presidents born in the eighteenth century, for eight generations of presidents born in the nineteenth century, and for nine generations of presidents born in the twentieth century. In each table the president is #1, his parents are #s2-3 (father #2, mother #3), his grandparents #s4-7 (paternal grandfather #4, paternal grandmother #5, maternal grandfather #6, maternal grandmother #7), great-grandparents #s8-15 (patrilineal great-grandfather #8, matrilineal great-grandmother #15), great-great-grandparents #s16-31, great-great-

great-grandparents #s32-63, great-great-great-great-grandparents #s64-127, great-great-great-great-great-grandparents #s128-255, and great-great-great-great-great-great-grandparents #s256-511. Males, other than the president himself, have even numbers; females, odd numbers. For the parents of any ancestor, double his or her number for the father, and then add one for the mother. For any ancestor's child, divide the ancestor's number by two and drop halves. Full dates and places are provided, when known, for the birth, death, and marriage of each ancestor (but note the exception below), places before dates. After each forebear, following a comma, is his or her birthplace, then birthdate, a dash, and then place and death date. After death dates for men follows a comma and then a marriage place and marriage date. Former or later wives of male ancestors are omitted; former or later husbands of female ancestors are included, since the latter often thus married or died bearing different surnames. Although no rigid pattern is followed and user convenience is here the guide, when towns are known counties are usually omitted (pertinent cited sources usually designate counties, however, in case two towns or areas in a single state may have the same name), and when towns or cities are listed repeatedly in the same table states are often omitted. Eighth generation ancestors of presidents born in the nineteenth century, and ninth generation ancestors of presidents born in the twentieth century, who usually lived themselves in the seventeenth or early eighteenth centuries (and if New Englanders married before 1700, are listed in Clarence Almon Torrey's **New England Marriages Prior to 1700**), receive somewhat condensed treatment. Following each such ancestor are birth and death years (in parentheses if both are known), principal place of residence, or if an immigrant, English or other place origin and eventual colonial residence, and then, following male ancestors, a marriage year. Little biographical information is given -- a few occupations or offices, some colleges, "Rev." for ministers but no military titles or indications of war service. Other notes -- dates of "flourishing" (fl.), of wills and/or probate if no death date is available, etc. -- should be self-explanatory. As for "slash years" (Jan.-Mar. pre-1752) and Quaker dating, I have followed my sources. When abstracting a major TAG ancestry table or the work of Raymond Martin Bell and a few others, I tried, on most other discretionary matters, likewise to follow the lead of my predecessors. Particularly frustrating, however, are dates without places. Some are undoubtedly taken from tombstones and family Bibles; other dates, with places, however, can undoubtedly be confirmed with further research, and such queries form probably half of the items I wish to check before publication of this book's "first edition."

As a final word to readers, I want to acknowledge the "dullness" of tables, bibliographies, and charts but say also that I think you will enjoy this book. For within these tables and charts lie not only clues perhaps to new lines in your own ancestry, but also, for genealogists who have traced many American forebears, probably various, and collectively millions, of kinships to presidents. Discovering and enjoying these kinships and then reflecting on some of the social patterns discussed in this introduction, you will, I hope, have further thoughts about your own genealogical connectedness, or "fit," into the country at large, and perhaps beyond. Happy hunting, and please let me know of all your corrections and additions to this work, plus whatever new research it inspires.

Gary Boyd Roberts

18 February 1989-29 September 1989

New England Historic
Genealogical Society
101 Newbury Street
Boston, Massachusetts 02116
(617) 536-5740

ANCESTOR TABLES

1. GEORGE WASHINGTON

1. GEORGE WASHINGTON, Pope's Creek, Westmoreland Co., Virginia 11 Feb. 1731/2-Mount Vernon, Fairfax Co., Va. 14 Dec. 1799, New Kent Co., Va. 6 Jan. 1759 Mrs. Martha Dandridge Custis, New Kent Co. 21 June 1731-Mount Vernon 22 May 1802, widow of Daniel Parke Custis

2. Augustine Washington, Wakefield, Westmoreland Co. c. 1694-Ferry Farm, King George Co., Va. 12 Apr. 1743, 6 Mar. 1731

3. Mary Ball, Lancaster Co., Va. c. 1708-09-Fredericksburg, Va. 25 Aug. 1789

4. Lawrence Washington, Westmoreland Co. Sept. 1659-Westmoreland Co. Feb. 1697/8, prob. Warner Hall, Gloucester Co., Va. c. 1689

5. Mildred Warner, prob. Warner Hall c. 1671-bur. Whitehaven, Cumberland, England 26 Mar. 1701, m. (2) George Gale of Whitehaven

6. Joseph Ball, England 24 May 1649-Epping Forest, Lancaster Co. between 25 June & 11 July 1711, c. 1707-8 (post 6 Feb. 1707)

7. Mrs. Mary Johnson, d. 1721, m. (3) Richard Hewes; very likely she was the Mary Bennett of West Chester, England who m. William Johnson of Norwich, Middlesex Co., Va. 10 Feb. 1688/9 & was probably a near kinswoman of a Thomas Bennett of Westmoreland Co., living 1738/9

8. John Washington, prob. Purleigh, Essex c. 1634-prob. Washington Parish, Westmoreland Co. c. 1677, Westmoreland Co. 1 Dec. 1658

9. Anne Pope, d. Westmoreland Co. c. 1668

10. Augustine Warner, Jr., prob. York Co., Va. 3 June 1642-prob. Warner Hall 19 June 1681, Speaker of the House of Burgesses, m. ante 1671

11. Mildred Reade, d. prob. Warner Hall c. 1694 (will dated 4 Jan. 1694/5)

12. William Ball, c. 1615-Millenbeck, Lancaster Co. 15 Oct.-Nov. 1680, London 2 July 1638

13. Hannah Atherold of London, c. 1615-prob. Lancaster Co. c. 1695

14-15. ---

16. Rev. Lawrence Washington, Sulgrave Manor, Northamptonshire c. 1602-bur. Malden, Essex 21 Jan. 1653, rector of Purleigh & Little Braxted, Essex, Fellow & lecturer of Brasenose College, Oxford, m. prob. Purleigh Mar.-Dec. 1633

17. Amphyllis Twigden, bp. Spratton, Northamptonshire 2 Feb. 1601/2-bur. Tring, Hertfordshire 19 Jan. 1654/5

18. Nathaniel Pope, to Maryland c. 1637, to Va. c. 1650, d. Cliffs, Westmoreland Co., Va. between 16 May 1659 & 26 Apr. 1660

19. Lucy ---, d. post 1660

20. Augustine Warner, prob. Hoveton or Norwich, Norfolk c. 28 Sept. 1611-Warner Hall 24 Dec. 1674, ante 13 May 1638

21. Mary Towneley, Stone Edge, Lancashire 13 May 1614-Warner Hall 11 Aug. 1662

22. George Reade, Linkenholt, Hampshire 25 Oct. 1608-prob. Gloucester Co., Va. ante 21 Nov. 1674, Secretary of the Colony & Acting Governor of Va. (1638-39), prob. Yorktown c. 1641

23. Elizabeth Martiau, prob. York Co., Va.-prob. Gloucester Co. c. 1686 (will dated 10 Feb. 1686)

24. (possibly) Dr. Richard Ball, D. D., of London, fl. 1613

25. ---

26. (possibly) Thomas Atherold, bp. Burgh, Suffolk 16 Aug. 1590-Burgh 6 May 1658

27. (possibly) Mary Vesey of Oldham, bur. Burgh May 1665, widow of William Herbert

28-31. ---

32. Lawrence Washington, prob. Sulgrave Manor c. 1568-Brington, Northamptonshire 13 Dec. 1616, Aston-le-Walls, Northamptonshire 3 Aug. 1588
33. Margaret Butler of Tyes Hall, Cuckfields, Sussex, ante 1568-c. 1652
34. John Twigden, d. Little Creaton, Northamptonshire between 8 Dec. 1610 & 26 Jan. 1610/1
35. Anne Dickens of Great Creaton, Northamptonshire, bur. Tring, Hertfordshire Apr. 1637, m. (2) Andrew Knowling of Tring
36-39. ---
40. (prob.) Thomas Warner, bp. Hoe, Norfolk 14 Mar. 1580/1, matriculated at Caius College, Cambridge 30 June 1597, later of Hoveton, Thorpe-by-Norwich & Norwich, m. St. Mary, Hellesdon, Norfolk 15 or 20 Oct. 1602
41. (prob.) Elizabeth Sotherton of Hellesdon, c. 1582-84-living 1629
42. Lawrence Towneley of Stone Edge, bur. Colne, Lancashire 12 Feb. 1654/5, ante 1597/8
43. Jennet Halstead of Windlehouse, prob. bur. Burnley, Lancashire 12 Aug. 1623
44. Robert Reade of Faccombe & Linkenholt, Hampshire, c. 1551(71?)-c. 1627 (will dated 10 Dec. 1619), St. Martin-in-the-Fields, Westminster (London) 31 July 1600
45. Mildred Windebank of Haines Hill, Hurst, Berkshire, c. 1584-will dated 15 Aug. 1630
46. Nicholas Martiau, French Huguenot settler of Elizabeth City, Charles City & York Cos., Va., c. 1591-prob. Yorktown between 1 Mar. 1656/7 & 24 Apr. 1657
47. --- (prob. an unknown first wife; G. H. S. L. Washington, however, thought she was Jane --- [widow of Edward Berkeley], who m. Martiau about 1625 & d. ante 1646)
48. (possibly) Lawrence Ball of Northamptonshire
49-51. ---
52. (possibly) Thomas Atherold of Burgh, Suffolk
53. ---
54. (possibly) Thomas Vesey of Aldham, Suffolk
55. (possibly) Elizabeth Church of Malden, Essex
56-63. ---
64. Robert Washington, prob. Sulgrave, Northamptonshire c. 1544-prob. Nether Boddington, Northamptonshire between 7 Feb. 1620 & 3 Jan. 1621, c. 1565
65. Elizabeth Light (Lyte) of Radway Grange, Warwickshire, d. c. 1599
66. William Butler of Tyes Hall, Cuckfields, Sussex, fl. 1588
67. Margaret Greeke of Palsters, Lancashire, & London
68. Thomas Twigden, d. Little Creaton, Northamptonshire between 2 Jan. 1579/80 & 22 Oct. 1580
69. --- Watts
70. William Dickens, d. Great Greaton between 15 Aug. 1583 & 30 Jan. 1583/4, Newnham, Northamptonshire 16 June 1573
71. Anne Thornton of Newnham, bur. Spratton, Northamptonshire 27 Dec. 1614, m. (2) Edward Twigden of Little Creaton
72-79. ---
80. (prob.) William Warner of Thompson, Hoveton, & Norwich, Norfolk, b. Hoe c. 1540-will proved 1610/1
81. (prob.) Mary ---, will proved 1616
82. (prob.) Augustine Sotherton of Hellesdon, bur. St. Andrew, Norwich 26 Mar. 1585, St. Michael at Plea, Norwich 22 Sept. 1572
83. (prob.) Ann Peck, bp. St. Michael at Plea 12 Apr. 1553
84. Lawrence Towneley, prob. Barnside, Lancashire-Stone Edge, Lancashire between 5 & 19 Jan. 1597/8, prob. Stone Edge ante 3 June 1563
85. Margaret Hartley of Stone Edge

86. John Halstead of Windlehouse, bur. Burnley 10 July 1601
87. Elizabeth ---, bur. Stone Edge 21 Sept. 1612
88. Andrew Reade, bur. Faccombe, Hampshire 8 July 1623
89. Alice Cooke, bur. Faccombe 6 Mar. 1606, prob. a sister of Richard Cooke of Beakesbourne, Kent
90. Sir Thomas Windebank of Haines Hill, Hurst, Berkshire & Westminster, Clerk of the Signet & Deputy Clerk of the Privy Council, knighted 23 July 1603, d. 24 Oct., bur. St. Martin-in-the-Fields, Westminster (London) 25 Nov. 1607, Scrivelsby, Lincolnshire 20 Aug. 1566
91. Frances Dymoke of Scrivelsby (daughter of Sir Edward Dymoke, Royal Champion at the coronations of Edward VI, Mary I & Elizabeth I, M.P. for Lincolnshire, & Anne Talboys)
92-107. ---
108. (possibly) Thomas Vesey of Aldham, Suffolk
109. (possibly) Elizabeth Gardiner of Suffolk
110. (possibly) John Church of Malden, Essex
111-127. ---

* * *

2. JOHN ADAMS, JR. and [6] JOHN QUINCY ADAMS

1. JOHN QUINCY ADAMS, Braintree, Mass. 11 July 1767-Washington, D. C. 23 Feb. 1848, London, England 26 July 1797 Louisa Catherine Johnson, London 12 Feb. 1775-Washington, DC 15 May 1852
2. JOHN ADAMS, JR., Braintree 19 Oct. 1735-Quincy, Mass. 4 July 1826, Weymouth, Mass. 25 Oct. 1764
3. Abigail Smith, Weymouth 23 Nov. 1744-Quincy 28 Oct. 1818
4. John Adams, Braintree 8 Feb. 1690/1-Braintree 25 May 1761, Brookline, Mass. 23 Nov. 1734
5. Susanna Boylston, Brookline 5 March 1708/9-Quincy 17 April 1797, m. (2) John Hall
6. Rev. William Smith, Jr., Charlestown, Mass. 29 Jan. 1706/7-Weymouth 17 Sept. 1783, Braintree 16 Oct. 1740
7. Elizabeth Quincy, bp. Braintree 17 Dec. 1721-Weymouth 1 Oct. 1775
8. Joseph Adams, Jr., Braintree 24 Dec. 1654-Braintree 12 Feb. 1736/7, c. 1688
9. Hannah Bass, Braintree 22 June 1667-Braintree 24 Oct. 1705
10. Peter Boylston, c. 1673-Brookline 10 Sept. 1743, c. 1704
11. Ann White, Brookline 4 July 1685-Mar. 1772
12. William Smith, Charlestown 24 Mar. 1666/7-Charlestown 3 June 1730, c. 1669
13. Abigail Fowle, Charlestown 7 Aug. 1679-post 1731
14. John Quincy, Boston, Mass. 21 July 1689-Braintree 13 July 1767, Hingham, Mass. 6 Oct. 1715
15. Elizabeth Norton, b. Hingham 15 Mar. 1695/6
16. Joseph Adams, Kingweston, Somerset, England 9 Feb. 1626-Braintree 6 Dec. 1694, Braintree 2 Nov. 1650
17. Abigail Baxter, Roxbury, Mass. Sept. 1634-Braintree 27 Aug. 1692
18. John Bass, bp. Saffron Walden, Essex, England 18 Sept. 1630-Braintree 12 Sept. 1716, Braintree 3 Feb. 1657/8
19. Ruth Alden, c. 1640-Braintree 12 Oct. 1674
20. Thomas Boylston, Jr., Watertown, Mass. 26 Jan. 1644/5-c. 1695, Charlestown 13 Dec. 1665
21. Mary Gardner, bp. Roxbury 9 April 1648-Brookline 8 July 1722
22. Benjamin White, c. 1626-Brookline 9 Jan. 1722/3, Ipswich, Mass. 21 Jan. 1681/2
23. Susanna Cogswell, Ipswich 5 Jan. 1657/8-post 1701
24. Thomas Smith, d. Charlestown 14 Feb. 1690, c. 1663

25. Sarah Boylston, Watertown 30 Sept. 1642-Charlestown 8 Aug. 1711
26. Isaac Fowle, c. 1648-Charlestown 15 Oct. 1718, Charlestown 30 Nov. 1671
27. Beriah Bright, Watertown 22 Sept. 1649-Charlestown 7 Oct. 1734
28. Daniel Quincy, Braintree 7 Feb. 1650/1-Boston 10 Aug. 1690, Boston 9 Nov. 1682
29. Anna Shepard, Charlestown 8 Sept. 1663-Braintree 24 July 1708, m. (2) Rev. Moses Fiske
30. Rev. John Norton, c. 1651-Hingham 3 Oct. 1716, Boston 29 Nov. 1678
31. Mary Mason, d. Braintree June 1740
32. Henry Adams, Barton St. David, Somerset 21 Jan. 1583-bur. Braintree 6 Oct. 1646, Charlton Mackrell, Somerset 19 Oct. 1609
33. Edith Squire, bp. Charlton Mackrell 29 May 1587-Medfield, Mass. 21 Jan. 1672/3, m. (2) John Fussell
34. Gregory Baxter, d. Braintree 21 June 1659, ante 1632
35. Margaret Paddy, d. Braintree 13 Feb. 1661/2, sister of William Paddy of Plymouth and Boston
36. Samuel Bass, d. Braintree 30 Dec. 1694, Saffron Walden, Essex 25 April 1625
37. Ann Savell or Savil, bp. Saffron Walden 26 April 1601-Braintree 5 Sept. 1693
38. John Alden (possibly of Harwich, Essex & possibly a grandson of Spanish captive [in 1586] John Alden, whose [likely second] wife, Elizabeth Russell, was a sister of Robert Russell, step-father of Mayflower Master Christopher Jones), d. Duxbury 12 Sept. 1687, Mayflower passenger, m. ante 1624
39. Priscilla Mullins, Mayflower passenger, d. post 1680
40. Thomas Boylston, bp. St. Dionis Backchurch, London 12 Feb. 1614/5, of Watertown, d. 1653, c. 1639
41. Sarah ---, d. Watertown 14 Sept. 1704, m. (2) John Chinery
42. Thomas Gardner, Jr., d. Roxbury 15 July 1689, Charlestown 4 July 1641
43. Lucy Smith, d. Roxbury 4 Nov. 1687
44. John White, d. Brookline 15 Apr. 1691, int. Brookline 10 Apr. 1640
45. Frances Jackson, d. Brookline 26 Feb. 1696
46. William Cogswell, bp. Westbury Leigh, Wiltshire, England Mar. 1618/9-Ipswich 15 Dec. 1700, c. 1649
47. Susanna Hawkes, Charlestown 13 Aug. 1633-ante 1696
48-49. ---
50. same as 40
51. same as 41
52. George Fowle, probably bp. Wittersham, Kent, England 27 Jan. 1610-Charlestown 19 Sept. 1682, c. 1634
53. Mary ---, c. 1613-Charlestown 15 Feb. 1676/7
54. Henry Bright, bp. St. James, Bury St. Edmunds, Suffolk, England 29 Dec. 1602-Watertown 9 Oct. 1686, c. 1634
55. Anna Goldstone, bp. Wickham Skeith, Suffolk, England 16 May 1615
56. Edmund Quincy, Jr., bp. Achurch, Northamptonshire, England 15 Mar. 1627/8-Braintree 7 Jan. 1697/8, Braintree 26 July 1648
57. Joanna Hoar, bp. St. Michael's, Gloucester, England June 1624-Braintree 16 May 1680
58. Rev. Thomas Shepard, Jr., London, England, 5 April 1635-Charlestown 22 Dec. 1677, Charlestown 3 Nov. 1656
59. Anna Tyng, Boston 6 Jan. 1639/40-Milton, Mass. 5 Aug. 1709
60. William Norton, d. Ipswich 30 April 1694, c. 1649
61. Lucy Downing, d. Ipswich 5 Feb. 1697/8
62. Arthur Mason, c. 1630-Boston 4 Mar. 1707/8, Boston 5 July 1655

63. Joanna Parker, Boston 1 June 1635-Boston 2 Jan. 1704/5

64. John Adams, c. 1555-Barton St. David shortly ante 22 March 1603/4, c. 1576

65. Agnes (possibly Stone), bur. Barton St. David 15 Jan. 1615/6

66. Henry Squire, b. c. 1563, of Charlton Mackrell & Kingweston, m. c. 1586

67-73. ---

74. William Savil of Saffron Walden

75-77. ---

78. William Mullins, Mayflower passenger, nuncupative will dated at Plymouth 21 Feb. 1620/1

79. Alice ---, d. Plymouth winter 1620/1

80. Edward Boylston, citizen & pewterer of London, bur. St. Dionis Backchurch 22 Aug. 1625, c. 1613

81. Anne Bastian, c. 1595-bur. St. Dionis Backchurch 11 May 1621

82-83. ---

84. Thomas Gardner, bur. Roxbury Nov. 1638

85. ---, bur. Roxbury 7 Oct. 1658

86-91. ---

92. John Cogswell, c. 1592-Ipswich 29 Nov. 1669, Westbury Leigh 10 Sept. 1615

93. Elizabeth Thompson, d. Ipswich 2 June 1676

94. Adam Hawkes, bp. Hingham, Norfolk, England 26 Jan. 1605-Lynn, Mass. 13 Mar. 1671/2

95. Mrs. Ann (possibly Brown) Hutchinson, c. 1595-Lynn 4 Dec. 1669

96-99. ---

100. same as 80

101. same as 81

102-103. ---

104. (probably) Myles Fowle, c. 1562-bur. Tenterden, Kent 22 Jan. 1620, Wittersham, Kent 8 June 1599

105. (probably) Iden Thorlton, bp. Kenardington, Kent 19 Jan. 1577, bur. Wittersham 23 Jan. 1611

106-107. ---

108. Henry Bright, bp. St. James, Bury St. Edmunds 20 Sept. 1560-1609

109. Mary ---, d. post 1618, m. (2) William Cole

110. Henry Goldstone, bp. Wickham Skeith 17 July 1591-Watertown 25 July 1638, c. 1614

111. Anne ---, c. 1591-Watertown 26 Apr. 1670, m. (2) John George

112. Edmund Quincy, bp. Lilford, Northamptonshire 30 May 1602-c. 1637, Lilford 14 July 1623

113. Judith Pares of Bythorne, Huntingdonshire, England, d. Boston 29 Mar. 1654, m. (2) Moses Paine, (3) Robert Hull

114. Charles Hoar, Alderman of Gloucester, d. Sept.-Dec. 1638

115. Joanna Hincksman, d. Braintree 21 Dec. 1661

116. Rev. Thomas Shepard, Towcester, Northamptonshire 5 Nov. 1605-Cambridge, Mass. 25 Aug. 1649, c. 1632

117. Margaret Touteville (Stouteville, Estouteville), bp. Humanby, Yorkshire, England 3 Aug. 1606-Cambridge Feb. 1635/6

118. William Tyng, c. 1605-Braintree 18 Jan. 1652/3, c. 1636-7

119. Elizabeth Coytmore, c. 1617-between Jan. 1642/3 & Jan. 1648/9

120. William Norton, b. prob. Sharpenhoe, Bedfordshire, England, c. 1575

121. Alice Bownest or Bonus of Buckland, Hertfordshire, England

122. Emanuel Downing, bp. St. Lawrence, Ipswich, Suffolk 12 Aug. 1585-c. 1660 (of Salem, Mass., 1638-1654), Groton, Suffolk 10 Apr. 1622

123. Lucy Winthrop (sister of Gov. John Winthrop of Massachusetts Bay), Groton, Suffolk 9 Jan. 1600/1-London 19 Apr. 1679; a son of Emanuel and Lucy was Sir George Downing, 1st Bt. (c. 1623-1684),

soldier & politician, for whom Downing Street is named

124-125. ---

126. Nicholas Parker of Roxbury & Boston, d. post 1655, c. 1629

127. Ann ---

128. Henry Adams, Barton St. David c. 1531-Barton St. David shortly ante 12 Aug. 1596

129. (possibly) Rose ---, bur. Barton St. David 20 Sept. 1598

130. (possibly) John Stone, d. Barton St. David shortly ante 27 May 1597

131. (possibly) Agnes ---, d. post 27 May 1597

132. (probably) Rev. William Squire, rector of Charlton Mackrell, Somerset, d. prob. c. 1567

133-159. ---

160. Henry Boylson or Boylston, d. Newton Solney, Derbyshire between 12 & 15 Sept. 1592

161. ---, d. prob. ante 12 Sept. 1592

162. Thomas Bastian or Baston, citizen & Draper of London, d. c. 1597, m. St. Andrew Undershaft, London 30 Nov. 1588

163. Sara Wright, bp. St. Andrew Undershaft 14 Feb. 1559/60-St. Dionis Backchurch, London prob. 3 Nov. 1607, widow of Ralph Shittleworth. She m. (3) John Dudley

164-183. ---

184. Edward Cogswell, d. Westbury Leigh, Wiltshire between 23 June 1615 & 12 Jan. 1615/6

185. Alice ---, d. Westbury Leigh between 25 June 1615 & 11 May 1616

186. Rev. William Thompson, rector of Westbury Leigh, Wiltshire post 1603, d. there 1623

187. Phyllis ---, bur. Westbury Leigh 19 July 1608

188. John Hawke of Hingham, Norfolk

189. ---

190. (possibly) Edward Brown of Inkbarrow, Worcestershire, fl. 1590/1-1612/3

191. (possibly) Jane Lide

Note: Numbers 1, 2, 6, 14, 30 and 58 were Harvard graduates of 1787, 1755, 1725, 1708, 1671, and 1653 respectively.

* * *

3. THOMAS JEFFERSON

1. THOMAS JEFFERSON, Shadwell, Goochland (now Albemarle) Co., Virginia 2 Apr. 1743-Monticello, Albemarle Co., Va. 4 July 1826, The Forest, Charles City Co., Va. 1 Jan. 1772 Mrs. Martha Wayles Skelton, Charles City Co. 19 Oct. 1748-Monticello 6 Sept. 1782, widow of Bathurst Skelton

2. Peter Jefferson, prob. Osborne's, Chesterfield Co., Va. 29 Feb. 1707/8-Shadwell 17 Aug. 1757, Goochland Co. (bond 3 Oct.) 1739

3. Jane Randolph, bp. St. Paul's Church, Shadwell, London 20 Feb. 1720-Monticello 31 Mar. 1776

4. Thomas Jefferson, Jr., prob. Henrico Co., Va. c. 1679-prob. Osborne's 15 Feb. 1730/1, Henrico Co. 20 Nov. 1697

5. Mary Field, Henrico Co. 3 Feb. 1679/80-prob. Henrico Co. 13 Aug. 1715

6. Isham Randolph, Turkey Island, Henrico Co. Jan. 1685-Dungeness, Goochland Co. Nov. 1742, White Chapel, London c. 1718

7. Jane Rogers, c. 1695-1700-Dungeness between 5 Dec. 1760 & 21 July 1761

8. Thomas Jefferson, d. Henrico Co. ante 7 Dec. 1697, m. c. 1678/9

9. Mary (sometimes called Martha) Branch, m. (2) Joseph Mattox

10. Peter Field of Charles City, Henrico & New Kent Cos., Va. c. 1647-St. Peter's Parish, New Kent Co. 24 July 1707, "Chickahominy,"

Va. 21 Oct. 1678

11. Judith Soane, prob. Litlington, Sussex c. 1646-prob. Henrico Co. c. 1703, widow of Henry Randolph, Jr.

12. William Randolph, prob. Moreton Morell, Warwickshire c. 1648-Turkey Island, Henrico Co., Va. 21 Apr. 1711, ante 1678

13. Mary Isham, c. 1660-post 1713/4

14. Charles Rogers, d. post 1704, m. c. 1694

15. Jane Lilburne of Newcastle-upon-Tyne, Durham, d. post 1724, m. (2) William or John Linton

16-17. ---

18. Christopher Branch, Jr., Henrico Co. c. 1627-prob. Charles City Co. c. 1665

19-21. ---

22. Henry Soane, bp. Brighton, Sussex 17 Nov. 1622-James City Co., Va. c. 1661/2, (lic. Lewes, Sussex) 17 Feb. 1642/3

23. Judith Fuller of Southover Church, Lewes-Va. post 1695

24. Richard Randolph, bp. Little Houghton, Northamptonshire 24 Feb. 1621/2-May 1678, of Moreton Morrell, Warwickshire

25. Elizabeth Ryland (Riland)

26. Henry Isham, prob. Pytchley, Northamptonshire c. 1628-prob. Bermuda Hundred, Henrico Co., Va. c. 1675, c. 1659

27. Katherine Banks of Canterbury, Kent c. 1630-Henrico Co., Va. between 10 Oct. & 1 Dec. 1686, widow of Joseph Royall

28-29. ---

30. William Lilburne, c. 1636-Newcastle-upon-Tyne 17 Jan. 1681/2, St. Nicholas Parish, Newcastle 21 Aug. 1662

31. Elizabeth Nicholson, will dated 1715 & proved 1721

32-35. ---

36. Christopher Branch, c. 1602-03-Henrico Co., Va. between 20 June 1678 & 20 Feb. 1681/2, St. Peter's, Westcheap, London (lic. 2) Sept. 1619

37. Mary Addie of Darton, Yorkshire

38-43. ---

44. (almost certainly) Henry Soane of Rottingdean, Sussex, d. between 6 Feb. & 16 Mar. 1632, Brighton, Sussex 5 Nov. 1621

45. (almost certainly) Elizabeth Worger, d. post 1632

46-47. ---

48. William Randolph, possibly bur. Moreton Morrell 1657, prob. Courteenhall or Cotton End, Northamptonshire 30 Mar. 1619

49. Dorothy Lane, bp. Courteenhall 4 Sept. 1589, widow of Thomas West

50. John Ryland (Riland)

51. ---

52. William Isham, bp. Braunston, Northamptonshire 20 Mar. 1587/8, Toddington, Bedfordshire 15 Aug. 1625

53. Mary Brett, c. 1604-ante 22 Dec. 1682

54-59. ---

60. George Lilburne of Sunderland-by-the-Sea, Durham, c. 1585-post 1681, prob. Whitburn or Stockton, Durham 13 Apr. 1629

61. Eleanor Hicks, bur. 23 Oct. 1677, widow of Ralph Lambert

62. Christopher Nicholson, bp. Hawkshead Hall, Lancashire 30 Nov. 1602-Newcastle 29 Sept. 1670, merchant & alderman of Newcastle

63. Jane Butler, bp. St. Nicholas, Newcastle 8 Oct. 1611

64-71. ---

72. Lionel Branch, bp. Abingdon, Berkshire 18 Aug. 1566-c. 1605, St. Martin, Ludgate, London 8 July 1596

73. Valentia Sparkes

74. Francis Addie of Darton, Yorkshire

75-95. ---

96. Robert Randolph of Hams (Hamsey, near Lewes), Sussex

97. ---

98. Richard Lane of Courteenhall, Northamptonshire

99. Elizabeth Vincent of Harpole, Northamptonshire

100-103. ---

104. Sir Euseby Isham, 26 Feb. 1552/3-Pytchley, Northamptonshire 11 June 1626, knighted by King James I 11 May 1603

105. Anne Borlase of Little Marlow, Buckinghamshire, d. prob. Pytchley Dec. 1627

106. William Brett, prob. London c. 1562-prob. Toddington, Bedfordshire between 4 June & 20 Sept. 1624, brother of Sir Edward Brett of Blendenhall, Bexley, Kent (whose 1682 will mentions the two daughters of his nephew Henry Isham, late of Va.)

107. Mary ---, d. post 1624

108-119. ---

120. John Lilburne of Thickley Punchardon, Durham

121. Isabel Wortley

122. John Hicks, rector of Whitburn, Durham, will dated 1631, Lamesley, Durham 20 Feb. 1603/4

123. Alice Blaikston

124. Alan Nicholson, bur. Hawkshead Hall, Lancashire 7 Oct. 1616, c. 1595

125. Susan Hechstetter of Keswick, Cumberland, bur. Hawkshead Hall 4 Mar. 1642 (daughter of Daniel & Radigunda Hechstetter, the former from Augsburg, Germany, in Keswick by 1572)

126. John Butler, merchant of Newcastle-upon-Tyne, d. 1643, m. St. Nicholas, Newcastle 14 Nov. 1609

127. Jane Huntley

* * *

4. JAMES MADISON, JR.

1. JAMES MADISON, JR., Port Conway, King George Co., Virginia 5 Mar. 1750/1-Montpelier, Orange Co., Va. 28 June 1836, "Harewood" near Charlestown, Jefferson Co., Va. 15 Sept. 1794 Mrs. Dorothea (Dolly) Payne Todd, Guilford Co., North Carolina 20 May 1768-Washington, D. C. 12 July 1849, widow of John Todd, Jr.

2. James Madison, prob. Orange Co., Va. 27 Mar. 1723-Montpelier 27 Feb. 1801, 13 Sept. 1749

3. Eleanor Rose "Nelly" Conway, Caroline Co., Va. 9 Jan. 1731-Montpelier 11 Feb. 1829

4. Ambrose Madison, d. prob. Spotsylvania Co., Va. 27 Aug. 1732, m. prob. Orange Co., Va. 24 Aug. 1721

5. Frances Taylor, c. 1700-25 Nov. 1761

6. Francis Conway, Richmond Co., Va. 15 Sept. 1696-will proved Caroline Co. 12 Apr. 1733, 21 Oct. 1717

7. Rebecca Catlett, prob. Essex Co., Va. c. 1700-between 6 Nov. 1759 & 6 Mar. 1760, m. (2) John Moore

8. John Madison, Jr. of St. Stephen's Parish, King & Queen Co., Va., fl. 1683-1717, Sheriff of King & Queen Co. 1704

9. Isabella, usually called Todd but not a daughter of Capt. Thomas Todd & Anne Gorsuch, d. post 1706

10. James Taylor, Jr., prob. King & Queen Co. 14 Mar. 1674/5-prob. Orange Co. 23 June 1729, prob. New Kent or King & Queen Co. 23 Feb. 1699

11. Martha Thompson, c. 1679-c. 1762

12. Edwin Conway, Jr., c. 1653-54-Richmond Co., Va. between 19 Mar. & 7 Sept. 1698, Richmond Co. 21 May 1695

13. Elizabeth Thornton, Richmond Co. 3 Jan. 1674-will proved King George Co., Va. 2 Dec. 1732, m. (2) Jonathan Gibson

14. John Catlett, Jr., prob. Rappahannock Co., Va. ante 1670-Essex Co. between 18 Nov. 1724 & 19 Jan. 1724/5

15. (said to be) Elizabeth Gaines

16. John Madison of St. Stephens Parish, New Kent Co., ship carpenter, d. ante 16 Apr. 1683

17-19. ---

20. James Taylor, said to be from Carlisle, England, d. King & Queen Co. 30 Apr. 1698

21. Frances ---, d. prob. New Kent Co. 23 Sept. 1680

22. (almost certainly) Roger Thompson of New Kent Co., living 1704

23. ---

24. Edwin Conway, prob. Worcestershire c. 1610-Lancaster Co., Va. c. 1675, c. 1640

25. Martha Eltonhead of Eltonhead, Lancashire, d. prob. Va. post 1652

26. Francis Thornton, prob. Gloucester Co., Va. 5 Nov. 1651-prob. King George Co. c. 1726, Richmond Co. 13 Apr. 1674

27. Alice Savage, prob. d. ante 1701

28. John Catlett, prob. Sittingbourne, Kent c. 1629 (or ante)-c. 1670 (allegedly killed by Indians at a fort that later became Fort Royal), of Rappahannock Co., prob. Rappahannock Co. ante 5 Jan. 1663/4

29. Elizabeth Underwood, c. 1632-will proved Rappahannock Co. 7 Mar. 1673, widow of Dr. James Taylor & Francis Slaughter, Sr., m. (4) Rev. Amory Butler

30. (said to be) Daniel Gaines, d. Rappahannock Co. between 18 Aug. 1682 & 1 Oct. 1684 (his will mentions no daughter Elizabeth)

31. (said to be) Margaret ---, d. post 1686, m. (2) John Daingerfield

32-49. ---

50. Richard Eltonhead of Eltonhead, Lancashire, c. 1582-post 1664

51. Ann Sutton of Rushton Spencer, Staffordshire

52. William Thornton of Gloucester & Stafford Cos., d. post 1708

53. ---

54. Anthony Savage of Gloucester & Richmond Cos., will proved Richmond Co. 5 June 1695

55-57. ---

58. --- Underwood, d. c. 1647

59. Margaret ---, d. prob. Rappahannock Co. 1663-69, m. (2) John Upton, (3) Thomas Lucas

60-99. ---

100. William Eltonhead of Eltonhead, Lancashire

101. Ann Bowers of Brierly, Yorkshire

102. Edward Sutton of Rushton Spencer, Staffordshire

103-107. ---

108. (possibly) Anthony Savage of Broadway, Worcestershire, 2nd son of Francis Savage of Elmley Castle (will proved 1558) & Anne Sheldon of Beoley Court, & father of a 4th son Anthony & grandfather of an Anthony bp. 1623 (son of Charles Savage of Tetbury, Gloucestershire & Elizabeth Abington) who might be 54 above

109. (possibly) Elizabeth Hall of Idlecott, Warwickshire

110-127. ---

* * *

5. JAMES MONROE

1. JAMES MONROE, Westmoreland Co., Virginia 28 Apr. 1758-New York, New York 4 July 1831, New York City 16 Feb. 1786 Elizabeth Kortright, New York City 30 June 1768-Oak Hill, Loudoun Co., Va. 23 Sept. 1830

2. Spence Monroe, c. 1727-will dated 1774, of Westmoreland Co., Va., c. 1752

3. Elizabeth Jones, b. prob. King George Co., Va.

4. Andrew Monroe, d. 1735, of Westmoreland Co.

5. Christian Tyler, widow of Spence Monroe, 1st cousin of Andrew; she m. (3) Richard Fry

6. James Jones, will proved King George Co., Va. 1 June 1744
7. Hester ---
8. William Monroe, Westmoreland Co. c. 1666-will dated 1737, c. 1689
9. Margaret Bowcock
10. Charles Tyler, perhaps Maryland to Westmoreland Co. by 1690-ante 1723
11. Jane ---, d. prob. ante 1737/8, m. (2) William Woffendall
12-15. ---
16. Andrew Monroe, Scotland to St. Mary's Co., Md. by 1642, of Westmoreland Co., Va. by 1650, d. 1668, c. 1652
17. Elizabeth --- (sometimes called Alexander), d. post 1686/7, m. (2) George Horner, m. (3) Edward Mountjoy
18. Thomas Bowcock of Westmoreland Co.
19. Jane ---, m. (2) Thomas White
20-127. ---

* * *

7. ANDREW JACKSON, JR.

1. ANDREW JACKSON, JR., Waxhaws, South Carolina 15 March 1767-Nashville, Tennessee 8 June 1845, Natchez, Mississippi Aug. 1791 (& Nashville 17 Jan. 1794) Rachel Donelson, Pittsylvania Co., Virginia 15 June 1767-The Hermitage, near Nashville 22 Dec. 1828, divorced wife of Lewis Robards
2. Andrew Jackson, Carrickfergus, Antrim, Ireland to Waxhaws, S. C. by 1760-1, d. Waxhaws c. 1 Mar. 1767, Carrickfergus ante 1760
3. Elizabeth Hutchinson of Carrickfergus, d. Charleston, S. C. Nov. 1781
4. Hugh Jackson of Carrickfergus, d. c. 1782
5. ---
6. --- Hutchinson of Carrickfergus
7. (said to be) --- Leslie
8. Thomas Jackson of Ballyregan in Dundonald, Down, Ireland, living 1761
9-127. ---

* * *

8. MARTIN VAN BUREN

1. MARTIN VAN BUREN, Kinderhook, New York 5 Dec. 1782-Kinderhook 24 July 1862, Catskill, N. Y. 21 Feb. 1807 Hannah Hoes (his first cousin once removed), Kinderhook 8 Mar. 1783-Albany, N. Y. 5 Feb. 1819
2. Abraham Van Buren, bp. Albany 27 Feb. 1737-Kinderhook 8 Apr. 1817, c. 1776
3. Maria Hoes, Claverack, N. Y. 16 Jan. 1747/8-Kinderhook 16 Feb. 1817, widow of Johannes Van Alen
4. Martin Van Buren, bp. Albany 28 Sept. 1701, m. 7 Nov. 1729
5. Dirkje Van Alstyne, bp. 30 Apr. 1710
6. Johannes Dircksen Hoes, bp. Albany 12 May 1700, m. Albany by license dated 20 Apr. 1723
7. Jannetje Laurense Van Schaick, bp. Albany 5 Apr. 1707
8. Pieter Martense [Van Buren], c. 1670-prob. ante 1743, Albany 15 Jan. 1693
9. Adriaantje Barentse [Meynders]
10. Abraham Janse Van Alstyne of Kinderhook, living 1742, Albany 17 Jan. 1694
11. Marritje Teuwisse (Mateuisse) Van Deusen, b. c. 1674
12. Dirk Janse Hoes of Kinderhook, c. 1675-between 1 June & 5 Aug. 1732, c. 1697

13. Elizabeth Luycassen Wyngaart
14. Laurens Van Schaick, m. Albany 19 Dec. 1699
15. Jannetje Oothout
16. Marten Cornelisz [Van Buren], Houton, Netherlands c. 1638-9-13 Nov. 1703, c. 1662
17. Marritje Quackenbush, b. prob. Oestgeest near Leyden, Netherlands c. 1646
18. Barent Meynders, d. Albany c. 1679
19. Eytie ---
20. Jan Martense Van Alstyne, Meppel, province of Drenthe, Netherlands c. 1623-Kinderhook c. 1698
21. Dircken Hermanse, c. 1623-c. 1682
22. Teuwis (Matheeus or Matthew) Abrahamse Van Deusen of Albany & Claverack, b. c. 1631, m. c. 1653
23. Helena Robberts
24. Jan Tyssen Hoes, c. 1630-Kinderhook 31 May 1695
25. Christyntje Van Hoesen
26. Luykas Gerritsen Wyngaart
27. Anna Janse Van Hoesen
28. Claas Gerritse Van Schaick of Rensselaerswyck, living 1677
29. (Jannetje?) ---
30. Jan Janse Oothout, d. Greenbush, N. Y. c. 1695/6
31. Hendrickje Cornelisse van Ness
32. Cornelis Maessen [Van Buren], from Buurmalsem, Gelderland, d. Papsknee near Greenbush, N. Y. c. 1648, c. 1635-6
33. Catalyntje Martense, d. Papsknee near Greenbush c. 1648
34. (prob.) Pieter Quackenbush (Quackenbosch), also known as Pieter Bont, fl. Albany 1650s-80s
35. (prob.) Marritje ---
36-43. ---
44. Abraham Pietersz [Van Deusen, Van Deursen], bp. Haarlem, Netherlands 3 Sept. 1599, Haarlem int. 25 Nov. 1629
45. Tryntje Melchiors, b. Groningen, Netherlands
46-49. ---
50, 54. Jan Franssen Van Hoesen of Albany, d. c. 1703
51, 55. Volkertje Jurrianse
52-53, 56-61. ---
62. Cornelis Hendrickse van Ness of Rensselaerswyck, d. post 1684, prob. Sianen, Netherlands shortly before 31 July 1625
63. Marijen Hendricks van den Burchgraeff, d. ante 1664
64-87. ---
88. Pieter Jans [Van Duersen in Brabant], b. Doersen, Netherlands, Haarlem int. 15 Jan. 1591
89. Pauline Vincke, b. Rensselaer, Netherlands
90-125. ---
126. Hendrick Adriaensz van den Burchgraeff, d. ante 1635
127. Annetje Jans of Scherperswijk near Leksmond, living 1635

* * *

9. WILLIAM HENRY HARRISON and [23] BENJAMIN HARRISON

1. BENJAMIN HARRISON, North Bend, Ohio 20 Aug. 1833-Indianapolis, Indiana 13 Mar. 1901, (1) Oxford, Ohio 20 Oct. 1853 Caroline Lavinia Scott, Oxford 1 Oct. 1832-The White House, Washington, D. C. 25 Oct. 1892, (2) New York, New York 6 Apr. 1896 Mrs. Mary Scott Lord Dimmick (niece of his first wife), Honesdale, Pennsylvania 30 Apr. 1858-New York City 5 Jan. 1948, widow of Walter Erskine Dimmick
2. John Scott Harrison, Vincennes, Ind. 4 Oct. 1804-Point Farm, near North Bend 25 May 1878, 12 Aug. 1831
3. Elizabeth Ramsey Irwin, Mercersburg, Pa. 18 July 1810-North Bend 15 Aug. 1850

4. WILLIAM HENRY HARRISON, Berkeley (plantation), Charles City Co., Virginia 9 Feb. 1773-The White House, Washington, D. C. 4 Apr. 1841, North Bend, Ohio 22 Nov. 1795

5. Anna Tuthill Symmes, Flatbrook, New Jersey 25 July 1775-North Bend 25 Feb. 1864

6. Archibald Irwin, III, Mercersburg 13 Feb. 1772-Mercersburg 3 Mar. 1840, Franklin Co., Pa. 11 Oct. 1798

7. Mary Ramsey, Franklin Co. 30 Mar. 1781-Mercersburg 10 Feb. 1813

8. Benjamin Harrison, V, Governor of Virginia, signer of the Declaration of Independence, Berkeley, Charles City Co., c. Apr. 1726-Berkeley 24 Apr. 1791, c. 1748

9. Elizabeth Bassett, Eltham, New Kent Co., Va. 13 Dec. 1730-Berkeley c. 1792

10. John Cleves Symmes, Congressman, Ohio pioneer, Southold, L. I., N. Y. 21 July 1742-Cincinnati, Ohio 26 Feb. 1814, 30 Oct. 1760

11. Anna Tuthill, Oct. 1741-25 July 1776

12. Archibald Irwin, Jr., prob. Ireland c. 1734-Mercersburg, Pa. 23 Jan. 1798, c. 1757

13. Jane McDowell, Franklin Co., Pa. 19 Apr. 1736-6 Aug. 1814

14. James Ramsey, Jr., prob. York Co., Pa. 8 June 1751-Ligonier, Pa. 17 Mar. 1810, 15 Feb. 1776

15. Elizabeth Porter, b. 6 Nov. 1754, m. (2) Gen. Charles Campbell

16. Benjamin Harrison, IV, c. 1695-Berkeley 12 July 1745, c. 1722

17. Anne Carter, prob. Corotoman, Lancaster Co., Va. c. 1702-prob. Berkeley between 17 Oct. 1743 & Aug. 1745

18. William Bassett, IV, prob. Eltham, New Kent Co., Va. 8 July 1709-ante 1752, 29 Jan. 1729

19. Elizabeth Churchill, c. 1710-Eltham 16 Apr. 1779, m. (2) William Dawson, President of the College of William and Mary

20. Rev. Timothy Symmes, Jr., Harvard graduate of 1733, Scituate, Massachusetts 27 May 1714-Ipswich, Mass. 6 Apr. 1756, Aquebogue, L. I., N. Y. c. 1740

21. Mary Cleves, d. Aquebogue c. 1746

22. Henry Tuthill, III, Southold, L. I. ante Dec. 1715-prob. Aquebogue 17 Sept. 1793, 16 Mar. 1738

23. Phoebe Horton, c. 1722-3 Nov. 1793

24. Archibald Irwin of Peters, Cumberland Co., Pa. (later Mercersburg, Franklin Co.)

25. ---

26. William McDowell of Chester & Franklin Cos., Pa., c. 1680-c. 1759, c. 1715

27. Mary ---, d. prob. Peters, Pa. 18 Feb. 1782

28. James Ramsey, c. 1725 or Glasgow, Scotland 20 Sept. 1722-York Co., Pa. 16 Apr. 1757, said to be 2 Oct. 1746

29. (said to be) Mary Porter

30. (said to be) William Porter

31. (said to be) Sarah (?) Percival

32. Benjamin Harrison, III, c. 1673-Berkeley 10 Apr. 1710

33. Elizabeth Burwell, c. 1678-prob. Berkeley 30 Dec. 1734

34. Robert "King" Carter, Colonial official & landowner, Lancaster Co., Va. c. 1663-Corotoman 4 Aug. 1732, c. 1701

35. Elizabeth Landon, Credenhill, Herefordshire, England c. 1684-Williamsburg, Va. 3 July 1719, widow of Richard Willis

36. William Bassett, III, New Kent Co., Va. c. 1671-Eltham 11 Oct. 1723, prob. Carter's Creek, Gloucester Co. 23 Nov. 1693

37. Joanna Burwell, c. 1675-prob. Eltham 7 Oct. 1727

38. William Churchill, bp. North Aston, Oxfordshire, England 2 Dec. 1649-prob. Bushy Park, Middlesex Co., Va. between 18 Nov. 1710 & 10 Mar. 1710/1, prob. Rosegill, Middlesex Co. 5 Oct. 1703

39. Elizabeth Armistead, d. prob. Bushy Park 16 Nov. 1716, widow

of Ralph Wormeley, Secretary of the Colony of Virginia

40. Timothy Symmes, Charlestown, Mass. c. 1683-Scituate, Mass. c. 1765, Scituate 31 July 1710

41. Elizabeth Collamore, Scituate 11 Dec. 1679-Scituate 18 Jan. 1758, widow of Jeremiah Rose

42. John Cleves (prob. Jr.) of Southold & Aquebogue, L. I., c. 1686-Southold 25 May 1750, c. 1717

43. (prob.) Mary ---, c. 1697-Southold 16 Jan. 1784

44. Henry Tuthill, Jr., Southold c. 1690-Southold 1 Sept. 1775

45. Hannah (Crouch?), c. 1693-Southold 1 Dec. 1715

46. Caleb Horton, Southold 22 Dec. 1687-Roxbury (now Chester), N. J. 6 Aug. 1772, Southold 10 Dec. 1714

47. Phebe Terry, Southold c. 1698-Roxbury, N. J. 24 Dec. 1776

48-55. ---

56. (possibly) George Ramsey of Glasgow

57. (possibly) Isabel Littlejohn

58-63. ---

64. Benjamin Harrison, Jr., Southwark, Surry Co., Va. 20 Sept. 1645-Wakefield, Surry Co. 30 Jan. 1712/3

65. Hannah ---, 13 Feb. 1651/2-Surry Co. 16 Feb. 1698/9

66. Lewis Burwell, Jr., prob. Gloucester Co., Va. c. 1647-prob. Carter's Creek, Gloucester Co. 19 Dec. 1710

67. Abigail Smith, prob. Colchester, Essex, England 11 Mar. 1656-prob. Gloucester Co., Va. 12 Nov. 1692

68. John Carter, c. 1613-Corotoman 10 June 1669, c. 1662 (his fourth wife)

69. Sarah Ludlow, prob. Wiltshire, England c. 1635-prob. Corotoman c. 1668

70. Thomas Landon of Credenhill, Herefordshire & Middlesex Co., Va., d. between 9 Nov. 1700 & 3 Feb. 1700/1

71. Mary ---

72. William Bassett, Jr., prob. Newport, Isle of Wight to Blissland, New Kent Co., Va., d. between 28 Aug. 1671 & 4 Jan. 1671/2, c. 1670

73. Bridget Cary, d. prob. Warwick Co., Va. c. 1652

74. same as 66

75. same as 67

76. John Churchill of North Aston, Oxfordshire, b. 1591, m. 1626

77. Dorothy ---

78. John Armistead, prob. Elizabeth City Co., Va., c. 1640-prob. Gloucester Co. post 1688

79. Judith ---

80. William Symmes, bp. Dunstable, Bedfordshire, England 10 Jan. 1626/7-Charlestown, Mass. 22 Sept. 1691, c. 1675

81. Mary Chickering, Dedham, Mass. Apr. 1648-Weymouth, Mass. 12 Mar. 1720/1, m. (2) Rev. Samuel Torrey

82. Anthony Collamore, prob. Northam, Devon, England-Scituate, Mass. 16 Dec. 1693, Scituate 14 June 1666

83. Sarah Chittenden, Scituate 25 Feb. 1646/7-Scituate 25 Oct. 1703

84. (prob.) John Cleves, d. Southold 19 Jan. 1707

85. (possibly) Eliza ---, c. 1665-Southold 1 Feb. 1740

86-87. ---

88. Henry Tuthill, Southold 1 May 1665-Southold 4 Jan. 1750, ante 1690

89. Bethia Horton, Southold c. 1674-Southold 16 Mar. 1744

90-91. ---

92. Barnabas Horton, Cutchogue, L. I., N. Y. 23 Sept. 1666-Southold Dec. 1696, c. 1686

93. Sarah Wines, Southold c. 1668-70-Southold 16 Apr. 1733, m. (2) Eleazer Luce

94. Nathaniel Terry, b. Southold Jan. 1656, m. Cutchogue 31 [sic] Nov. 1682

95. Mary Horton, b. Cutchogue

96-127. ---

128. Benjamin Harrison, poss. bp. St. Giles, Northamptonshire, England Dec. 1594-prob. Wakefield, Surry Co., Va. or Jamestown between 1643 & 1649

129. Mary ---, d. between 1 Mar. 1687/8 & 29 May 1688, m. (2) Benjamin Sidway

130-131. ---

132. Lewis Burwell, bp. Ampthill, Bedfordshire 5 Mar. 1621-prob. Carter's Creek, Gloucester Co., Va. 18 Nov. 1653, c. 1646

133. Lucy Higginson, c. 1626-Va. 26 Nov. 1675, m. (2) William Bernard, (3) Philip Ludwell, Virginia councilor & Governor of the Carolinas

134. Anthony Smith of Colchester, Essex, d. between 29 Aug. 1662 & 13 May 1667, c. 1651

135. Martha Bacon of Burgate, Suffolk, half-sister of Acting Governor Nathaniel Bacon of Virginia

136. (possibly) John Carter, citizen & vintner of London, c. 1574-between 23 Apr. & 6 May 1630

137. (possibly) Bridget Benion, d. ante 1630 (bur. Christchurch, Newgate St., London)

138. Gabriel Ludlow, bp. Dinton, Wiltshire 10 Feb. 1587-between 1639 & 1646

139. Phyllis ---, d. between 12 Sept. & 18 Dec. 1657

140. Sylvanus Landon of Credenhill, Herefordshire, d. between 30 July & 15 Aug. 1681

141. Anne ---

142-143. ---

144. William Bassett, yeoman, bur. Newport, Isle of Wight 4 Dec. 1646

145. Anne ---, living at Newport 1671, m. (2) --- Dickeson

146. Miles Cary, bp. All Saints Church, Bristol, England 30 Jan. 1622, of Windmill Point, Warwick Co., Va., d. Va. 10 June 1667

147. Anne Taylor of Warwick Co.

148. same as 132

149. same as 133

150. same as 134

151. same as 135

152. Henry Churchill of North Aston, Oxfordshire, 1565-1628, m. 1589

153. Bridget ---, 1565-1625

154-155. ---

156. William Armistead, bp. All Saints Church, Kirkdeighton, Yorkshire 3 Aug. 1610, of Elizabeth City & Gloucester Cos., Va., d. ante 1666, Giggleswick, Yorkshire, England 1632

157. Ann Ellis

158-159. ---

160. Rev. Zachariah Symmes (1599-1670/1), St. George's, Canterbury to Charlestown, Mass., graduate of Emmanuel College, Cambridge, in 1620, = 1622

161. Sarah Baker (d. 1676), Southwark, Surrey to Charlestown

162. Francis Chickering (d. 1658), Ringsfield, Suffolk to Dedham, Mass.

163. Anne Fiske (1610-1649), South Eltham, Suffolk to Dedham

164. (prob.) John Collamore (1608-prob. 1657), Northam, Devon, = 1637

165. (prob.) Mary Nicholl

166. Isaac Chittenden (c. 1625-1676), Scituate, Mass., = 1646

167. Martha Vinal (b. c. 1628)

168-175. ---

176. John Tuthill (1635-1717), Southold, L. I., = 1657

177. Deliverance King (1641-1688/9), Salem, Mass. to Southold

178. Jonathan Horton (c. 1648-1707, brother of Caleb Horton, 184

below), Southold, = c. 1672
179. Bethia Wells (c. 1655-1733)
180-183. ---
184. Caleb Horton (c. 1640-1702, brother of Jonathan Horton, 178 above), Southold & Cutchogue, L. I., = 1665
185. Abigail Hallock (d. 1697)
186. Barnabas Wines, Jr. (c. 1636-c. 1711), Watertown, Mass. to Southold
187. Mary --- (c. 1638-1727)
188. Richard Terry (1618-1676), England to New Haven to Southold, L. I.
189. Abigail --- (d. post 1676)
190. same as 184 above
191. same as 185 above
192-255. ---
256. (possibly) Thomas Harrison of Gobion's Manor, Northamptonshire, d. ante 1616, c. 1581
257. (possibly) Elizabeth Bernard of Abington, Northamptonshire, m. (2) Henry Travel of Coventry, Warwickshire; she was an aunt of the immigrant double first cousins Richard Bernard of Purton, Gloucester Co., Va. & William Bernard of Nansemond & Isle of Wight Cos., Va., & a great-great-aunt of Sir Francis Bernard, 1st Bt., colonial governor of Massachusetts & New Jersey
258-263. ---
264. Edward Burwell, prob. bp. Toddington, Bedfordshire 24 Aug. 1579-between 18 Oct. & 9 Nov. 1626, of Houghton Park, Ampthill, & Harlington, Bedfordshire
265. Dorothy Bedell of Great Catworth, Huntingdonshire, d. post 1635/6, sometime of Va., m. (2) Roger Wingate, treasurer of the Virginia Colony, 1639-41
266. Robert Higginson of Berkeswell, Warwickshire, London, & Va., d. Va. Aug. 1649, c. 1625
267. Joanna Tokesy
268-269. ---
270. Rev. James Bacon, rector of Burgate, Suffolk, d. 9 Nov. 1649, great-nephew of Sir Nicholas Bacon (1509-1579), Elizabethan statesman, & first cousin once removed of Francis Bacon, 1st Viscount St. Albans (1561-1626), lord chancellor, philosopher & scientist
271. Martha Woodward of Upton, Buckinghamshire, m. (2) Rev. Robert Pecke of Hingham, Norfolk
272. (possibly) Thomas Carter of Watford & Aldenham, Hertfordshire, b. c. 1528
273-275. ---
276. Thomas Ludlow, prob. Hill Deverill, Wiltshire c. 1555-bur. Dinton, Wilts. 25 Nov. 1607, c. 1582
277. Jane Pyle or Pile of Bubton, Wilts., d. post 1607
278-279. ---
280. (prob.) John Landon, yeoman
281-291. ---
292. John Cary, draper, bp. St. Nicholas, Bristol, England 10 Apr. 1583-bur. All Saints Church, Bristol 13 Feb. 1661
293. Alice Hobson of Bristol
294. Thomas Taylor, mariner, of Elizabeth City & Warwick Cos., Va., fl. 1626-43
295. ---
296-303. same as 264-271
304. Richard Churchill of North Aston, Oxfordshire, 1524-1592
305-311. ---
312. Anthony Armistead of Kirkdeighton, Yorkshire, b. c. 1587, mar. lic. 1608
313. Frances Thompson
314-319. ---

* * *

10. JOHN TYLER

1. JOHN TYLER (IV), Greenway, Charles City Co., Virginia 29 Mar. 1790-Richmond, Va. 18 Jan. 1862, (1) Cedar Grove, New Kent Co., Va. 29 Mar. 1813 Letitia Christian, Cedar Grove 12 Nov. 1790-The White House, Washington, D. C. 10 Sept. 1842, (2) New York City 26 June 1844 Julia Gardiner, Gardiner's Island, N. Y. 4 May 1820-Richmond, Va. 10 July 1889

2. John Tyler (III), Governor of Virginia, Yarmouth, Va. 28 Feb. 1747-Greenway 6 Jan. 1813, c. 1776

3. Mary Marot Armistead, prob. York Co., Va. c. 1761-Greenway 5 Apr. 1797

4. John Tyler, Jr., prob. Williamsburg, Va. c. 1710-15-prob. Williamsburg between 24 July & 20 Sept. 1773

5. Anne Contesse

6. Robert Booth Armistead, prob. York Co. 1737 or earlier-prob. York Co. ante 21 July 1766, c. 1760

7. Anne Shields, b. Williamsburg (Bruton Parish) 31 July 1742, m. (2) Frederick Bryan, Jr.

8. John Tyler, prob. York Co. c. 1685-prob. Williamsburg c. 1727

9. Elizabeth Jarrett

10. Dr. Louis Contesse, French Huguenot physician, d. Williamsburg 11 Sept. 1729

11. Mary Morris

12. Ellyson Armistead, prob. York Co.-will proved York Co. 19 Dec. 1757

13. ---

14. James Shields, Jr., prob. James City Co. c. 1700-York Co. c. 1750

15. Anne Marot, widow of James Inglis, m. (3) Henry Wetherburn

16. Henry Tyler, Jr., prob. York Co. c. 1660-prob. Williamsburg between 2 July & 15 Dec. 1729, c. 1683

17. Elizabeth Chiles, d. Williamsburg 19 Jan. 1702/3

18. John Jarrett, d. prob. 1697-1704, "nephew" of William Sherwood, lawyer, of Jamestown, d. 1697

19. Joanna Lowe, housekeeper at Westover (plantation of William Byrd II)

20-23. ---

24. Robert Armistead of York & Elizabeth City Cos., Va., will proved Elizabeth City Co. 19 May 1742

25. --- Booth, b. prob. York Co. c. 1694

26-27. ---

28. James Shields, innkeeper, d. Williamsburg 2 June 1727

29. Hannah ---

30. Jean Marot, French Huguenot (to Va. 1700), innkeeper & secretary of William Byrd II, c. 1677-Williamsburg between 31 Aug. & 17 Dec. 1717

31. Anne ---, d. post 1717

32. Henry Tyler, possibly Shropshire, England c. 1604-York Co., Va. 13 Apr. 1672, c. shortly post 1655

33. Ann ---, d. York Co. 2 Apr. 1679, widow of John Orchard, m. (3) Martin Gardner

34. Walter Chiles, Jr., d. Jamestown, Va. ante 25 Nov. 1671

35. Mary Page

36-37. ---

38. Michael Lowe

39-47. ---

48. Anthony Armistead of Elizabeth City Co., d. ante 26 Oct. 1726

49. Hannah Ellyson, d. Elizabeth City Co. between 26 Oct. 1726 &

19 Oct. 1728

50. Robert Booth, Jr., d. York Co. c. 1695, m. c. 1693

51. Ann Bray, widow of Peter Temple, Jr. (d. 1692), m. (3) Munro Inglis

52-67. ---

68. Walter Chiles, almost certainly bp. St. Mary Redcliffe, Bristol, England 20 Mar. 1608/9-prob. Jamestown c. 1653

69. Elizabeth ---

70. John Page, prob. Belfont, Middlesex c. 1626-Williamsburg 23 Jan. 1691/2

71. Alice Lukin, England c. 1625-Williamsburg 22 June 1698

72-95. ---

96. William Armistead, bp. All Saints Church, Kirkdeighton, Yorkshire 3 Aug. 1610, of Elizabeth City & Gloucester Cos., Va., d. ante 1666, m. Giggleswick, Yorkshire 1632

97. Ann Ellis

98. Dr. Robert Ellyson of St. Mary's Co., Md. & James City Co., Va., d. ante 1688

99. ---

100. Robert Booth of York Co., d. c. 1657

101. Frances ---, b. c. 1609

102. James Bray of James City & York Cos., d. Williamsburg 24 Oct. 1691

103. Angelica ---

104-127. ---

* * *

11. JAMES KNOX POLK

1. JAMES KNOX POLK, Mecklenburg Co., North Carolina 2 Nov. 1795-Nashville, Tennessee 15 June 1849, Murfreesboro, Tennessee 1 Jan. 1824 Sarah Childress, near Murphreesboro 4 Sept. 1803-Nashville 14 Aug. 1891

2. Samuel Polk, prob. Tryon Co., N. C. 5 July 1772-Columbia, Tenn. 5 Nov. 1827, Hopewell, N. C. 25 Dec. 1794

3. Jane Knox, sometimes called Jean Gracy Knox, prob. Iredell Co., N. C. 13 Nov. 1776-Columbia, Tenn. 11 Jan. 1852

4. Ezekiel Polk, Cumberland Co., Pennsylvania (near present Carlisle) 7 Dec. 1747-near Bolivar, Tenn. 31 Aug. 1824, Mecklenburg Co., N. C. c. 1769

5. Mary Wilson, d. near Pineville, N. C. 1791

6. James Knox, Rowan Co., N. C. c. 1752-Hopewell 10 Oct. 1794, bond Rowan Co. 4 Nov. 1772

7. Lydia Gillespie

8. William Polk, Jr., prob. "White Hall" (on the eastern shore of) Maryland c. 1700-N. C. "west of the Yadkin" c. 1753

9. Margaret Taylor

10. Samuel Wilson, c. 1710-Mecklenburg Co., N. C. 13 Mar. 1778

11. Mary Winslow

12. John Knox, Scotland c. 1708-Rowan Co., N. C. 12 Oct. 1758

13. Jean Gracy, c. 1708-Rowan Co., N. C. 18 Sept. 1772

14. Thomas Gillespie, Cecil Co., Md. or New London, Pa. c. 1719-Rowan Co., N. C. will dated 15 Nov. 1796, c. 1740

15. Naomi ---, d. post 15 Nov. 1796

16. William Polk, prob. Co. Donegal, Ireland c. 1664-Md. c. 1739 (will proved 24 Feb. 1739/40)

17. Mrs. Nancy Knox Owens, widow

18-21. ---

22. Benjamin Winslow, fl. N. C. 1752-8

23-25. ---

26. --- Gracy

27. Jean Sinclair

28-31. ---

32. Robert Pollock or Polk, from Co. Donegal to the eastern shore of Md., d. 1699-1704

33. Magdalen Tasker, who inherited Moneen, an estate in the Barony of Rafo, parish of Lyford, Donegal, will dated 7 Apr. 1726 (filed in Somerset Co., Md.)

34-127. ---

* * *

12. ZACHARY TAYLOR

1. ZACHARY TAYLOR, Montebello, Orange Co., Virginia 24 Nov. 1784-The White House, Washington, D. C. 9 July 1850, Jefferson Co., Kentucky 21 June 1810 Margaret Mackall Smith, Calvert Co., Maryland 21 Sept. 1788-East Pascagoula, Mississippi 14 Aug. 1852

2. Richard Taylor, Orange Co., Va. 3 Apr. 1744-near Lexington, Ky. 19 Jan. 1829, prob. Orange Co. 20 Aug. 1779

3. Sarah Dabney Strother, prob. Orange Co. 14 Dec. 1760-13 Dec. 1822

4. Zachary Taylor, 17 Apr. 1707-Orange Co. ante 29 Mar. 1768, prob. Northumberland Co., Va., ante 23 Feb. 1737/8

5. Elizabeth Lee of Northumberland Co., widow of Swan Jones

6. William Strother, prob. Hanover Co., Va. c. 1725-Woodford Co., Ky. c. 1808, ante 20 Feb. 1752

7. Sarah Bayly of Urbana, Middlesex Co., Va., c. 1720-Orange Co. between 23 Aug. & 22 Dec. 1774, widow of William Pannill of Culpeper Co., Va.

8. James Taylor, Jr., prob. King & Queen Co., Va. 14 Mar. 1674/5-prob. Orange Co. 23 June 1729, prob. New Kent or King & Queen Co. 23 Feb. 1699

9. Martha Thompson, c. 1679-prob. Orange Co. 19 Nov. 1762

10. Hancock Lee, prob. Northumberland Co. c. 1653-Ditchley, Northumberland Co. 25 May 1709, c. 1700

11. Sarah Allerton, prob. Northumberland Co. c. 1671-Ditchley 17 May 1731

12. Francis Strother, prob. Richmond Co., Va.-prob. St. Mark's Parish, Culpeper Co. between 17 Apr. 1751 & --- 1752

13. Susannah Dabney, d. post 1752

14-15. ---

16. James Taylor, said to be from Carlisle, England, d. King & Queen Co. 30 Apr. 1698

17. Frances ---, d. prob. New Kent Co. 23 Sept. 1680

18. (almost certainly) Roger Thompson of New Kent Co., living 1704

19. ---

20. Richard Lee, bp. Worcester Saint Martin, Worcestershire 22 Mar. 1617/8-Cobbs Hall, Northumberland Co., Va. between 6 Feb. 1663/4 & 20 Apr. 1664, prob. Jamestown, Va. c. 1641

21. Anne Constable, d. post 1663/4

22. Isaac Allerton, Jr., Plymouth, Massachusetts c. May 1627-1630, Harvard graduate of 1650-prob. Westmoreland Co., Va. between 25 Oct. & 3 Dec. 1702, post 8 Sept. 1662

23. Elizabeth Willoughby, prob. Elizabeth City Co., Va. c. 1635, living Apr. 1672, widow of Simon Overzee & George Colclough

24. William Strother, Jr., prob. Rappahannock Co., Va. c. 1665-75-King George Co., Va. ante 26 July 1726

25. Margaret Thornton, prob. Richmond Co., Va. 2 April 1678-living 1727

26-39. ---

40. John Lee, clothier, bur. Worcester Saint Martin, Worcestershire, 23 Feb. 1629/30, m. ante 1616

41. Jane Hancock, bur. Worcester Saint Martin 24 Feb. 1638/9, m.

(2) John Maninge

42-43. ---

44. Isaac Allerton, Mayflower pilgrim, Co. Suffolk, England c. 1585-New Haven, Connecticut between 1 & 12 Feb. 1658/9, Plymouth, Mass. c. 1626

45. Fear Brewster, d. Plymouth shortly ante Dec. 1634

46. Thomas Willoughby, c. 1598-1601/2-All Hallows, Barking, London ante 15 April 1657, sometime of Elizabeth City & Lower Norfolk Cos.

47. Alice ---

48. William Strother, d. Richmond Co., Va. between 30 Dec. 1700 & 4 Nov. 1702

49. Dorothy ---, living 1716

50. Francis Thornton, prob. Gloucester Co., Va. 5 Nov. 1651-prob. King George Co. c. 1726, Richmond Co. 13 Apr. 1674

51. Alice Savage, prob. d. ante 1701

52-79. ---

80-81. ---

82. Edward Hancock of Twining, Gloucestershire, will proved 26 Jan. 1620/1

83. Alice Jeffreys

84-89. ---

90. William Brewster, Mayflower pilgrim, prob. Scrooby, Nottinghamshire c. 1565-7-Plymouth, Mass. 10 Apr. 1644, c. 1590

91. Mary ---, d. Plymouth 17 Apr. 1627, once thought to be Mary Wentworth, daughter of Thomas & Grace (Gascoigne) Wentworth of Scrooby, she is now thought by John G. Hunt (a conjecture disputed by others) to be Mary Wyrall, daughter of Thomas & Frances (Mallory) Wyrall of Loversall, Yorkshire

92-95. ---

96. (said to be) William Strother of Kirknewton & Canno Mill, Northumberland c. 1597-8-will dated 1667

97. (said to be) Elizabeth ---

98-99. ---

100. William Thornton of Gloucester & Stafford Cos., d. post 1708

101. ---

102. Anthony Savage of Gloucester & Richmond Cos., will proved Richmond Co. 5 June 1695

103-127. ---

* * *

13. MILLARD FILLMORE

1. MILLARD FILLMORE, Locke (now Summerhill), N. Y. 7 Jan. 1800-Buffalo, N. Y. 8 March 1874, (1) Moravia, N. Y. 5 Feb. 1826 Abigail Powers, Stillwater, N. Y., 13 Mar. 1798-Washington, D. C. 30 March 1853, (2) Albany, N. Y. 10 Feb. 1858 Mrs. Caroline Carmichael McIntosh, Morristown, N. J., 21 Oct. 1813-Buffalo 11 Aug. 1881, widow of Ezekiel C. McIntosh.

2. Nathaniel Fillmore, Jr., Bennington, Vt. 19 April 1771-Aurora, N. Y. 28 Mar. 1863, (1) Bennington c. 1796-7

3. Phoebe Millard, Pittsfield, Mass. 12 Aug. 1781-Aurora 2 Apr. 1831

4. Nathaniel Fillmore, Franklin, Ct. 20 Mar. 1739/40-Bennington 7 Sept. 1814, Bennington 28 Oct. 1767

5. Hepzibah Wood, Franklin 14 Apr. 1747-Bennington 11 May 1783

6. Abiathar Millard, Rehoboth, Mass. 22 June 1744-Penfield, N. Y. 1811, Amenia, N. Y. 30 Sept. 1761

7. Tabitha Hopkins, b. Harwinton, Conn. 16 Oct. 1745

8. John Fillmore, Jr., Ipswich, Mass. 18 March 1702-Norwich, Ct. 22 Feb. 1777, Attleboro, Mass. 26 June 1735

9. Dorcas Day, Attleboro 2 Feb. 1714/5-Norwich 22 Mar. 1759

10. Ebenezer Wood, Jr., Norwich 15 Nov. 1726-Bennington 1796, Norwich 10 Dec. 1745
11. Philippa Story, Ipswich 21 May 1726-post 1796
12. Robert Millard, Rehoboth, Mass 20 Apr. 1702-Pawling, N. Y. c. 1784, Norton, Mass. 7 Mar. 1725/6
13. Hannah Eddy, b. c. 1704
14. Ebenezer Hopkins, Jr., Hartford, Ct. 24 June 1699-Shaftsbury, Vt. c. 1784, Hartford 7 June 1727
15. Susannah Messenger, b. Wallingford, Ct. 30 Nov. 1704
16. John Fillmore, c. 1676-c. 1708-11, m. Ipswich, Mass. or Hampton Falls, N. H., 19 June 1701
17. Abigail Tilton, Ipswich 1 Apr. 1679-Norwich, Ct. 13 Nov. 1727, m. (2) Robert Bell
18. Nathaniel Day, Gloucester, Mass. 9 April 1665-Attleboro, Mass. 5 Feb. 1775, Gloucester 13 Feb. 1689/90
19. Ruth Rowe, Gloucester 26 June 1671-Attleboro 10 May 1736
20. Ebenezer Wood, Bradford, Mass. 8 Sept. 1698-Norwich, Ct. 1744, Norwich 12 Mar. 1718
21. Mary Rudd, Norwich 3 Feb. 1695-post 1757
22. Stephen Story, Ipswich, Mass. 7 Oct. 1697-Bennington, Vt. 13 Dec. 1766, Ipswich 23 Sept. 1721
23. Mary Emerson, Ipswich 20 Apr. 1704-Bennington 13 July 1777
24. Nehemiah Millard, Rehoboth 6 June 1668-Rehoboth 23 July 1751, Rehoboth 3 Mar. 1696/7
25. Phoebe Shore, Lynn, Mass. 20 Apr. 1674-Rehoboth 11 Mar. 1717/8
26. Eleazer Eddy, Taunton, Mass. 16 Oct. 1681-Norton 8 Dec. 1739, Taunton 27 Mar. 1701
27. Elizabeth Randall, possibly the Elizabeth b. Scituate, Mass. 3 July 1673
28. Ebenezer Hopkins, Hartford, Ct., July 1668-Hartford 1711, Hartford 21 Jan. 1691/2
29. Mary Butler, c. 1670-Waterbury, Ct. 17 May 1744
30. Daniel Messenger, c. 1683-Harwinton, Ct. c. 1751, Wallingford, Ct. 28 Jan. 1703/4
31. Lydia Royce, Wallingford 28 May 1680-between 1747 & 1751
32-33. ---
34. Abraham Tilton, c. 1638-42-Ipswich 28 Mar. 1728
35. Deliverance Littlefield, d. 1730-33 (prob. Ipswich May 1732)
36. Anthony Day, c. 1624-27-Gloucester, Mass. 23 Apr. 1707, c. 1650
37. Susannah Matchett, c. 1623-Gloucester 10 Dec. 1717
38. Hugh Rowe, c. 1645-Gloucester 11 Dec. 1696, Gloucester 10 June 1667
39. Rachel Langton of Ipswich, d. Gloucester 7 Mar. 1673/4
40. John Wood, Rowley 2 Nov. 1656-(prob. Littleton, Mass.) post 1738/9, Rowley 16 Jan. 1680/1
41. Isabel Hazen, Rowley 21 July 1662-post 1726
42. Nathaniel Rudd, c. 1652-Bozrah, Ct. Apr. 1727, Norwich, Ct. 16 Apr. 1685
43. Mary Post, Norwich Nov. 1662-Norwich Nov. 1705
44. Samuel Story, Ipswich, Mass. c. 1658-60-Norwich 1726
45. Elizabeth ---
46. Thomas Emerson, Ipswich c. 1671-Ipswich 14 Apr. 1738, Ipswich 20 Nov. 1685
47. Philippa Perkins, Ipswich 28 Nov. 1670-Ipswich 26 Apr. 1738
48. Robert Millard, c. 1632-Rehoboth, Mass. 16 March 1699, Rehoboth 24 Dec. 1662
49. Elizabeth Sabin, Rehoboth c. 1642-3-Rehoboth 7 Feb. 1717/8, m. (2) Samuel Hayward
50. Jonathan Shore, bp. Boston 29 April 1649, Charlestown, Mass. 15 Jan. 1668/9

51. Priscilla Hathorne, bp. Salem 22 July 1649
52. John Eddy, d. Taunton 27 Nov. 1695, Taunton 1 May 1672
53. Deliverance Owen, Braintree, Mass. 15 Feb. 1654/5-Norton, Mass. 3 May 1726, m. (2) Nathaniel Smith
54. (possibly) Joseph Randall, bp. Scituate, Mass. 23 Nov. 1645-Scituate 21 Feb. 1723, Scituate Oct. 1672
55. (possibly) Hannah Macomber of Marshfield
56. Stephen Hopkins, c. 1635/6-Hartford Sept.-Nov. 1689, ante 1657
57. Dorcas Bronson, bp. Earl's Colne, Essex 19 Dec. 1633-Hartford 13 May 1697
58. Samuel Butler, c. 1641-Wethersfield, Ct. 31 Dec. 1692
59. Elizabeth Olmstead, d. Wethersfield 12 Oct. 1681
60. Samuel Messenger, ante 1650-Jamaica, Long Island 1685
61. Susannah ---
62. Nehemiah Royce, c. 1636-Wallingford, Ct. Nov. 1706, New London, Ct. 20 Nov. 1660
63. Hannah Morgan, Roxbury, Mass. 18 July 1642-Wallingford, Ct. 12 Dec. 1706
64-67. ---
68. William Tilton, c. 1589-Lynn, Mass. 1653
69. Susannah ---, d. Hampton, N. H. 28 Jan. 1654/5, m. (2) Roger Shaw
70. Francis Littlefield, bp. Tichfield, Hampshire 17 June 1619-Wells, Me. c. Jan. 1712/3, by 1649
71. Rebecca ---, b. 31 Jan. 1630, living 1683
72-75. ---
76. John Rowe, d. Gloucester, Mass. 9 Mar. 1661/2
77. Bridget (possibly Jeggles) of Salem, d. Gloucester, Mass. 2 May 1680, m. (2) William Colman
78. Joseph Langton of Ipswich, Mass., m. by July 1652
79. Rachel Parsons or Varney, d. Gloucester 15 Feb. 1707, m. (1) Thomas Cook, (2) as above, (3) William Vinson, imprisoned for witchcraft at Ipswich, 1692
80. Thomas Wood, c. 1633-Rowley Sept. 1687, Rowley 7 June 1654
81. Ann ---, c. 1637-Rowley 29 Dec. 1714
82. Edward Hazen, bp. Cadney, Lincolnshire 14 Dec. 1614-Rowley, Mass. 22 July 1683, Rowley Mar. 1650
83. Hannah Grant, bp. Cottingham, Yorkshire 16 Oct. 1631-Haverhill, Mass. Feb. 1715/6, m. (2) George Browne
84. Jonathan Rudd, d. Saybrook, Ct. 1658, "Bridebrook," Ct. 1647
85. ---
86. John Post, c. 1626/7-Norwich, Ct. 10 Feb. 1710/1, Saybrook Mar. 1652
87. Hester (Esther) Hyde, d. Norwich 13 Nov. 1703
88. William Story, c. 1614-Ipswich ante Jan. 1702/3
89. Sarah Foster, b. c. 1620
90-91. ---
92. Nathaniel Emerson, c. 1631-Ipswich, Mass. 29 Dec. 1712
93. Sarah ---, d. Ipswich 3 Aug. 1670
94. Jacob Perkins, Ipswich, Mass. c. 1646-Ipswich 26 Nov. 1719, Ipswich 25 Dec. 1667
95. Sarah Wainwright, d. Ipswich 3 Feb. 1688
96. John Millard, d. Rehoboth, Mass. 1684-9
97. ---
98. William Sabin, d. Rehoboth Feb. 1686/7, perhaps c. 1639
99. --- Wright, d. c. 1661
100. Sampson Shore of Boston, Mass., fl. 1641-79, c. 1639
101. Abigail Purchase, bp. Holy Trinity Church, Dorchester, Dorset 4 July 1624
102. John Hathorne, bp. Binfield, Berkshire 20 Apr. 1621-Lynn, Mass. 12 Dec. 1676, c. 1643

103. Sarah ---, d. post 1676
104-105. ---
106. William Owen, d. Braintree, Mass. 17 Jan. 1702, Braintree 29 Sept. 1650
107. Elizabeth Davis, c. 1634-Braintree 3 June 1702
108. (possibly) William Randall, c. 1615-Scituate, Mass. 13 Oct. 1693, c. 1640
109. (possibly) Elizabeth Barstow, d. post 1692, sister of Michael, William, George, and John Barstow, and of Mrs. Susan Barstow Perry, all immigrants to New England
110. (possibly) William Macomber, c. 1610-Marshfield, Mass. ante 1670, Bridport, Dorset 16 Jan. 1633/4
111. (possibly) Ursula Cooper, d. post 1670
112. John Hopkins, d. Hartford, Ct. ante 1654
113. Jane ---, d. c. 1679, m. (2) Nathaniel Ward, (3) Gregory Wolterton
114. John Bronson (Brownson, Brunson), bp. Lamarsh, Essex 21 Sept. 1602-Farmington, Ct. 1680, Halstead, Essex 19 Nov. 1626
115. Frances Hills, d. post 1680
116. Richard Butler, d. Hartford, Ct. 6 Aug. 1684
117. Elizabeth ---, d. Hartford 1691
118. Nicholas Olmstead, bp. Fairstead, Essex 15 Feb. 1612-Hartford, Ct. 31 Aug. 1684, c. ante 1640
119. Sarah Loomis, c. 1617/8-Hartford, Ct. 1667
120. Andrew Messenger of Jamaica, Long Island, d. ante 1681
121. ---, d. post. 1681
122-123. ---
124. Robert Royce, d. New London, Ct. 1676
125. Mary --- (not Sims), d. Wallingford, Ct. 1696
126. James Morgan, c. 1607-New London, Ct. 1685, Roxbury 6 Aug. 1640
127. Margery Hill
128-139. ---
140. Edmund Littlefield (1592-1661), Tichfield, Hampshire to Wells, Me., = 1614
141. Agnes (Anne, Annis) Austen (1596/7-1677/8)
142-153. ---
154. (possibly) William Jeggles (c. 1590-1659), Salem, Mass., = c. 1614
155. (possibly) Mary ---
156. Roger Langton, d. ante 1671, Haverhill, Mass.
157. Joan ---, d. 1669
158. --- Parsons or William Varney (c. 1600-1653/4) of Ipswich, the two husbands of 159
159. Bridget --- (c. 1600-1672), m. (1) c. 1625 --- Parsons, (2) c. 1635 William Varney
160. Edward Wood (1598-1642), Nuneaton, Warwickshire to Charlestown, Mass., = 1619/20
161. Ruth Lee, d. 1642
162-163. ---
164. Thomas Hassen (1580/1-1628), Grasby, Lincolnshire
165. Elizabeth ---, prob. d. 1647, prob. m. (2) Thomas Sewell
166. Thomas Grant (1600-ante 1643), Hessle, Yorkshire to Rowley, Mass., = 1624
167. Jane Haborne (1602-1696), Cottingham, Yorkshire to Rowley, Mass.
168-171. ---
172. Stephen Post, d. 1659, Otham, Kent to Saybrook, Ct., = 1625
173. Elinor Panton, d. 1670
174. William Hyde, d. 1681/2, Norwich, Ct.
175-177. ---
178. Renald Foster, d. 1680/1, Theydon Garnon, Essex to Ipswich, Mass., = 1619
179. Judith Wignol, d. 1664

180-183. ---
184. Thomas Emerson (1584-1666), Bishop's Stortford, Hertfordshire, to Ipswich, Mass., = 1611
185. Elizabeth Brewster, d. post 1666
186-187. ---
188. John Perkins, Jr. (1609-1686), Ipswich, Mass., = c. 1635
189. Elizabeth ---, d. 1684
190. Francis Wainwright (c. 1620-1692), Salem, Mass., = c. 1647
191. Philippa Sewell (1628/9-1669), Halstead, Essex to Ipswich, Mass.
192-197. ---
198. Richard Wright, b. c. 1598, Seekonk, Mass.
199-201. ---
202. Aquila Purchase, d. 1633, perhaps en route to New England, from Kingweston, Somerset, = 1613/4
203. Ann Squire (1591-1662), Charlton Mackrell, Somerset to Boston, m. (2) Thomas Oliver
204. William Hathorne (c. 1576-1650), Binfield, Berkshire, = c. 1605
205. Sarah ---, d. 1655
206-213. ---
214. --- Davis
215. Margaret (Margery) --- (c. 1603-1669), Braintree, Mass., m. (2) Charles Grice (Grise)
216-227. ---
228. Roger Brownson (1576-1635), Earl's Colne, Essex, = 1600
229. Mary Underwood (1585/6-1522/3)
230-235. ---
236. James Olmstead (1580-1640), Great Leighs, Essex to Hartford, Ct., = 1605
237. Joyce Cornish, d. 1621
238. Joseph Loomis, d. 1658, Braintree, Essex to Windsor, Ct., = 1614
239. Mary White (1590-1652), Shalford, Essex to Windsor, Ct.
240-255. ---

* * *

14. FRANKLIN PIERCE

1. FRANKLIN PIERCE, Hillsboro[ugh], New Hampshire 23 Nov. 1804-Concord, N. H. 8 Oct. 1869, Amherst, N. H. 19 Nov. 1834 Jane Means Appleton, Hampton, N. H. 12 Mar. 1806-Andover, Mass. 2 Dec. 1863
2. Benjamin Pierce, Jr., Governor of New Hampshire, Chelmsford, Mass. 25 Dec. 1757-Hillsboro 1 Apr. 1839, 1 Feb. 1790
3. Anna Kendrick, Amherst, N. H. 30 Oct. 1768-prob. Hillsboro 7 Dec. 1838
4. Benjamin Pierce, Chelmsford 25 Nov. 1726-Chelmsford 16 June 1764, Methuen, Mass. 2 Aug. 1746
5. Elizabeth Merrill, b. Methuen 22 Feb. 1727/8, m. (2) Oliver Bowers
6. Benjamin Kendrick, Newton, Mass. 30 Jan. 1723/4-Amherst, N. H. 13 Nov. 1812, prob. Hollis, N. H. 1 Mar. 1750
7. Sarah Harris, Littleton, Mass. 22 Jan. 1729/30-Amherst, N. H. 27 May 1818 [henceforth unless indicated all towns are in Mass.]
8. Stephen Pierce, Jr., Chelmsford c. 1679-Chelmsford 9 Sept. 1749, Chelmsford 5 Jan. 1707
9. Esther Fletcher, Chelmsford c. 1681-prob. Chelmsford 21 Sept. 1767
10. Abel Merrill, Newbury c. 1690-Methuen 29 Mar. 1753, Haverhill 15 Nov. 1714
11. Sarah Bodwell, Andover 1 Dec. 1694-Methuen 4 Feb. 1737

12. Caleb Kendrick, Newton 8 Mar. 1694-Newton 31 Mar. 1771, 14 or 15 Sept. 1721
13. Abigail Bowen, Roxbury 5 July 1700-Groton 16 Sept. 1775
14. Stephen Harris, Rowley 10 June 1700-prob. Hollis, N. H. 1775, prob. ante 1729
15. Mary ---, 1705-1781
16. Stephen Pierce, Woburn 16 July 1651-Chelmsford 10 June 1733, Chelmsford 18 Nov. 1676
17. Tabitha Parker, Chelmsford 28 Feb. 1658/9-Chelmsford 31 Jan. 1741/2
18. William Fletcher, Jr., Chelmsford 21 Feb. 1656/7-Chelmsford 23 May 1712, Chelmsford 19 Sept. 1677
19. Sarah Richardson, Chelmsford 25 Mar. 1659/60-Dunstable 30 Jan. 1748
20. John Merrill, Newbury 16 Feb. 1662/3-Haverhill 15 May 1705
21. Lucy Webster, Newbury 19 Dec. 1664-living 1718
22. Henry Bodwell, c. 1652-Methuen 1 June 1745, Newbury 4 May 1681
23. Bethia Emery, Newbury 15 Oct. 1658-living 1726
24. John Kendrick, Jr., Boston 3 Oct. 1641-Newton 30 Sept. 1721, 23 Oct. 1673
25. Esther Green, c. 1753-Newton 14 Sept. 1723, widow of John Hall
26. John Bowen, Roxbury 1 Sept. 1662-will proved 24 Nov. 1718, by 1696
27. Hannah Brewer, Roxbury 5 July 1665-post 1706
28. Timothy Harris, Rowley 1 Dec. 1657-Rowley 24 Mar. 1722/3, Rowley 24 Aug. 1682
29. Phebe Pearson, Rowley 13 April 1660-Rowley 15 or 16 Oct. 1732
30-31. ---
32. Thomas Pierce, Jr., c. 1608/18?-Woburn 6 Nov. 1683, Charlestown 6 May 1635
33. Elizabeth Cole, d. Woburn 5 March 1688
34. Jacob Parker, d. Malden ante 1669
35. Sarah ---, c. 1626-Malden 13 Jan. 1707/8
36. William Fletcher, c. 1622-Chelmsford 6 Nov. 1677, Concord 7 Oct. 1645
37. Lydia (Fairbanks?), poss. bp. Boston, Lincolnshire 13 June 1622-Chelmsford 12 Oct. 1704, widow of Edward Bates
38. Josiah Richardson, bp. Charlestown 7 Nov. 1635-Chelmsford 22 June 1695, Concord 6 June 1659
39. Remembrance Underwood, Concord 25 Feb. 1639/40-Chelmsford 20 Feb. 1718/9
40. Nathaniel Merrill, Jr., c. 1634-Newbury 1 Jan. 1682/3, Newbury 15 Oct. 1661
41. Joanna Ninian/Ninny/Nanny/Kenney/Kinney?, c. 1627-8 Feb. 1717/8
42. John Webster, Jr., c. 1632-post 1716, Newbury 13 June 1653
43. Ann Batt, 7 Apr. 1635-Newbury 13 June 1653
44-45. ---
46. John Emery, Jr., bp. Romsey, Hampshire 3 Feb. 1629-post 1693, ante 1650
47. Mary ---, d. Newbury 3 Feb. 1709
48. John Kendrick, c. 1604-Cambridge 29 Aug. 1686
49. Anna Smith, d. 1656
50. John Green
51. Elizabeth ---
52. Henry Bowen, c. 1633/4-Woodstock, Ct. 13 Mar. 1724, 20 Dec. 1658
53. Elizabeth Johnson, Roxbury 24 Dec. 1637-13 Aug. 1683
54. Daniel Brewer, Jr., c. 1624-Roxbury 8 Jan. 1708, Roxbury 5 Nov. 1652

55. Hannah Morrill, Roxbury 12 or 16 Sept. 1636-Roxbury 6 Oct. 1717
56. John Harris, c. 1607-Rowley 15 Feb. 1694/5, c. 1644
57. Bridget (almost certainly) Angier, prob. Dedham, Essex c. 1607-bur. Rowley 4 Aug. 1672
58. John Pearson, d. Rowley 22 Dec. 1693
59. Dorcas ---, d. Rowley 12 Jan. 1702/3
60-63. ---
64. Thomas Pierce, c. 1583/4-Charlestown 7 Oct. 1666
65. Elizabeth ---, c. 1595/6?-post 1666/7
66. Rice (Ryce) Cole, d. Charlestown 15 May 1646
67. Arrold ---, d. Charlestown 20-25 Dec. 1661
68-71. ---
72. Robert Fletcher, c. 1592-Concord 3 Apr. 1677
73. --- (poss. --- Hartwell)
74. (possibly) Richard Fairbanks
75. ---
76. Ezekiel Richardson, prob. Westmill, Hertfordshire c. 1604-Woburn 21 Oct. 1647
77. Susanna ---, d. Woburn 16 Sept. 1681, m. (2) Henry Brooks
78. William Underwood, c. 1615-Chelmsford 12 Aug. 1697
79. Sarah ---, d. Chelmsford 5 Nov. 1684
80. Nathaniel Merrill, bp. Wherstead, Suffolk 4 May 1601-Newbury 16 Mar. 1654/5, c. 1630
81. Susanna ---, d. Newbury 25 Jan. 1672, m. (2) Stephen Jordan
82-83. ---
84. John Webster, c. 1605-Ipswich c. 1645/6, c. 1630
85. Mary Shatswell, c. 1610-Newbury 28 Apr. 1694, m. (2) John Emery (92 below)
86. Nicholas Batt of St. John's, Devises, Wiltshire, d. Newbury 6 Dec. 1679
87. Lucy ---, d. Newbury 26 Jan. 1678/9
88-91. ---
92. John Emery, prob. Romsey, Hampshire 29 Sept. 1598-Newbury 3 Nov. 1683
93. (possibly) Mary ---
94-103. ---
104. Griffith Bowen, prob. Langwith, Gower, Wales c. 1600-England c. 1675/6, c. 1627, sometime of Boston
105. Margaret Fleming of Gellihir, Gower, Wales
106. Isaac Johnson of Roxbury, d. Great Swamp Fight 19 Dec. 1675, 20 Jan. 1636/7
107. Elizabeth Porter, d. Roxbury 13 Aug. 1683
108. Daniel Brewer, d. Roxbury 28 Mar. 1646
109. Joanna ---, c. 1602-Roxbury 7 Feb. 1688/9
110. Isaac Morrill, c. 1588-Roxbury 20 Dec. 1661
111. Sarah ---, c. 1600-Roxbury 9 Jan. 1672
112. Thomas Harris (Williams alias Harris) of Hatherup, Gloucestershire and Charlestown, d. ante 1634
113. Elizabeth ---, c. 1577/8-Charlestown 16 Feb. 1670, m. (2) William Stetson
114. Edmund Angier of Wiston, Suffolk, d. 1677/8
115. Bridget Rogers of Dedham, Essex, living 1678
116-151. ---
152. Thomas Richardson, d. 1633/4, Westmill, Hertfordshire, = 1590
153. Katherine Duxford (c. 1565-70-1631/2)
154-159. ---
160. Nathaniel Merrill (c. 1570-1626/7) Wherstead, Suffolk, = 1592/3
161. Mary Blacksoll, d. 1624, of Belstead, Suffolk
162. ---
163. (possibly) Susanna --- (c. 1587-1662), 1st known wife of

Gregory Wolterton/Wilterton/Walterton/Winterton of Hartford
164-169. ---
170. (possibly) William Shatswell of Ipswich, Mass.
171. ---
172. Richard Batt, d. 1612/3, of St. John's, Devises, Wiltshire
173. Agnes ---, d. post 1612
174-183. ---
184. (probably) John Emery of Romney, Hampshire
185. (probably) Agnes ---
186-207. ---
208. Francis Bowen of Langwith, Gower, Wales
209. Ellen Franklyn, living 1638
210. Henry Fleming of Llanrimdian, Gower, Wales, living 1650
211. Alice Dawkins of Gellihir
212. John Johnson, d. 1659, Herne, Kent to Roxbury, Mass.
213. Margery --- (Scudder? Heath?), d. 1655
214-223. ---
224. William Harris, d. 1599, Hatherup, Gloucestershire, = 1579
225. Agnes Mason
226-227. ---
228. William Angier (c. 1550-1620/2), Dedham, Essex
229. ---
230. John Rogers, minister of Dedham, Essex, d. 1636, = c. 1595
231. Bridget Ray, bp. 1576, of Stradishall, Suffolk
232-255. ---

* * *

15. JAMES BUCHANAN, JR.

1. JAMES BUCHANAN, JR., Stony Batter near Mercersburg, Pennsylvania 23 Apr. 1791-Wheatland, Lancaster, Pa. 1 June 1868, unm.
2. James Buchanan, Ramelton (Rathmelton), Donegal, Ireland c. 1761-Mercersburg, Pa. 11 June 1821, South Mountain, Pa. (between Chambersburg & Gettysburg) 16 Apr. 1788
3. Elizabeth Speer, Lancaster Co., Pa. c. 1767-Greensburg, Pa. 14 May 1833
4. John Buchanan of The Cairn, Ramelton, m. c. 1751
5. Jane Russell of The Ards near Ramelton
6. James Speer, Ireland to Lancaster Co. to South Mountain
7. Mary Patterson, d. ante 1788
8. --- Buchanan
9. ---
10. Samuel Russell of The Ards near Ramelton, m. prob. late 1720s
11. Mary Watt
12-15. ---
16. (said to be) Thomas Buchanan of Ramelton, b. c. 1685
17-31. ---
32. (perhaps) George Buchanan of Blairlusk & Deroran, Tyrone, Ireland, b. c. 1648, Ireland 1675
33. (perhaps) Elizabeth Mayne
34-63. ---
64. (perhaps) John Buchanan of Blairlusk, d. 1662
65. (perhaps) --- (unknown first wife)
66-127. ---
128. (perhaps) George Buchanan of Gartincaber, living 1629
129. (perhaps) Elizabeth Leckie of Disheour, Stirlingshire
130-255. ---

* * *

16. ABRAHAM LINCOLN

1. **ABRAHAM LINCOLN**, Sinking Spring Farm, near Hodgenville, Kentucky 12 Feb. 1809-Washington, D. C. 15 Apr. 1865, Springfield, Illinois 4 Nov. 1842 Mary Ann Todd, Lexington, Ky. 13 Dec. 1818-Springfield, Ill. 16 July 1882

2. **Thomas Lincoln**, Augusta (now Rockingham) Co., Virginia 6 Jan. 1778-near Farmington, Ill. 17 Jan. 1851, Beech Creek, Washington Co., Ky. 12 June 1806

3. **Nancy Hanks**, Campbell Co., Va. 5 Feb. 1784-near Gentryville, Indiana 5 Oct. 1818

4. **Abraham Lincoln**, Berks Co., Pennsylvania 13 May 1744-killed by Indians Jefferson Co., Ky. prob. May 1786, license Augusta Co., Va. 9 July 1770

5. **Bathsheba** (said to be Herring), c. 1750-c. 1836

6. **James Hanks** of North Carolina (according to Louis A. Warren & Ralph E. Pearson), or **Abraham Hanks**, of Fauquier, Prince William & Campbell Cos., Va., c. 1759-c. 1810 (according to Adin Baber), or **Thomas Hanks**, of Ross & Washington Cos., Ohio, c. 1759-c. 1810 (according to David S. Keiser), or --- Hanks of Va., c. 1757-c. 1785 (according to R. M. Bell)

7. **Lucy Shipley**, of Va., N. C. & Ky., c. 1765-1825, who m. (2) Henry Sparrow (according to Warren & Pearson), or **Sarah Harper** of Prince William Co., Va., d. c. 1790 (according to Baber), or **Mary Berry**, d. c. 1788 (according to Keiser), or --- Berry of Va., c. 1761-c. 1785 (according to Bell)

8. **John Lincoln**, Freehold, New Jersey 3 May 1716-Linville's Creek, Rockingham Co., Va. Nov. 1788, prob. Berks Co., Pa. 5 July 1743

9. **Rebecca Flowers**, 30 March 1720-prob. Linville's Creek 20 July 1806, widow of James Morris

10. (said to be) **Alexander Herring (Herron), Jr.**, c. 1708-Rockingham Co., Va. c. June 1778, ante 1735

11. (said to be) **Abigail Harrison**, Smithtown, Long Island, New York c. 1710-Rockingham Co., Va. c. 1780

12. (prob., according to Warren, Pearson, Keiser & Bell) **Joseph Hanks**, Va. c. 1722-Nelson Co., Ky. c. 1793

13. (prob.) **Nanny ---**, b. c. 1728

14. **Robert Shipley, Jr.**, bp. Howard Co., Maryland 19 Oct. 1713, to Mecklenburg Co., N. C. from Lunenburg Co., Va. 1771, m. Md. ante 1737 (according to Warren & Pearson), or **George Harper** of Prince William Co., Va. (according to Baber), or **Richard Berry**, c. 1734-c. 1798, Md. to Mercer Co., Ky. (according to Keiser & Bell)

15. **Sarah** (said to be Dorsey) (according to Warren & Pearson), or **Elizabeth** (prob.) **Shipley** (according to Baber), or **Rachel Shipley**, b. Md. c. 1740, daughter of Robert Shipley & Sarah (said to be Dorsey) (according to Keiser & Bell)

16. **Mordecai Lincoln, Jr.**, Hingham, Massachusetts 24 Apr. 1686-Amity, Pa. 12 May 1736, prob. Monmouth Co., N. J. ante 14 Sept. 1714

17. **Hannah Salter**, d. c. 1727

18. **Enoch Flowers**, b. c. 1693, of Berks Co., Pa., Concord, Pa. (Quaker Meeting) shortly ante 8 Apr. 1713

19. **Rebecca Barnard**

20. (said to be) **Alexander Herring (Herron)**, d. Sussex Co., Delaware c. 1735

21. (said to be) **Margaret ---**, d. post 1735

22. (said to be) **Isaiah Harrison**, c. 1666-Sussex Co., Del. c. 1738 (earlier of Oyster Bay & Smithtown, L. I.), c. 1700

23. (said to be) **Abigail ---** (poss. Smith), d. Sussex Co., Del. c. 1732

24. (prob., according to Warren, Pearson, Keiser & Bell) **Luke Hanks**, Richmond Co., Va. c. 1686-Lancaster Co., Va. ante Feb. 1757 (according to Baber he should be #12)

25. (prob.) Elizabeth ---, b. c. 1694
26-27. ---
28. (prob., according to Warren & Pearson; according to Keiser & Bell 28 & 29 should be 60 & 61) Robert Shipley, Annapolis, Md. c. 1678-Anne Arundel (now Howard) Co., Md. c. Feb. 1763, c. 1710
29. (prob.) Elizabeth Stevens of Anne Arundel Co., Md.
30-31. ---
32. Mordecai Lincoln, Hingham, Mass. 14 June 1657-Scituate, Mass. 28 Nov. 1727, prob. Hull, Mass. c. 1685
33. Sarah Jones, d. ante 17 Feb. 1701/2
34. Richard Salter, d. post 1728, lawyer, judge & colonial legislator, of Monmouth Co., N. J.
35. Sarah Bowne, Gravesend, L. I., N. Y. 27 Nov. 1669-post 1714
36. William Flower of Marcus Hook, Pa., Concord, Pa. (Quaker Meeting) shortly post 10 Oct. 1692
37. Elizabeth Moris
38. Richard Barnard, Kingston, Wiltshire, England to Chester (now Delaware) Co., Pa., d. c. 1698, care of Chippenham (Quaker) Meeting, Wiltshire 1678
39. Frances Lambe, m. (2) Thomas Bowater
40-47. ---
48. (prob.) William Hanks, c. 1650-Richmond Co., Va. ante 7 Feb. 1704
49. (prob.) Sarah ---, m. (2) Richard White
50-55. ---
56. (prob.) Adam Shipley of Anne Arundel Co., Md. fl. 1668-1687
57. (prob.) Lois --- (poss. Howard), c. 1655-c. 1725
58. (prob.) Charles Stevens, Jr., c. 1645-Anne Arundel Co., Md. c. 1703, c. 1670
59. (prob.) Elizabeth ---, m. (2) Thomas Browne
60-63. ---
64. Samuel Lincoln, perhaps b. 1619, bp. Hingham, Norfolk, England 24 Aug. 1622-Hingham, Mass. 26 May 1690
65. Martha Lyford, prob. Ireland ante 1624-Hingham, Mass. 10 Apr. 1693
66. Abraham Jones, c. 1630-Hull, Mass. 25 Jan. 1718, c. 1656
67. Sarah Whitman, d. Hull 11 June 1718
68-69. ---
70. John Bowne, c. 1630-Monmouth Co., N. J. 1684
71. Lydia Holmes, d. post 1693
72-77. ---
78. Richard Lambe of Kingston, St. Michael's, Wiltshire
79. Lucy Baillie
80-95. ---
96. (poss.) Thomas Hanks of Gloucester Co., Va., d. post 1674
97. (poss.) Elizabeth ---
98-115. ---
116. (prob.) Charles Stevens, c. 1615-Anne Arundel Co., Md. c. 1658
117. (prob.) Susannah (prob. Norwood), b. c. 1620, m. (2) John Howard
118-127. ---
128. Edward Lincoln (c. 1575-1639/40), Hingham, Norfolk, = c. 1600
129. Bridget Gilman
130. Rev. John Lyford, d. ante 10 Oct. 1634, a graduate of Magdalen College (A.B. 1597, A.M. 1602), minister at Leverlegkish near Laughgaid, Armagh, Ireland, at Plymouth, Hull, Cape Ann & Salem, Mass., & in Va.
131. Sarah ---, m. (2) Edmund Hubbard
132. Thomas Jones (c. 1602-1680/1), Hingham & Manchester, Mass.
133. Ann ---, d. ante 1657
134. John Whitman (c. 1603-1692), Weymouth, Mass.

135. Ruth ---, d. 1662
136-139. ---
140. William Bowne, d. c. 1677, Salem, Mass., Gravesend, L. I., & Middletown, N. J.
141. Ann ---
142. Rev. Obadiah Holmes (1609/10-1682), minister of the First Baptist Church at Newport, R. I., Didsbury, Lancashire to Newport, = 1630
143. Katherine Hyde
144-233. ---
234. (prob.) John Norwood, d. post 1662, Va. & Anne Arundel Co., Md.; Harry Wright Newman in **To Maryland from Oversees** (1982), p. 130, states that English research commissioned by a Norwood descendant in 1961 established that this John Norwood was born in Wykeham, Spalding, Lincolnshire, the son of Tyringham Norwood (1575-1625); however, A. R. Maddison's **Lincolnshire Pedigrees**, vol. 2 (Harleian Society Publications, Visitations Series, vol. 51, 1902), p. 729, lists four sons of Tyringham Norwood, d. 1621, and Anne Butler: Anthony, Henry, Nicholas & Charles - but no John.
235-255. ---

* * *

17. ANDREW JOHNSON

1. ANDREW JOHNSON, Raleigh, North Carolina 29 Dec. 1808-Carter's Station, Tennessee 31 July 1875, Greene Co., Tenn. 17 May 1827 Eliza McCardle, Greeneville, Tenn. 4 Oct. 1810-Carter Co., Tenn. 15 Jan. 1876
2. Jacob Johnson, 17 Apr. 1778-Raleigh 4 Jan. 1812, Raleigh 9 Sept. 1801
3. Mary "Polly" McDonough, prob. Beaufort Co., N. C. 17 July 1782-Greene Co., Tenn. 13 Feb. 1856, m. (2) Turner Daughtrey
4-5. ---
6. Andrew McDonough, Jr., Beaufort Co., N. C. 30 Nov. 1759-Marion Co., Tenn. 20 Jan. 1846, also of Tyrrell & Wake Cos., N. C., & Bledsoe Co., Tenn.
7. --- (first wife)
8-11. ---
12. Andrew McDonough (McDonah, MacDonnack) of Beaufort Co., will dated 28 Nov. 1787
13. Mary ---, d. post 1787 (mentioned in husband's will, poss. not the mother of Andrew, Jr.)
14-255. ---

* * *

18. ULYSSES SIMPSON GRANT

1. ULYSSES SIMPSON GRANT, originally Hiram Ulysses Grant, Point Pleasant, Ohio 27 Apr. 1822-Mount McGregor (near Saratoga), New York 23 July 1885, St. Louis, Missouri 22 Aug. 1848 Julia Boggs Dent, St. Louis 26 Jan. 1826-Washington, D. C. 14 Dec. 1902
2. Jesse Root Grant, near Greensburg, Pennsylvania 23 Jan. 1794-Covington, Kentucky 29 June 1873, Point Pleasant, Ohio 24 June 1821 (or 1820?)
3. Hannah Simpson, Horsham, Pa. 23 Nov. 1798-Jersey City, New Jersey 11 May 1883
4. Noah Grant (III), Tolland, Connecticut 20 June 1748-Maysville, Ky. 14 Feb. 1819, Greensburg, Pa. 4 Mar. 1792
5. Rachel Kelley, sometimes called Mrs. Rachel Miller Kelley, d. Deerfield (Maysville), Ohio 10 Apr. 1805
6. John Simpson, Jr., c. 1767-Tate, Ohio 20 Jan. 1837, Harts-

ville, Pa. 17 Oct. 1793

7. Rebecca Weir, b. c. 1801-1802

8. Noah Grant, Jr., Tolland, Conn. 12 July 1719-in military service 20 Sept. 1756, Tolland 5 Nov. 1746

9. Susanna Delano, Tolland 23 June 1724-Coventry, Conn. perhaps 16 Aug. 1806

10-11. ---

12. John Simpson, b. Northern Ireland c. 1738, of Horsham, Pa. d. Aug. 1804, Philadelphia 25 Nov. 1762

13. Hannah Roberts, d. Doylestown, Pa. 1820-1821

14. Samuel Weir, b. c. 1731, d. New Britain, Pa. 1811

15. Mary ---, d. ante 1796

16. Noah Grant, Windsor, Conn. 11 Dec. 1693-Tolland 10 Oct. 1727, Tolland 20 June 1717

17. Martha Huntington, Norwich, Conn. 6 Dec. 1696-Tolland prob. 26 Aug. 1779, m. (2) Peter Buell

18. Jonathan Delano, Jr., Dartmouth, Mass. 30 Jan. 1680-Tolland, Conn. 25 Mar. 1752, Falmouth, Mass. 20 June 1704

19. Amy Hatch, Falmouth 15 July 1684-Tolland 1 June 1762

20-23. ---

24. William Simpson, Northern Ireland c. 1710-Buckingham, Pa. 15 May 1794

25. Jane Hines

26. Lewis Roberts

27. Mary ---

28-31. ---

32. Samuel Grant, Jr., Windsor, Conn. 20 Apr. 1659-8 May 1710, Windsor 11 Apr. 1688

33. Grace Miner, Stratford, Conn. 20 Sept. 1670-16 Apr. 1753

34. John Huntington, Norwich 15 Mar. 1666-between 1695 & 1703, Norwich 9 Dec. 1686

35. Abigail Lathrop, b. May 1665

36. Jonathan Delano, Duxbury, Mass. c. 1648-Dartmouth, Mass. 23 Dec. 1720, Plymouth, Mass. 28 Feb. 1678

37. Mercy Warren, Plymouth 20 Feb. 1658-post 1727

38. Joseph Hatch, 7 Mar. or 10 June 1654-Falmouth, Mass. 16 Feb. 1737/8, Falmouth 7 Dec. 1683

39. Amy Allen, Sandwich, Mass. 15 Aug. 1663-(Falmouth 24 Feb. 1710/11?)

40-47. ---

48. Thomas Simpson, Northern Ireland c. 1683-Paxtang, Pa. June 1761

49-63. ---

64. Samuel Grant, Dorchester, Mass. 12 Nov. 1631-Windsor, Conn. 10 Sept. 1718, 27 May 1656

65. Mary Porter, b. c. 1638

66. John Miner, bp. Charlestown, Mass. 30 Aug. 1635-Woodbury, Conn. 17 Sept. 1719, Stratford, Conn. 19 (or 21) Oct. 1658

67. Elizabeth Booth, Stratford, Conn. 10 Sept. 1641-Woodbury, Ct. 24 Oct. 1732

68. Christopher Huntington, c. 1626-Norwich, Conn. 1691, Windsor 7 Oct. 1652

69. Ruth Rockwell, b. Dorchester, Mass. Aug. 1633

70. Samuel Lathrop, c. 1622-Norwich, Conn. 29 Feb. 1700, Barnstable, Mass. 28 Nov. 1644

71. Elizabeth Scudder, d. ante 1690, sister of John Scudder of Barnstable

72. Philip Delano or de Lannoy, bp. Leyden, Holland 6 Nov. 1603-Bridgewater, Mass. c. 1681, Duxbury, Mass. 19 Dec. 1634

73. Hester (Esther) Dewsbury

74. Nathaniel Warren, Plymouth, Mass. c. 1624/5-Plymouth 1667, Plymouth 19 Nov. 1645

75. Sarah Walker, bp. St. Olave, Southwark, London 10 Nov. 1722-

Plymouth 24 Nov. 1700

76. Jonathan Hatch, c. 1625-Falmouth, Mass. Dec. 1710, Barnstable, Mass. 11 Apr. 1646

77. Sarah Rowley

78. James Allen, c. 1637-Chilmark, Mass. 25 July 1714

79. Elizabeth Partridge, d. Chilmark 7 Aug. 1722

80-95. ---

96. (poss.) John Simpson, Scotland to Northern Ireland, b. c. 1660

97-127. ---

128. Matthew Grant (1601-1681), Windsor, Conn., = 1625

129. Priscilla --- (1601-1644)

130. John Porter, d. 1648, Felsted, Essex to Windsor, Conn., = 1620

131. Ann White (1600-1648), Messing, Essex to Windsor

132. Thomas Miner (1608-1690), Chew Magna, Somerset to Stonington, Conn., = 1634

133. Grace Palmer, d. 1690

134. Richard Booth (c. 1607/8-post 1688), Stratford, Conn.

135. Elizabeth (Hawley?)

136. Simon Huntington, d. prob. on the voyage to New England 1633

137. Margaret Barrett, Norwich, England to Windsor, Conn., = (2) Thomas Stoughton

138. William Rockwell (1590/1-1640), Fitzhead, Somerset to Windsor, Conn., = 1624

139. Susanna Capen (c. 1602-1664), = (2) Matthew Grant (128 above)

140. Rev. John Lathrop (1584-1653), Etton, Yorkshire to Barnstable, Mass., graduate of Queen's College, Cambridge = 1610

141. Hannah House, d. London 1633, of Eastwell, Kent

142-143. ---

144. Jean de Lannoy (Jan de Lano) of Tourcoing, France, a Walloon, d. c. 1604, betrothed at Leyden 13 Jan. 1596

145. Marie le Mahieu of Lille, France, m. (2) Robert Mannoo

146-147. ---

148. Richard Warren, d. 1628, Mayflower passenger, London to Plymouth, Mass.

149. Elizabeth --- (c. 1583-1673)

150. William Walker, draper of Southwark, London

151. --- Clark

152. Thomas Hatch (c. 1603-1661), Cornwall to Barnstable, Mass.

153. Grace ---

154. Henry Rowley of Plymouth, Mass.

155. --- Palmer, d. ante 1633

156. Samuel Allen, d. 1669, Braintree, Mass.

157. Ann ---, d. 1641

158. George Partridge of Duxbury, Mass., = 1638

159. Sarah Tracy

160-255. ---

* * *

19. RUTHERFORD BIRCHARD HAYES

1. RUTHERFORD BIRCHARD HAYES, Delaware, Ohio 4 Oct. 1822-Fremont, Ohio 17 Jan. 1893, Cincinnati, Ohio 30 Dec. 1852 Lucy Ware Webb, Chillicothe, Ohio 28 Aug. 1831-Fremont, Ohio 25 June 1889

2. Rutherford Hayes, Jr., Brattleboro, Vt. 4 Jan. 1787-Delaware, Ohio 20 July 1822, Wilmington, Vt. 13 Sept. 1813

3. Sophia Birchard, Wilmington, Vt. 15 Apr. 1792-Columbus, Ohio 30 Oct. 1866

4. Rutherford Hayes, Branford, Conn., 29 July 1756-West Brattleboro, Vt. 25 Sept. 1836, early 1779

5. Chloe Smith, South Hadley, Mass. 10 Nov. 1762-Brattleboro, Vt. 17 Feb. 1847

6. Roger Cornwall alias Birchard, Mansfield, Conn. 25 Dec. 1756-Wilmington, Vt. 22 Aug. 1805, Wilmington 2 Dec. 1790

7. Drusilla Austin, prob. Suffield, Conn. 3 Apr. 1762-Wilmington, Vt. 3 Mar. 1813

8. Ezekiel Hayes, Simsbury, Conn. 21 Oct. or 21 Nov. 1724-New Haven, Conn. 17 Oct. 1817, Branford, Conn. 26 Dec. 1749

9. Rebecca Russell, New Haven, Conn. 6 Feb. 1723-New Haven 27 May 1773

10. Israel Smith, Granby, Mass. 2 Apr. 1739-Bainbridge, N. Y. 7 June 1811, perhaps Enfield, Conn. c. 1761

11. Abigail Chandler, Enfield, Conn. 11 Sept. 1741-Bainbridge, N. Y. Oct. 1791

12. --- Cornwall (father, illegitimately, of 6)

13. Sarah Jacob, Mansfield, Conn. 13 Dec. 1735, who m. at Mansfield 25 Jan. 1758 Elias Birchard, whose surname was assumed by Sarah's illegitimate son

14. Daniel Austin, Suffield, Conn. 28 Apr. or 9 May 1720-Wilmington, Vt. 24 June 1804, Wilmington 21 Dec. 1749

15. Abigail Phelps, 11 Nov. 1731-Wilmington, Vt., Jan. 1816

16. Daniel Hayes, Windsor, Conn., 26 Apr. 1686-Simsbury (now Granby), Conn., 23 Sept. 1756, Simsbury 4 May 1721

17. Sarah Lee of Westfield, 24 Apr. 1692-Simsbury, Conn. 13 July 1738

18. John Russell, Branford, Conn. (or perhaps Deerfield, Mass.) 24 Jan. 1687-Branford 4 July 1757, New Haven, Conn. 17 Dec. 1707

19. Sarah Trowbridge, New Haven 26 Nov. 1686-New Haven 23 Jan. 1761

20. John Smith (III), Hadley, Mass. 1 Feb. 1697-Brattleboro, Vt. 1784, early 1727

21. Elizabeth Smith (her husband's first cousin), Northampton, Mass. 5 May 1703-Brattleboro, Vt. 12 Jan. 1778

22. Isaac Chandler, Andover, Mass. c. 1717-Enfield, Conn. 5 June 1787, 28 Feb. 1740/1

23. Abigail Hale, Enfield, Conn. 3 July 1718-18 June 1796

24-25. ---

26. Joseph Jacob, Jr., Lynn, Mass. 3 Aug. 1705-Mansfield, Conn. 15 Dec. 1790

27. Mary Storrs, b. May 1710

28. Nathaniel Austin, Suffield, Conn. 20 May 1678-Suffield 12 Dec. 1760, Suffield 27 Jan. 1701

29. Abigail Hovey, Hadley, Mass. 8 Jan. 1682-Enfield, Conn. 9 Jan. 1764

30. Timothy Phelps, Northampton, Mass c. 1697-5 Dec. 1788, Springfield, Mass. 18 Jan. 1725/6

31. Abigail Merrick, Springfield, Mass. 5 Apr. 1702-Suffield, Conn. 16 Aug. 1791

32. George Hayes, c. 1655-Simsbury, Conn. 2 Sept. 1725, c. 1685

33. Abigail Dibble, Windsor, Conn. 19 Jan. 1666/7-Simsbury, Conn. post 1725

34. John Lee, Northampton, Mass. 2 Jan. 1657-Westfield, Mass. 13 Nov. 1711, c. 1686

35. Elizabeth Crampton, b. Guilford, Conn. 1662/7

36. Rev. Samuel Russell, Hadley, Mass. 4 Nov. 1660-Branford, Conn. 24 June 1731, c. 1686 or earlier, Harvard graduate of 1681

37. Abigail Whiting, c. 1665-7 May 1733

38. Thomas Trowbridge (III), New Haven, Conn. 14 Feb. 1663/4-New Haven 15 Sept. 1711, 16 Oct. 1685

39. Mary Winston, New Haven 24 June 1667-New Haven 16 Sept. 1742

40. John Smith, Jr., 15 May 1665-Hadley, Mass. 20 Jan. 1724, c. 1687

41. Mary Root, 22 Sept. 1667-1724 (post 20 Jan.)

42. Benjamin Smith, 10 Jan. 1673-1754/5, Wethersfield, Conn. 14 Mar. 1699/1700
43. Ruth Buck, Wethersfield, Conn. 4 Dec. 1681-ante 1754
44. Henry Chandler, Andover, Mass. 28 May 1667-Enfield, Conn. 27 Aug. 1737, Andover 28 Nov. 1695
45. Lydia Abbott, 31 Sept. 1675-Enfield 11 Mar. 1748/9
46. John Hale, Hadley, Mass. 2 Nov. 1680-Enfield, Conn. 24 May 1753, 21 Nov. 1716
47. Abigail Gleason, Enfield, Conn. 14 March 1692-19 Apr. 1721
48-51. ---
52. Joseph Jacob, c. 1673-Mansfield, Conn. 26 Dec. 1764, Lynn, Mass. 18 Dec. 1693
53. Sarah Lindsey, b. Lynn, Mass. 2 Mar. 1674/5
54. Samuel Storrs, Jr., Barnstable, Mass. 17 May 1677-9 Aug. 1727, Windham, Conn. 31 Oct. 1700
55. Martha Burgess, c. 1671-Sept. 1728
56. Anthony Austin, England Jan.-Mar. 1636-Suffield, Conn. 22 Aug. 1708, Rowley, Mass. 19 Oct. 1664
57. Esther Huggins, Hampton, N. H. c. 1642/3-7 Mar. 1697/8
58. Thomas Hovey, Ipswich, Mass. c. 1648-Hadley, Mass. 4 Mar. 1739, Nov. 1677
59. Sarah Cooke, 31 Jan. 1662-post 10 Apr. 1739
60. Nathaniel Phelps, Jr., Windsor, Conn. 2 June 1653-Northampton, Mass. 20 June 1719, Northampton 11 Aug. 1676
61. Grace Martin, c. 1656-Northampton 2 Aug. 1727
62. John Merrick, Springfield, Mass. 9 Nov. 1658-Springfield 10 Apr. 1748, 4 Feb. 1687
63. Mary Day, Springfield, Mass. 15 Dec. 1666-Springfield 29 Apr. 1723
64-65. ---
66. Samuel Dibble, Windsor, Conn. 19 Feb. 1643/4-Windsor 5 Mar. 1709/10, c. 1666
67. --- Graves, d. ante 1668
68. Walter Lee, d. 9 Feb. 1717/8
69. Mary ---, d. 29 Feb. 1695/6
70. Dennis Crampton, d. Guilford, Conn. 31 Jan. 1689/90, Guilford 16 Sept. 1660
71. Mary Parmelee, d. Guilford 16 or 31 Mar. 1667
72. Rev. John Russell, Jr., c. 1627-Hadley, Mass. 20 Dec. 1692, c. 1651, Harvard graduate of 1651
73. Rebecca Newberry
74. Rev. John Whiting, c. 1635-Hatfield, Mass. 8 Sept. 1689, Cambridge, Mass. c. 1654, Harvard graduate of 1653
75. Sybil Collins, c. 1638-Hartford (or New Haven), Conn. 3 June 1672
76. Thomas Trowbridge, Jr., bp. Exeter, Devon 11 Dec. 1631-New Haven, Conn. 22 Aug. 1702, New Haven 24 June 1657
77. Sarah Rutherford, New Haven 31 July 1641-New Haven 5 Jan. 1687
78. John Winston, c. 1621-New Haven 21 Feb. 1696/7
79. Elizabeth ---, c. 1617-New Haven 19 Oct. 1680
80. John Smith, Wethersfield, Conn. c. 1637-Hatfield, Mass. 30 May 1676, 12 Nov. 1673
81. Mary Partridge, c. 1638-20 May 1683, m. (2) Peter Montague
82. John Root, Jr., Farmington, Conn. c. 1642-Westfield, Mass. 24 Sept. 1687, 18 Oct. 1664
83. Mary Ashley, b. Springfield, Mass. 6 Apr. 1644
84. same as 80
85. same as 81
86. Henry Buck, c. 1625/6-Wethersfield, Conn. 7 July 1712, 31 Oct. 1660
87. Elizabeth Churchill, b. Wethersfield 15 May 1642
88. Thomas Chandler, bp. Bishop's Stortford, Hertfordshire

1628-Andover, Mass. 15 Jan. 1702/3

89. Hannah Brewer, c. 1630-Andover, Mass. 25 Oct. 1717

90. George Abbott, Jr., c. 1631-Andover 22 Mar. 1688/9, Ipswich, Mass. 26 Apr. 1658

91. Sarah Farnum, b. prob. Mass. c. 1638

92. Thomas Hale, Jr., bp. Hartford, Conn. 19 Jan. 1650/1-Enfield, Conn. 7 Apr. 1725, 18 Nov. 1675

93. Priscilla Markham, c. 1654-Enfield 18 Apr. 1682

94. Isaac Gleason, Watertown, Mass. c. 1654-Enfield, Conn. 14 May 1698, Windsor, Conn. 26 June 1684

95. Hester Eggleston, b. Windsor, Conn. 1 Dec. 1663

96-105. ---

106. John Lindsey, c. 1640-Lynn, Mass. c. 1705, Lynn 6 June 1667

107. Mary Alley, Lynn 6 Jan. 1641/2-Lynn 2 Jan. 1680/1

108. Samuel Storrs, bp. Sutton-cum-Lound, Nottinghamshire 7 Dec. 1640, 6 Dec. 1666

109. Mary Huckins, bp. Barnstable, Mass.-Barnstable 24 Sept. 1683

110. John Burgess of Yarmouth, Mass., m. Sandwich, Mass. 8 Sept. 1657

111. Mary Worden

112. Richard Austin, prob. Bishopstoke, Hampshire c. 1598-Charlestown, Mass. shortly post 1638

113. ---

114. John Huggins, c. 1609-Hampton, N. H. 7 June 1670

115. Bridget ---, c. 1615-Springfield, Mass. 7 May 1695, m. (2) John Clifford

116. Daniel Hovey, bp. Waltham Abbey, Essex 9 Aug. 1618-Ipswich, Mass. 24 April 1692

117. Abigail Andrews, d. 24 June 1655

118. Aaron Cooke (III), bp. Windsor, Conn. 21 Feb. 1640/1-Hadley, Mass. 16 Sept. 1716, 30 May 1661

119. Sarah Westwood, c. 1644-Hadley 24 Mar. 1730

120. Nathaniel Phelps, c. 1627-Northampton, Mass. 27 May 1702, Windsor, Conn. 17 Sept. 1650

121. Elizabeth Copley, widow?, d. Northampton 6 Dec. 1712

122. William Martin, m. Widford, Essex 17 Nov. 1645

123. Lydia Marsh, c. 1624-post 1658, sister of John Marsh of Hadley, Mass.

124. Thomas Merrick, c. 1620-Springfield, Mass. 7 Sept. 1704, Springfield 21 Aug. 1653

125. Elizabeth Tilley, d. Springfield 21 Aug. 1684

126. Thomas Day, c. 1638-Springfield 27 Dec. 1711, Springfield 27 Oct. 1659

127. Sarah Cooper, prob. Windsor, Conn. c. 1642-Springfield 21 Nov. 1726

128-131. ---

132. Thomas Dibble (c. 1613-1700), Windsor, Conn.

133. --- (Miriam?)

134. William Graves, d. c. 1679, Newtown, Long Island

135-141. ---

142. John Parmelee of New Haven, will dated 1659

143. (Hannah ---?)

144. John Russell (1597/8-1680), Crettingham, Suffolk to Hadley, Mass.

145. Phebe Collins (1604/5-1642), Bramford, Suffolk to Cambridge, Mass., sister of 150 below

146. Thomas Newberry (1594-1635/6), Yarcombe, Devon to Dorchester, Mass., = c. 1630

147. Jane --- (perhaps Dabinott, a second wife)

148. William Whiting, d. 1643-7, Hartford, Conn.

149. Susanna ---, d. 1673, m. (2) Samuel Fitch, (3) Alexander Bryan

150. Edward Collins (1603-1689), Bramford, Suffolk to Charlestown, Mass., brother of 145 above
151. Martha --- (1609-1699/1700)
152. Thomas Trowbridge (1597/8-1672/3), Taunton, Somerset to Dorchester, Mass. & New Haven, Conn., back to Taunton =1627
153. Elizabeth Marshall (1602/3-1641), Exeter, Devon to New Haven
154. Henry Rutherford, d. 1668, New Haven
155. Sarah ---, d. 1673, m. (2) Governor William Leete of Conn.
156-159. ---
160. Samuel Smith (c. 1601/2-1680), near Hadleigh, Suffolk to South Hadley, Mass. =1624
161. Elizabeth Smith (c. 1602-1686), Whatfield, Suffolk to South Hadley
162. William Partridge, d. 1668, possibly Berwick-on-Trent to Hadley, Mass. =1644
163. Mary Smith (c. 1625-1680) (not a kinswoman of 160 or 161)
164. John Root (prob. 1608-1684), probably Badby, Northamptonshire to Farmington, Conn., = c. 1641
165. Mary Kilbourn (c. 1619-1697), Wood Ditton, Cambridgeshire to Farmington
166. Robert Ashley, d. 1682, Springfield, Mass. =1641
167. --- (widow of Thomas Horton)
168. same as 160
169. same as 161
170. same as 162
171. same as 163
172-173. ---
174. Josiah Churchill, d. 1685/6, Wethersfield, Conn., = c. 1638
175. Elizabeth Foote (1617/8-1700), Shalford, Essex to Wethersfield
176. William Chandler (1595-1641/2), Bishop's Stortford, Hertfordshire to Roxbury, Mass. =1625
177. Annis (Agnes, Hannah) Bayford (1603-1682/3), Farnham, Essex to Sudbury, Mass., m. (2) John Dane, (3) John Parmenter
178. (prob.) Daniel Brewer, d. 1646, Roxbury, Mass.
179. (prob.) Joanna --- (c. 1592-1689)
180. George Abbott, d. 1647, Rowley, Mass.
181. ---
182. Ralph Farnum (c. 1601-ante 1648), possibly London to Andover, Mass.
183. Alice ---, b. c. 1607, m. (2) Solomon Martin
184. Thomas Hale (1610-1679), Watton-at-Stone, Hertfordshire to Norwalk, Conn. =1639/40
185. Jane Lord, d. ante 1659
186. William Markham (c. 1621-1689), Hadley, Mass.
187. Priscilla Graves, d. ante 1658
188. Thomas Gleason (c. 1607-1686), Cambridge, Mass.
189. Susanna Page, d. 1691
190. James Eggleston, d. 1679, Windsor, Conn.
191. Esther/Hester --- (c. 1636-1720), m. (2) James Eno, poss. (3) John Williams
192-211. ---
212. Christopher Lindsey, d. 1669, Lynn, Mass.
213. Margaret ---, d. 1688
214. Hugh Alley (c. 1608-1674), Lynn, Mass.
215. Mary ---
216. Thomas Storrs, b. 1605, Sutton-cum-Lound, Nottinghamshire
217. Mary ---
218. Thomas Huckins (c. 1617-1679), Barnstable, Mass., = c. 1642
219. Mary Wells, d. 1648
220. Thomas Burgess, d. 1684/5, possibly Tanfield, Durham to Sandwich, Mass., possibly 1628

221. Dorothy (possibly Waynes), d. 1686/7
222. Peter Worden, d. 1680/1, Yarmouth, Mass.
223. Mary ---, d. 1687
224-231. ---
232. Richard Hovey, d. 1676/7, Waltham Abbey, Essex
233. ---, prob. d. 1683
234. Robert Andrews, d. 1644/6, Ipswich, Mass.
235. Elizabeth ---
236. Aaron Cooke, Jr. (1613/4-1690), Bridport, Dorset to Windsor, Conn. =ante 1637
237. Mary Cooke, living 1645
238. William Westwood (c. 1603/6-1669), Essex, England to Hadley, Mass., = 1630
239. Bridget Kerrington (1602-1676), Glemsford, Suffolk to Hadley
240. William Phelps, d. 1672, Windsor, Conn.
241. Elizabeth ---, d. ante 1636
242-245. ---
246. John Marsh (c. 1586-will dated 1627), Braintree, Essex, England
247. Grace Baldwin, will proved 1667
248-251. ---
252. Robert Day (c. 1604-1648), Hartford, Conn. =ante 1637
253. Editha Stebbing, d. 1688, m. (2) John Maynard, (3) Elizur Holyoke
254. Thomas Cooper (c. 1617-1675), Springfield, Mass.
255. Sarah (Slye?), d. 1688, m. (2) William Clarke

* * *

20. JAMES ABRAM GARFIELD

1. JAMES ABRAM GARFIELD, Orange, Ohio 19 Nov. 1831-Elberon, New Jersey 19 Sept. 1881, Hiram, Ohio 11 Nov. 1853 Lucretia Rudolph, Garrettsville, Ohio 19 Apr. 1832-South Pasadena, California 13 Mar. 1918
2. Abram Garfield, Worcester, New York 28 Dec. 1799-Otsego Co., N. Y. 3 May 1833, Zanesville, Ohio 3 Feb. 1820
3. Eliza Ballou, Richmond, New Hampshire 21 Sept. 1801-Mentor, Ohio 21 Jan. 1888
4. Thomas Garfield, Westminster, Massachusetts 19 Mar. 1773-Worcester, N. Y. 1801, c. 1794
5. Asenath Hill of Schoharie Co., N. Y., c. 1778-Newberg, Ohio 5 Feb. 1851, m. (2) Amos Boynton (she was a likely sister of Josiah Hill [c. 1776-c. 1864] of Worcester & Cherry Valley [now Roseboom], N. Y.)
6. James Ballou (IV), Cumberland, Rhode Island 25 Apr. 1761-Richmond, N. H. 30 Apr. 1808, Richmond 5 Nov. 1786
7. Mehitable Ingalls, Cumberland, R. I. 21 July 1764-Perry, Ohio 4 Dec. 1821
8. Solomon Garfield, Lincoln, Mass. 18 July 1743-Worcester, N. Y. 1807, Sudbury, Mass. 22 Aug. 1769
9. Sarah Bryant (widow of James Stimpson), d. post 1785, who prob. belonged to, but cannot be placed among, the progeny of the immigrant Abraham Bryant of Reading, Mass.
10-11. ---
12. James Ballou (III), Wrentham, Mass. (later Cumberland, R. I.) 10 Dec. 1723-Richmond, N. H. 21 Jan. 1812, Wrentham 7 June 1744
13. Tamasin Cook, Wrentham 16 June 1725-Richmond, N. H. 25 Apr. 1804
14. Henry Ingalls, Cumberland, R. I. 12 Oct. 1738-Otsego Co., N. Y. c. 1811, Rehoboth, Mass. 31 Dec. 1761
15. Sybil Carpenter, b. Rehoboth 26 Feb. 1739

16. Thomas Garfield, Jr., 28 Feb. 1713-Lincoln, Mass. 3 Jan. 1774, Lunenburg, Mass. 21 Oct. 1742
17. Rebecca Johnson, Lunenburg 2 Nov. 1719-3 Feb. 1763
18-23. ---
24. James Ballou, Jr., Providence (later Smithfield), R. I. 1 Nov. 1684-Cumberland, R. I. 10 Feb. 1764, Providence 25 Jan. 1713
25. Catherine Arnold
26. Daniel Cook, Mendon, Mass. 18 Aug. 1703-will proved 11 Apr. 1786
27. Susanna ---, d. post 1786
28. Ebenezer Ingalls, Rehoboth 14 July 1711-ante 1771, Rehoboth 5 June 1735
29. Elizabeth Wheeler, b. Rehoboth 9 June 1717
30. Jotham Carpenter, Jr., Rehoboth 1 Aug. 1708-Cumberland, R. I. 10 May 1777, Rehoboth 11 May 1728
31. Mehitable Thompson, Rehoboth 17 May 1701-Rehoboth 10 Feb. 1747
32. Thomas Garfield, Watertown, Mass. 12 Dec. 1680-Weston, Mass. 4 Feb. 1752, Watertown 2 Jan. 1706/7
33. Mercy Bigelow, Watertown c. 1686-Weston 28 Feb. 1744/5
34. Samuel Johnson of Lunenburg, Mass.
35. Rebecca ---, d. Lunenburg 29 Aug. 1731
36-47. ---
48. James Ballou, Providence, R. I. c. 1652-post 1744, Providence 25 July 1683
49. Susanna Whitman, Providence 28 Feb. 1658-c. 1725
50-51. ---
52. Nicholas Cook, Weymouth, Mass. 9 Feb. 1659/60-Bellingham, Mass. 7 Dec. 1730, 4 Nov. 1684
53. Joanna Rockwood, Mendon, Mass. 25 Aug. 1669-c. 1710
54-55. ---
56. Edmund Ingalls, d. Rehoboth, Mass., m. 29 Nov. 1705
57. Eunice Ludden, b. Weymouth, d. post 1726
58. James Wheeler, Jr., Rehoboth 27 Mar. 1697-Rehoboth 1740 or 1753, Rehoboth 8 Mar. 1716
59. Elizabeth West, b. Rehoboth 30 Nov. 1694
60. Jotham Carpenter, Swansea, Mass. 1 June 1682-Rehoboth, Mass. c. 1760, Rehoboth 10 July 1707
61. Desire Martin, Rehoboth 20 Mar. 1684/5-Rehoboth 12 Sept. 1727
62. John Thompson, Reading, Mass. 24 Mar. 1660/1, later of Rehoboth
63. Elizabeth ---
64. Benjamin Garfield, Watertown c. 1643-Watertown 28 Nov. 1717, Watertown 17 Jan. 1677/8
65. Elizabeth Bridge, b. Cambridge, Mass. 17 Aug. 1659, m. (2) Daniel Harrington
66. Joshua Bigelow, Watertown 5 Nov. 1655-Westminster, Mass. 1 Feb. 1745, Watertown 20 Oct. 1676
67. Elizabeth Flagg, Watertown 22 Mar. 1656-Watertown 9 Aug. 1729
68-95. ---
96. Maturin Ballou, d. Providence, R. I. 1661-1673
97. Hannah Pike, d. Providence 1718/9
98. Valentine Whitman, d. Providence 26 Jan. 1701, c. 1650-1651
99. Mary ---, d. Providence 31 May 1718
100-103. ---
104. Walter Cooke, d. Mendon, Mass. 5 Jan. 1695/6
105. Catharine ---, d. Mendon 2 Jan. 1695/6
106. John Rockwood, Braintree, Mass. 1 Dec. 1641-Mendon 1724, Braintree 15 Sept. 1662
107. Joanna Ford
108-111. ---

112. John Ingalls, prob. Skirbeck, Lincolnshire c. 1626-Rehoboth, Mass. 31 Dec. 1721, Lynn, Mass. 26 May 1667
113. Elizabeth Barrett of Salem, d. ante 1718
114. Benjamin Ludden of Weymouth, Mass. c. 1650-on expedition to Canada 28 Jan. 1690/1, c. 1678
115. Eunice Holbrook, b. Weymouth 12 May 1658
116. James Wheeler, Salisbury, Mass. 27 May 1667-Rehoboth, Mass. 1740 or 1753, c. 1690
117. Grizell Squire, Boston, Mass. 14 May 1668-ante 1738
118. John West of Swansea and Rehoboth, Mass.
119. Mehitable ---, d. post 1694
120. Benjamin Carpenter, Rehoboth 15 Jan. 1658-Swansea 22 May 1727, c. 1679
121. Renew Weeks, Dorchester, Mass. 12 Aug. 1660-Swansea 29 July 1703
122. John Martin, bp. Ottery St. Mary, Devon 20 Jan. 1652/3-Rehoboth 28 Aug. 1720, Rehoboth 27 June 1681
123. Mercy Billington, Plymouth, Mass. prob. 25 Feb. 1651/2-Rehoboth 28 Sept. 1718
124. George Thompson, c. 1638-Reading, Mass. 7 Sept. 1674
125. Sarah ---, d. post 1674
126-127. ---
128. Edward Garfield (c. 1575?-1672), Watertown, Mass., = c. 1634
129. Rebecca --- (c. 1606-1661)
130. Matthew Bridge (c. 1615-1700), Lexington, Mass., = 1643
131. Anna Danforth (bp. 1622-1704), Framlingham, Suffolk to Lexington
132. John Bigelow (c. 1617-1703), Watertown, Mass., = 1642
133. Mary Warren (1624-1691), Nayland, Suffolk to Watertown
134. Thomas Flagg (prob. 1621-1697/8), prob. Hardingham, Norfolk to Watertown
135. Mary ---, d. 1703
136-193. ---
194. Robert Pike, d. c. 1674, Providence, R. I.
195. Catharine ---, d. 1679-1685/6
196-211. ---
212. Richard Rockwood, d. ante 1660, Braintree, Mass., = c. 1636/7
213. Agnes --- (c. 1607-1643), widow of Zachary Bicknell
214-223. ---
224. Edmund Ingalls (c. 1590-1648) Skirbeck, Lincolnshire to Lynn, Mass., = c. 1618
225. Ann ---, living 1649
226-227. ---
228. James Luddin (c. 1611-1692/3), Weymouth, Mass., = 1636
229. Mary Johnson, b. c. 1614
230. John Holbrook (1618-1699), Glastonbury, Somerset to Weymouth, Mass.
231. Elizabeth Stream (c. 1624-1688)
232. Henry Wheeler (c. 1635-ante 1696), Salisbury, England to Salisbury, Mass., = c. 1659
233. Abigail Allen (1640-post 1696)
234. Philip Squire, d. 1692/3, Boston, Mass., = c. 1664
235. Rachel Ruggles
236-239. ---
240. Joseph Carpenter (c. 1634-1675), Swansea, Mass., = 1655
241. Margaret Sutton (c. 1635-1700)
242. William Weeks (c. 1628/9-1677), Dorchester, Mass., = c. 1649/50
243. Elizabeth --- (c. 1631-1709/10)
244. Richard Martin (1609-1694/5), Ottery St. Mary, Devon to Rehoboth, Mass., = 1631

245. Elizabeth Salter
246. Francis Billington (c. 1606-1684), prob. Spalding or Cowbit, Lincolnshire to Middleboro, Mass., son of Mayflower passenger & murderer John Billington & Elinor ---, = 1634
247. Christian Penn (c. 1606-c. 1684), widow of Mayflower passenger Francis Eaton
248-255. ---

* * *

21. CHESTER ALAN ARTHUR

1. CHESTER ALAN ARTHUR, Fairfield, Vermont 5 Oct. 1830-New York, New York 18 Nov. 1886, New York City 25 Oct. 1859 Ellen Lewis Herndon, Culpeper, Virginia 30 Aug. 1837-New York City 12 Jan. 1880
2. Rev. William Arthur, "the Draen," near Ballymena, Antrim, Ireland 5 Dec. 1796-Newtonville (near Albany), N. Y. 27 Oct. 1875, Dunham, Quebec 12 Apr. 1821
3. Malvina Stone, Berkshire, Vt. 29 Apr. 1802-Newtonville, N. Y. 16 Jan. 1869
4. Alan Arthur of "the Draen," near Ballymena, b. c. 1766
5. Eliza McHarg
6. Rev. George Washington Stone, Piermont, New Hampshire 22 Feb. 1777-Dunham, Quebec 12 Jan. 1854, 23 Mar. 1800
7. Judith Stevens, Newbury, Vt. 26 Oct. 1771-Dunham, Quebec 28 Dec. 1855
8. Gavin Arthur of "the Draen," near Ballymena, b. c. 1735
9. Jane Campbell
10-11. ---
12. Uriah Stone, Haverhill, Mass. 1 Dec. 1744-Piermont, N. H. 7 Apr. 1807, Hampstead, N. H. 24 Nov. 1763
13. Hepzibah Hadley, Amesbury, Mass. 25 July 1744-East Berkshire, Vt. 4 May 1732
14. Simeon Stevens, Hampton Falls, N. H. 29 Apr. 1735-Newbury, Vt. 6 July 1788, Hampstead, N. H. 16 Dec. 1762
15. Sarah Hadley, Amesbury, Mass. 13 Feb. 1736/7-Newbury, Vt. 1779
16-23. ---
24. Benjamin Stone, bp. Andover, Mass. 2 May 1714, later of Haverhill, Mass., m. Gloucester, Mass. 26 or 28 Apr. 1734
25. Mary Nichols
26. Samuel Hadley (III), Amesbury, Mass. 5 May 1707-Hampstead, N. H. 3 Mar. 1761, Amesbury 22 Oct. 1768
27. Judith Flanders, b. Amesbury 4 Feb. 1711/2
28. Otho Stevens, prob. England or Wales c. 1702-Hampstead, N. H. 4 Apr. 1771, Gloucester, Mass. 21 Mar. 1722/3
29. Abigail Kent, Gloucester 9 July 1697-Hampstead 4 Mar. 1771
30-31. same as 26-27
32-47. ---
48. Hugh Stone, Jr., b. Andover, Mass. 3 Aug. 1682
49. Dorothy ---
50-51. ---
52. Samuel Hadley, Jr., prob. Amesbury, Mass.-Amesbury 14 Dec. 1747, Amesbury 20 Jan. 1703/4
53. Dorothy Colby, Rowley, Mass. 15 June 1677-Amesbury 18 May 1756
54. Daniel Flanders, Salisbury, Mass. 16 Mar. 1674/5-Amesbury ante 1 Apr. 1735, Amesbury 1 May 1700
55. Sarah Colby, d. 1720-1724
56-57. ---
58. Josiah Kent, Gloucester, Mass. 31 Mar. 1659/60-Gloucester 19 May 1725, Gloucester 17 Apr. 1689
59. Mary Lovekin or Lufkin, b. c. 1670-Gloucester 1730

60-63. same as 52-55
64-95. ---
96. Hugh Stone, executed Andover, Mass., prob. 1689, m. Andover 15 Oct. 1667
97. Hannah Foster, murdered by her husband Andover 20 Apr. 1689
98-103. ---
104. Samuel Hadley, c. 1652-prob. Amesbury, Mass. post 1734
105. Jane Martin, Salisbury, Mass. 2 Nov. 1656-post 1703/4
106. Isaac Colby, Salisbury 6 July 1640-Amesbury Mar.-Apr. 1684
107. Martha Parratt, Rowley 9 Oct. 1649-Amesbury 13 July 1730
108. Steven Flanders, Jr., (recorded at Salisbury) 8 Mar. 1646-Salisbury ante 1689, Salisbury 28 Dec. 1670
109. Abigail Carter, Salisbury 11th mo. 1652, living 1747
110. John Colby, Jr., Salisbury 19 Nov. 1656-Amesbury 6 Apr. 1719, Amesbury 27 Dec. 1675
111. Sarah Eldridge, d. Amesbury post 1692
112-115. ---
116. Thomas Kent, Jr., c. 1635-Gloucester, Mass. 3 Aug. 1696, Gloucester 28 Mar. 1658/9
117. Joan Penney
118. Thomas Lufkin, d. Gloucester 3 Mar. 1708
119. Mary ---, c. 1644-Gloucester Dec. 1730
120-127. same as 104-111
128-193. ---
194. Andrew Foster (c. 1580?-1685), Andover, Mass.
195. Ann ---, d. 1692
196-207. ---
208. George Hadley of Ipswich & Rowley, Mass., = c. 1651
209. Mary Proctor (c. 1634-ante 1668)
210. George Martin (c. 1618-c. 1686), Salisbury & Amesbury, Mass., = 1646
211. Susanna North (c. 1620-1625-executed for witchcraft at Salem 19 July 1692)
212. Anthony Colby, d. 1660/1, Salisbury, Mass.
213. Susanna ---, d. 1689, m. (2) William Whitridge
214. Francis Parratt (c. 1610-c. 1656), Rowley, Mass. (d. England)
215. Elizabeth Northend, b. c. 1612, m. (2) Thomas Tenney
216. Steven Flanders, d. 1684, Salisbury, Mass.
217. Jane ---, d. 1683
218. Thomas Carter, will dated 1676, Salisbury, Mass.
219. Mary ---, d. post 1676
220. John Colby (1633-1673/4), Amesbury, Mass. (son of 212-213), = 1655/6
221. Frances Hoyt (c. 1635-1720/1)
222-231. ---
232. Thomas Kent, d. 1658, Gloucester, Mass.
233. --- ---, d. 1671
234. Thomas Penney, d. c. 1692, Gloucester, Mass.
235. Ann ---, d. 1667
236-239. ---
240-255. same as 208-223

* * *

22. [& 24.] (STEPHEN) GROVER CLEVELAND

1. (STEPHEN) GROVER CLEVELAND, Caldwell, New Jersey 18 Mar. 1837-Princeton, N. J. 24 June 1908, Washington, D. C. (The White House) 2 June 1886 Frances Folsom, Buffalo, New York 21 July 1864-Baltimore, Maryland 29 Oct. 1947 (she m. [2] Thomas Jex Preston, Jr.)
2. Rev. Richard Falley Cleveland, Norwich, Connecticut 19 June

1804-Holland Patent, N. Y. 1 Oct. 1853, Baltimore, Md. 10 Sept. 1829

3. Anne Neal, Baltimore, Md. 4 Feb. 1806-Holland Patent, N. Y. 19 July 1882

4. William Cleveland, Norwich, Conn. 20 Dec. 1770-Black Rock (near Buffalo), N. Y. 18 Aug. 1837, Westfield, Mass. 19 Dec. 1793

5. Margaret Falley, Westfield, Mass. 25 Nov. 1766-Black Rock 10 Aug. 1850

6. Abner Neal, Ireland-Baltimore c. 1826

7. Barbara Reel, d. Baltimore c. 1832, German Quakeress of Germantown, Pa.

8. Rev. Aaron Cleveland (IV), East Haddam, Conn. 2 Feb. 1744-New Haven, Conn. 21 Sept. 1815, Norwich, Conn. 12 April 1768

9. Abiah Hyde, Norwich 27 Dec. 1749-Norwich 23 Aug. 1788

10. Richard Falley, Jr., Lower Settlement, St. Georges' River (now Cushing), District of Maine 31 Jan. 1740-Westfield, Mass. 3 Sept. 1808, Springfield, Mass. 14 Jan. 1762

11. Margaret Hitchcock, Springfield 25 May 1741-Volney (now Fulton), N. Y. 20 Mar. 1820

12-15. ---

16. Rev. Aaron Cleveland (III), prob. Cambridge, Mass. 29 Oct. 1715-Philadelphia, Pa. 11 Aug. 1757, Harvard graduate of 1735, Medford, Mass. 4 Aug. 1739

17. Susanna Porter, Medford 26 Apr. 1716-Salem, Mass. 1 Mar. 1788

18. James Hyde, Norwich, Conn. 28 Feb. 1707-Norwich 24 Apr. 1793, Norwich 26 Dec. 1743

19. Sarah Marshall, Norwich 12 Apr. 1720-Norwich 3 Nov. 1773

20. Richard Falley, Isle of Guernsey c. 1711/2-Westfield, Mass. 7 Aug. 1756, St. Georges' River, District of Maine c. 1739

21. Ann Lamb, Dublin, Ireland c. 1722-Westfield 29 Apr. 1758

22. Samuel Hitchcock, Springfield, Mass. 9 June 1717-Springfield 22 Apr. 1777, Springfield 11 June 1738

23. Ruth Stebbins, Springfield 16 Oct. 1722-Springfield 20 Feb. 1775

24-31. ---

32. Aaron Cleveland, Jr., Woburn, Mass. 9 July 1680-Cambridge (now Medford), Mass. or Norwich, Conn. c. 1 Dec. 1755, Woburn 1 Jan. 1701/2

33. Abigail Waters, Woburn 29 Nov. 1683-prob. Norwich, Conn. 6 Jan. 1761

34. Rev. Aaron Porter, Hadley, Mass. 19 July 1689-Medford, Mass. 24 Jan. 1721/2, Harvard graduate of 1708, Salem, Mass. 22 Oct. 1713

35. Susanna Sewall, Salem 24 Oct. 1691-22 July 1747

36. John Hyde, Norwich, Conn. Dec. 1667-Norwich 26 July 1727, Norwich 3 Mar. 1698

37. Experience Abell, Norwich Dec. 1674-Norwich 24 Oct. 1763

38. Abiel Marshall, d. Norwich 1 June 1758, m. 18 Nov. 1708

39. Abiah Hough, New London, Conn. 30 Oct. 1690-Norwich, Conn. post 1720

40-41. ---

42. Richard Lamb of Dublin, d. at sea en route to Boston, Mass. between 12 Aug. 1736 & 4 July 1737

43. ---

44. John Hitchcock, Jr., Springfield, Mass. 13 Apr. 1670-Springfield 4 July 1751, Springfield 24 Sept. 1691

45. Mary Ball, Springfield 12 July 1673-Springfield 14 Oct. 1760

46. Thomas Stebbins, Springfield 7 Mar. 1686/7-Springfield 4 Dec. 1758, Springfield 1 Mar. 1711

47. Mary Ely, Springfield 25 July 1689-Springfield 9 Apr. 1770

48-63. ---

64. Aaron Cleveland, Woburn, Mass. 10 Jan. 1654/5-Woburn 14

Sept. 1716, Woburn 26 Sept. 1675

65. Dorcas Wilson, 29 Jan. 1657-Cambridge, Mass. 29 Nov. 1714

66. Samuel Waters, Lancaster, Mass. 14 Jan. 1651/2-Woburn 2 May 1729, Lancaster 21 Mar. 1672/3

67. Mary Hudson, Lancaster 7 Sept. 1653-Woburn 10 Dec. 1721

68. Samuel Porter, Jr., Hadley, Mass. 6 Apr. 1660-Hadley 29 July 1722, Hadley 22 Feb. 1683

69. Joanna Cooke, Hadley 10 July 1665-Hadley 13 Nov. 1713

70. Stephen Sewall, Baddesley, Hampshire 10 Aug. 1657-Salem, Mass. 17 Oct. 1725, 13 June 1682

71. Margaret Mitchell, c. 1664-Boston, Mass. 20 Jan. 1735/6

72. Samuel Hyde, Hartford, Conn. c. 1637-Norwich, Conn. 1667, June 1659

73. Jane Lee, bp. Rusper, Sussex 12 Sept. 1640

74. Caleb Abell, prob. Rehoboth, Mass. c. 1646-Norwich, Conn. 17 Aug. 1731, Norwich July 1669

75. Margaret Post, Saybrook, Conn. 21 Feb. 1653-Norwich Nov. 1700

76-77. ---

78. John Hough, New London, Conn. 17 Oct. 1655-New London 26 Aug. 1715, 17 Jan. 1680

79. Sarah Post, b. Saybrook, Conn. 6 Nov. 1659

80-87. ---

88. John Hitchcock, Wethersfield, Conn. 27 Sept. 1642-Springfield, Mass. 9 Feb. 1711/2, Springfield 27 Sept. 1666

89. Hannah Chapin, Springfield 2 Dec. 1644-Springfield 21 May 1719

90. Samuel Ball, Springfield 6 Mar. 1647/8-Northampton, Mass. 13 Sept. 1689, prob. Hadley, Mass. 15 June 1671

91. Mary Graves, Hatfield, Mass. c. 1654-Springfield 21 May 1727, m. (2) Benjamin Stebbins, m. (3) James Warriner

92. Edward Stebbins, Springfield 14 Apr. 1656-Springfield 31 Oct. 1712, Springfield 12 Apr. 1679

93. Sarah Graves, Hatfield c. 1659-Springfield 12 June 1700

94. Joseph Ely, Springfield 20 Aug. 1663-West Springfield, Mass. 28 Apr. 1755, Springfield 9 July 1685

95. Mary Riley, Springfield 2 June 1665-West Springfield 19 May 1736

96-127. ---

128. Moses Cleveland (c. 1624-1701/2), Woburn, Mass., = 1648

129. Ann Winn (c. 1626-ante 1682)

130. John Wilson (c. 1611-1687), Woburn, Mass.

131. Hannah James, m. (2) Thomas Fuller of Danvers, Mass.

132. Laurence Waters (c. 1603-1687), Charlestown, Mass., = c. 1632

133. Ann Linton (c. 1614-1680)

134. Daniel Hudson (1620-1697), Epping, Essex to Lancaster, Mass.

135. Joanna ---, d. 1697

136. Samuel Porter (1635-1689), Hadley, Mass., = c. 1659

137. Hannah Stanley (c. 1640-1708)

138. Aaron Cooke (III) (1640/1-1716), Hadley, Mass., = 1661

139. Sarah Westwood (c. 1644-1730)

140. Henry Sewall, Jr. (1615-1700), Baddesley, Hampshire to Newbury, Mass., = 1646

141. Jane Dummer, b. c. 1628, Bishopstoke, Hampshire to Newbury

142. Rev. Jonathan Mitchell (1624-1668, Harvard graduate of 1647), Cambridge, Mass., = 1650

143. Margaret Borodell, widow of Rev. Thomas Shepard

144. William Hyde, d. 1681/2, Norwich, Conn.

145. ---

146. Thomas Lee, d. en route to New England, = c. 1639

147. Phoebe Browne, b. 1620, Rusper, Sussex to Norwich, Conn.

148. Robert Abell (c. 1605-1663), Stapenhill, Derbyshire to Rehoboth, Mass.
149. Joanna ---, d. post 1682, Norwich, Conn.
150. John Post (c. 1626/7-1710/1), Norwich, Conn., = 1652
151. Hester (Esther) Hyde, d. 1703 (daughter of 144-145 above)
152-155. ---
156. William Hough (c. 1619-1683), New London, Conn., = 1645
157. Sarah Calkins
158. same as 150
159. same as 151
160-175. ---
176. Luke Hitchcock, d. 1659, Wethersfield, Conn., = prob. by 1642
177. Elizabeth Gibbons, d. 1696, Springfield, Mass., m. (2) William Warriner, m. (3) Joseph Baldwin
178. Samuel Chapin (1598-1675), Paignton, Devon to Springfield, Mass., = 1623/4
179. Cecily Penny (1601-1682/3), Paignton to Springfield
180. Francis Ball (c. 1620-1648), Springfield, Mass., = 1644
181. Abigail Burt (c. 1623-1707), Harberton, Devon to Springfield, m. (2) Benjamin Munn, m. (3) Thomas Stebbins, 184 below
182. John Graves (c. 1622-1677), Hatfield, Mass., = c. 1650
183. Mary Smith (c. 1630-1668), Wethersfield, Conn.
184. Thomas Stebbins (1619/20-1683), Springfield, Mass., = (1) 1645
185. Hannah Wright, d. 1660
186. same as 182
187. same as 183
188. Samuel Ely, d. 1691/2, Springfield, Mass., = 1659
189. Mary Day (c. 1641-1725), Hatfield, Mass., m. (2) Thomas Stebbins, Jr. (son of 184-185 above), m. (3) John Coleman
190. John Riley, d. 1684, Springfield, Mass.
191. Margaret ---, d. 1689
192-255. ---

* * *

25. WILLIAM McKINLEY, JR.

1. WILLIAM McKINLEY, JR., Niles, Ohio 29 Jan. 1843-Buffalo, New York 14 Sept. 1901, Canton, Ohio 25 Jan. 1871 Ida Saxton, Canton 8 June 1847-Canton 26 May 1907
2. William McKinley, Wolf Creek, Pennsylvania 15 Nov. 1807-Canton 24 Nov. 1892, New Lisbon, Ohio 6 Jan. 1829
3. Nancy Campbell Allison, Columbiana Co., Ohio (near New Lisbon) 22 April 1809-Canton 12 Dec. 1897
4. James Stevenson McKinley, Wolf Creek 19 Sept. 1783-South Bend, Indiana 20 Aug. 1847, Mercer Co., Pa. c. 1805
5. Mary Rose, prob. Hunterdon Co., New Jersey or Bucks Co., Pa. 10 or 15 Nov. 1788-South Bend, Ind. 20 Aug. 1847 (on the same day as her husband)
6. Abner Allison, c. 1769-Centre, Ohio 10 Sept. 1827, c. 1798
7. Ann Campbell, 3 Jan. 1774-6 Nov. 1846
8. David McKinley, Chanceford, Pa. 16 May 1755-Chatfield, Ohio 8 Aug. 1840, Westmoreland Co., Pa. 19 Dec. 1780
9. Sarah Gray, 10 May 1760-6 Oct. 1814, of Lancaster Co., Pa.
10. Andrew Rose, Sr., ante 1755-Mercer Co., Pa. 1815-17, 5 Mar. 1774
11. Hannah Chapman, 1 or 15 Aug. 1757-Chatfield, Ohio 1840
12. (said to be) Gavin Allison
13. ---
14. (said to be) Obadiah Campbell, b. ante 1755, of Carmichael, Pa. in 1800

15. (said to be) Abigail ---
16. John McKinlay, c. 1728-Chanceford, Pa. 18 Feb. 1779
17. Margaret ---, d. ante 1782, m. (2) Thomas McColtagh
18. John Gray of Lancaster Co., Pa. (Donegal Presbyterian Church near Mt. Joy)
19. Hannah Stevenson/Stephenson
20. (prob.) John Rose, d. Hunterdon Co., N. J. c. 1788
21-31. ---
32. David McKinlay, Ireland c. 1705-Chanceford, Pa. 1760-61, ante 1728
33. Esther ---
34-37. ---
38. James Stevenson/Stephenson of Lancaster Co., Pa. (Donegal Presbyterian Church near Mt. Joy)
39. Elizabeth ---
40-255. ---

* * *

26. THEODORE ROOSEVELT, JR.

1. THEODORE ROOSEVELT, JR., New York City (NYC), New York 27 Oct. 1858-Sagamore Hill, Oyster Bay, Long Island, N. Y. 6 Jan. 1919, (1) Brookline, Massachusetts 27 Oct. 1880 Alice Hathaway Lee, Chestnut Hill (Boston), Mass. 29 July 1861-NYC 14 Feb. 1884, (2) London, England 2 Dec. 1886 Edith Kermit Carow, Norwich, Connecticut 6 Aug. 1861-Sagamore Hill 30 Sept. 1948
2. Theodore Roosevelt, NYC 22 Sept. 1831-NYC 9 Feb. 1878, Roswell, Georgia 22 Dec. 1853
3. Martha Bulloch, Hartford, Connecticut 8 July 1834-NYC 12 Feb. 1884
4. Cornelius Van Schaack Roosevelt, NYC 30 Jan. 1794-Oyster Bay 17 July 1871, c. 1822
5. Margaret Barnhill, 13 Dec. 1799-23 Jan. 1861
6. James Stephens Bulloch, b. prob. Savannah, Ga. c. 1793-18 Feb. 1849, 8 May 1831
7. Martha Stewart, bp. 15 Aug. 1799-c. 1862-4, widow of John Elliott
8. James J. (Jacobus) Roosevelt, bp. NYC 25 Oct. 1759-NYC 12 or 13 Aug. 1840, Kinderhook, N. Y. 8 Mar. 1793
9. Maria Van Schaack, bp. Kinderhook 8 Dec. 1773-NYC 3 Feb. 1845
10. Robert Barnhill, 31 Jan. 1754-12 Aug. 1814, prob. Sussex Co., New Jersey 22 Sept. 1778
11. Elizabeth Potts, prob. Moreland, Pennsylvania 27 Jan. 1750-20 Aug. 1807
12. James Bulloch, Ga. c. 1765-Ga. 9 Feb. 1806, 13 Apr. 1786
13. Anne Irvine, 14 Jan. 1770-post 1810, m. (2) James Powell
14. General Daniel Stewart, Newport, Liberty Co., Ga. 20 Oct. or Dec. 1761-17 May 1829, (bond) Liberty Co. 18 Jan. 1786
15. Susannah Oswald, Newport, Ga. 2 Nov. 1770-20 Dec. 1807
16. Jacobus Roosevelt, bp. NYC 9 Aug. 1724-Red Hook, N. Y. 12 Mar. 1777, NYC 4 Dec. 1746
17. Annetje Bogert, bp. NYC 18 Aug. 1728-NYC 9 July 1773
18. Cornelius Van Schaack, Jr., bp. Kinderhook 15 Sept. 1734-18 Mar. 1797, 1 Dec. 1772
19. Angeltje (Angelica) Yates, b. Albany, N. Y. 6 July 1752
20. John Barnhill, d. 27 Feb. 1797
21. Sarah Craig
22. Thomas Potts, c. 1729-prob. Chelsea Forge, N. J. 29 July 1776, (Abington, Pa., 2nd int. 12-25-1752) 16 Jan. 1753
23. Elizabeth Lukens of Horsham & Upper Dublin, m. (2) Dr. John Rockhill
24. Archibald Bulloch, first President of the Provincial Con-

gress of Georgia, delegate to the Continental Congress, Charleston, South Carolina c. 1729-30-Savannah 22 Feb. 1777, Argyle Island, Ga. 9 Oct. 1764

25. Mary De Veaux of Shaftsbury, Ga., Ga. (26?) Jan. 1748-Savannah 26 May 1818

26. Dr. John Irvine, Scotland 15 Sept. 1742-Ga. 15 Oct. 1808, Sunbury, Ga. 5 or 19 Sept. 1765

27. Ann Elizabeth Baillie, 27 Sept. 1749-Chatham Co., Ga. 23 July 1807

28. John Stewart, Jr., Dorchester, S. C. 13 Feb. 1725/6-Midway, Ga. 4 Sept. 1776

29. Susannah (Bacon?), d. Midway 21 Oct. 1766

30. Joseph Oswald, d. Liberty Co., Ga. 1786-8

31. Ann ---, d. post 1796

32. Johannes Roosevelt, bp. Kingston, N. Y. 3 Mar. 1689-NYC 4 Apr. 1750, NYC 25 Sept. 1708

33. Heyltje Sioerts, bp. NYC 2 Sept. 1688-prob. NYC between 11 July 1751 & 5 Mar. 1752

34. John Bogert, NYC (or Harlem) 1 May 1697-NYC 7 Nov. 1775, NYC 10 Mar. 1716

35. Hannah Peeck, NYC 12 June 1696-NYC 8 Oct. 1769

36. Cornelius Van Schaack, Kinderhook 17 Oct. 1705-Kinderhook 13 Oct. 1776, Kinderhook 6 Oct. 1728

37. Lydia Van Dyck, Albany 16 July 1704-Kinderhook 10 June 1785

38. Johannes G. Yates, Albany 14 Oct. 1716-prob. Albany between 27 Dec. 1775 & 4 June 1776, Albany 28 Nov. 1737

39. Rebecca Waldron, bp. Albany 30 Aug. 1719

40. Robert Barnhill of Bucks Co., Pa.

41. Sarah ---

42. Daniel Craig, d. prob. Bucks Co., Pa., m. c. 1776

43. Margaret ---, d. post 1776

44. John Potts, prob. Bristol, Pa. 8 8th Mo. 1696-Upper Dublin, Pa. shortly post 28 Sept. 1766, Abington, Pa. between 27 4th Mo. & 25 5th Mo. 1726

45. Elizabeth McVeagh, c. 1699-5 1st Mo. 1791

46. William Lukens, prob. Germantown, Pa. 22 Feb. 1688/9-prob. Upper Dublin between 15 June 1739 & 26 Feb. 1739/40, (Abington, Pa. 2nd int.) 27 Nov. 1710

47. Elizabeth Tyson, Germantown 7 Oct. 1690-bur. 18 Feb. 1765

48. James Bulloch, prob. Glasgow, Scotland c. 1701-Ga. 25 Oct. 1780, S. C. c. 1729

49. Jean Stobo, b. prob. S. C. c. 1710

50. James De Veaux, prob. France c. 1710-23 Nov. 1785, prob. Charleston, S. C. c. 1730

51. Anne Fairchild, prob. Charleston-Savannah, Ga. 8 Mar. 1765

52. Charles Irvine of Over Boddam, Bieldside & possibly Cults, near Aberdeen, Scotland c. 1696-28 Mar. 1779, 7 June 1733

53. Euphemia Douglas of Tilquhillie, c. 1711-21 Dec. 1766

54. Kenneth Baillie of Balrobert & Torbreck, Scotland-St. John Parish, Ga. 10 July 1766

55. Elizabeth Mackay

56. John Stewart of Dorchester Co., S. C. & St. John's Parish, Ga.

57. Hannah ---, prob. d. St. George's Parish, Berkeley Co., S. C. c. 1780

58-63. ---

64. Nicholas Roosevelt, bp. NYC 2 Oct. 1658-NYC 30 July 1742, NYC 26 Dec. 1682

65. Heyltje Jans Kunst, b. Albany, living 1730/1

66. Olfert Sioerts, Heerenveen, Holland c. 1661-NYC c. 1710, NYC 9 Sept. 1682

67. Margaret Clopper, bp. NYC 28 Nov. 1660-ante 22 May 1703

68. Claes Bogart, Bedford, L. I. c. 1668-NYC 5 Jan. 1727, NYC 26 or 28 June 1695

69. Belitje Van Schaick, bp. NYC 2 Apr. 1672-NYC 7 Feb. 1707
70. Johannes Peeck, bp. New Amsterdam (later NYC) 12 Oct. 1653, m. NYC 18 July 1683
71. Elizabeth Van Imbroch, b. Albany c. 1659
72. Emanuel Van Schaack, prob. Kinderhook c. 1680-Kinderhook 19 Nov. 1706, prob. Albany 11 June 1703
73. Maria Wyngaart, bp. Albany 15 Feb. 1685
74. Dr. Hendrick Van Dyck, Albany c. 1665-Albany 11 Apr. 1707, Albany 3 Feb. 1689
75. Maria Schuyler, Albany 29 Sept. 1666-Kinderhook 7 June 1742
76. Christoffel (Christopher) Yates, Albany 16 Apr. 1684-bur. Albany 26 Feb. 1754, Albany 12 July 1706
77. Catelyntje (Catherine) Winne, b. Albany c. 1691
78. Pieter Waldron, bp. NYC 25 June 1675-bur. Albany 3 May 1725, NYC 9 Sept. 1698
79. Tryntje Cornelis Van Den Bergh, prob. Rensselaerswyck c. 1684-3 Mar. 1753
80-87. ---
88. David Potts, perhaps Llangirrig, Montgomeryshire, Wales c. 1670-Philadelphia Co. (prob. Bristol), Pa. 16 Nov. 1730, Philadelphia Co. 26 11th Mo. or 22 1st Mo. 1693/4
89. Alice Croasdale, (New Hay?), Yorkshire 26 7th Mo. or 3 8th Mo. 1673-prob. ante 16 Nov. 1730
90. Edmond McVeagh of Lower Dublin, Pa., will proved 3 Nov. 1739
91. Alice Dickinson, living 1727
92. Johann Lucken, prob. Dahlen or Wickrath in the Lower Rhineland 1650s-d. Germantown, Pa. between 9 Oct. 1741 & 24 Jan. 1744
93. Merken Gastes
94. Rynear Tyson (Reiner Theissen), prob. Kaldenkirchen in the Lower Rhineland c. 1659-Abington, Pa. 27 Sept. 1745
95. Margaret (Streypers?), d. prob. ante 27 Sept. 1745
96. (probably) William Balloch, m. 1687 or James Balloch, m. 1690, both of Glasgow, Scotland, brothers
97. (probably) Jean Reid (m. William) or Margaret Leckie (m. James)
98. Rev. Archibald Stobo, Scotland-will dated Colleton Co., S. C. 25 Feb. 1736/7
99. Elizabeth Park of Edinburgh, living S. C. 1747
100. Andre De Veaux of St. Andrew's Parish, S. C., will dated 1754
101. ---
102. Richard Fairchild, d. Charleston Oct. 1721
103. Ann Bellinger of Charleston, will dated 17 Feb. 1721/2
104. Robert Irvine of Cults, c. 1639-c. 1728
105. Margaret Coutts, c. 1665-c. 1710, widow of Alexander Irvine of Drum (nephew of 104)
106. John Douglas of Tilquhillie
107. Agnes Horn
108. John Baillie "of Balrobert" who is probably John Baillie of Torbreck or his brother-in-law John Baillie (in 1721 also of Torbreck, d. c. 1747), who m. 18 Dec. 1718
109. Jean Baillie (wife of John Baillie, d. c. 1747, & sister of John Baillie of Torbreck; John, d. c. 1747, also m. Mary Baillie, a niece of this Jean & of John of Torbreck)
110-127. ---
128. Claes Martenszen Van Rosenvelt, d. 1658-60, Holland to New Amsterdam, = ante 1650
129. Jannetje Tomas or Samuels, d. 1660
130. Jan Barentsen Kunst, living 1670, Germany or North Holland to Kingston & Hurley, N. Y.
131. Jannetje Adriaens, d. ante 1663
132. Sioert Olfertsen, d. 1702, Heerenveen to NYC
133. Itie Roelofs
134. Cornelius Jansen Clopper, d. ante 1686, Bergen-op-Zoom or

North Holland to NYC, = 1657

135. Heyltje Pieters, d. c. 1700, Amsterdam, Holland to NYC, m. (2) Sioert Olfertsen, #132 above

136. Jan Louwe Bogert (c. 1630-post 1707), Schoonderwoert, Holland to NYC

137. Cornelia Everetse (Everts), d. post 1707

138. Hendrick Cornelisen Van Schaick (1646-c. 1709), NYC, = 1669

139. Neeltje Cornelis [Stille], b. 1648

140. Jan Peeck, d. post 1664, New Amsterdam, = 1650

141. Maria du Trieux (1617-post 1670/1), Leyden, Holland to New Amsterdam, widow of Cornelis Volckertsen [Viele]

142. Dr. Gysbert Van Imbroch, d. 1665, NYC & Ulster Co., N. Y.

143. Rachel de La Montagne (c. 1634-1664)

144. Claas Gerritse Van Schaick, living 1677, Holland to Rensselaerswyck

145. (Jannetje ---?)

146. Luykas Gerritse Wyngaart, will dated 1709, Albany

147. Anna Janse Van Hoesen

148. Dr. Cornelis Van Dyck (1642-1686/7), Albany, = c. 1663

149. Elizabeth Laeckens, d. ante 1682

150. David Pietersz Schuyler (1636-1690), Amsterdam, Holland to Albany, = 1657

151. Catalyntie (Catalina) Ver Planck

152. Joseph Yates (poss. 1647-1730), possibly Leeds, England to Albany

153. Huybertsie Marselis Van Bommel, d. 1730, Albany

154. (probably) Adam Winne (c. 1663-c. 1691), Albany, = c. 1683

155. (probably) Anna Loockermans, b. c. 1664, m. (2) 18 Oct. 1691 Jacob Tennise Van Woert

156. Willem Waldron, b. 1647, Amsterdam, Holland to NYC, = 1671

157. Engeltie Van Stoutenburg, b. 1653, NYC

158. Cornelis Gysbertse Van Den Bergh (c. 1650-1717), Rensselaerswyck, = c. 1684

159. Cornelia Wynantse Van Der Poel, b. c. 1660, Albany

160-177. ---

178. Thomas Croasdale (prob. ante 1644-1682), prob. Newah, Yorkshire to Middletown, Pa., = 1664

179. Agnes Hathornthwaite, d. 1684, Lancashire to Middletown

180-183. ---

184. Wilhelm Lucken, b. Dahlen c. 1620-prob. Krefeld in the Lower Rhineland post 1694

185. Adelheid (Alletgen) ---, b. Dahlen c. 1623-post 29 Aug. 1694

186-187. ---

188. Theis Doors, b. Kaldenkirchen

189. Agnes ---, b. Kaldenkirchen

190-191. ---

192. (probably) James Balloch of Glasgow, = 1671

193. (probably) Christian MacGie

194-197. ---

198. James Park of Edinburgh, = 1673

199. Jean Scott

200-205. ---

206. Edmund Bellinger, Landgrave, Surveyor General of the two Carolinas, fl. 1674-1700, James Island, S. C., = c. 1680

207. Sarah Cartwright

208. John Irvine of Murthill, d. post 1672

209. --- Irvine of Fortrie, her husband's cousin

210-211. ---

212. John Douglas of Inchmarlo, = 1666

213. Grizel Forbes

214. Rev. James Horn of West Hall, Vicar of Elgin, fl. 1656-1674

215. Isabel Leslie of Pitcaple

216 or 218. Alexander Baillie, 9th laird of Dunain, d. 1679, = 1665

217 or 219. Jean Mackenzie of Coul, living 1700, m. (2) William Fraser of Erchit [216/8 & 217/9 were parents of John Baillie of Torbreck & of Jean Baillie, wife of John Baillie, d. c. 1747]; or

216. William Baillie, Commissary of Inverness (brother of Alexander Baillie, 9th laird of Dunain

217. Magdalen Stuart [216 & 217 were parents of John Baillie, d. c. 1747, who m. Jean Baillie, his 1st cousin]

220-255. ---

* * *

27. WILLIAM HOWARD TAFT

1. WILLIAM HOWARD TAFT, Cincinnati, Ohio 15 Sept. 1857-Washington, D. C. 8 Mar. 1930, Cincinnati 19 June 1886 Helen (Nellie) Herron, Cincinnati 2 June 1861-Washington, D. C. 22 May 1943

2. Alphonso Taft, Townshend, Vt. 5 Nov. 1810-San Diego, Calif. 21 May 1891, Jurist, U. S. Secretary of War & Attorney General, diplomat, Millbury, Massachusetts 26 Dec. 1853

3. Louisa Maria Torrey, Boston, Mass. 11 Sept. 1827-Millbury 8 Dec. 1907

4. Peter Rawson Taft, Uxbridge, Mass. 14 Apr. 1785-Cincinnati 1 Jan. 1867, 5 Dec. 1810

5. Sylvia Howard, Townshend, Vt. 17 Feb. 1792-1866

6. Samuel Davenport Torrey, Mendon, Mass. 14 Apr. 1789-Millbury 23 Dec. 1877, Millbury 27 Jan. 1824

7. Susan Holman Waters, Apr. 1803-Millbury 3 Feb. 1866

8. Aaron Taft, Uxbridge 28 May 1743-Townshend 26 Mar. 1808, Uxbridge 1 June 1769

9. Rhoda Rawson, Uxbridge 4 Oct. 1749-Townshend 9 June 1827

10. Levi Howard (Hayward), 15 Sept. 1752-Townshend 14 May 1833, Mendon 28 May 1776

11. Bethiah Chapin, Mendon 12 Mar. 1755-Townshend 6 Oct. 1829

12. William Torrey, Mendon 23 Nov. 1754-Mendon 16 Sept. 1817, Mendon 20 July 1788

13. Anna Davenport, Mendon 8 Sept. 1765-Mendon 1 Aug. 1842, m. (2) Peter Holbrook

14. Asa Waters, Jr., Sutton, Mass. 2 Oct. 1769-Millbury 24 Dec. 1841, Sutton 19 May 1802

15. Susan Trask Holman, Sutton 22 Feb. 1784-Millbury 28 Nov. 1849

Henceforth all towns, unless otherwise designated, are in Massachusetts.

16. Peter Taft, c. 1715-Uxbridge 12 Dec. 1783, Medfield 20 Apr. 1736

17. Elizabeth Cheney, Medfield 21 Sept. 1707-Uxbridge 21 Sept. 1783

18. Abner Rawson, Uxbridge 27 April 1721-Uxbridge 14 Nov. 1794, Medway 17 May 1745

19. Mary Allen, Medway 22 July 1722-Uxbridge 19 Aug. 1790

20. Benjamin Hayward, Jr., (Mendon 23 Aug. 1715?)-(Jamaica, Vermont 29 Oct. 1783), Mendon 13 Feb. 1734/5

21. Mary Wheaton, b. Mendon 23 Oct. 1718

22. John Chapin, Jr., Mendon 7 Oct. 1730-Heath 16 or 17 July 1815, Mendon 28 May 1754

23. Rhoda Albee, Mendon 1 June 1731-Heath 18 or 19 July 1819

24. Joseph Torrey, c. 1727-Mendon 29 Nov. 1760, Mendon 6 Sept. 1752

25. Deborah Holbrook, Uxbridge 24 Feb. 1731/2-Uxbridge 13 Sept. 1775, m. (2) Gershom Chapin

26. Seth Davenport, Milton 2 Nov. 1739-Mendon 28 Mar. 1813, Mendon 20 Nov. 1764

27. Chloe Daniel, Mendon 13 Sept. 1745-Mendon 19 May 1823
28. Asa Waters, Sutton 11 Jan. 1741/2-Millbury 2 Nov. 1813, Sutton 11 June 1764
29. Sarah Goodale, Sutton 8 Mar. 1745/6-Millbury 28 Aug. 1828
30. Jonathan Holman, Sutton 13 Aug. 1732-Millbury 25 Feb. 1814, Sutton 10 July 1783
31. Susanna Trask, Sutton 11 Oct. 1759-Millbury 25 Feb. 1843
32. Joseph Taft, c. 1680-Uxbridge 18 July 1747, c. 1708
33. Elizabeth Emerson, Ipswich 6 Mar. 1686/7-Uxbridge 10 Mar. 1760
34. Josiah Cheney, Medfield 27 July 1685-Medfield 16 Mar. 1754, c. 1706
35. Hannah ---, d. Medfield 22 Apr. 1717
36. Edmund Rawson, Mendon 8 July 1689-Uxbridge 20 May 1765, Uxbridge 22 May 1717
37. Elizabeth Hayward, Bridgewater 16 Apr. 1683-Uxbridge 15 June 1759
38. Ebenezer Allen, Medfield 25 Sept. 1694-(Medway 2 Apr. 1778?), Medway 19 July 1719
39. Mary Hill, Medfield 15 July 1696-Medway 9 Feb. 1785?
40. Benjamin Hayward, b. Mendon 14 Feb. 1689, c. 1711
41. Hannah ---
42. Samuel Wheaton, b. Rehoboth 20 Aug. 1693, Mendon 24 Feb. 1717/8
43. Mary Rockwood, b. Mendon 31 July 1690
44. John Chapin, Mendon 13 May 1695-Mendon 3 Aug. 1770, c. 1719
45. Dorcas ---, 4 Oct. 1694-Mendon 22 Aug. 1767
46. Obadiah Albee, b. Mendon 29 Oct. 1705, c. 1729
47. Jean or Jane ---
48. William Torrey, Bristol, Rhode Island 17 Dec. 1700-Mendon 1 Mar. 1779, Bristol, R. I. 29 Dec. 1724
49. Susanna Giddings, Ipswich 2 Oct. 1704-Mendon 15 Jan. 1794
50. William Holbrook, Mendon 28 Mar. 1693/4-1776?, Mendon 9 Apr. 1722
51. Hopestill Read, Mendon 1 Apr. 1698-Uxbridge 15 Mar. 1762
52. Samuel Davenport, Dorchester 20 Oct. 1697-Mendon 29 June 1773, ante 1726
53. Rebecca Holbrook, Roxbury 9 Feb. 1699-Mendon 23 Sept. 1777
54. David Daniel, Mendon 4 or 5 July 1710-Mendon 21 May 1776, Upton 25 Jan. 1737/8
55. Huldah Taft, b. Mendon 28 June 1718
56. Jonathan Waters, bp. Salem 31 July 1715-Sutton 13 Sept. 1786, Salem 10 Aug. 1738
57. Mehitable Giles, 1716?-Sutton 29 Apr. 1799
58. Samuel Goodale, Jr., bp. Salem 13 June 1708-Sutton 13 Apr. 1769, Sutton 20 Oct. 1743
59. Silence Holbrook, b. Sherborn 23 Mar. 1723/4
60. Solomon Holman, Jr., Newbury 25 Nov. 1697-Sutton 17 April 1785, Oxford 28 Aug. 1729
61. Mercy Waters, bp. Salem 24 July 1697-post 1785
62. Samuel Trask, Salem 17 Dec. 1721-Sutton 7 Mar. 1790, Sutton 6 Jan. 1757
63. Anna Bond, Weston 9 Nov. 1732-c. 1784
64. Robert Taft, c. 1640-Mendon 8 Feb. 1725, c. 1670?
65. Sarah ---, c. 1640-Nov. 1725
66. James Emerson, d. prob. Mendon 1756, c. 1686
67. Sarah ---, c. 1663-Mendon 13 Oct. 1732
68. Joseph Cheney, Roxbury 6 June 1647-16 Sept. 1704, Medfield 12 Mar. 1667/8
69. Hannah Thurston, Dedham 28 Apr. 1650-Medfield 29 Dec. 1690
70-71. ---
72. Rev. Grindall Rawson, 23 Jan. 1659-Mendon 6 Feb. 1714/5, Medfield 30 Aug. 1682

73. Susanna Wilson, Medfield 1 Dec. 1664-Mendon 8 July 1748
74. John Hayward of Bridgewater, d. 1710, m. c. ante 1661
75. Sarah Mitchell, b. 1641-post 1731
76. Nathaniel Allen, Dedham 29 Aug. 1648-1718, Medfield 10 Apr. 1677
77. Mary Frizzell, 16 May 1656-Medfield 18 Mar. 1745/6
78. Samuel Hill, c. 1656-1723, Medfield 4 Nov. 1679
79. Hannah Twitchell, c. 1661-1690
80. Samuel Hayward, d. Mendon 29 July 1713, Medfield 28 Nov. 1666
81. Mehitable Thompson, d. ante 1711
82-83. ---
84. Benjamin Wheaton of Rehoboth, Feb. 1661/2-1726?, ante 1693
85. Margaret ---
86. Joseph Rockwood, Mendon 27 May 1671-1713?, c. 1689?
87. Mary Hayward, b. c. 1672?
88. Seth Chapin, Braintree? 4 Aug. 1668-Mendon 1 Apr. 1746
89. Bethiah Thurston, b. Medfield 30 Apr. 1672
90-91. ---
92. Benjamin Albee of Mendon, m. ante 1694
93. Abial ---
94-95. ---
96. Angel Torrey, Weymouth 10 June 1657-Bristol, R. I. 1724 or 1725, c. 1688
97. Hannah ---
98. Joseph Giddings, Jr., b. Ipswich 9 June 1672, m. Ipswich 25 Dec. 1701
99. Grace Wardwell
100. Peter Holbrook, Braintree 7 May 1655/6-Mendon 3 May 1712, ante 1679
101. Alice Godfrey, d. Mendon 29 Apr. 1705
102. Samuel Read, Jr., Mendon 3 Nov. 1669-Mendon 14 Feb. 1724/5, c. 1693
103. Deborah Chapin, b. Mendon 12 Feb. 1675/6
104. John Davenport, Dorchester 20 Oct. 1664-Milton 21 Mar. 1725, c. 1694
105. Naomi ---
106. Daniel Holbrook, b. Roxbury 15 Mar. 1676, m. Roxbury 29 May 1698
107. Abigail Crafts, Roxbury 1 Dec. 1673-Roxbury 5 Nov. 1702
108. Eleazer Daniel, Mendon 9 Mar. 1681-Mendon 28 Mar. 1772, Scituate 28 July 1709
109. Mary Holbrook, Scituate 2 Nov. 1686-Mendon 11 Mar. 1759
110. Israel Taft, Mendon 26 Apr. 1698/9-c. 1753?, Mendon 19 Dec. 1717
111. Mercy Aldrich, b. Mendon 21 June 1700
112. Nathaniel Waters, Salem 6 Feb. 1671/2-1718?, 12 Dec. 1699
113. Elizabeth King, b. Salem Feb. 1671/2?
114. John Giles, Salem 31 Aug. 1681-post 1738, Salem 7 Nov. 1706
115. Ann Andrews
116. Samuel Goodale, b. Salem 3 Dec. 1669, m. Salem 25 Dec. 1697
117. Mary Buxton, b. Salem 3 Sept. 1669
118. John Holbrook, Jr., Sherborn 22 Mar. 1694-Grafton 6 May 1756, Sherborn 13 Mar. 1718/9
119. Ruth Hill, d. Grafton 12 May 1747
120. Solomon Holman, d. Newbury 7 May 1753, ante 1694
121. Mary Barton, c. 1673-Newbury 18 Oct. 1736
122. Richard Waters, Salem 19 Nov. 1669-(?Feb. 1725/6), Salem 3 Mar. 1697/8
123. Martha Reed
124. John Trask of Salem, b. c. 1678, m. 26 Nov. 1701
125. Hannah Osborn, b. 2 Dec. 1679
126. Josiah Bond, Watertown 20 Jan. 1695/6-Sutton 1781, Newton

13 or 31 Jan. 1719/20
127. Elizabeth Fuller, Newton 1 July 1701-Sutton 1786
128-131. ---
132. Rev. Joseph Emerson (1620-1679/80), Concord, = ante 1652
133. Elizabeth Woodmansey, d. ante 1665
134-135. ---
136. William Cheney (c. 1604-1667), Roxbury, = c. 1626
137. Margaret ---, d. 1686
138. John Thurston (1601-1685), Medfield, = ante 1633
139. Margaret --- (c. 1605-1662)
140-143. ---
144. Edward Rawson (1615-1693), London to Boston
145. Rachel Perne, d. 1677
146. Rev. John Wilson, Jr. (1621-1691), Medfield, = c. 1647
147. Sarah Hooker (c. 1620-1725)
148. Thomas Hayward, d. 1681, Aylesford, Kent to Bridgewater, = ante 1627
149. Susanna (Towne?), d. ante 1678
150. Experience Mitchell, d. 1689, Leyden, Holland to Bridgewater
151. Mary ---
152. James Allen, d. 1676, Medfield, = 1637/8
153. Anne Guild, d. 1672/3
154. James Frizzell (c. 1626-1716), Roxbury, = ante 1656
155. Sarah Busketh, d. 1712/3
156. John Hill, Jr. (c. 1630-1717/8), Sherborn, = c. 1653
157. Hannah ---, d. 1690
158. Benjamin Twitchell, d. 1680, Medfield, = ante 1659
159. Mary Riggs
160. William Hayward, d. 1659, Braintree, = c. 1637
161. Margery ---, d. 1676
162. John Thompson (1619?-1685), Mendon, = 1641?
163. Sarah ---
164-167. ---
168. Robert Wheaton, d. 1696?, Rehoboth, = c. 1636
169. Alice Bowen, m. (2) --- Darling
170-171. ---
172. John Rockwood (1641-1724), Braintree, = 1662
173. Joanna Ford
174. same as 80 above
175. same as 81 above
176. Josiah Chapin (c. 1634-1726), Mendon, = 1658
177. Mary King (1639-1676)
178. John Thurston, Jr. (1635-1711/2), Medfield (son of 138 & 139 above), = c. 1660
179. Mary Wood (1642-1726)
180-183. ---
184. James Albee, d. post 1717, Medfield, = 1671
185. Hannah Cooke
186-191. ---
192. William Torrey, d. 1690, Weymouth, = ante 1641
193. Elizabeth Frye
194-195. ---
196. Joseph Giddings, d. 1691, Ipswich, = 1671
197. Susanna Rindge
198. Uzal Wardwell (1639-1742), Boston, = c. 1678
199. Grace ---
200. Thomas Holbrook, Jr., d. 1697, Weymouth, = ante 1651
201. Joan Kingman (1624-post 1697)
202. Richard Godfrey, d. 1691, Taunton, = ante 1651
203. Jane (Turner?)
204. Samuel Read (c. 1645-1717), Mendon, = 1665
205. Hopestill Holbrook, d. 1705/6

206. same as 176 above
207. same as 177 above
208. Thomas Davenport, d. 1685, Dorchester, = c. 1642
209. Mary ---, d. 1691
210-211. ---
212. John Holbrook (c. 1639-1678), Roxbury, = 1663
213. Elizabeth Hemingway, b. 1645
214. Samuel Crafts, b. 1637, Roxbury, = 1661
215. Elizabeth Seaver (1643-1731)
216. Joseph Daniel (c. 1637-1715), Medway, = 1665
217. Mary Fairbanks (1647-1682)
218. Samuel Holbrook (c. 1643-1712), Scituate, = 1675
219. Mary Pierce, d. 1735
220. Robert Taft, Jr. (c. 1674-1748), Uxbridge (son of 64 and 65 above), = c. 1694/5
221. Elizabeth Woodward (1671?-post 1748)
222. Jacob Aldrich, b. 1677, Mendon, = 1699
223. Margery Hayward (daughter of 80 & 81, 174 & 175 above)
224. John Waters (1640-1707) Salem, = 1663
225. Sarah Tompkins (1642/3-post 1707)
226. John King, b. 1638, Salem, = 1660
227. Elizabeth Goldthwaite, b. 1642
228. Eleazer Giles, b. 1640, Salem, = 1678
229. Elizabeth Bishop, b. 1657
230. John Andrews, Jr. (c. 1648-ante 1706/7), Salem, = ante 1685
231. Ann Jacobs, d. post 1711/2
232. Zachariah Goodale (b. 1640), Salem, = 1666
233. Elizabeth Beacham, b. 1648
234. John Buxton (c. 1644-1715), Salem, = 1668
235. Mary Small, d. 1675/6
236. John Holbrook (c. 1667-1740/1), Sherborn, = 1692/3
237. Silence Wood (1675/6-1756)
238. Eleazer Hill, Sherborn, = c. 1687
239. Sarah Breck
240-241. ---
242. William Barton, d. 1700?, Cape Porpoise, Maine?, = 1673
243. Anne Greene, m. (2) Walter Pennel
244. same as 224
245. same as 225
246-247. ---
248. William Trask, Jr. (1640-1691), Salem, = c. 1677
249. Anna ---
250. William Osborn, Salem, = 1672/3
251. Hannah Burton
252. Jonas Bond, b. 1664, Watertown, = 1688/9
253. Grace Coolidge (1663-1699)
254. Joseph Fuller (1652-1739/40), Newton, = 1678/9
255. Lydia Jackson (c. 1655-1725/6)

* * *

28. (THOMAS) WOODROW WILSON

1. (THOMAS) WOODROW WILSON, Staunton, Virginia 28 Dec. 1856-Washington, D. C. 3 Feb. 1924, (1) Savannah, Georgia 24 June 1885 Ellen Louise Axson, Savannah 15 May 1860-White House, Washington, D. C. 6 Aug. 1914, (2) Washington, D. C. 18 Dec. 1915, Mrs. Edith Bolling Galt, Wytheville, Virginia 15 Oct. 1872-Washington, D. C. 28 Dec. 1961, widow of Norman Galt

2. Rev. Joseph Ruggles Wilson, Steubenville, Ohio 28 Feb. 1822-Princeton, New Jersey 21 Jan. 1903, 7 June 1849

3. Janet Woodrow, Carlisle, England 20 Dec. 1826-Clarksville, Tennessee 15 Apr. 1888

4. James Wilson, Strabane, Down, Ireland 20 Feb. 1787-Steubenville, Ohio 17 Oct. 1850, Philadelphia 1 Nov. 1808

5. Mary Anne Adams, b. c. 1791, of co. Antrim or co. Down, Ireland

6. Rev. Thomas Woodrow, Paisley, Scotland 15 Mar. 1793-Columbus, Ohio 25 Apr. 1877, graduate, University of Glasgow Theological Academy, 1819, Presbyterian missionary at Brockville, Canada & Chillicothe, Ohio, m. Feb. 1820

7. Marion Williamson, 1791-Paisley, Scotland 16 Feb. 1836

8-11. ---

12. John Wodrow, artificer, maker of Paisley shawls, b. 7 June 1765, m. Leigh Kirk, Low Paisley, Scotland 27 Sept. 1787

13. Janet Morton

14. Robert Williamson, m. 1774

15. Marion Wright, 1754-Oct. 1797

16-23. ---

24. John Wodrow, m. 12 Jan. 1751

25. Jean Slater (Sclatters)

26-47. ---

48. John Wodrow, b. 25 May 1695, m. 19 Mar. 1725

49. Sofia Douglas

50-95. ---

96. Rev. James Wodrow, 2 Jan. 1637-25 Sept. 1707, professor at the University of Glasgow, m. Sept. 1692

97. Janet Luke, d. 1733

98-191. ---

192. Robert Wodrow, c. 1600-22 July 1672

193. Agnes Dunlop of Polnoon Milne, d. 14 July 1653

194. John Luke, merchant of Glasgow

195-255. ---

* * *

29. WARREN GAMALIEL HARDING

1. WARREN GAMALIEL HARDING, Blooming Grove (sometime Corsica), Ohio 2 Nov. 1865-San Francisco, California 2 Aug. 1923, Marion, Ohio 8 July 1891 Florence Mabel Kling, Marion 15 Aug. 1860-Marion 21 Nov. 1924, divorced wife of Henry (Pete) De Wolfe

2. George Tyron Harding, Blooming Grove, Ohio 12 June 1844-Santa Ana, Calif. 19 Nov. 1928, Galion, Ohio 7 May 1864

3. Phoebe Elizabeth Dickerson, near Blooming Grove 21 Dec. 1843-Marion 20 May 1910

4. Charles Alexander Harding, Clifford, Pennsylvania 8 Apr. 1820-Blooming Grove 3 Apr. 1878, 28 May 1840

5. Mary Ann Crawford, prob. Washington Co., Pa. 26 Aug. 1823-Blooming Grove 11 Mar. 1895

6. Isaac Haines Dickerson, prob. New Jersey c. 1802-Blooming Grove 1867, 5 Oct. 1826

7. Charity Malvina Van Kirk, prob. Washington Co., Pa. c. 1803-Blooming Grove 1878

8. George Tyron Harding, Pittston, Pa. 15 June 1790-Blooming Grove 9 Jan. 1860, 1 May 1816

9. Elizabeth Madison, 26 July 1800-6 Feb. 1866

10. Joshua Crawford of Baltimore, Maryland & Washington Co., Pa., m. 1821

11. Sophia Stevens, b. Pa. Mar. 1802

12. (prob.) Joseph Dickerson, N. J. 23 Dec. 1776-1837, Washington Co., Pa. c. 1800

13. (prob.) Abigail Hines (Hinds, Haines) of N. J.

14. William Van Kirk, N. J. 17 Feb. 1763-Morris, Pa. 18 Feb. 1826, c. 1783

15. Deborah Watters

16. Amos Harding, Orange Co., N. Y. 19 Mar. 1764-Blooming Grove 10 July 1839, prob. Pittston 21 Aug. 1784
17. Phoebe Tripp, Orange Co., N. Y. 17 Aug. 1767-La Porte Co., Ind. 2 Nov. 1844
18. (said to be) William Madison, 1776-1849, c. 1799
19. (said to be) Mary Hooper
20-23. ---
24. (prob.) Joshua Dickerson (Jr.), N. J. c. 1740-Washington Co., Pa. 1802-3
25. (prob.) Abigail ---, living 1810
26. (prob.) Benjamin Hines (Hinds, Haines)
27. (prob.) Mary Breese, b. N. J. c. 1740
28. Henry Van Kirk, Jr., N. J. 17 Dec. 1740-Amwell, Pa. 3 Apr. 1798, c. 1762
29. ---
30. Thomas Watters of Maidenhead, N. J., will proved 16 Feb. 1767
31. Priscilla ---, of Lebanon, N. J., inventory dated 9 Apr. 1806
32. Abraham Harding, Jr., prob. New London, Connecticut 14 Apr. 1744, to Pittston, Pa. 1772, d. post 1778, m. Conn. 9 July 1762
33. Huldah Tryon
34. William Tripp, b. c. 1738, m. c. 1756
35. Sarah Slocum, prob. West Greenwich, Rhode Island 5 Nov. 1738-Luzerne Co., Pa. 18 Oct. 1808
36. (said to be) Rev. John Madison, Baptist minister, 1729-1813, c. 1750
37. (said to be) Jane Giddings
38-47. ---
48. (poss.) Joshua Dickerson, Southold, Long Island, New York, 1718-25-prob. Morris Co., N. J., 1770-7, Southold 30 Oct. 1740
49. (poss.) Mehitable Dickerson
50-53. ---
54. (prob.) John Breese, c. 1713-Barnard, N. J. 4 Mar. 1803
55. (prob.) Dorothy Riggs, c. 1713-prob. Barnard 23 Nov. 1803
56. Henry Van Kirk, c. 1700-will proved 3 Apr. 1776, Freehold, N. J. to Hopewell, N. J.
57. Dorothy Morgan, c. 1703-c. 1745
58-63. ---
64. Abraham Harding, Providence, R. I. c. 1714-Susquehanna Co., Pa., 1806, New London, Conn. c. 1741
65. Mercy Vibber, New London 9 Jan. 1715-between 1755 & 1779
66-67. ---
68. Isaac Tripp, c. 1704-killed by Indians during the Wyoming (Pa.) massacre 16 Dec. 1778, c. 1732
69. Susannah Spencer, living 1775
70. Joseph Slocum, Newport, R. I. 30 Jan. 1706-prob. Pa. post 1768, Newport 27 Sept. 1724
71. Patience Carr, prob. Jamestown, R. I. c. 1705-prob. West Greenwich c. 1742-3
72. (said to be) Joseph Madison, Jr., 1701-1773, c. 1720
73. (said to be) Eliza Stone
74-95. ---
96. (poss.) Thomas Dickerson, Southold, L. I. between 1686 & 1698-Southold 12 Sept. 1725, Southold 13 Jan. 1715
97. (poss.) Abigail Reeve, Southold ante 1686-post 1737, m. (2) Charles Wager
98. (poss.) John Dickerson, Southold, L. I. c. 1686-will proved 23 May 1758, Southold 25 Dec. 1710
99. (poss.) Abigail Reeve, Southold post 1686-post 1758
100-111. ---
112. John Van Kirk, Jr., Kings Co., N. Y. c. 1664, of Freehold, N. J., inventory dated 28 Jan. 1724, c. 1697

113. Alsey ---, b. c. 1675, m. (2) Thomas Hankinson
114-127. ---
128. Stephen Harding (c. 1677-post 1734-5), Providence, R. I. to Waterford, Conn., = c. 1700
129. Jemima ---, d. post 1734
130. John Vibber (1689-post 1754), New London, Conn., = 1711
131. Joanna Williams (c. 1684-1754)
132-135. ---
136. Job Tripp (c. 1663-1751), North Kingston, R. I.
137. ---
138. William Spencer, will proved 1748, North Kingston, R. I.
139. ---
140. Giles Slocum (1680-ante 1724), Newport, R. I., = 1704
141. Mary Paine, b. c. 1684
142. Caleb Carr, Jr. (1679-post 1750), Jamestown & West Greenwich, R. I., = 1701
143. Joanna Slocum (1680/1-1708/9)
144. (said to be) Joseph Madison (1672-1763), = 1693
145. (said to be) Sarah Hall
146-191. ---
192. (poss.) Peter Dickerson (1648-1721/2), Salem, Mass. to Southold, L. I., = ante 1686
193. (poss.) Naomi Mapes (1666/7-1725)
194. (perhaps) John Reeve, d. 1712, Southold, = c. 1678
195. (perhaps) Hannah Browne, d. 1698/9
196. (poss.) same as 192
197. (poss.) same as 193
198. (perhaps) Joseph Reeve (c. 1656-1736), Southold (brother of 194)
199. (perhaps) Abigail ---, d. 1707
200-223. ---
224. Jan Janszen Verkerk (John Van Kirk) (c. 1630-will dated 1688), Buren, Gelderland, Netherlands to New Utrecht, N. Y.
225. Mayke Gysberts, prob. d. 1688
226-255. ---

* * *

30. (JOHN) CALVIN COOLIDGE, JR.

1. (JOHN) CALVIN COOLIDGE, JR., Plymouth, Vermont 4 July 1872-Northampton, Massachusetts 5 Jan. 1933, Burlington, Vt. 4 Oct. 1905 Grace Anna Goodhue, Burlington 3 Jan. 1879-Northampton 8 July 1957
2. John Calvin Coolidge, Plymouth, Vt. 31 Mar. 1845-Plymouth 18 Mar. 1926, Plymouth 6 May 1868
3. Victoria Josephine Moor, Plymouth, Vt. 14 Mar. 1846-Plymouth 14 Mar. 1885
4. Calvin Galusha Coolidge, Plymouth, Vt. 22 Sept. 1815-Plymouth 15 Dec. 1878, Plymouth 3 Mar. 1844
5. Sarah Almeda Brewer, Ludlow, Vt. 17 Dec. 1823-Plymouth 2 Jan. 1906, m. (2) George W. Putnam
6. Hiram D. Moor, prob. Rockingham, Vt. 26 Dec. 1812-Guthrie Center, Iowa 9 Jan. 1888, Plymouth, Vt. 5 Dec. 1838
7. Abigail Franklin, Plymouth, Vt. 18 Apr. 1811-Plymouth 3 Oct. 1892
8. Calvin Coolidge, Plymouth, Vt. 27 Mar. 1780-Plymouth 30 Apr. 1853, Plymouth 9 Dec. 1814
9. Sarah Thompson, Chester, Vt. 3 Apr. 1789-Plymouth, Vt. 19 Nov. 1856
10. Israel C. Brewer, Paxton, Mass. c. 1797-Columbia Co., Wisconsin 1873
11. Sally Brown, Plymouth, Vt. 4 Feb. 1801-1884
12. John Moor, b. prob. Salem, New York c. 1785, m. Rockingham,

Vt. 9 Sept. 1811

13. Mary Davis, b. Rockingham, Vt. 14 Dec. 1787

14. Luther Franklin, Guilford, Vt. 5 Mar. 1780-Plymouth, Vt. 18 Apr. 1861, Guilford, Vt. 5 Dec. 1799

15. Priscilla Pinney, Guilford, Vt. c. 1778-Plymouth, Vt. 18 Oct. 1811

16. John Coolidge, Bolton, Mass. c. 1756-Plymouth, Vt. 23 March 1822, Lancaster, Mass. 8 Sept. 1779

17. Hannah Priest of Marlboro, Mass. c. 1751-Plymouth, Vt. 2 May 1829

18. William Thompson, Jr., Wilmington, Mass. 30 June 1754-Plymouth, Vt. 23 Oct. 1830, Reading, Mass. 25 Feb. 1774

19. Dorcas Eaton, Reading, Mass. 31 July 1754-Plymouth, Vt. 3 Feb. 1845

20. Eliab Brewer, Rutland, Vt. 6 Apr. 1760-Ludlow, Vt. 24 Sept. 1835, Rutland 18 Feb. 1782

21. Sally Rice, c. 1761-Ludlow, Vt. 3 Jan. 1835

22. Israel Putnam Brown, Moultonborough, New Hampshire 2 Nov. 1781-Plymouth, Vt. 9 Nov. 1867, Plymouth 7 Oct. 1799

23. Sally Briggs, prob. Putney, Vt. c. 1783-Plymouth, Vt. 18 June 1869

24-25. ---

26. Nathaniel Davis, Jr., Mass. 15 Mar. 1754-Rockingham, Vt. 10 June 1835, Rockingham 14 Aug. 1780

27. Lydia Harwood, prob. Ware, Mass. c. 1761-Rockingham, Vt. 19 Mar. 1838

28. Jabez Franklin, Scituate, Rhode Island c. 1759-Guilford, Vt. 26 Feb. 1829

29. Sarah Starr, Killingly, Connecticut 28 Nov. 1760-Guilford, Vt. 20 Aug. 1805

30. Jonathan Pinney, c. 1754-Plymouth, Vt. 1812, Guilford, Vt. c. 1775

31. Priscilla Grover, Killingly, Conn. 2 Apr. 1757-Plymouth, Vt. 1820

Henceforth all towns, unless otherwise designated, are in Massachusetts.

32. Josiah Coolidge, Watertown 17 July 1718-Lancaster 25 Dec. 1780, Brookline 26 Apr. 1742

33. Mary Jones

34. James Priest, b. prob. Watertown c. 1720, (int.) Woburn 8 Sept. 1750

35. Hannah Lawrence, b. Charlestown 25 Feb. 1721/2

36. William Thompson, Wilmington 19 Oct. 1723-Chester, Vt. May 1808, Wilmington 24 Nov. 1747

37. Abigail Jones, Wilmington 29 June 1729-Wilmington 15 Sept. 1757

38. Thomas Eaton, Reading 17 Feb. 1724/5-Reading 14 Oct. 1774, c. 1747

39. Betsey Boutwell, b. Reading 24 Mar. 1723/4

40. Samuel Brewer, b. Framingham 4 Nov. 1716, Framingham 10 Mar. 1740

41. Martha Bent, b. Framingham 7 Mar. 1719/20

42-43. ---

44. Adam Brown, Jr., c. 1748-perhaps ante 1837, Ipswich 3 Dec. 1772

45. Priscilla Putnam, Sutton 22 Aug. 1751-Plymouth, Vt. 6 Oct. 1837

46. Asa Briggs, Berkley 22 June 1755-Kalamazoo, Michigan 1834, Berkley 27 Dec. 1777

47. Elizabeth Paul, c. 1754-Kalamazoo, Mich.

48-51. ---

52. Nathaniel Davis, Concord 3 Nov. 1715-Rockingham, Vt. 5 Jan. 1802, Bedford 16 April 1741

53. Susanna Lane, b. Billerica 8 Apr. 1720

54. John Harwood, Jr., Hardwick 25 June 1736-Rockingham, Vt. 12 Mar. 1800, c. 1760

55. Mary Pulsipher, Pomfret, Conn. 19 Jan. 1744-Rockingham, Vt. 19 Jan. 1827

56. Aaron Franklin, b. 1729, m. c. 1755

57. Margaret ---

58. Comfort Starr (III), Killingly, Conn. 10 Aug. 1731-Guilford, Vt. 30 Nov. 1812, Killingly, Conn. 22 Dec. 1754

59. Judith Cooper, Killingly, Conn. 14 Feb. 1736/7-Guilford, Vt. 2 Sept. 1815

60-61. ---

62. Eleazer Grover, Killingly, Conn. 31 Jan. 1728-Guilford, Vt., m. c. 1756

63. Elizabeth ---

64. Obadiah Coolidge, Jr., Watertown 27 Aug. 1695-post 1737, Watertown 24 July 1717

65. Rachel Goddard, b. Watertown 18 Apr. 1699

66-67. ---

68. Joseph Priest, Jr., Boston 18 Mar. 1678/9-Waltham 28 Apr. 1756, Watertown 25 Dec. 1701

69. Margaret Childs, b. c. 1680

70. Jonathan Lawrence, Groton 14 June 1696-prob. Woburn 1773, c. 1720

71. Joanna Phillips, b. Charlestown 8 Sept. 1697

72. James Thompson, Jr., Woburn May 1680-Wilmington 3 July 1763, c. 1716

73. Abigail Hamlet, Woburn 25 Mar. 1689-Wilmington 17 Mar. 1759

74. Ebenezer Jones, Woburn 18 June 1699-Fort William Henry, N. Y. 20 July 1758, Woburn 18 Nov. 1719

75. Elizabeth Dale, Woburn 10 Dec. 1693-1737/46

76. John Eaton, Reading 31 Jan. 1696/7-Reading 1758/9, Reading 28 Dec. 1721

77. Abigail Roberts, c. 1701-post 1758

78. John Boutwell, Jr., b. Reading 28 Apr. 1702, Charlestown 30 Apr. 1723

79. Elizabeth Parker, b. Reading Jan. 1705/6

80. Jonathan Brewer, Sudbury 21 June 1689-Framingham c. 1753, c. 1715/6

81. Arabella Goulding, poss. Hadley c. 1692/3-Framingham c. 1774

82. John Bent (III), Sudbury 29 Nov. 1689-Framingham 1759, Framingham 15 Nov. 1711

83. Hannah Rice, b. Sudbury 5 Jan. 1691/2

84-87. ---

88. Adam Brown, bp. Ipswich 16 Apr. 1721-Moultonborough, N. H. 20 July 1775, Ipswich 4 Aug. 1743

89. Esther Parkman, b. Wenham 17 July 1724

90. Tarrant Putnam, Jr., Salem 3 Apr. 1716-Sutton 27 Aug. 1794, Boxford 9 Dec. 1742

91. Priscilla Baker, Topsfield 4 Aug. 1724-Sutton 16 Mar. 1812

92. Silas Briggs, Dighton 17 Apr. 1732-Barre, Vt. 9 Sept. 1813, Berkley 31 Oct. 1754

93. Esther Soper, Bridgewater 10 May 1738-Barre, Vt. 9 July 1812

94. James Paul, Dighton c. 1725-Westminster, Vt. c. 1814, Dighton 16 Nov. 1749

95. Sarah White, Dighton 19 Feb. 1729-Dighton c. 1789

96-103. ---

104. Daniel Davis, Concord 26 March 1673-Bedford 10 Feb. 1740/1, Concord 27 Apr. 1699

105. Mary Hubbard, b. Concord 3 June 1682

106. John Lane, Jr., Billerica 20 Oct. 1691-Bedford 23 Sept. 1763, Billerica 31 Dec. 1714

107. Katherine Whiting, Billerica c. 1691-Bedford 1 Apr. 1731
108. John Harwood, b. Chelmsford 27 May 1703, c. 1729
109. Mary ---
110. David Pulsipher, Jr., b. Boston 7 May 1708, Pomfret, Conn. 2 Oct. 1740
111. Elizabeth Stowell, Newton 21 Aug. 1719-prob. Rockingham, Vt.
112. Philip Franklin, Swansea 25 Feb. 1707-Guilford, Vt. 5 Feb. 1797, Rehoboth 31 Mar. 1728
113. Rachel Horton, Rehoboth 8 June 1706-Guilford, Vt. 24 Feb. 1791
114-115. ---
116. Comfort Starr, Jr., Dedham 9 Aug. 1696-13 Feb. 1775, c. 1725
117. Elizabeth Perley, Boxford 10 Oct. 1705-Thompson, Conn. 4 Mar. 1742
118. Timothy Cooper, b. Lexington 9 Apr. 1706, c. 1730
119. Sarah Guile, b. Haverhill 20 Jan. 1694/5, widow of Samuel Davis
120-123. ---
124. Stephen Grover, Jr., Charlestown c. 1682-Killingly, Conn. c. 1730, Charlestown 2 July 1705
125. Elizabeth Bateman, Charlestown 11 July 1688-post 1730
126-127. ---
128. Obadiah Coolidge (1663-1707), Watertown, = 1686/7
129. Elizabeth Rose (prob. 1665-ante 1732)
130. Josiah Goddard, d. 1720, Watertown, = 1695/6
131. Rachel Davis (1672-1740)
132-135. ---
136. Joseph Priest, b. c. 1650, Watertown, = c. 1677
137. Hannah Hagar (1649-1702)
138. Richard Child (c. 1635-1694), Watertown, = 1678
139. Hannah Train, b. 1657
140. Nathaniel Lawrence, Jr. (1661-1736/7), Woburn, = c. 1689
141. Anna Fiske (1656/7-ante 1725)
142. Andrew Phillips, Jr. (c. 1662-1717), Charlestown, = 1683
143. Sarah Smith, b. 1661, m. (2) Nathaniel Lawrence, Sr., father of 140 above
144. James Thompson (1649-1693), Woburn, = 1674
145. Hannah Walker (1648-1686)
146. Jacob Hamlet, b. c. 1641, Cambridge, = c. 1679
147. Mary Adford, b. 1651, widow of Abraham Jaquith
148. Samuel Jones (1672-1753), Woburn, = c. 1695
149. Abigail Snow (1677-post 1753)
150. Robert Dale, d. 1700, Woburn, = 1680
151. Joanna Farrar (1661-1733)
152. Jonathan Eaton (1655-1743), Reading, = 1691
153. Mary ---
154. Abraham Roberts (c. 1655-1731), Woburn, = 1700
155. Susanna Thompson (1661-1725/6)
156. John Boutwell (1671-1713), Reading, = 1695
157. Grace Eaton, b. 1677
158. John Parker, Jr. (1668-1740/1), Reading, = 1691
159. Elizabeth Goodwin (1673-1731)
160. John Brewer, Jr. (1642-1690/1), Sudbury, = c. 1668
161. Elizabeth Rice (1648-1739/40)
162. Peter Goulding (c. 1630-1703), Sudbury, = 1672
163. Sarah ---
164. John Bent, Jr. (1636-1717), Framingham, = c. 1688
165. Martha Rice, b. 1657
166. David Rice, b. 1659 (brother of 161 above), Sudbury, = 1687
167. Hannah Walker (1669/70-1704)
168-175. ---
176. Jacob Brown (c. 1680-1767), Ipswich, = 1707/8

177. Sarah Burnham (c. 1679-1729)
178. John Parkman (1693-1727), Boston, = 1718
179. Abigail Fairfield, b. 1698
180. Tarrant Putnam (1688-1732/3), Salem, = 1715
181. Elizabeth Bacon (1695-1761)
182. Thomas Baker, Jr. (1687/8-1725), Topsfield, = 1709/10
183. Mary Capen, b. 1688/9, m. (2) John Griffin
184. Seth Briggs (c. 1708/10-1780 or later), Putney, Vt. = (1) 1726
185. Ann Whitmarsh (1702/3-1750), Berkley
186. Samuel Soper, Jr. (1709-ante 1751), Boston, = 1731
187. Esther Littlefield, b. 1714, m. (2) Seth Briggs, 184 above
188. William Paul (c. 1691-1732), Dighton, = c. 1716
189. Mary Whitmarsh, b. 1698, sister of 185 above, m. (2) William Mitchell
190. John White, d. 1752/3, Dighton, = 1716
191. Elizabeth Hathaway (1690-1753 or later)
192-207. ---
208. Samuel Davis, Concord, = 1665/6
209. Mary Meddowes, b. c. 1644
210. Jonathan Hubbard (1659-1728), Concord, = 1681
211. Hannah Rice (1659-1747)
212. John Lane (1660-1714/5), Billerica, = 1683
213. Susannah Whipple (1662-1713)
214. Samuel Whiting (III) (1662/3-1714/5), Billerica, = c. 1686
215. Elizabeth Read, b. c. 1665, m. (2) William Patten
216. James Harwood (c. 1655-1719), Littleton, = 1678
217. Lydia Barrett, b. 1659
218-219. ---
220. David Pulsipher, b. 1685, Ipswich, = c. 1707
221. Susanna ---
222. David Stowell, Jr. (c. 1693-ante 1763), Willington, Conn., = 1716
223. Patience Herrington (1697-1724), Newton
224. James Franklin, Jr., b. 1682, Dartmouth, = c. 1706
225. Martha Ormsby, b. 1680
226. Thomas Horton, Jr. (1677-1746), Rehoboth, = 1700
227. Hannah Garnsey, b. 1676
228-231. ---
232. Comfort Starr (1661/2-1729), Dedham, = 1683
233. Mary Stone (1664/5-1735)
234. Isaac Perley (c. 1680-1711/2), Ipswich, = c. 1704
235. Frances ---, d. 1710
236. John Cooper, b. 1675, Killingly, Conn., = 1697/8
237. Elizabeth Winter, b. 1678
238. Ephraim Guile, b. 1661/2, Haverhill, = 1686
239. Martha Bradley, b. 1667
240-247. ---
248. Stephen Grover, d. 1694, Charlestown, = c. 1680
249. Sarah ---
250. Eleazer Bateman (c. 1660-1751), Killingly, Conn., = 1686
251. Elizabeth Wright, b. 1664
252-255. ---

* * *

31. HERBERT CLARK HOOVER

No assumption should be made whether or not the dates below represent Quaker months, or whether the month represents old or new style, until the original records have been consulted.

1. HERBERT CLARK HOOVER, West Branch, Iowa 10 Aug. 1874-New

York, New York 20 Nov. 1964, Monterey, California 10 Feb. 1899 Lou Henry, Waterloo, Iowa 29 Mar. 1874-New York, N. Y. 7 Jan. 1944

2. Jesse Clark Hoover, Stillwater, Ohio 2 Sept. 1846-West Branch 13 Dec. 1880, Iowa 12 Mar. 1870

3. Hulda Randall Minthorn, Norwich, Canada 4 May 1848-West Branch, Iowa 22 Feb. 1884

4. Eli Hoover, Miami Co., Ohio 17 July 1820-Hubbard, Iowa 24 July 1892, Miami Co. 20 Feb. 1840

5. Mary Davis, 26 Oct. 1820-Miami Co., Ohio 3 Mar. 1853

6. Theodore Minthorn, Younge Street, Toronto, Canada 11 Oct. 1817-West Branch, Iowa Oct. 1866, Younge Street 4 Jan. 1842

7. Mary Wasley, Younge Street 1 Sept. 1818-Newberg, Oregon 11 June 1903

8. Jesse Hoover, Uwharrie, North Carolina 20 June 1799-West Branch, Iowa 15 Nov. 1856, West Milton, Ohio 18 Apr. 1819

9. Rebecca Yount, Kentucky 3 Nov. 1801-West Branch, Iowa 13 Aug. 1895

10. John Davis, prob. Georgia 2 May 1781-4 Mar. 1853, Miami Co., Ohio 7 Nov. 1810

11. Lydia Coate, 23 Nov. 1793-12 Aug. 1826

12. John Minthorn, near Hartford, Connecticut 4 Oct. 1768 (or 1769)-Canada (bur. near Oakwood, Ontario) 17 Dec. 1859, Canada c. 1811

13. Lucinda Sherwood, 13 Oct. 1794-17 Apr. 1854

14. Henry Wasley, Bucks Co., Pennsylvania, 19 April 1793-Toronto, Canada 21 Sept. 1864

15. Ann Tool, 14 Nov. 1790-14 Sept. 1872

16. John Hoover, Uniontown, Maryland c. 1760-West Milton, Ohio 18 Nov. 1831, Randolph Co., N. C. c. 1784

17. Sarah Burkhart, 20 Sept. 1767-Ohio 29 Dec. 1843

18. John Yount, prob. N. C. 23 Sept. 1768-Ohio 1 Dec. 1822

19. Mary Lowe, 28 Mar. 1771-22 July 1842

20. Abiather Davis, Wrightsborough, Ga. to West Branch, Iowa, Wrightsborough c. 1778

21. Lydia Embree, b. N. C. 10 Feb. 1754, to West Milton, Ohio

22. Henry Coate, 18 Aug. 1770-prob. Miami Co., Ohio, 26 Nov. 1840, South Carolina Feb. 1793

23. Mary Hasket

24. William Minthorn (III), bp. Hartford, Conn. 24 Mar. 1744/5-Younge Street, Toronto c. 1830

25. Mrs. Hannah Eldridge Lewis, widow

26. Thomas (or Isaac) Sherwood of Younge Street, d. c. 1844

27. Endymia Winn, b. 4 Sept. 1775

28. Francis Wasley, Jr., c. 1751-c. 1831, Muncy, Pa. to Younge Street, Toronto, m. Younge Street

29. Hannah Scott of Norwich, Ontario, 14 Jan. 1762-prob. Younge Street 21 May 1835

30. Aaron Tool, Bucks Co., Pa. to Toronto, Canada, St. Paul's Church 7 June 1790

31. Rachel Haworth, b. 7 Jan. 1766

32. Andrew Hoover (Andreas Huber), Ellerstadt in the Palatinate, Germany 29 Jan. 1723-Randolph Co., N. C. c. 1783, c. 1745

33. Anna Margreta (Margaret) Pfautz, prob. Zweibruecken in the Palatinate c. 1725-N. C. 1797

34. Christian Burkhard (numerous variant spellings), prob. Switzerland-prob. Miami Co., Ohio, m. Pa. c. 1753

35. Anna Barbara Graeff

36. George Yount, Alsace c. 1740-Union, Ohio 23 Apr. 1810, Randolph Co., N. C.

37. Rosannah Waywire, Germany c. 1751-Montgomery Co., Ohio 16 Aug. 1814

38-39. ---

40. Samuel Davis of Pa., 3 Aug. 1734-1787

41. Mary ---
42. John Embree of Cane Creek, 12 Nov. 1721-post 1768
43. Mary ---
44. Marmaduke Coate, b. perhaps S. C. 13 June 1738-Miami Co., Ohio 25 Sept. 1822, c. 1754
45. Mary Jane Coppock
46. Isaac Hasket, 18 Apr. 1744-1782
47. Lydia Elliot
48. William Minthorn, Jr., England c. 1716-prob. New Hartford, Conn. c. 1805
49. Mary Gilbert, bp. Hartford 14 Dec. 1712
50. James Eldridge (of Conn.?)
51. Elizabeth ---
52-53. ---
54. Jacob Winn (III), 20 Oct. 1744-prob. East Guillimbury, Upper Canada 10 Apr. 1809
55. Phoebe Grout, Charlestown, New Hampshire 1 Apr. 1751-1819
56. Francis Wasley of Falls, Pa., m. 5 Dec. 1749
57. Phebe Bunting, b. c. 1726
58. Henry Scott, b. c. 1739, of Lycoming Co., Pa., m. 16 March 1761
59. Mary Dean, c. 1741-1782
60. John Tool, Jr., c. 1756-13 Mar. 1791
61. Ruth Rankin
62. John Haworth, c. 1715-Delaware Co., Pa. 9 Nov. 1776
63. Mary Garner of Bucks Co., Pa.
64. Gregor Jonas Huber, Oberkulm, Switzerland 6 July 1668-Ellerstadt in the Palatinate 23 Apr. 1741, c. 1698
65. Anna Maria Kruetzer, c. 1675/6-Ellerstadt 12 Apr. 1756
66. Jacob Pfautz, to Pa. 1727?
67. Maria Elizabeth ---
68. Johannes Burkhart, Switzerland c. 1710-prob. Lancaster Co., Pa. c. 1756
69-71. ---
72. Andrew Yount, Alsace c. 1717, to Pa. 1751
73. ---
74. John Rudolph Waywire, Hanover, Germany c. 1725-Randolph Co., N. C. 1801
75-83. ---
84. Moses Embree of Hempstead, N. Y. & elsewhere, d. 1748
85. Mary ---
86-87. ---
88. William Coate, Jr. of Philadelphia, b. c. 1703, m. 1722
89. Rachel Ann Budd, b. c. 1705
90. Moses Coppock, Chester Co., Pa. to Newberg District, S. C.
91. Martha Scarr
92. William Hasket
93. Mary ---
94. (poss.) Joseph Elliot, will proved Perquimans Co., N. C. Apr. 1788 (father or uncle of Mrs. Lydia Elliot Hasket)
95. (poss.) Hannah Gordon, wife of Joseph Elliot
96. William Minthorn, d. en route to New England
97. Mary ---, d. en route to N. E.
98. Joseph Gilbert, Hartford, Conn. 3 Apr. 1666-Hartford June 1751, Hartford 7 May 1695
99. Elizabeth Smith, Hartford Nov. 1672-Hartford 15 July 1756
100-107. ---
108. Jacob Winn, Jr.
109. Sarah Buck, b. Woburn, Massachusetts 16 Apr. 1716
110. John Grout, Jr., Lunenburg, Mass. 13 June 1731, later of Charlestown, N. H., Lunenburg 22 Oct. 1750
111. Phoebe Spofford, b. Rowley, Mass. 1 July 1733
112-113. ---

114. Samuel Bunting of Falls, Pa., c. 1692-c. 1759
115. Priscilla Burgess
116. John Scott, Jr., b. Longhamroe, Yorkshire, England 30 3rd Mo. 1693, later of Falls & Abington, Pa., m. 21 Jan. 1731
117. Hannah Merrick, b. c. 1707
118-119. ---
120. John Tool
121. Elizabeth Pugh
122-123. ---
124. George Haworth, Lancashire, England c. 1681-Buckingham, Pa. 28 Nov. 1724, Bucks Co., Pa. 28 Sept. 1710
125. Sarah Scarborough, Solesbury, Pa. 4 Feb. 1694-4 Mar. 1748
126. Hans Garner, Germany to Bucks Co., Pa.
127. ---
128. Johann Heinrich Huber (c. 1644-c. 1706), Oberkulm, Switzerland to Ellerstadt in the Palatinate
129. Maria Margaretta Hoffman
130-131. ---
132. Hans Michael Pfautz, d. 1741/2, to Pa. 1727
133. Ursula --- (c. 1682-c. 1772)
134-135. ---
136. Emmanual Burkhardt
137-143. ---
144. Hans George Jundt (Yount), b. c. 1691, to Pa. 1731
145. Anna Maria ---, b. c. 1691
146-175. ---
176. William Coate (c. 1684-c. 1749), Burlington Co., N. J., = 1702
177. Rebecca Sharpe, b. c. 1687, m. (2) Joseph Lippincott
178-183. ---
184. Anthony Hasket of Albemarle Co., N. C.
185. Martha ---
186-187. ---
188. Thomas Elliot of Va.
189. Margaret ---
190-195. ---
196. John Gilbert (c. 1626-1690), Hartford, Conn., = 1647
197. Amy Lord, b. 1626, Towcester, Northamptonshire to Hartford
198. Joseph Smith, d. 1689/90, Hartford, Conn., = 1656
199. Lydia Huit
200-215. ---
216. (perhaps) Jacob Winn (1681-post 1737), Woburn, Mass., = 1704
217. (perhaps) Prudence Wyman (1683-ante 1737)
218. Samuel Buck, b. 1682, Woburn, Mass., = c. 1708
219. Hannah ---
220. John Grout (1704-1771), Jaffrey, N. H., = 1727
221. Joanna Boynton, b. 1712
222. John Spofford (IV) (1703/4-post 1757), Rowley, Mass., = 1728
223. Hannah Tyler, b. 1710
224-227. ---
228. Job Buntin, d. 1703, Matlock, Derbyshire to Bucks Co., Pa., = 1689
229. Rachel Baker, b. 1669, Hindley, Lancashire to Bucks Co., Pa.
230. Samuel Burgess, Falls, Pa.
231. Elinor ---
232. John Scott (1654-1700), Longhamroe, Yorkshire to Bucks Co., Pa., = 1687
233. Jane Bond (1664-post 1707), Chipping, Lancashire to Bucks Co., = (2) John Whittaker (Whitacre)
234. John Merrick (1654-will dated 1732), Herefordshire to Philadelphia Co., Pa.
235. Mrs. Eleanor Kellet Smith, b. c. 1665

236-247. ---
248. James Haworth, d. 1684, Rockliffe, Lancashire
249. Isabel ---, d. c. 1710
250. John Scarborough, Jr. (c. 1667-1727), Solesbury, Pa.
251. Mary Pierson (c. 1676-1751)
252-255. ---

* * *

32. FRANKLIN DELANO ROOSEVELT

1. FRANKLIN DELANO ROOSEVELT, Hyde Park, New York 30 Jan. 1882-Warm Springs, Georgia 5 Apr. 1945, New York City 17 Mar. 1905 (Anna) Eleanor Roosevelt (his fifth cousin once removed), NYC 12 Oct. 1884-NYC 7 Nov. 1962

2. James Roosevelt, Hyde Park, N. Y. 16 July 1828-Hyde Park 8 Dec. 1900, Algonac (near Newburgh), N. Y. 7 Oct. 1880

3. Sara Delano, Algonac 21 Sept. 1854-Hyde Park 7 Sept. 1941

4. Isaac Roosevelt, NYC 21 Apr. 1790-Hyde Park 23 Oct. 1863, 26 Tpr. 1827

5. Mary Rebecca Aspinwall, NYC 20 Dec. 1809-NYC 24 Feb. 1886

6. Warren Delano, Jr., Fairhaven, Mass. 13 July 1809-Algonac, N. Y. 17 Jan. 1898, Northampton, Mass. 1 Nov. 1843

7. Catherine Robbins Lyman, Northampton, Mass. 12 Jan. 1825-Algonac 10 Feb. 1896

8. James Roosevelt, NYC 10 Jan. 1760-NYC 6 Feb. 1847, NYC 15 Nov. 1786

9. Maria Eliza Walton, NYC 15 Mar. 1769-NYC 22 Mar. 1810

10. John Aspinwall, Jr., NYC 10 Feb. 1774-NYC 6 Oct. 1847, NYC 27 Nov. 1803

11. Susan Howland, Norwich, Connecticut 20 May 1779-NYC 12 or 23 Dec. 1852

12. Warren Delano, Fairhaven, Mass. 28 Oct. 1779-Fairhaven 25 Sept. 1866, Fairhaven 6 Nov. 1808

13. Deborah Church, Fairhaven 21 Mar. 1783-Fairhaven 7 Aug. 1827

14. Joseph Lyman (III), Northampton, Mass. 22 Oct. 1767-Northampton 11 Dec. 1847, Milton, Mass. 27 Oct. 1811

15. Anne Jean Robbins, prob. Milton, Mass. 3 July 1789-Somerville, Mass. 25 May 1867

16. Isaac Roosevelt, NYC 8 Dec. 1726-NYC 13 Oct. 1794, NYC 22 Sept. 1752

17. Cornelia Hoffman, Kingston, N. Y. 13 Aug. 1734-NYC 13 Nov. 1789

18. Abraham Walton, NYC c. 1739-NYC 21 Dec. 1796, c. 1766

19. Grace Williams, b. c. 1745

20. John Aspinwall, c. 1705/6-NYC 15 July 1774, Stamford, Conn. 5 June 1766

21. Rebecca Smith, c. 1734/5-Flushing, L. I. 25 Nov. 1809

22. Joseph Howland, Boston, Mass. 30 Sept. 1749-NYC 11 Mar. 1836, Norwalk, Conn. 26 May 1772

23. Lydia Bill, Norwich, Conn. 7 July 1753-NYC 1 May 1838

24. Ephraim Delano, Dartmouth, Mass. 25 Aug. 1733-Dartmouth (now Fairhaven) 4 July 1815, Dartmouth 27 Nov. 1760 (or 3 July 1768)

25. Elizabeth Cushman, Dartmouth 29 July 1739-Dartmouth (now Fairhaven) 24 Nov. 1809

26. Joseph Church, Dartmouth 14 Dec. 1752-prob. Fairhaven c. 1839, Dartmouth 19 Apr. 1777

27. Deborah Perry, Dartmouth 14 Oct. 1754-c. 1808

28. Joseph Lyman, Jr., Northampton 4 May 1731-Northampton 21 Oct. 1804, Northampton 5 Aug. 1756

29. Mary Sheldon, Northampton c. 1731-Northampton 18 Oct. 1805

30. Edward Hutchinson Robbins, Lt. Gov. of Mass., Milton 19 Feb.

1758-Milton 29 Dec. 1829, Nov. 1785

31. Elizabeth Murray, North Carolina 14 Mar. 1756-Milton 17 Dec. 1837

32. James (Jacobus) Roosevelt, NYC 28 Feb. 1692-NYC 4 or 5 May 1776, NYC 31 Jan. 1713

33. Catharina Hardenbroeck, NYC 20 Feb. 1694-post 1739

34. Martin Hoffman, Kingston, N. Y. 6 Feb. 1706/7-NYC 29 Aug. 1772, NYC 19 Oct. 1733

35. Tryntje (Catharine) Benson, Kingston, N. Y. 30 May 1712-prob. Dutchess Co., N. Y. 31 Mar. 1765

36. Jacob Walton, NYC 3 July 1703-NYC 17 Oct. 1749, NYC 14 May 1726

37. Maria Beekman, NYC or Flatbush 10 Jan. 1704-NYC c. 1794

38. Charles Williams, c. 1700-NYC 2 July 1773

39. Sarah Elizabeth ---

40. Joseph Aspinwall, Muddy River (Brookline), Mass. 9 Oct. 1673-c. 1743, lic. NYC 13 July 1700

41. Hannah Dean

42. William Henry Smith, Manor of St. George, Setauket, Long Island 29 Oct. 1708-prob. Setauket 2 Oct. 1776 (last Lord of St. George's Manor), Manor of Queen's Village, Lloyd's Neck, L. I. 19 Dec. 1732

43. Margaret Lloyd, Lloyd's Neck 1 June 1713-Brookhaven, L. I. 25 Sept. 1756

44. Nathaniel Howland, Jr., b. Plymouth, Mass. 9 June 1705, m. Boston 22 Nov. 1739

45. Abigail Burt, Boston 28 Mar. 1718-Boston 22 July 1766, widow of Richard Lane

46. Ephraim Bill, New London, Conn. 15 Aug. 1719-Norwich 24 Nov. 1802, Norwich 3 Apr. 1746

47. Lydia Huntington, Norwich 15 Mar. 1727-Norwich 23 Sept. 1798

48. Thomas Delano, b. Dartmouth, Mass. 10 May 1704, m. Dartmouth 4 Nov. 1727 (1729?)

49. Jean Peckham, b. Dartmouth 23 Jan. 1702/3

50. James Cushman, Plymouth, Mass. c. 1695-prob. Dartmouth, Plymouth 24 Dec. 1722

51. Sarah Hatch

52. Caleb Church, Little Compton, Rhode Island 28 Apr. or July 1728-prob. Dartmouth c. 1771, Dartmouth 21 Sept. 1751

53. Mercy Pope, Dartmouth 26 Jan. 1729/30-prob. Dartmouth ante 8 Dec. 1780

54. Samuel Perry, Sandwich, Mass. 27 June 1731-New Bedford, Mass. 15 Apr. 1805, Dartmouth 14 Apr. 1754

55. Susannah Swift, c. 1734-New Bedford 8 June 1806

56. Joseph Lyman, Northampton, Mass. 22 Aug. 1699-Northampton 30 Mar. 1763, c. 1727

57. Abigail Lewis, Farmington, Conn. 15 Nov. 1701-Northampton c. 1776

58. Benjamin Sheldon, Northampton c. 1697-Northampton 28 Aug. 1773, Northampton 12 June 1723

59. Mary Strong, Northampton 16 Jan. 1701-Northampton 26 May 1770 (1776?)

60. Rev. Nathaniel Robbins, Cambridge, Mass. 12 Apr. 1726-Milton 19 May 1795, Milton 21 July 1757

61. Elizabeth Hutchinson, Boston, Mass. 31 Dec. 1731-Milton 2 May 1793

62. James Murray, Ewes, Dumfries, Scotland 9 Aug. 1713-Halifax, Nova Scotia 8 Nov. 1781 (sometime of N. C. and Boston, Mass.), Chesters, Ancrum, Roxburgh, Scotland 14 May 1744

63. Barbara Bennet (her husband's first cousin), Ancrum 29 Nov. 1724-N. C. Feb. 1758

64. Nicholas Roosevelt, bp. New Amsterdam (later NYC) 2 Oct.

1658-NYC 30 July 1742, NYC 26 Dec. 1682

65. Heyltje Jans Kunst, b. Albany, living 1730/1

66. Johannes Hardenbroeck, bp. Amsterdam, Netherlands 25 Sept. 1665-prob. NYC 1710-14, NYC 16 June 1686

67. Sara Van Laer, prob. bur. NYC 17 Nov. 1743

68. Nicholas Hoffman, Kingston, N. Y. c. 1680-Kingston 31 Dec. 1750, Kingston 30 Dec. 1704

69. Jannetje Crispel, bp. Hurley, N. Y. 7 Feb. 1686-prob. Kingston, N. Y. 14 Feb. 1752

70. Robert Benson, bp. Albany, N. Y. 1 Jan. 1686-prob. NYC c. 1715, Albany or NYC 14 Mar. 1708

71. Cornelia Roos, bp. Albany 6 May 1688-c. 1760, m. (2) Anthony Rutgers

72. William Walton, N. Y. c. 1675-NYC 23 May 1747, NYC 7 Sept. 1698

73. Mary Santvoort, bp. NYC 27 Nov. 1678-NYC 3 Sept. 1768

74. Gerardus Beekman, bp. New Amsterdam 17 Aug. 1653-NYC 10 Oct. 1723, Flatbush, L. I. 29 Aug. 1677

75. Magdalena Abeel, b. prob. Albany c. 1657-prob. NYC 20 Oct. 1745

76-79. ---

80. Peter Aspinwall of Toxteth Park (now part of Liverpool), England c. 1612-Brookline, Mass. 1 Dec. 1687, Boston 12 Feb. 1661

81. Remembrance Palfrey, bp. Salem, Mass. 16 Sept. 1638-ante 4 Apr. 1701

82. Christopher Dean, d. 1689

83. ---

84. Henry Smith, Tangier, Africa 19 Jan. 1678/9-Manor of St. George, Setauket, L. I. 31 Oct. 1766, Charlestown, Mass. 9 Jan. 1704/5

85. Anna Shepard, Charlestown, Mass. 30 Jan. 1684/5-Manor of St. George, Setauket 7 May 1735

86. Henry Lloyd, Boston, Mass. 28 Nov. 1685-Lloyd's Neck, L. I., N. Y. 18 Mar. 1763, Lord of the Manor of Queen's Village, m. Boston 27 Nov. 1708

87. Rebecca Nelson, Boston 15 Nov. 1688-Lloyd's Neck 27 July 1728

88. Nathaniel Howland, Plymouth, Mass. c. 1671-Plymouth 29 Dec. 1746, Plymouth 3 Mar. 1696/7

89. Martha Cole, 1669-Plymouth 11 Aug. 1718

90. John Burt, b. Boston, Mass. 5 Jan. 1692, m. Boston 3 June 1714

91. Abigail Cheever, b. Boston 20 May 1690

92. Samuel Bill, Jr., New London, Conn. c. 1690-prob. New London or at sea ante 1 Mar. 1753

93. Hannah ---, c. 1692-New London 7 May 1740

94. Joshua Huntington, Norwich, Conn. 30 Dec. 1698-Norwich 26 Aug. 1745, Norwich 16 Oct. 1718

95. Hannah Perkins, Norwich 7 July 1701-Norwich 1745

96. Jonathan Delano, Duxbury, Mass. c. 1648-Dartmouth, Mass. 23 Dec. 1720, Plymouth 28 Feb. 1678

97. Mercy Warren, Plymouth 20 Feb. 1658-Dartmouth post 1727

98. Stephen Peckham, prob. Newport, R. I.-Dartmouth 23 Apr. 1724, prob. Newport

99. Mary ---

100. Eleazer Cushman, Plymouth, Mass. 20 Feb. 1656/7-Plympton, Mass. post 1723, Plymouth 12 Jan. 1687/8

101. Elizabeth Coombs, Boston 30 Nov. 1662-post 1723

102-103. ---

104. Nathaniel Church, Little Compton, R. I. 8 Feb. 1693-perhaps Dartmouth, Mass., Little Compton 14 Mar. 1717

105. Innocent Head of Little Compton

106. Lemuel Pope, Dartmouth 21 Feb. 1696-Dartmouth 23 May 1771,

Dartmouth 4 Feb. 1718/9

107. Elizabeth Hunt, Weymouth, Mass. c. 1697-Dartmouth 2 July 1782

108. Ebenezer Perry, Sandwich, Mass. 5 Mar. 1705/6-prob. Hardwick, Mass. post 1775, c. 1728

109. Abigail Presbury, prob. Watertown, Mass. c. 1703-Sandwich 25 June 1749

110. Jireh Swift, Jr., prob. Wareham, Mass. 23 Nov. 1709-Acushnet, Mass. 16 Mar. 1782, Dartmouth 9 Oct. 1730

111. Deborah Hathaway, Dartmouth 10 July 1713-Acushnet 7 Jan. 1794

112. Benjamin Lyman, Northampton 10 Aug. 1674-Northampton 14 Oct. 1723, Northampton 27 Oct. 1698

113. Thankful Pomeroy, Northampton 31 May 1679-Northampton 18 Sept. 1773, m. (2) Nathaniel Lewis, #114

114. Nathaniel Lewis, Farmington, Conn. 1 Oct. 1676-Farmington 24 Feb. 1752, 25 Nov. 1699

115. Abigail Ashley, Westfield, Mass. 27 Apr. 1681-Farmington 11 Apr. 1723

116. Thomas Sheldon, Northampton 6 Aug. 1661-Northampton 7 June 1725, Northampton c. 1685

117. Mary Hinsdale, Medfield, Mass. 22 July 1665-Northampton Sept. 1738

118. Ebenezer Strong, Jr., Northampton 2 Aug. 1671-Northampton 12 Nov. 1729, Northampton 25 Oct. 1695

119. Mary Holton, Northampton 22 July 1678-Northampton 8 Dec. 1705

120. Thomas Robbins, Cambridge, Mass. 11 Aug. 1703-Lexington, Mass. 30 Jan. 1791, Woburn, Mass. 2 May 1723

121. Ruth Johnson, c. 1703-Cambridge 27 June 1737

122. Edward Hutchinson, Boston, Mass. 18 June 1678-1752, Boston 10 Oct. 1706

123. Lydia Foster, b. Boston c. 1687

124. John Murray of Unthank, Ewes, Dumfries, 1 or 4 Feb. 1677-27 Feb. 1728, Ancrum, Roxburgh 20 Apr. 1712

125. Ann Bennet of Chesters, 20 Nov. 1694-13 Apr. 1737

126. Andrew Bennet of Chesters, Ancrum, Roxburgh (brother of Ann), c. 1696-July 1745, Ancrum 29 Dec. 1719

127. Dorothy Collingwood of Little Ryle, Whittingham, Northumberland, England, c. 1695-July 1736

128. Claes Martenszen van Rosenvelt, d. 1658-60, Holland to New Amsterdam, = ante 1650

129. Jannetje Tomas or Samuels, d. 1660

130. Jan Barentsen Kunst, living 1670, Germany or North Holland to Kingston & Hurley, N. Y.

131. Jannetje Adriaens, d. ante 1663

132. Andries Hardenbroeck, bp. 1634, Amsterdam, Holland, = 1663

133. Aeffe Jans Sijbrantsz, b. 1637

134. Stoffel Gerritszen Van Laer (c. 1639/40-living 1665), Germany to New Amsterdam, = 1660

135. Catharina Jans

136. Martin Hermanzen Hoffman (c. 1625-living 1688), Revel, Sweden (now U.S.S.R.) to Kingston & New Amsterdam, = 1664

137. Emmerentje Claesen de Witte, Esens, Germany to New Amsterdam

138. Antoine Crispel (1635-1707), St. Guin, Artois, France to Kingston & Hurley, N. Y., = c. 1680

139. Petronella DuMond (or LeMan)

140. Samson Benson (1652-1730), NYC, = 1673

141. Tryntje Van Deursen, b. c. 1654

142. Johannes Roos, d. 1695, Albany, N. Y.

143. Cornelia ---

144. Thomas Walton, d. 1689, Staten Island, N. Y., = 1671

145. Mary Lawrence, b. c. 1640s, Newtown, L. I., prob. m. (2) --- White
146. Jacob Abrahamsen Santvoort, living 1685, Vianen, Holland to New Amsterdam, = 1677
147. Magdaleentje Van Vleck, living 1699, Bremen, Germany to New Amsterdam
148. Wilhelmus Hendrickse Beekman (1623-1707), Hasselt, Overys-sel, Holland to New Amsterdam, = 1649
149. Catalina (Catharine) de Boogh, Albany
150. Stoffel Janse Abeel (1621-1684), Amsterdam, Holland to Albany, = 1660
151. Neeltje Janse Croom (c. 1630-c. 1681), Holland to Albany, = 1660
152-161. ---
162. Peter Palfrey, d. 1663, Reading, Mass.
163. Edith ---
164-167. ---
168. William Smith (1654/5-1704/5), Lord of the Manor of St. George, Newton Bromswold, Northamptonshire to Tangier, Africa to Setauket, L. I., N. Y., = 1675
169. Martha Tunstall (1652-1709), Putney, Surrey to Setauket
170. Rev. Thomas Shepard (III) (1658-1685), Charlestown, Mass., = 1682
171. Mary Anderson (ante 1654-1717), widow of Thomas Lynde, m. (3) Samuel Hayman
172. James Lloyd (c. 1653-1693), Bristol, England to Boston, Mass., = 1676
173. Grizzell Sylvester, d. 1688-91, of Shelter Island, N. Y.
174. John Nelson (1654-1734), London to Boston, Mass., see Dict. Amer. Biog.
175. Elizabeth Tailer (1667-1734)
176. Joseph Howland, d. 1703/4, Plymouth, Mass., = 1664
177. Elizabeth Southworth, d. 1717
178. James Cole, Jr. (c. 1625/6-1712), London to Plymouth, Mass., = 1652
179. Mary Tilson
180. William Burt of Boston
181. Elizabeth ---
182. Rev. Thomas Cheever (1658-1749), Malden & Chelsea, Mass., = ante 1685
183. Sarah Bill (c. 1658-1704/5)
184. Samuel Bill (c. 1665-c. 1729/30) of New London & Groton, Conn., a first cousin of Sarah, 183 above
185. Mercy Haughton of New London
186-187. ---
188. Simon Huntington (III) (1659-1736), Norwich, Conn., = 1683
189. Lydia Gager (1663-1737)
190. Jabez Perkins (1677-1741/2), Ipswich, Mass. to Norwich, Conn., = 1698
191. Hannah Lathrop (1677-1721)
192. Philip Delano or De Lannoy (1603-1681), Leyden, Holland to Duxbury & Bridgewater, Mass., = 1634
193. Hester (Esther) Dewsbury
194. Nathaniel Warren (c. 1624/5-1667), Plymouth, Mass., = 1645
195. Sarah Walker (1622-1700), London to Plymouth, Mass.
196. John Peckham (c. 1600-c. 1681), Newport, R. I., = ante 1648
197. Eleanor ---
198-199. ---
200. Thomas Cushman (1607/8-1691), Canterbury, Kent to Plymouth, Mass., = c. 1636
201. Mary Allerton (1616-1699), Leyden, Holland to Plymouth
202. John Coombs, Jr. (c. 1632-1668), Plymouth, Boston & Hing-ham, Mass., = 1661/2

203. Elizabeth (Royall?), d. c. 1671/2, widow of Thomas Barlow, m. (3) John Warren
204-207. ---
208. Joseph Church, Jr. (1663-1715), Little Compton, R. I., = 1688
209. Grace Shaw (c. 1666-1737)
210. Henry Head (c. 1647-1716), Little Compton, R. I., = c. 1677
211. Elizabeth --- (c. 1654-1748)
212. Seth Pope (1648-1727), Plymouth to Dartmouth, Mass., = c. 1675
213. Deborah Perry (1654-1710/1), Sandwich to Dartmouth, Mass.
214. Ephraim Hunt, Jr. (c. 1650-1713), Weymouth, Mass., = c. 1678
215. Joanna Alcock (1660-1746), Boston to Acushnet, Mass.
216. Samuel Perry (1667-1751, brother of Deborah Perry, 213 above), Sandwich, Mass., = 1689
217. Esther Taber (1671-1749/50), Dartmouth to Sandwich, Mass.
218. Stephen Presbury (c. 1666-1730), Edgartown, Mass., = c. 1693
219. Deborah Skiffe (1668-1743) Sandwich to Edgartown, Mass.
220. Jireh Swift (c. 1665-1749), Sandwich & Wareham, Mass., = 1697
221. Abigail Gibbs (c. 1677-ante 1741)
222. Jonathan Hathaway (c. 1671-1727), Dartmouth, Mass., = 1701
223. Susannah Pope (1681-1760), daughter of 212 & 213 above
224. John Lyman (1623-1690), High Ongar, Essex to Northampton, Mass., = 1655
225. Dorcas Plum, Wethersfield & Branford, Conn. to Northampton
226. Medad Pomeroy (1638-1716), Windsor, Conn. to Northampton, = 1661
227. Experience Woodward (1643-1686), Dorchester to Northampton, Mass.
228. William Lewis, Jr. (c. 1622-1690), Farmington, Conn., = 1671
229. Mary Cheever (1640-1728, half-sister of Rev. Thomas Cheever, 182 above), New Haven to Farmington, Conn.
230. David Ashley (1642-1718), Springfield to Westfield, Mass., = 1663
231. Hannah Glover (1646-1722), New Haven, Conn. to Westfield
232. Isaac Sheldon (c. 1629/30-1708), prob. Ashwell, Bakewell, Derbyshire to Windsor, Conn. & Northampton, Mass., = c. 1653
233. Mary Woodford (c. 1635-1684), Hartford, Conn. to Northampton
234. Samuel Hinsdale (c. 1641/2-1675), Dedham to Medfield to Hadley to Deerfield, = 1660
235. Mehitable Johnson (1644-1689), Roxbury to Deerfield, Mass., m. (2) John Root, (3) John Coleman
236. Ebenezer Strong (c. 1643-1729), Northampton, Mass., = 1668
237. Hannah Clapp, b. 1646, Dorchester to Northampton, Mass.
238. William Holton, Jr. (c. 1644-1711), Hartford, Conn. to Northampton, Mass. to Lebanon & Hartford, Conn., = 1676
239. Sarah Marshfield, b. 1656, Springfield, Mass.
240. Nathaniel Robbins, Jr. (1677/8-1741/2), Cambridge, Mass., = c. 1695
241. Hannah Chandler (1673-1718), Andover to Cambridge, Mass.
242. William Johnson, Jr. (1656/7-1729/30), Charlestown & Woburn, Mass., = ante 1686
243. Esther Gardner (1659-1706)
244. Elisha Hutchinson (1641-1717), Boston, Mass., = 1677
245. Elizabeth Clarke (1642-1713), widow of John Freake
246. John Foster (c. 1648-1711), Aylesbury, England to Boston, = ante 1678 or 1679
247. Lydia Turell (1660-ante 1688)
248. John Murray, d. 1712, of Bowhill, Scotland, a senator in the

College of Justice

249. Margaret (or Jean) Scott of Ancrum, sister of John Scott of New York

250. Archibald Bennet, living 1712, Laird of Chesters, Ancrum, Roxburgh, = 1682

251. Barbara Rutherford, d. ante 1705, of Edgerston, Jedburgh, Roxburgh

252. same as 250

253. same as 251

254. Alexander Collingwood (c. 1665-1745/6) of Little Ryle, Whittingham, Northumberland, = 1691/2

255. Dorothy Lawson of Brayton

Numbers 30, 60, 170 & 182 were Harvard graduates of 1775, 1747, 1676 and 1677 respectively; numbers 1 & 2 were Harvard graduates of 1903 and 1852 respectively, and number 14 was a Yale graduate of 1783.

* * *

33. HARRY S TRUMAN

1. HARRY S TRUMAN, Lamar, Missouri 8 May 1884-Kansas City, Mo. 26 Dec. 1972, Independence, Mo. 28 June 1919 Elizabeth (Bess) Virginia Wallace, Independence 13 Feb. 1885-Independence 18 Oct. 1982

2. John Anderson Truman, Jackson Co., Mo. 5 Dec. 1851-Kansas City, Mo. 3 Nov. 1914, Jackson Co. 28 Dec. 1881

3. Martha Ellen Young, Parish Farm (now Kansas City), Jackson City, Mo. 25 Nov. 1852-Grandview, Mo. 26 July 1949

4. Anderson Shipp Truman, Shelby Co., Kentucky 27 Feb. 1816-Grandview, Mo. 3 July 1887, Shelby Co. 13 Aug. 1846

5. Mary Jane Holmes, Shelby Co. 15 Mar. 1821-Jackson Co. 15 Feb. 1879

6. Solomon Young, Shelby Co., Ky. 24 Apr. 1815-Grandview, Mo. 26 Jan. 1892, Shelby Co. (lic.) 9 Jan. 1838

7. Harriet Louisa Gregg, Shelby Co. 15 Oct. 1818-Grandview 9 Dec. 1909

8. William Truman, Jr., Virginia 15 Jan. 1783-Shelby Co., Ky. 28 Nov. 1863, Woodford Co., Ky. 28 Aug. 1807

9. Emma Grant Shipp, St. Mary's Parish, Caroline Co., Va. 29 Oct. 1787-prob. Shelby Co., Ky. 21 June 1872

10. Jesse Holmes, Fauquier Co., Va. 17 Dec. 1775-Shelby Co., Ky. 8 May 1840, Shelby Co. (lic.) 17 Nov. 1803

11. Ann Drusilla (Nancy) Tyler, Boone's Station, Ky. 4 Apr. 1780-Kansas City, Mo. 8 July 1875

12. Jacob Young, Mecklenburg Co., North Carolina c. 1764-Tampico, Indiana 24 Aug. 1836, Mercer Co., Ky. 16 Dec. 1792

13. Rachel Goodnight, Mecklenburg Co. 15 or 25 Apr. 1771 or 1776-Shelby Co., Ky. 22 Nov. 1828

14. David Gregg, 20 Dec. 1767-Shelby Co., Ky. 25 June 1828, Jefferson Co., Ky. 19 Oct. 1795

15. Sarah Scott, 24 July 1775 or 1776-Jefferson or Shelby Co., Ky. 13 Sept. 1823

16. William Truman of Bedford & Franklin Cos., Va.

17. Nancy ---

18. Richard Shipp, St. Mary's Parish, Caroline Co., Va. 12 Nov. 1747-Woodford Co., Ky. c. 1828, Feb. 1774

19. Elizabeth Doniphan, King George Co., Va. June 1759-Woodford Co., Ky. c. 1812

20. James Holmes, Jr., Prince William Co., Va. 18 Sept. 1745-Shelby Co., Ky. 7 June 1833, 18 Sept. 1764

21. Margaret Lewis, Fauquier Co., Va. 9 May 1743-Shelby Co., Ky. 25 Mar. 1832

22. Robert Tyler, Frederick Co., Va. 19 Aug. 1751-Shelby Co., Ky. 6 Apr. 1815, c. 1772

23. Margaret ---, Va. 15 Mar. 1775-Shelby Co., Ky. 14 Oct. 1840

24. John Young (Jung), prob. Germany ante 1740-Mecklenburg Co., N. C. late 1789

25. Ann ---

26. Hans Michael Goodnight (Gutknecht), Germany ante 1730-near Harlan's Station, Ky. (killed by Indians) 1 Sept. 1781, to Philadelphia 1752, m. Va. or N. C. 19 Feb. 1762

27. Mary Landis or Landers, m. (2) --- Flanigan

28. John Gregg of Jefferson Co., Ky.

29. ---

30. William Scott, 1 Feb. 1747-Jefferson Co., Ky. between 30 Dec. 1823 & 12 April 1824

31. (probably) Margaret ---, d. post 1824

32-35. ---

36. Thomas Shipp, Jr., St. Anne's Parish, Essex Co., Va. c. 1727-Caroline Co., Va. between 14 Aug. & 13 Nov. 1777, c. early 1747

37. Rachel ---

38. Anderson Doniphan, c. 1718-20-Brunswick Parish, King George Co., Va. between 4 Dec. 1760 & 5 March 1761

39. Magdalin Monteith, d. post 1792, m. (2) Jonathan Finnall of Stafford Co.

40. James Holmes of Prince William Co., Va., d. ante 1782

41. Elizabeth ---, d. prob. Prince William Co. c. 1803-05

42. (prob.) James Lewis of Fauquier Co., Va.

43. ---

44. Edward Tyler, Jr., Queen Anne Parish, Prince Georges Co., Maryland 18 Jan. 1719/20-Jefferson Co., Ky. 20 May 1802, prob. Frederick Co., Va. c. 1750

45. Ann (Nancy) Langley, prob. Md. c. 1732-prob. Jefferson Co., Ky. 31 July 1820

46-71. ---

72. Thomas Shipp, St. Anne's Parish, Essex Co., Va. c. 1707-Caroline Co., Va. shortly ante Sept. 1752, c. 1725

73. Elizabeth ---

74-75. ---

76. Mott Doniphan, d. prob. Overwharton Parish, Stafford Co., Va. c. 1776, c. 1710

77. Rosanna Anderson of Potomac Creek, Stafford Co., d. ante 1776

78. Thomas Monteith, Glasgow, Scotland to King George Co., Va. c. 1694-c. 1747, ante 1737

79. Phillis Gallop

80. John Holmes of Stafford & Prince William Cos., Va. d. between 2 Feb. 1732/3 & 24 Mar. 1739

81. Mary ---, d. post 1739

82-87. ---

88. Edward Tyler, Queen Anne Parish, Prince Georges Co., Md. 2 Oct. 1696-Prince Georges Co. c. 1726, Prince Georges Co. c. 1713-14

89. Elizabeth Duvall, prob. Anne Arundel Co., Md. c. 1696-post 1770

90-143. ---

144. Richard Shipp (c. 1685-1724), St. Anne's Parish, Essex Co., Va.

145. Mary ---

146-151. ---

152. Alexander Doniphan (c. 1653-1717), Westmoreland & Richmond Cos., Va., = ante 1692

153. Margaret Mott

154. George Anderson, living 1707, Stafford Co., Va.

155. Mary Mathews, d. ante 1707

156-157. ---

158. Robert Gallop, d. c. 1720, Prince George & Richmond Cos., Va.
159-175. ---
176. Robert Tyler, Jr. (c. 1671-c. 1738), Calvert & Prince Georges Cos., Md., = c. 1695
177. Susanna Duvall (c. 1676-c. 1716/7), sister of 178
178. Samuel Duvall (c. 1667-1741/2), Anne Arundel & Prince Georges Cos., Md., brother of 177, = 1697
179. Elizabeth Ijams (c. 1671-74-ante 1741), widow of Daniel Clarke
180-255. ---

* * *

34. DWIGHT DAVID EISENHOWER

1. DWIGHT DAVID EISENHOWER, Denison, Texas 14 Oct. 1890-Washington, D. C. 28 Mar. 1969, Denver, Colorado 1 July 1916 Mamie Geneva Doud, Boone, Iowa 14 Nov. 1896-Washington, D. C. 31 Oct. 1979
2. David Jacob Eisenhower, Elizabethville, Pennsylvania 23 Sept. 1863-Abilene, Kansas 15 Mar. 1942, Hope, Kansas 23 Sept. 1885
3. Ida Elizabeth Stover, Mount Sidney, Virginia 1 May 1862-Abilene, Kansas 11 Sept. 1946
4. Jacob Frederick Eisenhower, Elizabethville, Pa. 19 Sept. 1826-Abilene, Kansas 20 May 1906, Elizabethville, Pa. 25 Feb. 1847
5. (Margaret?) Rebecca Matter, Pa. 18 Mar. 1825-Abilene, Kansas 22 June 1890
6. Simon P. Stover, Augusta Co., Va. 28 Sept. 1822-Augusta Co. 11 Dec. 1873, Augusta Co. 31 Dec. 1848
7. Elizabeth Ida (Juda) Link, Augusta Co. 19 Nov. 1822-Augusta Co. 28 Mar. 1867
8. Frederick Eisenhower, prob. near Linglestown, Pa. 15 July 1794-Abilene, Kansas 13 Mar. 1884, c. 1816
9. Barbara Miller, 27 May 1789-Elizabethville, Pa. 1 Jan. 1862
10. Henry Matter, 26 Dec. 1796-1 Oct. 1868
11. Anna Mary Dietrich, 16 Mar. 1803-11 Nov. 1865
12. Daniel Stover, Jr., c. 1780-Augusta Co., Va. 18 Jan. 1862, Augusta Co. 30 Mar. 1803
13. Mary Hannah, c. 1781-c. 1852
14. William Link, Augusta Co., Va. 24 Oct. 1795-Augusta Co. 21 June 1879, Augusta Co. 10 June 1818
15. Esther Charlotte Schindler, 16 Apr. 1796-Augusta Co. 1 Nov. 1874
16. Johann Peter Eisenhauer, Forbach, Lorraine 15 Mar. 1722-Lower Paxton, Pa. c. 1802, Stouchsburg, Berks Co., Pa. 29 Jan. 1777
17. Ann Dissinger, d. post Nov. 1815
18. John Miller
19. Susanna Raysor
20. Michael Matter, 3 Oct. 1763-12 Feb. 1852
21. Anna Maria Romberger, 12 June 1771-18 Mar. 1866
22. Jacob Dietrich
23. Anna Magdalena ---
24. Daniel Stover, c. 1750-Augusta Co., Va. c. 1822, ante 1773
25-27. ---
28. Peter Link, Frederick Co., Maryland 26 May 1765-Augusta Co., Va. 1 Mar. 1825, Augusta Co. 11 Mar. 1788
29. Judith Burkett (Burkhardt), Frederick Co. 24 June 1769-Augusta Co. 13 Aug. 1829
30. Adam Schindler of Augusta Co., Va.
31. ---
32. Johann Nicol Eisenhauer, prob. Darmstadt, Germany c. 1695, to Philadelphia 1741, later of Bethel, Pa., d. post Mar. 1760, m. 1721 or earlier

33. Anna Margaretha Strubel
34. Peter Dissinger of Stumpstown (now Fredericksburg), Pa., fl. 1776-81
35-39. ---
40. John Matter, c. 1737-May 1802
41. Anna Catharina ---
42. Henry Romberger
43. Elizabeth ---
44-47. ---
48. (prob.) Abraham Stover of Franklin Co., Va., b. post 1720
49-55. ---
56. John Matthias Link, Berks Co., Pa. 11 Feb. 1737-Augusta Co., Va. 8 Feb. 1815
57. Anna Mary Christina Schmit, prob. Frederick Co., Md. c. 1746-Augusta Co. 12 June 1817
58. Daniel Burkett (Burkhardt) of Frederick Co., Md., c. 1740-post 1788
59-63. ---
64. Johann Friedrich Eisenhauer, c. 1659-Karlsbrunn, Saar, Germany 28 Feb. 1729
65-95. ---
96. (prob.) Jacob Stover (Stuber, Stowber), c. 1688-Augusta Co., Va. Mar. 1741, Philadelphia 15 Mar. 1715
97. (prob.) Sarah Boone, Bradninch, Devon 18 Feb. 1691/2-ante 1744
98-111. ---
112. Johann Jacob Link, Grossgartach, Germany 20 Oct. 1682-Berks Co., Pa. Apr. 1738, Biberach, Germany 3 Sept. 1720
113. Anna (Maria) Magdalena Neuwirth, b. Biberach 13 Aug. 1692
114-193. ---
194. (prob.) George Boone, bp. Stoke Canon, Devon 19 Mar. 1666-Exeter, Pa. 27 July 1744, c. 1689
195. (prob.) Mary Maugridge, b. Bradninch, Devon c. 1669
196-223. ---
224. Hans Bernhard Linckh, Grossgartach, Germany c. 24 May 1647-ante 26 Nov. 1708, Grossgartach 3 May 1681
225. Anna Catharina Schuhmann, b. Grossgartach 15 July 1657
226. Jeremias Neuwirth, c. 1653-Biberach 16 Feb. 1725, Biberach 20 Jan. 1674
227. Margareta Christ
228-255. ---

* * *

35. JOHN FITZGERALD KENNEDY

1. JOHN FITZGERALD KENNEDY, Brookline, Massachusetts 29 May 1917-Dallas, Texas 22 Nov. 1963, Newport, Rhode Island 12 Sept. 1953 Jacqueline Lee Bouvier, b. Southampton, Long Island, New York 28 July 1929, who m. (2) Aristotle Socrates Onassis
2. Joseph Patrick Kennedy, financier, diplomat, Boston, Mass. 6 Sept. 1888-Hyannis Port, Mass. 18 Nov. 1969, Boston 7 Oct. 1914
3. Rose Elizabeth Fitzgerald, b. Boston 21 July 1890, created a papal countess by Pope Pius XII
4. Patrick Joseph Kennedy, Boston 14 Jan. 1858-Boston 18 May 1929, Boston 23 Nov. 1887
5. Mary Augusta Hickey, Boston 6 Dec. 1857-Boston 20 May 1923
6. John Francis Fitzgerald ("Honey Fitz"), Mayor of Boston, Boston 11 Feb. 1863-Boston 2 Oct. 1950, Concord, Mass. 18 Sept. 1889 his second cousin (dispensation for consanguity in 3rd degree)
7. Mary Josephine Hannon, Acton, Mass. 31 Oct. 1865-Boston 8 Aug. 1964
8. Patrick Kennedy, Dunganstown, Wexford, Ireland c. 1823-

Boston 22 Nov. 1858, Boston 26 Sept. 1849

9. Bridget Murphy, Ireland c. 1821-Boston 20 Dec. 1888

10. James Hickey, prob. Clonakilty Bay, Cork, Ireland c. 1836-Boston 22 Nov. 1900

11. Margaret M. Field, Rosscarbery, Cork, Ireland 26 Jan. 1835-Boston 5 June 1911

12. Thomas Fitzgerald, prob. Lough Gur, Limerick, Ireland c. 1822-Boston 19 May 1885, Boston 15 Nov. 1857

13. Rosanna Cox, Ireland c. 1835-Boston 10 Mar. 1879

14. Michael Hannon, Lough Gur 29 Sept. 1832-Acton, Mass. 1 Feb. 1900, Boston 12 Feb. 1854

15. Mary Ann Fitzgerald, Bruff, Limerick, Ireland 27 May 1834-Concord 1 July 1904

16. (alleged) Patrick Kennedy of Dunganstown

17. (alleged) Mary Johanna ---

18. Richard Murphy

19. Mary ---

20. Michael Hickey of Clonakilty Bay

21. Catherine Hasset

22. Patrick Field, m. Rosscarbery, Cork, Ireland 6 Feb. 1825

23. Mary Sheehy

24. Michael Fitzgerald of Lough Gur, d. Ireland

25. Ellen Wilmouth, Ireland c. 1797-Boston 17 Nov. 1875

26. Philip Cox

27. Mary ---

28. John Hannon, d. Lough Gur 22 July 1835

29. Ellen Noonan or Newman, Ireland c. 1793-Acton 28 Nov. 1877

30. Edmund Fitzgerald, prob. Lough Gur or Bruff, Limerick 21 Aug. 1798-Boston 27 Oct. 1883

31. Mary Linnehan, d. Ireland

32-47. ---

48. James Fitzgerald

49. Hannah ---

50. Thomas Wilmouth

51. Bridget ---

52-57. ---

58. Daniel Noonan or Newman

59. ---

60. same as 48

61. same as 49

62-255. ---

* * *

36. LYNDON BAINES JOHNSON

1. LYNDON BAINES JOHNSON, Stonewall, Texas 27 Aug. 1908-en route via helicopter between LBJ Ranch, Stonewall, & San Antonio, Tex. 22 Jan. 1973, San Antonio 17 Nov. 1934 Claudia Alta ("Lady Bird") Taylor, b. Karnack, Tex. 22 Dec. 1912

2. Samuel Ealy Johnson, Jr., Texas State Representative, Buda, Tex. 11 Oct. 1877-Austin, Tex. 23 Oct. 1937, Fredericksburg, Tex. 20 Aug. 1907

3. Rebekah Baines, McKinney, Tex. 26 June 1881-Austin 12 Sept. 1958

4. Samuel Ealy Johnson, Randolph Co., Alabama 12 Nov. 1838-Stonewall 25 Feb. 1915, Lockhart, Tex. 11 Dec. 1867

5. Eliza Jane Bunton, near Russellville, Kentucky 24 June 1849-Stonewall, Tex. 31 Jan. 1917

6. Joseph Wilson Baines, Mount Lebanon, Louisiana 24 Jan. 1846-Fredericksburg, Tex. 18 Nov. 1906, Rowlett, Tex. 12 Sept. 1869

7. Ruth Ament Huffman, near Rowlett 10 Dec. 1854-San Antonio 13 Feb. 1936

8. Jesse Johnson, Oglethorpe Co., Georgia 28 Apr. 1795-Lockhart 15 May 1856, Greene Co., Ga. 14 Nov. 1817

9. Lucy Webb Barnett, prob. Elbert Co., Ga. 14 Jan. 1798-Lockhart 13 Mar. 1857

10. Robert Holmes Bunton, Sumner Co., Tennessee 7 Sept. 1818-near Stonewall 22 Aug. 1895, Logan Co., Ky. 1 Sept. 1840

11. Priscilla Jane McIntosh, Fulton, Ky. 8 July 1821-near Stonewall 28 Apr. 1905

12. Rev. George Washington Baines, Perquimans Co., North Carolina 29 Dec. 1809-Belton, Tex. 28 Dec. 1882, Carroll Co., Arkansas 20 Oct. 1840

13. Melissa Ann Butler, N. C. 2 June 1824-Fairfield, Tex. 21 Jan. 1865

14. John (Smith) Huffman, Jr., Bourbon Co, Ky. 7 May 1824-near Rowlett 22 June 1865, prob. Collin Co., Tex. c. 1848

15. Mary Elizabeth Perrin, Russellville, Ky. 27 June 1826-Merkel, Tex. 12 July 1916

16. John Johnson (III), Southampton Co., Virginia 28 Mar. 1764-Oglethorpe Co., Ga. 14 Feb. 1828, c. 1786

17. Ann Eley (Ealy), Southampton Co. 14 Sept. 1763-Oglethorpe Co. 5 Jan. 1815

18. Leonard Barnett, St. Paul's Parish, Ga. c. 1773-living Greene Co., Ga. 1828

19. Nancy Statham

20. Joseph Robert Bunton, Rowan Co., N. C. 1770-82-Logan Co., Ky. 19 Jan. 1844, prob. Tenn. c. 1803

21. Phoebe Ann Desha, Davidson Co., N. C. (later Sumner Co., Tenn.) c. 1784-near Mountain City, Hays Co., Tex. 22 Dec. 1861

22. John William McIntosh of Russellville, Ky.

23. Julia Ann Miller

24. Rev. Thomas Baines, Edenton, N. C. 4 July 1787-Mississippi Dec. 1836, Perquimans Co., N. C. 13 Feb. 1808

25. Mary McCoy, Perquimans Co. c. 1783 (or 1794?)-Fairfield, Tex. c. 1864

26. Nealy Butler, N. C. 15 Jan. 1796-Stone Co., Missouri c. 1880

27. Amy Ogier, N. C. 28 Feb. 1799-Stone Co., Mo. c. 1875

28. John (Smith) Huffman, Bourbon Co., Ky. 2 Nov. 1794-near Plano, Tex. 8 Oct. 1879, Bourbon Co. 12 Mar. 1816

29. Susan Ament, Bourbon Co. 12 Oct. 1800-Bourbon Co. 18 May 1831

30. William Perrin, Logan Co., Ky. 15 Oct. 1800-Collin Co., Tex. c. 1856, Logan Co., Ky. c. 1820

31. Dycie Kirby, Logan Co. c. 1798-1802-Collin Co., Tex. c. 1856-57

32. John Johnson, Jr., Isle of Wight Co., Va. c. 1724-Franklin Co., N. C. between 22 May & June 1829, prob. Southampton Co., Va. ante 19 June 1763

33. Elizabeth Carr of Nottoway Parish, Southampton Co., d. ante 28 Oct. 1815

34. Samuel Eley, Isle of Wight Co., Va. c. 1736-Bute (now Franklin) Co., N. C. ante Nov. 1771, prob. Southampton Co. c. 1760

35. Mary Hillsman, living 1784, m. (2) --- Baker

36. Nathan Barnett, New Kent Co., Va. c. 1729-Greene Co., Ga. c. 1805, Va. c. 1757

37. Lucy Webb, b. Va. c. 1731

38. John Statham of Elbert Co., Ga.

39. ---

40. John Bunton, Jr., will dated Sumner Co., Tenn. 14 June 1803, m. Rowan Co., N. C. 16 Jan. 1769 (or 1767)

41. Mary McClure of Rowan Co.

42. Robert Desha, Jr., prob. Bucks Co., Pennsylvania c. 1738-Sumner Co., Tenn. between 6 May & Nov. 1816, Pa. c. 1758

43. Elinor Wheeler, prob. Bucks Co. c. 1740-Sumner Co., Tenn.

post Oct. 1793

44-47. ---

48. George Bains, 26 Jan. 1741-Edenton, N. C. 19 May 1802, 28 May 1769

49. Mary Creecy, 28 Jan. 1749-post 1802

50. William McCoy, will proved Perquimans Co., N. C. 18 Mar. 1795

51. Julia ---, d. post 1795

52-53. ---

54. Louis Ogier, Jr., London, c. 1753-Charleston, South Carolina 13 Nov. 1820, 2 Oct. 1783

55. Susan[nah] Martin, c. 1764-Charleston 14 Nov. 1827

56. John Huffman, Jr., (now) Washington Co., Maryland c. 1770 [RBJ (LBJ's mother) has 31 May 1766]-prob. Mo. (or Shelby Co., Ky.) 23 July 1826, c. 1790

57. Catharine Lyter, Frederick Co., Md. 2 Feb. 1771-near Floydsburg, Shelby Co. 15 Dec. 1831

58. Philip Ament, prob. Berks Co., Pa. c. 1755-Bourbon Co., Ky. c. 1836

59. Margaret ---

60. Charles Perrin, d. Russellville, Ky. c. 1850, m. Russellville c. 1792

61. Catherine Jameson, b. Franklin Co., Va. 20 Aug. 1773

62. George Kirby, m. Franklin Co. 10 Oct. 1795

63. Helen (Eleanor) Jameson, Franklin Co. c. 1775-c. 1816

64. John Johnston, Isle of Wight Co., Va. c. 1696-Southampton Co. between 30 Jan. & 8 May 1783

65. ---

66. Robert Carr of Nottoway Parish, Southampton Co., Va.

67. Sarah ---

68. Eli Eley of Isle of Wight Co., d. ante 10 Apr. 1753

69. Ann ---

70. Bennett Hillsman, d. Franklin Co., N. C. between 26 Dec. 1784 & Mar. 1789

71. ---

72. Frank Barnett (according to RBJ)

73. Sukey Johnson (according to RBJ)

74. John Webb (according to RBJ)

75. Peggy --- (according to RBJ)

76-79. ---

80. John Bunton or Buntine of Rowan Co., N. C., fl. 1762

81-83. ---

84. Robert Desha, b. c. 1715, d. prob. Smithfield, Pa., of French Huguenot background

85. Mary Everfieldt, d. prob. Northampton Co., Pa.

86. Joseph Wheeler of Fishing Creek, near Bloomsburg, Pa., c. 1720-Feb. 1787

87. Maria Holmes

88-97. ---

98. Levi Creecy (according to RBJ)

99. ---

100. James McCoy (according to RBJ)

101-107. ---

108. Louis Ogier, silk merchant, Moncoutant, Lower Poitou, France 16 July 1726-Ashley River, Charleston, S. C. 8 Oct. 1780, London 18 July 1751

109. Catherine Creuzé, London 12 Dec. 1732-Clapton, Hackney, London 17 July 1808

110. Rev. William (or John) Martin, d. ante 2 Oct. 1783

111. ---

112. John Huffman, prob. Germany c. 1738-Culpeper Co., Va. c. 1802, Hagerstown, Md. c. 1768

113. Catherine ---

114. Henry Lyter, bp. Maschwanden, Canton Zurich, Switzerland 13 Mar. 1740-near Lexington, Ky. 28 Oct. 1807, c. 1764
115. Catharine Beaver, prob. Bucks Co., Pa. 15 July 1743-prob. Bourbon Co., Ky. 13 Mar. 1823
116-121. ---
122. Thomas Jameson, York Co., Pa. 7 Nov. 1732-Jefferson Co., Indiana 6 Apr. 1830, Albemarle Co., Va. c. 1764
123. Hannah Taggart, Ireland 2 Apr. 1740-Jefferson Co. 10 Jan. 1830
124-125. ---
126. same as 122
127. same as 123
128. James Johnston of Currowaugh in Nansemond & Isle of Wight Cos., Va., c. 1622-Isle of Wight Co., Va. between 30 Jan. 1745/6 & 11 June 1747, c. 1692
129. Mary Johnson, Isle of Wight Co. c. 1674-post 1747
130-159. ---
160. (possibly) William Bunting, d. Chester Co., Pa. ante 1733
161-215. ---
216. Pierre Ogier, silk weaver, Sigournois, Lower Poitou, France c. 1680-London Dec. 1740, c. 1710
217. Catherine Rabaud, Moncoutant c. 1688-London c. 1744
218. Pierre Francois Creuzé, jeweller, St. Symphorien, Saintonge, France 30 July 1690-Clapton, Hackney, London 24 Jan. 1758, Spitalfields, London 25 Nov. 1722
219. Elizabeth Giboreau, London 11 Jan. 1704-London 30 Aug. 1766
220-223. ---
224. Hans Peter Huffman, prob. Germany c. 1705-Frederick Co., Md. c. 1748
225. Mary Appolonia (prob. Loy), prob. Germany c. 1709-post 1757, widow (prob.) of Tabell Troud & Frederick Unseld, m. (4) John A. Ochs
226-227. ---
228. Melchior Leutert, Ottenbach, Canton Zurich, Switzerland 22 Aug. 1706-near Middletown, Md. 24 June 1771, Maschwanden 23 Jan. 1737
229. Barbara Frick, Maschwanden 9 Oct. 1712-en route to Pa. 2 Sept. 1749
230. Peter Beaver, Jr., prob. Hirschland, Germany c. 1718-living Frederick Co., Md. 1782, prob. Bucks Co., Pa.
231. Elizabeth ---, living Frederick Co. 1782
232-243. ---
244. John Jameson, Galway, Ireland c. 1680-prob. York Co., Pa. c. 1736
245. Margaret White
246-251. ---
252. same as 244
253. same as 245
254-257. ---
258. Robert Johnson (c. 1643-1732/3), Isle of Wight Co., Va., = c. 1662
259. Katherine Allen (c. 1645-c. 1693)
260-431. ---
432. Pierre Ogier (Auger) (c. 1645-55-c. 1697), Chassay l'Eglise & Benêtre in Sigournois, France, = c. 1678
433. Jeanne Bernardin (c. 1658-c. 1738), Moncoutant, France (& England?)
434-435. ---
436. Francois Creuzé, b. c. 1650, of St. Symphorien, Saintonge, France, = c. 1682
437. Marie Laidain
438. Jean Giborceau, living 1704, flour dealer, Beauce, France to Stepney, London

439. Susanne le Bailly
440-449. ---
450. (probably) George Loy
451-455. ---
456. Rudolff (Ruodeli) Leutert (1670-1728), Ottenbach & Maschwanden, Switzerland, = 1693
457. Barbel (Barbara) Haberling (1675-1757)
458. Hans Jacob Frick of Maschwanden
459. Anna ---
460. Peter Beaver of Hirschland, Germany, living 1733
461-487. ---
488. James Jameson, b. c. 1650, Glasgow, Scotland to York Co., Pa. c. 1700
489-503. ---
504. same as 488
505-511. ---

* * *

37. RICHARD MILHOUS NIXON

1. RICHARD MILHOUS NIXON, b. Yorba Linda, California 9 Jan. 1913, Riverside, Calif. 21 June 1940 Thelma Catherine (Pat) Ryan, b. Ely, Nevada 16 Mar. 1912
2. Francis Anthony Nixon, Elk, Ohio 3 Dec. 1878-La Habra, Calif. 4 Sept. 1956, Whittier, Calif. 25 June 1908
3. Hannah Milhous, near Butlerville, Ind. 7 Mar. 1885-Whittier 30 Sept. 1967
4. Samuel Brady Nixon, Atlasburg, Pa. 9 Oct. 1847-Vinton Co., Ohio 28 April 1914, Hocking Co., Ohio 10 Apr. 1873
5. Sarah Ann Wadsworth, Hocking Co. 15 Oct. 1852-Vinton Co. 18 Jan. 1886
6. Franklin Milhous, near Colerain, Ohio 4 Nov. 1848-Whittier 2 Feb. 1919, Jennings Co., Ind. 16 Apr. 1879
7. Almira Park Burdg, Columbiana Co., Ohio 16 Sept. 1849-Whittier 23 July 1943
8. George Nixon III, Washington, Pa. c. 1821-Gettysburg, Pa. 14 July 1863, Washington Co., Pa. 10 Jan. 1843
9. Margaret Ann Trimmer, Smith, Pa. c. 1826-Vinton Co., Ohio 18 Mar. 1865
10. Thomas Wiley Wadsworth, Harford Co., Md. 10 Feb. 1826-Hocking Co., Ohio 11 Sept. 1879, Morgan Co., Ohio 30 May 1850
11. Mary Louise Moore, Morgan Co. 24 Dec. 1832-18 Nov. 1918, m. (2) George Amerine
12. Joshua Vickers Milhous, Colerain, Ohio 31 Dec. 1820-Bigger, Ind. 15 Apr. 1893, Washington Co., Pa. 23 Dec. 1847
13. Elizabeth Price Griffith, West Pike Run, Pa. 28 Apr. 1827-Whittier 3 May 1923
14. Oliver Burdg, Jefferson, Pa. 28 Sept. 1821-Whittier 11 June 1908, 29 Apr. 1846
15. Jane M. Hemingway, Mahoning Co., Ohio 30 Aug. 1824-Jennings Co., Ind. 5 Apr. 1890
16. George Nixon, Jr., Brandywine, Del. Dec. c. 1784-post 1860, Washington, Pa. c. 1806
17. Hannah Wilson, c. 1790-Washington, Pa. c. 1827
18. Anthony Trimmer, Fermanagh, Pa. c. 1781-Smith, Pa. 1841, Smith 21 Sept. 1824
19. Margaret Hunt, Smith c. 1804-Vinton Co., Ohio 1876, m. (2) Richard Howard
20. Robert Wadsworth, Baltimore or Harford Co., Md. 5 Nov. 1785-Washington, Ohio 18 Oct. 1867, Md.
21. Elizabeth Lytle, 27 Aug. 1794-Harford Co. 18 Apr. 1831
22. Joseph Dickinson Moore, Centre Co., Pa. 21 Oct. 1794-

Indianola, Iowa 1860, Perry Co., Ohio 23 June 1825

23. Jane Brown, Perry Co. 16 Mar. 1807-Indianola 26 Feb. 1886

24. William Milhous, Jr., Chester Co., Pa. 4 June 1783-Belmont Co., Ohio 15 Mar. 1874, 10 June 1807

25. Martha Vickers, 27 Mar. 1786-29 May 1873

26. Amos Griffith, Washington Co., Pa. c. 1798-Columbiana Co., Ohio 10 Sept. 1871, Md. 7 Dec. 1820

27. Edith Price, Gunpowder, Md. 9 May 1801-Short Creek, Ohio 11 Feb. 1873

28. Jacob Burdg, Jr., Shrewsbury, N. J. 28 Jan. 1783-near Butlerville, Ind. 1 Dec. 1862, Redstone, Pa. 9 Dec. 1807

29. Miriam Matthews, Baltimore Co., Md. 11 Aug. 1786-post 1860

30. James Hemingway, Jr., N. J. 23 July 1801-Mo. 28 Jan. 1893, Columbiana Co., Ohio 1823

31. Hope Malmsbury, Burlington Co., N. J. 7 Sept. 1804-near West Branch, Iowa 10 May 1865

32. George Nixon, Brandywine, Del. c. 1752-Colona, Ill. 5 Aug. 1842, Wilmington, Del. 17 Aug. 1775

33. Sarah Seeds

34. William Wilson, Del. c. 1764-Washington, Pa. 12 Nov. 1837, New Castle Co., Del. 4 Feb. 1790

35. Elenor Scothorn, c. 1764-22 Nov. 1819

36. Paul Trimmer, Morris Co., N. J. c. 1750-Robinson, Pa. c. 1834, Fermanagh, Pa. c. 1780

37. Jane McElwain of Lancaster Co., Pa.

38. William Hunt of Smith, Pa., fl. 1803-1817

39. Margaret Andover, b. Washington Co., Pa.

40. Thomas Wadsworth, Jr., Md. 19 Mar. 1747-prob. post 1830, Joppa, Md. 18 Aug. 1768

41. Mary Wiley

42. George Lytle, b. c. 1759, d. Baltimore Co., Md.

43. Elizabeth McComas

44. Joseph Moore, Salisbury, Pa. 15 Dec. 1759-Morgan Co., Ohio 18 Feb. 1832, Boos, Pa. 10 Jan. 1782

45. Mary Clemson, 3 Mar. 1763-17 Jan. 1817

46. Isaac Brown, Ireland 16 Apr. 1771-Perry Co., Ohio 1 Mar. 1853, 27 Oct. 1795

47. Mary Clayton, 18 Feb. 1777-Ohio 27 Jan. 1822

48. William Milhous, Chester Co., Pa. 12 June 1738-Belmont Co., Ohio 24 Jan. 1826, 22 Oct. 1767

49. Hannah Baldwin, 4 Nov. 1748-20 Oct. 1825

50. Thomas Vickers, Jr., Plumstead, Pa. 8 Mar. 1757-East Caln, Pa. 25 Dec. 1829, 30 June 1779

51. Jemima Mendenhall, 9 Dec. 1757-5 Dec. 1851

52. Jacob Griffith, Warrington, Pa. 27 Feb. 1757-Clover Hill, Pa. 2 Apr. 1841, 16 April 1778

53. Lydia Hussey, York Co., Pa. 27 Mar. 1757-Washington Co., Pa. 21 Sept. 1843

54. Daniel Price, 22 Oct. 1761-Gunpowder Forest, Md. 2 Aug. 1846, 17 Dec. 1783

55. Elizabeth Hussey, Pa. 3 Nov. 1759-26 Mar. 1847

56. Jacob Burdg, Shrewsbury, N. J. 5 4th Mo. 1743-ante 1797, 1768

57. Judith Smith, 9 May 1751-Upper Springfield, Ohio 5 Mar. 1836

58. William Matthews, Mar. 1755-Baltimore Co., Md., 20 Feb. 1844

59. Ann Griffith, 1 Feb. 1754-6 July 1792

60. James Hemingway, Framingham, Massachusetts 12 April 1760-now Mahoning Co., Ohio 15 July 1822

61. Elizabeth Armstrong, N. J. 17 Mar. 1757-Springfield, Ohio 15 Jan. 1837

62. Benjamin Malmsbury, Burlington Co., N. J. 6 Nov. 1779-Goshen, Ohio 3 June 1854, 1801

63. Jane Cattell, 22 Apr. 1780-29 Mar. 1853
64. James Nixon of Brandywine, Del., will probated 26 June 1775
65. Mary ---, d. post 1821
66. (possibly) John Seeds, Jr. (1725-1753) or Joseph Seeds (1722-1754) of Wilmington
67-69. ---
70. Nathan Scothorn, Jr., Upper Darby, Pa. c. 1730-Christiana Hundred, Del. c. 1764, 29 Oct. 1759
71. Hannah Twiggs
72. Anthony Trimmer, c. 1724-Roxbury, N. J. Nov. 1754, c. 1749
73. Elizabeth ---, 1723-1781, m. (2) Thomas Faircloe
74. Moses McElwain, d. Lancaster Co., Pa. 1760
75. Agnes Miller, living 1762
76-77. ---
78. Christopher Andover, Pa. 1755-present Brooke Co., W. Va. 1831, Chester Co., Pa. c. 1780
79. Margaret ---
80. Thomas Wadsworth, m. Baltimore Co., Md. Jan. 1741
81. Rebecca Passmore
82. (probably) Matthew Wiley, b. 16 Nov. 1730
83. ---
84. Guy Lytle, d. Baltimore Co., Md. 20 Mar. 1764, 25 Mar. 1751
85. Elizabeth Webster, b. 1 Nov. 1723
86. Alexander McComas, Jr., m. Baltimore Co., Md. 27 July 1747
87. Deborah Hartley
88. James Moore, Ballymoney, Antrim, Ireland-Sadsbury, Pa. 1777, Sadsbury 5 4th Mo. 1759
89. Elizabeth Dickinson, b. 13 July 1739
90. Thomas Clemson, Delaware Co., Pa. c. 1710-Salisbury, Pa. 30 10th Mo. 1785, 30 9th Mo. 1747
91. Elizabeth Strode
92. Alexander Brown, from Ireland c. 1773, d. Hampshire Co., Va. (now W. Va.) Sept. 1816
93. Mary Bradford
94. Thomas Clayton, Jr., possibly Monmouth Co., N. J. c. 1745-Clayton, Ohio, 1813, c. 1772
95. Mary (Walker?)
96. Thomas Milhous, Carrickfergus, Antrim, Ireland 14 3rd Mo. 1699-Pikeland, Pa. 1770, Timahoe, Kildare, Ireland 1 4th Mo. 1721
97. Sarah Miller, Maghera, Londonderry, Ireland 16 10th Mo. 1701-26 Aug. 1775
98. Joshua Baldwin, Chester, Pa. 13 11th Mo. 1721/2-East Caln, Pa. 13 5th Mo. 1800, 17 9th Mo. 1747
99. Mercy Brown, 12 1st Mo. 1722-22 1st Mo. 1784
100. Thomas Vickers, Plumstead, Pa. c. 1720-East Caln 30 12th Mo. 1793, 13 9th Mo. 1746
101. Rebecca Dillon
102. Joshua Mendenhall, 11 11th Mo. 1727/8-East Caln 5 Feb. 1816, 1755
103. Lydia Mendenhall
104. William Griffith, Jr., New Castle Co., Del. 1714-20 9th Mo. 1778
105. Esther Davis, c. 1722-18 4th Mo. 1762
106. Recond Hussey, d. Warrington, Pa. 5 Apr. 1784, 6 Sept. 1756
107. Miriam Harry, d. 19 Mar. 1809
108. Samuel Price, 28 2nd Mo. 1739-Gunpowder Forest, Md. 16 Apr. 1825, 25 10th Mo. 1760
109. Ann Moore, 16 2nd Mo. 1744-16 Sept. 1784
110. John Hussey (III), post 1713-Newberry, Pa. 1770, (2) c. 1750
111. Elizabeth ---
112. Joseph Burdg of Monmouth Co., N. J., living 1777, 1739 or ante
113. Sarah Morris

114. Anthony Smith, Cape May, N. J. 26 July 1723-Morgan, Pa. 1810, lic. Monmouth Co. 16 May 1746
115. Lydia Willets, b. 16 Jan. 1726
116. Oliver Matthews, 28 Nov. 1721-Gunpowder, Md. 17 Jan. 1824
117. Hannah Johns, c. 1728-15 Nov. 1791
118. Isaac Griffith, Richland, Pa. 5 1st Mo. 1720/1-Gunpowder, Md., m. 9th Mo. 1744
119. Ann Burson, b. 9 2nd Mo. 1721
120. Isaac Hemingway, Framingham, Mass. 17 July 1730-Framingham 31 Jan. 1778, Framingham 28 Nov. 1754
121. Elizabeth Haven, b. Framingham 2 Sept. 1736, m. (2) Israel Leadbetter
122. Ephraim Armstrong, d. Northampton, N. J. 1788, c. 1753
123. Elizabeth McCulley
124. John Malmsbury, Jr., Burlington Co., N. J. 7 June 1744-post 1797, c. 1771
125. Rebecca Doane, b. 5 Apr. 1754
126. James Cattell, Jr., Burlington Co., N. J. 16 5th Mo. 1743-Evesham, N. J. 1806, 27 July 1763
127. Hope Gaskill, b. 3 Aug. 1743
128-131. ---
132. (possibly) John Seeds of Wilmington, Del., d. ante 1738, c. 1722
133. (possibly) Britta Laican, c. 1700-7 May 1756, m. (2) Thomas Milner
134-139. ---
140. Nathan Scothorn, Darby, Pa. 10 Nov. 1705-Darby 10 Jan. 1731, c. 1730
141. Mary --- (possibly Lewis), d. Newport, Del. May 1778, m. (2) Thomas Phillips, (3) John Twiggs (142 below)
142. John Twiggs, d. Del. 1760, 16 Feb. 1721
143. Eleanor Thomasson, d. ante 1758
144. John Trimmer, d. Amwell, N. J. 1750, c. 1721
145. Mary ---
146-147. ---
148. Robert McElwain, d. West Salisbury, Pa. 1760
149. Isabel ---
150. James Miller
151-155. ---
156. Joseph Andover, m. Philadelphia 1 July 1751
157. Mary Reames
158-163. ---
164. Luke Wiley of Baltimore Co., Md., 1706-c. 1771
165. Kezia ---
166-167. ---
168. George Lytle, d. Baltimore Co., Md. 1757
169. ---
170. Michael Webster, d. Baltimore Co., Md. 1764
171. Elizabeth Giles
172. Alexander McComas, c. 1695-Baltimore Co., Md. Jan. 1761, 19 Nov. 1713
173. Elizabeth Day
174-175. ---
176. James Moore, d. Ballymoney, Antrim 1759, 7 5th Mo. 1714
177. Susanna Forster
178. Joseph Dickinson, Edenderry, Ireland 27 12th Mo. 1706/7-post 1780, 25 8th Mo. 1732, of Caln, Pa.
179. Elizabeth Miller, 7 5th Mo. 1713-post 1771
180. James Clemson, Birmingham, England c. 1660-Philadelphia 18 July 1718, c. 1698
181. Sarah ---
182. John Strode, d. West Marlborough, Pa. 1744
183. Magdalen James

184-187. ---
188. (probably) Thomas Clayton, c. 1710-c. 1757, of Monmouth Co., N. J.
189. (probably) Hannah ---
190-191. ---
192. John Milhous, Antrim, Ireland 6th Mo. 1669-Timahoe, Kildare 10 5th Mo. 1710, Ballinderry, Antrim 25 1st Mo. 1696
193. Sarah Mickle, b. Magheragall, Antrim 13 10th Mo. 1675
194. James Miller, Scorry, Antrim 24 4th Mo. 1669-Leacock, Pa. 1749, Waterstown, West Meath 13 12th Mo. 1700
195. Catharine Lightfoot of Hillsborough, d. Philadelphia 1729
196. John Baldwin (III), 10 4th Mo. 1697-Chester Co., Pa. 1728, 11 4th Mo. 1719
197. Hannah Johnson, m. (2) Joseph Cloud
198. Samuel Brown, 11 9th Mo. 1694-Falls, Pa. 3 10th Mo. 1769, 5 9th Mo. 1717
199. Ann Clark
200. Abraham Vickers, Shrewsbury, N. J. 11 9th Mo. 1691-Plumstead, Pa. 1756
201. Mary France
202. Nicholas Dillon, d. Bedminster, Pa. 1773
203. Mary ---
204. Benjamin Mendenhall, Jr., 5 3rd Mo. 1691-N. C. 13 5th Mo. 1743 (of Concord, Pa.), 9 3rd Mo. 1717
205. Lydia Roberts, b. Wales c. 1694, m. (2) William Hammans
206. Aaron Mendenhall, 20 9th Mo. 1690-East Caln, Pa. 30 4th Mo. 1765, 16 4th Mo. 1715
207. Rose Pierson, 1693-1771
208. William Griffith, b. Wales, of Warrington, Pa.
209-211. ---
212. same as 110 (John Hussey [III]), m. (1) 1733
213. Margaret Record
214. John Harry, d. Chester Co., Pa. 1763, 1732
215. Frances ---
216. Mordecai Price, Jr., b. c. 1698-Baltimore Co., Md. 28 Apr. 1724
217. Elizabeth White, b. 1708
218. Walter Price, d. Gunpowder Forest, Md. 1782
219. Ann ---, Pa. 10 Sept. 1710-Md. 11 Nov. 1783
220. John Hussey, Jr., Hampton, N. H. 18 Jan. 1676-Christiana Hundred, Del. 1733, 1703
221. Ann Inskeep
222-223. ---
224. Jonathan Burdg, Long Island, c. 1693-post 1762, of Freehold, N. Y.
225. (possibly) Sarah Ellison
226. Richard Morris, c. 1690-Middletown, N. J. 1763
227. ---
228. Thomas Smith, c. 1672-Cape May, N. J. 1732, c. 1717
229. Mary Allen, b. Sandwich, Mass. 15 Nov. 1681, m. (1) Daniel Wells, who d. 1715
230. Timothy Willets of Shrewsbury, N. J., 25 Dec. 1687/8-post 1755
231. Judith ---
232. Thomas Matthews, 29 Mar. 1693-Gunpowder, Md. 19 Dec. 1766, 28 July 1718
233. Sarah Thomas, widow
234-235. ---
236. Abraham Griffith, Wales 1680-Richland, Pa. 3 10th Mo. 1760, Abington, Pa. 1708
237. Hannah Lester, 1686-Md. post 1769
238. Joseph Burson, Abington, Pa. 25 12th Mo. 1689-post 1751 (when of Fairfax, Va.)

239. Rachel Potts
240. Joshua Hemingway (III), Framingham, Mass. 2 Apr. 1697-Framingham, Mass. 30 Jan. 1754, Framingham 1 July 1718
241. Abigail Morse, Watertown, Mass. 1 Jan. 1696-Framingham 25 May 1739
242. James Haven, b. Framingham 4 Mar. 1709/10
243. Sarah ---, d. Framingham 19 Dec. 1762
244-245. ---
246. John McCulley, d. Mt. Holly, N. J. 1773
247. ---
248. John Malmsbury of Bucks Co., Pa., c. 1710-living 1767 Mansfield, N. J., New Hanover, N. J. 18 Sept. 1736
249. Mary Bowker, d. ante 1746
250. John Doane, Bucks Co., Pa. 11 1st Mo. 1716/7-Haycock, Pa. ante 1788, 13 12th Mo. 1739
251. Hannah Wilson
252. James Cattell, 1716-Chester, N. J. 1783, 18 May 1738
253. Ann Rogers, widow
254. Jonathan Gaskill, c. 1705-Springfield, N. J. 1754, 4 5th Mo. 1732
255. Jane Shinn
256-265. ---
266. (possibly) Neils Laican (1666-1721), Sweden to Northern Liberties (Township, Philadelphia Co.), Pa.
267. (possibly) Mary ---
268-279. ---
280. Robert Scothorn (1659-1708), Oxton, Nottinghamshire to Darby, Pa., = 1692
281. Mary Gibbons, d. 1730, m. (2) Roger Ball
282. (possibly) Thomas Lewis
283. (possibly) Jane Thomas
284-285. ---
286. Paul Thomasson, d. 1707, New Castle Co., Delaware
287. Felicia ---
288-339. ---
340. John Webster (1662-1753), Kent Island & Baltimore Co., Md.
341. Hannah Butterworth, d. ante 1735
342. Nathaniel Giles
343. ---
344. Daniel McComas, d. 1697, Scotland to Baltimore (now Harford) Co., Md., = c. 1687
345. (Elizabeth ---?)
346. Nicholas Day, d. 1705, Baltimore Co., Md.
347. Sarah ---
348-351. ---
352. (probably) James Moore of Ballymoney, Antrim, Ireland
353-355. ---
356. Daniel Dickinson, b. 1674, Sample, Cumberland, England-Edenderry, Ireland 1709, 1698
357. Elizabeth Scott of Balleyhorn at Mountmellick, Queens Co., Ireland
358. Gayen Miller, d. 1742, Ireland to Chester Co., Pa., = c. 1695
359. Margaret ---
360-363. ---
364. George Strode, Milbrook, Hampshire to Concord, Pa. ante 1682
365. Margaret ---
366. Morgan James, d. 1737, Chester Co., Pa., = 1694
367. Elizabeth Prothero
368-375. ---
376. (probably) Zebulon Clayton (1663-1744), Monmouth Co., N. J., = c. 1697

377. (probably) Mary Hartshorne, b. 1676
378-383. ---
384. Thomas Milhous, living 1669 Co. Antrim
385. Elizabeth ---, d. 1708, Timahoe, Kildare
386. Robert Mickle, Quaker, living 1696, Brookville, Magheragall & Magheralin, Cos. Antrim & Down
387. Mary ---
388. Robert Miller of Scorry, Antrim
389. Elizabeth ---
390. Thomas Lightfoot (c. 1640-1725), Cambridgeshire (?) to Darby, Pa.
391. Mary ---, d. prob. ante 1695
392. John Baldwin, Jr., d. 1731, Aston, Pa., = 1689
393. Catharine Carter (of Pleebdolglen?), widow of Edward Turner
394. Joshua Johnson, d. 1747, Philadelphia, Pa.
395. Mary ---, d. 1757
396. George Brown (1644-1726), Leicestershire to New Castle, Del. & Falls, Pa.
397. Mercy ---
398. John Clark, d. 7 6th Mo. 1724
399. Martha Wheeler
400. Thomas Vickers, d. 1695/6, Shrewsbury, N. J.
401. Esther ---, d. 1693
402-407. ---
408. Benjamin Mendenhall (1662-1740), Concord, Pa., brother of 412, = 1689
409. Ann Pennell, 1667-5th Mo. 1709
410. Owen Roberts, living 1716, Gwynedd, Pa.
411. Mary ---, widow of --- Lewis, Dolgelly, Merionethshire, Wales
412. John Mendenhall (1659-1758), Delaware Co., Pa., brother of 408, = 1685
413. Elizabeth Maris (1665-ante 1708)
414. Thomas Pierson, d. 1722, Bristol, England to New Castle Co., Del. & Caln, Pa., = 1690
415. Rose Dixson
416-423. ---
424. same as 220
425. same as 221
426-427. ---
428. Hugh Harry (Harris), d. 1708, Machynlleth, Montgomeryshire, Wales to Birmingham, Pa., = 1686
429. Elizabeth Brinton (1685-post 1708), Worcestershire, England
430-431. ---
432. Mordecai Price (c. 1660-1715), Anne Arundel Co., Md.
433. Mary Parsons, d. 1718
434. Guy White, Jr., d. 1712, Prince Georges Co., Md.
435. Elizabeth Griffith, d. 1752, Calvert Co., Md.
436-439. ---
440. John Hussey (1636-1707), Hampton, New Hampshire to New Castle Co., Del., = 1659
441. Rebecca Perkins
442. John Inskeep, b. c. 1650, Fulford, Staffordshire, England
443-447. ---
448. David Burdg (c. 1660-ante 1724), Hempstead, L. I. to Middletown, N. J., = c. 1684
449. ---
450. Richard Ellison, Jr. (1660-1719), Braintree, Mass. to Freehold, N. J.
451. Else ---
452. Lewis Morris (c. 1655-1694/5), Middletown, N. J.
453. Elizabeth Almy (1663-post 1711/2), Portsmouth, Rhode Island

to Monmouth Co., N. J., m. (2) John Leonard

454-455. ---

456. Abraham Smith, Jr., b. c. 1647, Hempstead, L. I. to Cape May, N. J.

457. Margery ---

458. Jedediah Allen (1646/7-1711/2), Sandwich, Mass. to Shrewsbury, N. J., = c. 1668

459. Elizabeth Howland, living 1711/2, Duxbury, Mass.

460. Hope Willets (1652-1703), Hempstead, L. I.

461. Mercy Langdon

462-463. ---

464. Oliver Matthews, England to New Castle Co., Del.

465. Elizabeth ---

466-471. ---

472. Howell Griffith, d. 1710, Wales to Philadelphia

473. ---

474. Peter Lester, d. c. 1742, Leicestershire to Richland, Pa., = 1685

475. Mary Duncalf

476. George Burson, d. 1715, Scarborough, England & Montgomery Co., Pa., = c. 1687

477. Hannah (possibly Gould, b. 1664)

478. Jonas Potts, fl. 1686-1754, Philadelphia

479. Mary ---

480. Joshua Hemingway, Jr. (1668-post 1754), Roxbury & Framingham, Mass., = c. 1694-6

481. Rebecca Stanhope, b. 1670, Sudbury, Mass.

482. Joseph Morse (1671-1709), Watertown, Mass., = 1691

483. Elizabeth Sawtelle, b. 1671, Watertown & Framingham, m. (2) Benjamin Nourse

484. Nathaniel Haven (1664-1746), Lynn & Framingham, Mass., = c. 1689

485. Elizabeth Travers, b. 1667/8, Gloucester & Brookfield, Mass.

486-497. ---

498. William Bowker of New Hanover, N. J., d. post 1725

499. Hannah Slade, 1679-ante 1710

500. Eleazer Doane (1691/2-1757), Eastham, Mass. to Wrightstown, Pa., = c. 1715

501. Susanna ---, d. ante 1731

502-503. ---

504. Jonas Cattell (c. 1690-1731), Deptford, N. J., = 1714

505. Mary Pearce, d. ante 1727

506-507. ---

508. Josiah Gaskill (1678-1761), Salem, Mass. to Northampton, N. J., = 1704

509. Rebecca Lippincott (1684-ante 1748)

510. John Shinn, Jr., d. 1736, England to Springfield, N. J., = 1707

511. Mary ---

* * *

38. GERALD RUDOLPH FORD, JR.

1. GERALD RUDOLPH FORD, JR., whose name was changed from LESLIE LYNCH KING, JR., b. Omaha, Nebraska 14 July 1913, m. Grand Rapids, Michigan 15 Oct. 1948 Mrs. Elizabeth Ann Bloomer Warren, b. Chicago, Illinois 8 Apr. 1918, divorced wife of William G. Warren

2. Leslie Lynch King, Chadron, Nebr. 25 July 1881 (or perhaps 1886)-Tucson, Arizona 1941, (1) Harvard, Ill. 7 Sept. 1912 (he m. [2] Margaret Atwood, later Mrs. Roy Mather)

3. Dorothy Ayer Gardner, Harvard, Ill. July 1892-Grand Rapids,

Mich. 17 Sept. 1967, m. (2) Gerald Rudolf (not Rudolph) Ford

4. Charles Henry King, Pennsylvania 12 Mar. 1853-Los Angeles, California 27 Feb. 1930

5. Martha Alice Porter, Indiana 17 Nov. 1853-Glendale, Calif. 14 July 1930

6. Levi Addison Gardner, Ill. 24 Apr. 1861-Grand Rapids, Mich. 8 May 1916, Harvard, Ill. 3 Oct. 1884

7. Adele Augusta Ayer, b. Youngstown, Ohio Dec. 1867

8. Lynch King of Pa.

9. Rebecca Shepherd of Virginia (West Virginia?)

10-11. ---

12. Alexander Gardner, Jr., Scotland 1812-Woodstock, Ill. 6 June 1875, 1834 (or 1837?)

13. Sally Miller, N. Y. 18 Apr. 1819-Woodstock, Ill. 30 Jan. 1873

14. George Manney Ayer, b. Wisconsin Mar. 1840, c. 1864/5

15. Amy Gridley Butler, b. New York 1848

16-23. ---

24. Alexander Gardner, b. Scotland 28 Feb. 1782, to Dundee, Quebec, m. 27 Feb. 1805

25. Mary Brodie, b. 1782

26-27. ---

28. John Varnum Ayer, Haverhill, Massachusetts 3 Jan. 1812-Chicago, Ill. c. 1877

29. Elida Vanderburgh Manney, Poughkeepsie, N. Y. 1 Jan. 1802 (or a later child of the same name?)-Chicago, Ill. c. 1877

30. George Selden Butler, 1820-1907, of Chicago, m. 1843

31. Elizabeth Ely Gridley, Clinton, N. Y. c. 1819-living 1912

32-47. ---

48. John Gardner, m. Kilmalcolm, Renfrewshire, Scotland 20 Jan. 1781

49. Janet Hartridge

50. Robert Brodie, c. 1735-22 Feb. 1836, of Kilburne, Ayrshire, Scotland

51. Margaret Burns, c. 1744-c. 1789

52-55. ---

56. Samuel Ayer, Plaistow, New Hampshire 13 Dec. 1777-Kenosha, Wisc. 12 Dec. 1847, Haverhill, Mass. 28 Nov. 1805

57. Polly Chase, Haverhill 15 Aug. 1784-Kenosha, Wisc. Aug. 1854

58. John Manney, Poughkeepsie, N. Y. 27 Dec. 1763-Ghent, N. Y. 25 June 1839, Poughkeepsie 1 Sept. 1796

59. Elizabeth Collins of Beekman, N. Y. 8 Jan. 1774-27 Oct. 1851

60. Daniel Butler of Montpelier, Vermont & Rockport, N. Y.

61. Betsey Comstock, Lyme, Connecticut 13 July 1795-prob. Rockport, N. Y. 10 Apr. 1857

62. Theodore Gridley, Farmington, Conn. c. 1757-Clinton, N. Y. c. 1826, Clinton c. 1818

63. Amy Ely, prob. Lyme, Conn. c. 1777-c. 1876

64-97. ---

98. Alexander Hartridge

99. Margaret Scott

100. William Brodie of Lockwinnow, Renfrewshire, m. c. 1720

101. Janet Orr

102. John Burns

103-111. ---

112. Daniel Ayer, Haverhill, Mass. 28 Jan. 1743-Plaistow, N. H. 6 June 1805, Rowley, Mass. 12 Oct. 1769

113. Sarah Adams, b. Rowley 3 Sept. 1743

114. William Chase, Haverhill 12 Apr. 1756-Haverhill 8 or 9 Dec. 1838, Kensington, N. H. 1 Oct. 1783

115. Abigail Gove, Hampton Falls, N. H. 23 Sept. 1761-Haverhill 29 Nov. 1844

116. Wines Manney, Poughkeepsie, N. Y. 22 Mar. 1730-Poughkeepsie 26 Nov. 1811, Poughkeepsie 16 Sept. 1758

117. Aeltje (Alida) Vanderburgh, prob. Poughkeepsie 7 Dec. 1741-Poughkeepsie 18 Feb. 1817

118. Hezekiah Collins, Jr., Westerly, Rhode Island 1 Dec. 1739-prob. N. Y. c. 1828, prob. Dartmouth, Mass. 19 Dec. 1765

119. Rhoda Ricketson, Dartmouth, Mass. 8 Aug. 1748-prob. N. Y. c. 1828

120-121. ---

122. Anselm Comstock, Lyme, Conn. 25 Aug. 1762-Sweden, N. Y. 28 July 1845, 13 Jan. 1790

123. Elizabeth Jewett, East Haddam, Conn. 28 Feb. 1771-Sweden, N. Y. 8 Mar. 1860

124. Jonathan Gridley, Jr., b. Farmington, Conn. 12 Dec. 1726, m. Farmington 18 Oct. 1750

125. Martha Adams

126. Wells Ely, Lyme, Conn. c. 1729-Lyme ante 1 Sept. 1804, c. 1754

127. Rebecca Selden, b. c. 1730-35

128-201. ---

202. William Orr

203-223. ---

224. William Ayer, Haverhill, Mass. 18 June 1716-living 1765, Haverhill 28 July 1741

225. Sarah Little, Haverhill 11 Nov. 1717-prob. Plaistow, N. H. 11 Dec. 1807

226. William Adams, Newbury, Mass. 8 May 1706-Rowley (now Georgetown) winter 1765-66, Newbury 22 Apr. 1728

227. Elizabeth Noyes, Newbury 16 Jan. 1708-prob. Rowley 1787

228. Ezra Chase, Newbury 9 July 1717-Haverhill 3 Mar. 1793, Haverhill 2 Dec. 1740

229. Judith Davis, Haverhill 12 Mar. 1721/2-Haverhill 28 Feb. 1808

230. Nathaniel Gove, Hampton, N. H. 24 June 1721-Kensington, N. H. 15 April 1793, Newbury, Mass. 14 Sept. 1743

231. Susanna Stickney, Newbury 10 Apr. 1724-Kensington, N. H. post 1769

232. John Many or Manney, bp. New York City 31 Aug. 1698, m. Southold, L. I., N. Y., 23 Jan. 1729

233. Ann Wines

234. Henry Vanderburgh, Jr., bp. Poughkeepsie 3 Apr. 1717-prob. Poughkeepsie week ante 5 Apr. 1792, United Empire Loyalist, lived in New Brunswick 1783-87, m. c. 1739

235. Sarah Van Kleeck, bp. Poughkeepsie 21 Nov. 1722

236. Hezekiah Collins, Westerly, R. I. 18 Aug. 1707-Hopkinton, R. I. 10 10th Mo. 1775, Westerly 6 Nov. 1735

237. Catherine Gifford, prob. R. I. 15 June 1718-Hopkinton, R. I. 13 5th Mo. 1801, m. (2) Benjamin Hoxie

238. Jonathan Ricketson, Jr., prob. Dartmouth, Mass. 3rd Mo. 1725/6-prob. Great Nine Partners, N. Y. 21 2nd Mo. 1772, Dartmouth 12 Oct. 1747

239. Meribah Wilbur, Dartmouth 22 Aug. 1729-Beekman, N. Y. 6 Nov. 1825

240-243. ---

244. Abner Comstock, Lyme, Conn. c. 1727-Lyme 27 Mar. 1811, Lyme 12 Dec. 1751

245. Eunice Goodspeed, Barnstable, Mass. 6 Apr. 1731-Lyme 3 Dec. 1809

246. David Jewett, North Lyme, Conn. 27 Oct. 1736-East Haddam, Conn. c. 1780, East Haddam 3 Nov. 1757

247. Sarah Selden, Lyme 15 Nov. 1735-East Haddam 16 May 1811

248. Jonathan Gridley, Farmington, Conn. Oct. 1690-prob. Farm-

ington 16 Nov. 1778, Farmington 17 Nov. 1714

249. Mary Pinney, prob. b. Windsor, Conn. 4 Mar. 1690

250-251. ---

252. Daniel Ely, Lyme, Conn. c. 1693-Lyme 14 Mar. 1776, East Hartford 5 Jan. 1725/6

253. Ruth Wells, Hartford, Conn. 29 Jan. 1697-Lyme 2 Apr. 1731

254. Samuel Selden, Hadley, Mass. 17 May 1695-Lyme, Conn. 28 Feb. 1745, c. 1721

255. Deborah Dudley, Saybrook, Conn. 15 Nov. 1701-Lyme 8 Mar. 1800, m. (2) Noadiah Brainerd

256-447. ---

448. James Ayer (1686-1771), Haverhill, Mass., = 1711

449. Mary White (1690-1777)

450. Daniel Little (1692-1777), Haverhill, Mass. & Hampstead, N. H., = 1712

451. Abiah Clement (1692-1766)

452. Abraham Adams, Jr. (1676-1763), Newbury, Mass., = 1703

453. Anne Longfollow (1683-1758)

454. John Noyes, Jr. (1677/8-1719), Newbury, Mass., = 1703/4

455. Mary Thurlo (1682-1747)

456. Jacob Chase (c. 1690-95-1754), Newbury & Haverhill, Mass., = 1716

457. Joanna Davis (1697-post 1754)

458. William Davis (1675-1753), Haverhill, Mass., = 1700

459. Mary Kelly (1678-1747), Newbury, Mass.

460. Edward Gove (1696-1765), Hampton & Hampton Falls, N. H., = 1718/9

461. Bethiah Clark (1697-1727)

462. Moses Stickney (1677-1756), Newbury & Hampton, N. H., = 1707

463. Sarah Wardwell

464. Jean Magny, d. c. 1703, Huguenot, Meschers, Saintonge, France to R. I. & New York City

465. Jeanne Machet, d. c. 1705-08

466. (prob.) Samuel Wines (c. 1683-1739), Southold, L. I.

467. (prob.) Abigail ---, d. post 1739

468. Henry Vanderburgh (c. 1685-c. 1750), NYC to Poughkeepsie, = c. 1710

469. Magdalena Knight of Brooklyn

470. Johannes van Kleeck (c. 1680-1754), Poughkeepsie, = ante 1709

471. Aeltje Terbosch or Ter Boss, bp. 1692, Kingston

472. John Collins, Jr. (1679-1755), Lynn, Mass. to Charlestown, R. I., = 1703/4

473. Susanna Daggett (1685-1753), Saco, Maine

474. Jabez Gifford (1686/7-1761), Falmouth, Mass. to Charlestown, R. I. & Dutchess Co., N. Y., = 1716

475. Dinah Sheldon (1697-post 1761), Kingstown, R. I.

476. Jonathan Ricketson (1688-1768), Dartmouth, Mass., = 1710

477. Abigail Howland (1686-1769)

478. Benjamin Wilbur (Wildbore) (1670-1729), Portsmouth, R. I. & Dartmouth, Mass., = 1710

479. Elizabeth Head (1682-1734), Little Compton, R. I.

480-487. ---

488. John Comstock, Jr. (1676-1747/8), Lyme, Conn., = 1712

489. Mary Colt

490. Samuel Goodspeed, b. 1701, Barnstable, Mass., = ante 1725

491. Rebecca ---, d. post 1739

492. Nathan Jewett (1710-1762), Rowley, Mass. & Lyme, Conn., = 1729

493. Deborah Lord (c. 1698-1777), Lyme, Conn.

494. same as 254

495. same as 255

496. Thomas Gridley, Jr. (c. 1650-1742), Hartford & Farmington,

Conn., = 1679

497. Elizabeth Clark, d. 1696, Farmington, Conn.
498. Isaac Pinney (1663-1709), Windsor, Conn., = 1685
499. Sarah Clark (1663-post 1722)
500-503. ---
504. William Ely (1647-1717), Plymouth, England to Lyme, Conn., = 1681
505. Elizabeth Smith (c. 1662-1750), Hartford & Haddam, Conn.
506. Samuel Welles (1662-1733), Hartford, Conn.
507. Ruth Judson (1664-1744), Stratford, Conn.
508. Joseph Selden (1651-1724), Hartford & Lyme, Conn., = 1676/7
509. Rebecca Church (c. 1654-1726), Hadley, Mass.
510. Joseph Dudley (1674-c. 1743), Saybrook, Conn., = 1697
511. Sarah Pratt, b. 1680

* * *

39. JAMES EARL CARTER, JR.

1. JAMES EARL CARTER, JR., b. Plains, Georgia 1 Oct. 1924, m. Plains 7 July 1946 (Eleanor) Rosalynn Smith, b. Plains 18 Aug. 1927
2. James Earl Carter, Calhoun Co., Ga. 12 Sept. 1894-Plains 22 July 1953, Sumter Co., Ga. 27 Sept. 1923
3. Bessie Lillian Gordy, Richland, Ga. 15 Aug. 1898-Americus, Ga. 30 Oct. 1983
4. William Archibald Carter, Sumter Co., Ga. 12 Nov. 1858-Arlington, Ga. 4 Sept. 1903, Abbeville Co., South Carolina 8 Sept. 1885
5. Nina Pratt, Abbeville Co. 5 Dec. 1863-Plains 8 March 1939
6. James Jackson Gordy, Chattahoochee Co., Ga. 25 Oct. 1853-Americus 16 Jan. 1948, Chattahoochee Co. 6 Sept. 1888
7. Mary Ida Nicholson, Chattahoochee Co. 10 Feb. 1871-Chattanooga, Tennessee 16 May 1951
8. Littleberry Walker Carter, c. 1832-Sumter Co., Ga. 27 or 28 Nov. 1873, Warren Co. 5 Jan. 1851
9. Mary Ann Diligent Seals, c. 1838-Sumter Co. 27 or 28 Nov. 1873 (same night as her husband)
10. James E. Pratt, Abbeville Co., S. C. 11 Dec. 1830-Abbeville Co. 31 Aug. 1911, Abbeville Co. c. 1854
11. Sophronia C. Cowan, Abbeville Co. 5 Oct. 1835-Abbeville Co. 11 Nov. 1865
12. James Thomas Gordy, Baldwin Co., Ga. 13 Nov. 1828-Chattahoochee Co. 10 Oct. 1889, Chattahoochee Co. 26 Oct. 1854
13. Harriet Emily Helms, 28 July 1836-Chattahoochee Co. 14 Feb. 1884
14. Nathaniel Nunn Nicholson, prob. Wilkinson Co., Ga. c. 1812-Chattahoochee Co. 2 July 1891, Chattahoochee Co. 5 May 1870
15. Mary Elizabeth Dawson, 10 Sept. 1836-9 Dec. 1909, widow of Dr. Daniel L. John(s)
16. Wiley Carter, c. 1798-Schley Co., Ga. 4 Mar. 1864, Warren Co. 18 Feb. 1821
17. Ann Ansley, Warren Co., Ga. c. 1801-Warren Co. c. 1848
18. William Archibald Seals, Warren Co. c. 1814-Glascock Co., Ga. c. 1860, Warren Co. 9 Feb. 1834
19. Eliza Harris, Warren Co. c. 1815-Glascock Co. c. 1886
20. John Pratt, Abbeville Co. 12 Jan. 1808-Abbeville Co. 18 Nov. 1888, Abbeville Co. c. 1829-30
21. Mary Kay, Abbeville Co. 30 Nov. 1809-Abbeville Co. 12 Jan. 1892
22. John Cowan, Abbeville Co. 16 Mar. 1805-Abbeville Co. 27 Dec. 1874, Abbeville Co. c. 1830
23. Sarah B. Clinkscales, Abbeville Co. 9 Nov. 1811-Abbeville Co. 6 Mar. 1852

24. Wilson Gordy, Hancock Co., Ga. 30 Jan. 1801-Chattahoochee Co. 21 June 1890, Baldwin Co. 20 Nov. 1825

25. Mary Scott, Sussex Co., Delaware 10 Mar. 1809-Chattahoochee Co., Ga. 1 Apr. 1881

26. Pamly Uriah Helms, prob. Mecklenburg Co., North Carolina c. 1791-Sumter Co., Ga. c. 1848

27. Elizabeth Fisher, Mecklenburg Co. c. 1792-living 1860 in Chattahoochee Co.

28. John Nicholson, prob. N. C. c. 1790-prob. Muscogee Co., Ga. c. 1843-47

29. Frances Nunn, prob. Chester Co., S. C. c. 1782-90-Muscogee Co. c. 1846-47

30. Malekiah Dawson, Ga. c. 1808-living 1875, Jones Co., Ga. c. 1830

31. Mary Marcus Brown, prob. Jones Co., Ga. c. 1812-living 1859

32. James Carter, c. 1773-Schley Co. 19 July 1858, Columbia Co., Ga. 31 Jan. 1798

33. Eleanor "Nellie" Duckworth, b. prob. Wilkes or Richmond Co., Ga. c. 1780, living 1820

34. Abel Ansley, Monmouth Co., New Jersey c. 1761-62-Warren Co., Ga. between 7 Mar. & May 1822, Richmond Co., Ga. 30 Jan. 1790

35. Lydia Morris, Monmouth Co. c. 1770-75-Warren Co. Fall 1838

36. Spencer Seals, prob. Virginia c. 1780-Talladega Co., Alabama c. 1847, Warren Co., Ga. 25 Nov. 1805

37. Elizabeth Burnley, Charlotte Co., Va. c. 1786-prob. Warren Co. ante 1831

38. Nathan Harris, d. Feb. 1822, m. Warren Co. 1 June 1805

39. Rhoda Champion, d. 1850

40. James Pratt, prob. Abbeville Co. 11 Mar. 1788-Abbeville Co. 14 Sept. 1828, Abbeville Co. c. 1807

41. Sara Lindsay, prob. Abbeville Co. 14 Sept. 1790-Abbeville Co. 25 April 1840

42. Rev. James Kay, prob. Prince William Co., Va. 13 or 30 June 1787-Abbeville Co. 25 or 27 May 1857, Abbeville Co. c. 1807

43. Elizabeth Ann Clinkscales, prob. Charles Co., Maryland 4 June or Aug. 1788-Abbeville Co. 15 July or 5 Aug. 1850 (not 1830)

44. Isaac Cowan, Abbeville Co. c. 1765-Abbeville Co. 25 Dec. 1831, Abbeville Co.

45. Jane Seawright, Abbeville Co. 31 Jan. 1771-Abbeville Co. 11 Mar. 1859

46. Francis Bucher Clinkscales, prob. Charles Co., Md. 3 Oct. 1786-Abbeville Co. 19 Sept. 1858

47. Eleanor "Ally" Brownlee, Abbeville Co. c. 1791-Abbeville Co. 28 Aug. 1831

48. Peter Gordy, III, prob. Worcester Co., Md.-Muscogee Co., Ga. c. 1844, ante 1801

49. Ruth Wilson, d. post 1844, widow of --- Burras

50. John R. Scott, Sussex Co., Del. 8 Feb. 1776-Chattahoochee Co., Ga. 2 Feb. 1860, prob. Sussex Co. 21 Nov. 1802

51. Rebecca Radney, 15 Oct. 1773-Chattahoochee Co. 3 Mar. 1851

52. George Helms, Jr., prob. Anson or Mecklenburg Co., N. C. c. 1758-Mecklenburg Co. between 1837 & Mar. 1838

53. Sarah Pressley, d. prob. ante 1837

54. William Fisher, prob. Mecklenburg Co. c. 1760-Wilcox Co., Ala. between 12 June & 20 July 1835, prob. Mecklenburg Co. by 1780

55. Nancy Phillips, d. ante 23 Mar. 1849

56-57. ---

58. John Nunn, prob. Orange Co., N. C. c. 1745-46-Wilkinson Co., Ga. c. 1836, prob. Orange Co. c. 1765-70

59. Eliza Pratt

60. Jonathan Dawson, Jr., b. Wilmington, N. C. c. 1750, living 1824 in Upson Co., Ga.

61. Repsy Nicholson of Edgefield Co., S. C.

62. Hollinger Brown, Ga. 31 Dec. 1785-Stewart Co., Ga. 22 Dec. 1859, Baldwin Co., Ga. 29 Dec. 1808

63. Sarah Cassandra (Sally) Marcus, Edgefield Co., S. C. 16 May 1789-Stewart Co. 26 Aug. 1851

64. Kindred Carter, prob. N. C. c. 1750-Columbia (now McDuffie) Co., Ga. c. 1800

65. ---

66. Jeremiah Duckworth, Orange Co., N. C. to Warren & Columbia Cos., Ga.

67. Christiana Ramsey of Columbia Co.

68. Thomas Ansley, bp. Monmouth Co., N. J. 20 Mar. (or May) 1737-Warren Co., Ga. 14 Jan. 1809, lic. Monmouth Co. 1 Nov. 1760

69. Rebecca Cox or Cocke, prob. Upper Freehold, N. J. c. 1733-Warren Co. 9 May 1814

70. Job Morris, Monmouth Co., N. J. c. 1740-Shrewsbury, N. J. between 28 June & 25 Aug. 1786, lic. Monmouth Co. 17 May 1760

71. Mary Ansley, Monmouth Co. c. 1745-Warren Co., Ga. c. 1815-17

72. William Seals, Va.-Hancock Co., Ga. c. 1827

73. Judith (Powell?)

74. Henry Burnley, prob. Hanover Co., Va. c. 1756-Columbia Co., Ga. between 13 July 1831 & 5 Mar. 1835, Charlotte Co., Va. 13 July 1782

75. Lucy Barksdale, Va. c. 1756-Warren Co., Ga. c. 1803, widow of John Smith Davenport

76-77. ---

78. (probably) John Champion of Wilkes & Warren Cos., Ga.

79. ---

80. William Pratt, c. 1734-administration in Abbeville Co., S. C. 28 March 1797, prob. Abbeville Co. 28 Jan. 1783

81. (probably) Mary Drennan, d. post 1797

82. Robert Lindsay of Abbeville Co.

83. ---

84. James Kay, c. 1760-prob. Abbeville Co. post 1820

85. Grace Elgin, c. 1758-prob. Abbeville Co. post 1820

86. Francis Clinkscales, Charles Co., Md. c. 1748-Anderson Co., S. C. Oct. 1837, Charles Co. c. early 1786

87. Mary Carpenter, d. prob. ante 11 Nov. 1831

88. Andrew Cowan, c. 1742-Abbeville Co. between 6 Nov. 1786 & 1 May 1789, c. 1763

89. Ann ---, c. 1745-Abbeville Co. c. 1831

90. James Seawright, c. 1745-Abbeville Co. between 29 Oct. 1789 & 6 Apr. 1790

91. Elizabeth McCullough, d. ante 29 Oct. 1789

92. same as 86

93. same as 87

94. George Brownlee, County Antrim, Ireland c. 1757-Abbeville Co. 17 Feb. 1836, prob. Abbeville Co. ante 1787

95. Sarah Caldwell, c. Jan. 1758-Abbeville Co. 13 Apr. 1826

96. Peter Gordy, Jr., d. Worcester Co., Md. shortly ante 25 July 1788

97. Ellinor ---, d. by 1797

98. Samuel Wilson, d. Ga. between 11 Oct. 1799 & 15 Jan. 1803

99. ---

100. Perry Scott, b. Sussex Co., Del. Dec. 1755, m. c. 1775

101. Barbara ---

102-103. ---

104. George Helms, c. 1720-25 (prob. Bethlehem, Bucks Co., Pa., to Anson Co., N. C. c. 1748-49)-Anson or Mecklenburg Co., N. C. post 1800, Anson Co. c. 1755

105. Mary Margaret Falkenborough, b. c. 1735

106. Thomas Pressley, d. 1808

107. Sarah ---

108. Charles Fisher, will dated Mecklenburg Co., N. C. 1 June 1814
109. Barbara ---
110. William Phillips, c. 1730-will dated Mecklenburg Co. 8 Oct. 1815
111. Lussy ---
112-115. ---
116. William Nunn, c. 1713 (later of Craven & Orange Cos., N. C., & Chester Co., S. C.)-prob. Ga. post Jan. 1787, prob. Craven Co. c. 1743
117. Elizabeth Loftin
118-119. ---
120. Jonathan Dawson of Wilmington, N. C., d. c. 1750
121. Frances Rouse, m. (2) --- Williams of S. C.
122. Wright Nicholson, c. 1740-Edgefield Co., S. C. between 14 Jan. & 23 Oct. 1807
123. --- (a 2nd wife, probably not the mother of 61, was Mary Douglass, who d. Edgefield Co. between 6 Oct. 1821 & 30 Aug. 1825)
124. John Brown, prob. Va. c. 1760-Baldwin Co., Ga. c. 1814, Charlotte Co., Va. 1 Feb. 1779
125. Mildred "Milly" Gaines, b. Goochland Co., Va. 1 Jan. 1761
126. Daniel Marcus, N. C. c. 1763-Baldwin Co. c. 1818
127. Mary ---, living Jones Co., Ga. 1832
128. Isaac Carter of Bertie Co., N. C., d. post 1790, m. c. 1742
129. Sarah Browne, widow of John Battle of Bertie Co.
130-133. ---
134. John Ramsey, d. 1805, Orange Co., N. C. to Little Kiokee Creek, Columbia Co., Ga.
135. ---
136. William Ansley, d. Freehold, N. J. shortly ante 27 Mar. 1773, m. c. 1735-36
137. Rebecca ---, d. prob. Freehold 1750s
138. Thomas Cox (III), Monmouth Co., N. J. (prob. Middletown) 23 June 1700-Cream Ridge, N. J. 5 June 1783
139. Rebecca Potts, Burlington Co., N. J. c. 1702-prob. Monmouth Co. ante 1754
140. Richard Morris, Monmouth Co. c. 1690-Middletown, N. J. between 10 May 1762 & 3 May 1763
141. ---
142. same as 136
143. same as 137
144-147. ---
148. Israel Burnley, c. New Kent or Hanover Co., Va. c. 1715-25-Wilkes Co., Ga. between 14 Nov. 1787 & 25 Jan. 1791, Hanover Co. c. 1748-50
149. Hannah Terrell, Va. c. 1724-25-Wilkes Co. c. 1792
150. Collier Barksdale, Va. c. 1715-20-Charlotte Co., Va. between 1 July 1766 & 3 Oct. 1774, c. 1739
151. Sarah ---, d. post 1 July 1766
152-155. ---
156. (possibly) Henry Champion of Wilkes & Warren Cos.
157-167. ---
168. Robert Kay, d. Old Pendleton District (now Anderson Co.), S. C. between 1804 & 26 Jan. 1808
169. Priscilla ---, d. Old Pendleton District between 26 Jan. & 25 Apr. 1808 (or possibly Elizabeth Strother, perhaps a 1st wife, who m. a Robert Kay in St. Paul's Parish, King George Co., Va. 12 Feb. 1765)
170-171. ---
172. Adam Clinkscales, Jr. c. 1720/1-Charles Co., Md. c. 1794
173. Ann ---, d. post 1795
174-179. ---
180. Andrew Seawright, Ireland c. 1712-near Donalds, S. C. c.

1777, to S. C. 1762-63, m. Ireland
181. Mary Eleanor Dickson
182-183. ---
184. same as 172
185. same as 173
186-187. ---
188. John Brownlee, d. Abbeville Co., S. C. between 25 Feb. & 12 June 1802
189. Alley ---, d. post 25 Feb. 1802
190-191. ---
192. Peter Gordy, Somerset Co., Md.-Worcester Co. between 22 June 1772 & 15 July 1775
193. Catherine ---, d. post 22 June 1772
194-199. ---
200. William Scott of Sussex Co., Del., fl. 1758
201-209. ---
210. (probably) Jacob or Isaac (sons of Henry) Falkenborough of Orange Co., Va. (1738) & Anson Co., N. C. (1748)
211-219. ---
220. Robert Phillips, will proved Mecklenburg Co., N. C. 23 Jan. 1797
221. Jean ---, d. Mecklenburg Co. c. 1799
222-231. ---
232. Francis Nunn, d. Craven Co., N. C. c. 1738
233. ---
234. Cornelius Loftin of Craven Co., N. C.
235-247. ---
248. William Brown of Locust Thicket, Campbell Co., Va.
249. ---
250. Richard Gaines, Jr., prob. King William or Culpeper Co., Va. c. 1726-will proved Charlotte Co., Va. 1 Feb. 1802, c. 1747
251. Mildred Hollinger
252. Ellis Marcus, of Granville Co., N. C. in 1744, d. Edgefield Co., S. C. between 19 Sept. & 13 Oct. 1788
253. Mary ---, d. post 19 Sept. 1788
254-255. ---
256. Moore Carter (c. 1680-c. 1741), Isle of Wight Co., Va. & Bertie Co., N. C.
257. Jane ---
258. Samuel Browne, d. Isle of Wight Co., Va. between 17 Oct. 1739 & 23 June 1740
259-275. ---
276. Thomas Cox, Jr. (c. 1669-1722/3), Middletown & Freehold, N. J., = ante 1695
277. Mary (prob. Wright) (c. 1671-c. 1760)
278. Thomas Potts, Jr. (1677-1754), Chesterfield, Derbyshire to (as infant) Burlington Co., N. J., = 1698
279. Mary Records, d. post 1754
280. Lewis Morris (c. 1655-1694/5), Middletown, N. J.
281. Elizabeth Almy (1663-post 1711/2), Portsmouth, R. I. to Monmouth Co., N. J., m. (2) John Leonard
282-295. ---
296. (prob.) John Burnley (c. 1675-c. 1765), New Kent & Hanover Cos., Va., = c. 1705
297. (prob.) Phoebe Davies
298. Joel Terrell (c. 1692-95-1758), New Kent & Hanover Cos., Va., = c. 1716-18
299. Sarah Oxford
300. (prob.) William Barksdale, d. 1771?, Charlotte Co., Va.
301-343. ---
344. Adam Clinkscales, d. c. 1727-30, Glasgow, Scotland to Charles Co., Md. by 1718
345. Mary (Preston?), d. c. 1760, m. (2) --- Crawford

346-359. ---
360. William Seawright, Ireland c. 1675-prob. near Beaver Creek, Orangeburg (now Calhoun) Co., S. C. c. 1749-50, to S. C. 1735-36, m. Ireland
361. Esther Thompson
362-367. ---
368. same as 344
369. same as 345
370-399. ---
400. (said to be) Joseph Scott of Ballymacran, Derry, Ireland
401-419. ---
420. (prob.) Henry Falkenborough of Orange Co., Va.
421-499. ---
500. (prob.) Richard Gaines (c. 1686/91-c. 1755/6) of Culpeper Co., Va.
501-511. ---

Note: In the ancestor table above no distinction is made between Abbeville County, Abbeville District or "Old Ninety-six."

* * *

40. RONALD WILSON REAGAN

1. RONALD WILSON REAGAN, b. Tampico, Illinois 6 Feb. 1911, m. (1) Glendale, California 24 Jan. 1940 (div. July 1949) Sarah Jane Folks, actress, known after 1937 as Jane Wyman, b. St. Joseph, Missouri 4 Jan. 1914, divorced wife of Myron Futterman (m. [3] & [4] Fred Karger), (2) North Hollywood, Calif. 4 Mar. 1952 Nancy Davis, actress, born Anne Francis Robbins in New York, New York 6 July 1921
2. John Edward Reagan, Fulton, Ill. 13 July 1883-Hollywood, Calif. 18 May 1941, Fulton 8 Nov. 1904
3. Nelle Clyde Wilson, Fulton 24 July 1883-Santa Monica, Calif. 24 July 1962
4. John Michael Reagan, Peckham, England c. 1854-5-Fulton, Ill. 10 Jan. 1889, Fulton 27 Feb. 1878
5. Jennie Cusick, Dixon, Ill. c. 1856-7-Whiteside Co., Ill. shortly after 19 Nov. 1886
6. Thomas Wilson, Clyde, Ill. 28 April 1844-Whiteside Co. 12 Dec. 1909, Morrison, Ill. 25 Jan. 1866
7. Mary Ann Elsey, Epsom, Surrey, England 28 Dec. 1843-Whiteside Co., Ill. 6 Oct. 1900
8. Michael Reagan, poss. the Michael Reagan or Ryan bp. Ballyporeen, Tipperary, Ireland 3 Sept. 1829-Fairhaven, Ill. 2 Mar. 1884 (to U. S. A. via Canada c. 1858), Southwark, London, England 31 Oct. 1852
9. Catherine Mulcahey, Ireland Aug. 1829-post 1906?
10. Patrick Cusick, Ireland c. 1825-6-shortly before 17 June 1891
11. Sarah Higgins, Ireland or N. Y. c. 1835-ante 1870
12. John Wilson, Paisley, Renfrewshire, Scotland 9 Feb. 1812-Clyde, Ill. 9 Mar. 1883 (to Canada c. 1832, to Clyde Sept. 1839), Whiteside Co. 28 Nov. 1841
13. Jane Blue, Nova Scotia Apr. 1821-Morrison, Ill. 3 June 1894
14. Robert Elsey, painter, bp. Epsom 19 Jan. 1817-1850-5 (in U. S.?), Kennington, Surrey, England 25 Dec. 1838
15. Mary Baker, England c. 1819-20-post 1860, to U. S. c. 1850, m. (2) --- Wesley
16. Thomas Reagan, possibly the Thomas Reagan or Ryan of Ballyporeen whose son Michael was baptized as above, d. ante 31 Oct. 1852
17. (poss.) Margaret Murphy, mother of the Michael Reagan or Ryan baptized as above
18. Patrick Mulcahey of Ireland, d. post 31 Oct. 1852

19-25. ---

26. Donald Blue, Argyllshire, Scotland 18 Jan. 1799-Whiteside Co., Ill. 14 Jan. 1888, Scotland 15 Jan. 1815

27. Catharine McFarlain, Scotland 1 Jan. 1801-Whiteside Co. 21 Feb. 1883

28. Henry Elsey, painter, c. 1776-7-Epsom, Surrey 16 Apr. 1844

29. Susannah ---, d. ante 1 July 1837?

30. John Baker, bricklayer, prob. the John Baker b. c. 1797, d. Epsom, Surrey 23 May 1858

31. (prob.) Ann ---, wife of John Baker, identified above, who survived her husband

32-511. ---

* * *

41. GEORGE HERBERT WALKER BUSH

1. GEORGE HERBERT WALKER BUSH, b. Milton, Massachusetts 12 June 1924, Rye, New York 6 Jan. 1945 Barbara Pierce, b. Rye 8 June 1925

2. Prescott Sheldon Bush, U. S. Senator from Connecticut, Columbus, Ohio 15 May 1895-New York City, N. Y. 8 Oct. 1972, Kennebunkport, Maine 6 Aug. 1921

3. Dorothy Walker, b. near Walker's Point, York Co., Me. 1 July 1901

4. Samuel Prescott Bush, Brick Church, New Jersey 4 Oct. 1863-Columbus, Ohio 8 Feb. 1948, Columbus 20 June 1894

5. Flora Sheldon, Franklin Co., Ohio 17 Mar. 1872-"Watch Hill," Rhode Island, 4 Sept. 1920

6. George Herbert Walker, St. Louis, Missouri 11 June 1875-New York, N. Y. 24 June 1953, 17 Jan. 1899

7. Lucretia [Loulie] Wear, St. Louis, Mo. 17 Sept. 1874-Biddeford, Me. 28 Aug. 1961

8. Rev. James Smith Bush, Rochester, N. Y. 15 June 1825-Ithaca, N. Y. 11 Nov. 1889, New York, N. Y. 24 Feb. 1859

9. Harriet Eleanor Fay, Savannah, Georgia 29 Oct. 1829-Boston, Mass. 27 Feb. 1924

10. Robert Emmet Sheldon, Tiffin, Ohio 1 June 1845-Columbus 21 Jan. 1917, Columbus 24 Feb. 1869

11. Mary Elizabeth Butler, Columbus 15 July 1850-Columbus 16 Jan. 1897

12. David Davis Walker, near Bloomington, Illinois 19 Jan. 1840-Kennebunkport 4 Oct. 1918, St. Louis, Mo. 25 Dec. 1862

13. Martha Adela Beaky, Emmitsburg, Maryland 1 June 1841-living 1906

14. James Hutchenson Wear (II), Otterville, Mo. 30 Sept. 1838-St. Louis, Mo. 14 June 1893, St. Louis 4 Dec. 1866

15. Nannie E. Holliday, c. 1848-25 Feb. 1942

16. Obadiah Newcomb Bush, 28 Jan. 1797-en route from California c. 1851, Rochester 8 Nov. 1821

17. Harriet Smith, Cambridge, N. Y. 12 May 1800-Cincinnati, Ohio 21 June 1867

18. Samuel Howard Fay, Cambridge, Mass. 21 July 1804-Brooklyn, N. Y. 16 Aug. 1847, Savannah, Ga. 5 July 1825

19. Susan Shellman, Savannah, Ga. 20 Feb. 1808-12 Jan. 1887

20. Thomas H. Sheldon, Providence, R. I. 12 May 1818-Franklin Co., Ohio 22 Nov. 1854, Franklin Co. 21 Jan. 1844

21. Martha Uncles, Columbus, Ohio 7 Jan. 1824-Columbus 9 July 1912, m. (2) William Merion, Jr.

22. Courtland Philip Livingston Butler, Clinton, N. Y. 8 March 1813-Columbus 9 Aug. 1891, Buffalo, N. Y. 16 Dec. 1840

23. Elizabeth Slade Pierce, Providence, R. I. 22 March 1822-Columbus 1 Mar. 1901

24. George E. Walker, prob. Burlington, N. J. c. 1797-near Bloomington, Ill. 28 Oct. 1864, Baltimore, Md. 22 May 1821

25. Harriet Mercer, Md. c. 1802-near Bloomington 24 Oct. 1869

26. Joseph Ambrose Beaky, Emmitsburg, Md. 14 June 1818-on the Mississippi River (on the steamship "Minnehaha") 27 Jan. 1858, Philadelphia, Pennsylvania 1 June 1840

27. Mary Ann Bangs, Philadelphia 15 June 1817-living 1876, m. (2) Joachim Elder

28. William Gault Wear, b. Blount Co., Tennessee 11 Dec. 1817, m. Cooper Co., Missouri, 2 Nov. 1837

29. Sarah Amanda Yancey, Glasgow, Kentucky 11 June 1819-Cooper Co. 4 Dec. 1879

30. John James Holliday, Pike Co., Mo. 23 July 1819-St. Louis 18 Sept. 1881, Randolph Co., Mo. 9 May 1843

31. Lucretia Green Foree, b. Ky. c. 1824

32. Timothy Bush, Jr., prob. Lebanon, Conn. 1 Apr. 1766-Rochester 4 May 1850, Penfield, N. Y. 26 July 1791

33. Lydia Newcomb, 28 Apr. 1763-Penfield 14 Sept. 1835

34. Dr. Sanford Smith, Stonington, Conn. 27 Feb. 1760-Scipio, N. Y. 15 June 1815

35. Priscilla Whippo, Cambridge, N. Y. c. 1763-Pottstown, Pa. 26 Aug. 1838

36. Samuel Prescott Phillips Fay, Concord, Mass. 10 Jan. 1778-Concord 18 May 1856, Cambridge, Mass. (int.) 31 July 1803

37. Harriet Howard, Boston 27 Mar. 1782-Cambridge, Mass. 27 July 1847

38. John Shellman, Jr., Fredericktown, Md. 5 May 1756-Savannah, Ga. 17 April 1838, Savannah 19 June 1794

39. Clarissa Montfort, b. Amelia Co., Va., d. 1845

40. Michael Sheldon (according to Thomas H. Sheldon's burial record)

41. Mary --- (according to Thomas H. Sheldon's burial record)

42. James Uncles, Bradford, England 5 Aug. 1794-Columbus 25 Jan. 1835, Franklinton, Ohio 26 Sept. 1816

43. Elizabeth (Betsey) Criswell/Kiswell, b. Lancaster, Pa.

44. Samuel Herrick Butler, Bennington, Vt. 12 Feb. 1785-Columbus 13 Dec. 1851, Waterford, N. Y. 26 June 1806

45. Judith Livingston, Poughkeepsie, N. Y. 4 Sept. 1785-Columbus 28 Feb. 1858

46. Levi Pierce, Rehoboth, Mass. 8 June 1797-1838, Rehoboth 9 Mar. 1818

47. Betsey S(lade?) Wheeler, Rehoboth 30 May 1800-Columbus 23 Feb. 1881

48. Thomas Walker, of Philadelphia & Burlington, N. J., d. c. 1798-1800, m. St. Andrew's Church, Clifton, Bristol, England 22 Feb. 1785

49. Catharine McLelland, m. (2) Robert Hodgson

50. John Mercer, m. Cecil Co., Md. (license) 11 Oct. 1793

51. Rebecca Davis

52. Joseph Beaky of Emmitsburg, Md.

53. Catharine Shriner, b. Pa.

54. Elijah Keeler Bangs, Stratford, Conn. 4 June 1780-Philadelphia 13 Sept. 1856, Philadelphia 29 Oct. 1807

55. Esther Stackhouse, Philadelphia 17 Oct. 1787-Philadelphia 27 Sept. 1819

56. James Hutchenson Weir, 30 Sept. 1789-Mo. Apr. 1832, Knoxville, Tenn. 27 Oct. 1812

57. Elizabeth Gault

58. David Yancey of Barren Co., Ky., m. Albemarle Co., Va. 27 March 1815

59. Mildred Field

60. Joseph Holliday, Ky. 15 Sept. 1789-Monroe Co., Mo. 17 Dec. 1870, Bourbon Co., Ky. 18 March 1816

61. Nancy R. McCune, Bourbon Co. 16 June 1799-Mo. 1834
62. Peter Foree, m. Henry Co., Ky. 18 May 1816
63. Eliza Dawson
64. Timothy Bush, d. Springport, N. Y. c. 1815, Hebron, Conn. 12 Apr. 1759
65. Deborah House, Lebanon, Conn. 6 Apr. 1742-Springport c. 1819
66. Daniel Newcomb, Hebron 29 Nov. 1729-Hebron ante 1789, Wethersfield, Conn. c. 1754
67. Elizabeth May, very prob. Wethersfield 3 Dec. 1730-Hebron shortly post 1789
68. Ephraim Smith, Stonington 5 Oct. 1704-Stonington 24 Mar. 1774, Stonington 3 Jan. 1743/4
69. Lucy Stevens, Stonington c. 1717-Pottstown 4 May 1806
70-71. ---
72. Jonathan Fay, Jr., Westboro, Mass. 21 Jan. 1752-Concord 1 June 1811, Concord 6 Dec. 1776
73. Lucy Prescott, Concord 24 Apr. 1757-Concord 10 Oct. 1792, sister of Dr. Samuel Prescott (1751-c. 1777), who completed Paul Revere's "Midnight Ride" of 19 Apr. 1775
74. Samuel Howard, Boston, Mass. c. 1752-Boston Jan. 1797, Boston int. 3 Apr. 1777
75. Anna Lillie, Boston c. 1760-Andover, Mass. Dec. 1804
76. John Shellman/Schellman, Germany c. 1723-Frederick Co., Md. 25 Sept. 1816, Frederick Co. c. 1748
77. Maria Margareth Fout/Fought/Fauth, Frederick Co., Md. 14 Jan. 1732-Frederick Co. 6 Oct. 1795
78. Robert Munford/Montfort, d. Amelia Co., Va. between 9 Sept. 1771 & 1778; m. Amelia Co. (bond) 11 Feb. 1755
79. Anne Brodnax of Charles City Co., Va., d. post 1780-82
80-87. ---
88. Rev. Nathaniel Butler (so identified in DAR application paper 134906), Cumberland, R. I. 14 June 1761-29 Sept. 1829, 12 June 17--
89. Sarah Herrick (so identified in DAR application paper 134906), 21 Feb. 1764?-c. 1823
90. Gilbert James Livingston, Poughkeepsie, N. Y. 14 Oct. 1758-Rome, N. Y. 7 April 1833, Troy, N. Y. 28 Feb. 1779
91. Susannah Lewis, prob. Poughkeepsie 25 Mar. 1761-Saratoga, N. Y. 27 July 1822
92. Isaac Pierce, Rehoboth, Mass. 22 Sept. 1763-Rehoboth 26 Nov. 1849, Rehoboth 7 Oct. 1782
93. Anna Fitch, Swansea, Mass. 1 Mar. 1763-Rehoboth 15 Nov. 1809
94. Jarvis Wheeler, Rehoboth 22 Sept. 1774-Rehoboth 3 Mar. 1852, Rehoboth 12 Feb. 1797
95. Sarah Horton, Rehoboth 28 Dec. 1777-Rehoboth 13 May 1856
96-99. ---
100. Robert Mercer, Jr., b. St. Stephen's, Cecil Co., Md. 22 Dec. 1737
101. ---
102. Richard Davis, b. Cecil Co., Md. c. 1745 (acc. to Pittman & Walker)
103. ---
104. Victor Emanuel Bechi of Md. (acc. to Pittman & Walker)
105-107. ---
108. Lemuel Bangs, Harwich, Mass. 31 Dec. 1739-Portage, N. Y. 9 May 1824, c. 1774-75
109. Rebecca Keeler, Ridgefield, Conn. 29 Apr. 1751-Grand River, Upper Canada 24 Feb. 1812
110. Amos Stackhouse, 4 5th Mo. 1757-5 4th Mo. 1825, Mt. Holly, N. J. 14 1st Mo. 1779
111. Mary Powell, 9 7th Mo. 1763-15 7th Mo. 1841
112. Jonathan Weir, c. 1750-60-Blount Co., Tenn. c. 1832

113. Mary ---, c. 1758-Dade Co., Mo. c. 1848
114. Jonathan Gault of Knoxville, Tenn.
115. ---
116. Jechonias Yancey, m. Albemarle Co., Va. 14 Oct. 1793
117. Mildred Wood
118. John Field, m. Albemarle Co., Va. 11 Sept. 1795
119. Sally Wood
120. William Holliday, Rathfriland, Down, Ireland c. 1755-Harrison Co., Ky. between 20 Dec. 1811 & Apr. 1812
121. (probably) Martha Patton
122-125. ---
126. Samuel Dawson (acc. DAR 19316, 23452)
127. --- Montjoy or Mountjoy (acc. DAR 19316, 23452)
128. (possibly) Richard Bush, d. Bristol, R. I. 27 Sept. 1732, int. 25 Jan. 1726
129. (possibly) Mary Fairbanks, 22 Aug. 1699-Bristol 7 May 1743
130. John House, Little Compton, R. I. 8 Dec. 1715-Hebron 4 July 1805, Lebanon 6 Sept. 1739
131. Deborah Guile, 26 June 1715-15 Aug. 1783
132. Obadiah Newcomb, Edgartown, Mass. c. 1695-Hebron 4 May 1761
133. Abigail ---, c. 1693-Hebron 9 May 1757
134. Hezekiah May, Roxbury, Mass. 14 Dec. 1696-Wethersfield 5 Sept. 1783, Wethersfield 27 Apr. 1721
135. Anna Stillman, Hadley, Mass. 6 Apr. 1699-Wethersfield 7 Nov. 1767
136. John Smith, Watertown, Mass. 13 July 1672-Stonington 8 May 1739, ante 1695
137. Susanna ---, c. 1669-Stonington 28 Sept. 1746
138. Henry Stevens, Jr., Stonington 20 Nov. 1681-living 1749/50, Plainfield, Conn. 2 Mar. 1708/9
139. Elizabeth Fellows, Ipswich, Mass. 14 Sept. 1685-living 1741
140-143. ---
144. Jonathan Fay, Westboro, Mass. 21 Nov. 1724-Westboro 3 Mar. 1800, 25 June 1746
145. Joanna Phillips, Stoneham, Mass. 17 May 1729-Westboro 10 June 1788
146. Dr. Abel Prescott, Concord 7 Apr. 1718-Concord 22 Oct. 1805, c. 1742
147. Abigail Brigham, Sudbury, Mass. 31 Dec. 1723-ante 12 June 1777
148. Ebenezer Howard, Boston 12 Oct. 1730-Boston between 15 June 1782 & 13 Apr. 1784, int. Boston 26 Apr. 1750
149. Martha Goffe, d. Boston shortly ante 25 Apr. 1808
150. John Lillie, Boston 8 Aug. 1728-will proved Boston 19 Apr. 1765, Boston 16 Aug. 1754
151. Abigail Breck, Boston 19 June 1732-Boston 28 Oct. 1819, m. (2) Samuel Harris
152-153. ---
154. Baltis/Balthazar Fout/Fought/Fauth, d. Frederick Co., Md. between 29 Apr. & 23 May 1751, c. 1721
155. Susanna Bocher, Lomersheim, Wuerttemberg 25 July 1703-Frederick Co., Md. 11 Feb. 1773, m. (2) Caspar Apple
156. James Munford, d. Amelia Co., Va. between 16 Mar. & 25 Apr. 1754, = 1727/8
157. Elizabeth Bolling, Prince George Co., Va. 17 Dec. 1709-post 1754, prob. m. (2) John Bannister
158. Edward Brodnax, d. prob. Charles City Co., Va. c. 1749
159. Mary Brown
160-175. ---
176. Benjamin Butler, Barnstable, Mass. 18 Dec. 1727-Middletown Springs, Vt. c. 1800, Cumberland, R. I. 14 Jan. 1757
177. Susanna Whiting, b. Wrentham, Mass. 14 Sept. 1734
178. Samuel Herrick (so identified in DAR application paper

134906), Coventry, Conn. 2 April 1732-Springfield, N. Y. c. 1797-98, Norwich, Conn. 26 Feb. 1754

179. Silence Kingsley (so identified in DAR application paper 134906), b. Easton, Mass. 30 Aug. 1727

180. James Livingston, Esopus, N. Y. 29 March 1728-prob. Poughkeepsie, N. Y. 2 June 1790, Poughkeepsie 11 Nov. 1751

181. Judith Newcomb, Lebanon, Conn. 31 May 1733-31 Aug. 1808

182. Richard Lewis of Poughkeepsie, m. c. 1758

183. Susanna Vanderburgh, bp. Poughkeepsie 1 June 1725

184. Rev. Nathan Pierce, Swansea, Mass. 21 Feb. 1716-14 Apr. 1793, Rehoboth 6 Oct. 1737

185. Lydia Martin, Rehoboth 17 July 1718-21 Dec. 1798

186. William Fitch, m. Swansea 26 Apr. 1752

187. Hannah Bourn, b. Swansea 8 Oct. 1730

188. Jeremiah Wheeler, Rehoboth 23 Mar. 1731-Rehoboth 26 Feb. 1811, Rehoboth 4 Jan. 1753

189. Submit Horton, d. Rehoboth 18 Apr. 1778

190. Comfort Horton, Rehoboth 29 Mar. 1743-Rehoboth 14 June 1805, 8 Dec. 1768

191. Joanna Wood, Swansea 29 Aug. 1750-29 Apr. 1813

192-199. ---

200. Robert Mercer, b. Cecil Co., Md. 19 Dec. 1696-living 1727, St. Stephen's, Cecil Co. 1 Aug. 1727

201. Ann Mounce, b. Cecil Co. 9 Jan. 1702

202-203. ---

204. Thomas Davis, b. Cecil Co. c. 1710, m. St. Stephen's, Cecil Co. 9 Jan. 1734/5

205. Rebecca Gregory

206-215. ---

216. Joseph Bangs, Harwich, Mass. 30 Jan. 1713-Oblong, N. Y. c. 1757, Barnstable, Mass. 18 Sept. 1735

217. Thankful Hamblen, Barnstable 6 Aug. 1715-living 1768

218. Elijah Keeler, Ridgefield, Conn. 17 Mar. 1727-living 1790

219. Sarah ---

220. James Stackhouse, Bucks Co., Pa. 11 11th Mo. 1725/6-Philadelphia 16 8th Mo. 1759, Philadelphia 13 9th Mo. 1750

221. Martha Hastings, 27 4th Mo. 1722-23 6th Mo. 1806

222. John Powell

223. Susanna Bryan

224. (prob.) Hugh Weir of Rockbridge Co., Virginia, will dated 3 Aug. 1779

225-231. ---

232. Jeremiah Yancey of Albemarle Co., Va. c. 1748-c. 1788

233. Margaret (said to be Mullins)

234. William Wood, d. Albemarle Co., Va. between 15 Apr. & Sept. 1808, brother of Jesse Wood, 238 below

235. Martha ---, d. post 15 Apr. 1808

236. Robert Field of Albemarle Co., Va.

237. (said to be) --- Green

238. Jesse Wood, Sr., will dated Albemarle Co. 2 Jan. 1824, brother of William Wood, 234 above

239. ---

240. Samuel Holliday of Rathfriland, Down, Ireland, b. c. 1710

241. Janet Adair, b. Roth, Down, Ireland c. 1714

242-251. ---

252. Henry Dawson (acc. DAR 19316, 23452, but prob. not Henry Dawson, 1748-c. 1811-15, of Tyrone, Pa., Maysville, Ky., & Champaign & Clark Cos., Ohio)

253. --- Sandford (acc. DAR 19316, 23452)

254-257. ---

258. (possibly) Jeremiah Fairbanks (1674-1735), Dedham, Mass. & Bristol, R. I., = 1698

259. (possibly) Mary Penfield, b. 1678, Lynn, Mass.

260. Nathaniel House, d. 1763, Lebanon, Conn., = 1710
261. Hannah Davenport (1686-1769), Little Compton, R. I.
262. Israel Guild (1690-1766), Dedham, Mass. & Lebanon, Conn., = 1715
263. Sarah George (c. 1695-post 1732), Dorchester, Mass.
264. Simon Newcomb (c. 1665-1744/5), Kittery, Me., Edgartown, Mass., & Lebanon, Conn., = c. 1687
265. Deborah --- (c. 1664-1756)
266-267. ---
268. John May, Jr. (1663-c. 1729-30), Roxbury, Mass., = 1684
269. Prudence Bridge (1664-1723)
270. George Stillman (c. 1654-1728), Hadley, Mass. & Wethersfield, Conn., = c. 1686
271. Rebecca Smith (c. 1668-1750)
272. Daniel Smith, Jr. (1642-1681), Watertown, Mass., = 1668
273. Mary Grant, d. post 1681
274-275. ---
276. Henry Stevens, d. c. 1726, Stonington, Conn.
277. Elizabeth Gallup, living 1736
278. Ephraim Fellows (c. 1641-post 1710), Ipswich, Mass., & Plainfield, Conn., = c. 1683-84
279. Anne Cross (c. 1651-post 1710), widow of Thomas Marshall
280-287. ---
288. John Fay (III) (1700-1732), Westboro (earlier Marlboro, later Northboro), Mass., = 1721
289. Hannah Child (c. 1700-02-1788), Watertown, Mass., m. (2) Samuel Lyscomb
290. Ebenezer Phillips (1695-1745/6), Charlestown & Southboro, Mass.
291. Mary Smith (1697/8-post 1745/6)
292. Dr. Jonathan Prescott, Jr. (1677-1729), Concord, Mass., = 1701
293. Rebecca Bulkeley, b. 1681
294. John Brigham, Jr. (1680-1729), Marlboro & Sudbury, Mass.
295. Martha ---, d. 1734
296. Amos Howard, b. prob. 1696, prob. Lynn & Boston, Mass., = 1721
297. Judith Wallingford, b. 1699/1700, Bradford, Mass.
298. prob. John, b. 1678, Samuel, b. 1683, Joseph, b. 1685, William, b. 1687, or Ebenezer, b. 1692/3, sons of John & Hannah (Sumner) Goffe of Boston, Mass.
299. ---
300. Theophilus Lillie (1690-1760), Boston, Mass., = 1725
301. Hannah Ruck (1702-c. 1767)
302. John Breck (III) (1705-1761), Boston, Mass., = 1727
303. Margaret Thomas (1708/9-1765)
304-309. ---
310. George Bocher of Lomersheim, Wuerttemberg (& Pa. & Md.?)
311. Margareth ---
312. Robert Munford, d. prob. Prince George Co., Va. c. 1735, = c. 1701
313. Martha Kennon of Conjuror's Neck, Henrico Co., Va.
314. Robert Bolling, Jr., Charles City Co., Va. 25 Jan. 1682-Prince George Co. post 1728 (son of Robert Bolling & his 2nd wife, Anne Stith; the 1st wife of Robert Bolling, Sr., was Jane Rolfe, granddaughter of Pocahontas), Charles City Co. 27 Jan. 1706
315. Anne Cocke, Charles City Co. c. 1688-Prince George Co. c. 1749
316. William Brodnax, Godmersham, Kent 28 Feb. 1675-Charles City Co. 16 Feb. 1727, = post 1700
317. Rebecca Champion, c. 1677-Charles City Co. 19 Dec. 1723, widow of Edward Travis
318-351. ---

352. Israel Butler (c. 1696-ante 1757), Tisbury, Mass., = 1725
353. Elizabeth Blossom (1705-1734/5), Barnstable
354. Ephraim Whiting (1699-1788), Wrentham, Mass. to Cumberland, R. I., = 1731
355. Abigail Mason, d. 1749, Norton to Wrentham
356. Daniel Herrick, b. 1708, Preston & Coventry, Conn., = 1731
357. Elizabeth Rust (1713-1741), Coventry
358. Samuel Kingsley (III) (ante 1693-c. 1730), Bridgewater & Easton, Mass., = c. 1714
359. Mary ---
[352-359 depend on the identifications of 88-89 & 178-79 in DAR application paper 134906]
360. Gilbert Livingston (1690-1746), Kingston, N. Y., = 1711
361. Cornelia Beekman (1693-1742)
362. Thomas Newcomb (c. 1691-92-c. 1761), Edgartown, Mass. to Lebanon, Conn. to Pleasant Valley, N. Y., = 1720
363. Judith Woodworth, b. c. 1701, Little Compton, R. I. to Lebanon
364-365. ---
366. Henry Vanderburgh (c. 1685-c. 1750), NYC to Poughkeepsie, = 1710
367. Magdalena Knight of Brooklyn
368. Mial Pierce (1692-1786), Rehoboth, = 1711
369. Judith Round (c. 1687-1744), Swansea
370. Ephraim Martin (1676-1734), Swansea & Rehoboth, = 1699
371. Thankful Bullock (1681-1762), Rehoboth
372-373. ---
374. William Bourn, Jr. (1704-post 1752), Rehoboth & Swansea, = 1729
375. Mary Sheffield, b. 1701, Tiverton, R. I.
376. James Wheeler, Jr. (1697-1740 or 1753), Rehoboth, = 1716
377. Elizabeth West, b. 1694
378. Thomas Horton (1698?-1733), brother of 380 below, Swansea & Rehoboth, = 1721
379. Keziah Carpenter (1697-1763), m. (2) John Barney
380. Jonathan Horton (c. 1695-1774), brother of 378 above, Rehoboth, = 1725
381. Ann Millard (1708-1751)
382. Rev. Jabez Wood, Jr. (1719/20-1793), Middleborough, Mass. to Warren, R. I. to Guilford, Vt., = 1748
383. Joanna Short, b. 1715, Rehoboth & Swansea
384-399. ---
400. Thomas Mercer, of Cecil Co., Md. by 1671
401. Elizabeth ---
402. Christopher Mounce of Cecil Co., Md.
403. Martha ---
404-407. ---
408. William Davis of Cecil Co., Md.
409. --- Angell
410-431. ---
432. Samuel Bangs (1680-1750), Harwich, Mass., = 1703
433. Mary Hinckley (1678-1741)
434. Ebenezer Hamblen (1683-1736), Barnstable, Mass., = 1710
435. Thankful Hamblen (1689-1768)
436. Joseph Keeler (c. 1683-1757), Norwalk & Ridgefield, Conn., = c. 1705
437. Elizabeth Whitney (c. 1684-1763)
438-439. ---
440. Robert Stackhouse (1692-1788), Bristol & Berwick, Pa.
441. Margaret Stone
442. Samuel Hastings
443. Mary Hill
444. Isaac Powell, = 1729

445. Elizabeth Perdue
446-471. ---
472. (said to be) Col. John Field, Culpeper Co., Va.-Battle of Point Pleasant 10 Nov. 1774, c. 1748
473. (said to be) Anna Clark, not a sister, as often alleged, of the explorers George Rogers Clark and William Clark
474-479. ---
480. Adam Holliday of Rathfriland, Down, Ireland, b. c. 1680
481. Jane Macomson, b. c. 1688
482-503. ---
504. (perhaps, although doubtful) George Dawson, b. c. 1704, Montgomery Co., Va. & Tyrone, Pa., = c. 1740
505. (perhaps, although doubtful) Anne Lowe of "Bowlingly," Queenstown, Md.
506-511. ---

* * *

LIST OF ABBREVIATIONS

AB N. G. Parke II & D. L. Jacobus, The Ancestry of Lorenzo Ackley & His Wife Emma Arabella Bosworth (1960)
AL W. G. Davis, The Ancestry of Abel Lunt (1963)
ALR Carl Boyer, 3rd, Ancestral Lines Revised (1981)
APP Virginia M. Meyer & J. F. Dorman, Adventurers of Purse & Person, Virginia, 1607-1624/5, 3rd ed. (1987)
AR 6 F. L. Weis & W. L. Sheppard, Jr., Ancestral Roots of 60 New England Colonists, 6th ed. (1988)
AS W. G. Davis, The Ancestry of Annis Spear (1945)
AT ancestor table
BG E. B. Sumner, Ancestry of Edward Wales Blake & Clarissa Matilda Glidden with 90 Allied Families (1948)
BH W. G. Davis, The Ancestry of Bethia Harris (1934)
BMV C. E. Banks, The History of Martha's Vineyard, Dukes County, Massachusetts, Volume III, Family Genealogies (1925, reprint 1966)
BP Belle Preston, Bassett-Preston Ancestors (1930)
BPF2 Burke's Presidential Families of the United States of America, 2nd ed. (1981)
BTGC Boston Transcript Genealogical Column
BW Henry Bond, Genealogies of the Families & Descendants of the Early Settlers of Watertown, Massachusetts, 2nd ed., 1860 (reprint 1978)
CCAD L. E. deForest, Our Colonial & Continental Ancestors: the Ancestry of Mr. & Mrs. Louis William Dommerich (1930)
CFSSA S. P. Hardy, Colonial Families of the Southern States of America, 2nd ed. (1958, reprint 1965)
CH W. G. Davis, The Ancestry of Charity Haley (1916)
CP Vicary Gibbs, etc., The [New] Complete Peerage, 13 vols. (1910-1959)
CW G. W. Chamberlain, History of Weymouth, Massachusetts, vols. 3 & 4 (1923), reprinted as Genealogies of the Early Families of Weymouth, Massachusetts (1984)
DAB Dictionary of American Biography, 20 vols. plus index, 1928-1937, & eight supplements (to deaths through 1970) & index guide, 1944-1988
DG1,2 Mary Walton Ferris, Dawes-Gates Ancestral Lines, vol. 1 (1943), vol. 2 (1931)
DSGRM The Detroit Society for Genealogical Research Magazine
DSSAY Dutch Settlers Society of Albany Yearbooks
DW W. G. Davis, The Ancestry of Dudley Wildes (1959)
EA The Essex Antiquarian
EIHC Essex Institute Historical Collections
EO1,2 English Origins of New England Families from The New England Historical & Genealogical Register, 1st Ser. (3 vols., 1984), 2nd Ser. (3 vols., 1985)
ESR G. B. Blodgette & A. E. Jewett, Early Settlers of Rowley, Massachusetts (1933, reprint 1981)
FCW Frederick Chester Warner, The Ancestry of Samuel, Freda & John Warner (typescript, 1949, bound at NEHGS in 5 vols.)
FD Julia L. F. Bunce, Some of the Ancestors of the Rev. John Selby & His Wife Clara Winchester Dana (1948)
FM E. E. Salisbury, Family Memorials, 2 vols. (plus an appendix vol. of charts) (1885)
FNE Ernest Flagg, Genealogical Notes on the Founding of New England (1926, reprint 1973)
FSA Jonathan Pearson, Contributions for the Genealogies of the First Settlers of the Ancient County of Albany, 1630-1800 (1872, reprint 1978, originally vol. 4 of Joel Munsell, Collections on the History of Albany, 1871)

GAF E. F. Waterman & D. L. Jacobus, The Granberry Family & Allied Families (1945)

GDMNH C. T. Libby, Sybil Noyes, & W. G. Davis, Genealogical Dictionary of Maine & New Hampshire (1928-1929, reprint 1972)

GDNE James Savage, A Genealogical Dictionary of the First Settlers of New England, 4 vols. (1860-62, last reprint 1986)

GDRI J. O. Austin, The Genealogical Dictionary of Rhode Island (1887, reprint with additions & corrections from TAG, 1969)

GGE H. F. Waters, Genealogical Gleanings in England (1901-1907, reprint 1969)

GKFFC Genealogies of Kentucky Families from The Filson Club History Quarterly (1981)

GKFR Genealogies of Kentucky Families from The Register of the Kentucky Historical Society, 2 vols. (1981)

GLIF Genealogies of Long Island Families from The New York Genealogical & Biographical Record, 2 vols. (1987)

GM F. F. Starr, Various Ancestral Lines of James Goodwin & Lucy (Morgan) Goodwin of Hartford, Connecticut, 2 vols. (1915)

GMF Genealogies of Mayflower Families from The New England Historical & Genealogical Register, 3 vols. (1985)

GMNJ Genealogical Magazine of New Jersey

GPFPGM Genealogies of Pennsylvania Families from The Pennsylvania Genealogical Magazine, 3 vols. (1982)

GPFPM Genealogies of Pennsylvania Families from the Pennsylvania Magazine of History & Biography, 1 vol. (1981)

GVFT Genealogies of Virginia Families from Tyler's Quarterly Historical & Genealogical Magazine, 4 vols. (1981)

GVFVM Genealogies of Virginia Families from the Virginia Magazine of History & Biography, 5 vols. (1981)

GVFWM Genealogies of Virginia Families from the William & Mary College Quarterly Magazine, 5 vols. (1982)

GWF C. W. Bowen, The History of Woodstock, Connecticut: Genealogies of Woodstock Families, vols. 2-3 (1930), 4 (1932), 5 (1933), 6 (1936), 7-8 (1943)

HB E. B. Sumner, Ancestry & Descendants of Amaziah Hall & Betsey Baldwin (1954)

HGM J. E. Stillwell, Historical & Genealogical Miscellany: Early Settlers of New Jersey & their Families, 5 vols. (1903-1932, reprint 1970)

HH D. L. Jacobus & E. F. Waterman, Hale, House & Related Families Mainly of the Connecticut River Valley (1952, reprint 1978)

HSA David W. Hoyt, The Old Families of Salisbury & Amesbury, Massachusetts, vols. 1-4 (1897-1919, reprint in one vol., 1982)

HSF J. B. Boddie, Historical Southern Families, 23 vols. (1957-1980)

HSPVS Harleian Society Publications, Visitations Series

HVG Rev. Horace Edwin Hayden, Virginia Genealogies (1891, reprint 1959)

JIC N. D. Thompson & R. C. Anderson, A Tribute to John Insley Coddington on the Occasion of the Fortieth Anniversary of the American Society of Genealogists (Association for the Promotion of Scholarship in Genealogy, Ltd., Occasional Publication No. One, 1981)

JN W. G. Davis, Ancestry of Joseph Neal (1945)

KW J. C. Frost, Ancestry of Evelyn Wood Keeler, Wife of Willard Underwood Taylor (1939) (known as the Keeler-Wood genealogy)

LBNS DAR Lineage Book, National Society of the Daughters of the American Revolution, 166 vols. (1895-1939, covering members who joined through 1921)

LDBR H. H. d'Angerville, Living Descendants of Blood Royal, 5 vols. (1959-1973)

MAF L. E. & A. L. deForest, Moore & Allied Families: the Ancestry of William Henry Moore (1938)

MCS 3 Arthur Adams, Frederick Lewis Weis & Walter Lee Sheppard, Jr., The Magna Charta Sureties, 1215, 3rd ed. (1979)

MD The Mayflower Descendant

MF1-3 Mayflower Families Through Five Generations: Descendants of the Pilgrims Who Landed at Plymouth, Mass. December 1620, vol. 1 (L. M. Kellogg, ed. 1975: Eaton, S. Fuller, White), vol. 2 (R. M. Sherman, ed. 1978: Chilton, More, Rogers), vol. 3 (A. B. Harding, ed. 1980: Soule)

MFIP Mayflower Families in Progress (four generation pamphlets of Mayflower progeny to c. 1720, 1986-present) (covering to date, among presidential forebears, Billington, Cooke, Priest & Warren)

MP Mayflower passenger

MQ The Mayflower Quarterly

MSR Mayflower Source Records: Primary Data Concerning Southeastern Massachusetts, Cape Cod, & the Islands of Nantucket & Martha's Vineyard, from The New England Historical & Genealogical Register (1986)

N&Q Notes & Queries

NAW Notable American Women, 1607-1950, A Biographical Dictionary, 3 vols. (1971), & Notable American Women: the Modern Period: a Biographical Dictionary (1980)

NCAB National Cyclopaedia of American Biography, 76 vols. (1-63 [63-N], & current volumes A-M), 1888-1984

ND W. G. Davis, The Ancestry of Nicholas Davis (1956)

NEHGR The New England Historical & Genealogical Register

NGSQ National Genealogical Society Quarterly

NH D. L. Jacobus, Families of Ancient New Haven, 3 vols. (originally published as New Haven Genealogical Magazine, vols. 1-8, 1922-33), 1974

NYGBR The New York Genealogical & Biographical Record

OF1-3 D. L. Jacobus, History & Genealogy of the Families of Old Fairfield, vol. 1 (17th century) (1930), vols. 2-3 (18th cent.) (1932) (reprint 1976)

PA M. L. Holman, Ancestry of Charles Stinson Pillsbury & John Sargent Pillsbury, 2 vols. (1938)

PC E. A. Stratton, Plymouth Colony: Its History & People, 1620-1691 (1986)

PCG L. R. Paige, History of Cambridge, Massachusetts 1630-1877 (1877), & M. I. Gozzaldi, Supplement & Index (1930) (both reprinted 1986)

PG N. G. Parke II & D. L. Jacobus, The Ancestry of Rev. Nathan Grier Parke & His Wife Ann Elizabeth Gildersleeve (1959)

PGM Pennsylvania Genealogical Magazine

PH W. G. Davis, The Ancestry of Phoebe Tilton (1947)

PHSVS Publications of the Harleian Society, Visitations Series

PK presidential kinsmen

PM Putnam's Monthly Historical Magazine

PMHB The Pennsylvania Magazine of History & Biography

PS Sidney Perley, The History of Salem, Massachusetts, vol. 1, 1626-1637 (1924), vol. 2, 1638-1670 (1926), vol. 3, 1671-1716 (1928)

PW ancestor shared by The Princess of Wales

RD royal descent

RM Josephine C. Frost, Ancestors of Welding Ring & His Wife Ida Malvina Mailler (1935)

SAW H. R. Stiles, The History & Genealogies of Ancient Windsor, Connecticut, 1635-1891, vol. 2, Genealogies & Biographies (1892, reprint 1976)

SAWE H. R. Stiles, The History of Ancient Wethersfield, Connecticut, vol. 2, Genealogies & Biographies (1904, reprint 1975

SB W. C. Sprague, Genealogies of the Families of Braintree, Massachusetts, 1640-1850, Including the Modern Towns of Randolph & Holbrook & the City of Quincy (microfilm, NEHGS, 1984)

SE1,2 Nora E. Snow & Myrtle M. Jillson, The Snow-Estes Ancestry, 2 vols. (1939)

SH W. G. Davis, The Ancestry of Sarah Hildreth (1958)

SHG J. L. Sibley, Biographical Sketches of Graduates of Harvard University, vols. 1-3 (1642-89) (1873-1885), & Sibley's Harvard Graduates, vols. 4-17 (1690-1771) (1933-1975)

SM1,2 M. L. & W. L. Holman, Ancestry of John Harrington Stevens & His Wife Frances Helen Miller, 2 vols. (1948-1952)

SP Sir J. B. Paul, The Scots Peerage, 9 vols. (1904-1914)

SS James William Hook, Lieut. Samuel Smith, His Children & One Line of Descendants & Related Families (1953)

TAG The American Genealogist

TCB Dwight Brainerd & D. L. Jacobus, Ancestry of Thomas Chalmers Brainerd (1948)

TF E. B. Sumner, Descendants of Thomas Farr of Harpswell, Maine, & 90 Allied Families (1959)

TG The Genealogist (New York & Salt Lake City, 1980-present)

TGM The Genealogical Magazine

TM R. M. Tingley, Some Ancestral Lines; Ancestors of Guilford Solon Tingley & His Wife Martha Pamelia Meyers (1935)

TVG The Virginia Genealogist

UGHM The Utah Genealogical & Historical Magazine

VGE Lothrop Withington, Virginia Gleanings in England: a Consolidation of Articles from the Virginia Magazine of History & Biography (1980)

VHG J. B. Boddie, Virginia Historical Genealogies (1954)

VVR Virginia Vital Records from The Virginia Magazine of History & Biography, The William & Mary College Quarterly, & Tyler's Quarterly (1982)

VWR Virginia Will Records from The Virginia Magazine of History & Biography, The William & Mary College Quarterly, & Tyler's Quarterly (1982)

WB Josephine C. Frost, Ancestors of James Wickham & His Wife Cora Prudence Billard (1935)

WC T. B. Wyman, The Genealogies & Estates of Charlestown, Massachusetts, 1629-1818 (2 vols., 1879, reprint 1982)

WCPDD G. E. McCracken, The Welcome Claimants: Proved, Disproved & Doubtful, with an Account of Their Descendants (Publications of the Welcome Society of Pennsylvania, Number 2) (1970)

WV Clayton Torrence, Winston of Virginia & Allied Families (1927)

* * *

BIBLIOGRAPHY

George Washington

TAG 51 (1975):167-71, 52 (1976):87-88, 53 (1977):15 & BPF2:14-15 (AT & patrilineal descent, all by G. H. S. L. Washington, the leading recent authority on this family, for a listing of some of whose myriad Washington articles, together with some items on this "first" American family by earlier scholars, see T. F. Beard's "Foreward" to A. L. Langston & J. O. Buck, Jr., comp., Pedigrees of Some of the Emperor Charlemagne's Descendants, vol. 2 [1974], p. xcvi & EO2:1: viii-ix); Burke's Landed Gentry, 1939 ed. (reprinted in 1971 as Prominent Families in America with British Ancestry), pp. 2959-63, HSF 4:149-52, 154, 160-63, NEHGR 129 (1975):106-32, Hertfordshire Life July 1975:18-21, Northamptonshire & Bedfordshire Life June 1976:24-27 (Washington, the last three by Peter Walne); GGE 709-15 (Washington, Light); N&Q New Ser. 19 (1972):171-72, 24 (1977):499 (Butler, Greeke), Rev. H. I. Longden, The Visitation of the County of Northampton in the Year 1681 (PHSVS 87, 1935), pp. 32-33 (Butler) & H. S. London & S. W. Rawlins, Visitation of London 1568 (PHSVS 109-110, 1963), pp. 99-100 (Greeke); NEHGR 94 (1940):251-77, 322-46, 96 (1942):194-196, 97 (1943):195-97 (Twigden, Dickens, Thornton, Wilmer, Spencer, etc.), W. C. Metcalfe, ed., The Visitations of Northamptonshire Made in 1564 & 1618-19 (1887), p. 142, & George Baker, The History & Antiquities of the County of Northampton, vol. 1 (1822), p. 115 (Thornton, Newnham); GVFWM 4:153-54, 168-69 (Pope); M. E. Sorley, Lewis of Warner Hall (1935, reprint 1979), pp. 31-53 (Martiau, Reade, Warner), GVFVM 5:538-90 (Warner, Sotherton, Peck, Towneley, Halstead), HSF 2:174-94 & York Lowry Wilson, A Carolina-Virginia Genealogy (1962), pp. 94-96, 251-335 (Reade, Cooke, Windebank, Dymoke), APP (Martiau, Reade, Warner, Washington) & J. B. Stoudt, Nicholas Martiau: The Adventurous Huguenot, the Military Engineer, & the Earliest American Ancestor of George Washington (1932); Sir G. J. Armitage, Bart., ed., Middlesex Pedigrees as Collected by Richard Mundy (PHSVS 65, 1914), p. 123 (Windebank), A. R. Maddison, Lincolnshire Pedigrees, vol. 4 (PHSVS 55, 1906), pp. 1202-5 (Dymoke) & Burke's Landed Gentry, 18th ed., vol. 1 (1965), pp. 220-21 (Dymoke); GVFVM 1:16-22 (also by Peter Walne), HVG 47-53, 56-59, 79-82, & GVFWM 3:194-95 (Ball, Mrs. Mary Bennett Johnson); W. C. Metcalfe, ed., The Visitations of Suffolk (1882), p. 172 (Vesey).

RD - George Reade, John Washington of Westmoreland County, Mrs. Mary Towneley Warner

Queen Elizabeth the Queen Mother-Augustine Jr. & Mildred (Reade) Warner

PK - Coolidge, F. D. Roosevelt, Bush (Spencer-English)

* * *

John Adams, Jr. and John Quincy Adams

TAG 21 (1944-45):167-69 (an ancestor list, without dates, places, or references, by C. A. Torrey), plus Torrey's full AT (1-127, 238-39, with full dates, places, and some references, to printed Massachusetts vital records esp.) in his MSS. collection at NEHGS, confirmed & sometimes extended by A. N. Adams, A Genealogical History of Henry Adams of Braintree, Massachusetts, & His Descendants (1898), J. G. Bartlett, Henry Adams of Somersetshire, England & Braintree, Massachusetts, His English Ancestry & Some of His Descendants (1927), Enid E. Adams, Ancestors & Descendants of Jeremiah Adams, 1794-1883 (1974), & SB (Adams, Baxter, Bass, Quincy);

NEHGR 107 (1953):218-20 (Bass, Savil, reprinted in EO 1:3:179-81); MQ 42 (1976):87-90, MD 39 (1989):111-22 (Alden), H. K. Shaw & A. C. Williams, Families of the Pilgrims: John Alden, William Mullins (1986), pp. 1-4, 9-10 (Alden, Bass, Adams), & PC 232-33, 331-32 (Alden, Mullins); "Ye Books of ye Boylstons", n. a., n. d., MSS. at NEHGS, & "The Boylston Family in England & Their Connection with the Pipe Family," an unpublished article by Mr. Don Charles Stone of Philadelphia; FD (Gardner) & DW 1 (Gardner, Cogswell); NEHGR 52 (1898): 421-23 & EIHC 83 (1947):14 (White); E. O. Jameson, The Cogswells in America (1884), pp. vii-xv, 1-7, 9-12, 23, E. F. Smith, Adam Hawkes of Saugus, Mass., 1605-1672: the First Six Generations in America (1980), pp. 1-31, & NEHGR 103 (1949):182 (Browne, reprinted in EO 1:3:764); WC (Smith, Boylston, Fowle) & the forthcoming George Fowle of Charlestown genealogy by Eugene Chambers Fowle (to be published by NEHGS); BW (Bright, Goldstone) & J. B. Bright, The Brights of Suffolk, England (1858); NEHGR 92 (1936):30-32 (Quincy, reprinted in EO 2:2:344-78) & 53 (1899):92-101, 186-98, 289-300 (Hoar, reprinted in EO 2:2:344-78); G. F. Shepard & D. L. Jacobus, The Shepard Families of New England, Volume 3, Additional Family Groups (1973), pp. 293-97, 300-1; NEHGR 100 (1946):73 (reprinted in EO 2:3:206) & Yorkshire Genealogist 1 (1888):92-94 (Estouteville, Robertson); TAG 32 (1956):9-23, reprinted somewhat rearranged, in JIC 136-49 (Tyng, Coytmore), & TAG 50 (1974):92-93, TGM 1 (1905-6):134 & PM 2 (1893-94):170-71 (Tyng); TAG 16 (1939-40):101-15 (Norton); R. C. Winthrop, Jr., Evidences of the Winthrops of Groton, Co. Suffolk, England, & of Families in & near that County with Whom They Intermarried, 1894-96 (later part of J. J. Muskett, Suffolk Manorial Families, vol. 1 (1900) (Downing, Winthrop, Sharpe, Browne); GDNE 3, 166 (Arthur Mason), 355 (Nicholas Parker). See also SHG, volumes for 1755 (John Adams, Jr.), 1725 (Rev. William Smith), 1708 (John Quincy), & 1653 (Rev. Thomas Shepard, Jr.). In addition to royal descent through Mrs. Elizabeth Coytmore Tyng, Mrs. Abigail Smith Adams and John Quincy Adams also have likely baronial and royal ancestors through Mrs. Margaret (Es)Touteville Shepard. I am unable, however, to trace her Fitzwilliam of Sprotsborough line from readily available printed sources.

RD - Mrs. Elizabeth Coytmore Tyng (J. Q. Adams only)

MP - John & Priscilla (Mullins) Alden, William & Alice (---) Mullins

PW - William & Susanna (Hawkes) Cogswell

PK - Fillmore, Taft, Coolidge (Squire); Coolidge (Cogswell, Bass); two Harrisons (J. Q. only, Wyngate); Coolidge, FDR (J. Q. only, Miles/Myles)

* * *

Thomas Jefferson

Dumas Malone, Jefferson & His Time, vol. 1, Jefferson the Virginian (1948), pp. 3-20, 426-31; GVFT 2:432-41, 450-55 (Jefferson; there is no provable kinship to the Jeaffreson family well treated in M. T. Jeaffreson, Pedigrees of the Jeaffreson Family with Notes & Memoirs, 1922); APP, Alvahn Holmes, The Farrar's Island Family & its English Ancestry, vol. 2 (1979), p. 127 esp. (but the RD of Christopher Branch outlined on pp. 121-22 of this work is erroneous; for the correct such line see the royal descents section of this work), & GVFVM 1:208-32 (Branch); VMHB 4 (1896-7):10-11, GVFWM 4:229-31, HSF 5:86-90, & Dabney N. McLean, Henry Soane, Progenitor of Thomas Jefferson (1985) (Field, Soane); R. I. Randolph, The Randolphs of Virginia: A Compilation of the Descendants of William Randolph of Turkey Island & His Wife Mary Isham of

Bermuda Hundred (1937), pp. 11, 107, 114-15; H. W. Brainard, A Survey of the Ishams in England & America (1938), pp. 81-89 (Randolph), 12-19, 21-22, 32-35, 44-45, 50-55 (Isham); GVFVM 5:27-29, 52-61 (Isham, Randolph, Rogers, Lilburne); MCS3, line 71 (Randolph, Lane); John Nichols, The History & Antiquities of the County of Leicester, vol. 4, part II (1811), p. 870 (Vincent); The Genealogist, New Ser. 2 (1885):229-30 esp. (Borlase); GVFWM 1:453-54 & VGE 369-70 (Brett); Joseph Foster, ed., Pedigrees Recorded at the Heralds' Visitations of the County of Northumberland [1615 & 1666] (1890?), pp. 79 (Lilburne), 93 (Nicholson), 22 (Butler); Robert Surtees, History & Antiquities of the County Palatine of Durham, vol. 2 (1820), p. 54 (Hicks), vol. 3 (1823), p. 49 (Butler), & Transactions of the Cumberland & Westmorland Antiquarian & Archaeological Society, 11, part I (1891), chart opposite p. 24 (Nicholson) & New Ser., 10 (1910):385-86 (Hechstetter). The Lilburne-Hicks-Nicholson-Butler ancestry of Jefferson's immigrant maternal grandmother, Mrs. Jane Rogers Randolph, deserves further investigation for the possibility of royal descent.

RD - William Randolph, Henry Isham, Christopher Branch

* * *

James Madison, Jr.

GVFWM 3:522-26, VVR 695-99 (Madison), WV (Madison, Taylor), GVFVM 5:417-20, GVFT 3:557-59, & VMHB 32 (1924):16-17 (Taylor, Thompson); HVG 671-72, 225-34, 244, 255-59 (Taylor, Conway, Eltonhead); G. H. S. King, Marriages of Richmond County, Virginia, 1668-1853 (1964, abstracts with extensive notes), pp. 43-44, 77, 210, 248, addenda pages B & C (Conway, Thornton), GVFWM 5:19-21 (Thornton), GVFT 3:471-79 (Savage), & W. D. Ligon, Jr., The Ligon Family and Connections, vol. 1 (1947, reprint 1988), pp. 40-41 (Savage, Thornton, Conway); D. A. Avant, Jr., Florida Pioneers and Their Alabama, Georgia, Carolina, Maryland and Virginia Ancestors (1974), pp. 170-76, 431-38 & VMHB 3 (1895-96):60-66 (Catlett, Gaines, Underwood), & APP 564 (Mrs. Elizabeth Underwood Taylor Slaughter Catlett Butler). The identification of the second wife of Edwin Conway, Jr., as Elizabeth Thornton (not Thompson, as in HVG 231-32) is based, finally, on the Francis Thornton, Sr. Bible record at the Virginia Historical Society. For a discussion of Madison's once believed Todd-Gorsuch descent, now very doubtful, see TAG 59 (1983):3.

RD - Mrs. Martha Eltonhead Conway, Anthony Savage (unproved)
PK - Taylor (Taylor, Thornton)

* * *

James Monroe

GVFWM 3:742-52 (from WM 2:13 [1933])(Monroe) & GVFT 3:800-5 (from T 5+8 [1924, 1927])(Tyler & Jones, pp. 800, 803 esp.); TAG 46 (1970):182-84 (Monroe). Proof that the president's great-great-grandfather, Andrew Monroe/Munro of St. Mary's Co., Md. 1642-47, & later of Westmoreland Co., Va., was not the younger "Mr." Andrew Munro, second son of David Munro of Katewell & Agnes Munro of Durness, & rector of St. Luke's Church, Newport Parish, Isle of Wight Co., Va., who died intestate in 1719, is found in Clan Munro Magazine, No. 6, 1959-60, pp. 14-18 ("An Unsolved Problem: President James Monroe's Scottish Ancestry" by George H. S. King, author also of the WM & TAG articles cited above). Andrew Monroe/Munro of St. Mary's Co. is of unknown origin although some affiliation with the Munros of Foulis was believed by the president & seems likely.

* * *

Andrew Jackson

NGSQ 53(1965):251-62, 55(1967):21-28, 253-57, 57(1969):298-303, 59(1971):89-90, & EIHC 8(1866):118-23 (Jackson); Marion Emerson Murphy, **Early Leslies in York County, South Carolina, Their Migrations to Tennessee, Missouri, & Arkansas, Their Ancestry & Descendants**, 3rd ed., 1976, pp. 7-11b (Hutchinson, Leslie). Also useful, but not without likely errors (as regards the president's patrilineal connections esp.), is Appendix I, Genealogical Charts, of **The Papers of Andrew Jackson, Volume I, 1770-1803** (1980), S. B. Smith & H. C. Owsley, eds.

* * *

Martin Van Buren

TAG 35(1959):73-75 (G. E. McCracken), which cites 1913 Van Buren, 1912 Van Deursen, 1909 Quackenbush & 1939 Waterman (vol. 1, for Van Buren patrilineal kindred with the surname Bloemendaal) genealogies by H. C. W. Van Buren Peckham, A. H. Van Deusen, A. S. Quackenbush & E. F. Waterman (& D. L. Jacobus) respectively, plus NYGBR articles on Van Buren (vol. 28:1897), Van Deursen (30:1899 & 65:1934), Hoes (31:1900), Van Hoesen (51:1920), & Van Ness-Van Den Burchgraeff (72:1941), TAG 33 (1957) on Meynders, & **Americana** 27 (1933) on Van Schaick. The 1913 Van Buren genealogy contains extensive Hoes, Van Alstyne, Van Deusen & Van Ness data, & the 1912 Van Deusen genealogy, extensive Hoes, Van Alstyne & Van Buren data. See also FSA 155 esp. (Wyngaart), NYGBR 109(1978):215-16 (Van Deursen Dutch origins), Lester Van Alstine, **Van Alstyne-Van Alstine Family History**, vol. 3 (1981), pp. 27-28, 38, 115 esp., & G. R. Quackenbush, **The Quackenbush Family in America** (1987), pp. 3-8.

PK - T. Roosevelt (Van Schaick, Wyngaart, Van Hoesen); F. D. Roosevelt (Van Deu[r]sen)

* * *

William Henry Harrison and Benjamin Harrison

C. P. Keith, **The Ancestry of Benjamin Harrison** (1893), much expanded or amplified in GVFVM 3:687-947, esp. 687-92, 695-98, 708-16, 718-21, 729-45, 766-68, 807, 810, 936-47 (Harrison, 1922-32, 1946); Walter C. Metcalfe, **The Visitations of Northamptonshire Made in 1564 & 1618-19, with Northamptonshire Pedigrees from Various Harleian MSS** (1887), pp. 98 (Harrison of Gobions Manor), 3 (Bernard of Abington) & Mrs. Napier Higgins, **The Bernards of Abington & Nether Winchendon: A Family History**, 2 vols. (1903), esp. vol. 1, p. 39; WV (Burwell, Higginson, Smith, Bacon, with Bedell & Woodward notes, Bassett, Cary) & APP (Burwell, Taylor-Cary); R. R. Carter & R. I. Randolph, **The Carter Tree** (1951), pp. 3, 77-79 (President Benjamin Harrison is #541355) & Noel Currer-Briggs, **The Carters of Virginia: Their English Ancestry** (1979), pp. 102-04 esp.; H. F. Seversmith, **Colonial Families of Long Island, New York, & Connecticut**, vol. 5 (**The Ancestry of Roger Ludlow**, vol. 1) (1964), pp. 2095-2100; VMHB 2(1894-95):430-33 & VGE 651-52 (Landon); Fairfax Harrison, **The Virginia Carys** (1919, well abstracted for the Bassett-Harrison descent in WV & APP);

GVFWM 1:813-19 (Churchill), 105-8 (Armistead) & HSF 2:3-7 (Armistead) (ancestry of W. H. Harrison); J. A. Vinton, The Symmes Memorial (1873), pp. 1-24, 33-34, 44-45, 61-64, 89-92, 119-20 & TAG 12(1935-36):67-69 (Symmes), AB (Chickering, Fiske), Charles Hatch, Genealogy of the Descendants of Anthony Collamer of Scituate, Massachusetts (1915), pp. 9, 21 esp., plus further English Collamore research by Mr. Douglas Richardson of Bethany, Oklahoma; Hamilton Wilson Welch, "Early Families of Scituate & Neighboring Towns," MSS. at NEHGS (Thomas & Isaac Chittenden) & NEHGR 6(1852):186 (Anna Vinal[l], reprinted in MSR 535); C. B. Moore, Town of Southold, Long Island, Personal Index Prior to 1698 & Index of 1698 (1868), p. 66 esp. (Cle[a]ves), NYGBR 29(1898):123-27, 217-18 (Tuthill, reprinted in GLIF 2:481-85, 488-89) & 33(1902):71-73 (King, reprinted in GLIF 1:493-95), RM (Tuthill, King, Horton, Wells, Hallock), WB (Wines, Terry), H. D. & A. H. White, The Hortons in America (1929), pp. 1, 137-39, 407-8, L. H. Hallock, A Hallock Genealogy (1920), pp. 532-33, 621, 145, NGSQ 63(1975):22-24, & C. E. W. Jacques & A. W. C. Kappenberg, Luce on Long Island (1979), pp. 4-5 (the last two items on Mrs. Sarah Wines Horton Luce; collectively the ancestry of Mrs. W. H. Harrison); Biographical Annals of Franklin County, Pennsylvania (1905), pp. 80, 84-85, 91-92, 102, 106-7 (McDowell, Irwin, Harrison) & Your Family Tree [a central Pa. journal] 24(1978):85-86 (McDowell). Note also that Rev. Timothy Symmes was a 1733 graduate of Harvard College.

RD - Mrs. Sarah Ludlow Carter, Anthony Collamore (highly probable, not fully proved, a forebear of Benjamin only)
PK - J. Q. Adams (Wyngate); Tyler (Armistead); Carter? (Carter); Taft, Harding (King-Benjamin only); Coolidge (Fiske-Benjamin only); Ford (Wines-Benjamin only)

* * *

John Tyler (IV)

L. G. Tyler, The Letters & Times of the Tylers, vol. 3 (1896), Appendix H, pp. 209-21 esp. (Tyler, Armistead, Shields, Marot), considerably amplified and extended by GVFT 3:776-77 (Tyler); GVFVM 1:784-89 & Omnibus 7 (1986, journal of the Augustan Society):102-9 (Chiles); R. C. M. Page, Genealogy of the Page Family in Virginia, 2nd ed. (1893), pp. 9-26 & APP (Lukin, Page, Chiles, Tyler); WM 1st Ser. 17 (1908-09):264-67 & VGE 43-44 (Jarrett, Lowe); CFSSA (Armistead, Shields) & GVFWM 1:105-7, 120-21, 132-33 (Armistead), 447, 449-50 (Bray, Booth), 4:430-33 (Shields, Marot). See also HSF 2:3-5, 10 (Armistead), VWR 871-76 (Sherwood, Jarrett), 431 (Marot), & VVR 74 (Booth).

PK - Harrisons (Armistead)

* * *

James Knox Polk

NEHGR 77 (1923):133-37, 140-45, 221-23, 78 (1924):329 (Polk); Hattie S. Goodman, The Knox Family: A Genealogical & Biographical Sketch of the Descendants of John Knox of Rowan County, North Carolina, & Other Knoxes (1905), pp. 30-37, 113-18, 121-25. For Mary Wilson, the President's paternal grandmother, see Rev. Jethro Rumple, A History of Rowan County, North Carolina (1881, reprint 1974), pp. 123-25, J. B. Alexander, Biographical Sketches of the Early Settlers of the Hopewell Section (1897), pp. 65-69, & Worth S. Lay, The Mecklenburg Signers & Their Neighbors [part III of The

Lost Tribes of North Carolina] (1946, reprint 1962), pp. 503-11, 533, all three of which contain errors. The Mecklenburg Winslows were not Beverly descendants (see John McGill, The Beverley Family of Virginia [1956], pp. 812, 821 esp.), & no descent from the noted Massachusetts family can be proved, although a Joseph Winslow "of Boston, mariner" was associated with Perquimans Co., N. C. (see MF 2:19-20). For Lydia Gillespie, Polk's maternal grandmother, & her parents (Thomas & Naomi [--] Gillespie) see W. L. Lingle, Thyatira Presbyterian Church, Rowan County, N. C. (1753-1948) (n. d.), pp. 21-22, R. W. Ramsey, Carolina Cradle: Settlement of the Northwest Carolina Frontier, 1747-1762 (1964), pp. 40-41, Brent H. Holcomb, Marriages of Rowan County, North Carolina, 1753-1868 (1981), p. 229, & Jo White Linn, Abstracts of Wills & Estate Records of Rowan County, North Carolina, 1753-1805, & Tax Lists of 1759 & 1778 (1980), pp. 90, 144. The ancestry of the immigrant Capt. Robert Pollock or Polk & his wife Magdalen Tasker should be investigated further for possible noble, royal, or ancient Scottish descent.

* * *

Zachary Taylor

HVG 671-73, 675-77, 683-84, GVFVM 5:417-20, GVFT 3:557-59 & WV (Taylor); VMHB 32 (1924):16-17 (Taylor, Thompson); E. J. Lee, Lee of Virginia, 1642-1892 (1895, reprint 1974), pp. 49-65, 518-31, DAB (Richard Lee), VMHB 62 (1954):3-49, NGSQ 76(1988):253-67 (William Thorndale on the Lee English origins), & Walter C. Metcalfe, ed., The Visitation of the County of Worcester, 1682/1683 (1883), p. 53 (Hancock); TVG 32(1988):83-89, 176-78, 295-96, & forthcoming installments, & MQ 47(1981):14-18 (Allerton); E. C. B. Jones, The Brewster Genealogy, 1566-1907, vol. 1 (1908), pp. 3-7, 24-26, 38-39, 52-53, 81-82, 132-33, 251-53 & M. E. Terry & A. B. Harding, A Notebook on the Descendants of Elder William Brewster of Plymouth Colony (1985), pp. 1-2, 7, 28, TAG 41 (1965):1-7, 63 & J. G. Hunt, Of Mary Brewster, the Identity of Mary, Wife of Elder William Brewster of the Mayflower, 2 vols. (1984-85, on whether she might be Mary Wentworth or Mary Wyrall, hypotheses that remain unproved & perhaps unlikely); APP (Willoughby, Allerton, Lee, Taylor); Thomas McAdory Owen, William Strother of Virginia & His Descendants (1898) (from Publications of the Southern History Association for April, 1898), pp. 27-32, 37-40, 43-45 (& Dabney note pp. 37-38 esp.), GVFT 3:371-78, 380-82, 385-87, HSF 5:290-91, Lineage Book, Descendants of the Illegitimate Sons & Daughters of the Kings of Britain, No. 76, & The [New] History of Northumberland, vol. 11 (1922), pp. 132-34 (Strother, including alleged English ancestry & royal descent); GVFWM 5:19-21 (Thornton), GVFT 3:471-79 (likely Savage English origins, which also may lead to a royal descent), & W. D. Ligon, The Ligon Family & Connections, vol. 1 (1947, reprint 1988), pp. 40-41 (Savage, Thornton, Strother).

RD - William Strother, Anthony Savage (both unproved)
MP - Isaac Allerton, William & Mary (--) Brewster
PK - Madison (Taylor, Thornton), FDR (Allerton)

* * *

Millard Fillmore

TAG 63 (1988):46-55 (G. B. Roberts), the most recent TAG presidential AT, & sources cited therein, esp. Charles L. Fillmore, So Soon Forgotten: Three Thousand Fillmores (1984), PT (Tilton) & AS (Littlefield), TM (Day, Rowe, Jeggles, Langton, Varney, not authoritative), Dorothy Rudd DuMond, Some Ancestors & Descendants of **Joseph Rudd, Jr., 1740-1818, & His Wife, Sarah Story, 1744-1842, of Bennington, Vt.** (1982) (Wood, Hazen, Rudd, Post, Hyde, Story, Foster, Emerson, Perkins, & Wainwright, covering, but not authoritatively, the entire known American ancestry of Mrs. Hepzibah Wood Fillmore, the president's paternal grandmother), DSGRM 23 (1959-60):5-10, 57-58, 95-97, 26 (1962):22-24, 51-52 (Millard, by F. D. McTeer, F. C. Warner, & R. K. Lee), Ruth S. D. Eddy, **The Eddy Family in America** (1930), Timothy Hopkins, **John Hopkins of Cambridge, Mass., 1634, & Some of His Descendants** (1932), & NH 1181 (Messenger), 1549-52 (Royce). Other pivotal sources are TG 9(1988):90-159 (Wood), T. E. Hazen & D. L. Jacobus, **The Hazen Family in America** (1947), GAF (Rudd, Morgan), DG2 (Post, Olmstead, Loomis), DW (Foster, Perkins, Hathorne), AB (Butler), NEHGR 67 (1913):248-60 (Hathorne), 262-29 (Sewell) (reprinted in EO 1:1:267-79, 281-88), 36 (1882):52 (Sabin), 99 (1945):242-44 (Wright), 122 (1968):274-77 (Royce, reprinted in EO 2:3:42-45), TAG 21 (1944-45):123-33, 30 (1954):100-3 (Hunt), 38 (1962):193-204 (Bronson, by J. I. Coddington), 40(1964):188-89 (Post), 60 (1984):27-32 (Mrs. Elizabeth Olmstead Butler, by R. D. Joslyn), & UGHM 20 (1929):56-61 (Loomis, Lingwood, Marlar). Noble connections might be traced through Fillmore's probable Loomis, Lingwood & Marlar descents or the possible Swallow, Grey & Whitbred forebears of Mrs. Philippa Sewell Wainwright.

PW - James & Margery (Hill) Morgan
PK - 2 Adamses, Taft, Coolidge (Squire); Grant, Cleveland, Ford (White); Cleveland, Ford (Hyde); Coolidge, FDR (Perkins); Hoover, Ford (Wood); Coolidge (Littlefield); Taft (Emerson); Bush (Millard)

* * *

Franklin Pierce

TAG 55 (1979):142-45 (Edward F. Holden), undoubtedly taken, at least in part, from F. B. Pierce & F. C. Peirce, **Pierce Genealogy, Being the Record of the Posterity of Thomas Pierce, an Early Inhabitant of Charlestown** (1882), pp. 17-23, 27, 38, 55-57, 91-100, 166-70; SE 1:257-98 (Pierce, Cole, Parker, Fletcher, Bates, Richardson & Underwood, the entire known American ancestry of Benjamin Pierce, the president's grandfather), Winifred Lovering Holman, "Descendants of Robert Fletcher: The First Six Generations" (1950), typescript at NEHGS, pp. 1-17, 36-48, 93-104, SH (Richardson, Underwood), & NEHGR 139 (1985):147-48 (Duxford); Samuel Merrill, **A Merrill Memorial**, vol. 1 (1917-28), pp. 159-64, 173-74, 212; PA (Merrill, Webster, Shatswell, Emery), BG (Bodwell, Emery, Shatswell), J. E. Burns, **The Revised Genealogical Records of the Descendants of John Emery of Newbury, Massachusetts** (1982), pp. 16-19, 21-22, 33, 58, NEHGR 52 (1898):51, 321 (Batt, reprinted in EO 2:1:145-46), & TAG 17 (1940-41):96-99 (Emery) & 32 (1956):197-201 (Wolterton); I. B. Dodge, **Kenrick, Kendrick, Kindrick, Some of the Descendants of John Kenrick the Immigrant** (1894), pp. 2-7; E. A. Bowen, **Lineage of the Bowens of Woodstock, Connecticut** (1897), pp. 3-95, 100-112, GWF 2:502-7 (Bowen), GWF 7:147-49 (Johnson), SM 1 (Johnson), DG 1 (Brewer), & FCW (Morrill); **Records of Littleton, Mass.** (1900), p. 35 (Harris), BH (Harris, Mason), ESR 272-74 (Pearson), AL (Angier), GGE 209-10, etc. (Rogers), & NEHGR 64 (1910):51-61 (reprinted in EO 1:1:56-66) (Ray).

RD - Griffith & Margaret (Fleming) Bowen
PK - Hayes, Bush (Brewer); Hoover?, Coolidge (Richardson); Hoover (Pearson); FDR (Johnson)

* * *

James Buchanan, Jr.

G. T. Curtis, Life of James Buchanan, Fifteenth President of the United States, vol. 1 (1883), pp. 1-4, & Philip S. Klein, President James Buchanan, a Biography (1962), pp. 1-4, 431 (this last a partial genealogical bibliography); NGSQ 24(1936):85-87, 25 (1937):14-15, 67, & John Guthrie Smith, Strathendrick & Its Inhabitants from Early Times (1896), pp. 283-86, 309-10, 346-47, 350-52 (the traditional patrilineal descent, which is undocumented, passes through one unknown generation, a --- Buchanan, possible son of Thomas of Ramelton or Rathmelton & possible father of John of Ramelton or Rathmelton, the president's grandfather, & requires further research) & The Parish of Strathbane (1886), pp. 104-10. See also TAG 52 (1976): 27, 59 (1983): 3, 61 (1985-86): 172 (& sources cited therein), plus, for the highly probable royal descent of the Buchanans of Carbeth, Gartincaber, Blairlusk & Ramelton/Rathmelton, an unpublished AT for John Buchanan of Cartincaber, b. 1545 (son of Thomas Buchanan of Carbeth & Janet Buchanan of that Ilk), prepared by Charles F. H. Evans & Andrew B. W. MacEwen. For Jane Russell, the president's paternal grandmother, see Russell Register 6 (1983-84):763-64; further data is being collected by Mr. George Ely Russell of Middletown, Md.

RD - James Buchanan (father, unproved)

* * *

Abraham Lincoln

The Lincoln Kinsman, Nos. 1-54 (1938-42), esp. nos. 1 (July 1938-Lincoln), 3 (Sept. 1938-Herring, Harrison) & 23 (May 1940-Salter, Bowne, Holmes) & DSGRM 3 (1939-40):97-100, 4 (1940-41):93-96 (Lincoln's known ancestry to that time); Waldo Lincoln, History of the Lincoln Family (1923), pp. 1-9, 14-23, 43-53, 92-103, 193-204, 333-42, 464-71, J. H. Lea & J. R. Hutchinson, The Ancestry of Abraham Lincoln (1909), esp. pp. 61-62, TAG 11 (1934-35):137-38, 193-94 (Lincoln-Gilman), AL 151-58 (Gilman), & NYGBR 60 (1929):115-17 (Lincoln-Lyford); Lincoln Herald 79 (1977):146-49 (Lyford), 63 (1961):134-37 (Flowers, Barnard-both articles by David S. Keiser); NEHGR 113 (1959):42-45 (Jones), 143 (1989): 125-29, 131-33 (Jones, Lincoln, by Ethel F. Smith), & C. H. Farnam, History of the Descendants of John Whitman of Weymouth, Mass. (1889), pp. 1-13; HGM 4:176-87 (Salter, Lincoln), 3:29-36, 51 (Bowne), TAG 19 (1942-43):166-67 (Bowne), J. T. Holmes, The American Family of Rev. Obadiah Holmes (1915), pp. 11-77, ALR (Holmes), NEHGR 64 (1910):237-39, 67 (1913):21-23 (Holmes, reprinted in EO 1:1:76-80), & F. L. Weis, The Colonial Clergy & the Colonial Churches of New England (1936), pp. 108, 130 (Holmes, Lyford); J. H. Harrison, Settlers by the Long Grey Trail: Some Pioneers to Old Augusta County, Virginia, & Their Descendants, of the Family of Harrison & Allied Lines (1935, reprint 1975), pp. 269-90, 122-23 (Herring, Harrison); Adin Baber, The Hanks Family of Virginia & Westward (1965, the last and most comprehensive of Mr. Baber's various books on the Nancy Hanks ancestry), #s 2, 4, 11, 16, 17, 22, 25, 29, 33, 37, 43, 45, 47-49 of The Lincoln Kinsman, edited by Louis A. Warren, & correspondence from R. M. Bell, D. S. Keiser & Ralph E. Pearson (Hanks); L. P. Shipley, The Shipleys of Maryland (1968), pp. 5-9, 371-74, & Indiana Magazine of History 29 (1933):203-12 (Shipley); W. K. & A. C. Z. Rutherford, Genealogical History of Our Ancestors, vol. 1 (1977), pp. 737-38, 740-43, 769-73 (Shipley, Stevens), J. D. Warfield, The Founders of Anne

Arundel & Howard Counties, Maryland (1905, reprint 1980), pp. 69, 161 (Stevens, Norwood), H. W. Newman, To Maryland from Overseas (1982), p. 130, & A. R. Maddison, Lincolnshire Pedigrees, vol. 2 (PHSVS 51, 1903), p. 729 (Norwood). The ancestry of both Nancy Hanks & Bathsheba (Herring?), Lincoln's mother and paternal grandmother, is conjectural, and the AT herein merely reports the opinions of leading authorities. Lincoln's Shipley, Stevens & Norwood lines are possible, perhaps even likely, but I can find no evidence at all of Dorsey or Howard descent.

PK - Ford, Bush (Gilman)

* * *

Andrew Johnson

Jerry L. Cross, The Andrew Johnson Birthplace: a Documentary Research Report (with data on parents), prepared for the Raleigh Historical Properties Commission, 1976 (available at the Research Branch, Archaeology & Historic Preservation Section, Division of Archives & History, North Carolina Department of Cultural Resources, Raleigh), which supersedes two typescripts also at NCDCR, "The Genealogy of Andrew Johnson, the Seventeenth President of the United States, November 1958," compiled by Ferol Frost Hubbs, & "Andrew Johnson, 17th President of the United States: Records of Hazel Graves Hansrote," 1959. The president's father, Jacob Johnson, is of unknown origin; the origin given for him in W. S. & M. Y. Junkin, The Henckel Genealogy, 1500-1960 (1964), pp. 227-28, 269, was disproved in the Henckel Genealogical Bulletin (Mrs. Bert Harter, ed.), vol. 4, #2, Fall 1973, pp. 153-60. For the parents (Andrew McDonough, Jr. & ---) & paternal grandparents (Andrew McDonough & possibly Mary ---) of Mary "Polly" McDonough, the president's mother, see The North Carolina Genealogical Society Journal 7 (1981):160-62.

* * *

Ulysses Simpson Grant

TAG 51 (1975):231-41, 52 (1976):88-90, 248, 53 (1977):216 (G. E. McCracken), which cites, among other sources, the 1898 Grant, 1927 Simpson, 1915 Huntington, 1884 Lo-Lathrop, & 1899 Delano genealogies by A. H. Grant, H. A. Simpson, E. B. Huntington (author of both the Huntington & Lo-Lathrop works) & J. A. Delano, respectively. Since publication of McCracken's next-to-last presidential AT there have appeared K. W. Bate, The Ebenezer Hanks Story (1982) (Delano, Mahieu, Warren, Walker, Clark, Hatch, Rowley, Allen, Partridge, Tracy, Lee, the entire known ancestry of Mrs. Susanna Delano Grant), J. A. Miner, Thomas Minor Descendants, 1608-1981 (1981), pp. 15-19, NEHGR 138 (1984):182-85 or NYGBR 115 (1984):163-65 (Minor English origins), R. S. Wakefield, J. A. Beebe & others, Richard Warren of the Mayflower & His Descendants for Four Generations, 3rd ed. (a MFIP pamphlet) (1989), pp. 1, 5-6, 27-28, 115-16 (Warren, Delano), & NEHGR 143(1989):195-200. For other New England ancestors of Grant see TAG 16 (1939-40):49-53, 122, 17 (1940-41):86-87, 18 (1941-42):56-60 (Porter), TCB (White, Lathrop, House, Scudder), H. W. Palmer, "Palmer Families in America" (typescript, n. d.), pp. 1-10, D. L. Jacobus, The Genealogy of the Booth Family (1952), pp. 1-3, HH (Huntington, Baret or Barrett), S. C. Millett, Pedigree of Rockwell & Allied Families (1973?), C. A. Hayden, The Capen Family (1929), pp. 11-15, GGE 1068-70 (Capen, Purchase), & W. P. W. Phillimore, E. R. Nevill & T. M. Blagg, Dorset Parish Registers: Marriages, vol. 7 (1914), p. 3

(Oliver Purchas & Thomesin Harris). Note also the Grant & Rockwell sections of Burton W. Spear, **Search for the Passengers of the Mary & John, 1630**, 10 vols. (1985-87).

MP - Richard Warren
PK - Fillmore, Cleveland, Ford (White); FDR, Bush (Lathrop, Mahieu); FDR (Delano, Huntington); Coolidge (Capen)

* * *

Rutherford Birchard Hayes

TAG 56 (1980):160-169, 230-36, the most authoritative TAG AT by G. E. McCracken, based largely on SS, which covers the bulk of the American ancestry of Hayes' father, esp. the Hayes, Russell, Whiting, Trowbridge, Rutherford, Smith, Chandler & Hale families; **TAG** 52 (1976):140-41 (R. C. Anderson on the illegitimate Roger Cornwall alias Birchard, Hayes' maternal grandfather); & **FCW** (covering the entire known American ancestry of Mrs. Drusilla Austin Birchard, Hayes's maternal grandmother). Also notable, & cited by either McCracken or in my original bibliography, are 1884 Hayes, 1910 Russell, 1908 Trowbridge, 1883 Chandler, 1952 Hale-House & 1969 Austin genealogies (by C. W. Hayes, G. W. Russell, F. B. Trowbridge, George Chander, E. F. Waterman & D. L. Jacobus, & Edith Austin Moore respectively), & M. P. Kuhns, **The "Mary and John": a Story of the Founding of Dorchester, Mass., 1630** (1943), pp. 154, 156-57 (Phelps, Merrick, Day), this last much expanded & improved in Burton W. Spear, **Search for the Passengers of the Mary & John, 1630**, 10 vols. (1985-87). For the ancestry of Sarah Jacob, mother of Roger Cornwall alias Birchard see the Mansfield, Conn. vital records (Jacob), M. L. Atkinson, **Annual Report of the Lindsay Family Association of America for 1912** (1913?), pp. 209-11, 214 (Lindsey), EA 3 (1899):49 (Alley), FCW (Storrs, Huckins, Wells, Worden), Ebenezer Burgess, **Burgess Genealogy** (1865), pp. 9-12, 18, & **TAG** 61 (1985-86):69. Note also **TAG** 57 (1981):31-33 (on Hayes' royal descent through Thomas Trowbridge of Conn.) & 58 (1982):223-28 (Mrs. Grace Martin Phelps).

RD - Thomas Newberry (unproved) & Thomas Trowbridge
PW - Mrs. Elizabeth Charde Cooke Ford
PK - Taft, Nixon, Bush (Foote); Pierce, Bush (Brewer); Cleveland, FDR (Charde); Cleveland, Bush (S. Smith); Cleveland (Day); FDR (Ashley, Burgess, Chandler); Ford (Newberry, Farnum)

* * *

James Abram Garfield

Proceedings of the Massachusetts Historical Society 19 (1881-82):83-94 (reprinted as **Concerning President Garfield's Ancestry, a Communication from the Rev. Edward G. Porter**, 1881) & G. F. Hoar, **President Garfield's New England Ancestry** (1882); W. D. Bridge, **Genealogy of the John Bridge Family in America, 1632-1924** (1924), pp. 413-24, 2-5, 28-43 (Garfield, Bridge), NGSQ 27 (1939):65-69 (Edward Garfield), DG 1 (Danforth), Patricia Bigelow, ed. **The Bigelow Family Genealogy, Volume 1** (1986), pp. 4-10, 13-14, 29-30, & AB (Bigelow, Warren, Flagg); W. A. Davis, **The Early Records of the Town of Lunenburg, Massachusetts...1719-1764** (1896), pp. 229, 250, 306, 347 (Johnson) & **NEHGR** 137 (1983):326 (on Mrs. Sarah Bryant Stimpson Garfield, the president's great-grandmother, whose parentage cannot be proved & who was probably not, as has been alleged, the Sarah Bryant born at Stoneham, Mass. 2 Nov. 1741, daughter of Joseph & Sarah [Gould] Bryant). The parentage of

Garfield's paternal grandmother, Mrs. Asenath Hill Garfield Boynton, also cannot be proved; for initial "clues for further research," however, see J. F. & C. H. Boynton, The Boynton Family (1897), pp. 222-23, Biographical Review Publishing Co., Biographical Sketches of the Leading Citizens of Otsego County, New York (1893), pp. 188-90 (biography of Jacob B. Hill, a great-nephew), & Crisfield Johnson, History of Cuyahoga County, Ohio (1879), pp. 495-97 (biography of Amos Boynton, Asenath's second husband). The known ancestry of Garfield's mother is treated in Adin Ballou, History & Genealogy of the Ballous in America (1898), pp. 3-17, 22-25, 39-43, 78-81, 182-87, 431-33; GDRI (Pike, Whitman); E. S. Arnold, The Arnold Memorial (1935), p. 86 & Rhode Island Genealogical Register 3(1980-81):239, which show that the Catherine Arnold, born at Pawtucket, R. I. 28 Feb. 1690, daughter of Elisha Arnold & Susanna Carpenter, married Ebenezer Bates, not James Ballou, Jr.; Myrtle M. Jillson, "Walter Cook[e] Genealogy" (1940) (typescript at NEHGS), pp. 1-3, 5, 16 & SB (Rockwood); Charles Burleigh, The Genealogy & History of the Ingalls Family in America (1903, reprint 1984), pp. 17-20, 24, 31-32, 46-47, TM (Ludden), JN (Holbrook), H. S. Cole, Hayden Samuel Cole & His Ancestry (1935), pp. 60-63 (Wheeler, Squire, West), PA (Ingalls, Dominick Wheeler), MAF (William Allen, Goodale), & E. J. Paul, The Ancestry of Katharine Choate Paul, Now Mrs. William J. Young, Jr. (1914), p. 179 (Squire); A. B. Carpenter, A Genealogical History of the Rehoboth Branch of the Carpenter Family in America (1898), pp. 38-43, 45-46, 58, 74, 123-24, 238, ALR (Carpenter), & SM 1 (Carpenter, Weeks, Clapp); MQ 46 (1980):14-15, 196, 49 (1983):174-78 (Martin, Billington), Harriet Woodbury Hodge, John Billington of the Mayflower & His Descendants for Five Generations (1988, a MFIP pamphlet), pp. 1-6, 13-14, 27, 77-78 (Billington, Martin, Carpenter), CCAD (George Thompson), & Rehoboth vital records (family of John & Elizabeth [---] Thompson)

MP - John, Elinor & Francis Billington

PK - Hoover, Ford, Bush (Wheeler); Taft, Bush (Holbrook); Taft (W. Cooke, Rockwood); Coolidge (Martin); Bush (Carpenter)

* * *

Chester Alan Arthur

Proceedings of the Vermont Historical Society, New Ser., 9 (1941):3-13 & Vermont History 38 (1970):177-88, 291-304 (on Arthur's birthplace, parents, & patrilineal Scots-Irish background); James A. B. Stone, The Piermont Branch of the Stone Family, n. d., pp. 1-2, 5, & R. C. Stevens, Ancestry of the Children of Robert Croll Stevens & Jane Eleanor (Knauss) Stevens, vol. 1: The Genealogy of Otho Stevens, 1702-1771, Together with Kent, Hills, Hastings, Smith, Proctor, Sproule, & Associated Lines (1982), pp. xxx (a chart of Arthur's ancestry for five generations by David Curtis Dearborn, who collected Arthur ancestral data for several years & first introduced me to several of the sources herein cited), 1.1-1.11, 1.14-1.16, 2.1-2.4, 3.1-3.2, 4.1-4.3 (Stevens, Kent, Penny, Lufkin, authoritatively covering the entire known ancestry of Capt. Simeon Stevens, Arthur's mother's mother's father, based in part on research undertaken by Mrs. Winifred Lovering Holman Dodge for Robert Hastings Stevens & now part of the Holman Dodge MSS. collection at NEHGS); Charlotte Helen Abbott, "Early Records of Families in Andover," (typescript in 14 vols. at NEHGS, original at the Andover Historical Society), Stone & Foster sections (vols. 13 & 6 respectively), plus Andover, Gloucester & Haverhill VRs (Hugh, Jr., Benjamin & Uriah Stone); S. P. Hadley, Genealogical Record of the Descendants of Moses Hadley

& Rebecca Page of Hudson, N. H. (1887), pp. 7-22, 25-26, 28 & L. H. Proctor, John Proctor of Ipswich & Some of His Descendants (1985), pp. 6-7; TAG 58 (1982):193-204, 59 (1983):17-18 (D. L. Greene on Salem "witch" Mrs. Susanna North Martin), F. L. Weis, The Colby Family in Early America (1970), pp. 3-4, 7-10, 15-16, 27-28, 45-46, E. F. Dunbar, The Flanders Family from Europe to America (1935), pp. 23-26, 42-44, HSA (esp. Carter & Hoyt), & PA (Colby, Parratt, Northend)

Salem "witch" ancestor - Mrs. Susanna North Martin
Salem "wizard" connection - Mrs. Mary Proctor Hadley, sister of "wizard" John Proctor, Jr.

* * *

(Stephen) Grover Cleveland

Eben Putnam, New England Ancestry of Grover Cleveland, President of the United States of America (1892), first published in PM 1 (1892-93):153-65, esp. charts I-VI, which does not, however, cover the forebears of Caleb Abell, Abiel Marshall (whose parentage remains unknown), or Mrs. Ruth Stebbins Hitchcock, & which is either based upon, or much amplified by, E. J. & H. G. Cleveland, The Genealogy of the Cleveland & Cleaveland Families, 3 vols. (1899), pp. 23-32, 36-39, 60-62, 108-16, 227-32, 504-5, 1088-89, 1782-92, 2420-21 (Cleveland, Winn, with notes on various maternal lines); Josephine C. Frost, Ancestors of Frank Herbert Davol & His Wife Phebe Downing Willits (1925), pp. 198-99 & Floyd E. Neikirk, "Ohio Descendants of Seventeenth Century Ancestors: a Sequel to 'The Genealogy of Clark Rathbun Cleveland'," typescript at NEHGS (1960?), pp. 100-1 esp., which cites Leyden betrothal records edited by D. Plooig & J. R. Harmes for the marriage of Roger Wilson, grandfather of Mrs. Dorcas Wilson Cleveland, & Elizabeth Williams (not --- Fuller); SM 1 (Waters, Linton), TAG 56 (1980):25-28 (Hudson), & NEHGR 71 (1917):236-51 (Josselyn, reprinted in EO 1:1:476-91); TAG 16 (1939-40):49-53, 122, 17 (1940-41):86-87, 18 (1941-42):56-60, 29 (1953):210 (Porter), GM 2 (Robert White), H. P. Andrews, The Descendants of John Porter of Windsor, Conn., 1635-39, 2 vols (1893), pp. 1-5, 16-17, 67-68, 184, 339-41, 492-93, 685-86 (with notes on the ancestry of various Porter & Cleveland spouses), & NEHGR 129 (1975):198-220 (Porters of Hadley); I. P. Warren, The Stanley Families of America, (1887), pp. 285-90, FNE 299, 341-45 (Stanley, Tritton), & D. L. Jacobus & A. B. Dayton, The Early Daytons & Descendants of Henry, Jr. (1959), pp. 3-4; FCW & TAG 56 (1980):166, 230 (Hayes AT #s 118-19, 236-39; Cooke, Westwood); FM (Sewall, Pyldren-Dummer), M. Halsey Thomas, ed., The Diary of Samuel Sewall, 1674-1729, Volume II, 1709-1729 (1973), Genealogical Appendix, pp. 1071-75, 1080-81, & NEHGR 35 (1881):254-71, 321-31 (Dummer, reprinted in EO 2:1:699-727); PG (Mitchell) & G. F. Shepard & D. L. Jacobus, The Shepard Families of New England, Volume III, Additional Family Groups (1973), p. 293 (Mrs. Margaret Borodell Shepard Mitchell); R. H. Walworth, Hyde Genealogy, 2 vols. (1864), pp. 1-6, 12-13, 23, 65, 95-96, 401-2 & TAG 15 (1938-39):84-86 (Lee, Browne); H. A. & L. P. Abell, The Abell Family in America (1940), pp. 39-46, 49-52, 58 & TG 5 (1984):158-71 (Abell); TAG 63 (1988), 51, 53 (Fillmore AT #s 86-87, 172-75; Post, Hyde), N. L. Major, C. W. Post - The Hour and the Man: a Biography with Genealogical Supplement (1963), pp. 227-37, 241-45, & TAG 40 (1964):188-89 (Post); E. P. & T. C. Huff, M. M. B. Uzzell & W. H. Wiegand, The Hough &/or Huff Families in England & America (1962), pp. 67-70 & Mrs. Turney Sharps, "Genealogy of the Calkins Family" (typescript at NEHGS, n. d.), #1 (Hugh & Ann --- Caulkins); NEHGR 108 (1954):39-46, 96-105 (Falley); Mrs.

Edward Hitchcock, The Genealogy of the Hitchcock Family (1894), pp. 203-13, 219, 234-35, G. W. Chapin, The Chapin Book, 2 vols. (1924), pp. 2, 7, 27-28, 116, 327, 719, 1309-10, 1895-96, & SM 1 (Ball, Burt, March, Graves, Samuel Smith); R. S. & R. L. Greenlee, The Stebbins Genealogy, 2 vols. (1904), pp. 51-74, 98-99, 154-56, 198-99, 285-86, 448-49, 715-16, BG (Samuel Wright), HH (Ely, Day, Riley), & TAG 31 (1955):193-201 (Stebbing). I can find no confirmation, & am thus dubious, of Douglas Merritt's tentative identification, in Coxe & Connected Families, 2nd ed. (1915), p. 20, of Abiel Marshall (d. 1758) of Norwich, Conn., as a son of Samuel Marshall (b. 1652) & Rebecca Newberry (1655-1718) of Northampton, Mass. For Cleveland's three ancestors who were Harvard graduates, Revs. Aaron Cleveland III (class of 1735), Aaron Porter (1708) & Jonathan Mitchell (1647), see the appropriate volumes of SHG.

RD - Robert Abell
PW - Mrs. Elizabeth Charde Cooke Ford
PK - Fillmore, Grant, Ford (White); Fillmore, Ford (Hyde, Post or Lee); Hayes, FDR (Charde); Hayes, Bush (S. Smith); Hayes (Day); FDR (Wright); Ford (Sewall); Bush (Stanley); Taft (Chapin); Hoover? (Winn)

* * *

William McKinley, Jr.

William M. Duncan, The North East Duncans: Their Kith & Kin, 1769-1932 (1932), pp. 5-8, 52-61, Duncan-McKinley-Deetrick-Park-Allison chart, & photostatic copies of the Bible records of David, William (Sr.) & William (Jr.) McKinley (a work that completely supersedes The Gathering of the Clan McKinlay at Chicago, Illinois, U. S. A., September 13, 1893 (1894?), E. A. Claypool, The Scotch Ancestors of William McKinley, President of the United States (1897), & the 1897 newspaper articles by Robert C. Bair of York, Pa.); J. L. Ziegler, An Authentic History of Donegal Presbyterian Church Located in East Donegal Township, Lancaster Co., Pa. (1902), pp. 64-66 (McKinley, Gray & Stephenson); Christine Rose, Andrew Rose Family of Bucks County, Pennsylvania & Mercer County, Pennsylvania: the First Five Generations in America (1977), pp. 1-7, 17-18; Ohio Records & Pioneer Families 19 (1978):180-81 (Allison, Campbell); & further material collected by the McKinley Memorial Library, Niles, Ohio, & by Mr. Roger D. Joslyn of New Windsor, N. Y. The president's patrilineal descent beyond David McKinley of York Co., Pa., d. 1760/1, is unknown.

* * *

Theodore Roosevelt, Jr.

NYGBR 85 (1954):196-205 (Howard K. Beale) & sources cited therein (including some of the following, which considerably amplify Mr. Beale's essay & chart), 64 (1933):139-42, 72 (1941):24-26, TAG 19 (1942-43):210-11, & NYGBR 118 (1987):193-99, 201-2, 119 (1988):22-24 (Roosevelt, the last [two] arcticle[s] by T. F. Beard & H. B. Hoff), & C. B. Whittlesey, The Roosevelt Genealogy, 1649-1902 (1902), pp. 3-4, 6-7, 10-12, 21-22, 36-37, 49-50, 68-72, 91-95 (with notes on ancestors of the several Roosevelt wives); Dingman Versteeg, trans., P. R. Christoph, Kenneth Scott, & Kenn Stryker-Rodda, eds., Kingston Papers, vol. 2 (part of the New York Historical Manuscripts: Dutch Series) (1976), pp. 643-44 (Kunst); J. R. Witcraft, Cornelius Jansen Clopper & His Descendants (1912), pp. 1-3 & E. N. Clopper, An American Family (1950), passim, esp. pp. 9, 13-14, 19; H. S. Ackerman, Five Bogert Families, vol. 1 (1950), pp. 171, 174, 182, 201; NYGBR 7(1876):49-50, 53-56 (Van Schaick, Stille) & M. W. Van Scoyoc, Descendants of Cornelis Aertsen Van Schaick, vol. 2, 1st ed. (1982-86), pp. 1037-38; NYGBR 57 (1926):208-17, 338-39, NYGBR 58(1927):76-78 (duTrieux, Peeck); N. B. Sylvester, History of Ulster County, New York (1880), pp. 48-49 (Van Imborch) & Mrs. Robert W. deForest, A Walloon Family in America: Lockwood deForest & His For[e]bears, 1500-1848, 2 vols. (1914), esp. vol. 2, pp. 283-85; Americana 27 (1933):417-19 (Claas Van Schaick) & FSA (Van Schaick, Wyngaart); DSSAY 32-33 (1956-58):9-11, 13 (Van Dyck), & NYGBR 82(1951):51 (Van Dyck), 69 (1938):3-24 (Schuyler), 24 (1893):39-40 (Ver Planck), Florence Christoph, Schuyler Genealogy (1987), pp. 2-8, 32, & W. E. Ver Planck, The History of Abraham Isaacse Ver Planck & His Male Descendants in America (1892), pp. 9-38; FSA (Yates), NYGBR 114(1983):228-35 (Joseph Yates), DSSAY 40 (1964-66):9-10 (Winne), & NYGBR 8(1877):11 & ALR (Loockermans); J. H. Slipper, Resolved Waldron's Descendants: Vanderpoel Branch (1910), pp. 46-47 esp., & W. G. Eliot, Hon. Pieter Van Stoutenburgh & His Descendants (charts, 1916); DSSAY 44(1972-74);23-24, 30 (Van Den Bergh), 41 (1966-68):9-10 (Vanderpoel); T. M. Potts, Historical Collections Relating to the Potts Family (1901), pp. 441-49, 451-54, 461-62, 474, WCPDD (Croasdale), J. G. Leach, Chronicle of the Yerkes Family (1904), pp. 14-15 (McVeagh), & C. V. Roberts, Ancestry of Clarence V. Roberts & Frances A. (Walton) Roberts (1940), pp. 156-60 (Lukens), 270-73 (Tyson), PMHB 23(1899):270-71, 408 (reprinted in GPFPM 876-78) & PGM 31(1979-80):195-205 (reprinted in GPFPGM 3:500-510); Joseph G. B. Bulloch, A History & Genealogy of the Families of Bulloch & Stobo & of Irvine of Cults (1911) (Bulloch, Stobo, Park, Irvine), Genealogical & Historical Records of the Baillies of Inverness, Scotland, & Some of Their Descendants in the United States of America (1923) (Baillie, Bulloch), A History & Genealogy of the Families of Bellinger & De Veaux & Other Families (1895) (Bellinger, Fairchild, De Veaux), & History & Genealogy of the Stewart, Elliott, & Dunwoody Families (1895) (Stewart), The Scottish Antiquary 8 (1893-94):40-42, 88-89, 142, 185 (Douglas, Horn, Leslie), Alistair & Henrietta Tayler, The House of Forbes (1937), p. 416 (Grizel Forbes of Waterton, wife of John Douglas of Inchmarlo), & K. H. Leslie, Historical Records of the Family of Leslie from 1067 to 1868-9, vol. 3 (1869), p. 392 (Isabel Leslie of Pitcaple, wife of Rev. James Horn); The Georgia Genealogical Magazine No. 7 (Jan. 1963):403-4 & Stewart Clan Magazine 24, No. 8 (Feb. 1947):173-74 (Stewart); C. P. Wilson, Annals of Georgia, Volume I, Liberty County Records & a State Revolutionary Pay Roll (1928, reprint 1969), pp. 9, 33, 49, 51, 94-95 (Oswald).

RD - John Irvine, Kenneth Baillie (highly probable, unproved)

PK - Van Buren (C. Van Schaick, Wyngaart, Van Hoesen); FDR (Roosevelt, Vigne); Bush (Schuyler)

* * *

William Howard Taft

TAG 22(1945-46):205-10 (an ancestor list, without dates, places, or references, by C. A. Torrey), plus Torrey's full AT (#s 32-1789, with full dates, places & many references to a wide variety of sources) in his MSS. collection at NEHGS, plus, for disproof of his once accepted Mayflower descent from Francis Cooke, NEHGR 127 (1973):94-95 (reprinted in GMF 2:741-42), MQ 49 (1983):130-34, TAG 59 (1983):28-31, & R. V. Wood, Jr., Francis Cooke of the Mayflower: Four Generations (1986), pp. 6-7. For the immediate family &/or patrilineal descents of Taft's eight great-grandparents, plus data on their progeny, see Russell Smith Taft &

Russell Wales Taft, "Taft Family Genealogy," n. d., typescript in NEHGS MSS. collection, unpaged (note, esp. its coverage, under #100, Mrs. Huldah Taft Daniels, of the president's second Taft descent), E. B. Crane, The Rawson Family (1875), pp. 1-7, 12-14, 17, 36, 69-71, M. H. Kingsbury & I. I. Illingworth, "William Hayward of Weymouth & Braintree, Massachusetts," 1966?, typescript at NEHGS, pp. 1-4, 6-8, 13, 26-27, 52-53, G. W. Chapin, The Chapin Book, 2 vols. (1924), pp. 2, 5-6, 23-24, 94-95, 100, 282-83, 301, 625, 676, 1170, 1266, 1759, 2178, F. C. Torrey, The Torrey Families and Their Children in America, vol. 1 (1924), pp. 13-17, 34-35, 59-60, 108, 173-74, 247, vol. 2 (1929), pp. 120-22, 250, NEHGR 33 (1879):25-26, 28, 33, 132 & the Mendon, Mass. VRs (Davenport), & W. A. Benedict & H. A. Tracy, History of the Town of Sutton, Massachusetts, from 1704 to 1876 (1878, reprint 1966) (Waters, Holman), & D. E. Holman, The Holmans in America (1909), pp. 3-6, 13-15, 32, 71, 155-58, 218-21. For Taft's descents from Hartford founder Rev. Thomas Hooker & Salem "wizard" George Jacobs see Edward Hooker, The Descendants of Rev. Thomas Hooker, Hartford, Connecticut, 1586-1908 (1909), pp. 3, 9-10, 17-18, 31, TAG 58 (1982):65-72, 74-76 (Jacobs, Andrews, by D. L. Greene), & J. A. Vinton, The Giles Memorial (1864), pp. 4-11, 13-14 (Torrey undoubtedly makes Mrs. Mehitable Giles Waters a daughter of John Giles & Ann Andrews largely because her children included a John, an Anna, & an Andrus Waters).

RD - Mrs. Jane Lawrence Giddings
Salem "wizard" ancestor - George Jacobs
PW - Thomas & Margaret (Williams) Mitchell
PK - 2 Adamses, Fillmore, Coolidge (Squire); Hayes, Nixon, Bush (Foote); Coolidge, Nixon, Bush (Morse); Garfield, Bush (Holbrook); B. Harrison, Harding (King); Coolidge, FDR (Hooker); Hoover, Bush (Sherman); Garfield (W. Cooke, Rockwood); Coolidge (Coolidge, Waters, Tompkins, Trask); Hoover (Holyoke?); FDR (Cheney, Lawrence); Bush (Davenport, Ravens, Fairbanks?, Mitchell?, M. Pierce); Fillmore (Emerson); Cleveland (Chapin); Harding (Greene); Ford (Wardwell)

* * *

(Thomas) Woodrow Wilson

William E. Norman, Norman Genealogy: Ancestors & Descendants of George Norman I & Martha Mellish Norman, Somerset, England, with Descendant & Collateral Families of America (1976), pp. 250b-258. Wilson was the first president with no colonial ancestry; his paternal grandparents (James Wilson & Mary Anne Adams) were Scots-Irish immigrants, his maternal grandparents (Rev. Thomas Woodrow & Marion Williamson) Scottish immigrants, all to Ohio. Rev. Thomas Woodrow is listed in A. W. Innes Addison, A Roll of the Graduates of the University of Glasgow from 31st December, 1727 to 31st December, 1897, with Short Biographical Notes (1898), p. 658. For biographical detail on Wilson's parents & grandparents see chapter 1, "The Wilsons & the Woodrows" in R. S. Baker, Woodrow Wilson, Life & Letters: Youth, 1856-1890 (1927).

* * *

Warren Gamaliel Harding

Clara Gardner Miller, The Ancestry of President Harding & Its Relation to the Hardings of Wyoming Valley & Clifford, Pennsylvania (1928), reprinted in Proceedings & Collections of the Wyoming Historical & Genealogical Society 21 (1930):1-46; W. J. Harding, **The Hardings in America** (1925), esp. pp. 27-32, 35-36, 79-92, 117-19, 121, 124-31 (Harding & Madison esp.) & M. L. Holman, "Harding Ancestry," compiled 1924 for Edwin E. Cox of Los Angeles, pp. 1-20 (Stephen[1], Abraham[2], Stephen[3], Abraham[4],[5] Harding); H. A. Baker, **History of Montville, Connecticut** (1896), pp. 231-32, 458-59 (Vibber, Williams); ---, **Bacon & Allied Families: A Family Directory** (1958), p. 355 & Mrs. Martha Clapp Barner, **Tryon Family** (1950?), p. 21 (on Huldah Tryon, b. 1740, wife of Ebenezer Harding, not Abraham, the origin of whose wife, also called Huldah Tryon, is unknown); TG 4(1983):59-65, 72-73, 88-90, 109-21 (Tripp); HB & ALR (Anthony Paine) & GDRI (Sisson); C. E. Slocum, **A Short History of the Slocums, Slocumbs, & Slocombs of America** (1882), pp. 33-41, 45-49, 54, 68-69, 87-88 & NEHGR 70(1916):283-84, 78(1924):395-96, 110(1956):77-78 (Slocum, reprinted in EO 1:2:73-77); NEHGR 15(1861):235-36 (Ralph Paine) & 102(1948):203-6 (Carr); E. I. Carr, **The Carr Family Records** (1894), pp. 12-15, 24-25, 34, 54, & ALR (Carr); G. S. Greene & L. B. Clarke, **The Greenes of Rhode Island** (1903), pp. 38-40, 52-62, 75-77 & Walter & Ella Greene, **A Greene Family History: An Account of the Ancestors & Descendants of Nathan & Job Greene Who Pioneered the Settlement of St. Albans, Vermont** (1981), pp. 8-11, 16, 27-41; NEHGR 71(1917):310-22, 78 (1924):391-95 (Almy, reprinted in EO 1:2:69-73 & EO 2:1:19-31); Brown Thurston, **Thurston Genealogies, 1635-1892** (1892), pp. 518-20 & ALR (Thurston, Mott); H. H. Hain, **History of Perry County, Pennsylvania** (1922), pp. 609-10 (Crawford, Stevens - but there is no kinship, according to R. M. Bell, to Confederate Vice President Alexander H. Stephens); W. L. Baker, **Dickerson & Dickinson Descendants of Philemon Dickerson of Southold, Long Island, N. Y.** (1978), pp. 1-34, 42-52, 258-59, 309-13 & **Study of the Reeve Family of Southold, Long Island, N. Y.** (1970), pp. 114-15, 340-43, 347-48, 351-52, 357-59, 369-71; WB (Thomas Paine, Purrier), L. D. Mapes, **A Tentative Correction of the Mapes Family Line** (1941), pp. 1-3, NYGBR 31(1900):65-67 (Browne) & 33(1902):71-73 (King) (both reprinted in GLIF 1:163-65, 493-95); C. H. Batchelder, **The Ancestry of the Breese Family** (1934), pp. 1-3 (unfortunately neither J. H. Wallace, **Genealogy of the Riggs Family**, vol. 1 [1901] nor the Riggs section of PG cover the ancestry of Mrs. Dorothy Riggs Breese); R. M. Bell, **Some New Jersey Families: Bunn, Burdg, Clayton, Inskeep, Malmsbury, Trimmer, Van Kirk** (1983), pp. 25-26, **Western Pennsylvania Genealogical Society Quarterly** 10(1983):39-49 (Van Kirk), & GMNJ 41(1966):49-52, 102, 104 (Van Kirk also). Harding's Dickerson-Thomas Paine-Mapes-Purrier-Reeve-Brown-King-Hines-Breese-Riggs descent is problematic (probable or possible but unproved) & the sole source for the Madison line is an 1881 letter from Thomas Madison (b. 1800), brother of Mrs. Elizabeth Madison Harding.

PK - B. Harrison, Taft (King-problematic); Nixon, Carter (Almy); Taft (Greene); Ford (Mott)

* * *

John Calvin Coolidge, Jr.

TAG 53(1977):65-74, 160-67, 54(1978):141 (an authoritative AT by R. C. Anderson), plus, among sources published since, TAG 59(1983):47-48 & Christine Rose, **Descendants of Robert Rose of Wethersfield & Branford, Connecticut** (1983), pp. 1-11, 20-22, 33-34 (both on "Elizabeth Roose of Hartford," wife of Obadiah Coolidge & JCC ancestor #129, & both in agreement with Mr. Anderson's discussion of her identification in TAG 53:69, which Mrs. Rose cites), & TAG 62(1987):65-73, 164 (M. J. Wood on Mary Ravens, wife of John Coolidge, immigrant patrilineal ancestor of the president). The TAG AT cited Vermont & Massachusetts vital records, E. D. Coolidge, Descendants of John Coolidge of Watertown, Massachusetts, 1630 (1930), & B. B. Bryant & G. E. Baker, Early Settlers, Plymouth, Vermont, Including Their Genealogical Records (1975, with John Coolidge, Moses Priest, William Thompson, Adam Brown, Jr., Hiram D. Moor, Luther Franklin, & Jonathan Pinney chapters). These sources, plus L. S. Hayes, History of the Town of Rockingham, Vermont, 1753-1907, with Family Genealogies (1907) & (by F. S. & L. C. Lovell) 1907-1957 (1958) (Davis, Harwood, Pulsifer), Broad Brook Grange No. 151, Official History of Guilford, Vermont, 1678-1961, with Genealogies & Biographical Sketches (1961) (Franklin, Starr), B. B. Bryant, The Progenitors & Descendants of Thomas Page Brown & Sarah (Sally) Parker (1938), pp. 114-24 (covering much, but not all, of the known American ancestry of Mrs. Sarah Thompson Coolidge, esp. Thompson, Eaton & Boutwell), J. H. Temple, History of Framingham, Massachusetts, 1640-1880, with a Genealogical Register (1887) (Brewer, Bent), Killingly, Connecticut vital records (Grover), & J. P. Grover, Ancestry & Genealogy of Our Thomas Grover Family, 2 vols. (1966-67), p. 176, cover, although often not authoritatively, nos. 1-63 of the Coolidge AT. Confirmation & biographical expansion of much of the data for nos. 64-255 can be found in BW, WC, PCG, PS, CW, the above-cited history of Framingham, histories of Woburn, Mass. (1868, by Samuel Sewall), Reading (1874, by Lilly Eaton), & Billerica (1883, by H. A. Hazen), The Hammatt Papers: Early Inhabitants of Ipswich (1880-99, by Abraham Hammatt), & the MSS. collection on Sudbury families assembled by Mrs. William R. Dewey III of Wayland, Mass.

RD - Samuel & Judith (Everard) Appleton, William Goddard, & Mrs. Elizabeth St. John Whiting

PW - John & Elizabeth (Thompson) Cogswell

PK - 2 Adamses, Fillmore, Taft (Squire); Washington, FDR, Bush (Spencer-English); Taft, Nixon, Bush (Morse); 2 Adamses (Cogswell, Bass); J. Q. Adams, FDR (Miles, Myles); Fillmore, FDR (Perkins); Pierce, Hoover? (Richardson); Taft, FDR (Hooker); Taft, Bush (Ravens); Fillmore (Littlefield); Taft (Waters, Tompkins, Trask); Hoover? (Putnam); FDR (Hunt, Alcock); Ford (Coffin, Davis); Bush (Bulkeley, Phillips, Horton, Garnsey); Grant (Capen); B. Harrison (Fiske)

* * *

Herbert Clark Hoover

Hulda Hoover McLean (the president's niece), Genealogy of the Herbert Hoover Family (1967) & "Errata & Addenda" (1976), TAG 54(1978):12-14, & caveats as per TAG 55(1979):48-49. For Hoover's New England ancestry, via Mrs. Mary Gilbert Minthorn & Mrs. Endymia Winn Sherwood, see also H. W. Brainerd, H. S. Gilbert, & C. A. Torrey, The Gilbert Family: Descendants of Thomas Gilbert, 1582(?)-1659, of Mt. Wollaston (Braintree), Windsor, & Wethersfield (1953), pp. 9-24, 54-62, 92-93, Kenneth Lord, Genealogy of the Descendants of Thomas Lord (1946), pp. 1-6, 361, & CCAD (Joseph Smith, Huit); Samuel Sewall, The History of Woburn, Middlesex County, Mass. (1868) & Woburn VRs (Winn, Buck, Brooks, Mousall, esp. the 1743 marriage of Jacob Winn & Sarah Buck, & the 1716 birth of this latter), E. J. & H. G. Cleveland, The Genealogy of the Cleveland & Cleaveland Families, vol. 3 (1899), chapter 5 (Winn, esp. pp. 2420-27, wherein, however, no parentage is offered for Jacob Winn, husband of Sarah Buck, said by McLean, who admits to the difficulty of this line, to be a son of Jacob Winn, b. 1681, & Prudence Wyman), Mrs. Elizabeth S. Richards, Genealogy of the Buck Family (1913), pp. 7-10, 12-18, Samuel Buck, Buck History &

Genealogy: Supplement or Appendix (1924), pp. 74, 78 (a poor work - Samuel Buck's wife on these two pages is said to be firstly Abigail Wyman & then Hannah Farmer; the Sarah Buck born in 1716 in Woburn was a daughter of Samuel & Hannah), & NEHGR 58(1904):48-51 (Brooks, Buck), 47(1893):462-67 (Mousall, Brooks); Albert Annett & Alice E. E. Lehtinen, History of Jaffrey (Middle Monadnock), New Hampshire, vol. 2 (1934), pp. 354-57, 718-19 (Grout, Spofford), H. S. B. Osgood, A Family Affair Concerning Certain Descendants of Captain John Grout (1949-52), pp. 10-18, 20-34 (esp. 29), BW (Grout, Busby, Dix, Barnard), & ESR (Boynton, Swan, Jewett, Wood, Spofford, Wheeler, Hopkinson, Pearson); NEHGR 66(1912):87 (Busby, reprinted in EO 1:3:711), FCW (Dix), Mary E. N. Backus, The New England Ancestry of Dana Converse Backus (1949), p. 54 (Barnard), B. L. Stratton, Transatlantic Shermans (1969), passim, esp. 96-97 & charts at end (Barnard, Whiting, Sherman), ALR (Sherman, Lawrence), J. F. & C. H. Boynton, The Boynton Family (1897), pp. 44-47, 54-55, F. C. Jewett, History & Genealogy of the Jewetts of America, vol. 1 (1908), pp. 3-4, 13-17, 35, 56, TAG 63(1988):48, 51-52, 54 & sources cited therein (Fillmore AT #s 80-81, 160-61, 322-23; Wood, Mousall), Jeremiah & Aphia T. Spofford, A Genealogical Record of Descendants of John Spofford & Elizabeth Scott (1888), pp. 37-39, 41, 45-46, 59, NEHGR 99(1945):174-75 (Spofford, reprinted in EO 2:3:897, 768), PT (Scott), PA (Scott, Whatlock, Wheeler), & FCW (Wheeler, Wise); W. I. T. Brigham, The Tyler Genealogy: The Descendants of Job Tyler of Andover, Massachusetts, 1619-1700, vol. 1 (1912), pp. 3-23, 45-46, 79-80, L. M. F. & C. A. Woodson, The Woodson-Fenno Ancestry (1907), pp. 117-18 (Blake), Dean Dudley, History of the Dudley Family (1886-98), pp. 276, 659-75, & DAB (Governors Simon Bradstreet & Thomas Dudley), & NAW (Mrs. Anne Dudley Bradstreet) & sources cited therein. The ancestry of Hoover forebears Thomas (or Isaac) Sherwood, husband of Endymia Winn, & of Jacob Winn, husband of Sarah Buck, remains problematic, although both men were undoubtedly of New England ancestry; further research is desirable also on the Woburn Bucks. For the Yorkshire & Bucks Co. Scott family see TAG 54(1978):19-24 (an article brought to my attention by its author, Harry Hollingsworth) & Pennsylvania Vital Records from the Pennsylvania Genealogical Magazine & The Pennsylvania Magazine of History & Biography, vol. 1 (1983), p. 42.

RD - Gov. Thomas Dudley of Mass.

PK - Garfield, Ford, Bush (Wheeler); Fillmore, Ford (Wood); Pierce, Coolidge (Richardson-problematic); Taft, Bush (Sherman); Pierce (Pearson); Coolidge (Putnam-problematic); Ford (Lord); Cleveland (Winn-problematic); Taft (Holyoke-problematic); Nixon (Sawtelle-problematic)

* * *

Franklin Delano Roosevelt

Alvin Page Johnson, Franklin D. Roosevelt's Colonial Ancestors (1933), confirmed, expanded & occasionally corrected by a wide variety of sources, including, for the patrilineal descents of FDR's great-grandparents, NYGBR 64(1933):139-42, 72(1941):24-26, TAG 19(1942-43):210-11, NYGBR 118(1987):193-97, 199-202, 119(1988):27-29, & C. B. Whittelsey, The Roosevelt Genealogy, 1649-1902 (1902), pp. 3-4, 6-7, 12-14, 26-30, 44-46, 57-58, 79-80; Annette Townsend, The Walton Family of New York (1945), chapters 1-5 (pp. 10-52) & Bentley D. Hasell, Genealogical Chart Showing the Descent & Alliances from the Colonial Period of the Issue of Cruger, son of Henry Walton (1897); GWF 2:252-56, 259-60, 265-66 (Aspinwall, with a bibliography of earlier sources on p. 252); The

Howland Quarterly 28, Nos. 2 & 3 (Jan.-Apr. 1964):6-7, TAG 52(1976):198-205, & Franklyn Howland, A Brief Genealogical & Biographical History of Arthur, Henry, & John Howland (1885), pp. 315-24, 328-29, 335, 343-44, 356-57; TAG 52(1976):91-92, K. W. Bate, The Ebenezer Hanks Story (1982) (Delano, Mahieu, Warren, Walker, Clark), & J. A. Delano, The Genealogy, History, & Alliances of the American House of Delano, 1621 to 1899 (1899), pp. 99-102, 294-95 (but ignore the spurious English Warren ancestry), 484, 500, 504-5; LCF (Church, Shaw, Head) & J. A. Church, Descendants of Richard Church of Plymouth, Mass. (1913), pp. 7-16, 36-37, 48-49, 78, 119; SM 1 (Lyman), Lyman Coleman, Genealogy of the Lyman Family (1872), pp. 34-40, 391-95, Sylvester Judd & W. E. Corbin, "Early Families of Northampton" (in the W. E. Corbin MSS. collection at NEHGS), pp. 726, 728, 738-39, 744, 760, 774 (Lyman); & F. L. Weis, Richard Robbins (1610-1683) of Charlestown, Boston & Cambridge, Massachusetts, His Ancestry & Some of His Descendants (1933), pp. 3-6, 10-11, 21-24, 48-49, 71-72, 90-91, 109-10, 120. Sources covering other families (through AT #s 128-255) in the ancestry of FDR's eight great-grandparents include the following:

1. Roosevelt (maternal lines): Dingman Versteeg, trans., P. R. Christoph, Kenneth Scott, Kenn Stryker-Rodda, eds., Kingston Papers, vol. 2 (part of the New York Historical Manuscripts: Dutch Series) (1976), pp. 643-44 (Kunst); NYGBR 70(1939):128-30, 133, 373, 376-77, 117(1986):1-7 & Netherlandish research by Douglas Richardson that located the marriage intentions of Andries Hardenbroeck & Aefje Jans Sijbrantz, plus the latter's baptism; E. A. Hoffman, Genealogy of the Hoffman Family (1899), pp. 96-100, 106-12, 118-27, 147-48, 196-97, 262, 360-61; NYGBR 17(1886):251-53 (deWitt), K. E. Hasbrouck, The Crispell Family in America (1976), pp. 1-4, 8, 15; S. V. Talcott, Genealogical Notes of New York & New England Families (1883, reprint 1973), pp. 8-10, 13-14 & DSGRM 3(1939-40):170-71 (Benson); NYGBR 65(1934):62-66, 109(1978):215-16, & A. H. Van Deusen, Van Deursen Family, vol. 1 (1912), pp. 3-4, 7-8, 19-20; FSA 158 & NYGBR 90(1959):164-65 (Roos).

2. Walton: TAG 17(1940-41):74-78 (Lawrence); NYGBR 7(1876):118-19 (Santvoort); W. B. Aitken, Distinguished Families in America Descended from Wilhelmus Beekman & Jan Thomasse Van Dyke (1912), pp. 1-6, 53-55, 141; John Van Z. Cortelyou, The Ancestors of Two Sisters: Records of the Ancestors of Helen Robina Cortelyou & Carol Van Zandt Cortelyou (1954), pp. 107-8, 118-19, 121-23 (Beekman, Baudertis, de Boogh, Abeel, Kroom); NYGBR 103(1972):105 (abstract of obituary of Charles Williams, Esq., reprinted in Kenneth Scott, comp., Genealogical Data from Colonial New York Newspapers [1977], p. 175).

3. Aspinwall: E. A. Bowen, Lineage of the Bowens of Woodstock, Connecticut (1897), pp. 215, 218 (Palfrey); R. T. Smith & H. B. Hoff, The Tangier Smith Family: Descendants of Colonel William Smith of the Manor of St. George, Long Island, New York (The Order of Colonial Lords of Manors in America; publication No. 34) (1978), pp. 1-6, 10-12, 24, 58-66; G. F. Shepard & D. L. Jacobus, The Shepard Families of New England, Volume 3, Additional Family Groups (1973), pp. 293-97, 299-300; GGE 604-6 (Anderson); Dorothy C. Barck, ed., Papers of the Lloyd Family of the Manor of Queens Village, Lloyd's Neck, Long Island, New York, 1654-1826, Volume II, 1752-1826 (Collections of the New York Historical Society for the Year 1927) (1927), pp. 878-85, 887; Temple Prime, Descent of John Nelson & of His Children, with Notes on the Families of Tailer & Stoughton, 2nd ed. (1894), pp. 3-7, 51-52 esp.

4. Howland: S. G. Webber, A Genealogy of the Southworths (Southards), Descendants of Constant Southworth (1905), pp. 1-28, 33-35; E. B. Cole, The Descendants of James Cole of Plymouth, 1633 (1908), pp. 21-22, 25 & MQ 27(1925):41-44 (Cole); Boston VRs (for 1718 & 1692 births of Abigail & John Burt, & 1714 marriage of John

Burt & Abigail Cheever); S. W. V. Cheever, "Cheever Notes" (c. 1960, typescript at NEHGS), pp. 1-2, J. T. Hassam, **The Cheever Family** (1896), p. 5, & SHG 2 (Thomas Cheever); Ledyard Bill, **History of the Bill Family** (1867), pp. 25-44, 55-59, 68-69, 83-85, 122-26, 146-50, 175-78; F. M. Caulkins, **History of New London, Connecticut**, 2nd ed. (1860), pp. 299-300 (Haughton); HH (Huntington) & Huntington Family Association, **The Huntington Family in America: A Genealogical Memoir of the Known Descendants of Simon Huntington from 1633 to 1915** (1915), pp. 11-12, 419-21, 446, 532; GAF (Gager); DW (Perkins) & G. A. Perkins, **The Family of John Perkins of Ipswich, Massachusetts, Part III, Descendants of Sergeant Jacob Perkins** (1889), pp. 1-7, 13, 23; TCB (Lathrop, House, Scudder, Adgate).

5. **Delano:** S. F. Peckham, **Peckham Genealogy** (1922), pp. 207-16, 223-24; R. S. Wakefield, J. A. Beebe & others, **Richard Warren of the Mayflower & His Descendants for Four Generations**, 3rd ed. (a MFIP pamphlet) (1989), pp. 1, 3-6, 17, 21-22, 27-28, 72-73, 89-90, 113, 119 (Warren, Cooke, Church, Snow, Skiffe, Gibbs, Delano, Presbury, Swift); J. A. Cushman, **The First Seven Generations of the Cushman Family in New England** (1964), pp. 11-12, 15-16, 29, 66-67; TVG 32(1988):83-85 & MQ 47(1981):14-18 (Allerton); Mrs. C. D. Townsend, R. S. Wakefield & M. H. Stover, **Degory Priest of the Mayflower & His Descendants for Four Generations** (a MFIP pamphlet) (1987), pp. 1-3, 8-9, 25-26 (Priest, Coombs, Cushman).

6. **Church:** D. P. Worden, W. F. Langworthy, & B. P. Burch, **Genealogy of Thomas Pope (1608-1683) & His Descendants** (1917), pp. 9-17, 19-20; NEHGR 115(1961):86-91, 96-98, 192-93, 116(1962):30-31 (Perry, reprinted in GMF 3:4-9, 14-16, 29-30, 61-62); CW (Hunt); NEHGR 97(1943):10-14 (Alcock); R. V. Wood, Jr., **Francis Cooke of the Mayflower: Four Generations** (1986), pp. 1-5, 14, 17, 50, 60 (Cooke & Warren, Hathaway, Taber, Perry) & G. L. Randall, **Taber Genealogy: Descendants of Thomas Son of Philip Taber** (1924), pp. 5-7; BMV (Presbury, Skiffe); G. H. Swift, **William Swift of Sandwitch [sic] & Some of His Descendants, 1637-1899** (1900), pp. 1-4, 6-7, 14, NEHGR 123(1969):54-56, 58-60 (Gibbs, reprinted in GMF 2:1-3, 5-7); E. S. Versailles, **Hathaways of America, 1970 Edition** (1970), pp. 747-54.

7. **Lyman:** BP (Plum, Lewis); SM 1 (Pomeroy, Woodward, Sheldon, Woodford, Blott, John Johnson, Strong, Ford, Holton) & A. A. Pomeroy, **History & Genealogy of the Pomeroy Family** (1914), pp. 125-41, 151 esp.; William Lewis notes in M. L. Holman & W. L. Holman Dodge MMS. collection at NEHGS; F. B. Trowbridge, **The Ashley Genealogy: A History of the Descendants of Robert Ashley of Springfield, Massachusetts** (1896), pp. 3-18, 21-24; Judd & Corbin, "Early Families of Northampton," as above (for Lyman), pp. 1034, 1038, 1048 (Sheldon); TCB (Hinsdale) & S. C. Hinsdale, H. C. Andrews, & A. L. Holman, **Hinsdale Genealogy: Descendants of Robert Hinsdale of Dedham, Medfield, Hadley & Deerfield** (1906), pp. 59-62, 64-66, 71-72; B. W. Dwight, **The History of the Descendants of Elder John Strong of Northampton, Mass.** (1871, reprint 1975), pp. 14-19, 1120-22, 1125-26; TF (Clapp) & Ebenezer Clapp, **The Clapp Memorial** (1876), pp. 195-200 esp.; E. P. Holton & Harriet Scofield, "A Genealogy of the Descendants in America of William Holton (1610-1691) of Hartford, Conn. & Northampton, Mass.," 2nd ed., 1965 (typescript at NEHGS), pp. 1-7, 21, 33; FCW (Marshfield); BG (Samuel Wright).

8. **Robbins:** NEHGR 85(1931):133-45, 96(1942):301-2 (Chandler, Bayford, reprinted in EO 1:2:354-66, 732-33) & George Chandler, **The Chandler Family** (1883), pp. 1-4, 11-16, 35-36; NEHGR 59(1905):79-83 (Edward Johnson), C. L. Newhall, **The Record of My Ancestry** (1899), pp. 77-97, 99-100 (Johnson, Wiswall, Gardner), & WC (Gardner); NYGBR 45(1914):164-69 (Hutchinson) & W. H. Whitmore, **A Brief Genealogy of the Descendants of William Hutchinson &**

Thomas Oliver (1865), pp. 5-11 (see the royal descents section for sources for Anne Marbury & Catherine Hamby); GDMNH (Thomas Clarke); Estes Howe, Memoir of Hon. James Murray Robbins (n. d.), pp. 3-11 (Clarke & Foster, esp.); TF (Turrell, Colbron); N. M. Tiffany, Letters of James Murray, Loyalist (1901), pp. 292-95, 309 esp.; Sir Robert Douglas of Glenbervie, 6th Bt., The Baronage of Scotland (1798), pp. 104-6 (Murray), 302-6 (Scott); Miscellanea Genealogica et Heraldica, 4th Ser., vol. 2 (1906-7), pp. 166-67 (Bennet, Murray); T. H. Cockburn-Hood, The Rutherfords of That Ilk & Their Cadets (1884), chart in end pocket esp.; Northumberland County History Committee, A History of Northumberland, vol. 14 (1935), pp. 550-52 (Collingwood).

RD - James & Barbara (Bennet) Murray, John Nelson, Mrs. Anne Marbury Hutchinson, Dr. Richard Palgrave, Thomas Southworth (probable, unproved), Mrs. Elizabeth Coytmore Tyng, Mrs. Catherine Hamby Hutchinson, Thomas Lawrence (of Newtown, L. I.)

MP - Isaac & Mary (Norris) Allerton & Mrs. Mary Allerton Cushman, Francis & John Cooke, John & Elizabeth (Tilley) Howland, John & Joan (Hurst) Tilley, Degory Priest, Richard Warren (two descents from the Cookes, six descents from Warren)

PW - John & Elizabeth (Gore) Gager, Henry & Elizabeth (--) Woodward, Thomas & Mary (Blott) Woodford, John & Abigail (Ford) Strong, William & Mary (--) Holton

PK - Washington, Coolidge, Bush (Spencer-English); Nixon, Ford, Bush (Howland); J. Q. Adams, Coolidge (Miles/Coytmore); Fillmore, Coolidge (Perkins); Grant, Bush (Lathrop, Mahieu); Hayes, Cleveland (Charde/Cooke/Ford); Taft, Coolidge (Hooker); Grant (Delano, Huntington); Hayes (Ashley, Burgess, Chandler); Cleveland (Wright); T. Roosevelt (Roosevelt, Vigne); Taft (Cheney, Lawrence); Coolidge (Alcock, Hunt); Nixon (Swift); Ford (Head); Bush (Beekman, F. Cooke?, Hutchinson, Jenney, Palgrave, Pope, Richards); Van Buren (Van Deu[r]sen); Taylor (Allerton); Pierce (John Johnson)

Note 1: For various kinships between FDR & Sir Winston Leonard Spencer-Churchill see NYGBR 73(1942):159-62.

Note 2: A tenth immigrant ancestor of FDR with likely (but as yet unraveled) royal descent is Mrs. Margaret (Es)Touteville Shepard, also an ancestress of J. Q. Adams (for sources see the Adams bibliography).

* * *

Harry S Truman

GVFT 3:610-659 (Truman, Shipp, Doniphan, Holmes, Tyler, Duvall, Ijams, Cheney, etc., by G. H. S. King); TVG 11(1967):90 (Truman); R. D. Shipp, The Shipp Family Genealogy (1975), pp. 1-2, 10-13, 45-46, 48-49, 60-61, 69 & The Shipp Family Genealogy Revised (1985), pp. 32-39, 192-99, 208; GVFT 4:708-18 (Doniphan, Anderson, Matthews), G. H. S. King, Marriages of Richmond County, Virginia, 1668-1853 (1964), pp. 57, 136, 258 (Doniphan, Mott, Monteith), & H. W. Newman, Mareen Duvall of Middle Plantation (1952), pp. 20-56, 148-49, 161-69, 181-83, 190-91 (Duvall, Tyler); Elsie Spry Davis, Descendants of Jacob Young of Shelby County, Kentucky, Including President Harry S. Truman (1980), esp. pp. 1-55, 121, 125-50, GKFR 1:348-83 (Goodnight/Goodknight, Gutnecht), & GKFFC 841-59 (Holmes, Tyler, Gregg, Scott).

* * *

Dwight David Eisenhower

Look Magazine vol. 20 (Nov. 13, 1956), pp. 40-41 (a chart "tree" & brief comments); Fannie Belle Taylor-Richardson, Eisenhower Lineages & Reference, 1691-September 3, 1957 (1957?), pp. 1-12 (#1), 1-9, 17-18, 30-32, 56-57, 91-103 (#2); Heinz F. Friedrichs, President Dwight D. Eisenhower's Ancestors & Relations (1955, also published in German, & note the review by K. F. von Frank in Senftenegger Monatsblatt, Band IV, Heft 8 [1958]); PMG 22(1961-62):144-46, Saarlaendische Familienkunde 14(1981):151-59 (partly abstracted by R. M. Bell in NEHGR 136[1982]:66) & Archiv fuer Sippenforschung 50(1984):599-610 (on the Eisenhower patrilineal descent in Germany); Paxson Link, The Link Family: Ancestors & Descendants of John Jacob Link, 1417-1951 (1951), pp. 201, 203, 211, 230, 275, 374, 542-43 & Familie und Volk 2(1953):280-84 (a continental AT for Johann Jacob Link, 1682-1738, of Berks Co., Pa., & his wife Anna Maria Magdalena Neuwirth, b. 1692). For Eisenhower's probable Stover & Boone descents (his only likely non-German or non-Swiss ancestry is derived through Sarah Boone, b. 1691/2, aunt of the illustrious Daniel & wife of Jacob Stover of Philadelphia [now Berks] Co., Pa., & Augusta Co., Va.) see V. H. Walgreen, Through the Years: Your Family & Mine (1962), pp. 34-35, 51 esp. (Stover), H. A. Spraker, The Boone Family: A Genealogical History of the Descendants of George & Mary Boone Who Came to America in 1717 (1922, reprint 1974), pp. 19-24, & Boone Pioneer Echoes 16(1974):9, 20(1978):1. Further Stover material is being collected by Mrs. Sheila Spencer Stover (Mrs. Jack W. Stover) of Branford, Conn.

* * *

John Fitzgerald Kennedy

TAG 53(1977):145-46 (G. B. Roberts), corrected & extended in TAG 55(1979):50, 57(1981):89, 61(1985-86):173, BPF 2, Appendix C, Kennedy chart, NEHGR 139(1985):211-24 (reprinted in The Irish in New England [NEHGS, 1985], pp. 25-38), Harvey Rachlin, The Kennedys: A Chronological History, 1823-Present (1986), esp. the inside & back cover charts (which contain, however, a few typographical errors & omissions) & part one, & Doris Kearns Goodwin, The Fitzgeralds & the Kennedys (1987), charts preceding the table of contents (where Edmund Fitzgerald, 1798-1883, is mistakenly called Edward), chapter one, & pp. 88-89, 827 esp. Ms. Goodwin found the dispensation record for John Francis Fitzgerald & Mary Josephine Hannon (Dispensation Records, Consanguinity, 1889-1892, Archives, Archdiocese of Boston), which together with the death record of Edmund Fitzgerald (7 Murray Court, Boston, 27 Oct. 1883, age 85/2/6, trader, born Ireland, son of James Fitzgerald & Hannah ---, both also born in Ireland), establishes that Kennedy's maternal grandparents were second cousins, both great-grandchildren of the above (but only therein identified) James & Hannah Fitzgerald. Fitzgerald & Hannon family Bibles are in the Kennedy Library in Boston. Known Irish ancestral place origins include Dunganstown, co. Wexford for the Kennedys, Clonakilty Bay & Rosscarbery, co. Cork for the Hickeys & Fields respectively, Lough Gur, co. Limerick for the Hannons, & Lough Gur & Bruff, co. Limerick for the Fitzgeralds.

* * *

Lyndon Baines Johnson

BPF 2:550-51 (H. B. Johnston) & Rebeckah Baines Johnson, A Family

Album (1965); Eddis Johnson & H. B. Johnston, The Johnsons & Johnstons of Corrowaugh in Isle of Wight County, Virginia, Volume I, Robert Johnson, Planter, His Ancestry & Descendants, 1616-1979 (1979), pp. 3-10, 17-22, 29-41 & Alabama Genealogical Register 6(1964):3-15, 53-57, 139-66 (Johnson, Ealy, Hillsman, also by H. B. Johnston); R. W. Wilson & B. F. Duholm, Bunton-Buntin-Bunten-Bunting, Including Family of President Lyndon Baines Johnson Genealogy (1967), pp. 1-4, 6-10, 18-19, 33-38, 54-56, 76-77, 141-46; DeWitt C. Nogues, Desha Genealogy: A Survey (1983), pp. 1, 3-5, 18-19, 46-47, 91, 168, 275; NEHGR 121(1967):229-31 (Ogier); John A. Leiter, History & Genealogy of the Leiter, Lighter, Liter, Lyter Families, 2nd ed. (1977), pp. xii-xiii, 175-76, 187, 212-16 (Lyter, Beaver, Hoffman, Ament) & I. M. Beaver, History & Genealogy of the Bieber, Beaver, Biever, Beeber Family (1939), p. 923; Samuel K. Helms, The Helm Family of Virginia, vol. 1 (1985), passim, esp. pp. 628-42 (Jameson). A second volume of the Johnson/Johnston of Corrowaugh genealogy, covering the progeny of James & Mary (Johnson) Johnston of Isle of Wight Co., is expected.

* * *

Richard Milhous Nixon

R. M. Bell, The Ancestry of Richard Milhous Nixon (1972, revised 1976), partly abstracted in TAG 46(1970):85-91, 47(1971):114-16, 48(1972):99-101, 149, 54(1978):140-41, 242, with other amplification in NGSQ 62(1974):3-12 (R. M. Bell on tracing Nixon's ancestry generally), TAG 52(1976):114-16 (Bell on the Milhous[e] Irish origins), R. M. Bell, Some New Jersey Families: Bunn, Burdg, Clayton, Inskeep, Malmsbury, Trimmer, Van Kirk (1983) (Burdg, Clayton, Inskeep, Malmsbury & Trimmer are Nixon ancestors), M. J. F. Wadsworth, The Wadsworth Family in America, 1632-1977 (1978), pp. 355-56, 361, 375-76, ALR (Mendenhall, Pennell), J. M. Olsen, Lippincott: Five Generations of the Descendants of Richard & Abigail Lippincott (1982), pp. 19, 22-23, 35-36, 75, 214-15, & R. J. Harry, The Ancestors & Descendants of Hugh Harry & Elizabeth Brinton (1987), pp. 1-32, 105-6, 127-28, 146-47, 179-80, 232-33, 323. The widely recognized leading Nixon genealogical scholar is Raymond Martin Bell of Washington, Pa., formerly of Washington & Jefferson College, also cited under Lincoln, B. Harrison & Harding. In adding a few items to Mr. Bell's coverage of Nixon's New England ancestry, I used, in addition to sources listed by Bell & the Framingham vital records, J. H. Morse & E. W. Leavitt, Morse Genealogy (1903, reprint 1979), Joseph Morse section, pp. 17-18 esp., NEHGR 126(1972):6-7 (Sawtelle), & N. H. Daniels, Descendants of Henry Travers of London, England, & Newbury, Massachusetts (1903), pp. 27-34 esp.

RD - Hugh Harry
Mayflower connection - Henry Howland, brother of John
PW (probable) - John & Alice (Myres) Clayton
PK - Hayes, Taft, Bush (Foote); Taft, Coolidge, Bush (Morse); FDR, Ford, Bush (Howland); Harding, Carter (Almy); FDR (Swift); Ford (Batchiler/Batchelder); Hoover? (Sawtelle)

* * *

Gerald Rudolph Ford, Jr.

Born Leslie Lynch King, Jr.: TAG 53(1977):56-57, 55(1979):51, 61(1985-86):173-74, & sources listed therein, esp., for his immediate forebears, LBNSDAR, vol. 97 (1927), p. 213 (Mrs. Dorothy Gardner Ford, the president's mother, #96681), vol. 107 (1929), pp. 140-41 (Mrs. Adele Ayer Gardner, the president's maternal grandmother, #33603), the California death records of Charles Henry King & his wife Martha Alice Porter (the president's paternal grandparents), William F. Gardner, Alexander Gardner & His Wife Mary Brodie (n. d.) & correspondence with Joseph L. Druse (on the Gardner-Brodie-Miller ancestry of L. A. Gardner & the identification, with a very useful AT, of Elida Vanderburgh Manney esp.) & Kenneth B. Schoonmaker of the Magny Families Association on the Manney, Machet, Wines & Vanderburgh families, S. E. Titcomb, Early New England People (1882), pp. 179-85 (Ayer), plus Chase & Longfellow/Sewall chapters, G. W. Edes, William Ricketson & His Descendants, vol. 2 (1932), pp. 1-3, 11-12, 49-54 (Ricketson, Collins, Manney), & M. S. Beach, William Ely & G. B. Vanderpoel, The Ely Ancestry (1902), pp. 32-44, 51-54, 79, 136, 256 (Ely, Gridley, Butler). Sources covering families in the ancestry (through AT #s 448-511) of Ford's now-known New England or New York great-great-grandparents (Ayer, Manney, Butler & Gridley) can be listed as follows:

1. John Varnum Ayer: Haverhill, Mass. VRs (1812 birth of J. V. Ayer), Priscilla Hammond, Vital Records of Plaistow, New Hampshire (1937), pp. 32, 59, 87-88 (J. V., Samuel & Daniel Ayer), J. K. Graves, Some Seventeenth-Century New England Settlers: John Ayer, John Aires, Moses Eayers, Richard Ayres, Robert Ayars, Samuel Ayres, Simon Eyre & Others, Extended Four Generations (1963), John Ayer Family, #s 1, 3, 18 & 78, & G. W. Chamberlain, "The Genealogy of John Ayer of Haverhill, Massachusetts," MMS. at NEHGS, for #84 William[5] Ayer esp.; D. A. White, The Descendants of William White of Haverhill, Mass. (1889), pp. 7-13; G. T. Little, The Descendants of George Little (1882), pp. 1-7, 14-16, 30-31; P. W. Clement, M. L. Holman & C. C. Brown, Ancestors & Descendants of Robert Clements, vol. 1 (1927), pp. 1-9, 13-30, 47-57, 69-70, 122-23; A. N. Adams, A Genealogical History of Robert Adams of Newbury, Mass., & His Descendants, 1635-1900 (1900), pp. 1-8, 11-12, 25-27; M. Halsey Thomas, ed., The Diary of Samuel Sewall, 1674-1729, Volume II, 1709-1729 (1973), Genealogical Appendix, pp. 1071-75, 1083-84 (Sewall, Longfellow); Henry E. & Harriette E. Noyes, Genealogical Record of Some of the Noyes Descendants of James, Nicholas & Peter Noyes, Volume I, Descendants of Nicholas Noyes (1904), pp. 43-47, 52-56; SE 1 (Thorley), NEHGR 53(1899):121 (March, Thorley), & AL (March); J. C. Chase & G. W. Chamberlain, Seven Generations of the Descendants of Aquila & Thomas Chase (1928), pp. 29-34, 39-41, 51, 76, 148, & PA (Chase, Wheeler, Challis, Davis, Eaton); HSA (Samuel[2] & William[3] Davis, Barnes, Kelly, Knight); W. H. Gove, The Gove Book (1922), pp. 9-11, 13-51, 57-59, 65-66, 90-91; M. A. Stickney, The Stickney Family (1869), pp. 1-12, 17-22, 50-52; AS (Wardwell, where Mrs. Sarah Wardwell Stickney is omitted among the children of Elihu Wardwell & Elizabeth Wade).

2. Elida Vanderburgh Manney: Collections of the New York Historical Society for the Year 1892 (1893), p. 89, & For the Year 1893 (1894), pp. 7-8 (Machet); R. S. D. Eddy, The Eddy Family in America (1930), pp. 3-13, 21 (Eddy, Wines), WB (Wines, Eddy), NYGBR 80(1949):216-18 (Wines) & Wines folder, Bushnell carton (14), J. G. Bartlett MSS. collection (SG BAR 86-146) at NEHGS, which corrects C. B. Moore, Town of Southold, Long Island: Personal Index Prior to 1698 & Index of 1698 (1868), pp. 129-31 (Wines); "The Vanderburgh Ancestry of Presidents Gerald R. Ford, Jr., & George H. W. Bush," unpublished typescript by William J. Powers, Jr., of Acton, Mass., Wallace McLeod, The Family of Richard Vanderburgh of Richmond Hill (1797-1869) (1962), pp. 2-9, Tunis Van Kleeck, The Van Kleeck Family (1900), pp. 5-7, 10-17, 24-25, & J. G. Wood, "The Ter Bos Family" (typescript, 1939?), pp. 1-4 esp.; G. K. Collins, Descendants of John Collins of Charles-

town, R. I. & Susannah Daggett, His Wife (1901), pp. 7-10, 13; G. H. & S. B. Daggett, A Supplement to the Sections Entitled Thomas Doggett-Daggett of Marshfield, Massachusetts & William Daggett of Saco, Maine, from the 1894 Edition of "A History of the Doggett-Daggett Family" (1975), Section II, pp. 1-2; NEHGR 128(1974):241-50, 255-61, 129(1975):225-26 (Gifford); GDRI (John Sheldon of Kingstown); NGSQ 75(1987):105-9, 113-15, 219, 224 & The Howland Quarterly 28, Nos. 2 & 3 (Jan.-Apr. 1964):6-7 (Howland); NEHGR 112(1958):108-18, 184-90, 250-57, 113(1959):55-58, 94-104 (Wilbore, reprinted in EO 1:3:273-313), & J. R. Wilbor & B. F. Wilbour, The Wildbores in America, 2nd ed., vol. 1 (1933), pp. 35-36, 40-41; LCF (Wilbor, Head).

3. George Selden Butler: J. A. Comstock, A History & Genealogy of the Comstock Family in America (1949), pp. 2-3, 5, 11-12, 25; BTGC 17 Feb. 1933, #5938 & TAG 14(1937-38):87-96, 172-73 (Finch, Colt); NEHGR 82(1928):443-53, 84(1930):236, 105(1951):153 (Goodspeed, reprinted in EO 1:2:251-61) & W. A. Goodspeed, History of the Goodspeed Family, vol. 1 (1907), pp. 17-52, 79-87; F. C. Jewett, History & Genealogy of the Jewetts of America, vol. 1 (1908), pp. 3-4, 13-17, 35, 55, 104-5, 195, 331-32, CH (Jewett, Hibbert, Gibbins, Lewis), & AL (Gibbins, Lewis, Marshall, etc.); Kenneth Lord, Genealogy of the Descendants of Thomas Lord (1946), pp. 1-6, 71-74, 194, 227-28; S. S. Rogers, E. S. Lane, & E. Van D. Selden, Selden Ancestry: A Family History (1931), pp. 18-23, 25-32, 35-55, 63-70, 110-12 (Selden, Jewett, Ely, Gridley, Butler) & TCB (Selden, Wakeman, Church); TAG 10(1933-34):73-78 (Dudley, Roe); DG 2 (William Pratt) & F. W. Chapman, The Pratt Family (1864), pp. 53-54, 68-69, 71.

4. Elizabeth Ely Gridley: Oneida Chapter, N.S.D.A.R., Memorial to Revolutionary Soldiers, Clinton, New York (1938), pp. 23-24 (Theodore Gridley), Farmington VRs, Julius Gay MSS. collection on Farmington, Conn. families at the Connecticut Historical Society & the Farmington, Conn. genealogical collection of Wayne C. Hart (Gridley, Clark), W. L. Holman, "Brief Gridley Notes" (1948, typescript at NEHGS), & G. F. & W. T. R. Marvin, Descendants of Reinold & Matthew Marvin (1904), pp. 9-28, 287-98, 312-14 (Marvin, John Clark of Farmington); Burton W. Spear, Search for the Passengers of the Mary & John, 1630, vol. 7 (1987), pp. 101-4, 108-10 (Pinney); SAW (Pinney, Daniel Clark); KW (Simon Smith); HH (Marvin, Welles, Tomes, Tuttle); OF 1 (Judson); & Selden, Church, Dudley & Pratt sources as above.

RD - Thomas & Elizabeth (Marshall) Lewis, Thomas Newberry (unproved)

Salem "witch" connection - Robert Ayer (grandfather of 448), brother of Mrs. Mary Ayer Parker

PK - Fillmore, Grant, Cleveland (White); Garfield, Hoover, Bush (Wheeler); FDR, Nixon, Bush (Howland); Fillmore, Cleveland (Hyde); Fillmore, Hoover (Wood); Lincoln, Bush (Gilman); Hayes (Farnum, Newberry); Cleveland (Sewall); Coolidge (Coffin, Davis); Hoover (Lord); FDR (Head); Nixon (Batchilor/Batchelder); Bush (Vanderburgh); Taft (Wardwell); B. Harrison (Wines); Harding (Mott)

Note 1: Additional unpublished research into the ancestry of Lynch & Rebecca (Shepherd) King has been undertaken by Jerome E. Anderson of NEHGS.

Note 2: Another immigrant ancestor of Ford (in addition to Thomas & Elizabeth [Marshall] Lewis & Thomas Newberry) for whom royal descent has been proposed, but not proved, is Alice Tomes, first wife of Governor Thomas Welles of Connecticut; see AR 6, line 98.

* * *

James Earl Carter, Jr.

Georgia Life, vol. 3, #3 (Winter, 1976):40-41, 46 & vol. 6, #4 (Spring 1980-last issue):40-41, 43 & sources cited therein, plus much correspondence with the author of these articles, Kenneth H. Thomas, Jr., of Atlanta, esp. a longer version of his "Carter-Gordy: an Update," from which the second article was excerpted; Noel Currer-Briggs, The Carters of Virginia: Their English Ancestry (1979), which suggests patrilineal kinship to Robert "King" Carter, forebear of the Harrisons (see TAG 61[1985-86]:179); J. B. Boddie, Seventeenth Century Isle of Wight County, Virginia (1938), pp. 567-68, & B. A. Chapman, Wills & Administrations of Isle of Wight County, Virginia, 1647-1800, Book I (1938), pp. 79-80, 96, & Isle of Wight County Marriages, 1628-1800 (1933), p. 9 (Carter, Moore); Elizabeth Ramsey Ramsey, Links: Vol. II: A Family's Footprints in the History of Georgia & the Indian Territory of Oklahoma... (1983), passim (Carter, Duckworth, Ramsey); K. H. Thomas, Jr., The Rock House, McDuffie County, Georgia: An Analysis of an Historic Site (1974), pp. 28-51, 111-31, 138-51, Phyllis Ansley Griffin, A History of Descendants: Thomas Ansley, Warren County, Georgia, vol. 1 (1979), pp. 1-2, 6-13, 16-17, 20, 32-33, 35-36, 425-31, & GMNJ 26(1951):57 (Ansley); HGM 3:168-70, 173-74, 4:14, 25, 34-35, 39-41, 47-48 (Cox & Morris of N. J.); T. M. Potts, Historical Collections Relating to the Potts Family (1901), pp. 124-45, & J. W. Clay, ed., Familiae Minorum Gentium, vol. 4 (HSPVS 40, 1896), p. 1241 (Pott); R. M. Bell, The Ancestry of Richard Milhous Nixon (1972, revised 1976), pp. 50-51, 60, 68, 73, 56a, 78 (Morris, Almy, Cornell), TAG 61(1985-86):178 (Almy), & sources cited in both, plus GDRI (Almy, Cornell); Emma Dicken, Our Burnley Ancestors & Allied Families (1946), pp. 5-12, 75-85, 93-108, 115-18 & Terrell Genealogy (1952), pp. 14-20, 56-64, 79-82, 92-97; Sarah D. Hubert, Genealogy of Part of the Barksdale Family of America (1895), pp. 3, 20, 24-25, 31-32 & J. A. Barksdale, Barksdale Family History & Genealogy (1940), pp. 40-42, 49-55; Marion Horton Shook, Carolina Roundup: Kay-Clinkscales-Pratt & Related Families (1965), pp. 1-2, 20-21, 53-55, 58-60, 73, 84, 87-88, J. P. Lovelace, The Pratt Directory (1980), pp. 630, 292, 319, & H. A. Cook, Charles Cook of Generostee with the Johnson & Other Allied Families (1980), pp. 121-34 (Clinkscales); W. P. Young, Abstracts of Old Ninety-Six & Abbeville District Wills & Bonds (1950, reprint 1969), pp. 55, 60, 65, 391 (Cowan); L. R. & J. J. Mize, Threads of Ancestors: Telford-Ritchie-Mize (1956), pp. 184-86 & Forty-sixth Annual Wyatt Reunion Combined with Reunions of the Following Allied & Associated Families...Brownlee...Seawright... and All Descendants of These Families, Greenville Presbyterian Church, Donalds, South Carolina, Sunday June 15, 1952, n. d., p. 17 (Seawright); DAR lineage papers for George Brownlee, 1756-1836; W. L. Crawford, Jr., Ancestors & Friends (A History & Genealogy) (1978), pp. 342-50 (Gordy); N. K. Rogers, History of Chattahoochee County, Georgia (1933), pp. 144-47, 335-37, 362-63, 378-79 (Gordy, Nicholson, Scott); G. C. Helms, Tilman, George & Jonathan Helms, Brothers, 1720-1881: History & Genealogy of the Helms Family (1984), pp. 4, 6, 6a, 12, 31; W. L. Jones, The Fisher Scrap Book, 1730-1972 (1972), pp. 12-19, 312-15; Dorris & Alexander Nunn, Nunns of the South (1974), pp. 27-30, 45-50, 56-58, 60; Mrs. W. A. Simmons, Genealogy of Hollinger Daniel Brown, Jr, & Allied Families (1965), pp. 16-18, 88-93, etc. (Brown, Marcus); C. E. Sutherd, A Compilation of Gaines Family Data with Special Emphasis on the Lineage of William & Isabella (Pendleton) Gaines (2nd ed., 1972), pp. 33-42, 75, 82.

PK - two Harrisons (Carter); Harding, Nixon (Almy)

* * *

Ronald Wilson Reagan

BPF 2 (Reagan chapter, Reagan ancestor table, & addendum) & W. A. Reitwiesner, "The Family of Ronald Wilson Reagan" (5 March 1981), computerized compilation sent to & used in correspondence by the White House, based on research by Mr. Reitwiesner, Michael Pollock, myself, David G. Williamson of London (on the Elseys & Bakers of Epsom, Surrey), & esp. Nancy Gubb Frederick of Evanston, Illinois, who undertook extensive research in primary records in Illinois. Of the various articles in the early 1980s on "Reagan's Roots," the best is perhaps in the Deseret News of Salt Lake City, 9-10 July 1981, pp. B1 & B2. The Ballyporean, Tipperary origin of Michael Reagan, the president's patrilineal great-grandfather, was researched by Debrett's Peerage & Hugh Peskett, reported widely, notably in The Wall Street Journal on 2 Dec. 1980, pp. 1-2, & questioned by the British press at the time of Reagan's summer 1984 visit to Ireland (see The Sunday Times [London] of 3 June 1984, p. 3). A photograph of the Michael Reagan or Ryan 1829 Ballyporean baptismal record appeared in "Ron Reagan Traces the Presidential Family Tree," Signature [The Diner's Club Magazine], vol. 19, Jan. 1984, p. 42, & a Reagan pedigree prepared by the Chief Herald of Ireland appeared in the same article & in many newspapers (the article was distributed by the Los Angeles Times Syndicate), including The Boston Herald of Sunday, 11 March 1984, p. 20. For Reagan's maternal Wilson & Blue forebears see Charles Bent, History of Whiteside County, Illinois (1877), pp. 144-46.

* * *

George Herbert Walker Bush

NEHGS NEXUS 3(1986):124-25 (Bush's patrilineal descent, by Mrs. Elaine Bush Prince of Framingham, Mass.), & 6(1989):23-27, 156-59 (G. B. Roberts; an AT, #1-63, & general discussion), further notes of Mrs. Prince, & a more extended AT compiled by W. A. Reitwiesner of Washington, D. C., based upon, or amplified by, a large variety of sources. These last include, for families covered through AT numbers 258-505, NCAB N-63 (1984):221-23 (G. H. W. Bush), 57(1977):110-11 (P. S. Bush), 40(1955):333-34 (S. P. Bush), Obituary Record of Graduates of Yale University Deceased During the Academical Year Ending in June, 1890 (1890), pp. 574-75 (Rev. J. S. Bush), & M. E. Goddard & H. V. Partridge, A History of Norwich, Vermont (1905), pp. 178-80 (Timothy & Fairbanks Bush); L. S. Fairbanks, Genealogy of the Fairbanks Family in America (1897), pp. 31-34, 39-40, 54-55, TAG 37(1961):65-72 (Fairbanks), NH (Penfield), & NEHGR 101(1947):75-77 (Penfield, Lewis); HH 426-27, 429-31 (House) & LCF (House, Davenport); Charles Burleigh, The Genealogy & History of the Guild, Guile & Gile Family (1887), pp. 25-26, 33; Thomas Hills, "Genealogical Data Connected with the Name of George" (1909, MSS. at NEHGS), pp. 81-82, 87, 100-1; B. M. Newcomb, Andrew Newcomb, 1618-1686, & His Descendants (1923), pp. 9-27, 35-37, 45-46, 76-77; Samuel May, J. J. May, R. S. Edes, J. W. May & J. F. May, Descendants of John May of Roxbury, Mass., 1640, 2nd ed. (1978), pp. 1-5, 287 & DG 1 (May, Brewer, Bridge, Robinson); SAWE (Stillman); SS (Samuel & Philip Smith); BTGC 14 Feb. 1923, #471, 4 & 5 Nov. 1931, #2463, 12 May 1932, #3679 (Bush, Smith, Whipple/Whippo), BW (Daniel Smith, Sr. & Jr.), R. A. Wheeler, History of the Town of Stonington, County of New London, Connecticut (1900, reprint 1977), pp. 570-72, 574 (patrilineal descent of Mrs. Harriet Smith Bush); Plowdon Stevens, Stephens-Stevens Genealogy: Lineage from Henry Stephens or Stevens of Stonington, Connecticut, 1668 (1909), pp. 20-30, 36-39,

49; D. C. Gallup & J. M. Peck, Gallup Genealogy (1966), pp. 3-6, 9, 263; Myrtle M. Morris, Joseph & Philena (Elton) Fellows: Their Ancestry & Descendants (1940), pp. 24-49 & PT (Cross); O. P. Fay, Fay Genealogy (1898), pp. 19, 21-23, 25, 38, 68, 103, & J. W. Norcross, "The Genealogy of the Fay Family" (1887, MSS. at NEHGS), pp. 1-7, 10-11, 36-37, 116-17, 232, 289; Harrison Ellery & C. P. Bowditch, The Pickering Genealogy, vol. 2 (1897), p. 685 (a list of families in the ancestry of S. P. P. Fay & Harriet Howard), & Ancestor Tables for same (6 vols., MSS. at NEHGS), Sheets 201-300, VIII/283 for 50 VIII 555 (Richard Sullivan Fay); Elias Child, Genealogy of the Child, Childs & Childe Families (1881), pp. 494, 506-7 & the 1742 will of John Child of Waltham (Middlesex Co., Mass. Probate Records, vol. 25, pp. 218-22); A. M. Phillips, Phillips Genealogies (1885), pp. 97-98, WC (Ebenezer, Andrew Jr., & Andrew Phillips, Sr., Michael Smith, John Smith, Jr., & Thomas Cutler), & TAG 19(1942-43):231 (Phillips), 53(1977):70, 72 (Coolidge AT #s 142-43, 284-87); William Prescott, The Prescott Memorial (1870, reprint 1983), pp. 41-44, 46-47, 50-51, 65-66, 88-89, & SM 1 (Prescott, Platts alias Gawkroger); D. L. Jacobus, The Bulkeley Genealogy (1933), p. 2-51, 92-113, 129-31, 151, 210, 441-42 (Bulkeley, Prescott, Fay) & W. I. T. Brigham, The History of the Brigham Family, vol. 1 (1907), pp. 33-59, 70-77, 89-90, vol. 2 (E. E. Brigham [1927]), pp. 19-29, 34, 42-43; Boston VRs (1730 birth & 1750 marriage intention of Ebenezer Howard) & various Howard probate & deed records in Suffolk Co., Mass. (esp. the 1784 will & 1808 administration of Ebenezer & Martha [Goff] Howard, & a 1792 deed between Martha & Samuel Howard, mother & son; S. B. Shackford, "Wallingford Family Records" (1928, typescript at NEHGS), pp. for 1, 1-3, & 1-3-6 & GDMNH (Wallingford, Tuttle); Thomas Theodore Goff MSS. Collection at NEHGS, Box 11, Section 330, p. 693 & W. S. Appleton, Record of the Descendants of William Sumner of Dorchester, Mass., 1636 (1879), pp. 1-2 (Sumner, Goffe); E. L. Pierce, Major John Lillie, 1755-1801; the Lillie Family of Boston, 1663-1896 (1896), pp. 47-94, 106-14; John Wentworth, The Wentworth Genealogy, English & American, 2nd ed., vol. 1 (1878), p. 288 (Ruck) & W. H. Whitmore, A Brief Genealogy of the Descendants of William Hutchinson & Thomas Oliver (1865), pp. 6-10; Samuel Breck, Genealogy of the Breck Family (1889), pp. 11-16, 18-19; J. M. Raymond, Thomas Families of Plymouth Colony, Massachusetts, 1st ed. (1980), pp. 249-50; LBNSDAR, vol. 116 (1930), pp. 54-55 (John Shellman, Jr.); T. J. C. Williams & Folger McKinsey, History of Frederick County, Maryland (1910, reprint 1967), vol. 2, pp. 1313-14, G. L. Tracey & J. P. Dern, Pioneers of Old Monocacy: The Early Settlement of Frederick County, Maryland, 1721-1743 (1987), pp. 161-63, F. S. Weiser, Records of Marriages & Burials in the Monocacy Church in Frederick County, Maryland & in the Evangelical Lutheran Congregation in the City of Frederick, Maryland, 1743-1811 (National Genealogical Society Special Publication No. 38, 1972), pp. 87, 124, & Western Maryland Genealogy, 4(1988):157 (Shellman, esp. an obituary of John Shellman, Sr., & burial records for Mrs. Maria Margareth Fauth Schellman & Mrs. Susanna Bocher Fauth Apfelin); H. K. Lyon & M. H. Vesely, Montfort-Munford Family of Virginia & Georgia & Allied Families (1978), pp. 1-25 esp. & GVFT 2:739-50 (Munford); Zelma Wells Price, Of Whom I Came; From Whence I Came-Wells-Wise, Rish-Wise & Otherwise, vol. 6 (1963), part I, pp. 3-6 (Bolling), part II, pp. 146-52, 161 (Cocke), part III, pp. 319-20 (Kennon); GVFWM 1:455-61, 463 & GVFVM 1:435-38 (Brodnax); Historical Publishing Co., Franklin County at the Beginning of the Twentieth Century (1901), p. 131 & W. A. Taylor, Centennial History of Columbus & Franklin County, Ohio, vol. 2 (1909), pp. 197-99 (Robert E. Sheldon); fact sheet concerning the president's ancestors in Franklin Co., Ohio, prepared by Meg Scott of the Franklin County

Genealogical Society & available in various Columbus-area libraries, Franklin Co. data gathered by Meg Scott, Mrs. Ferdinand P. Schoedinger, Jr., & George S. Hoster, Jr., partly published in The Report (Journal of the Ohio Genealogical Society) 26(1986):125 & burial records of the Greenlawn Cemetery, Columbus, Ohio, microfilmed by the Franklin County Genealogical Society (Sheldon, Uncles, Butler); Marjorie Smith, Ohio Marriages Extracted from the Old Northwest Quarterly (1980), p. 322 (1816 marriage of James Unckles/Uncles & Betsey Kiswell) & Ohio Cemetery Records Extracted from The "Old Northwest" Genealogical Quarterly (1984), p. 253 (Samuel H. & Courtland P. L. Butler & their wives); LBNSDAR, vol. 8 (1899), p. 249 (Mrs. Harriet Livingston Butler Doty, #7739, sister of Mrs. Mary Elizabeth Butler Sheldon) & vol. 135 (1933), p. 287 (Mrs. Ella Nason Burrows, #134906, a great-granddaughter of S. H. Butler & Judith Livingston), plus the application paper for Mrs. Burrows, which contains various dates that confirm or lead to other sources, esp. the birth date of Rev. Nathaniel Butler; James N. Arnold, Vital Record of Rhode Island, 1636-1850, vol. 3, part 5 (1892), pp. 18, 87 (marriage record of Benjamin Butler & Susanna Whiting, & births of their children, including Nathaniel); LBNSDAR, vol. 143 (1935), pp. 154-55 (data on Benjamin Butler under 142470), BMV 47-48, 63 (Butler), TAG 63 (1988):65-77, 239-42 (Blossom) & T. S. Lazell, Whiting Genealogy (1902), pp. 5-13, 17, 28; TAG 14 (1937-38):96-98, DG 2 (Herrick), L. C. Herrick, Herrick Genealogy (1885), pp. 27, 73, 104, & Vital Records of Norwich, 1659-1848, part 1 (1913), p. 322 (Samuel Herrick & Silence Kingsley); A. D. Rust, Record of the Rust Family (1891), pp. 1-13, 25-31, 39-45; W. A. Kingsley, Kingsley Family of America (1980), pp. 418-19, 422-23 esp. (but the mother of Silence Kingsley was Mary ---, not Mary Packard), R. V. Wood, Jr., Francis Cooke of the Mayflower: Four Generations (1986), pp. 1-3, 6-7, 20-21, 84 & Mr. Wood's draft page for Samuel Kingsley (III), Silence's father, a 5th generation Cooke descendant; NYGBR 84(1953):4-6, 12, 85 (1954):25-26, 89(1958):240 (Livingston), & Florence Van Rensselaer, The Livingston Family in America & Its Scottish Origins (1949), pp. 3-77, 81-83, 89, 107; W. B. Aitken, Distinguished Families in America Descended from Wilhelmus Beekman & Jan Thomasse Van Dyke (1912), pp. 1-8 esp.; J. W. Behan, The Woodworth Family of America, vol. 1 (1988), pp. 1-12, 21-27; "The Vanderburgh Ancestry of Presidents Gerald R. Ford, Jr., & George H. W. Bush," unpublished typescript by William J. Powers, Jr., of Acton, Mass., & Wallace McLeod, The Family of Richard Vanderburgh of Richmond Hill (1797-1869) (1962), pp. 2-9; F. C. Pierce, Pierce Genealogy, No. IV, Being the Record of the Posterity of Captain Michael, John & Captain William Pierce (1889), pp. 33-36, 40-44, 49-50, 58, 89-91, 156-59, 255-58; H. L. Peter Rounds, The John Round Family of Swansea & Rehoboth, Massachusetts (1983), pp. 11-16, 37-41; MQ 49(1983):170-74, SE 2 (Martin), & M. B. Clarke, Bosworth Genealogy, Part IV (1931), p. 453 (Martin, Bullock); Sherrill R. Bourn, Jared Bourn: a Family History of One Line for Ten Generations (1987), pp. 1-27, 93-99; A. G. Wheeler, The Genealogical & Encyclopedic History of the Wheeler Family in America, vol. 1 (1914), pp. 394-96, 429-32, 434, H. S. Cole, Hayden Samuel Cole & His Ancestry (1935), pp. 60-63 (Wheeler, Squire, West), & PA (Dominick Wheeler); M. R. Jenks & F. C. Seymour, Thomas Horton of Milton & Rehoboth, Massachusetts, vol. 1 (1984), pp. 3-5, 8-9, 11-12, 27-28; SM 1 (Carpenter, Weeks, Clapp) & ALR (Carpenter); DSGRM 23(1959-60):5-10, 57-58, 97-100 (Millard); J. S. Wood, Sr., The Wood Family Index (1966), pp. 205, 98, 231, 256, & Mrs. N. M. P. Akeley & Mrs. Jessie A. Porter, "Carpenter Cemetery, Guildford, Vermont," typescript, n. d., p. 4 (epitaph of Rev. Jabez Wood, Jr.), plus, for various ancestors of Betsey S. Wheeler, Rehoboth, Swansea, Middleborough & Warren, R. I. vital records; Walker data collected by Christopher Thompson Walker of Woodbridge, Conn.; Mrs. H. D. Pittman & Mrs. R. K.

Walker, Americans of Gentle Birth & Their Ancestors, vol. 1 (1903, reprint 1970), pp. 312-24, 335 (Walker, Mercer, Davis, Beaky, Bangs, Hinckley, Stackhouse, Heaton, Powell, Wear, with some errors, as to English origins esp.); James Cox, Old & New St. Louis (1894), pp. 196-97, William Hyde & H. L. Conard, Encyclopedia of the History of St. Louis, vol. 4 (1899), p. 2395, & J. W. Leonard, ed., The Book of St. Louisans (1906), p. 590 (David Davis Walker); Capt. Jeremiah Baker Chapter, D.A.R., Cecil County, Maryland Marriage Licenses, 1777-1840 (1974), p. 14 (1793 license of John Mercer & Rebecca Davis) & Robert Barnes, comp., Maryland Marriages, 1634-1777 (1975), pp. 47 (Thomas Davis & Rebecca Gregory), 121 (Robert Mercer & Anne Mounce); Dean Dudley, History & Genealogy of the Bangs Family in America (1896), pp. 9-20, 22-26, 36, 55, 87-91, 153-58 & AB (Bangs, Hobart); E. Charles Hinckley, Hinckley Heritage & History, 3rd ed. (1982), pp. 40-41, 45; H. F. Andrews, History of the Hamlin Family, Part One (1894), pp. 43-53, 63-66, 68-69, 83-85, 116; Wesley B. Keeler, Keeler Family: Ralph Keeler of Norwalk, Ct., & Some of His Descendants (1985), pp. 1-4, 7-8, 15-16, 37-38; S. W. Phoenix, The Whitney Family of Connecticut & Its Affiliations (1878), vol. 1, pp. 1-12, 16-17, 31, 82-83, 239-40, 652, vol. 2, p. 1433, vol. 3, p. 2178; E. G. Stackhouse, Stackhouse: An Original Pennsylvania Family (1988), pp. 6-10, 39, 72, & correspondence from the author, WCPDD (Stackhouse), W. R. & W. F. Stackhouse, The Stackhouse Family (1935), pp. 87-96, & W. W. H. Davis, W. S. Ely & J. W. Jordan, History of Bucks County, Pennsylvania, vol. 3 (1905, reprinted as A Genealogical & Personal History of Bucks County, Pennsylvania, 1975), pp. 489-90 (Stackhouse, Hastings, Powell); O. G. Edwards & I. W. Roberts, Descendants of East Tennessee Pioneers [Wear] (1963), pp. 220-22, 226-27; LBNSDAR, vol. 20 (1905), p. 117 (Mrs. Minnie Holliday Nave, #19316, sister of the president's matrilineal great-grandmother) & vol. 24 (1907), p. 158 (Mrs. Mildred Wear [not Near] Kotany, #23452, the president's great-aunt); "Cooper County Cemeteries," manuscript at the State Historical Society of Missouri, p. 44 (Mrs. Sarah A. Y. Wear), A. M. Coppage III & D. F. Wulfeck, Virginia Settlers in Missouri (1966), p. 99, #6011 (Yancy-Field-Wear query), W. H. & J. H. Norwood & O. Y. Lacy, Genealogy of Yancey-Medearis & Related Lines (1958), pp. 1-2, Edgar Woods, Albemarle County in Virginia (1932), pp. 357-58 (Yancey), & D. F. Wulfeck, Marriages of Some Virginia Residents, 1607-1800, vol. 2 (1986), p. 321 (Jechonias Yancey & Mildred Wood); W. H. Miller, History & Genealogies of the Families of Miller, Woods, Harris, Wallace, Maupin, Oldham, Kavanaugh, & Brown (1907), p. 448 (Mullins); Wood-Woods Exchange 2(1948):6-7 (will abstracts for Jesse & William Wood); F. C. Pierce, Field Genealogy, vol. 2 (1901), pp. 1101-7, 1119, 1136; GKFFC 274 esp. (Clark); Hyde & Conard, op. cit. (see under D. D. Walker) (1899), p. 2477 (J. H. Wear) & vol. 2, pp. 1038-40 (Hollidays), W. S. Stevens, St. Louis: History of the Fourth City, 1763-1909, vol. 2 (1909), pp. 1045-46 (J. H. Wear) & Portrait & Biographical Record of Lafayette and Saline Counties, Missouri (1893), pp. 418-19 (W. H. Holliday); E. P. Ellsberry, Cemetery Records of Monroe County, Missouri, vol. 2, n. d., p. 43 (Joseph Holliday); A. W. Burns, Record of Marriages, Bourbon County, Paris, Kentucky (1931), p. 24 (Joseph Holliday & Nancy R. McCune), & Record of Marriage Bonds in Henry County, Kentucky for the Period of Years 1798 to 1851 Inclusive (1932), p. 20 (Peter Foree & Eliza Dawson), Mrs. W. B. Ardery, Kentucky Records (1926, reprint 1958), p. 51 (will abstract of William Holliday), & H. W. Miller, The Dawson Family in America Applicable to the Lineage of Clarinda Dawson Miller, n. d., C. C. Dawson, A Collection of Family Records...of Various Families & Individuals Bearing the Name Dawson (1873), pp. 229-32, & various DAR lineage papers concerning Henry Dawson, 1748-1811.

For tracing much of Bush's Southern & mid-Atlantic ancestry I am indebted to my colleagues Julie Helen Otto & Richard Andrew Pierce of NEHGS (especially for their skillful use, among numerous other sources, of census indexes & the International Genealogical Index for clues) & to W. A. Reitwiesner. I also wish to thank Eric G. Grundset of the DAR Library, Kenneth H. Thomas, Jr., Dr. J. Bradley Arthaud, Ronald D. Risley, & the above-mentioned Elaine Prince, Christopher Walker, Meg Scott & Mary Schoedinger. Still untraced is the parentage of Priscilla Whippo, Michael & Mary (--) Sheldon, James Uncles, Elizabeth Criswell or Kiswell, Thomas Walker, Catharine McLelland, & Catharine Shriner. The parents & maternal grandparents of Samuel Herrick Butler, moreover, are identified only in DAR application papers which are not fully documented; further proof, perhaps to be found in Bible or tombstone records or Vermont, New York, or Ohio primary sources, is much desired, for the alleged identifications lead to descent from **Mayflower** passenger Francis Cooke & Leyden residents Thomas & Margaret (Williams) Mitchell, whose almost certain daughter, Mrs. Constant Mitchell Fobes Briggs, is an ancestor of The Princess of Wales.

RD - Walter Aston, Rev. Peter & Jane (Allen) Bulkeley, Mrs. Anne Marbury Hutchinson & Mrs. Catherine Hamby Hutchinson, Robert Livingston the Elder, & Dr. Richard Palgrave.

MP - John & Elizabeth (Tilley) Howland, John & Joan (Hurst) Tilley; Francis Cooke (possible, unproved)

PW - Thomas & Margaret (Williams) Mitchell (possible, unproved)

PK - Washington, Coolidge, FDR (Spencer-English); Hayes, Taft, Nixon (Foote); Garfield, Hoover, Ford (Wheeler); Taft, Coolidge, Nixon (Morse); FDR, Nixon, Ford (Howland); Pierce, Hayes (Brewer); Lincoln, Ford (Gilman); Grant, FDR (Lathrop, Mahieu); Garfield, Taft (Holbrook); Hayes, Cleveland (S. Smith); Taft, Coolidge (Ravens); Taft, Hoover (Sherman); Garfield (Carpenter); Cleveland (Stanley); Taft (Davenport, Fairbanks?, Mitchell?, M. Pierce); Coolidge (Phillips, Bulkeley, Horton, Garnsey); FDR (Beekman, F. Cooke?, Hutchinson, Jenney, Palgrave, Pope, Richards); Ford (Vanderburgh); Fillmore (Millard); T. Roosevelt (Schuyler)

* * *

A note on the NEHGS "team" of researchers on presidential genealogy: Since the April 1989 publication of the preliminary edition of **Ancestors of American Presidents** I have coordinated the assembling of additions and corrections to the text and have received, and gratefully acknowledge, extensive new data or lesser but well documented items from Raymond Martin Bell, Kenneth H. Thomas, Jr., Henry Bainbridge Hoff, William J. Powers, Jr., Brice McAdoo Clagett, Jean Fletcher Yates, Dr. John Bradley Arthaud, Sherrill R. Bourn, Harry Hollingsworth, Joseph L. Druse, Teri Howden Freedman, Ronald D. Risley and Constance Mulholland, among others. This new data has been especially helpful on Hayes, Garfield, Benjamin Harrison, T. Roosevelt, Hoover, Truman, Nixon, Ford, Carter and Bush. My colleague Julie Helen Otto has drawn or (usually only slightly) corrected a dozen or more charts, several entirely new, based on these findings, and is much interested in Bush's Whippo ancestry; her article on Capt. Lawrence Hammond, a possible ancestor of the Long Island and Cambridge, N. Y. Whippos, appears in NEHGS **NEXUS** 6(1989):149-52. Of enormous value also have been the probings, in both printed and primary materials, by Richard Andrew Pierce, noted Boston genealogist and NEHGS volunteer, into some of the most difficult problems in presidential genealogy, including the Truman and Kennedy patrilineal ancestry, the patrilineal forebears of Coolidge's mother (the Moor line), Eisenhower's possible Scots-

Irish Hannah and Bush's McCune ancestry, the identity of Hayes' Cornwall great-grandfather, and Mrs. Asenath Hill Garfield Boynton. Given the difficulty of these problems, many of Mr. Pierce's findings to date are somewhat speculative, and some research, in the Kennedy home parish of Whitechurch, co. Wexford, especially, is continuing. Of particular interest, since it might lead to considerable new Connecticut ancestry for Garfield, is Richard's suggestion that Asenath Hill's father might be Hezekiah Hill, born in Middletown 25 Feb. 1735/6, son of Jonathan and Sarah, and seemingly a soldier in the French and Indian Wars and later resident of Lee, Mass. (1790) and Worcester, Otsego Co., N. Y. (1800). Possible sons of this Hezekiah Hill include Hezekiah (Jr.?), Amasa (see M. E. H. Steed, **Soldiers and Widows of the American Revolution Who Lived in Lake County, Ohio**, 1985, pp. 114-15) and Josiah.

# # #

PRESIDENTIAL ROYAL DESCENTS

The best line through each royally descended presidential immigrant ancestor

George Washington Through (1) George Reade

1 Edward III, King of England, d. 1377 = Philippa of Hainault
2 Lionel of Antwerp, Duke of Clarence = Elizabeth de Burgh
3 Philippa Plantagenet = Edmund Mortimer, 3rd Earl of March
4 Elizabeth Mortimer = Sir Henry "Hotspur" Percy
5 Henry Percy, 2nd Earl of Northumberland = Eleanor Neville
6 Henry Percy, 3rd Earl of Northumberland = Eleanor Poynings
7 Margaret Percy = Sir William Gascoigne
8 Elizabeth Gascoigne = Sir George Talboys
9 Anne Talboys = Sir Edward Dymoke
10 Frances Dymoke = Sir Thomas Windebank
11 Mildred Windebank = Robert Reade
12 George Reade of Va. = Elizabeth Martiau
13 Mildred Reade = Augustine Warner Jr.
14 Mildred Warner = Lawrence Washington
15 Augustine Washington = Mary Ball
16 George Washington, 1731/2-1799, 1st U. S. President
= Mrs. Martha Dandridge Custis

Sources: MCS 3, lines 86 & 108; LDBR 5:101-2; AR 6, lines 3, 5 & 19, plus sources cited in all three.

George Washington Through (2) John Washington

1 Edward I, King of England, d. 1307 = Margaret of France
2 Edmund of Woodstock, Earl of Kent = Margaret Wake
3 Joan Plantagenet = Thomas Holand, 1st Earl of Kent
4 Thomas Holand, 2nd Earl of Kent = Alice FitzAlan
5 Eleanor Holand = Edward Cherlton, 4th Baron Cherlton of Powis
6 Joyce Cherlton = John Tiptoft (Tibetot), 1st Baron Tiptoft
7 Joyce Tiptoft = Sir Edmund Sutton (or Dudley)
8 Sir John Sutton = --- Charroll
9 Margaret Sutton = John Butler
10 William Butler = Margaret Greeke
11 Margaret Butler = Lawrence Washington
12 Lawrence Washington = Amphyllis Twigden
13 John Washington of Va. = Anne Pope
14 Lawrence Washington = Mildred Warner
15 Augustine Washington = Mary Ball
16 George Washington, 1731/2-1799, 1st U. S. President
= Mrs. Martha Dandridge Custis

Sources: Burke's Landed Gentry of Great Britain, 1939 ed., reprinted in 1971 as Prominent Families in America with British Ancestry, pp. 2959-63; HSF 4:149-54; MCS 3, lines 30, 90, 94 & 114 (plus AR 6, lines 47 & 155, & LDBR 5:131-32, 135); & TAG 53(1977):15.

Note: Philippa Plantagenet & Edmund Mortimer, 3rd Earl of March (Reade, generation 3) were the paternal grandparents, & Eleanor Holand (Washington, generation 5) the mother (by Roger Mortimer, 4th Earl of March, her first husband), of Anne Mortimer, wife of Richard Plantagenet, Earl of Cambridge, & mother of Richard Plantagenet, 3rd Duke of York; see the first page of the John of Gaunt presidential descendants charts.

George Washington Through (3) Mrs. Mary Towneley Warner

1 William I the Lion, King of Scotland, d. 1214
2 Isabel of Scotland (illeg. by a dau. of Richard Avenal) = Robert de Ros, Magna Charta Surety
3 Sir William de Ros = Lucy FitzPiers
4 Sir William de Ros = Eustache Fitzhugh
5 Lucy de Ros = Sir Robert Plumpton
6 Sir William Plumpton = Christiana ---
7 Alice Plumpton = Sir Richard Sherburne
8 Margaret Sherburne = Richard Bayley
9 Richard Bayley alias Sherburne = Agnes Stanley
10 Richard Sherburne = Matilda Hamerton
11 Isabel Sherburne = John Towneley
12 Lawrence Towneley = ---
13 Henry Towneley = ---
14 Lawrence Towneley = Helen Hesketh
15 Lawrence Towneley = Margaret Hartley
16 Lawrence Towneley = Jennet Halstead
17 Mary Towneley of Va. = Augustine Warner
18 Augustine Warner, Jr. = Mildred Reade
19 Mildred Warner = Lawrence Washington
20 Augustine Washington = Mary Ball
21 George Washington, 1731/2-1799, 1st U. S. President = Mrs. Martha Dandridge Custis

Sources: GVFVM 5:538-90; Edward Baines, **History of the County Palatine & Duchy of Lancaster**, vol. 3 (1836), chart between pp. 572 & 573 (Sherburne); AR 6, line 170.

Thomas Jefferson Through (1) William Randolph

1 Edward III, King of England, d. 1377 = Philippa of Hainault
2 John of Gaunt, Duke of Lancaster = Catherine de Roet
3 Joan Beaufort = Ralph Neville, 1st Earl of Westmoreland
4 Edward Neville, 1st Baron Abergavenny = Catherine Howard
5 Catherine Neville = Robert Tanfield
6 William Tanfield = Isabel Stavely
7 Francis Tanfield = Bridget Cave
8 Anne Tanfield = Clement Vincent
9 Elizabeth Vincent = Richard Lane
10 Dorothy Lane = William Randolph
11 Richard Randolph = Elizabeth Ryland
12 William Randolph of Va. = Mary Isham
13 Isham Randolph = Jane Rogers
14 Jane Randolph = Peter Jefferson
15 Thomas Jefferson, 1743-1826, 3rd U. S. President = Mrs. Martha Wayles Skelton

Sources: MCS 3, lines 71, 47 & 45 (plus AR 6, lines 1 & 2, & LDBR 5:315-16), & sources cited therein.

Thomas Jefferson Through (2) Henry Isham

1 Henry II, King of England, d. 1189
2 William de Longespee (illeg. perhaps by Alix de Porhoet), Earl of Salisbury = Ela, Countess of Salisbury
3 Stephen de Longespee = Emmeline de Riddleford
4 Emmeline de Longespee = Maurice FitzMaurice
5 Juliana FitzMaurice = Thomas de Clare

6 Margaret de Clare = Bartholomew Badlesmere, 1st Baron Badlesmere
7 Margaret Badlesmere = John de Tibetot, 2nd Baron Tibetot
8 Robert de Tibetot, 3rd Baron Tibetot = Margaret Diencourt
9 Elizabeth de Tibetot = Sir Philip Despencer
10 Margery Despencer = Sir Roger Wentworth
11 Margaret Wentworth = Sir William Hopton
12 Margaret Hopton = Sir Philip Booth
13 Audrey Booth = Sir William Lytton
14 Sir Robert Lytton = Frances Cavalery
15 Anne Lytton = Sir John Borlase
16 Anne Borlase = Sir Euseby Isham
17 William Isham = Mary Brett
18 Henry Isham of Va. = Katherine Banks
19 Mary Isham = William Randolph
20 Isham Randolph = Jane Rogers
21 Jane Randolph = Peter Jefferson
22 Thomas Jefferson, 1743-1826, 3rd U. S. President = Mrs. Martha Wayles Skelton

Sources: LDBR 5:723-24; CP, Tibetot (Tiptoft) & Badlesmere articles; AR 6, lines 200, 54, 178, 31 & 30. See also H. W. Brainerd, A Survey of the Ishams in England and America, 1938, pp. 32-35, 44-45, 50-55; The Genealogist, New Ser., vol. 2 (1885), pp. 228-30 (Borlase); & Robert Clutterbuck, The History and Antiquities of the County of Hertford, vol. 2 (1821), p. 377 (Lytton).

Thomas Jefferson Through (3) Christopher Branch

1 Henry I, King of England, d. 1135
2 Robert of Caen (illegitimate), 1st Earl of Gloucester = Mabel FitzHamon
3 Maud of Gloucester = Ranulph de Meschines, 2nd Earl of Chester
4 Hugh Kevelioc, 3rd Earl of Chester
5 Amicia de Meschines (illegitimate) = Ralph de Mainwaring
6 Bertrade de Mainwaring = Henry de Audley
7 Emma de Audley = Gruffydd ap Madog, Prince of Powys Fadog
8 Margaret ferch Gruffydd ap Madog = Sir John Arderne
9 Agnes Arderne = Sir John Whetenhall
10 Margaret Whetenhall = Adam Bostock
11 Adam Bostock = Janet Bradshaw
12 Sir Ralph Bostock = Isabel Lawton
13 Sir Adam Bostock = Elizabeth Venables
14 Nicholas Bostock = Catherine Mobberly
15 Hugh Bostock = Joan Del Heath
16 George Bostock = Joan Horne
17 Joan Bostock = William Jennings
18 Thomas Jennings = Alice Bright
19 Catherine Jennings = William Branch
20 Lionel Branch = Valentia Sparkes
21 Christopher Branch of Va. = Mary Addie
22 Christopher Branch, Jr. = ---
23 Mary Branch = Thomas Jefferson
24 Thomas Jefferson, Jr. = Mary Field
25 Peter Jefferson = Jane Randolph
26 Thomas Jefferson, 1743-1826, 3rd U. S. President = Mrs. Martha Wayles Skelton

Sources: GVFVM 1:208-32 (Branch); W. H. Rylands, ed., The Four Visitations of Berkshire, vol. 2 (HSPVS, vol. 57, 1908), pp. 76-78 (Bostock, Jennings); George Ormerod, History of the County Palatine and City of Chester, 2nd ed. (Thomas Helsby, ed.), 1882, vol. 3, p. 259 (Bostock), vol. 2, p. 195 (Whetenhall), & vol. 2, pp. 85 & 77 (Arderne, Powys Fadog); John Ross Delafield, Delafield: The Family History, 1945, vol. 2, pp. 589-97 (Powys Fadog, Audley & Mainwaring); AR 6, lines 124-25.

James Madison, Jr., Through (1) Mrs. Martha Eltonhead Conway

1 Henry II, King of England, d. 1189
2 William de Longespee (illeg. perhaps by Alix de Porhoet), Earl of Salisbury = Ela, Countess of Salisbury
3 Stephen de Longespee = Emmeline de Riddleford
4 Ela de Longespee = Sir Roger la Zouche
5 Alan la Zouche, 1st Baron Zouche of Ashby = Eleanor de Segrave
6 Maud la Zouche = Robert Holand, 1st Baron Holand
7 Maud Holand = Sir Thomas Swinnerton
8 Sir Robert Swinnerton = Elizabeth Beke
9 Maud Swinnerton = Sir John Savage
10 Sir John Savage = Eleanor Brereton
11 (probably, although which Sir John Savage was Alice's father remains problematic) Alice (or Dulcia) Savage = Sir Henry Bold
12 Maud Bold = Thomas Gerard
13 Jennet Gerard = Richard Eltonhead (see next line)
14 William Eltonhead = Anne Bowers
15 Richard Eltonhead = Anne Sutton
16 Martha Eltonhead of Va. = Edwin Conway
17 Edwin Conway, Jr. = Elizabeth Thornton
18 Francis Conway = Rebecca Catlett
19 Eleanor Rose Conway = James Madison
20 James Madison, Jr., 1750/1-1836, 4th U. S. President = Mrs. Dorothea "Dolly" Payne Todd

Sources: HVG 227-29 (Eltonhead); Edward Baines, The History of the County Palatine & Duchy of Lancaster (James Croston, ed.), vol. 4, 1891, pp. 375-76 (Gerard) & vol. 5, 1893, pp. 25 (Bold) & 74 (Harington, see next line); various Savage sources, none satisfactory, including George Ormerod, The History of the County Palatine and City of Chester, 2nd ed. (Thomas Helsby, ed.), vol. 1, 1882, pp. 712-13, William Salt Archaeological Society, Collections for a History of Staffordshire, New Ser., vol. 12, 1909, p. 144, & Glover's & Flower's The Visitation of Cheshire, 1580 (HSPVS, vol. 18, 1882), p. 203; AR 6, lines 30-32 (above) & 34 (next line).

James Madison, Jr., Through (1) Mrs. Martha Eltonhead Conway
second line

1 Ethelred II the Unready, King of England, d. 1016 = Aelflede
2 Elgiva of England = Uchtred, Earl of Northumberland
3 Edith of Northumberland = Maldred of Scotland, Lord of Carlisle & Allerdale
4 Gospatrick, Earl of Northumberland & Dunbar = ---, sister of Edmund
5 Gunnilda = Orm, son of Ketel
6 Gospatrick, Lord of Workington = Egeline (Engaine?)
7 Thomas of Workington = Grace ---
8 Ada of Workington = William le Fleming
9 Sir Michael le Fleming = Agatha Fitz Henry
10 William le Fleming of Aldingham = ---
11 Eleanor le Fleming = Sir Richard Cansfield

12 Agnes Cansfield = Sir Robert Harington (de Haverington)
13 Sir John Harington = Joan (Dacre?)
14 Sir John Harington = Katherine Banastre
15 Sir Nicholas Harington = Isabel English
16 Nicholas Harington of Hoyton = Margaret Lathom
17 --- Harington (daughter) = Nicholas Eltonhead
18 John Eltonhead = Margaret Lancaster
19 John Eltonhead = Elizabeth Birkenhead
20 Richard Eltonhead = Jennet Gerard
21 William Eltonhead = Anne Bowers
22 Richard Eltonhead = Anne Sutton
23 Martha Eltonhead of Va. = Edwin Conway
24 Edwin Conway, Jr. = Elizabeth Thornton
25 Francis Conway = Rebecca Catlett
26 Eleanor Rose Conway = James Madison
27 James Madison, Jr., 1750/1-1836, 4th U. S. President = Mrs. Dorothea "Dolly" Payne Todd

James Madison Through (2) Anthony Savage (unproved)

1 Edward I, King of England, d. 1307 = Eleanor of Castile
2 Elizabeth Plantagenet = Humphrey de Bohun, 4th Earl of Hereford & Essex
3 William de Bohun, 1st Earl of Northampton = Elizabeth Badlesmere
4 Elizabeth de Bohun = Richard FitzAlan, 10th Earl of Arundel
5 Ellizabeth FitzAlan = Sir Robert Goushill
6 Joan Goushill = Thomas Stanley, 1st Baron Stanley
7 Catherine Stanley = Sir John Savage, son of Sir John Savage and Eleanor Brereton, see previous chart (generation 10 of Madison's first royal descent via Mrs. Martha Eltonhead Conway)
8 Sir Christopher Savage (whose maternity has been doubted) = Anne Stanley
9 Christopher Savage = Anne Lygon
10 Francis Savage = Anne Sheldon
11 Anthony Savage = Elizabeth Hall
12 Anthony Savage (or his nephew, another Anthony Savage bp. 1623, son of Charles Savage & Elizabeth Abington), possibly the immigrant to Va. = ---
13 Alice Savage = Francis Thornton
14 Elizabeth Thornton = Edwin Conway, Jr.
15 Francis Conway = Rebecca Catlett
16 Eleanor Rose Conway = James Madison
17 James Madison, Jr., 1750/1-1836, 4th U. S. President = Mrs. Dorothea "Dolly" Payne Todd

Sources: W. D. Ligon, The Ligon Family & Connections, vol. 1 (1947, reprint 1988), pp. 38-41; GVFT 3:474-79; AR 6, lines 57, 20, 15 & 6.

John Quincy Adams Through Mrs. Elizabeth Coytmore Tyng

1 Edward III, King of England, d. 1377 = Philippa of Hainault
2 John of Gaunt, Duke of Lancaster = Catherine de Roet
3 Henry Beaufort, Cardinal Beaufort
4 (illeg. by Alice FitzAlan, who = John Cherlton, 4th Baron Cherlton of Powis) Jane Beaufort = Sir Edward Stradling
5 Sir Henry Stradling = Elizabeth Herbert
6 Thomas Stradling = Janet Mathew
7 Jane Stradling = Sir William Griffith
8 Dorothy Griffith = William Williams

9 Jane Williams = William Coytmore
10 Rowland Coytmore = Mrs. Katherine Miles Gray of Mass.
11 Elizabeth Coytmore of Mass. = William Tyng
12 Anna Tyng = Thomas Shepard, Jr.
13 Anna Shepard = Daniel Quincy
14 John Quincy = Elizabeth Norton
15 Elizabeth Quincy = William Smith, Jr.
16 Abigail Smith = John Adams, Jr., 1735-1826, 2nd U. S. President
17 John Quincy Adams, 1767-1848, 6th U. S. President
= Louisa Catherine Johnson

Sources: AR 6, lines 199, 199A & 234, & TAG 32(1956):9-18, reprinted in JIC 136-43, 146-48.

William Henry Harrison & Benjamin Harrison
Through (1) Mrs. Sarah Ludlow Carter

1 Edward I, King of England, d. 1307 = Eleanor of Castile
2 Elizabeth Plantagenet = Humphrey de Bohun, 4th Earl of Hereford & Essex
3 Margaret de Bohun = Hugh Courtenay, 2nd Earl of Devon
4 Elizabeth Courtenay = Sir Andrew Luttrell
5 Sir Hugh Luttrell = Catherine Beaumont
6 Elizabeth Luttrell = John Stratton
7 Elizabeth Stratton = John Andrews
8 Elizabeth Andrews = Thomas Windsor
9 Andrews Windsor, 1st Baron Windsor = Elizabeth Blount
10 Edith Windsor = George Ludlow
11 Thomas Ludlow = Jane Pyle
12 Gabriel Ludlow = Phyllis ---
13 Sarah Ludlow of Va. = John Carter
14 Robert "King" Carter = Elizabeth Landon
15 Anne Carter = Benjamin Harrison (IV)
16 Benjamin Harrison (V), Signer of the Declaration of Independence = Elizabeth Bassett
17 William Henry Harrison, 1773-1841, 9th U. S. President
= Anna Tuthill Symmes
18 John Scott Harrison = Elizabeth Ramsey Irwin
19 Benjamin Harrison, 1833-1901, 23rd U. S. President
= (1) Caroline Lavinia Scott, (2) Mrs. Mary Scott Lord Dimmick

Sources: AR 6, lines 6 & 12 (& MCS 3, line 88); H. F. Seversmith, The Ancestry of Roger Ludlow (vol. 5 of Colonial Families of Long Island, New York, & Connecticut), 1964.

Benjamin Harrison Through (2) Anthony Collamore
(very probable, not fully proved)

1 Hugh Capet, King of France, d. 996 = Adeliza of Poitou
2 Edith of France = Rainier IV, Count of Hainault
3 Beatrix of Hainault = Ebles I, Count of Roucy
4 Alice of Roucy = Hildouin IV, Count of Montdidier
5 Margaret of Montdidier = Hugh I, Count of Clermont
6 Adeliza of Clermont = Gilbert de Clare
7 Richard de Clare = Adeliza de Meschines
8 Roger de Clare, 2nd Earl of Hertford = Maud de St. Hilaire
9 Aveline de Clare = Geoffrey FitzPiers
10 Hawise Fitz Geoffrey = Sir Reynold de Mohun
11 Alice de Mohun = Robert de Beauchamp

12 Sir Humphrey de Beauchamp = Sybil Oliver
13 Sir John Beauchamp = Joan Nonant
14 Sir John Beauchamp = Margaret Whalesburgh
15 Elizabeth Beauchamp = William Fortescue
16 William Fortescue = Matilda Falwell
17 John Fortescue = Joan Prutteston
18 Joan Fortescue = Thomas Hext
19 Thomas Hext = Wilmot Poyntz
20 Margery Hext = John Collamore
21 Peter Collamore = Edith ---
22 Thomas Collamore = Agnes Adams
23 John Collamore = Mary Nicholl
24 (very probably) Anthony Collamore of Mass. = Sarah Chittenden
25 Elizabeth Collamore = Timothy Symmes
26 Timothy Symmes, Jr. = Mary Cleves
27 John Cleves Symmes = Anna Tuthill
28 Anna Tuthill Symmes = William Henry Harrison, 1773-1841, 9th U. S. President
29 John Scott Harrison = Elizabeth Ramsey Irwin
30 Benjamin Harrison, 1833-1901, 23rd U. S. President = (1) Caroline Lavinia Scott, (2) Mrs. Mary Scott Lord Dimmick

Sources: AR 6, lines 106, 151, 246, 246B, 246E, TG 9(1988):7-9, 28-30 esp., & unpublished research of Douglas Richardson of Bethany, Oklahoma, based partly on J. L. Vivian, The Visitations of the County of Devon, 1895, pp. 216-17, Charles Hatch, Genealogy of the Descendants of Anthony Collamore of Scituate, Massachusetts, 1915, pp. 9-25, & the Northam, Devon, parish register.

Zachary Taylor Through (1) William Strother (unproved)

1 Edward III, King of England, d. 1377 = Philippa of Hainault
2 John of Gaunt, Duke of Lancaster = Catherine de Roet
3 Joan Beaufort = Ralph Neville, 1st Earl of Westmoreland
4 George Neville, 1st Baron Latymer = Elizabeth Beauchamp
5 Sir Henry Neville = Joanna Bourchier
6 Richard Neville, 2nd Baron Latymer = Anne Stafford
7 Dorothy Neville = Sir John Dawney
8 Anne Dawney = Sir George Conyers
9 Sir John Conyers = Agnes Bowes
10 Eleanor Conyers = Lancelot Strother
11 William Strother = Elizabeth ---
12 William Strother, allegedly the immigrant to Va. = Dorothy ---
13 William Strother, Jr. = Margaret Thornton
14 Francis Strother = Susannah Dabney
15 William Strother = Sarah Bayly
16 Sarah Dabney Strother = Richard Taylor
17 Zachary Taylor, 1784-1850, 12th U. S. President = Margaret Mackall Smith

Sources: Lineage Book, Descendants of the Illegitimate Sons and Daughters of the Kings of Britain, No. 76, which cites pp. 25-26 of a Strother manuscript the compiler cannot locate; CP, Latymer article, & AR 6, line 2. The above-given parentage & grandparentage of the immigrant William Strother first appeared, perhaps, in George Norbury Mackenzie's Colonial Families of the United States of America, vol. 5, 1915, reprint 1966, pp. 492-93.

Zachary Taylor Through (2) Anthony Savage (unproved)

Generations 1-13, from Edward I, King of England through Anthony Savage to his daughter Alice Savage, wife of Francis Thornton, see under James Madison, Jr.

14 Margaret Thornton = William Strother, Jr.
15 Francis Strother = Susannah Dabney
16 William Strother = Sarah Bayly
17 Sarah Dabney Strother = Richard Taylor
18 Zachary Taylor, 1784-1850, 12th U. S. President
= Mrs. Margaret Mackall Smith

Sources: as above, under James Madison, Jr.

Franklin Pierce Through (1) Griffith Bowen

1 Henry I, King of England, d. 1135
2 Robert of Caen (illegitimate), 1st Earl of Gloucester = Mabel FitzHamon
3 William Fitz Robert, 2nd Earl of Gloucester
4 Mabel (illegitimate) = Gruffyd ab Iforbach
5 Hywel Felyn = Sara le Sore
6 Madog = Iwerydd
7 Joan = Dafydd
8 Goleuddyeld = Rhys Llwyd ab Adam ap Rhys, who m. Gwladys ferch Llywelyn ap Hywel Felyn, 5 above
9 Gwilym = Margred
10 Gwenllian = Jenkin Gunter
11 Margred Gunter = Roger
12 John = Maud Aubrey
13 Alice = Owain
14 Gruffydd Bowen = Anne Berry
15 Philip Bowen = Elizabeth Vaughan
16 Francis Bowen = Ellen Franklyn
17 Griffith Bowen of Mass. = Margaret Fleming of Mass.
18 Henry Bowen = Elizabeth Johnson
19 John Bowen = Hannah Brewer
20 Abigail Bowen = Caleb Kendrick
21 Benjamin Kendrick = Sarah Harris
22 Anna Kendrick = Benjamin Pierce, Jr.
23 Franklin Pierce, 1804-1869, 14th U. S. President
= Jane Means Appleton

Sources: see next list.

Franklin Pierce Through (2) Griffith Bowen's Wife Margaret Fleming Bowen

1 Henry I, King of England, d. 1135
2 Robert of Caen (illegitimate), 1st Earl of Gloucester = Mabel FitzHamon
3 William Fitz Robert, 2nd Earl of Gloucester
4 Mabel (illegitimate) = Gruffyd ab Iforbach
5 Hywel Felyn = Sara le Sore
6 Madog = Iwerydd
7 Joan = Dafydd
8 Goleuddyeld = Rhys Llwyd
9 Isabel = Gruffydd
10 Mallt = Maredudd

11 Mabli = Gruffydd
12 Owain = Alison Malefaunt
13 Eleanor = William Barrett
14 William Barrett = Agnes
15 Henry Barrett = Catherine Morgan
16 Margaret Barrett = William Dawkins
17 Jenkin Dawkins = Elizabeth Jenkin
18 Alice Dawkins = Henry Fleming
19 Margaret Fleming of Mass. = Griffith Bowen of Mass.
20 Henry Bowen = Elizabeth Johnson
21 John Bowen = Hannah Brewer
22 Abigail Bowen = Caleb Kendrick
23 Benjamin Kendrick = Sarah Harris
24 Anna Kendrick = Benjamin Pierce, Jr.
25 Franklin Pierce, 1804-1869, 14th U. S. President
    = Jane Means Appleton

Sources (for this and ten [possibly twenty-one] other lines from Gruffyd ab Iforbach to either Griffith Bowen or his wife Margaret Fleming): AR 6, lines 179 & 124, NGSQ 67(1979):163-66, The Connecticut Nutmegger 19(1986-87):335-41, 588-96, & Lineage Book, Descendants of the Illegitimate Sons & Daughters of the King of Britain, No. 156; AT of Griffith Bowen & Margaret Fleming compiled by William Addams Reitwiesner of Washington, D. C., based largely on G. T. Clark's Limbus Patrum Morganiae et Glamorganiae, 1886 (pp. 386, 483 etc.), on Peter C. Bartrum's Welsh Genealogies, A. D. 300-1400, 8 vols., 1974, & Welsh Genealogies A. D. 1400-1500, 18 vols., 1983, & on correspondence among Bartrum, William C. Rogers & General Herman Nickerson, Jr. of Jacksonville, N. C. Note that on this chart the long pre-surname ap/ab & ferch patronymics are omitted, but the Welsh spelling of most given names is retained.

James Buchanan, Jr. Through His Father, James Buchanan (unproved)

1 Robert III, King of Scotland, d. 1406 = Annabella Drummond
2 Mary Stewart = Sir William Edmonstone
3 Sir William Edmonstone = Matilda Stewart
4 Sir Archibald Edmonstone = Janet Shaw
5 Margaret Edmonstone = George Buchanan of that Ilk
6 Janet Buchanan = Thomas Buchanan of Carbeth
7 John Buchanan of Gartincaber = ---
8 George Buchanan of Gartincaber = Elizabeth Leckie
9 John Buchanan of Blairlusk = ---
10 George Buchanan of Blairlusk = Elizabeth Mayne
11 Thomas Buchanan of Ramelton = ---
12 (probably) --- Buchanan = ---
13 John Buchanan of Ramelton (Rathmelton) = Jane Russell
14 James Buchanan of Pa. = Elizabeth Speer
15 James Buchanan, Jr., 1791-1868, 15th U. S. President, unm.

Sources: John Guthrie Smith, Strathendrick & Its Inhabitants from Early Times, 1896, pp. 346-47, 350-52 (copied in NGSQ 24[1936]:85-87, 25[1937]:14-15, 67) & The Parish of Strathbane, 1886, pp. 104-10; Sir Archibald Edmonstone, Genealogical Account of the Family of Edmonstone of Duntreath, 1875; correspondence from Mr. Andrew B. W. MacEwen of Stockton Springs, Maine.

Rutherford Birchard Hayes Through (1) Thomas Newberry (doubted by Sir A. R. Wagner)

1 Henry I, King of France, d. 1060 = Anne of Kiev
2 Hugh Magnus, Duke of France & Burgundy = Adelaide of Vermandois
3 Isabel of Vermandois = Robert de Beaumont, 1st Earl of Leicester
4 Isabel de Beaumont = Gilbert de Clare, 1st Earl of Pembroke
5 Richard de Clare ("Strongbow"), 2nd Earl of Pembroke = Eve of Leinster, of ancient Irish lineage
6 Isabel de Clare = William Marshall, 3rd Earl of Pembroke
7 Eva Marshall = William de Broase
8 Eva de Broase = William de Cantilupe
9 Milicent de Cantilupe = Eudo la Zouche
10 Elizabeth la Zouche = Nicholas Poyntz, 2nd Baron Poyntz
11 Hugh Poyntz, 3rd Baron Poyntz = Margaret (Paveley?)
12 Nicholas Poyntz, 4th Baron Poyntz = Eleanor (Erleigh?)
13 Margaret Poyntz = John de Newburgh
14 John Newburgh = Joan Delamere
15 John Newburgh = Alice Carent
16 Thomas Newburgh = Alice ---
17 Walter Newburgh = Elizabeth Birport
18 Richard Newborough = Elizabeth Horsey
19 Richard Newberry = Grace Matthew
20 Thomas Newberry of Mass. = Jane ---
21 Rebecca Newberry = John Russell
22 Samuel Russell = Abigail Whiting
23 John Russell = Sarah Trowbridge
24 Rebecca Russell = Ezekial Hayes
25 Rutherford Hayes = Chloe Smith
26 Rutherford Hayes, Jr. = Sophia Birchard
27 Rutherford Birchard Hayes, 1822-1893, 19th U. S. President = Lucy Ware Webb

Sources: AR 6, lines 253, 66 & 53, & sources cited therein, esp. J. Gardner Bartlett's **Newberry Genealogy: The Ancestors & Descendants of Thomas Newberry of Dorchester, Massachusetts, 1634, 920-1914**, 1914. Sir Anthony R. Wagner, former Garter King of Arms, is dubious of this particular patrilineal descent (generations 13-20) for Thomas Newberry of Dorchester, Mass., but thinks some derivation of the immigrant from the family that once held the earldom of Warwick may be likely. See **English Genealogy**, 3rd ed., 1983, p. 66.

Rutherford Birchard Hayes Through (2) Thomas Trowbridge

1 Hugh Capet, King of France, d. 996 = Adeliza of Poitou
2 Edith of France = Rainier IV, Count of Hainault
3 Beatrix of Hainault = Ebles I, Count of Roucy
4 Alice of Roucy = Hildouin IV, Count of Montdidier
5 Margaret of Montdidier = Hugh I, Count of Clermont
6 Adeliza of Clermont = Gilbert de Clare
7 Richard de Clare = Adeliza de Meschines
8 Roger de Clare, 2nd Earl of Hertford = Maud de St. Hilaire
9 Aveline de Clare = Geoffrey FitzPiers
10 Hawise FitzGeoffrey = Sir Reynold de Mohun
11 Alice de Mohun = Robert de Beauchamp
12 Sir Humphrey de Beauchamp = Sybil Oliver
13 Eleanor Beauchamp = John Bampfield
14 John Bampfield = Isabel Cobham
15 John Bampfield = Joan Gilbert
16 Thomas Bampfield = Agnes Coplestone

17 Agnes Bampfield = John Prowse
18 Richard Prowse = Margaret Norton
19 John Prowse = Joan Orchard
20 Robert Prowse = ---
21 John Prowse = Alice White
22 John Prowse = Elizabeth Collack alias Colwyck
23 Agnes Prowse = John Trowbridge
24 Thomas Trowbridge of Conn. = Elizabeth Marshall
25 Thomas Trowbridge, Jr. = Sarah Rutherford
26 Thomas Trowbridge (III) = Mary Winston
27 Sarah Trowbridge = John Russell
28 Rebecca Russell = Ezekiel Hayes
29 Rutherford Hayes = Chloe Smith
30 Rutherford Hayes, Jr. = Sophia Birchard
31 Rutherford Birchard Hayes, 1822-1893, 19th U. S. President = Lucy Ware Webb

Sources: TG 9(1988):3-39 (Charles Fitch-Northen), based in part on TAG 18(1941-42):129-37, 57(1981):31-33, & primary sources cited in both; printed sources cited in NEHGR 141 (1987):99; & AR 6, lines 106, 151, 246 & 246B.

Stephen Grover Cleveland Through Robert Abell

1 Edward I, King of England, d. 1307 = Eleanor of Castille
2 Joan Plantagenet = Gilbert de Clare, 3rd Earl of Gloucester, 7th Earl of Hertford
3 Margaret de Clare = Hugh de Audley, Earl of Gloucester
4 Margaret de Audley = Ralph Stafford, 1st Earl of Stafford
5 Katherine Stafford = Sir John Sutton
6 Sir John Sutton = Jane ---
7 Sir John Sutton = Constance Blount
8 John Sutton, 1st Baron Dudley = Elizabeth Berkeley
9 Jane Sutton = Thomas Mainwaring
10 Cecily Mainwaring = John Cotton
11 Sir George Cotton = Mary Onley
12 Richard Cotton = Mary Mainwaring, also descended (several times over) from Edward I, King of England
13 Frances Cotton = George Abell
14 Robert Abell of Mass. = Joanna ---
15 Caleb Abell = Margaret Post
16 Experience Abell = John Hyde
17 James Hyde = Sarah Marshall
18 Abiah Hyde = Aaron Cleveland (IV)
19 William Cleveland = Margaret Falley
20 Richard Falley Cleveland = Anne Neal
21 (Stephen) Grover Cleveland, 1837-1908, 22nd & 24th U. S. President = Frances Folsom

Sources: H. A. & L. P. Abell, The Abell Family in America, 1940, pp. 41-46 (& LDBR 5:141-42); AR 6, lines 9, 81 & 56A; TG 5(1984): 131-39, 150-51, 154-56, 158-71, 9(1988):89.

Theodore Roosevelt, Jr. Through (1) John Irvine

1 James I, King of Scotland, d. 1437 = Joan Beaufort
2 Joan Stewart = James Douglas, 1st Earl of Morton
3 Janet Douglas = Patrick Hepburn, 1st Earl of Bothwell
4 Janet Hepburn = George Seton, 3rd Baron Seton

5 George Seton, 4th Baron Seton = Elizabeth Hay
6 Beatrix Seton = Sir George Ogilvy of Dunlugas
7 Janet Ogilvy = William Forbes of Tolquhon
8 Thomas Forbes of Waterton = Jean Ramsay
9 Grizel Forbes = John Douglas of Inchmarlo
10 John Douglas of Tilquhillie = Agnes Horn
11 Euphemia Douglas = Charles Irvine of Over Boddam
12 John Irvine of Ga. = Ann Elizabeth Baillie
13 Anne Irvine = James Bulloch
14 James Stephens Bulloch = Martha Stewart
15 Martha Bulloch = Theodore Roosevelt
16 Theodore Roosevelt, Jr., 1858-1919, 26th U. S. President = (1) Alice Hathaway Lee, (2) Edith Kermit Carow

Sources: MCS 3, line 93; J. G. B. Bulloch, A History & Genealogy of the Families of Bulloch & Stobo & of Irvine of Cults, 1911, pp. 85-87; The Scottish Antiquary, vol. 8 (1893-94), pp. 40-42; Alistair & Henrietta Tayler, The House of Forbes, 1937, pp. 396-97, 416; SP, articles on Ogilvys (of Dunlugas, later Lords Banff), Setons (Lords Seton, later Earls of Winton), Hepburns (Earls of Bothwell) & Douglases (Earls of Morton).

Theodore Roosevelt, Jr. Through (2) Kenneth Baillie
(highly probable, unproved)

1 Edward III, King of England, d. 1377 = Philippa of Hainault
2 John of Gaunt, Duke of Lancaster = Catherine de Roet
3 John Beaufort, Marquess of Dorset & Somerset = Margaret Holand
4 Joan Beaufort = Sir James Stewart, "The Black Knight of Lorn"
5 John Stewart, 1st Earl of Atholl = Eleanor Sinclair
6 John Stewart, 2nd Earl of Atholl = Mary Campbell
7 Elizabeth Stewart = Sir Kenneth Mackenzie of Kintail
8 Colin Mackenzie of Kintail =
9 Alexander Mackenzie of Coul (illeg. by Mary MacKenzie) = Christian Munro
10 Sir Kenneth Mackenzie, 1st Bt. = Jean Chisolm
11 Jean Mackenzie = Alexander Baillie of Dunain
12 John Baillie "of Balrobert" (almost certainly son or son-in-law [the husband of Jean Baillie] of the above)
13 Kenneth Baillie of Ga. = Elizabeth Mackay
14 Ann Elizabeth Baillie = John Irvine
15 Anne Irvine = James Bulloch
16 James Stephens Bulloch = Martha Stewart
17 Martha Bulloch = Theodore Roosevelt
18 Theodore Roosevelt, Jr., 1858-1919, 26th U. S. President = (1) Alice Hathaway Lee, (2) Edith Kermit Carow

Sources: J. G. B. Bulloch, Genealogical & Historical Records of the Baillies of Inverness, Scotland, & Some of Their Descendants in the United States of America, 1923, pp. 3-6, 12-25, 40-46; G. E. Cokayne, Complete Baronetage, vol. 4 (1904), p. 296 (Mackenzie of Coul); SP, articles on Mackenzies (of Kintail, later Earls of Seaforth) & Stewarts (Earls of Atholl).

William Howard Taft Through Mrs. Jane Lawrence Giddings

1 Louis IV, King of France, d. 954 (probable grandson maternally of Edward the Elder, King of England, d. 924) = Gerberga, daughter of Henry I the Fowler, German emperor, d. 936
2 Charles, Duke of Lower Lorraine = Adelaide

3 Gerberga of Lower Lorraine = Lambert, Count of Louvain
4 Maud of Louvain = Eustace I, Count of Boulogne
5 Lambert, Count of Lens = Adeliza of Normandy, sister of William I, The Conqueror, King of England, & widow of Enguerrand II, Count of Ponthieu, for whose ancestry see G. A. Moriarty, The Plantagenet Ancestry (Ancestry of Edward III & Queen Philippa), MSS. widely available on microfilm, pp. 113-14, etc., & H. M. West Winter, The Descendants of Charlemagne (800-1400), part I, "Brandenburg Updated," generations I-XIV, 1987, XII 75a, etc. Enguerrand II was a son of Hugh III, Count of Ponthieu (& Bertha of Aumale), son of Enguerrand I, Count of Ponthieu (& Adela, possibly of Westfriesland), son of Hugh I, Count of Ponthieu & (almost certainly) Gisela, daughter of Hugh Capet, King of France, & Adela of Poitou.
6 Judith of Lens (paternity uncertain, possibly a daughter of Enguerrand; see Sir A. R. Wagner, Pedigree & Progress, 1975, p. 253, & sources cited therein) = Waltheof II, Earl of Huntington, Northampton & Northumberland
7 Matilda of Northumberland = Simon de St. Liz, Earl of Huntington & Northampton
8 Matilda de St. Liz = Robert de Clare
9 Walter Fitz Robert = Maud de Lucy
10 Alice Fitz Walter (sister of Robert Fitz Walter, leader of the Magna Charta Barons) = Gilbert Pecche
11 Hamon Pecche = Eve ---
12 Gilbert Pecche = Joan de Creye
13 Gilbert Pecche, 1st Baron Pecche = Iseult ---
14 Gilbert Pecche, 2nd Baron Pecche = Joan ---
15 Katherine Pecche = Thomas Notbeam
16 Margaret Notbeam = John Hinkley
17 Cecily Hinkley = Henry Caldebeck
18 Thomasine Caldebeck = Thomas Underhill
19 Anne Underhill = Thomas Knighton
20 Joan Knighton = Charles Bull
21 Richard Bull = Alice Hunt
22 Elizabeth Bull = John Lawrence
23 Thomas Lawrence = Joan Antrobus of Mass., who m. (2) John Tuttle
24 Jane Lawrence of Mass. = George Giddings
25 Joseph Giddings = Susanna Rindge
26 Joseph Giddings, Jr. = Grace Wardwell
27 Susanna Giddings = William Torrey
28 Joseph Torrey = Deborah Holbrook
29 William Torrey = Anna Davenport
30 Samuel Davenport Torrey = Susan Holman Waters
31 Louisa Maria Torrey = Alphonso Taft, diplomat, U. S. Secretary of War & Attorney General
32 William Howard Taft, 1857-1930, 27th U. S. President = Helen Herron

Sources: Unpublished, copyrighted research by David L. Greene, co-editor of TAG, based in part on AR 6, line 148, the Pecche article in CP (vol. 10, pp. 333-38), Joan Corder, ed., The Visitation of Suffolk, 1561, Part I (HSPVS, New Ser., vol. 2), 1981, pp. 78, 86, 88 esp. (Pecche to Knighton) & Walter C. Metcalf, ed., The Visitation of Hertfordshire in 1634 (HSPVS vol. 22), 1896, p. 34 (Bull). Mr. Greene's Lawrence monograph, to incorporate research in numerous English record sources, will appear in a future issue of TG.

(John) Calvin Coolidge, Jr. Through (1) William Goddard

1 Edward I, King of England, d. 1307 = Margaret of France
2 Thomas of Brotherton, Earl of Norfolk = Alice de Hales
3 Margaret Plantagenet, Duchess of Norfolk = John de Segrave, 4th Baron Segrave
4 Elizabeth de Segrave = John Mowbray, 4th Baron Mowbray
5 Eleanor Mowbray = John de Welles, 5th Baron Welles
6 Eleanor de Welles = Sir Hugh Poynings
7 Constance Poynings = Sir John Paulet
8 John Paulet = Eleanor Ros
9 Sir John Paulet = Alice Paulet
10 Eleanor Paulet = Sir William Gifford
11 John Gifford = Joan Bruges
12 Anne Gifford = Thomas Goddard
13 Richard Goddard = Elizabeth Walrond
14 Edward Goddard = Priscilla d'Oyley
15 William Goddard of Mass. = Elizabeth Miles
16 Josiah Goddard = Rachel Davis
17 Rachel Goddard = Obadiah Coolidge, Jr.
18 Josiah Coolidge = Mary Jones
19 John Coolidge = Hannah Priest
20 Calvin Coolidge = Sarah Thompson
21 Calvin Galusha Coolidge = Sarah Almeda Brewer
22 John Calvin Coolidge = Victoria Josephine Moor
23 (John) Calvin Coolidge (Jr.), 1872-1933, 30th U. S. President = Grace Anna Goodhue

Sources: MSS. autobiography of Edward Goddard (1675-1754) at the American Antiquarian Society in Worcester, Mass. (notably pp. 2-3); Frederick Arthur Crisp, Visitation of England & Wales, Notes, vol. 6 (1906), pp. 109-16, UGHM 21(1930):59-66, & W. Harry Rylands, Pedigrees from the Visitation of Hampshire (HSPVS, vol. 64), 1913, p. 16 (all three of which sources contain errors) (Goddard & Gifford); Miscellanea Genealogica et Heraldica 5th Ser., vol. 9 (1935-37), pp. 88-90, 142-46 (Paulet), 44-48 (Welles), 162-68 (Plantagenet, Segrave, Mowbray). A definitive monograph on the family of Gifford of Itchell, Hampshire, is badly needed.

(John) Calvin Coolidge (Jr.)
Through (2) Mrs. Elizabeth St. John Whiting

1 Edward I, King of England, d. 1307 = Eleanor of Castile
2 Joan Plantagenet = Gilbert de Clare, 3rd Earl of Gloucester, 7th Earl of Hertford
3 Margaret de Clare = Piers de Gaveston, Earl of Cornwall
4 Amy de Gaveston = John de Driby
5 Alice de Driby = Sir Anketil Malory
6 Sir William Malory = ---
7 Margaret Malory = Robert Corbet
8 Mary Corbet = Robert Charlton
9 Richard Charlton = Anne Mainwaring
10 Anne Charlton = Randall Grosvenor
11 Elizabeth Grosvenor = Thomas Bulkeley
12 Edward Bulkeley = Olive Irby
13 Sarah Bulkeley = Sir Oliver St. John
14 Elizabeth St. John of Mass. = Samuel Whiting
15 Samuel Whiting, Jr. = Dorcas Chester
16 Samuel Whiting (III) = Elizabeth Read
17 Katherine Whiting = John Lane, Jr.
18 Susanna Lane = Nathaniel Davis

19 Nathaniel Davis, Jr. = Lydia Harwood
20 Mary Davis = John Moor
21 Hiram D. Moor = Abigail Franklin
22 Victoria Josephine Moor = John Calvin Coolidge
23 (John) Calvin Coolidge (Jr.), 1872-1933, 30th U. S. President = Grace Anna Goodhue

Sources: AR 6, lines 85, 31, 29B, 16A & 9; TAG 35(1959):100-6, 37(1961):45-51, 40(1964):95-99, plus items listed in NEHGR 141 (1987):100.

(John) Calvin Coolidge (Jr.) Through (3) Samuel Appleton

1 John, King of England, d. 1216
2 Joan Plantagenet (illegitimate) = Llewelyn ab Iorwerth, Prince of Wales
3 Angharad of Wales (maternity uncertain, for the best alternate royal descent see note at generation 8, below) = Maelgwyn Fychan
4 Elen ferch Maelgwyn Fychan =Maredudd ap Owain — Margred ferch Maelgwyn Fychan = Owain ap Mareddud 4
5 Owain ap Mareddud = Angharad ferch Owain ap Mareddud 5
6 Llewelyn ap Owain = ---, daughter of Sir Robert de Vale
7 Thomas ap Llewelyn = --- (Eleanor ferch Philip ab Ivor?)
8 Elen ferch Thomas ap Llewelyn (great-aunt of Sir Owen Tudor, founder of the Tudor dynasty & husband of Katherine of France, widow of Henry V, King of England) = Gruffydd Fychan, son of Gruffyd ap Madog ap Gruffyd Maelor & Elizabeth le Strange, for whose descent from from Henry I, King of England, see AR 6, lines 249 & 124-26
9 Lowri ferch Gruffydd Fychan (sister of Owen Glendower, the Welsh rebel hero)
10 Angharad Puleston = Edwart (Iorwerth) Trevor ap Daffyd ap Ednyfed Gam
11 Rose Trevor = Sir Otewell Worsley
12 Margaret Worsley = Adrian Whetehill
13 Sir Richard Whetehill = Elizabeth Muston
14 Margery Whetehill = Edward Isaac
15 Mary Isaac = Thomas Appleton
16 Samuel Appleton of Mass. = Judith Everard
17 John Appleton = Priscilla Glover
18 Priscilla Appleton = Joseph Capen
19 Mary Capen = Thomas Baker, Jr.
20 Priscilla Baker = Tarrant Putnam, Jr.
21 Priscilla Putnam = Adam Brown, Jr.
22 Israel Putnam Brown = Sally Briggs
23 Sally Brown = Israel C. Brewer
24 Sarah Almeda Brewer = Calvin Galusha Coolidge
25 John Calvin Coolidge = Victoria Josephine Moor
26 (John) Calvin Coolidge (Jr.), 1872-1933, 30th U. S. President = Grace Anna Goodhue

Sources: AR 6, lines 249, 254 & 27 (& TG 1[1980]:80-95); Walter Goodwin Davis, The Ancestry of Mary Isaac, 1955.

(John) Calvin Coolidge (Jr.) Through (4) Mrs. Judith Everard Appleton

1 Louis IV, King of France, d. 954 (probable grandson maternally of Edward the Elder, King of England, d. 924) = Gerberga, daughter of Henry I the Fowler, German emperor, d. 936

2 Charles, Duke of Lower Lorraine = Adelaide
3 Gerberga of Lower Lorraine = Lambert, Count of Louvain
4 Maud of Louvain = Eustace I, Count of Boulogne
5 Lambert, Count of Lens = Adeliza of Normandy, sister of William I, The Conqueror, King of England, & widow of Enguerrand II, Count of Ponthieu, for whose ancestry see G. A. Moriarty, The Plantagenet Ancestry (Ancestry of Edward III & Queen Philippa), MSS. widely available on microfilm, pp. 113-14, etc., & H. M. West Winter, The Descendants of Charlemagne (800-1400), part I, "Brandenburg Updated," generations I-XIV, 1987, XII 75a, etc. Enguerrand II was a son of Hugh III, Count of Ponthieu (& Bertha of Aumale), son of Enguerrand I, Count of Ponthieu (& Adela, possibly of Westfriesland), son of Hugh I, Count of Ponthieu & (almost certainly) Gisela, daughter of Hugh Capet, King of France, & Adela of Poitou.
6 Judith of Lens (paternity uncertain, possibly a daughter of Enguerrand; see Sir A. R. Wagner, Pedigree & Progress, 1975, p. 253, & sources cited therein) = Waltheof II, Earl of Huntington, Northampton & Northumberland
7 Matilda of Northumberland = Simon de St. Liz, Earl of Huntington & Northampton
8 Matilda de St. Liz = Robert de Clare
9 Walter Fitz Robert = Maud de Lucy
10 Alice Fitz Walter (sister of Robert Fitz Walter, leader of the Magna Charta Barons) = Gilbert Pecche
11 Hamon Pecche = Eve ---
12 Gilbert Pecche = Joan de Creye
13 Gilbert Pecche, 1st Baron Pecche = Iseult ---
14 Sir Simon Pecche = Agnes Holme
15 Margaret Pecche = John Hunt
16 Iodena Hunt = Thomas Cornish
17 John Cornish = ---
18 John Cornish = Agnes Walden
19 Mary Cornish = Thomas Everard
20 Henry Everard = ---
21 Thomas Everard = Margaret Wiseman
22 John Everard = Judith Bourne
23 Judith Everard of Mass. = Samuel Appleton
24 John Appleton = Priscilla Glover
25 Priscilla Appleton = Joseph Capen
26 Mary Capen = Thomas Baker, Jr.
27 Priscilla Baker = Tarrant Putnam, Jr.
28 Priscilla Putnam = Adam Brown, Jr.
29 Israel Putnam Brown = Sally Briggs
30 Sally Brown = Israel C. Brewer
31 Sarah Almeda Brewer = Calvin Galusha Coolidge
32 John Calvin Coolidge = Victoria Josephine Moor
33 (John) Calvin Coolidge (Jr.), 1872-1933, 30th U. S. President = Grace Anna Goodhue

Sources: TAG 27(1951):208-210; FNE 315, 391-410; VHG 232-33 & HSF 1:338; Pecche article in CP & AR 6, line 148.

Herbert Clark Hoover Through Governor Thomas Dudley

1 Edward I, King of England, d. 1307 = Eleanor of Castille
2 Joan Plantagenet = Gilbert de Clare, 3rd Earl of Gloucester, 7th Earl of Hertford
3 Margaret de Clare = Hugh de Audley, Earl of Gloucester
4 Margaret de Audley = Ralph Stafford, 1st Earl of Stafford

5 Katherine Stafford = Sir John Sutton
6 Sir John Sutton = Jane ---
7 Sir John Sutton = Constance Blount
8 John Sutton, 1st Baron Dudley = Elizabeth Berkeley
9 John Dudley = Elizabeth Bramshot
10 Edmund Dudley, minister of Henry VII
11 Simon Dudley (illegitimate) = Emma Saunders
12 John Dudley = (1) Elizabeth Leighton
13 Roger Dudley (possibly illeg., no proof of parentage) = Susannah Thorne
14 Thomas Dudley, Governor of Mass. = Dorothy Yorke
15 Anne Dudley, known as Mrs. Anne Bradstreet, poet = Simon Bradstreet, Governor of Mass.
16 Dudley Bradstreet = Anne Wood
17 Margaret Bradstreet = Job Tyler
18 Hannah Tyler = John Spofford (IV)
19 Phoebe Spofford = John Grout, Jr.
20 Phoebe Grout = Jacob Winn (III)
21 Endymia Winn = Thomas Sherwood
22 Lucinda Sherwood = John Minthorn
23 Theodore Minthorn = Mary Wasley
24 Hulda Randall Minthorn = Jesse Clark Hoover
25 Herbert Clark Hoover, 1874-1964, 31st U. S. President = Lou Henry

Sources: MCS 3, lines 50 & 149B; AR 6, lines 9 & 81; TAG 44(1968):129-37; TG 5(1984):131-39, 150-51, 154-56. As the parentage of Roger Dudley remains unproved, the best royal descent of Gov. Thomas Dudley through his mother, Susanna Thorne, is outlined next.

1 John, King of England, d. 1216
2 Richard FitzRoy (illeg. by --- de Warren) = Rohese of Dover
3 Lorette de Dover = Sir William Marmion
4 John Marmion, 1st Baron Marmion = Isabel ---
5 John Marmion, 2nd Baron Marmion = Maud Furnival
6 Avice Marmion = John Grey, 1st Baron Grey of Rotherfield
7 Maud Grey = Sir Thomas Harcourt
8 Sir Thomas Harcourt = Jane Franceys
9 Sir Richard Harcourt = Edith St. Clair
10 Alice Harcourt = William Bessiles
11 Elizabeth Bessiles = Richard Fettiplace
12 Anne Fettiplace = Edward Purefoy
13 Mary Purefoy = Thomas Thorne
14 Susanna Thorne = Roger Dudley
15 Thomas Dudley, Governor of Mass. = Dorothy Yorke
16 Anne Dudley, known as Mrs. Anne Bradstreet, poet = Simon Bradstreet, Governor of Mass.
17 Dudley Bradstreet = Anne Wood
18 Margaret Bradstreet = Job Tyler
19 Hannah Tyler = John Spofford (IV)
20 Phoebe Spofford = John Grout, Jr.
21 Phoebe Grout = Jacob Winn (III)
22 Endymia Winn = Thomas Sherwood
23 Lucinda Sherwood = John Minthorn
24 Theodore Minthorn = Mary Wasley
25 Hulda Randall Minthorn = Jesse Clark Hoover
26 Herbert Clark Hoover, 1874-1964, 31st U. S. President = Lou Henry

Sources: AR 6, lines 50, 30, 219 & 218, & sources cited therein.

Franklin Delano Roosevelt Through (1) John Nelson

1 Edward III, King of England, d. 1377 = Philippa of Hainault
2 Lionel of Antwerp, Duke of Clarence = Elizabeth de Burgh
3 Philippa Plantagenet = Edmund Mortimer, 3rd Earl of March
4 Elizabeth Mortimer = Sir Henry "Hotspur" Percy
5 Henry Percy, 2nd Earl of Northumberland = Eleanor Neville
6 Henry Percy, 3rd Earl of Northumberland = Eleanor Poynings
7 Anne Percy = Sir Thomas Hungerford
8 Mary Hungerford = Edward Hastings, 2nd Baron Hastings
9 Anne Hastings = Thomas Stanley, 2nd Earl of Derby
10 Margaret Stanley = Robert Radcliffe, 1st Earl of Sussex
11 Jane Radcliffe = Anthony Browne, 1st Viscount Montagu
12 Hon. Anthony Browne = Mary Dormer
13 Dorothy Browne = Edmund Lee
14 Dorothy Lee = Sir John Temple
15 Mary Temple = Robert Nelson
16 John Nelson of Mass. = Elizabeth Tailer
17 Rebecca Nelson = Henry Lloyd
18 Margaret Lloyd = William Henry Smith
19 Rebecca Smith = John Aspinwall
20 John Aspinwall, Jr. = Susan Howland
21 Mary Rebecca Aspinwall = Isaac Roosevelt
22 James Roosevelt = Sara Delano
23 Franklin Delano Roosevelt, 1882-1945, 32nd U. S. President
= (Anna) Eleanor Roosevelt

Sources: TG 2(1981):123-28, & sources cited therein, especially the works of Temple Prime & John Alexander Temple.

Franklin Delano Roosevelt Through (2) James Murray and (3) His Wife Barbara Bennet

1 James II, King of Scotland, d. 1460 = Mary of Guelders
2 Mary Stewart = James Hamilton, 1st Baron Hamilton
3 James Hamilton, 1st Earl of Arran
4 Sir John Hamilton (illegitimate) = Janet Home
5 Margaret Hamilton = David Douglas, 7th Earl of Angus
6 Margaret Douglas = Sir Walter Scott
7 Mary Scott = William Elliot of Larriston;
Walter Scott, 1st Baron Scott of Buccleuth = Mary Kerr 7
8 Jean Eliot = Richard Rutherford of Edgerston;
Walter Scott, 1st Earl of Buccleuth = 8
9 Robert Rutherford of Edgerston = Marion Riddell;
Francis Scott of Mangerton (illegitimate) = --- 9
10 John Rutherford of Edgerston = Barbara Abernethy;
Elizabeth Scott = Sir John Scott, 1st Bt. 10
11 Barbara Rutherford = Archibald Bennet of Chesters;
Margaret Scott of Ancrum = John Murray of Bowhill 11
12 Andrew Bennet of Chesters = Dorothy Collingwood
12 Anne Bennet (sister of Andrew) = John Murray of Unthank 12
13 Barbara Bennet of N. C. = James Murray of N. C. & Mass. 13
14 Elizabeth Murray = Edward Hutchinson Robbins
15 Anne Jean Robbins = Joseph Lyman (III)
16 Catherine Robbins Lyman = Warren Delano, Jr.
17 Sara Delano = James Roosevelt
18 Franklin Delano Roosevelt, 1882-1945, 32nd U. S. President
= (Anna) Eleanor Roosevelt

Sources: N. M. Tiffany, Letters of James Murray, Loyalist, 1901, pp. 292-94 esp.; Miscellanea Genealogica et Heraldica, 4th Ser., vol. 2

(1906-7), p. 166; T. H. Cockburn-Hood, The Rutherfords of That Ilk & Their Cadets, 1884, chart at end esp.; Sir Robert Douglas of Glenbervie, 6th Bt., The Baronage of Scotland, 1798, p. 217 (Scott of Ancrum); SP, articles on the Scotts of Buccleuth, Douglases of Angus, and Hamiltons of Arran.

Franklin Delano Roosevelt
Through (4) Mrs. Elizabeth Coytmore Tyng

For generations 1-12 from Edward III, King of England through Mrs. Elizabeth Coytmore Tyng to her daughter, Anna Tyng, wife of Thomas Shepard, Jr., see under John Quincy Adams.

13 Thomas Shepard (III) = Mary Anderson
14 Anna Shepard = Henry Smith
15 William Henry Smith = Margaret Lloyd
16 Rebecca Smith = John Aspinwall
17 John Aspinwall, Jr. = Susan Howland
18 Mary Rebecca Aspinwall = Isaac Roosevelt
19 James Roosevelt = Sara Delano
20 Franklin Delano Roosevelt, 1882-1945, 32nd U. S. President = (Anna) Eleanor Roosevelt

Sources: as above under John Quincy Adams.

Franklin Delano Roosevelt
Through (5) Mrs. Anne Marbury Hutchinson

1 Edward I, King of England, d. 1307 = Eleanor of Castile
2 Joan Plantagenet = Gilbert de Clare, 3rd Earl of Gloucester, 7th Earl of Hertford
3 Eleanor de Clare = Hugh le Despencer, 1st Baron Despencer
4 Isabel Despencer = Richard FitzAlan, 9th Earl of Arundel
5 Isabel FitzAlan = John le Strange, 4th Baron Strange, of Blackmere
6 Ankaret le Strange = Richard Talbot, 4th Baron Talbot, a great-great-grandson of Elizabeth Plantagenet, wife of Humphrey de Bohun, 4th Earl of Hereford & Essex, & younger daughter of Edward I & Eleanor of Castile, see AR 6, lines 7, 13 & 14
7 Mary Talbot = Sir Thomas Greene
8 Sir Thomas Greene = Philippa Ferrers
9 Elizabeth Greene = William Raleigh
10 Sir Edward Raleigh = Margaret Verney
11 Edward Raleigh = Anne Chamberlayne
12 Bridget Raleigh = Sir John Cope
13 Elizabeth Cope = John Dryden
14 Bridget Dryden = Francis Marbury
15 Anne Marbury, known as Mrs. Anne Hutchinson, the religious reformer, heretic & founder of R. I. = William Hutchinson
16 Edward Hutchinson = Catherine Hamby
17 Elisha Hutchinson = Elizabeth Clarke
18 Edward Hutchinson = Lydia Foster
19 Elizabeth Hutchinson = Nathaniel Robbins
20 Edward Hutchinson Robbins = Elizabeth Murray
21 Anne Jean Robbins = Joseph Lyman (III)
22 Catherine Robbins Lyman = Warren Delano, Jr.
23 Sara Delano = James Roosevelt
24 Franklin Delano Roosevelt, 1882-1945, 32nd U. S. President = (Anna) Eleanor Roosevelt

and from generation 2 above:

2 Joan Plantagenet = Gilbert de Clare, 3rd Earl of Gloucester, 7th Earl of Hertford
3 Elizabeth de Clare = Hugh le Despencer, 1st Baron Despencer;
Margaret de Clare = Hugh de Audley, Earl of Gloucester 3
4 Sir Edward Despencer = Anne Ferrers;
Margaret de Audley = Ralph Stafford, 1st Earl of Stafford 4
5 Edward Despencer, 3rd Baron Despencer = Elizabeth Burghersh;
Elizabeth Stafford = John de Ferrers, 4th Baron Ferrers of Chartley 5
6 Margaret Despencer = Robert de Ferrers, 5th Baron Ferrers of Chartley 6
7 Philippa Ferrers = Sir Thomas Greene [8]

Sources: AR 6, lines 14, 8, 61, 9, 70 & 74; M. B. Colket, The English Ancestry of Anne Marbury Hutchinson & Katherine Marbury Scott, 1936; NEHGR 123(1969):180-81, reprinted in EO 2:2:483-84.

Franklin Delano Roosevelt Through (6) Thomas Southworth (probable but unproved)

1 Edward I, King of England, d. 1307 = Eleanor of Castile
2 Joan Plantagenet = Gilbert de Clare, 3rd Earl of Gloucester, 7th Earl of Hertford
3 Eleanor de Clare = Hugh le Despencer, 1st Baron Despencer;
Margaret de Clare = Hugh de Audley, Earl of Gloucester 3
4 Sir Edward Despencer = Anne Ferrers;
Margaret de Audley = Ralph Stafford, 1st Earl of Stafford 4
5 Edward Despencer, 3rd Baron Despencer = Elizabeth Burghersh;
Beatrix Stafford = Thomas de Ros, 5th Baron Ros of Helmsley 5
6 Elizabeth Despencer = John FitzAlan, 2nd Baron Arundel;
7 Margaret FitzAlan = William de Ros, 7th Baron Ros of Helmsley 6
8 Margaret de Ros = James Touchet, 2nd Baron Audley
9 Anne Touchet = Sir Thomas Sutton
10 Isabel Sutton = Sir Christopher Southworth
11 Sir John Southworth = Helen Langton
12 Sir Thomas Southworth = Margery Boteler, a descendant of Elizabeth Plantagenet, younger daughter of Edward I & Eleanor of Castile & wife of Humphrey de Bohun, 4th Earl of Hertford & Essex, see AR 6, lines 46, 20 & 15
13 Sir John Southworth = Mary Ashton
14 Thomas Southworth = Rosamond Lister
15 Edward Southworth, probably the Leyden Pilgrim = Alice Carpenter of Mass.
16 Thomas Southworth of Mass. = Elizabeth Reynor
17 Elizabeth Southworth = Joseph Howland
18 Nathaniel Howland = Martha Cole
19 Nathaniel Howland, Jr. = Abigail Burt
20 Joseph Howland = Lydia Bill
21 Susan Howland = John Aspinwall, Jr.
22 Mary Rebecca Aspinwall = Isaac Roosevelt
23 James Roosevelt = Sara Delano
24 Franklin Delano Roosevelt, 1882-1945, 32nd U. S. President = (Anna) Eleanor Roosevelt

Sources: AR 6, lines 8, 9, 21 & 74, & sources cited therein.

Franklin Delano Roosevelt Through (7) Richard Palgrave

1 Edward I, King of England, d. 1307 = Eleanor of Castile

2 Elizabeth Plantagenet = Humphrey de Bohun, 4th Earl of Hereford & Essex
3 William de Bohun, 1st Earl of Northampton = Elizabeth Badlesmere
4 Elizabeth de Bohun = Richard FitzAlan, 10th Earl of Arundel
5 Elizabeth FitzAlan = Sir Robert Goushill
6 Elizabeth Goushill = Sir Robert Wingfield
7 Elizabeth Wingfield = Sir William Brandon
8 Eleanor Brandon = John Glemham
9 Anne Glemham = Henry Pagrave
10 Thomas Pagrave = Alice Gunton
11 Edward Palgrave = ---
12 Richard Palgrave of Mass. = Anna ---
13 Sarah Palgrave = John Alcock
14 Joanna Alcock = Ephraim Hunt, Jr.
15 Elizabeth Hunt = Lemuel Pope
16 Mercy Pope = Caleb Church
17 Joseph Church = Deborah Perry
18 Deborah Church = Warren Delano
19 Warren Delano, Jr. = Catherine Robbins Lyman
20 Sara Delano = James Roosevelt
21 Franklin Delano Roosevelt, 1882-1945, 32nd U. S. President = (Anna) Eleanor Roosevelt

Sources: AR 6, line 15 & sources cited therein, esp. NEHGR 102(1948):87-98, 312-13, 103(1949):102-7, 287-95, 116(1962):79, all reprinted in EO 1:3:60-72, 82-96; MMS. notebooks of George Andrews Moriarty, Jr. at NEHGS.

Franklin Delano Roosevelt Through
(8) Mrs. Catherine Hamby Hutchinson

1 Henry I, King of England, d. 1135
2 Elizabeth (illegitimate) = Fergus, Lord of Galloway
3 Uchtred of Galloway = Gunnild of Dunbar, a descendant of Ethelred II, King of England, d. 1016
4 Roland, Lord of Galloway = Elena de Morville
5 Alan, Lord of Galloway = ---, daughter of Hugh de Lacy, Earl of Ulster
6 Helen of Galloway = Roger de Quincy, 2nd Earl of Winchester, a descendant of Henry I, King of France, d. 1060
7 Elizabeth de Quincy = Alexander Comyn, 2nd Earl of Buchan
8 Elizabeth Comyn = Gilbert de Umfreville, 1st Earl of Angus
9 Robert de Umfreville, 2nd Earl of Angus = Lucy de Kyme
10 Elizabeth de Umfreville = Gilbert de Boroughdon
11 Eleanor de Boroughdon, Baroness Kyme = Henry Talboys
12 Walter Talboys, Baron Kyme = Margaret ---;
Joan Talboys = Andrew Luttrell, 1st Baron Luttrell 12
13 Sir John Talboys = Agnes Cokefield;
Hawise Luttrell, Baroness Luttrell = Sir Godfrey Hilton 13
14 John Talboys = Katherine Cibthorpe;
Godfrey Hilton, Baron Luttrell = Margery --- 14
15 Margaret Talboys = John Ayscough;
Elizabeth Hilton = Richard Thimbleby 15
16 Elizabeth Ayscough = William Booth;
17 John Booth = Anne Thimbleby 16
18 Eleanor Booth = Edward Hamby
19 William Hamby = Margaret Blewett
20 Robert Hamby = Elizabeth Arnold
21 Catherine Hamby of Mass. = Edward Hutchinson
22 Elisha Hutchinson = Elizabeth Clarke

23 Edward Hutchinson = Lydia Foster
24 Elizabeth Hutchinson = Nathaniel Robbins
25 Edward Hutchinson Robbins = Elizabeth Murray
26 Anne Jean Robbins = Joseph Lyman (III)
27 Catherine Robbins Lyman = Warren Delano, Jr.
28 Sara Delano = James Roosevelt
29 Franklin Delano Roosevelt, 1882-1945, 32nd U. S. President = (Anna) Eleanor Roosevelt

Sources: A forthcoming article by Wayne H. M. Wilcox of Weymouth, Mass., based in part on Hamby of St. Matthew & Dallinghoo, Suffolk entries in the GSU International Genealogical Index (IGI) (baptisms of Catherine Hamby & her father); Walter C. Metcalf, ed., **The Visitations of Suffolk**, 1882, p. 194, & GGE 1266 (Hamby); A. R. Maddison, ed., **Lincolnshire Pedigrees** (HSPVS, vols. 50-52, 55), vol. 1 (1902), pp. 154 (Booth), 60 (Ayscough), vol. 3, pp. 945 (Talboys), 957 (Thimbleby); **The Genealogist** 5 (1881):114 (Thimbleby); Sir H. C. Maywell Lyte, **A History of Dunster & of the Families of Mohun & Luttrell**, vol. 2, 1909, p. 509 (Hilton, Luttrell); Kyme & Luterel articles in CP; AR 6, lines 224, 38, & 121B.

Franklin Delano Roosevelt Through (9) Thomas Lawrence

For generations 1-23 from Louis IV, King of France, to Thomas Lawrence, husband of Joan Antrobus of Mass. (who married secondly John Tuttle), see under William Howard Taft.

24 Thomas Lawrence of Newtown, L. I., N. Y. = Mary ---
25 Mary Lawrence (very probably, see TAG 17[1940-41]:74-78) = Thomas Walton
26 William Walton = Mary Santvoort
27 Jacob Walton = Maria Beekman
28 Abraham Walton = Grace Williams
29 Maria Eliza Walton = James Roosevelt
30 Isaac Roosevelt = Mary Rebecca Aspinwall
31 James Roosevelt = Sara Delano
32 Franklin Delano Roosevelt, 1882-1945, 32nd U. S. President = (Anna) Eleanor Roosevelt

Sources: As above under William Howard Taft.

Richard Milhous Nixon Through Hugh Harry

1 Edward III, King of England, d. 1377 = Philippa of Hainault
2 Edmund of Langley, 1st Duke of York = Isabel of Castile
3 Constance Plantagenet
4 Eleanor Holand (illegitimate by Edmund Holand, 4th Earl of Kent) = James Touchet, 2nd Baron Audley
5 Constance Touchet = Robert Whitney
6 Eleanor Whitney = John Poleston
7 Sir John Poleston = Gainor Roberts
8 Jane Puleston = Rhys Thomas
9 Gainor Thomas = Richard Pugh
10 Elizabeth Pugh = Rowland Owen
11 Thomas Owen = ---
12 Harry Thomas Owen = ---
13 Hugh Harry of Pa. = Elizabeth Brinton
14 John Harry = Frances ---
15 Miriam Harry = Record Hussey
16 Lydia Hussey = Jacob Griffith

17 Amos Griffith = Edith Price
18 Elizabeth Price Griffith = Joshua Vickers Milhous
19 Franklin Milhous = Almira Park Burdg
20 Hannah Milhous = Francis Anthony Nixon
21 Richard Milhous Nixon, b. 1913, 37th U. S. President
 = Thelma Catherine (Pat) Ryan

Sources: T. A. Glenn, Welsh Founders of Pennsylvania, vol. 1, 1911, reprint 1970, pedigree XX, pp. 136-38 & chart between pp. 138 & 139, & sources cited therein, data reprinted or absorbed in Robert Jesse Harry, The Ancestors & Descendants of Hugh Harry & Elizabeth Brinton, 1987.

Gerald Rudolph Ford, Jr.
Through (1) Mrs. Elizabeth Marshall Lewis

1 Edward I, King of England, d. 1307 = Eleanor of Castile
2 Joan Plantagenet = Gilbert de Clare, 3rd Earl of Gloucester, 7th Earl of Hertford
3 Margaret de Clare = Hugh de Audley, Earl of Gloucester
4 Margaret de Audley = Ralph Stafford, 1st Earl of Stafford
5 Katherine Stafford = Sir John Sutton
6 Sir John Sutton = Jane ---
7 Sir John Sutton = Constance Blount
8 John Sutton, 1st Baron Dudley = Elizabeth Berkeley
9 Eleanor Sutton = Sir Henry Beaumont
10 Constance Beaumont = John Mitton
11 Joyce Mitton = John Harpersfield
12 Edward Harpersfield alias Mitton = Anna Skrimshire
13 Katherine Mitton = Roger Marshall
14 Elizabeth Marshall of Maine = Thomas Lewis of Maine
15 Judith Lewis = James Gibbins
16 Hannah Gibbins = --- Hibbert
17 Mary Hibbert = Joseph Jewett
18 Nathan Jewett = Deborah Lord
19 David Jewett = Sarah Selden
20 Elizabeth Jewett = Anselm Comstock
21 Betsey Comstock = Daniel Butler
22 George Selden Butler = Elizabeth Ely Gridley
23 Amy Gridley Butler = George Manney Ayer
24 Adele Augusta Ayer = Levi Addison Gardner
25 Dorothy Ayer Gardner = (1) Leslie Lynch King, m. (2) Gerald Rudolf Ford
26 Leslie Lynch King, Jr., whose name was changed to Gerald Rudolph Ford, Jr., b. 1913, 38th U. S. President
 = Mrs. Elizabeth Ann (Betty) Bloomer Warren

Sources: AR 6, lines 9, 81, 221 & 17; ND 137-88; TG 5(1984):131-41, 150-51, 154-56.

Gerald Rudolph Ford, Jr. Through (2) Thomas Lewis

1 Cynfyn, Prince of Powys = Angharad II, Queen of Powys
2 Rhywallon, Prince of Powys, d. 1070 = ---
3 Sionet of Powys = Ednyfed ap Llywarch Gam
4 Rhys Sais = Efa ---
5 Elidir = ---
6 Sandde = ---
7 Hwfa = ---
8 Hwfa Gryg = ---

9 Hwfa Fychan = ---
10 Iorwerth = ---
11 Madog Foel =
12 Rheinallt ap Madog Foel (illegitimate) = ---
13 Owain ap Rheinallt = ---
14 Robert ab Owain = ---
15 William Coetmor = ---
16 Ievan Coetmor = ---
17 Lewis ab Ievan = Anne Wilson
18 Andrew Lewis = Mary Herring
19 Thomas Lewis of Maine = Elizabeth Marshall of Maine
20 Judith Lewis = James Gibbins
21 Hannah Gibbins = --- Hibbert
22 Mary Hibbert = Joseph Jewett
23 Nathan Jewett = Deborah Lord
24 David Jewett = Sarah Selden
25 Elizabeth Jewett = Anselm Comstock
26 Betsey Comstock = Daniel Butler
27 George Selden Butler = Elizabeth Ely Gridley
28 Amy Gridley Butler = George Manney Ayer
29 Adele Augusta Ayer = Levi Addison Gardner
30 Dorothy Ayer Gardner = (1) Leslie Lynch King, m. (2) Gerald Rudolf Ford
31 Leslie Lynch King, Jr., whose name was changed to Gerald Rudolph Ford, Jr., b. 1913, 38th U. S. President = Mrs. Elizabeth Ann (Betty) Bloomer Warren

Sources: NEHGR 101(1947):3-23, reprinted in EO 2:2:627-48; ND 105-25; Peter C. Bartrum, Welsh Genealogies, A. D. 300-1400, 1974: 1, 47; 4, 870, 887, 889, 890 (Tudor Trevor 1, 18, 20, 21) & Welsh Genealogies, A. D. 1400-1500, 1983, 10:1699 (Tudor Trevor 21[D2E]).

Gerald Rudolph Ford, Jr. Through (3) Thomas Newberry (doubted by Sir A. R. Wagner)

For generations 1-20, from Henry I, King of France, to Thomas Newberry of Mass., who married firstly Joan Dabinott (& had Mary below) & secondly Jane ---, see under Rutherford Birchard Hayes.

21 Mary Newberry = Daniel Clark
22 Sarah Clark = Isaac Pinney
23 Mary Pinney = Jonathan Gridley
24 Jonathan Gridley, Jr. = Martha Adams
25 Theodore Gridley = Amy Ely
26 Elizabeth Ely Gridley = George Selden Butler
27 Amy Gridley Butler = George Manney Ayer
28 Adele Augusta Ayer = Levi Addison Gardner
29 Dorothy Ayer Gardner = (1) Leslie Lynch King, m. (2) Gerald Rudolf Ford
30 Leslie Lynch King, Jr., whose name was changed to Gerald Rudolph Ford, Jr., b. 1913, 38th U. S. President = Mrs. Elizabeth Ann (Betty) Bloomer Warren

Sources: As above under Rutherford Birchard Hayes.

George Herbert Walker Bush Through (1) Mrs. Anne Marbury Hutchinson

For generations 1-17, from Edward I, King of England, through Mrs. Anne Marbury Hutchinson to her grandson, Elisha Hutchinson, see under Franklin Delano Roosevelt.

17 Elisha Hutchinson = Hannah Hawkins (his first wife)
18 Hannah Hutchinson = John Ruck
19 Hannah Ruck = Theophilus Lillie
20 John Lillie = Abigail Breck
21 Anna Lillie = Samuel Howard
22 Harriet Howard = Samuel Prescott Phillips Fay
23 Samuel Howard Fay = Susan Shellman
24 Harriet Eleanor Fay = James Smith Bush
25 Samuel Prescott Bush = Flora Sheldon
26 Prescott Sheldon Bush, U. S. Senator = Dorothy Walker
27 George Herbert Walker Bush, b. 1924, 41st U. S. President = Barbara Pierce

George Herbert Walker Bush Through (2) Richard Palgrave

For generations 1-12, from Edward I, King of England, to Richard Palgrave of Mass., who married Anna ---, see under Franklin Delano Roosevelt.

13 Mary Palgrave = Roger Wellington
14 Benjamin Wellington = Elizabeth Sweetman
15 Elizabeth Wellington = John Fay, Jr.
16 John Fay (III) = Hannah Child
17 Jonathan Fay = Joanna Phillips
18 Jonathan Fay, Jr. = Lucy Prescott
19 Samuel Prescott Phillips Fay = Harriet Howard
20 Samuel Howard Fay = Susan Shellman
21 Harriet Eleanor Fay = James Smith Bush
22 Samuel Prescott Bush = Flora Sheldon
23 Prescott Sheldon Bush, U. S. Senator = Dorothy Walker
24 George Herbert Walker Bush, b. 1924, 41st U. S. President = Barbara Pierce

George Herbert Walker Bush Through (3) Rev. Peter Bulkeley

For generations 1-11, from Edward I, King of England, to Edward Bulkeley, who married Olive Irby, see under (John) Calvin Coolidge (Jr.) Through (2) Mrs. Elizabeth St. John Whiting.

12 Rev. Peter Bulkeley of Mass. = Jane Allen
13 Edward Bulkeley = Lucian ---
14 Peter Bulkeley = Rebecca Wheeler
15 Rebecca Bulkeley = Jonathan Prescott, Jr.
16 Abel Prescott = Abigail Brigham
17 Lucy Prescott, sister of Dr. Samuel Prescott, who completed Paul Revere's "Midnight Ride" of 19 Apr. 1775 = Jonathan Fay, Jr.
18 Samuel Prescott Phillips Fay = Harriet Howard
19 Samuel Howard Fay = Susan Shellman
20 Harriet Eleanor Fay = James Smith Bush
21 Samuel Prescott Bush = Flora Sheldon
22 Prescott Sheldon Bush, U. S. Senator = Dorothy Walker
23 George Herbert Walker Bush, b. 1924, 41st U. S. President = Barbara Pierce

Sources for (1), (2) & (3): As above under Calvin Coolidge & F. D. Roosevelt.

George Herbert Walker Bush
Through (4) Robert Livingston the Elder

1 Robert II, King of Scotland, d. 1390 = Elizabeth Mure
2 Robert Stewart, 1st Duke of Albany = Margaret Graham, Countess of Menteith
3 Maria Stewart = Sir William Abernethy
4 Sir William Abernethy = Margaret Borthwick
5 Laurence Abernethy, 1st Baron Saltoun = Margaret ---
6 William Abernethy, 2nd Baron Saltoun = ---
7 --- Abernethy (daughter) = William Ogstoun
8 Elizabeth Ogstoun = Sir Adam Hepburn, also a descendant of Robert II, King of Scotland
9 Elizabeth Hepburn = Alexander Livingston of Duniplace
10 Thomas Livingston of Kirkland = Agnes Menteith
11 Alexander Livingston of the Halls of Airth = Marion Bryson
12 Agnes Livingston = William Livingston, also a descendant of Robert II, King of Scotland
13 John Livingston = Janet Fleming
14 Robert Livingston the Elder of N. Y., 1st Lord of Livingston Manor = Alida Schuyler
15 Gilbert Livingston = Cornelia Beekman
16 James Livingston = Judith Newcomb
17 Gilbert James Livingston = Susanna Lewis
18 Judith Livingston = Samuel Herrick Butler
19 Courtland Philip Livingston Butler = Elizabeth Slade Pierce
20 Mary Elizabeth Butler = Robert Emmet Sheldon
21 Flora Sheldon = Samuel Prescott Bush
22 Prescott Sheldon Bush, U. S. Senator = Dorothy Walker
23 George Herbert Walker Bush, b. 1924, 41st U. S. President = Barbara Pierce

Sources: MCS 3, line 42; Florence Van Rensselaer, The Livingston Family in America & Its Scottish Origins (1949), pp. 5-7, 67-68, 70-71, 73, 17; CP (Saltoun), SP (Hepburn, Earls of Bothwell, & Abernethy, Lords Saltoun). The patrilineal descent of the immigrant from the lords of Callender, as given by Florence Van Rensselaer but mistakenly doubted in SP 5:435, note 3 & MCS 3, may well be correct; see also E. B. Livingston, The Livingstons of Livingston Manor, 1910.

George Herbert Walker Bush Through (5) Mrs. Jane Allen Bulkeley

1 William I the Lion, King of Scotland, d. 1214
2 Isabel of Scotland (illeg. by a daughter of Richard Avenal) = Robert de Ros, Magna Charta Surety
3 Sir William de Ros = Lucy FitzPiers
4 Sir William de Ros = Eustache Fitzhugh
5 Lucy de Ros = Sir Robert Plumpton
6 Sir William Plumpton = Christiana ---
7 Alice Plumpton = Sir John Boteler
8 Alice Boteler = John Gerard
9 Constance Gerard = Sir Alexander Standish
10 Oliver Standish = ---
11 Grace Standish = Ralph Faircloth
12 Lawrence Faircloth = Elizabeth ---
13 Thomas Faircloth = Millicent Barr
14 Mary Faircloth = Thomas Allen
15 Jane Allen, who died in England = Rev. Peter Bulkeley of Mass.
16 Edward Bulkeley = Lucian ---
17 Peter Bulkeley = Rebecca Wheeler

18 Rebecca Bulkeley = Jonathan Prescott, Jr.
19 Abel Prescott = Abigail Brigham
20 Lucy Prescott, sister of Dr. Samuel Prescott, who completed Paul Revere's "Midnight Ride" of 19 Apr. 1775 = Jonathan Fay, Jr.
21 Samuel Prescott Phillips Fay = Harriet Howard
22 Samuel Howard Fay = Susan Shellman
23 Harriet Eleanor Fay = James Smith Bush
24 Samuel Prescott Bush = Flora Sheldon
25 Prescott Sheldon Bush, U. S. Senator = Dorothy Walker
26 George Herbert Walker Bush, b. 1924, 41st U. S. President = Barbara Pierce

Sources: Donald Lines Jacobus, The Bulkeley Genealogy, 1933, pp. 38-51; TAG 42(1966):129-35; F. L. Weis, The Families of Standish, Lancashire, England, 1959, pp. 14-15; AR 6, line 170.

George Herbert Walker Bush Through (6) Walter Aston

1 Henry II, King of England, d. 1189
2 William de Longespee (illeg. perhaps by Alix de Porhoet), Earl of Salisbury = Ela, Countess of Salisbury
3 Ida de Longespee = William de Beauchamp
4 Beatrice de Beauchamp = Sir Thomas FitzOtho or FitzOtes
5 Maud (or Matilda) FitzThomas = John de Botetourte, 1st Baron Botetourte, formerly thought to be an illegitimate son of Edward I, King of England, d. 1307, but see TAG 63(1988):145-53
6 Thomas de Botetourte = Joan de Somery
7 John de Botetourte, 2nd Baron Botetourte = Joyce La Zouche de Mortimer
8 Joyce de Botetourte = Sir Baldwin Freville
9 Sir Baldwin Freville = Maud ---
10 Joyce Freville = Sir Roger Aston
11 Sir Robert Aston = Isabella Brereton
12 John Aston = Elizabeth Delves
13 Sir John Aston = Joan Lyttleton, daughter of Sir William Lyttleton (& Ellen Walshe), son of Sir Thomas Lyttleton, author of Treatise on Tenures, & Joan Burley, daughter of William (not Sir John) Burley, speaker of the House of Commons, & Ellen Grendon (not Alice Grey as in MCS 3, line 101, & VHG 277). See William Salt Archaeological Society, Collections for a History of Staffordshire, New Ser., vol. 12, 1909, p. 90, a source brought to my attention by Timothy Field Beard.
14 Sir Edward Aston = Joan Bowles
15 Leonard Aston = Elizabeth Barton
16 Walter Aston = Joyce Nason
17 Walter Aston of Va. = Hannah Jordan
18 Mary Aston = Richard Cocke
19 Richard Cocke the Younger (of two brothers both named Richard) = Elizabeth (Littleberry?)
20 Anne Cocke = Robert Bolling, Jr.
21 Elizabeth Bolling = James Munford
22 Robert Munford/Montfort = Anne Brodnax
23 Clarissa Montfort = John Shellman, Jr.

24 Susan Shellman = Samuel Howard Fay
25 Harriet Eleanor Fay = James Smith Bush
26 Samuel Prescott Bush = Flora Sheldon
27 Prescott Sheldon Bush, U. S. Senator = Dorothy Walker
28 George Herbert Walker Bush, b. 1924, 41st U. S. President
= Barbara Pierce

Sources: MCS 3, line 101 & VHG 272-78 (but note the correction above); VGE 390-92; Sir Thomas Clifford, 1st Bt., & Arthur Clifford, A Topographical & Historical Description of the Parish of Tixall in the County of Stafford, 1817, pp. 146-49 (Aston); Genealogists' Magazine 21(1983-85):185-91 (Freville); AR 6, lines 216, 122A, & 30.

George Herbert Walker Bush Through
(7) Mrs. Catherine Hamby Hutchinson

For generations 1-21, from Henry I, King of England, to Catherine Hamby of Mass., wife of Edward Hutchinson, see under Franklin Delano Roosevelt.

22 Elisha Hutchinson = Hannah Hawkins (his first wife)
23 Hannah Hutchinson = John Ruck
24 Hannah Ruck = Theophilus Lillie
25 John Lillie = Abigail Breck
26 Anna Lillie = Samuel Howard
27 Harriet Howard = Samuel Prescott Phillips Fay
28 Samuel Howard Fay = Susan Shellman
29 Harriet Eleanor Fay = James Smith Bush
30 Samuel Prescott Bush = Flora Sheldon
31 Prescott Sheldon Bush, U. S. Senator = Dorothy Walker
32 George Herbert Walker Bush, b. 1924, 41st U. S. President
= Barbara Pierce

Sources: As above under F. D. Roosevelt.

# # #

SUMMARY OF ROYAL DESCENTS

President	Immigrant	Royal Ancestor
Washington	George Reade of VA	Edward III of England, d. 1377
	John Washington of VA	Edward I of England, d. 1307
	Mrs. Mary Towneley Warner of VA	William I of Scotland, d. 1214
Jefferson	William Randolph of VA	Edward III of England, d. 1377
	Henry Isham of VA	Henry II of England, d. 1189
	Christopher Branch of VA	Henry I of England, d. 1135
Madison	Mrs. Martha Eltonhead Conway of VA	Henry II of England, d. 1189
	*Anthony Savage of VA	Edward I of England, d. 1307
J. Q. Adams	Mrs. Elizabeth Coytmore Tyng of MA	Edward III of England, d. 1377
W. H. & B. Harrison	Mrs. Sarah Ludlow Carter of VA	Edward I of England, d. 1307
B. Harrison	*Anthony Collamore of MA	Hugh Capet of France, d. 996
Taylor	*William Strother of VA	Edward III of England, d. 1377
	*Anthony Savage of VA	Edward I of England, d. 1307
Pierce	Griffith Bowen &	Henry I of England, d. 1135
	Mrs. Margaret Fleming Bowen (his wife) of MA	Henry I of England, d. 1135
Buchanan	*James Buchanan of PA	Robert III Scotland, d. 1406
Hayes	*Thomas Newberry of MA	Henry I of France, d. 1060
	Thomas Trowbridge of CT	Hugh Capet of France, d. 996
Cleveland	Robert Abell of MA	Edward I of England, d. 1307
Theodore Roosevelt	John Irvine of GA	James I of Scotland, d. 1437
	*Kenneth Baillie of GA	Edward III of England, d. 1377
Taft	Mrs. Jane Lawrence	*Louis IV of France, d. 954
	Giddings of MA (or)	Hugh Capet of France, d. 996
Coolidge	William Goddard of MA	Edward I of England, d. 1307
	Mrs. Elizabeth St. John Whiting of MA	Edward I of England, d. 1307
	Samuel Appleton of MA	*John of England, d. 1216
	(or)	Henry I of England, d. 1135
	Mrs. Judith Everard Appleton of MA	*Louis IV of France, d. 954
	(or)	Hugh Capet of France, d. 996
Hoover	Gov. Thomas Dudley of MA	*Edward I of England, d. 1307
	(or)	John of England, d. 1216

President	Immigrant	Royal Ancestor
Franklin D. Roosevelt	John Nelson of MA	Edward III of England, d. 1377
	James Murray of NC	James II of Scotland, d. 1460
	Mrs. Barbara Bennet Murray of NC	James II of Scotland, d. 1460
	Mrs. Elizabeth Coytmore Tyng of MA	Edward III of England, d. 1377
	Mrs. Anne Marbury Hutchinson of RI	Edward I of England, d. 1307
	*Thomas Southworth of MA	Edward I of England, d. 1307
	Richard Palgrave of MA	Edward I of England, d. 1307
	Mrs. Catherine Hamby Hutchinson of MA	Henry I of England, d. 1135
	*Thomas Lawrence of LI, NY	*Louis IV of France, d. 954
	(or)	Hugh Capet of France, d. 996
Nixon	Hugh Harry of PA	Edward III of England, d. 1377
Ford	Mrs. Elizabeth Marshall Lewis of ME	Edward I of England, d. 1307
	Thomas Lewis of ME	Rhywallon, Prince of Powys, d. 1070
	*Thomas Newberry of MA	Henry I of France, d. 1060
Bush	Mrs. Anne Marbury Hutchinson of RI	Edward I of England, d. 1307
	Richard Palgrave of MA	Edward I of England, d. 1307
	Rev. Peter Bulkeley	Edward I of England, d. 1307
	of MA & Mrs. Jane Allen Bulkeley, his first wife	William I of Scotland, d. 1214
	Robert Livingston the Elder of NY	Robert II of Scotland, d. 1390
	Walter Aston of VA	Henry II of England, d. 1189
	Mrs. Catherine Hamby Hutchinson of MA	Henry I of England, d. 1135

Totals: Nineteen presidents, forty-one separate immigrants, eight lines from Edward III, King of England, d. 1377, sixteen lines from Edward I, King of England, d. 1307, one line from John, King of England, d. 1216, three lines from Henry II, King of England, d. 1189, five lines from Henry I, King of England, d. 1135, two lines from James II, King of Scotland, d. 1460, one line from James I, King of Scotland, d. 1437, one line from Robert III, King of Scotland, d. 1406, one line from Robert II, King of Scotland, d. 1390, two lines from William I, King of Scotland, d. 1214, two lines from Henry I, King of France, d. 1060, two lines from Hugh Capet, King of France, d. 996, three lines from Louis IV, King of France, d. 954, & one line from the Welsh Prince, Rhywallon of Powys, d. 1070, for a total of forty-eight in all. The best lines for seven presidents (Washington, Jefferson, J. Q. Adams, Taylor, the two Roosevelts & Nixon) are from Edward III, King of England, d. 1377 (with F. D. Roosevelt also from James II, King of Scotland, d. 1460, and T. Roosevelt from James I, King of Scotland, d. 1437); the best lines for eight presidents (Madison, the two Harrisons, Cleveland, Coolidge, Hoover, Ford & Bush) are from Edward I, King of England, d. 1307; the best line for Pierce is from Henry I, King of England, d. 1135; the best line for Buchanan is from Robert III, King of Scotland, d. 1406; the best line for Hayes is from Henry I, King of France, d. 1060; & the best line for Taft is from Louis IV, King of France, d. 954.

*Unproved descents or lines including problematic American generations. Before a sovereign an asterisk indicates that although some royal descent for the said immigrant is certain, his descent from this particular king may be problematic.

Note: The preceding charts outline the "best" royal descents, from the latest medieval king, for each presidential immigrant ancestor with such lineage. Thus descents from Edward III were preferred to those from Edward I, those from this latter to lines from King John, John to Henry II, Henry II to Henry I, & English sovereigns to Scottish (except James I or James II, the former of whom married a great-granddaughter of Edward III) or French Kings. Among descents from Edward III, those through Lionel of Antwerp, Duke of Clarence, were preferred to those through John of Gaunt, Duke of Lancaster, & lines through this latter to those through Edmund of Langley, 1st Duke of York. Among descents from Edward I, those through his younger sons, Thomas of Brotherton, Earl of Norfolk, & Edmund of Woodstock, 1st Earl of Kent, were preferred to those through his daughters Joan (Countess of Gloucester & Hertford, later Baroness Monthermer) & Elizabeth (Countess firstly of Holland, then of Hereford & Essex); Thomas was preferred to Edmund, and Joan to Elizabeth. Legitimate and illegitimate lines were considered equal.

ROYAL DESCENTS OF FIRST LADIES WHOSE HUSBANDS WERE NOT OF SUCH ANCESTRY

The best line through each royally descended immigrant ancestor

(Mrs. John Adams, Jr., Mrs. Ulysses Simpson Grant, Mrs. James Abram Garfield, Mrs. Chester Alan Arthur, both Mrs. [Thomas] Woodrow Wilsons, Mrs. Harry S Truman, Mrs. Dwight David Eisenhower, and the 2nd Mrs. Ronald Wilson Reagan)

This section is new to this edition.

ROYAL DESCENTS OF FIRST LADIES
WHOSE HUSBANDS WERE NOT OF SUCH ANCESTRY

The best line through each royally descended immigrant ancestor

(Mrs. John Adams, Jr., Mrs. Ulysses Simpson Grant, Mrs. James Abram Garfield, Mrs. Chester Alan Arthur, both Mrs. [Thomas] Woodrow Wilsons, Mrs. Harry S Truman, Mrs. Dwight David Eisenhower, and the 2nd Mrs. Ronald Wilson Reagan)

Mrs. John Adams, Jr.

(Mrs. Abigail Smith Adams - see under her son, John Quincy Adams)

Mrs. Ulysses Simpson Grant (Mrs. Julia Boggs Dent Grant)
Through (1) Gerard Fowke

1 Henry II, King of England, d. 1189
2 William de Longespee (illeg. perhaps by Alix de Porhoet), Earl of Salisbury = Ela, Countess of Salisbury
3 Ida de Longespee = William de Beauchamp
4 Beatrice de Beauchamp = Sir Thomas FitzOtho or FitzOtes
5 Maud (or Matilda) FitzThomas = John de Botetourte, 1st Baron Botetourte, formerly thought to be an illegitimate son of Edward I, King of England, d. 1307, but see TAG 63(1988):145-53
6 Thomas de Botetourte = Joan de Somery
7 John de Botetourte, 2nd Baron Botetourte = Joyce La Zouche de Mortimer
8 Joyce de Botetourte = Sir Baldwin Freville
9 Sir Baldwin Freville = Maud ---
10 Joyce Freville = Sir Roger Aston
11 Sir Robert Aston = Isabella Brereton
12 John Aston = Elizabeth Delves
13 Margaret Aston = John (or Thomas) Kinnersley
14 Isabel Kinnersley = John Bradshaw
15 Anne Bradshaw = John Fowke
16 Francis Fowke = Jane Raynsford
17 John Fowke = Dorothy Cupper
18 Roger Fowke = Mary Bayley
19 Gerard Fowke of Va. = Anne Thoroughgood
20 Elizabeth Fowke = William Dent
21 Peter Dent = Mary Brooke
22 Peter Dent, Jr. = Mary Eleanor ---
23 George Dent = Susannah Dawson
24 Frederick Fayette Dent = Ellen Bray Wrenshall
25 Julia Boggs Dent
= Ulysses Simpson Grant, 1822-1885, 18th U. S. President

Sources: AR 6, lines 216, 122A, & 30; Genealogists' Magazine 21(1983-85):185-91 (Freville); Sir Thomas Clifford, 1st Bt. & Arthur Clifford, A Topographical & Historical Description of the Parish of Tixall in the County of Stafford, 1817, pp. 146-48 (Aston); T. F. Kynnersley, A History of the Family of Kynnersley of Leighton, Shropshire, 1897, chart at end; Rev. Stebbing Shaw, History & Antiquities of Staffordshire, vol. 2, part 1, 1801, p. 60, VGE 583-85, & HVG 154-56, 743-44 (Fowke); H. W. Newman, The Maryland Dents, 1963, pp. 15-25, 36-42, 50-53, 69-70, 86-87.

Mrs. Ulysses Simpson Grant (Mrs. Julia Boggs Dent Grant) Through (2) Act. Gov. Robert Brooke

For generations 1-9 from Henry I, King of England through Robert de Umfreville, 2nd Earl of Angus, who married (2) Eleanor ---, see under Franklin Delano Roosevelt.

10 Thomas Umfreville = Joan de Roddam

11 Sir Thomas de Umfreville = Agnes (de Grey?)

12 Elizabeth de Umfreville = Sir William Elmeden

13 Joan Elmeden = Thomas Forster

14 Thomas Forster = Elizabeth de Etherstone

15 Thomas Forster = --- Fetherstonhaugh

16 Sir Roger Forster = Joan Hussey

17 Thomas Forster = Margaret Browning

18 Sir Thomas Forster = Susan Foster

19 Susan Foster = Thomas Brooke

20 Robert Brooke, Act. Gov. of Md. = Mary Baker

21 Thomas Brooke = Eleanor Hatton

22 Thomas Brooke, Jr. = Anne ---

23 Thomas Brooke (III) = Lucy Smith

24 Mary Brooke = Peter Dent

25 Peter Dent, Jr. = Mary Eleanor ---

26 George Dent = Susannah Dawson

27 Frederick Fayette Dent = Ellen Bray Wrenshall

28 Julia Boggs Dent
= Ulysses Simpson Grant, 1822-1885, 18th U. S. President

Sources: AR 6, lines 224, 38 & 121B, & MCS 3, lines 109 & 110; Bennet B. Browne, Pedigree Chart of Robert Brooke & Mary Baker, His First Wife, 1912; W. L. Sheppard, Jr., The Ancestry of Edward Carleton & Ellen Newton, His Wife, 1978 (microfilm at the Library of Congress & elsewhere - generations 1-11); Maryland Genealogies, vol. 1, 1980, pp. 91-96, 99-100, 104 (Brooke).

Mrs. James Abram Garfield (Mrs. Lucretia Rudolph Garfield) Through (1) Mrs. Anne Marbury Hutchinson and (2) Mrs. Catherine Hamby Hutchinson

For generations 1-15 from Edward I, King of England through Mrs. Anne Marbury Hutchinson of R. I., and for generations 1-21 from Henry I, King of England, to Catherine Hamby of Mass., wife of Edward Hutchinson, see under Franklin Delano Roosevelt.

15 Anne Marbury, known as Mrs. Anne Hutchinson, the religious reformer, heretic & founder of R. I. = William Hutchinson

16 Edward Hutchinson = Catherine Hamby of Mass., generation 21 under F. D. R.

Bridget Hutchinson = John Sanford, Act. Gov. of R. I. 16

17 Elizabeth Hutchinson = Edward Winslow

Peleg Sanford, Gov. of R. I. = Mary Coddington 17

18 Anne Winslow = John Taylor

Anne Sanford = John Mason 18

19 Elizabeth Taylor = Nathaniel Greene, Jr.

Peleg Sanford Mason = Mary Stanton 19

20 John Greene = Azubah Ward

21 Lucretia Greene = Elijah Mason, son of 19 above, right

22 Arabella Mason = Zebulon Rudolph

23 Lucretia Rudolph
= James Abram Garfield, 1831-1881, 20th U. S. President

Sources: As per F. D. Roosevelt-Hutchinson sources for generations

1-15; NEHGR 19(1865):14-15 (Hutchinson); MF 2:16-17, 43-44, 103 (Winslow, Taylor, Greene); NEHGR 103(1949):208-13 & 272-75, & J. M. Sanford, President John Sanford...& His Descendants, 1966, pp. 1-2, 7-9 (Sanford); G. S. Greene & L. B. Clarke, The Greenes of Rhode Island, 1903, pp. 149, 255-56, 417-21 (Greene, Mason, Rudolph); R. A. Wheeler, History of...Stonington...Connecticut, 1900 (reprint 1977), pp. 462, 464 (Mason). And for (2) Mrs. Catherine Hamby Hutchinson see under F. D. Roosevelt through (8) Mrs. Catherine Hamby Hutchinson, and immediately above for following generations.

Mrs. Chester Alan Arthur (Mrs. Ellen Lewis Herndon Arthur) Through Gov. Edward Digges

1 Edward III, King of England, d. 1377 = Philippa of Hainault
2 Lionel of Antwerp, Duke of Clarence = Elizabeth de Burgh
3 Philippa Plantagenet = Edmund Mortimer, 3rd Earl of March
4 Elizabeth Mortimer = Sir Henry "Hotspur" Percy
5 Henry Percy, 2nd Earl of Northumberland = Eleanor Neville
6 Henry Percy, 3rd Earl of Northumberland = Eleanor Poynings
7 Henry Percy, 4th Earl of Northumberland = Maud Herbert
8 Eleanor Percy = Edward Stafford, 3rd Duke of Buckingham, son of Henry Stafford, 2nd Duke of Buckingham, & Catherine Woodville, sister of Elizabeth Woodville, Queen of Edward IV
9 Mary Stafford = George Neville, 3rd Baron Abergavenny (their progeny shares the entire known ancestry of Elizabeth Plantagenet of York, Queen of Henry VII)
10 Ursula Neville = Sir Warham St. Leger
11 Anne St. Leger = Thomas Digges, mathematician
12 Sir Dudley Digges, diplomat, judge = Mary Kempe
13 Edward Digges, Gov. of Va. = Elizabeth Page
14 Catherine Digges = William Herndon
15 Edward Herndon = Mary Waller
16 Edward Herndon, Jr. = Elizabeth (Stubblefield?)
17 Joseph Herndon = Mary Minor
18 Dabney Herndon = Elizabeth Hull
19 William Lewis Herndon = Frances Elizabeth Hansbrough
20 Ellen Lewis Herndon = Chester Alan Arthur, 1829-1886, 21st U. S. President

Sources: MCS 3, lines 47, 48, 44, 36 & 161 & AR 6, lines 5, 19 & 3 & sources cited therein, especially CP (for generations 1-9), J. G. Herndon, The Herndon Family of Virginia, vol. 1 (The First Three Generations), 1947, pp. 1-10, 19-25, & vol. 2 (The Herndons of the American Revolution), part II, 1951, pp. 57, 70-73, 114-17.

The 1st Mrs. Woodrow Wilson (Mrs. Ellen Louise Axson Wilson) Through (1) John Throckmorton

1 Edward I, King of England, d. 1307 = Eleanor of Castile
2 Joan Plantagenet = Gilbert de Clare, 3rd Earl of Gloucester, 7th Earl of Hertford
3 Eleanor de Clare = Hugh le Despencer, 1st Baron Despencer
4 Isabel Despencer = Richard FitzAlan, 9th Earl of Arundel
5 Sir Edmund FitzAlan = Sybil Montagu
6 Philippa FitzAlan = Sir Richard Sergeaux
7 Philippa Sergeaux = Sir Robert Pashley
8 Anne Pashley = Edward Tyrrell
9 Philippa Tyrrell = Thomas Cornwallis
10 William Cornwallis = Elizabeth Stanford
11 Sir John Cornwallis = Mary Sulyard
12 Elizabeth Cornwallis = John Blennerhasset

13 Elizabeth Blennerhasset = Lionel Throckmorton
14 Bassingborne Throckmorton = Mary Hill
15 John Throckmorton of R. I. = Rebecca ---
16 John Throckmorton, Jr. = Alice Stout
17 Patience Throckmorton = Hugh Coward
18 John Coward = Alice Britton
19 Deliverance Coward = James FitzRandolph
20 Isaac FitzRandolph = Eleanor Hunter
21 Rebecca Longstreet FitzRandolph = Isaac Stockton Keith Axson
22 Samuel Edward Axson = Margaret Jane Hoyt
23 Ellen Louise Axson =
(Thomas) Woodrow Wilson, 1856-1924, 28th U. S. President

Sources: AR 6, line 208, NEHGR 98(1944):67-72, 111-23, 271-79, 117(1963):234 (Throckmorton, Blennerhasset), 110(1956):122-27 (Cornwallis), 109(1955):17-31, 236 (Tyrrell) (reprinted in EO 2:3:478-98, EO 1:2:765-73, 3:240-45, 204-19); MCS, lines 113A, 134, & 34; S. F. G. Sitherwood, Throckmorton Family History, 1930, pp. 45-62 esp.; HGM 3:165-66, 475-77 (Coward); L. A. Christian & H. S. FitzRandolph, Descendants of Edward FitzRandolph & Elizabeth Blossom, 1630-1950, 1950, pp. 27, 49, 84.

The 1st Mrs. Woodrow Wilson (Mrs. Ellen Louise Axson Wilson)
Through (2) Thomas Newberry (doubted by Sir A. R. Wagner)

For generations 1-21 from Henry I, King of France through Thomas Newberry of Mass. to his daughter Mary Newberry, wife of Daniel Clark, see under Rutherford Birchard Hayes & Gerald Rudolph Ford, Jr.

22 Mary Clark = John Gaylord
23 Mary Gaylord = Ebenezer Bliss
24 Jedediah Bliss = Miriam Hitchcock
25 Alexander Bliss = Abigail Williams
26 Margaret Bliss = Nathan Hoyt
27 Margaret Jane Hoyt = Samuel Edward Axson
28 Ellen Louise Axson
= (Thomas) Woodrow Wilson, 1856-1924, 28th U. S. President

Sources: As above under Hayes and Ford for generations 1-21; J. G. Bartlett, Newberry Genealogy, 1914, pp. 35-46 esp.; SAW 153 (Clark), 279 (Gaylord); A. T. & J. H. Bliss, Genealogy of the Bliss Family in America, vol. 1, 1982, pp. 51, 71, 120-21; D. W. Hoyt, Genealogical History of the Hoyt, Haight, & Hight Families, 1871 (reprint 1984), pp. 99, 162.

The 1st Mrs. Woodrow Wilson (Mrs. Ellen Louise Axson Wilson)
Through (3) Mrs. Margaret Wyatt Allyn

For generations 1-17 from Hugh Capet, King of France through John Fortescue, who married Joan Prutteston, see under Benjamin Harrison.

18 William Fortescue = Elizabeth Champernowne
19 Jane Fortescue = John Cobleigh
20 Margaret Cobleigh = Sir Roger Giffard
21 Jane Giffard = Amyas Chichester
22 Frances Chichester = John Wyatt
23 Margaret Wyatt of Conn. = Matthew Allyn
24 Thomas Allyn = Abigail Warham
25 Abigail Allyn = John Williams
26 Elijah Williams = Lydia Dwight
27 Abigail Williams = Thomas Williams, a cousin

28 Abigail Williams = Alexander Bliss
29 Margaret Bliss = Nathan Hoyt
30 Margaret Jane Hoyt = Samuel Edward Axson
31 Ellen Louise Axson
= (Thomas) Woodrow Wilson, 1856-1924, 28th U. S. President

Sources: AR 6, lines 52, 25, 246F, E & B, 246, 151 & 106; FNE 267-68, 221-22 (Allyn); George Sheldon, History of Deerfield, Massachusetts, with Genealogies, vol. 2, 1896, pp. 377-78, 380-81 (Williams); B. W. Dwight, The History of the Descendants of John Dwight of Dedham, Massachusetts, vol. 2, 1871, pp. 824-25 (Williams).

The 1st Mrs. Woodrow Wilson (Mrs. Ellen Louise Axson Wilson) Through (4) Edward FitzRandolph

1 Hugh Capet, King of France, d. 996 = Adelaide of Poitou
2 Edith of France = Rainier IV, Count of Hainault
3 Beatrix of Hainault = Ebles I, Count of Roucy
4 Alice of Roucy = Hildouin IV, Count of Clermont
5 Margaret of Montdidier = Hugh I, Count of Clermont
6 Adeliza of Clermont = Gilbert de Clare
7 Alice de Clare = Aubrey de Vere
8 Joliana de Vere = Hugh Bigod, 1st Earl of Norfolk
9 Roger Bigod, 2nd Earl of Norfolk = Ida ---
10 Mary Bigod = Ranulf FitzRobert
11 Ranulf FitzRanulf = Bertrama ---
12 Ralph FitzRanulf = Theophania (or Tiffany) de Lascelles
13 Ranulf FitzRalph = Isabel ---
14 John FitzRanulf = Maud de Campania
15 Randall FitzJohn = ---
16 Sir John FitzRandall = ---
17 Sir Ralph FitzRandall = Elizabeth ---
18 John FitzRandolph = Joan Conyers
19 John FitzRandolph = ---
20 Christopher FitzRandolph = Jane Langton
21 Christopher FitzRandolph = ---
22 Edward FitzRandolph = Frances Howis
23 Edward FitzRandolph of Mass. & N. J. = Elizabeth Blossom
24 Benjamin FitzRandolph = Sarah Dennis
25 Isaac FitzRandolph = Rebecca Seabrook
26 James FitzRandolph = Deliverance Coward
27 Isaac FitzRandolph = Eleanor Hunter
28 Rebecca Longstreet FitzRandolph = Isaac Stockton Keith Axson
29 Samuel Edward Axson = Margaret Jane Hoyt
30 Ellen Louise Axson
= (Thomas) Woodrow Wilson, 1856-1924, 28th U. S. President

Sources: MCS 3, lines 164 (& notes & sources therein), 154 & 155; AR 6, lines 246, 151 & 106; L. A. Christian & H. S. FitzRandolph, The Descendants of Edward FitzRandolph & Elizabeth Blossom, 1630-1950, 1950, pp. 5, 8, 14, 27, 49, 84.

The 2nd Mrs. Woodrow Wilson (Mrs. Edith Bolling Galt Wilson) Through (1) William Randolph, (2) Henry Isham, and (3) Christopher Branch

For generations 1-14, from Edward III, King of England through William Randolph of Va. to Jane Randolph, wife of Peter Jefferson; generations 1-21, from Henry II, King of England through Henry Isham of Va. to Jane Randolph, wife of Peter Jefferson; and generations 1-25, from Henry I, King of England through Christopher Branch of Va. to Peter Jefferson, husband of Jane Randolph, see under Thomas

Jefferson. The lines are continued with No. 15.

15 Mary Jefferson, sister of Thomas Jefferson, 3rd U. S. President = John Bolling III, a great-great-great grandson of Pocahontas & John Rolfe
16 Archibald Bolling = Catherine Payne
17 Archibald Bolling, Jr. = Anne E. Wigginton
18 William Holcombe Bolling = Sallie Spiers White
19 Edith Bolling = (1) Norman Galt
= (2) (Thomas) Woodrow Wilson, 1856-1924, 28th U. S. President

Sources: As above under Thomas Jefferson for generations 1-14, 1-21 & 1-25; R. I. Randolph, The Randolphs of Virginia, 1936, p. 114; M. D. Ackerly & L. E. J. Parker, "Our Kin": the Genealogies of Some of the Early Families...of Bedford County, Virginia, 1930, pp. 336-42 (Bolling).

The 2nd Mrs. Woodrow Wilson (Mrs. Edith Bolling Galt Wilson)
Through (4) Gov. John West

1 Edward III, King of England, d. 1377 = Philippa of Hainault
2 John of Gaunt, Duke of Lancaster = Catherine de Roet
3 John Beaufort, Marquis of Dorset & Somerset = Margaret Holand
4 Edmund Beaufort, 1st Duke of Somerset = Eleanor Beauchamp
5 Eleanor Beaufort = Sir Robert Spencer
6 Margaret Spencer = Thomas Cary
7 William Cary = Mary Boleyn, sister of Anne Boleyn, 2nd Queen of Henry VIII, & aunt of Elizabeth I, Queen of England
8 Mary Cary = Sir Francis Knollys
9 Anne Knollys = Thomas West, 2nd Baron Delaware (de la Warr)
10 John West, Gov. of Va. = Anne ---
11 John West, Jr. = Unity Croshaw
12 Nathaniel West = Martha Woodward
13 Unity West = William Dandridge, uncle of First Lady Mrs. Martha Dandridge Custis Washington
14 Nathaniel West Dandridge = Dorothea Spotswood
15 Martha Dandridge = Archibald Payne
16 Catherine Payne = Archibald Bolling
17 Archibald Bolling, Jr. = Anne E. Wigginton
18 William Holcombe Bolling = Sallie Spiers White
19 Edith Bolling = (1) Norman Galt
= (2) (Thomas) Woodrow Wilson, 1856-1924, 28th U. S. President

Sources: MCS 3, lines 4 & 80, & AR 6, line 1, & sources cited therein, esp. CP (generations 1-5 & 8-9); WV, West chart at end (West, Dandridge, Payne, Bolling), reprinted opposite p. 198 of A. W. Fox, The Noble Lineage of the Delaware-West Family of Virginia, 1958; APP (West, Dandridge).

The 2nd Mrs. Woodrow Wilson (Mrs. Edith Bolling Galt Wilson)
Through (5) Gov. Alexander Spotswood

1 Edward III, King of England, d. 1377 = Philippa of Hainault
2 John of Gaunt, Duke of Lancaster = Catherine de Roet
3 John Beaufort, Marquis of Dorset & Somerset = Margaret Holand
4 Joan Beaufort = Sir James Stewart, "The Black Knight of Lorn"
5 John Stewart, 1st Earl of Atholl = Eleanor Sinclair
6 John Stewart, 2nd Earl of Atholl = Janet Campbell
7 Jean Stewart = James Arbuthnott
8 Isabel Arbuthnott = Sir Robert Maule
9 William Maule = Bethia Guthrie

10 Eleanor Maule = Sir Alexander Morrison
11 Bethia Morrison = Sir Robert Spotswood
12 Robert Spotswood = Catherine Mercer
13 Alexander Spotswood, Gov. of Va. = Anne Butler Brayne
14 Dorothea Spotswood = Nathaniel West Dandridge
15 Martha Dandridge = Archibald Payne
16 Catherine Payne = Archibald Bolling
17 Archibald Bolling, Jr. = Anne E. Wigginton
18 William Holcombe Bolling = Sallie Spiers White
19 Edith Bolling = (1) Norman Galt
= (2) (Thomas) Woodrow Wilson, 1856-1924, 28th U. S. President

Sources: MCS 3, lines 43A, 111A, 91A, 91, 90, 161 & sources cited therein; M. S. Kennedy, Seldens of Virginia & Allied Families, vol. 2, 1911, pp. 99-112 (Spotswood) & 19-20 (Dandridge).

Mrs. Harry S Truman (Mrs. Elizabeth Virginia "Bess" Wallace Truman)
Through (1) Thomas Newberry (doubted by Sir A. R. Wagner)
Through (2) Mrs. Margaret Wyatt Allyn

For generations 1-20 from Henry I, King of France through Thomas Newberry of Mass., see under Rutherford Birchard Hayes. For generations 1-23 from Hugh Capet, King of France to Mrs. Margaret Wyatt Allyn of Conn., mother of Mary Allyn, wife of Benjamin Newberry, see under Benjamin Harrison and the first Mrs. (Thomas) Woodrow Wilson.

21 Benjamin Newberry, son of Thomas Newberry of Mass. & Jane, his 2nd wife = Mary Allyn
22 Mary Newberry = John Moseley
23 Joseph Moseley = Abigail Root
24 Abigail Moseley = John Lyman (III)
25 Mindwell Lyman = Ebenezer Pomeroy (III)
26 Eunice Pomeroy = Ebenezer Clark (III)
27 Jerusha Clark = Samuel Gates, Jr.
28 George Williams Gates (Vt. to Mo.) = Sarah D. Todd
29 George Porterfield Gates = Elizabeth Emery
30 Margaret (Madge) Gates = David Willick Wallace
31 Elizabeth Virginia "Bess" Wallace
= Harry S Truman, 1884-1972, 33rd U. S. President

Sources: As above under Hayes, Benjamin Harrison and the first Mrs. Wilson for Newberry generations 1-20 and Allyn 1-23; J. G. Bartlett, **Newberry Genealogy**, 1914, pp. 35-46, 50-54; SAW 508 (Moseley); Lyman Coleman, **Genealogy of the Lyman Family**, 1872, p. 243-44; A. A. Pomeroy, **History & Genealogy of the Pomeroy Family**, 1912, p. 197; Walter E. Corbin MSS. & microfilm collection at NEHGS, "Early Families [of] Northampton" (originally compiled by Sylvester Judd), vol. 1, pt. 1, p. 296 (Clark); Vermont Historical Society Miscellaneous File #831, Congregational Church Records of Lunenburg, kept by Rev. John Willard, 1802-22, typescript copy, p. 14 (marriage record of Samuel Gates, Jr. & Jerusha Clark, 31 July 1806); birth record of George Williams Gates (Lunenburg, Vt., 5 March 1807) at the Vital Records Dept., State House, Montpelier, Vt.; Howard L. Coward, ed., **Encyclopedia of the History of Missouri**, vol. 3, 1901, pp. 8-9 (for G. W. Gates & Sarah D. Todd); miscellaneous Gates & Wallace material on file at the Truman Library in Independence, Mo.

Mrs. Dwight David Eisenhower
(Mrs. Mamie Geneva Doud Eisenhower)
Through Mrs. Elizabeth Alsop Baldwin Fowler

(highly probable, not absolutely proved)

1 Edward I, King of England, d. 1307 = Margaret of France
2 Thomas of Brotherton, Earl of Norfolk = Alice de Hales
3 Margaret Plantagenet, Duchess of Norfolk = John de Segrave, 4th Baron Segrave
4 Elizabeth de Segrave = John Mowbray, 4th Baron Mowbray
5 Eleanor Mowbray = John de Welles, 5th Baron Welles
6 Eudo de Welles = Maud de Greystoke
7 Lionel de Welles, 6th Baron Welles = Joan Waterton
8 Margaret de Welles = Sir Thomas Dymoke
9 Margaret Dymoke = Thomas FitzWilliam
10 Elizabeth FitzWilliam = Robert Eyre
11 Jane Eyre = Thomas Meverell
12 Elizabeth Meverell = William Basset
13 Anne Basset (whose maternity as shown above is highly probable for chronological & other reasons, but unproved) = Thomas Alsop
14 Anne Alsop = John Alsop, a cousin
15 Anthony Alsop = Jane Smith
16 John Alsop = Temperance Gilbert
17 Elizabeth Alsop of Conn. = (1) Richard Baldwin, (2) William Fowler
18 Sarah Baldwin (by first husband) = Samuel Riggs
19 Ebenezer Riggs = Lois Hawkins
20 John Riggs = Hannah Johnson
21 John Riggs, Jr. = Abigail Peet
22 James Riggs = Sarah Clark
23 George Riggs = Phebe Caniff
24 Maria Riggs = Eli Doud
25 Royal Houghton Doud = Mary Cornelia Sheldon
26 John Sheldon Doud = Elivera Mathilda Carlson
27 Mamie Geneva Doud
= Dwight David Eisenhower, 1890-1969, 34th U. S. President

Sources: NEHGR 46(1892):366-69 (reprinted in EO 2:1:15-18) & **The Genealogist**, New Ser., 7(1890-91):1 (Alsop); Rev. Stebbing Shaw, **The History & Antiquities of Staffordshire**, vol. 2, part I, 1801, p. 13 (Basset of Blore); William Salt Archaeological Society, **Collections for a History of Staffordshire**, New Ser., 12(1909):167 (Meverell); Joseph Hunter, **Familiae Minorum Gentium**, vol. 2 (HSPVS, vol. 38, 1895), p. 551 (Eyre); Joseph Foster, **Pedigrees of the County Families of Yorkshire**, 2 vols., 1874-75 (FitzWilliam pedigree); A. R. Maddison, ed., **Lincolnshire Pedigrees**, vol. 4 (HSPVS, vol. 55, 1906), p. 1204 (Dymoke); AR 6, lines 202, 16; Susan Woodruff Abbott, **Families of Early Milford, Connecticut**, 1979, pp. 51-52 (Baldwin) & 620-21 (Riggs); J. H. Wallace, **Genealogy of the Riggs Family**, vol. 1, 1901, pp. 5-6, 8, 12, 22, 35, 67-68; T. C. Peet, **John Peet (1597-1684) of Stratford, Connecticut & His Descendants**, 1986, pp. 23-24; F. A. Virkus, **Compendium of American Genealogy** (an often unreliable source, largely correct, it seems, in this instance), vol. 6, 1937 (reprint 1987), p. 494 (Riggs, Doud); O. L. Doud, **Doud-Dowd & Allied Families**, 1976, pp. 7-12, 7-27-2.

The 2nd Mrs. Ronald Wilson Reagan (Mrs. Nancy Davis Reagan, born Anne Francis Robbins) Through (1) Thomas Newberry (doubted by Sir A. R. Wagner) Through (2) Mrs. Margaret Wyatt Allyn

For generations 1-22 from Henry I, King of France through Thomas Newberry of Mass. to his granddaughter, Mary Newberry, wife of John Moseley, see under Rutherford Birchard Hayes and Mrs. Harry S Truman. For generations 1-25 from Hugh Capet, King of France to Mrs. Margaret Wyatt Allyn of Conn. to her granddaughter, Mary Newberry, wife of John Moseley, see under Benjamin Harrison, the first Mrs. (Thomas) Woodrow Wilson, & Mrs. Harry S Truman.

23 Mary Moseley = Eleazer Weller, Jr.
24 Mary Weller = Daniel Sackett
25 Daniel Sackett, Jr. = Mehitable Cadwell
26 Mehitable Sackett = Luke Francis
27 Manning Francis = Elizabeth Robbins Root
28 Frederick Augustus Francis = Jessie Anne Stevens
29 Anne Ayers Francis = John Newell Robbins
30 Kenneth Seymour Robbins = Edith Luckett, who = (2) Dr. Loyal Edward Davis, who adopted his step-daughter,
31 Anne Francis Robbins, whose name was changed to Nancy Davis = Ronald Wilson Reagan, b. 1911, 40th U. S. President

Sources: As above under Hayes, Benjamin Harrison, the first Mrs. Wilson & Mrs. Truman for generations 1-22 & 1-25; TAG 34(1958):145 (Weller); Charles H. Weygant, The Sacketts of America: Their Ancestors & Descendants, 1630-1907, 1907, pp. 46, 96-97; B. W. Dwight, The History of the Descendants of John Dwight of Dedham, Mass., vol. 1, 1874, pp. 441-43 (generations 24-27); Charles E. Francis, Descendants of Robert Francis of Wethersfield, Conn., 1906, pp. 146, 148, 74; death record of Frederick Augustus Francis 30 Jan. 1913 (Mass. Vital Records, 1913, vol. 81, p. 339) & delayed birth record of Kenneth Seymour Robbins 23 Feb. 1894 (Delayed Mass. Vital Records, vol. 346, p. 470); Laurence Leamer, Make-Believe: The Story of Nancy & Ronald Reagan, 1983, passim.

# # #

EIGHTY-ONE CHARTS OUTLINING KINSHIPS AMONG AMERICAN PRESIDENTS

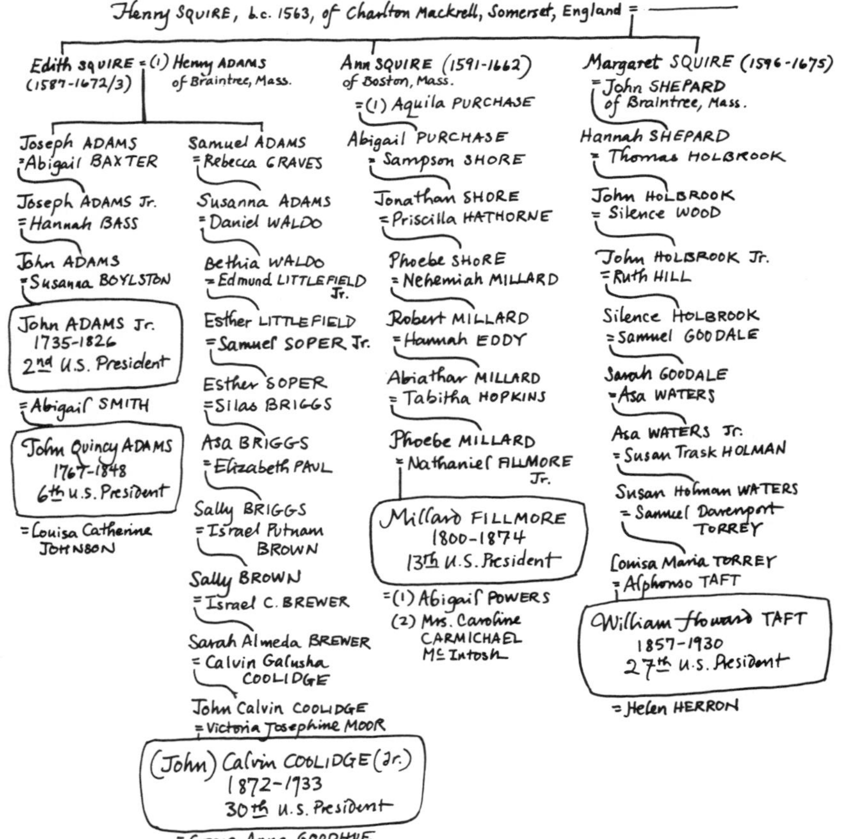
Henry SQUIRE, b.c. 1563, of Charlton Mackrell, Somerset, England = ———
Edith SQUIRE (1587-1672/3) = (1) Henry ADAMS of Braintree, Mass.
Joseph ADAMS = Abigail BAXTER
Joseph ADAMS Jr. = Hannah BASS
John ADAMS = Susanna BOYLSTON
John ADAMS Jr. 1735-1826 2nd U.S. President
= Abigail SMITH
John Quincy ADAMS 1767-1848 6th U.S. President
= Louisa Catherine JOHNSON
Samuel ADAMS = Rebecca GRAVES
Susanna ADAMS = Daniel WALDO
Bethia WALDO = Edmund LITTLEFIELD Jr.
Esther LITTLEFIELD = Samuel SOPER Jr.
Esther SOPER = Silas BRIGGS
Asa BRIGGS = Elizabeth PAUL
Sally BRIGGS = Israel Putnam BROWN
Sally BROWN = Israel C. BREWER
Sarah Almeda BREWER = Calvin Galusha COOLIDGE
John Calvin COOLIDGE = Victoria Josephine MOOR
(John) Calvin COOLIDGE (Jr.) 1872-1933 30th U.S. President
= Grace Anna GOODHUE
Ann SQUIRE (1591-1662) of Boston, Mass.
= (1) Aquila PURCHASE
Abigail PURCHASE = Sampson SHORE
Jonathan SHORE = Priscilla HATHORNE
Phoebe SHORE = Nehemiah MILLARD
Robert MILLARD = Hannah EDDY
Abiathar MILLARD = Tabitha HOPKINS
Phoebe MILLARD = Nathaniel FILLMORE Jr.
Millard FILLMORE 1800-1874 13th U.S. President
= (1) Abigail POWERS
(2) Mrs. Caroline CARMICHAEL McIntosh
Margaret SQUIRE (1596-1675)
= John SHEPARD of Braintree, Mass.
Hannah SHEPARD = Thomas HOLBROOK
John HOLBROOK = Silence WOOD
John HOLBROOK Jr. = Ruth HILL
Silence HOLBROOK = Samuel GOODALE
Sarah GOODALE = Asa WATERS
Asa WATERS Jr. = Susan Trask HOLMAN
Susan Holman WATERS = Samuel Davenport TORREY
Louisa Maria TORREY = Alphonso TAFT
William Howard TAFT 1857-1930 27th U.S. President
= Helen HERRON

Henry SPENCER of Badby, Northants., d. 1477/78 = Isabella LINCOLN

Thomas SPENCER
= Margaret SMITH

William SPENCER
= Agnes HERITAGE

Julian SPENCER
= William WILMER

Anne WILMER
= Henry THORNTON

Anne THORNTON
= William DICKENS

Anne DICKENS
= John TWIGDEN

Amphyllis TWIGDEN
= Lawrence WASHINGTON

John WASHINGTON (c.1634-c.1677) of Va.
= Anne POPE

Lawrence WASHINGTON
= Mildred WARNER

Augustine WASHINGTON
= Mary BALL

George WASHINGTON
1731/2-1799
1st U.S. President

= Mrs. Martha DANDRIDGE Custis

Thomas SPENCER = Dorothy SPENCER

Susan SPENCER = John TEMPLE

Sir Thomas TEMPLE, 1st Bt.
= Hester SANDYS

Sir John TEMPLE
= Dorothy LEE

Mary TEMPLE
= Robert NELSON

John NELSON (1654-1734) of Mass.
= Elizabeth TAILER

Rebecca NELSON
= Henry LLOYD

Margaret LLOYD
= William Henry SMITH

Rebecca SMITH
= John ASPINWALL

John ASPINWALL Jr.
= Susan HOWLAND

Mary Rebecca ASPINWALL
= Isaac ROOSEVELT

James ROOSEVELT = Sara DELANO

Franklin Delano ROOSEVELT
1882-1945
32nd U.S. President

= (Anna) Eleanor ROOSEVELT

William SPENCER
= Elizabeth EMPSON

Sir John SPENCER
= Isabel GRAUNT

Sir William SPENCER
= Susan KNIGHTLEY

Sir John SPENCER = Anne EMPSON
sister of Elizabeth & of Sir Richard EMPSON, minister of Henry VII.

Jane SPENCER = Sir William COPE

Sir John COPE
= Bridget RALEIGH

Elizabeth COPE
= John DRYDEN

Bridget DRYDEN
= Francis MARBURY

Anne MARBURY, (1591-c.1643), known as Mrs. Anne HUTCHINSON, religious reformer, "heretic" and a founder of R. I.)
= William HUTCHINSON

Edward HUTCHINSON
= Catherine HAMBY

Elisha HUTCHINSON = (1) Hannah HAWKINS
= (2) Elizabeth CLARKE

Edward HUTCHINSON
= Lydia FOSTER

Elizabeth HUTCHINSON
= Nathaniel ROBBINS

Edward Hutchinson ROBBINS
= Elizabeth MURRAY

Anne Jean ROBBINS
= Joseph LYMAN (III)

Catherine Robbins LYMAN
= Warren DELANO Jr.

Hannah HUTCHINSON
= John RUCK

Hannah RUCK
= Theophilus LILLIE

John LILLIE
= Abigail BRECK

Anna LILLIE
= Samuel HOWARD

Harriet HOWARD
= Samuel Prescott Phillips FAY

Samuel Howard FAY
= Susan SHELLMAN

Harriet Eleanor FAY
= James Smith BUSH

Samuel Prescott BUSH
= Flora SHELDON

Prescott Sheldon BUSH
= Dorothy WALKER

George Herbert Walker BUSH
b. 1924
41st U.S. President

= Barbara PIERCE

Sir Anthony COPE
= Jane CREWS

Edward COPE
= Elizabeth MOHUN

Ursula COPE
= John D'OYLY

Priscilla D'OYLY
= Edward GODDARD

William GODDARD (c.1630-1691) of Mass.
= Elizabeth MILES

Josiah GODDARD
= Rachel DAVIS

Rachel GODDARD
= Obadiah COOLIDGE Jr.

Josiah COOLIDGE
= Mary JONES

John COOLIDGE
= Hannah PRIEST

Calvin COOLIDGE
= Sarah THOMPSON

Calvin Galusha COOLIDGE
= Sarah Almeda BREWER

John Calvin COOLIDGE
= Victoria Josephine MOOR

(John) Calvin COOLIDGE (Jr.)
1872-1933
30th U.S. President

= Grace Anna GOODHUE

Robert WHITE, d. 1617, Messing, Essex, England = Bridget ALLGAR

Mary WHITE (1590-1652) of Windsor, Conn.
= Joseph LOOMIS

Sarah LOOMIS
= Nicholas OLMSTEAD

Elizabeth OLMSTEAD
= Samuel BUTLER

Mary BUTLER
= Ebenezer HOPKINS

Ebenezer HOPKINS Jr.
= Susannah MESSENGER

Tabitha HOPKINS
= Abiathar MILLARD

Phoebe MILLARD
= Nathaniel FILLMORE Jr.

Millard FILLMORE 1800-1874 13th U.S. President
= (1) Abigail POWERS
(2) Mrs. Caroline CARMICHAEL McIntosh

Anna WHITE (1600-1647) of Windsor, Conn.
= John PORTER

Mary PORTER
= Samuel GRANT

Samuel GRANT Jr.
= Grace MINER

Noah GRANT
= Martha HUNTINGTON

Noah GRANT Jr.
= Susanna DELANO

Noah GRANT (III)
= Rachel KELLEY

Jesse Root GRANT
= Hannah SIMPSON

Ulysses Simpson GRANT 1822-1885 18th U.S. President
= Julia Boggs DENT

Samuel PORTER
= Hannah STANLEY

Samuel PORTER Jr.
= Joanna COOK

Aaron PORTER
= Susanna SEWALL

Susanna PORTER
= Aaron CLEVELAND (III)

Aaron CLEVELAND (IV)
= Abiah HYDE

William CLEVELAND
= Margaret FALLEY

Richard Falley CLEVELAND
= Anne NEAL

Stephen Grover CLEVELAND 1837-1908 22nd & 24th U.S. President
= Frances FOLSOM

Sarah PORTER
= Joseph JUDSON

Ruth JUDSON
= Samuel WELLES

Ruth WELLES
= Daniel ELY

Wells ELY
= Rebecca SELDEN

Amy ELY
= Theodore GRIDLEY

Elizabeth Ely GRIDLEY
= George Selden BUTLER

Amy Gridley BUTLER
= George Manney AYER

Adele Augusta AYER
= Levi Addison GARDNER

Dorothy Ayer GARDNER
= (1) Leslie Lynch KING
(2) Gerald Rudolf FORD

Leslie Lynch KING Jr. whose name was changed to Gerald Rudolph FORD Jr. b. 1913 38th U.S. President
= Mrs. Elizabeth Ann (Betty) BLOOMER Warren

Robert FOOTE of Shalford, Essex, d. 1608/09 = Joan BROOKE

Nathaniel FOOTE, b. 1592 of Wethersfield, Conn., = Elizabeth (DEMING?)

Elizabeth FOOTE
= Josiah CHURCHILL
Elizabeth CHURCHILL
= Henry BUCK
Ruth BUCK
= Benjamin SMITH
Elizabeth SMITH
= John SMITH (III)
Israel SMITH
= Abigail CHANDLER
Chloe SMITH
= Rutherford HAYES
Rutherford HAYES Jr.
= Sophia BIRCHARD
Rutherford Birchard HAYES 1822-1893, 19th U.S. President
= Lucy Ware WEBB

Rebecca FOOTE
= Philip SMITH
Rebecca SMITH
= George STILLMAN
Anna STILLMAN
= Hezekiah MAY
Elizabeth MAY
= Daniel NEWCOMB
Lydia NEWCOMB
= Timothy BUSH Jr.
Obadiah Newcomb BUSH = Harriet SMITH
James Smith BUSH
= Harriet Eleanor FAY
Samuel Prescott BUSH = Flora SHELDON
Prescott Sheldon BUSH
= Dorothy WALKER
George Herbert Walker BUSH, b. 1924 41st U.S. President
= Barbara PIERCE

Mary FOOTE = John HEWES

Elizabeth HEWES = Ralph HEMINGWAY d. 1678, Roxbury, Mass.

Elizabeth HEMINGWAY
= John HOLBROOK
Daniel HOLBROOK
= Abigail CRAFTS
Rebecca HOLBROOK
= Samuel DAVENPORT
Seth DAVENPORT
= Chloe DANIEL
Anna DAVENPORT
= William TORREY
Samuel Davenport TORREY
= Susan Holman WATERS
Louisa Maria TORREY
= Alphonso TAFT
William Howard TAFT 1857-1930, 27th U.S. President
= Helen HERRON

Joshua HEMINGWAY
= Joanna EVANS
Joshua HEMINGWAY Jr.
= Rebecca STANHOPE
Joshua HEMINGWAY (III)
= Abigail MORSE
Isaac HEMINGWAY
= Elizabeth HAVEN
James HEMINGWAY
= Elizabeth ARMSTRONG
James HEMINGWAY Jr.
= Hope MALMSBURY
Jane M. HEMINGWAY
= Oliver BURDG
Almira Park BURDG
= Franklin MILHOUS
Hannah MILHOUS
= Francis Anthony NIXON
Richard Milhous NIXON, b. 1913, 37th U.S. President
= Thelma Catherine (Pat) RYAN

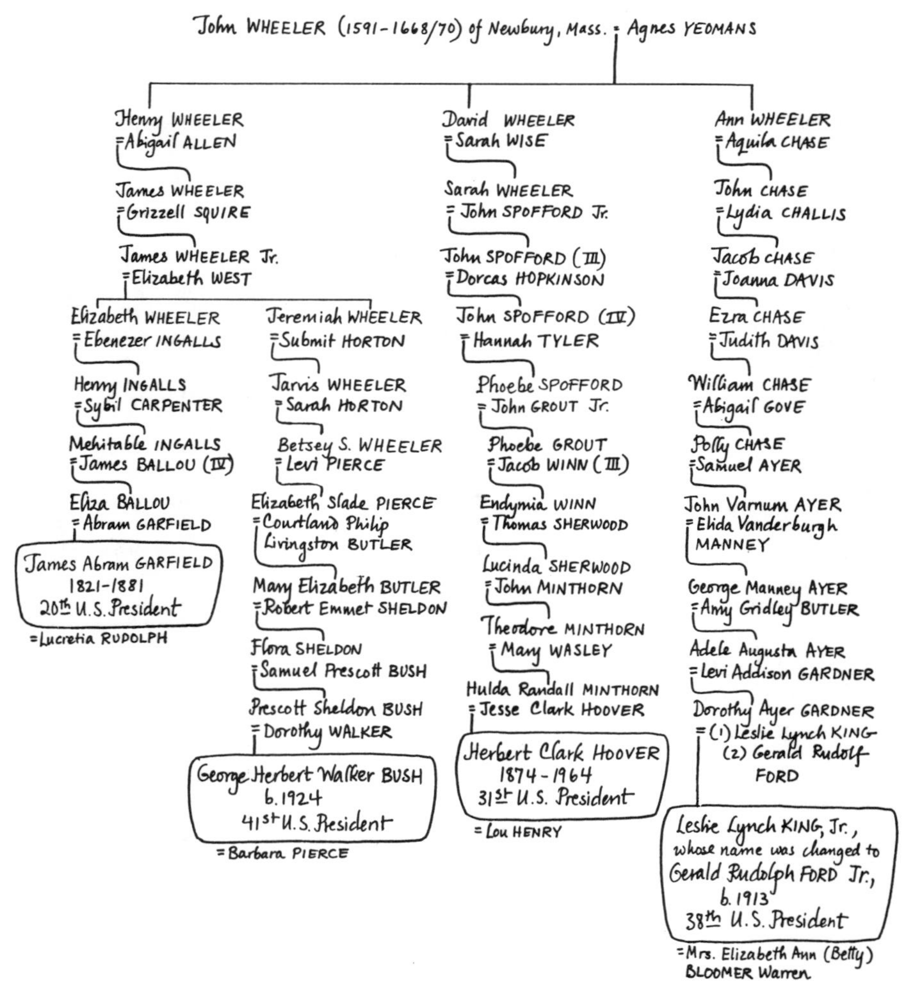
John WHEELER (1591-1668/70) of Newbury, Mass. = Agnes YEOMANS
Henry WHEELER
=Abigail ALLEN
James WHEELER
=Grizzell SQUIRE
James WHEELER Jr.
=Elizabeth WEST
Elizabeth WHEELER
=Ebenezer INGALLS
Henry INGALLS
=Sybil CARPENTER
Mehitable INGALLS
=James BALLOU (IV)
Eliza BALLOU
=Abram GARFIELD
James Abram GARFIELD
1821-1881
20th U.S. President
=Lucretia RUDOLPH
Jeremiah WHEELER
=Submit HORTON
Jarvis WHEELER
=Sarah HORTON
Betsey S. WHEELER
=Levi PIERCE
Elizabeth Slade PIERCE
=Courtland Philip Livingston BUTLER
Mary Elizabeth BUTLER
=Robert Emmet SHELDON
Flora SHELDON
=Samuel Prescott BUSH
Prescott Sheldon BUSH
=Dorothy WALKER
George Herbert Walker BUSH
b. 1924
41st U.S. President
=Barbara PIERCE
David WHEELER
=Sarah WISE
Sarah WHEELER
= John SPOFFORD Jr.
John SPOFFORD (III)
=Dorcas HOPKINSON
John SPOFFORD (IV)
=Hannah TYLER
Phoebe SPOFFORD
=John GROUT Jr.
Phoebe GROUT
=Jacob WINN (III)
Endymia WINN
=Thomas SHERWOOD
Lucinda SHERWOOD
=John MINTHORN
Theodore MINTHORN
=Mary WASLEY
Hulda Randall MINTHORN
=Jesse Clark HOOVER
Herbert Clark HOOVER
1874-1964
31st U.S. President
=Lou HENRY
Ann WHEELER
=Aquila CHASE
John CHASE
=Lydia CHALLIS
Jacob CHASE
=Joanna DAVIS
Ezra CHASE
=Judith DAVIS
William CHASE
=Abigail GOVE
Polly CHASE
=Samuel AYER
John Varnum AYER
=Elida Vanderburgh MANNEY
George Manney AYER
=Amy Gridley BUTLER
Adele Augusta AYER
=Levi Addison GARDNER
Dorothy Ayer GARDNER
=(1) Leslie Lynch KING
(2) Gerald Rudolf FORD
Leslie Lynch KING, Jr., whose name was changed to Gerald Rudolph FORD Jr.,
b. 1913
38th U.S. President
=Mrs. Elizabeth Ann (Betty) BLOOMER Warren

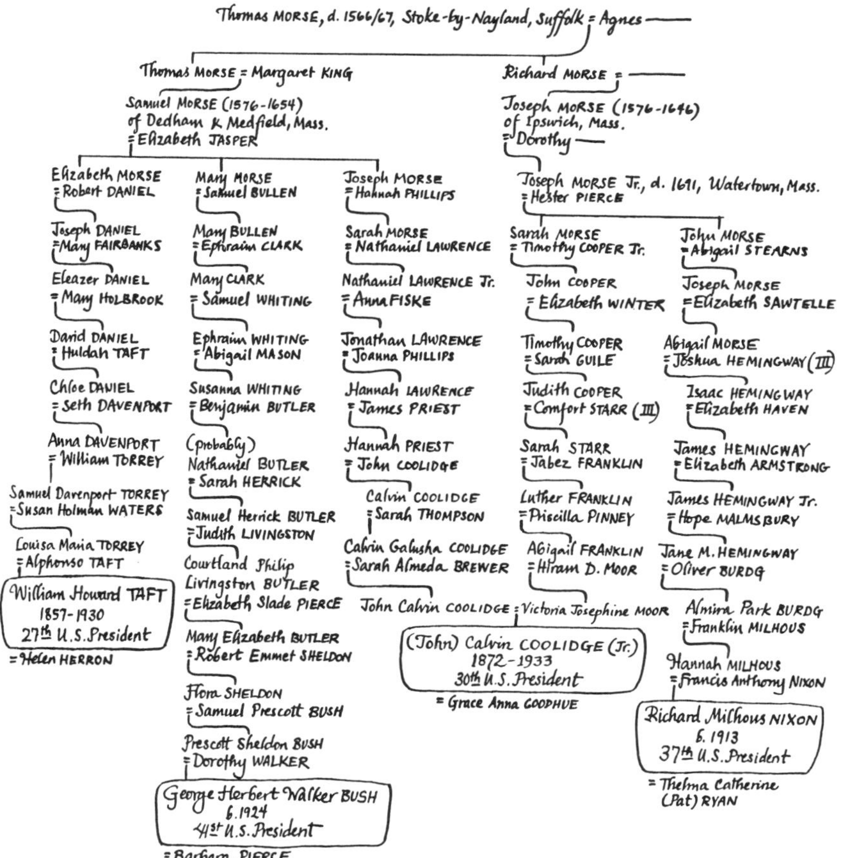
Thomas MORSE, d. 1566/67, Stoke-by-Nayland, Suffolk = Agnes
Thomas MORSE = Margaret KING
Richard MORSE =
Samuel MORSE (1576-1654) of Dedham & Medfield, Mass. = Elizabeth JASPER
Joseph MORSE (1576-1646) of Ipswich, Mass. = Dorothy
Elizabeth MORSE = Robert DANIEL
Mary MORSE = Samuel BULLEN
Joseph MORSE = Hannah PHILLIPS
Joseph MORSE Jr., d. 1691, Watertown, Mass. = Hester PIERCE
Joseph DANIEL = Mary FAIRBANKS
Mary BULLEN = Ephraim CLARK
Sarah MORSE = Nathaniel LAWRENCE
Sarah MORSE = Timothy COOPER Jr.
John MORSE = Abigail STEARNS
Eleazer DANIEL = Mary HOLBROOK
Mary CLARK = Samuel WHITING
Nathaniel LAWRENCE Jr. = Anna FISKE
John COOPER = Elizabeth WINTER
Joseph MORSE = Elizabeth SAWTELLE
David DANIEL = Huldah TAFT
Ephraim WHITING = Abigail MASON
Jonathan LAWRENCE = Joanna PHILLIPS
Timothy COOPER = Sarah GUILE
Abigail MORSE = Joshua HEMINGWAY (III)
Chloe DANIEL = Seth DAVENPORT
Susanna WHITING = Benjamin BUTLER
Hannah LAWRENCE = James PRIEST
Judith COOPER = Comfort STARR (III)
Isaac HEMINGWAY = Elizabeth HAVEN
Anna DAVENPORT = William TORREY
(probably) Nathaniel BUTLER = Sarah HERRICK
Hannah PRIEST = John COOLIDGE
Sarah STARR = Jabez FRANKLIN
James HEMINGWAY = Elizabeth ARMSTRONG
Samuel Davenport TORREY = Susan Holman WATERS
Samuel Herrick BUTLER = Judith LIVINGSTON
Calvin COOLIDGE = Sarah THOMPSON
Luther FRANKLIN = Priscilla PINNEY
James HEMINGWAY Jr. = Hope MALMSBURY
Louisa Maria TORREY = Alphonso TAFT
Courtland Philip Livingston BUTLER = Elizabeth Slade PIERCE
Calvin Galusha COOLIDGE = Sarah Almeda BREWER
Abigail FRANKLIN = Hiram D. MOOR
Jane M. HEMINGWAY = Oliver BURDG
William Howard TAFT 1857-1930 27th U.S. President
= Helen HERRON
Mary Elizabeth BUTLER = Robert Emmet SHELDON
John Calvin COOLIDGE = Victoria Josephine MOOR
Almira Park BURDG = Franklin MILHOUS
(John) Calvin COOLIDGE (Jr.) 1872-1933 30th U.S. President
= Grace Anna GOODHUE
Hannah MILHOUS = Francis Anthony NIXON
Flora SHELDON = Samuel Prescott BUSH
Richard Milhous NIXON b. 1913 37th U.S. President
= Thelma Catherine (Pat) RYAN
Prescott Sheldon BUSH = Dorothy WALKER
George Herbert Walker BUSH b. 1924 41st U.S. President
= Barbara PIERCE

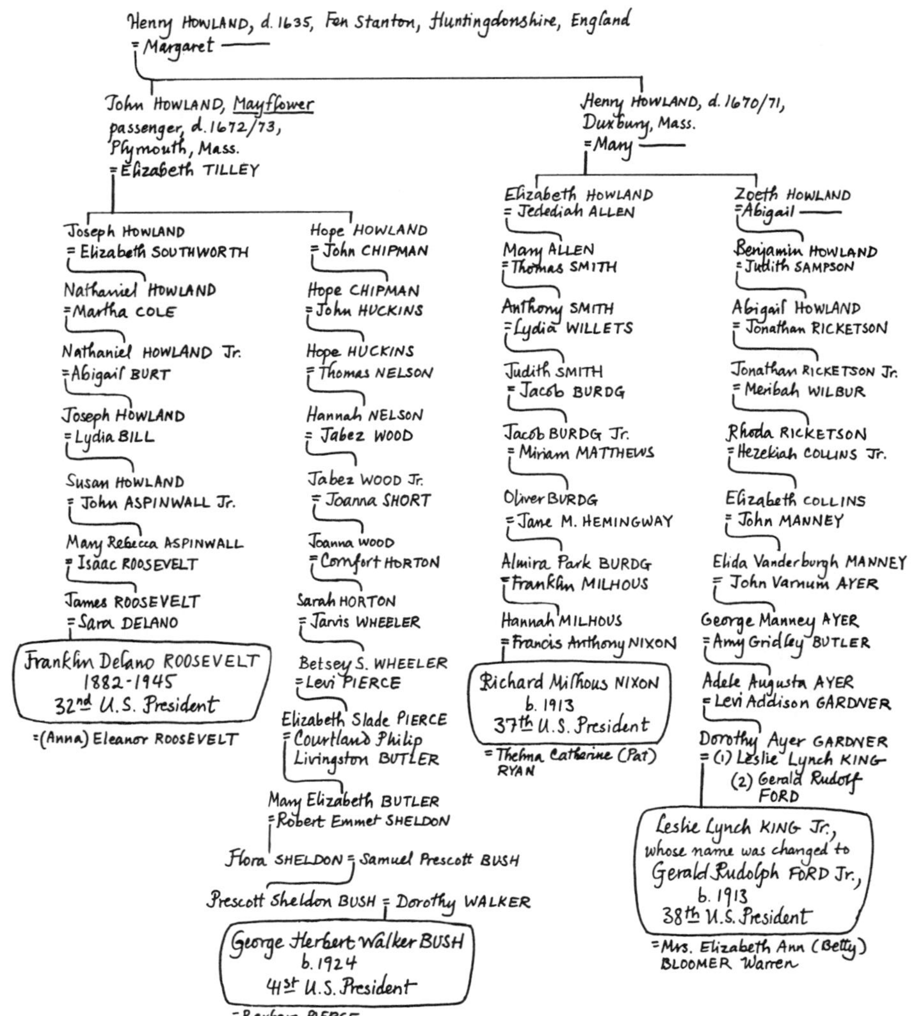
Henry HOWLAND, d. 1635, Fen Stanton, Huntingdonshire, England
= Margaret ——
John HOWLAND, Mayflower passenger, d. 1672/73, Plymouth, Mass.
= Elizabeth TILLEY
Henry HOWLAND, d. 1670/71, Duxbury, Mass.
= Mary ——
Joseph HOWLAND
= Elizabeth SOUTHWORTH
Nathaniel HOWLAND
= Martha COLE
Nathaniel HOWLAND Jr.
= Abigail BURT
Joseph HOWLAND
= Lydia BILL
Susan HOWLAND
= John ASPINWALL Jr.
Mary Rebecca ASPINWALL
= Isaac ROOSEVELT
James ROOSEVELT
= Sara DELANO
Franklin Delano ROOSEVELT
1882-1945
32nd U.S. President
=(Anna) Eleanor ROOSEVELT
Hope HOWLAND
= John CHIPMAN
Hope CHIPMAN
= John HUCKINS
Hope HUCKINS
= Thomas NELSON
Hannah NELSON
= Jabez WOOD
Jabez WOOD Jr.
= Joanna SHORT
Joanna WOOD
= Comfort HORTON
Sarah HORTON
= Jarvis WHEELER
Betsey S. WHEELER
= Levi PIERCE
Elizabeth Slade PIERCE
= Courtland Philip Livingston BUTLER
Mary Elizabeth BUTLER
= Robert Emmet SHELDON
Flora SHELDON = Samuel Prescott BUSH
Prescott Sheldon BUSH = Dorothy WALKER
George Herbert Walker BUSH
b. 1924
41st U.S. President
= Barbara PIERCE
Elizabeth HOWLAND
= Jedediah ALLEN
Mary ALLEN
= Thomas SMITH
Anthony SMITH
= Lydia WILLETS
Judith SMITH
= Jacob BURDG
Jacob BURDG Jr.
= Miriam MATTHEWS
Oliver BURDG
= Jane M. HEMINGWAY
Almira Park BURDG
= Franklin MILHOUS
Hannah MILHOUS
= Francis Anthony NIXON
Richard Milhous NIXON
b. 1913
37th U.S. President
= Thelma Catherine (Pat) RYAN
Zoeth HOWLAND
= Abigail ——
Benjamin HOWLAND
= Judith SAMPSON
Abigail HOWLAND
= Jonathan RICKETSON
Jonathan RICKETSON Jr.
= Meribah WILBUR
Rhoda RICKETSON
= Hezekiah COLLINS Jr.
Elizabeth COLLINS
= John MANNEY
Elida Vanderburgh MANNEY
= John Varnum AYER
George Manney AYER
= Amy Gridley BUTLER
Adele Augusta AYER
= Levi Addison GARDNER
Dorothy Ayer GARDNER
= (1) Leslie Lynch KING
(2) Gerald Rudolf FORD
Leslie Lynch KING Jr., whose name was changed to Gerald Rudolph FORD Jr.,
b. 1913
38th U.S. President
= Mrs. Elizabeth Ann (Betty) BLOOMER Warren

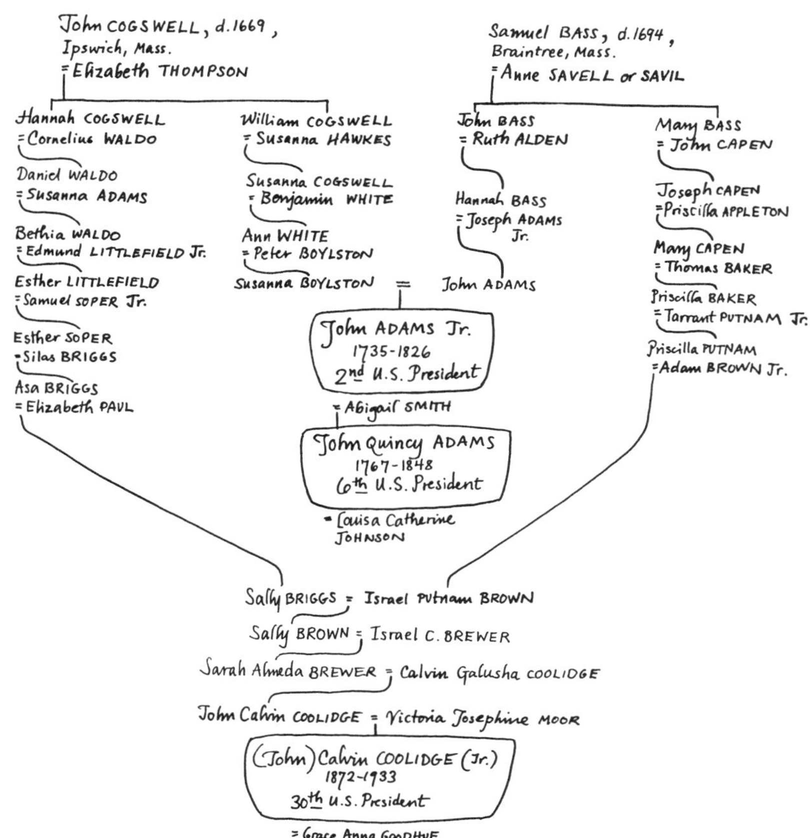
John COGSWELL, d.1669,
Ipswich, Mass.
= Elizabeth THOMPSON
Samuel BASS, d.1694,
Braintree, Mass.
= Anne SAVELL or SAVIL
Hannah COGSWELL
= Cornelius WALDO
William COGSWELL
= Susanna HAWKES
John BASS
= Ruth ALDEN
Mary BASS
= John CAPEN
Daniel WALDO
= Susanna ADAMS
Susanna COGSWELL
= Benjamin WHITE
Hannah BASS
= Joseph ADAMS Jr.
Joseph CAPEN
= Priscilla APPLETON
Bethia WALDO
= Edmund LITTLEFIELD Jr.
Ann WHITE
= Peter BOYLSTON
Mary CAPEN
= Thomas BAKER
Esther LITTLEFIELD
= Samuel SOPER Jr.
Susanna BOYLSTON = John ADAMS
Priscilla BAKER
= Tarrant PUTNAM Jr.
Esther SOPER
= Silas BRIGGS
John ADAMS Jr.
1735-1826
2nd U.S. President
Priscilla PUTNAM
= Adam BROWN Jr.
Asa BRIGGS
= Elizabeth PAUL
= Abigail SMITH
John Quincy ADAMS
1767-1848
6th U.S. President
= Louisa Catherine JOHNSON
Sally BRIGGS = Israel Putnam BROWN
Sally BROWN = Israel C. BREWER
Sarah Almeda BREWER = Calvin Galusha COOLIDGE
John Calvin COOLIDGE = Victoria Josephine MOOR
(John) Calvin COOLIDGE (Jr.)
1872-1933
30th U.S. President
= Grace Anna GOODHUE

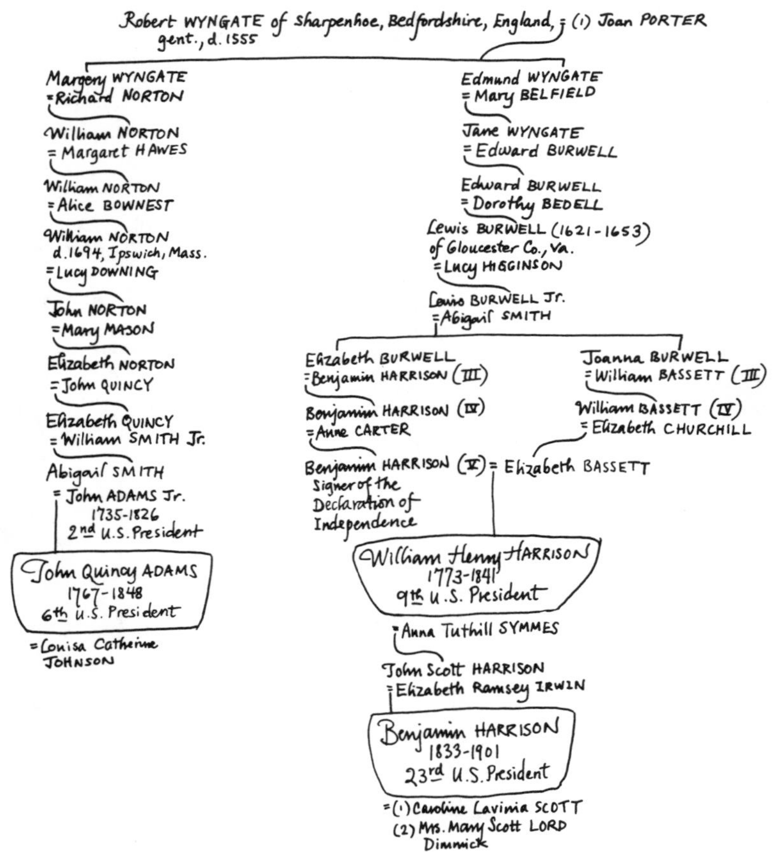
Robert WYNGATE of Sharpenhoe, Bedfordshire, England, gent., d. 1555 = (1) Joan PORTER
Margery WYNGATE
= Richard NORTON
William NORTON
= Margaret HAWES
William NORTON
= Alice BOWNEST
William NORTON
d. 1694, Ipswich, Mass.
= Lucy DOWNING
John NORTON
= Mary MASON
Elizabeth NORTON
= John QUINCY
Elizabeth QUINCY
= William SMITH Jr.
Abigail SMITH
= John ADAMS Jr.
1735-1826
2nd U.S. President
John Quincy ADAMS
1767-1848
6th U.S. President
= Louisa Catherine JOHNSON
Edmund WYNGATE
= Mary BELFIELD
Jane WYNGATE
= Edward BURWELL
Edward BURWELL
= Dorothy BEDELL
Lewis BURWELL (1621-1653)
of Gloucester Co., Va.
= Lucy HIGGINSON
Lewis BURWELL Jr.
= Abigail SMITH
Elizabeth BURWELL
= Benjamin HARRISON (III)
Benjamin HARRISON (IV)
= Anne CARTER
Benjamin HARRISON (V) = Elizabeth BASSETT
Signer of the Declaration of Independence
Joanna BURWELL
= William BASSETT (III)
William BASSETT (IV)
= Elizabeth CHURCHILL
William Henry HARRISON
1773-1841
9th U.S. President
= Anna Tuthill SYMMES
John Scott HARRISON
= Elizabeth Ramsey IRWIN
Benjamin HARRISON
1833-1901
23rd U.S. President
= (1) Caroline Lavinia SCOTT
(2) Mrs. Mary Scott LORD Dimmick

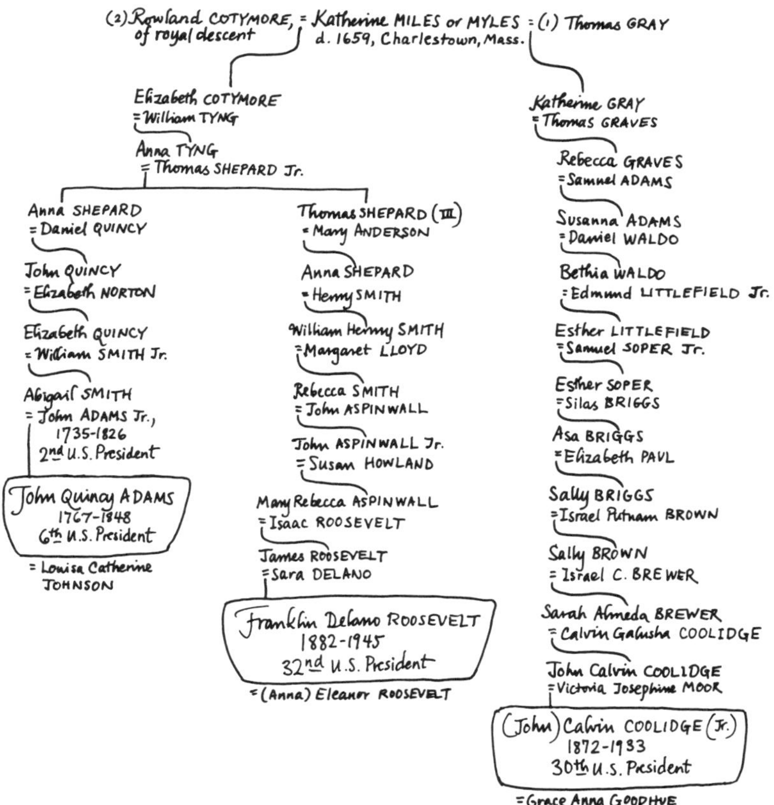
(2) Rowland COTYMORE, of royal descent = Katherine MILES or MYLES d. 1659, Charlestown, Mass. = (1) Thomas GRAY
Elizabeth COTYMORE
= William TYNG
Anna TYNG
= Thomas SHEPARD Jr.
Anna SHEPARD
= Daniel QUINCY
John QUINCY
= Elizabeth NORTON
Elizabeth QUINCY
= William SMITH Jr.
Abigail SMITH
= John ADAMS Jr., 1735-1826 2nd U.S. President
John Quincy ADAMS 1767-1848 6th U.S. President
= Louisa Catherine JOHNSON
Thomas SHEPARD (III)
= Mary ANDERSON
Anna SHEPARD
= Henry SMITH
William Henry SMITH
= Margaret LLOYD
Rebecca SMITH
= John ASPINWALL
John ASPINWALL Jr.
= Susan HOWLAND
Mary Rebecca ASPINWALL
= Isaac ROOSEVELT
James ROOSEVELT
= Sara DELANO
Franklin Delano ROOSEVELT 1882-1945 32nd U.S. President
= (Anna) Eleanor ROOSEVELT
Katherine GRAY
= Thomas GRAVES
Rebecca GRAVES
= Samuel ADAMS
Susanna ADAMS
= Daniel WALDO
Bethia WALDO
= Edmund LITTLEFIELD Jr.
Esther LITTLEFIELD
= Samuel SOPER Jr.
Esther SOPER
= Silas BRIGGS
Asa BRIGGS
= Elizabeth PAUL
Sally BRIGGS
= Israel Putnam BROWN
Sally BROWN
= Israel C. BREWER
Sarah Almeda BREWER
= Calvin Galusha COOLIDGE
John Calvin COOLIDGE
= Victoria Josephine MOOR
(John) Calvin COOLIDGE (Jr.) 1872-1933 30th U.S. President
= Grace Anna GOODHUE

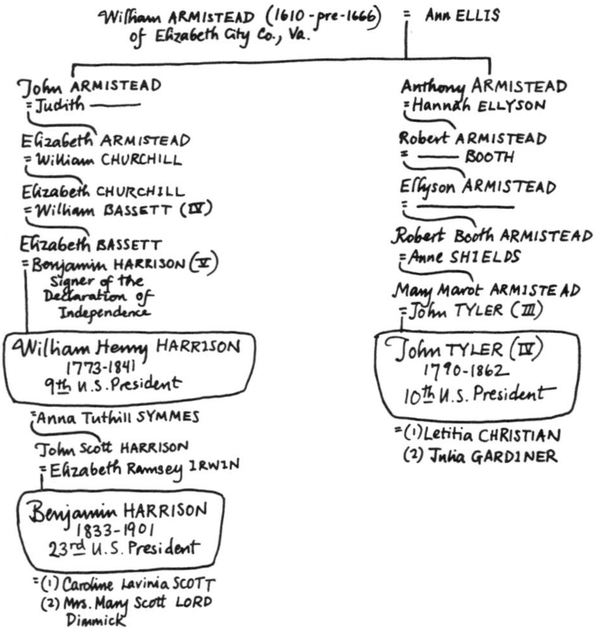
William ARMISTEAD (1610-pre-1666) of Elizabeth City Co., Va.
= Ann ELLIS
John ARMISTEAD
= Judith ———
Elizabeth ARMISTEAD
= William CHURCHILL
Elizabeth CHURCHILL
= William BASSETT (IV)
Elizabeth BASSETT
= Benjamin HARRISON (V)
Signer of the Declaration of Independence
William Henry HARRISON
1773-1841
9th U.S. President
= Anna Tuthill SYMMES
John Scott HARRISON
= Elizabeth Ramsey IRWIN
Benjamin HARRISON
1833-1901
23rd U.S. President
= (1) Caroline Lavinia SCOTT
(2) Mrs. Mary Scott LORD Dimmick
Anthony ARMISTEAD
= Hannah ELLYSON
Robert ARMISTEAD
= ——— BOOTH
Ellyson ARMISTEAD
= ————
Robert Booth ARMISTEAD
= Anne SHIELDS
Mary Marot ARMISTEAD
= John TYLER (III)
John TYLER (IV)
1790-1862
10th U.S. President
= (1) Letitia CHRISTIAN
(2) Julia GARDINER

John CARTER, d. 1630, of Christchurch, Newgate St., London. His sons Thomas and John may be, but have not been proved to have been, Thomas Carter of Isle of Wight Co., and John Carter of Corotoman, as below. = (2) Bridget BENION

John CARTER of Corotoman, Va., d. 1669
= Sarah LUDLOW

Robert "King" CARTER
= Elizabeth LANDON

Anne CARTER
= Benjamin HARRISON (IV)

Benjamin HARRISON (V)
Signer of the Declaration of Independence
= Elizabeth BASSETT

William Henry HARRISON
1773-1841
9th U.S. President

= Anna Tuthill SYMMES

John Scott HARRISON
= Elizabeth Ramsey IRWIN

Benjamin HARRISON
1833-1901
23rd U.S. President

= (1) Caroline Lavinia SCOTT
(2) Mrs. Mary Scott LORD Dimmick

Thomas CARTER of Isle of Wight Co., Va., d. 1660
= ———

Thomas CARTER Jr.
= Elinor ———

Thomas CARTER (III)
= Magdalene MOORE

(probably) Moore CARTER
= Jane ———

Isaac CARTER
= Ruth ———

Kindred CARTER = ———

James CARTER
= Eleanor DUCKWORTH

Wiley CARTER
= Ann ANSLEY

Littleberry Walker CARTER
= Mary Ann Diligent SEALS

William Archibald CARTER
= Nina PRATT

James Earl CARTER
= Bessie Lillian GORDY

James Earl CARTER Jr.
b. 1924
39th U.S. President

= (Eleanor) Rosalynn CARTER

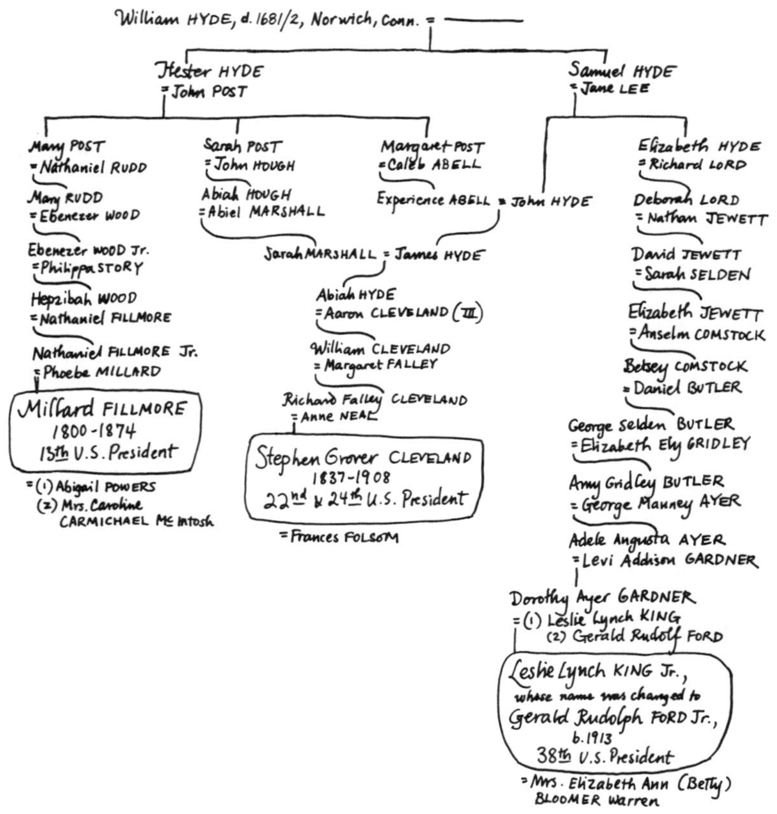
William HYDE, d. 1681/2, Norwich, Conn. =
Hester HYDE
= John POST
Samuel HYDE
= Jane LEE
Mary POST
= Nathaniel RUDD
Sarah POST
= John HOUGH
Margaret POST
= Caleb ABELL
Elizabeth HYDE
= Richard LORD
Mary RUDD
= Ebenezer WOOD
Abiah HOUGH
= Abiel MARSHALL
Experience ABELL = John HYDE
Deborah LORD
= Nathan JEWETT
Ebenezer WOOD Jr.
= Philippa STORY
Sarah MARSHALL = James HYDE
David JEWETT
= Sarah SELDEN
Hepzibah WOOD
= Nathaniel FILLMORE
Abiah HYDE
= Aaron CLEVELAND (III)
Elizabeth JEWETT
= Anselm COMSTOCK
Nathaniel FILLMORE Jr.
= Phoebe MILLARD
William CLEVELAND
= Margaret FALLEY
Betsey COMSTOCK
= Daniel BUTLER
Millard FILLMORE
1800-1874
13th U.S. President
Richard Falley CLEVELAND
= Anne NEAL
George Selden BUTLER
= Elizabeth Ely GRIDLEY
= (1) Abigail POWERS
(2) Mrs. Caroline CARMICHAEL McIntosh
Stephen Grover CLEVELAND
1837-1908
22nd & 24th U.S. President
Amy Gridley BUTLER
= George Mauney AYER
= Frances FOLSOM
Adele Augusta AYER
= Levi Addison GARDNER
Dorothy Ayer GARDNER
= (1) Leslie Lynch KING
(2) Gerald Rudolf FORD
Leslie Lynch KING Jr.,
whose name was changed to
Gerald Rudolph FORD Jr.,
b. 1913
38th U.S. President
= Mrs. Elizabeth Ann (Betty) BLOOMER Warren

John PERKINS (1583-1654) of Ipswich, Mass. = Judith GATER

John PERKINS Jr.
= Elizabeth ——
Jacob PERKINS
= Sarah WAINWRIGHT
Philippa PERKINS
= Thomas EMERSON
Mary EMERSON
= Stephen STORY
Philippa STORY
= Ebenezer WOOD Jr.
Hepzibah WOOD
= Nathaniel FILLMORE
Nathaniel FILLMORE Jr.
= Phoebe MILLARD
Millard FILLMORE
1800-1874
13th U.S. President
= (1) Abigail POWERS
(2) Mrs. Caroline CARMICHAEL McIntosh

Jacob PERKINS
= Elizabeth WHIPPLE

Judith PERKINS
= Nathaniel BROWN
Jacob BROWN
= Sarah BURNHAM
Adam BROWN
= Esther PARKMAN
Adam BROWN Jr.
= Priscilla PUTNAM
Israel Putnam BROWN
= Sally BRIGGS
Sally BROWN
= Israel C. BREWER
Sarah Almeda BREWER
= Calvin Galusha COOLIDGE
John Calvin COOLIDGE
= Victoria Josephine MOOR
(John) Calvin COOLIDGE (Jr.)
1872-1933
30th U.S. President
= Grace Anna GOODHUE

Jabez PERKINS
= Hannah LATHROP
Hannah PERKINS
= Joshua HUNTINGTON
Lydia HUNTINGTON
= Ephraim BILL
Lydia BILL
= Joseph HOWLAND
Susan HOWLAND
= John ASPINWALL Jr.
Mary Rebecca ASPINWALL
= Isaac ROOSEVELT
James ROOSEVELT
= Sara DELANO
Franklin Delano ROOSEVELT
1882-1945
32nd U.S. President
= (Anna) Eleanor ROOSEVELT

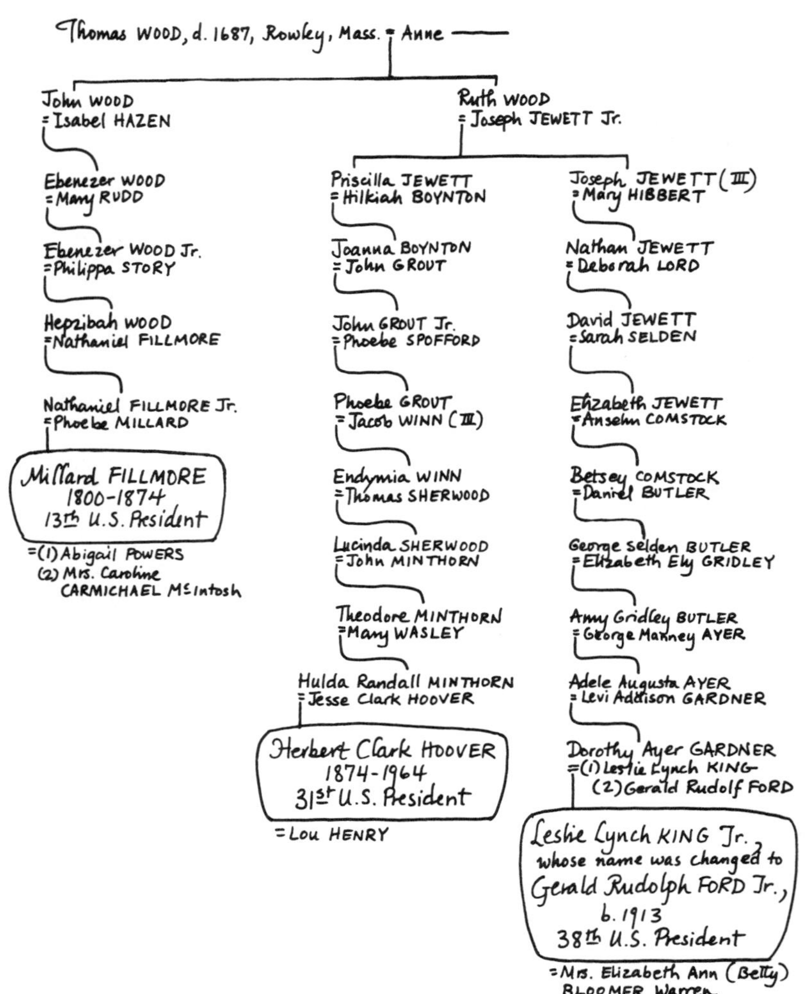
Thomas WOOD, d. 1687, Rowley, Mass. = Anne ——
John WOOD
= Isabel HAZEN
Ebenezer WOOD
= Mary RUDD
Ebenezer WOOD Jr.
= Philippa STORY
Hepzibah WOOD
= Nathaniel FILLMORE
Nathaniel FILLMORE Jr.
= Phoebe MILLARD
Millard FILLMORE
1800-1874
13th U.S. President
= (1) Abigail POWERS
(2) Mrs. Caroline CARMICHAEL McIntosh
Ruth WOOD
= Joseph JEWETT Jr.
Priscilla JEWETT
= Hilkiah BOYNTON
Joanna BOYNTON
= John GROUT
John GROUT Jr.
= Phoebe SPOFFORD
Phoebe GROUT
= Jacob WINN (III)
Endymia WINN
= Thomas SHERWOOD
Lucinda SHERWOOD
= John MINTHORN
Theodore MINTHORN
= Mary WASLEY
Hulda Randall MINTHORN
= Jesse Clark HOOVER
Herbert Clark HOOVER
1874-1964
31st U.S. President
= Lou HENRY
Joseph JEWETT (III)
= Mary HIBBERT
Nathan JEWETT
= Deborah LORD
David JEWETT
= Sarah SELDEN
Elizabeth JEWETT
= Anselm COMSTOCK
Betsey COMSTOCK
= Daniel BUTLER
George Selden BUTLER
= Elizabeth Ely GRIDLEY
Amy Gridley BUTLER
= George Manney AYER
Adele Augusta AYER
= Levi Addison GARDNER
Dorothy Ayer GARDNER
= (1) Leslie Lynch KING
(2) Gerald Rudolf FORD
Leslie Lynch KING Jr., whose name was changed to Gerald Rudolph FORD Jr.,
b. 1913
38th U.S. President
= Mrs. Elizabeth Ann (Betty) BLOOMER Warren

Daniel BREWER, d. 1646, Roxbury, Mass. = Joanna ———

Daniel BREWER Jr.
= Hannah MERRILL
Hannah BREWER = John BOWEN
Abigail BOWEN = Caleb KENDRICK
Benjamin KENDRICK
= Sarah HARRIS
Anna KENDRICK = Benjamin PIERCE Jr.
Franklin PIERCE
1804-1869
14th U.S. President
= Jane Means APPLETON

(probably) Hannah BREWER
= Thomas CHANDLER
Henry CHANDLER = Lydia ABBOTT
Isaac CHANDLER = Abigail HALE
Abigail CHANDLER = Israel SMITH
Chloe SMITH = Rutherford HAYES
Rutherford HAYES Jr.
= Sophia BIRCHARD
Rutherford Birchard HAYES
1822-1893
19th U.S. President
= Lucy Ware WEBB

Sarah BREWER = John MAY Jr.
John MAY (III) = Prudence BRIDGE
Hezekiah MAY = Anna STILLMAN
Elizabeth MAY = Daniel NEWCOMB
Lydia NEWCOMB = Timothy BUSH Jr.
Obadiah Newcomb BUSH = Harriet SMITH
James Smith BUSH = Harriet Eleanor FAY
Samuel Prescott BUSH = Flora SHELDON
Prescott Sheldon BUSH = Dorothy WALKER
George Herbert Walker BUSH
b. 1924
41st U.S. President
= Barbara PIERCE

Thomas RICHARDSON, d. 1633/4, Westmill, Hertfordshire, England = Katherine DUXFORD

Ezekiel RICHARDSON
d. 1647, Woburn, Mass.
= Susanna ———

Josiah RICHARDSON
= Remember UNDERWOOD

Sarah RICHARDSON
= William FLETCHER Jr.

Esther FLETCHER
= Stephen PIERCE Jr.

Benjamin PIERCE
= Elizabeth MERRILL

Benjamin PIERCE Jr.
= Anna KENDRICK

Franklin PIERCE
1804–1869
14th U.S. President

= Jane Means APPLETON

Thomas RICHARDSON
(1608–1651) of
Woburn, Mass.
= Mary ———

Sarah RICHARDSON
= Michael BACON Jr.

Jonathan BACON
= Elizabeth GILES

Elizabeth BACON
= Tarrant PUTNAM

Tarrant PUTNAM Jr.
= Priscilla BAKER

Priscilla PUTNAM
= Adam BROWN Jr.

Israel Putnam BROWN
= Sally BRIGGS

Sally BROWN
= Israel C. BREWER

Sarah Almeda BREWER
= Calvin Galusha COOLIDGE

John Calvin COOLIDGE
= Victoria Josephine MOOR

(John) Calvin COOLIDGE (Jr.)
1872–1933
30th U.S. President

= Grace Anna GOODHUE

Elizabeth RICHARDSON
= Francis WYMAN (WIMANT)

Francis WYMAN (1619–1699)
of Woburn, Mass.
= Abigail READ

William WYMAN
= Prudence PUTNAM

Prudence WYMAN
= Jacob WINN

Jacob WINN Jr. *
= Sarah BUCK

Jacob WINN (III)
= Phoebe GROUT

Endymia WINN
= Thomas SHERWOOD

Lucinda SHERWOOD
= John MINTHORN

Theodore MINTHORN
= Mary WASLEY

Hulda Randall MINTHORN
= Jesse Clark HOOVER

Herbert Clark HOOVER
1874–1964
31st U.S. President

= Lou HENRY

* The parentage of Jacob WINN, (Jr.?), husband of Sarah BUCK, is subject to doubt.

Edward GILMAN, bp. 1557, of Caston, Norfolk and Hingham, (England) = ——

Bridget GILMAN
= Edward LINCOLN

Samuel LINCOLN
d. 1690, Hingham, Mass.
= Martha LYFORD

Mordecai LINCOLN
= Sarah JONES

Mordecai LINCOLN Jr.
= Hannah SALTER

John LINCOLN
= Rebecca FLOWERS

Abraham LINCOLN
= Bathsheba (HERRING?)

Thomas LINCOLN
= Nancy HANKS

Abraham LINCOLN
1809-1865
16th U.S. President

= Mary Ann TODD

Edward GILMAN = Mary CLARK
d. 1655, Exeter, N.H.

John GILMAN
= Elizabeth TREWORGYE

Lydia GILMAN = John WHITE Jr.

Mary WHITE = James AYER

William AYER = Sarah LITTLE

Daniel AYER = Sarah ADAMS

Samuel AYER = Polly CHASE

John Varnum AYER
= Elida Vanderburgh MANNEY

George Manney AYER
= Amy Gridley BUTLER

Adela Augusta AYER
= Levi Addison GARDNER

Dorothy Ayer GARDNER
(= (1) Leslie Lynch KING
(2) Gerald Rudolf FORD

Leslie Lynch KING Jr.,
whose name was
changed to Gerald
Rudolph FORD Jr., b. 1913
38th U.S. President

= Mrs. Elizabeth Ann (Betty)
BLOOMER Warren

Mary GILMAN, d. 1681, Hingham, Mass.
= (1) Nicholas JACOB

Deborah JACOB = Nathaniel THOMAS Jr.

William THOMAS = Abigail RUCK

Margaret THOMAS = John BRECK (III)

Abigail BRECK = John LILLIE

Anna LILLIE = Samuel HOWARD

Harriet HOWARD = Samuel Prescott Phillips FAY

Samuel Howard FAY = Susan SHELLMAN

Harriet Eleanor FAY = James Smith BUSH

Samuel Prescott BUSH = Flora SHELDON

Prescott Sheldon BUSH = Dorothy WALKER

George Herbert Walker BUSH
b. 1924
41st U.S. President

= Barbara PIERCE

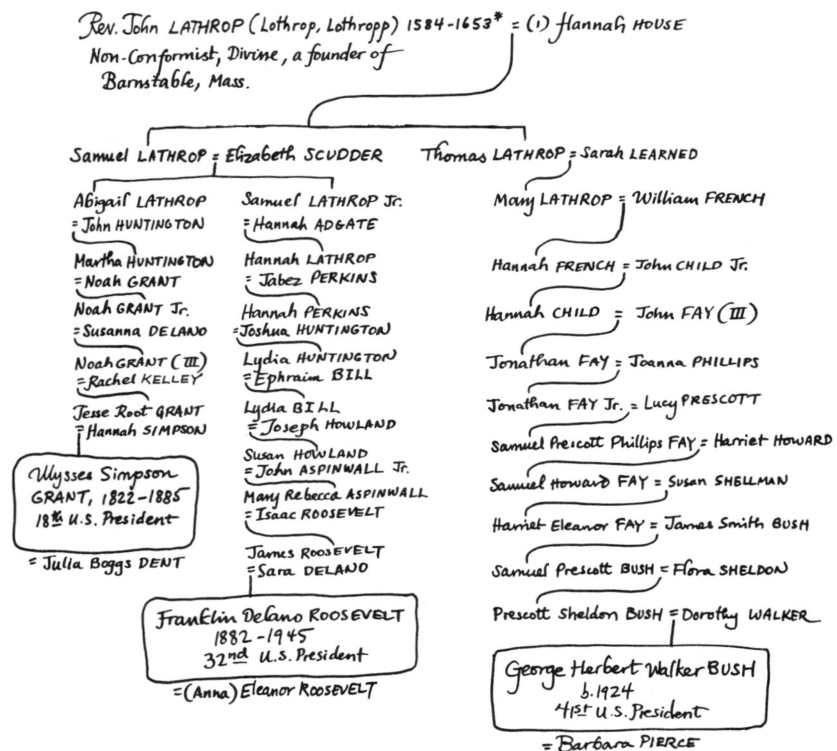

*For Rev. LATHROP, see Dictionary of American Biography and Dictionary of National Biography (British).

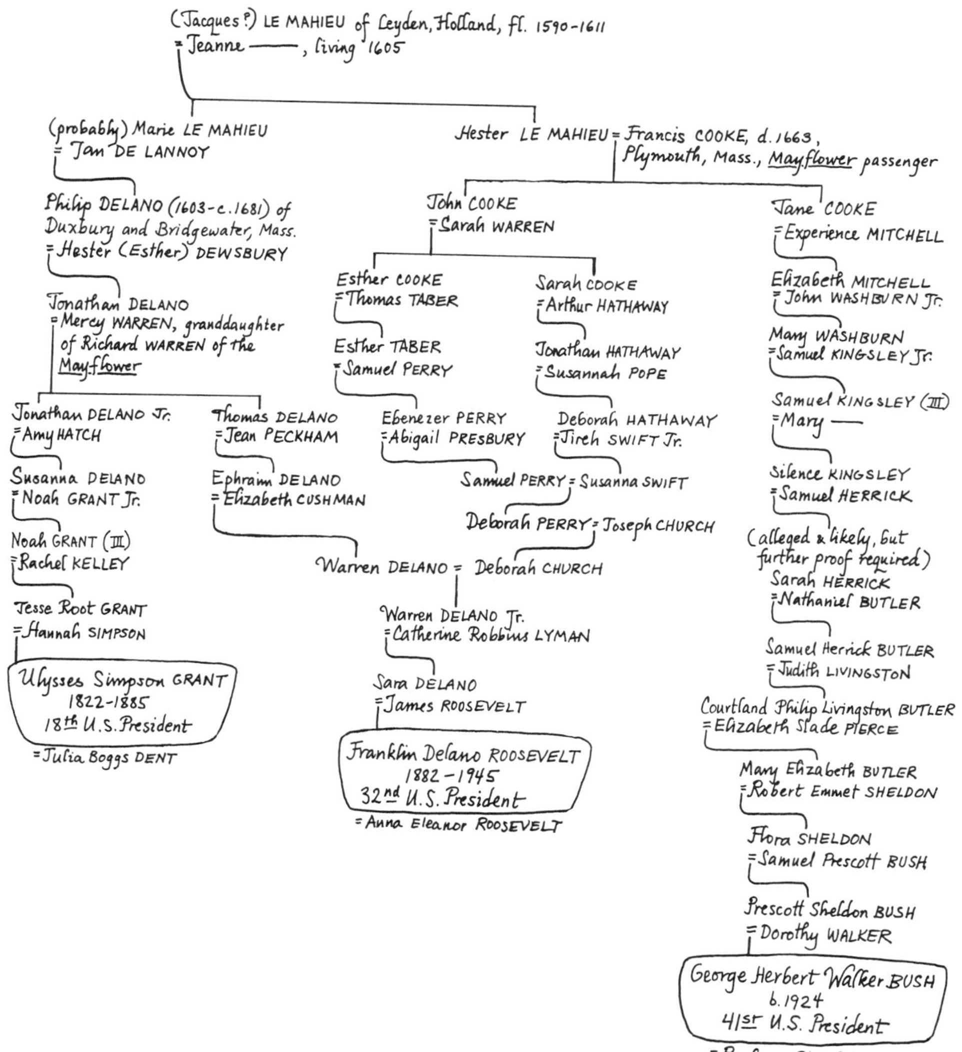
(Jacques?) LE MAHIEU of Leyden, Holland, fl. 1590-1611
= Jeanne ——, living 1605
(probably) Marie LE MAHIEU
= Jan DE LANNOY
Hester LE MAHIEU = Francis COOKE, d. 1663, Plymouth, Mass., Mayflower passenger
Philip DELANO (1603-c.1681) of Duxbury and Bridgewater, Mass.
= Hester (Esther) DEWSBURY
John COOKE
= Sarah WARREN
Jane COOKE
= Experience MITCHELL
Jonathan DELANO
= Mercy WARREN, granddaughter of Richard WARREN of the Mayflower
Esther COOKE
= Thomas TABER
Sarah COOKE
= Arthur HATHAWAY
Elizabeth MITCHELL
= John WASHBURN Jr.
Esther TABER
= Samuel PERRY
Jonathan HATHAWAY
= Susannah POPE
Mary WASHBURN
= Samuel KINGSLEY Jr.
Samuel KINGSLEY (III)
= Mary ——
Jonathan DELANO Jr.
= Amy HATCH
Thomas DELANO
= Jean PECKHAM
Ebenezer PERRY
= Abigail PRESBURY
Deborah HATHAWAY
= Jireh SWIFT Jr.
Susanna DELANO
= Noah GRANT Jr.
Ephraim DELANO
= Elizabeth CUSHMAN
Samuel PERRY = Susanna SWIFT
Silence KINGSLEY
= Samuel HERRICK
Deborah PERRY = Joseph CHURCH
Noah GRANT (III)
= Rachel KELLEY
Warren DELANO = Deborah CHURCH
(alleged & likely, but further proof required)
Sarah HERRICK
= Nathaniel BUTLER
Jesse Root GRANT
= Hannah SIMPSON
Warren DELANO Jr.
= Catherine Robbins LYMAN
Samuel Herrick BUTLER
= Judith LIVINGSTON
Ulysses Simpson GRANT
1822-1885
18th U.S. President
= Julia Boggs DENT
Sara DELANO
= James ROOSEVELT
Courtland Philip Livingston BUTLER
= Elizabeth Slade PIERCE
Franklin Delano ROOSEVELT
1882-1945
32nd U.S. President
= Anna Eleanor ROOSEVELT
Mary Elizabeth BUTLER
= Robert Emmet SHELDON
Flora SHELDON
= Samuel Prescott BUSH
Prescott Sheldon BUSH
= Dorothy WALKER
George Herbert Walker BUSH
b. 1924
41st U.S. President
= Barbara PIERCE

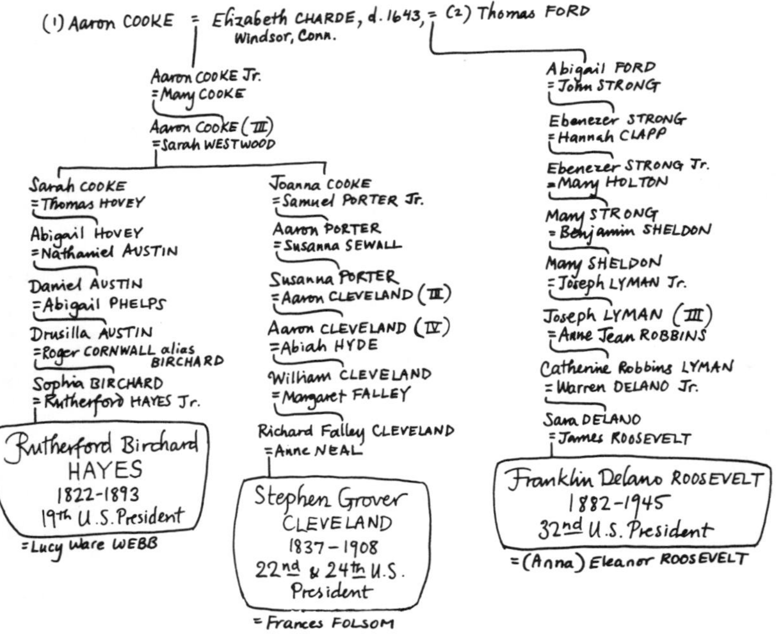
(1) Aaron COOKE = Elizabeth CHARDE, d. 1643, = (2) Thomas FORD
Windsor, Conn.
Aaron COOKE Jr.
=Mary COOKE
Aaron COOKE (III)
=Sarah WESTWOOD
Sarah COOKE
=Thomas HOVEY
Abigail HOVEY
=Nathaniel AUSTIN
Daniel AUSTIN
=Abigail PHELPS
Drusilla AUSTIN
=Roger CORNWALL alias BIRCHARD
Sophia BIRCHARD
=Rutherford HAYES Jr.
Rutherford Birchard HAYES
1822-1893
19th U.S. President
=Lucy Ware WEBB
Joanna COOKE
=Samuel PORTER Jr.
Aaron PORTER
=Susanna SEWALL
Susanna PORTER
=Aaron CLEVELAND (III)
Aaron CLEVELAND (IV)
=Abiah HYDE
William CLEVELAND
=Margaret FALLEY
Richard Falley CLEVELAND
=Anne NEAL
Stephen Grover CLEVELAND
1837-1908
22nd & 24th U.S. President
=Frances FOLSOM
Abigail FORD
=John STRONG
Ebenezer STRONG
=Hannah CLAPP
Ebenezer STRONG Jr.
=Mary HOLTON
Mary STRONG
=Benjamin SHELDON
Mary SHELDON
=Joseph LYMAN Jr.
Joseph LYMAN (III)
=Anne Jean ROBBINS
Catherine Robbins LYMAN
=Warren DELANO Jr.
Sara DELANO
=James ROOSEVELT
Franklin Delano ROOSEVELT
1882-1945
32nd U.S. President
=(Anna) Eleanor ROOSEVELT

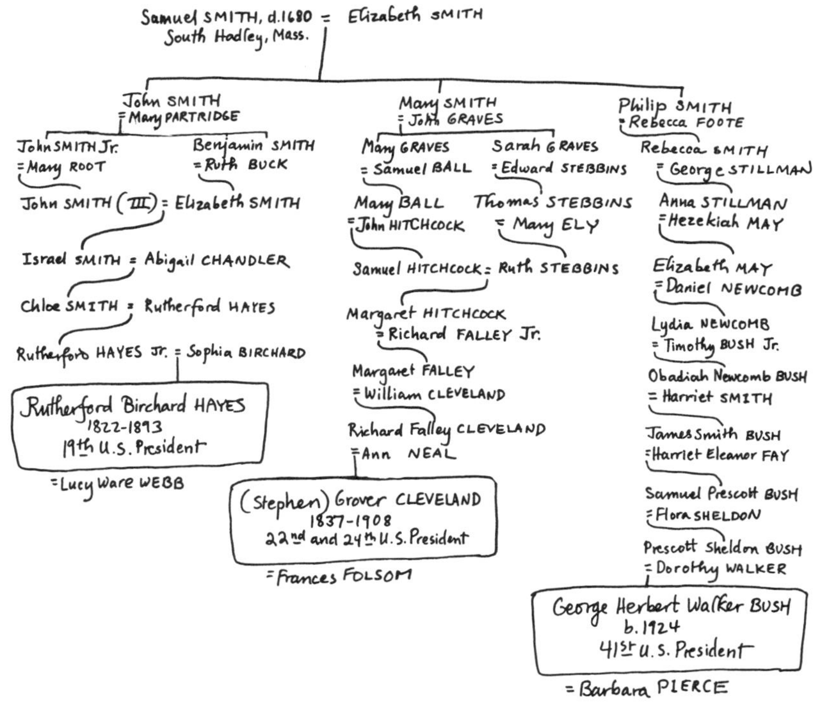

Samuel SMITH, d.1680 = Elizabeth SMITH
South Hadley, Mass.
John SMITH
= Mary PARTRIDGE
Mary SMITH
= John GRAVES
Philip SMITH
= Rebecca FOOTE
John SMITH Jr.
= Mary ROOT
Benjamin SMITH
= Ruth BUCK
John SMITH (III) = Elizabeth SMITH
Israel SMITH = Abigail CHANDLER
Chloe SMITH = Rutherford HAYES
Rutherford HAYES Jr. = Sophia BIRCHARD
Rutherford Birchard HAYES
1822-1893
19th U.S. President
= Lucy Ware WEBB
Mary GRAVES
= Samuel BALL
Sarah GRAVES
= Edward STEBBINS
Mary BALL
= John HITCHCOCK
Thomas STEBBINS
= Mary ELY
Samuel HITCHCOCK = Ruth STEBBINS
Margaret HITCHCOCK
= Richard FALLEY Jr.
Margaret FALLEY
= William CLEVELAND
Richard Falley CLEVELAND
= Ann NEAL
(Stephen) Grover CLEVELAND
1837-1908
22nd and 24th U.S. President
= Frances FOLSOM
Rebecca SMITH
= George STILLMAN
Anna STILLMAN
= Hezekiah MAY
Elizabeth MAY
= Daniel NEWCOMB
Lydia NEWCOMB
= Timothy BUSH Jr.
Obadiah Newcomb BUSH
= Harriet SMITH
James Smith BUSH
= Harriet Eleanor FAY
Samuel Prescott BUSH
= Flora SHELDON
Prescott Sheldon BUSH
= Dorothy WALKER
George Herbert Walker BUSH
b. 1924
41st U.S. President
= Barbara PIERCE

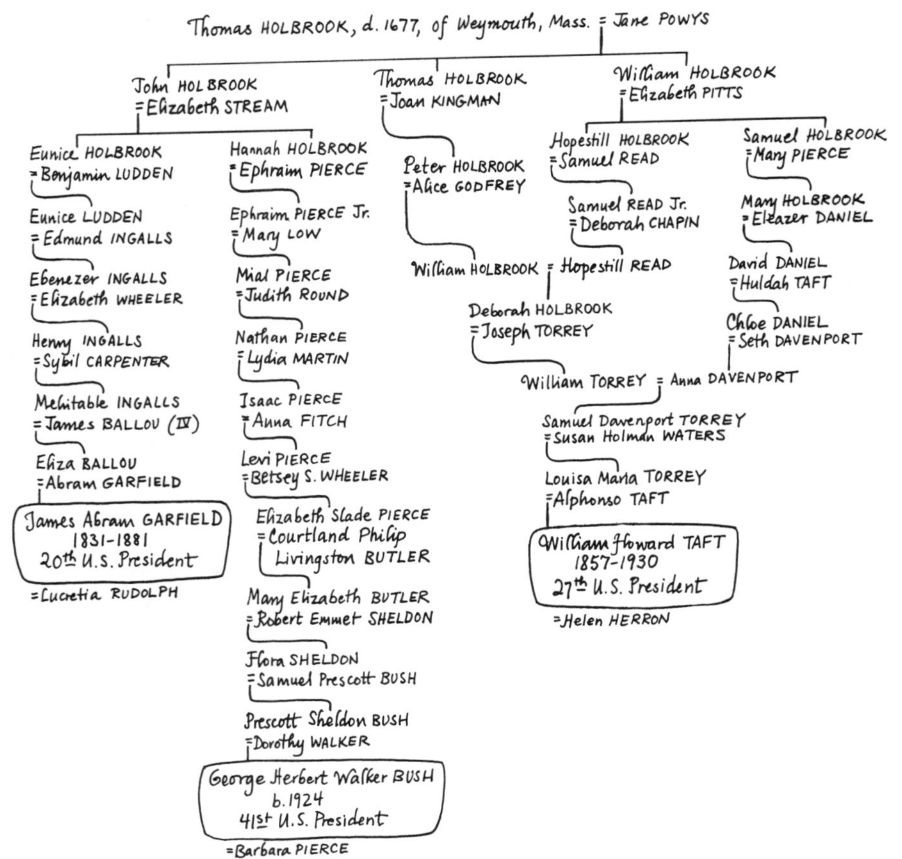
Thomas HOLBROOK, d. 1677, of Weymouth, Mass. = Jane POWYS
John HOLBROOK
=Elizabeth STREAM
Thomas HOLBROOK
=Joan KINGMAN
William HOLBROOK
=Elizabeth PITTS
Eunice HOLBROOK
=Benjamin LUDDEN
Hannah HOLBROOK
=Ephraim PIERCE
Peter HOLBROOK
=Alice GODFREY
Hopestill HOLBROOK
=Samuel READ
Samuel HOLBROOK
=Mary PIERCE
Eunice LUDDEN
=Edmund INGALLS
Ephraim PIERCE Jr.
=Mary LOW
Samuel READ Jr.
=Deborah CHAPIN
Mary HOLBROOK
=Eleazer DANIEL
Ebenezer INGALLS
=Elizabeth WHEELER
Mial PIERCE
=Judith ROUND
William HOLBROOK = Hopestill READ
David DANIEL
=Huldah TAFT
Henry INGALLS
=Sybil CARPENTER
Nathan PIERCE
=Lydia MARTIN
Deborah HOLBROOK
=Joseph TORREY
Chloe DANIEL
=Seth DAVENPORT
Mehitable INGALLS
=James BALLOU (IV)
Isaac PIERCE
=Anna FITCH
William TORREY = Anna DAVENPORT
Eliza BALLOU
=Abram GARFIELD
Levi PIERCE
=Betsey S. WHEELER
Samuel Davenport TORREY
=Susan Holman WATERS
James Abram GARFIELD
1831-1881
20th U.S. President
=Lucretia RUDOLPH
Elizabeth Slade PIERCE
=Courtland Philip Livingston BUTLER
Louisa Maria TORREY
=Alphonso TAFT
William Howard TAFT
1857-1930
27th U.S. President
=Helen HERRON
Mary Elizabeth BUTLER
=Robert Emmet SHELDON
Flora SHELDON
=Samuel Prescott BUSH
Prescott Sheldon BUSH
=Dorothy WALKER
George Herbert Walker BUSH
b. 1924
41st U.S. President
=Barbara PIERCE

William KING (c.1595 - c.1650/51) of Salem, Mass. = Dorothy HAYNE

Deliverance KING
= John TUTHILL

Henry TUTHILL
= Bethia HORTON

Henry TUTHILL Jr.
= Hannah (CROUCH?)

Henry TUTHILL (III)
= Phoebe HORTON

Anna TUTHILL
= John Cleves SYMMES

Anna Tuthill SYMMES
= William Henry HARRISON
1773-1841, 9th U.S. President

John Scott HARRISON
= Elizabeth Ramsey IRWIN

Benjamin HARRISON
1833-1901
23rd U.S. President

= (1) Caroline Lavinia SCOTT
(2) Mrs. Mary Scott LORD Dimmick

John KING
= Elizabeth GOLDTHWAITE

Elizabeth KING
= Nathaniel WATERS

Jonathan WATERS
= Mehitable GILES

Asa WATERS
= Sarah GOODALE

Asa WATERS Jr.
= Susan Trask HOLMAN

Susan Holman WATERS
= Samuel Davenport TORREY

Louisa Maria TORREY
= Alphonso TAFT

William Howard TAFT
1857-1930
27th U.S. President

= Helen HERRON

Hannah KING
= Richard BROWNE

Hannah BROWNE
= John REEVE

Abigail REEVE
= (probably) Thomas DICKERSON

Joshua DICKERSON
= Mehitable DICKERSON

(probably) Joshua DICKERSON Jr.
= Abigail ———

Joseph DICKERSON
= Abigail HINES (HINDS, HAINES)

(probably) Isaac Haines DICKERSON
= Charity Malvina VAN KIRK

Phoebe Elizabeth DICKERSON
= George Tryon HARDING

Warren Gamaliel HARDING
1865-1923
29th U.S. President

= Mrs. Florence Mabel KLING De Wolfe

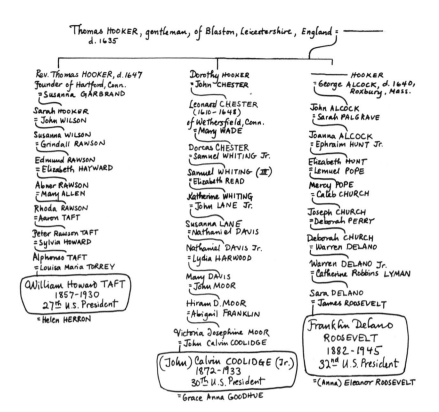

Thomas HOOKER, gentleman, of Blaston, Leicestershire, England = ———
d. 1635

Rev. Thomas HOOKER, d. 1647
Founder of Hartford, Conn.
= Susanna GARBRAND

Sarah HOOKER
= John WILSON

Susanna WILSON
= Grindall RAWSON

Edmund RAWSON
= Elizabeth HAYWARD

Abner RAWSON
= Mary ALLEN

Rhoda RAWSON
= Aaron TAFT

Peter Rawson TAFT
= Sylvia HOWARD

Alphonso TAFT
= Louisa Maria TORREY

William Howard TAFT
1857-1930
27th U.S. President

= Helen HERRON

Dorothy HOOKER
= John CHESTER

Leonard CHESTER
(1610-1648)
of Wethersfield, Conn.
= Mary WADE

Dorcas CHESTER
= Samuel WHITING Jr.

Samuel WHITING (III)
= Elizabeth READ

Katherine WHITING
= John LANE Jr.

Susanna LANE
= Nathaniel DAVIS

Nathaniel DAVIS Jr.
= Lydia HARWOOD

Mary DAVIS
= John MOOR

Hiram D. MOOR
= Abigail FRANKLIN

Victoria Josephine MOOR
= John Calvin COOLIDGE

(John) Calvin COOLIDGE (Jr.)
1872-1933
30th U.S. President

= Grace Anna GOODHUE

——— HOOKER
= George ALCOCK, d. 1640,
Roxbury, Mass.

John ALCOCK
= Sarah PALGRAVE

Joanna ALCOCK
= Ephraim HUNT Jr.

Elizabeth HUNT
= Lemuel POPE

Mercy POPE
= Caleb CHURCH

Joseph CHURCH
= Deborah PERRY

Deborah CHURCH
= Warren DELANO

Warren DELANO Jr.
= Catherine Robbins LYMAN

Sara DELANO
= James ROOSEVELT

Franklin Delano
ROOSEVELT
1882-1945
32nd U.S. President

= (Anna) Eleanor ROOSEVELT

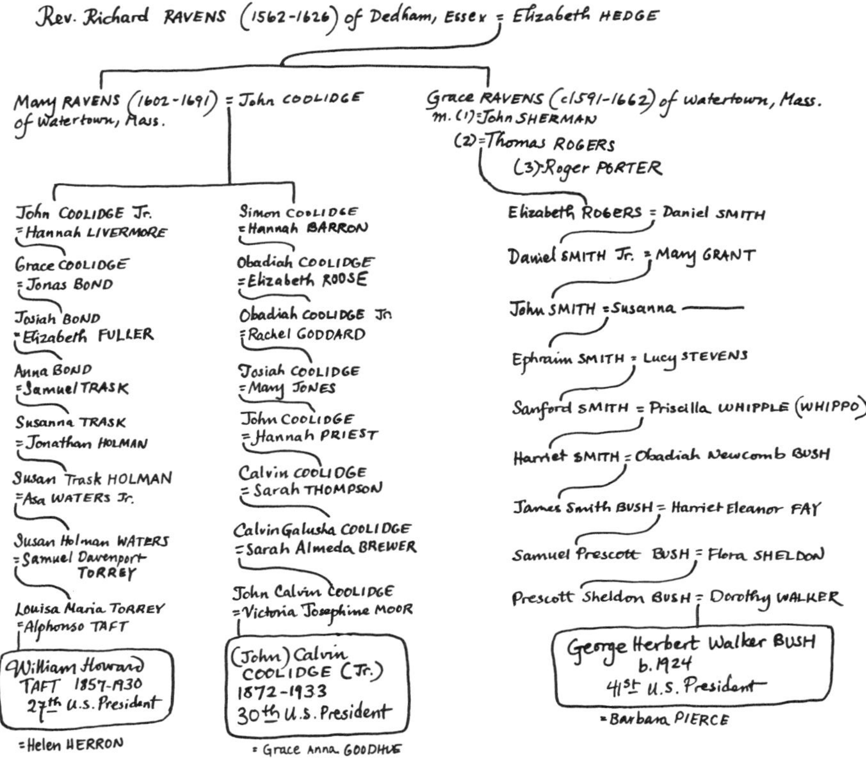
Rev. Richard RAVENS (1562-1626) of Dedham, Essex = Elizabeth HEDGE
Mary RAVENS (1602-1691) of Watertown, Mass. = John COOLIDGE
Grace RAVENS (c1591-1662) of Watertown, Mass.
m. (1) = John SHERMAN
(2) = Thomas ROGERS
(3) = Roger PORTER
John COOLIDGE Jr. = Hannah LIVERMORE
Grace COOLIDGE = Jonas BOND
Josiah BOND = Elizabeth FULLER
Anna BOND = Samuel TRASK
Susanna TRASK = Jonathan HOLMAN
Susan Trask HOLMAN = Asa WATERS Jr.
Susan Holman WATERS = Samuel Davenport TORREY
Louisa Maria TORREY = Alphonso TAFT
William Howard TAFT 1857-1930 27th U.S. President
= Helen HERRON
Simon COOLIDGE = Hannah BARRON
Obadiah COOLIDGE = Elizabeth ROOSE
Obadiah COOLIDGE Jr. = Rachel GODDARD
Josiah COOLIDGE = Mary JONES
John COOLIDGE = Hannah PRIEST
Calvin COOLIDGE = Sarah THOMPSON
Calvin Galusha COOLIDGE = Sarah Almeda BREWER
John Calvin COOLIDGE = Victoria Josephine MOOR
(John) Calvin COOLIDGE (Jr.) 1872-1933 30th U.S. President
= Grace Anna GOODHUE
Elizabeth ROGERS = Daniel SMITH
Daniel SMITH Jr. = Mary GRANT
John SMITH = Susanna ———
Ephraim SMITH = Lucy STEVENS
Sanford SMITH = Priscilla WHIPPLE (WHIPPO)
Harriet SMITH = Obadiah Newcomb BUSH
James Smith BUSH = Harriet Eleanor FAY
Samuel Prescott BUSH = Flora SHELDON
Prescott Sheldon BUSH = Dorothy WALKER
George Herbert Walker BUSH b. 1924 41st U.S. President
= Barbara PIERCE

Henry SHERMAN (ca. 1510/11-1590) of Dedham, Essex, England = Agnes (BUTTER?)

Edmund SHERMAN
= Anne PELLATTE

Edmund SHERMAN, d. 1641, Wethersfield, Conn.
= Joan ———

Grace SHERMAN
= John LIVERMORE

Hannah LIVERMORE
= John COOLIDGE Jr.

Grace COOLIDGE
= Jonas BOND

Josiah BOND
= Elizabeth FULLER

Anna BOND
= Samuel TRASK

Susanna TRASK
= Jonathan HOLMAN

Susan Trask HOLMAN
= Asa WATERS Jr.

Susan Holman WATERS
= Samuel Davenport TORREY

Louisa Maria TORREY
= Alphonso TAFT

William Howard TAFT
1857-1930
27th U.S. President
= Helen HERRON

Henry SHERMAN
= Susan LAWRENCE

Anne SHERMAN
= Anthony WHITING

Phoebe WHITING, d. 1685, Watertown, Mass.
= John BARNARD

Elizabeth BARNARD
= John DIX

Abigail DIX
= Jonathan GROUT

John GROUT
= Joanna BOYNTON

John GROUT Jr.
= Phoebe SPOFFORD

Phoebe GROUT
= Jacob WINN (III)

Endymia WINN
= Thomas SHERWOOD

Lucinda SHERWOOD
= John MINTHORN

Theodore MINTHORN
= Mary WASLEY

Hulda Randall MINTHORN
= Jesse Clark HOOVER

Herbert Clark HOOVER
1874-1964
31st U.S. President
= Lou HENRY

Samuel SHERMAN
= Philippa (WARD?)

Philip SHERMAN (1610-1687), First Secretary of the Colony of Rhode Island
= Sarah ODDING

John SHERMAN
= Sarah SPOONER

Hannah SHERMAN
= William BOURN

William BOURN Jr.
= Mary SHEFFIELD

Hannah BOURN
= William FITCH

Anna FITCH
= Isaac PIERCE

Levi PIERCE
= Betsey S. WHEELER

Elizabeth Slade PIERCE
= Courtland Philip Livingston BUTLER

Mary Elizabeth BUTLER
= Robert Emmet SHELDON

Flora SHELDON
= Samuel Prescott BUSH

Prescott Sheldon BUSH
= Dorothy WALKER

George Herbert Walker BUSH
b. 1924
41st U.S. President
= Barbara PIERCE

William ALMY, d. by 23 April 1677, of Portsmouth, R.I. = Audrey BARLOW

- Anne ALMY = John GREENE Jr.
  - Phillip(pa) GREENE = Caleb CARR
    - Caleb CARR Jr. = Joanna SLOCUM
      - Patience CARR = Joseph SLOCUM
        - Sarah SLOCUM = William TRIPP
          - Phoebe TRIPP = Amos HARDING
            - George Tryon HARDING = Elizabeth MADISON
              - Charles Alexander HARDING = Mary Anne CRAWFORD
                - George Tryon HARDING = Phoebe Elizabeth DICKERSON
                  - **Warren Gamaliel HARDING, 1865-1923, 29th U.S. President** = Mrs. Florence Mabel KLING De Wolfe
- Christopher ALMY = Elizabeth CORNELL
  - Elizabeth ALMY = Lewis MORRIS
    - Richard MORRIS = ———
      - Sarah MORRIS = Joseph BURDG
        - Jacob BURDG = Judith SMITH
          - Jacob BURDG Jr. = Miriam MATTHEWS
            - Oliver BURDG = Jane M. HEMINGWAY
              - Almira Park BURDG = Franklin MILHOUS
                - Hannah MILHOUS = Francis Anthony NIXON
                  - **Richard Milhous NIXON, b. 1913, 37th U.S. President** = Thelma Catherine (Pat) RYAN
      - Job MORRIS = Mary ANSLEY
        - Lydia MORRIS = Abel ANSLEY
          - Ann ANSLEY = Wiley CARTER
            - Littleberry Walker CARTER = Mary Ann Diligent SEALS
              - William Archibald CARTER = Nina PRATT
                - James Earl CARTER = Bessie Lillian GORDY
                  - **James Earl CARTER, Jr., b. 1924, 39th U.S. President** (Eleanor) Rosalynn SMITH

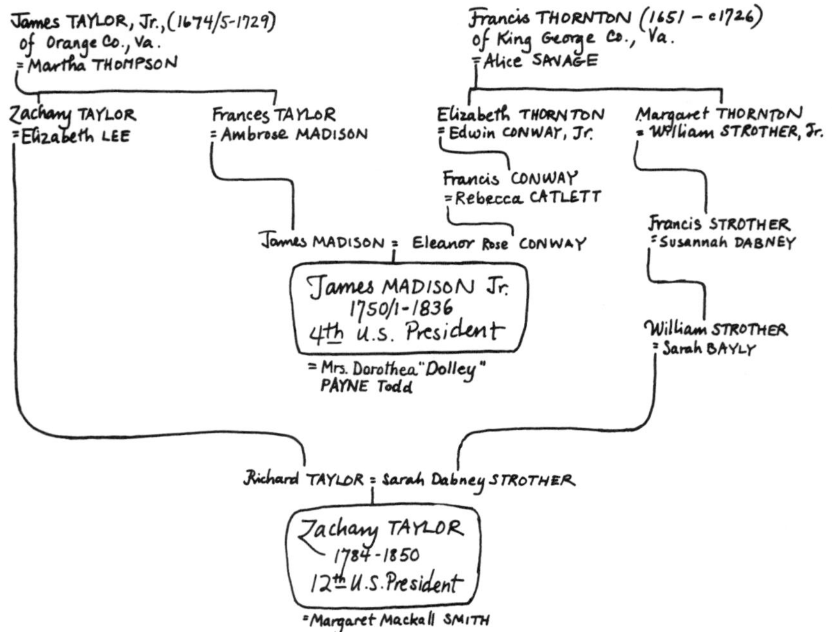
James TAYLOR, Jr., (1674/5-1729)
of Orange Co., Va.
= Martha THOMPSON
Francis THORNTON (1651 – c1726)
of King George Co., Va.
= Alice SAVAGE
Zachary TAYLOR
= Elizabeth LEE
Frances TAYLOR
= Ambrose MADISON
Elizabeth THORNTON
= Edwin CONWAY, Jr.
Margaret THORNTON
= William STROTHER, Jr.
Francis CONWAY
= Rebecca CATLETT
James MADISON = Eleanor Rose CONWAY
Francis STROTHER
= Susannah DABNEY
James MADISON Jr.
1750/1-1836
4th U.S. President
= Mrs. Dorothea "Dolley" PAYNE Todd
William STROTHER
= Sarah BAYLY
Richard TAYLOR = Sarah Dabney STROTHER
Zachary TAYLOR
1784-1850
12th U.S. President
= Margaret Mackall SMITH

Claas Gerritse VAN SCHAICK
of Albany, N.Y., living 1677 = ? Jannetje
Jan Franssen VAN HOESEN of Albany, N.Y.,
d.c. 1703
= Volkertje Jurrianse
Christyntje VAN HOESEN
= Jan Tyssen HOES
Anna Janse VAN HOESEN
= Luykas Gerritsen
WYNGAART, living 1709
Laurens VAN SCHAICK
= Jannetje OOTHOUT
Dirk Janse HOES = Elizabeth Luycassen WYNGAART
Jannetje Laurense VAN SCHAICK = Johannes Dircksen HOES
Maria HOES
= Abraham VAN BUREN
Dirck HOES
= Christina VAN ALEN
Martin VAN BUREN
1782-1862
8th U.S. President
John Dircksen HOES
= Maria QUACKENBOSS
= Hannah HOES
Emanuel VAN SCHAACK = Maria Luykassen WYNGAART
Cornelius VAN SCHAACK = Lydia VAN DYCK
Cornelius VAN SCHAACK Jr. = Angeltje (Angelica) YATES
Maria VAN SCHAACK = James J. (Jacobus) ROOSEVELT
Cornelius Van Schaack ROOSEVELT = Margaret BARNHILL
Theodore ROOSEVELT = Martha BULLOCH
Theodore ROOSEVELT Jr.
1858-1919
26th U.S. President
=(1) Alice Hathaway LEE
(2) Edith Kermit CAROW

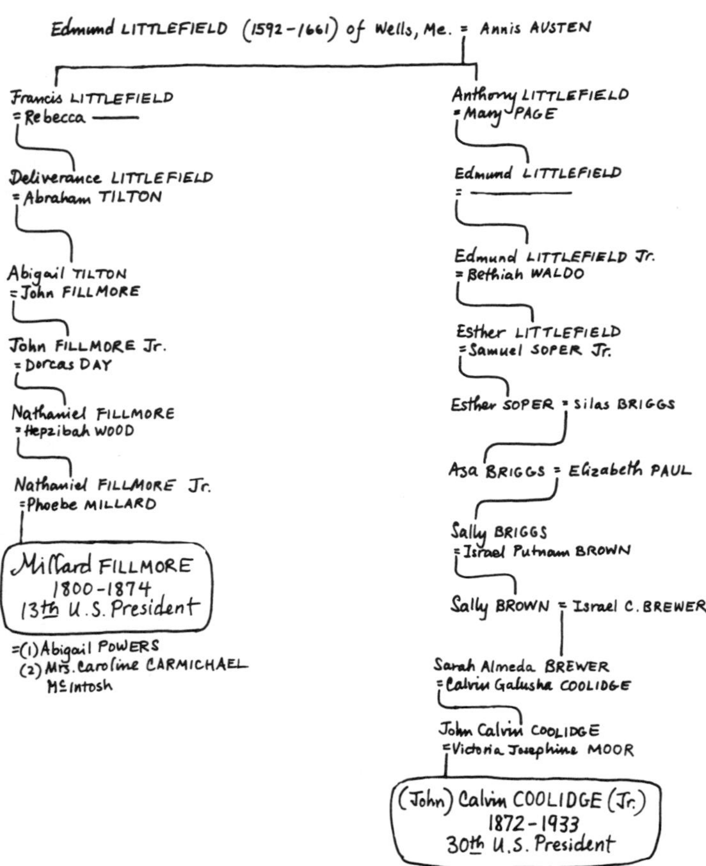

Edmund LITTLEFIELD (1592-1661) of Wells, Me. = Annis AUSTEN
Francis LITTLEFIELD
= Rebecca ——
Deliverance LITTLEFIELD
= Abraham TILTON
Abigail TILTON
= John FILLMORE
John FILLMORE Jr.
= Dorcas DAY
Nathaniel FILLMORE
= Hepzibah WOOD
Nathaniel FILLMORE Jr.
= Phoebe MILLARD
Millard FILLMORE
1800-1874
13th U.S. President
= (1) Abigail POWERS
(2) Mrs. Caroline CARMICHAEL McIntosh
Anthony LITTLEFIELD
= Mary PAGE
Edmund LITTLEFIELD
= ——
Edmund LITTLEFIELD Jr.
= Bethiah WALDO
Esther LITTLEFIELD
= Samuel SOPER Jr.
Esther SOPER = Silas BRIGGS
Asa BRIGGS = Elizabeth PAUL
Sally BRIGGS
= Israel Putnam BROWN
Sally BROWN = Israel C. BREWER
Sarah Almeda BREWER
= Calvin Galusha COOLIDGE
John Calvin COOLIDGE
= Victoria Josephine MOOR
(John) Calvin COOLIDGE (Jr.)
1872-1933
30th U.S. President
= Grace Anna GOODHUE

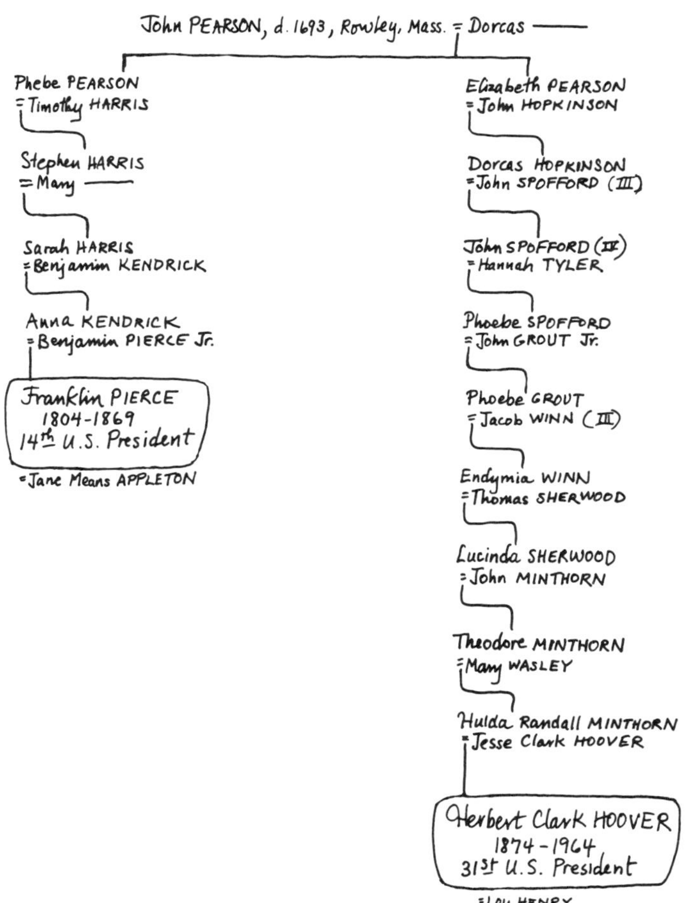
John PEARSON, d. 1693, Rowley, Mass. = Dorcas ——
Phebe PEARSON
= Timothy HARRIS
Stephen HARRIS
= Mary ——
Sarah HARRIS
= Benjamin KENDRICK
Anna KENDRICK
= Benjamin PIERCE Jr.
Franklin PIERCE
1804-1869
14th U.S. President
= Jane Means APPLETON
Elizabeth PEARSON
= John HOPKINSON
Dorcas HOPKINSON
= John SPOFFORD (III)
John SPOFFORD (IV)
= Hannah TYLER
Phoebe SPOFFORD
= John GROUT Jr.
Phoebe GROUT
= Jacob WINN (III)
Endymia WINN
= Thomas SHERWOOD
Lucinda SHERWOOD
= John MINTHORN
Theodore MINTHORN
= Mary WASLEY
Hulda Randall MINTHORN
= Jesse Clark HOOVER
Herbert Clark HOOVER
1874-1964
31st U.S. President
= Lou HENRY

Simon HUNTINGTON, d. 1633 = Margaret BARRETT of Windsor, Conn.

Christopher HUNTINGTON
= Ruth ROCKWELL

John HUNTINGTON
= Abigail LATHROP

Martha HUNTINGTON
= Noah GRANT

Noah GRANT Jr.
= Susanna DELANO

Noah GRANT (III)
= Rachel KELLEY

Jesse Root GRANT
= Hannah SIMPSON

Ulysses Simpson GRANT
1822–1885
18th U.S. President
= Julia Boggs Dent

Simon HUNTINGTON Jr.
= Sarah CLARK

Simon HUNTINGTON (III)
= Lydia GAGER

Joshua HUNTINGTON
= Hannah PERKINS

Lydia HUNTINGTON
= Ephraim BILL

Lydia BILL
= Joseph HOWLAND

Susan HOWLAND
= John ASPINWALL Jr.

Mary Rebecca ASPINWALL
= Isaac ROOSEVELT

James ROOSEVELT
= Sara DELANO

Franklin Delano ROOSEVELT
1882–1945
32nd U.S. President
= Anna Eleanor ROOSEVELT

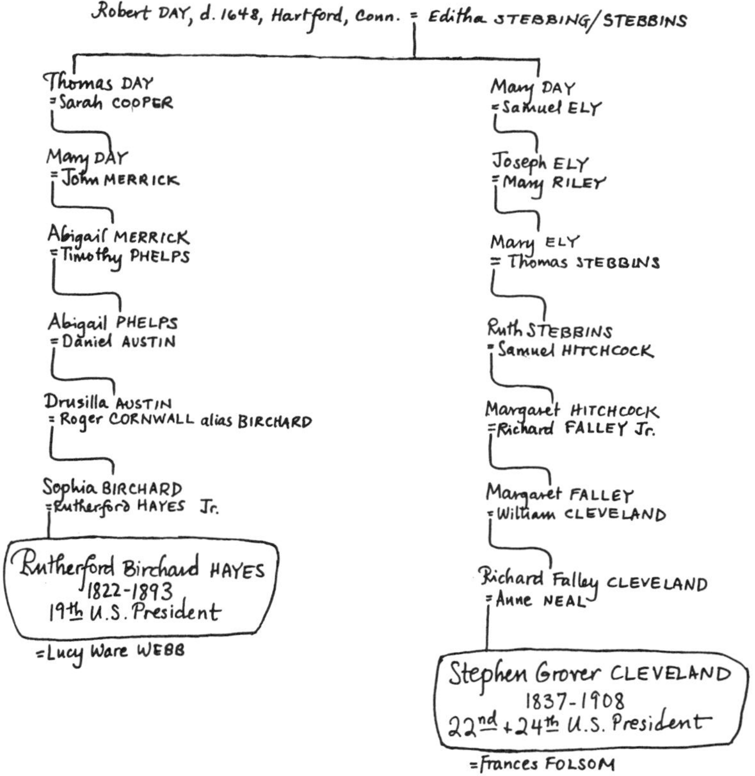
Robert DAY, d. 1648, Hartford, Conn. = Editha STEBBING/STEBBINS
Thomas DAY
=Sarah COOPER
Mary DAY
=John MERRICK
Abigail MERRICK
=Timothy PHELPS
Abigail PHELPS
=Daniel AUSTIN
Drusilla AUSTIN
= Roger CORNWALL alias BIRCHARD
Sophia BIRCHARD
=Rutherford HAYES Jr.
Rutherford Birchard HAYES
1822-1893
19th U.S. President
=Lucy Ware WEBB
Mary DAY
=Samuel ELY
Joseph ELY
=Mary RILEY
Mary ELY
= Thomas STEBBINS
Ruth STEBBINS
=Samuel HITCHCOCK
Margaret HITCHCOCK
=Richard FALLEY Jr.
Margaret FALLEY
=William CLEVELAND
Richard Falley CLEVELAND
=Anne NEAL
Stephen Grover CLEVELAND
1837-1908
22nd + 24th U.S. President
=Frances FOLSOM

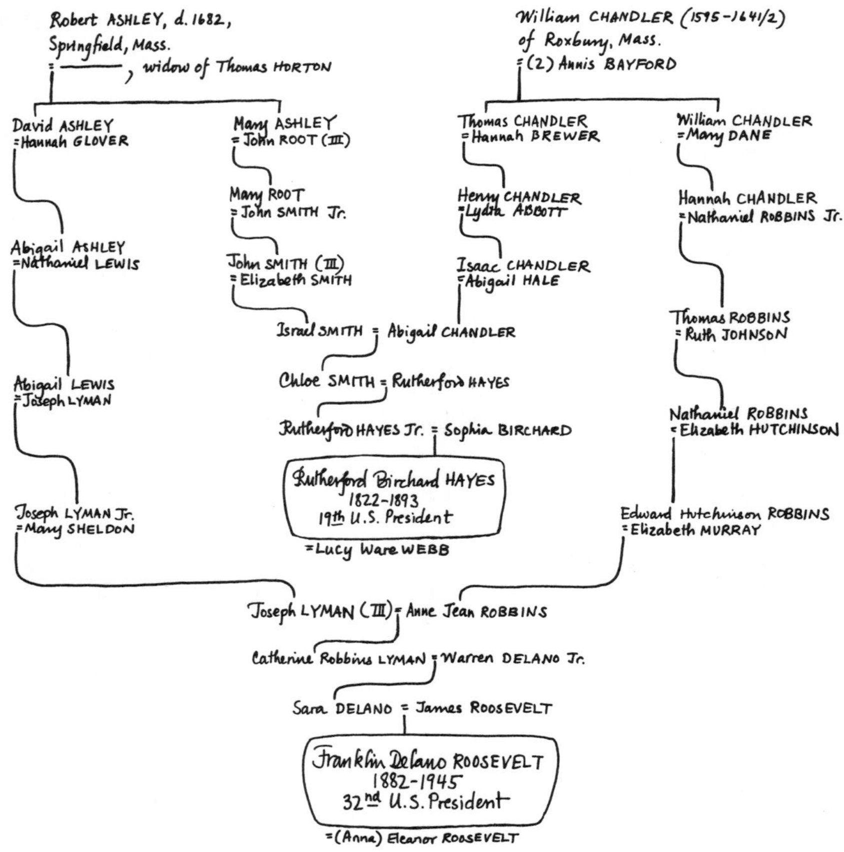
Robert ASHLEY, d. 1682,
Springfield, Mass.
= ———, widow of Thomas HORTON
William CHANDLER (1595-1641/2)
of Roxbury, Mass.
= (2) Annis BAYFORD
David ASHLEY
= Hannah GLOVER
Mary ASHLEY
= John ROOT (III)
Thomas CHANDLER
= Hannah BREWER
William CHANDLER
= Mary DANE
Mary ROOT
= John SMITH Jr.
Henry CHANDLER
= Lydia ABBOTT
Hannah CHANDLER
= Nathaniel ROBBINS Jr.
Abigail ASHLEY
= Nathaniel LEWIS
John SMITH (III)
= Elizabeth SMITH
Isaac CHANDLER
= Abigail HALE
Thomas ROBBINS
= Ruth JOHNSON
Israel SMITH = Abigail CHANDLER
Abigail LEWIS
= Joseph LYMAN
Chloe SMITH = Rutherford HAYES
Nathaniel ROBBINS
= Elizabeth HUTCHINSON
Rutherford HAYES Jr. = Sophia BIRCHARD
Rutherford Birchard HAYES
1822-1893
19th U.S. President
= Lucy Ware WEBB
Joseph LYMAN Jr.
= Mary SHELDON
Edward Hutchinson ROBBINS
= Elizabeth MURRAY
Joseph LYMAN (III) = Anne Jean ROBBINS
Catherine Robbins LYMAN = Warren DELANO Jr.
Sara DELANO = James ROOSEVELT
Franklin Delano ROOSEVELT
1882-1945
32nd U.S. President
= (Anna) Eleanor ROOSEVELT

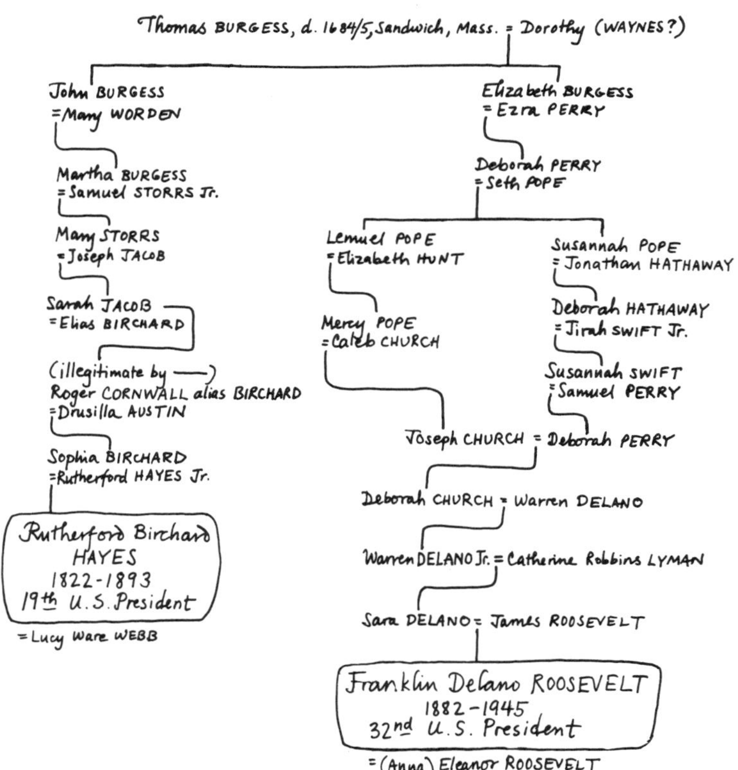
Thomas BURGESS, d. 1684/5, Sandwich, Mass. = Dorothy (WAYNES?)
John BURGESS
=Mary WORDEN
Elizabeth BURGESS
= Ezra PERRY
Martha BURGESS
= Samuel STORRS Jr.
Deborah PERRY
= Seth POPE
Mary STORRS
= Joseph JACOB
Lemuel POPE
= Elizabeth HUNT
Susannah POPE
= Jonathan HATHAWAY
Sarah JACOB
= Elias BIRCHARD
Mercy POPE
= Caleb CHURCH
Deborah HATHAWAY
= Jirah SWIFT Jr.
(illegitimate by —)
Roger CORNWALL alias BIRCHARD
= Drusilla AUSTIN
Susannah SWIFT
= Samuel PERRY
Joseph CHURCH = Deborah PERRY
Sophia BIRCHARD
= Rutherford HAYES Jr.
Deborah CHURCH = Warren DELANO
Rutherford Birchard HAYES 1822-1893 19th U.S. President
= Lucy Ware WEBB
Warren DELANO Jr. = Catherine Robbins LYMAN
Sara DELANO = James ROOSEVELT
Franklin Delano ROOSEVELT 1882-1945 32nd U.S. President
= (Anna) Eleanor ROOSEVELT

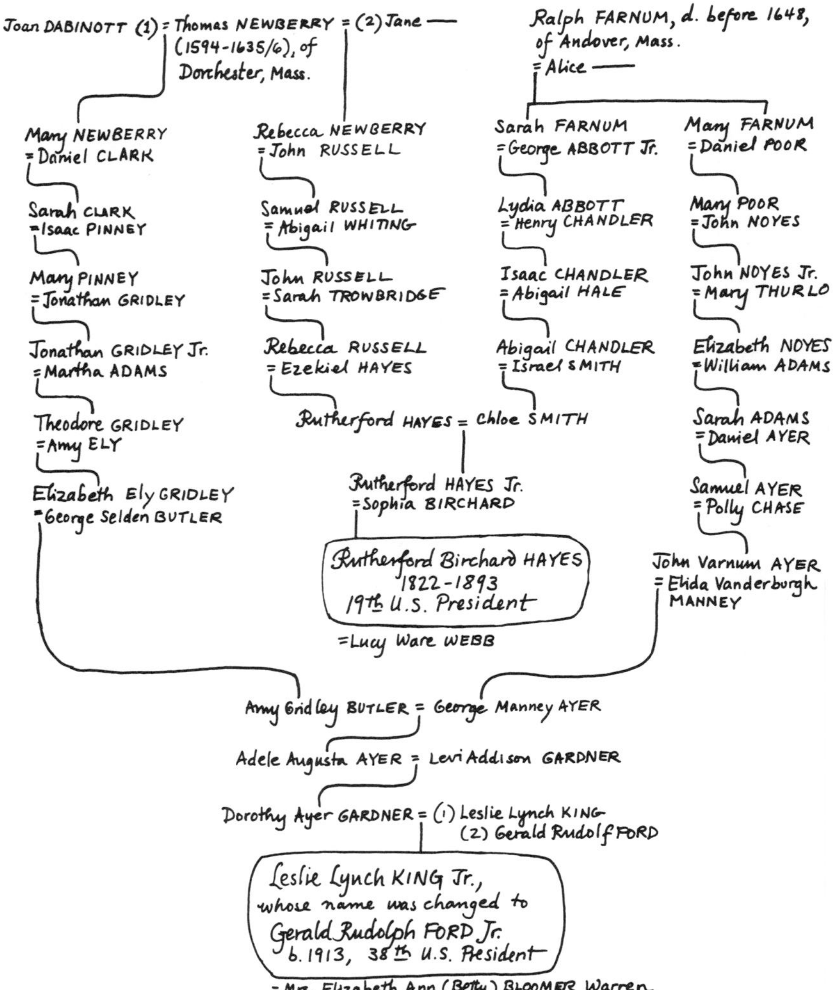
Joan DABINOTT (1) = Thomas NEWBERRY = (2) Jane ——
(1594-1635/6), of
Dorchester, Mass.
Ralph FARNUM, d. before 1648,
of Andover, Mass.
= Alice ——
Mary NEWBERRY
= Daniel CLARK
Rebecca NEWBERRY
= John RUSSELL
Sarah FARNUM
= George ABBOTT Jr.
Mary FARNUM
= Daniel POOR
Sarah CLARK
= Isaac PINNEY
Samuel RUSSELL
= Abigail WHITING
Lydia ABBOTT
= Henry CHANDLER
Mary POOR
= John NOYES
Mary PINNEY
= Jonathan GRIDLEY
John RUSSELL
= Sarah TROWBRIDGE
Isaac CHANDLER
= Abigail HALE
John NOYES Jr.
= Mary THURLO
Jonathan GRIDLEY Jr.
= Martha ADAMS
Rebecca RUSSELL
= Ezekiel HAYES
Abigail CHANDLER
= Israel SMITH
Elizabeth NOYES
= William ADAMS
Theodore GRIDLEY
= Amy ELY
Rutherford HAYES = Chloe SMITH
Sarah ADAMS
= Daniel AYER
Elizabeth Ely GRIDLEY
= George Selden BUTLER
Rutherford HAYES Jr.
= Sophia BIRCHARD
Samuel AYER
= Polly CHASE
Rutherford Birchard HAYES
1822-1893
19th U.S. President
= Lucy Ware WEBB
John Varnum AYER
= Elida Vanderburgh
MANNEY
Amy Gridley BUTLER = George Manney AYER
Adele Augusta AYER = Levi Addison GARDNER
Dorothy Ayer GARDNER = (1) Leslie Lynch KING
(2) Gerald Rudolf FORD
Leslie Lynch KING Jr.,
whose name was changed to
Gerald Rudolph FORD Jr.
b. 1913, 38th U.S. President
= Mrs. Elizabeth Ann (Betty) BLOOMER Warren

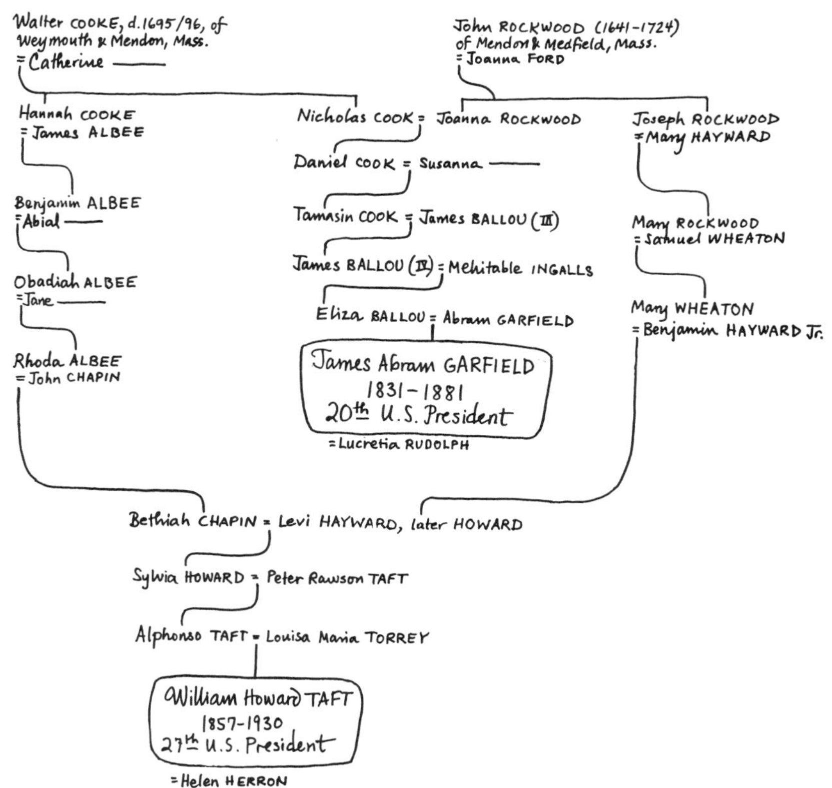
Walter COOKE, d.1695/96, of Weymouth & Mendon, Mass.
= Catherine ——
John ROCKWOOD (1641-1724) of Mendon & Medfield, Mass.
= Joanna FORD
Hannah COOKE
= James ALBEE
Nicholas COOK = Joanna ROCKWOOD
Joseph ROCKWOOD
= Mary HAYWARD
Daniel COOK = Susanna ——
Benjamin ALBEE
= Abial ——
Tamasin COOK = James BALLOU (III)
Mary ROCKWOOD
= Samuel WHEATON
James BALLOU (IV) = Mehitable INGALLS
Obadiah ALBEE
= Jane ——
Eliza BALLOU = Abram GARFIELD
Mary WHEATON
= Benjamin HAYWARD Jr.
Rhoda ALBEE
= John CHAPIN
James Abram GARFIELD
1831-1881
20th U.S. President
= Lucretia RUDOLPH
Bethiah CHAPIN = Levi HAYWARD, later HOWARD
Sylvia HOWARD = Peter Rawson TAFT
Alphonso TAFT = Louisa Maria TORREY
William Howard TAFT
1857-1930
27th U.S. President
= Helen HERRON

Benjamin CARPENTER (1658-1727) of Swansea, Mass.
= Renew WEEKS

Jotham CARPENTER
= Desire MARTIN

Jotham CARPENTER Jr.
= Mehitable THOMPSON

Sybil CARPENTER
= Henry INGALLS

Mehitable INGALLS
= James BALLOU (IV)

Eliza BALLOU
= Abram GARFIELD

James Abram GARFIELD
1821-1881
20th U.S. President

= Lucretia RUDOLPH

Keziah CARPENTER
= Thomas HORTON

Submit HORTON
= Jeremiah WHEELER

Jarvis WHEELER
= Sarah HORTON

Levi PIERCE
= Betsey S. WHEELER

Elizabeth Slade PIERCE
= Courtland Philip Livingston BUTLER

Mary Elizabeth BUTLER
= Robert Emmet SHELDON

Flora SHELDON
= Samuel Prescott BUSH

Prescott Sheldon BUSH
= Dorothy WALKER

George Herbert Walker BUSH
b.1924
41st U.S. President

= Barbara PIERCE

Samuel WRIGHT, d. 1665, Northampton, Mass. = Margaret ——

(probably) Hannah WRIGHT
= Thomas STEBBINS

Edward STEBBINS
= Sarah GRAVES

Thomas STEBBINS
= Mary ELY

Ruth STEBBINS
= Samuel HITCHCOCK

Margaret HITCHCOCK
= Richard FALLEY Jr.

Margaret FALLEY
= William CLEVELAND

Richard Falley CLEVELAND
= Anne NEAL

Stephen Grover CLEVELAND
1837-1908
22nd & 24th U.S. President

= Frances FOLSOM

Hester WRIGHT
= Samuel MARSHFIELD

Sarah MARSHFIELD
= William HOLTON Jr.

Mary HOLTON
= Ebenezer STRONG Jr.

Mary STRONG
= Benjamin SHELDON

Mary SHELDON
= Joseph LYMAN Jr.

Joseph LYMAN (III)
= Anne Jean ROBBINS

Catherine Robbins LYMAN
= Warren DELANO Jr.

Sara DELANO
= James ROOSEVELT

Franklin Delano ROOSEVELT
1882-1945
32nd U.S. President

= (Anna) Eleanor ROOSEVELT

Henry SEWALL Jr. (1615-1700) of Newbury, Mass.
=Jane DUMMER

Stephen SEWALL
=Margaret MITCHELL

Susanna SEWALL
=Aaron PORTER

Susanna PORTER
=Aaron CLEVELAND (III)

Aaron CLEVELAND (IV)
=Abiah HYDE

William CLEVELAND
=Margaret FALLEY

Richard Falley CLEVELAND
=Anne NEAL

Stephen Grover CLEVELAND
1837-1908
22nd & 24th U.S. President

=Frances FOLSOM

Anne SEWALL
=William LONGFELLOW

Anne LONGFELLOW
=Abraham ADAMS Jr.

William ADAMS
=Elizabeth NOYES

Sarah ADAMS
=Daniel AYER

Samuel AYER
=Polly CHASE

John Varnum AYER
=Elida Vanderburgh MANNEY

George Manney AYER
=Amy Gridley BUTLER

Adele Augusta AYER
=Levi Addison GARDNER

Dorothy Ayer GARDNER
=(1) Leslie Lynch KING
(2) Gerald Rudolf FORD

Leslie Lynch KING Jr.,
whose name was changed to
Gerald Rudolph FORD Jr.,
b. 1913
38th U.S. President

=Mrs. Elizabeth Ann (Betty) BLOOMER Warren

John STANLEY of Ashford, Kent, England = (1590) Susan LANCOCK

Thomas STANLEY (1597-1663) of Hartford, Conn. and Hadley, Mass.
= Bennett TRITTON

Hannah STANLEY = Samuel PORTER

Samuel PORTER Jr. = Joanna COOKE

Aaron PORTER = Susanna SEWALL

Susanna PORTER = Aaron CLEVELAND (III)

Aaron CLEVELAND (IV) = Abiah HYDE

William CLEVELAND = Margaret FALLEY

Richard Falley CLEVELAND = Anne NEAL

(Stephen) Grover CLEVELAND
1837-1908
22nd and 24th U.S. President
= Frances FOLSOM

Timothy STANLEY (1599/1600-1648) of Hartford, Conn.
= Elizabeth ———

Elizabeth STANLEY = Mark ST. JOHN

Sarah ST. JOHN = Samuel KEELER

Joseph KEELER = Elizabeth WHITNEY

Elijah KEELER = Sarah ———

Rebecca KEELER = Lemuel BANGS

Elijah Keeler BANGS = Esther STACKHOUSE

Mary Anne BANGS = Joseph Ambrose BEAKY

Martha Adela BEAKY = David Davis WALKER

George Herbert WALKER = Lucretia WEAR

Dorothy WALKER = Prescott Sheldon BUSH

George Herbert Walker BUSH
b. 1924
41st U.S. President
= Barbara PIERCE

Barnabas WINES, Jr. (c.1636 – c.1711) of Southold, L.I. = Mary ——

Sarah WINES
= Barnabas HORTON

Caleb HORTON
= Phebe TERRY

Phoebe HORTON
= Henry TUTHILL (III)

Anna TUTHILL
= John Cleves SYMMES

Anna Tuthill SYMMES
= William Henry HARRISON
1773-1841, 9th U.S. President

John Scott HARRISON
= Elizabeth Ramsey IRWIN

Benjamin HARRISON
1833-1901
23rd U.S. President

= (1) Caroline Lavinia SCOTT
(2) Mrs. Mary Scott LORD Dimmick

Samuel WINES
= Abigail ——

(probably) Ann WINES
= John MANY or MANNEY

Wines MANNEY
= Alida VANDERBURGH

John MANNEY
= Elizabeth COLLINS

Elida Vanderburgh MANNEY
= John Varnum AYER

George Manney AYER
= Amy Gridley BUTLER

Adele Augusta AYER
= Levi Addison GARDNER

Dorothy Ayer GARDNER
= (1) Leslie Lynch KING
(2) Gerald Rudolf FORD

Leslie Lynch KING, Jr.,
whose name was changed to
Gerald Rudolph FORD, Jr.
b. 1913
38th U.S. President

= Mrs. Elizabeth Ann (Betty) BLOOMER Warren

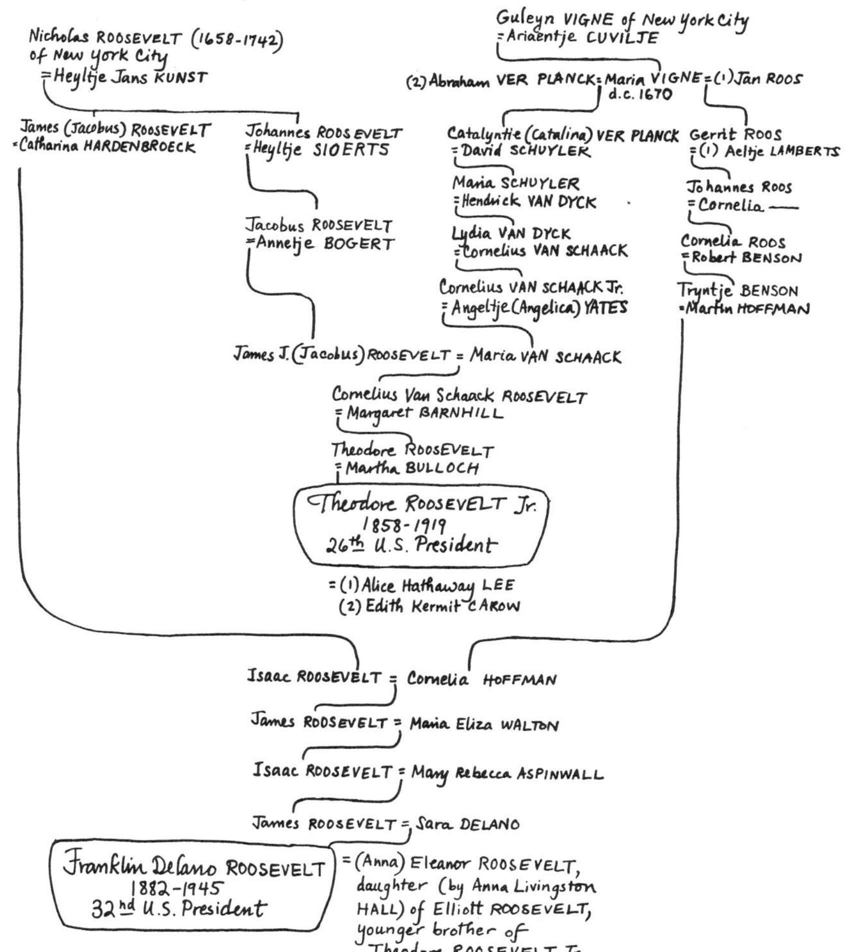

Nicholas ROOSEVELT (1658-1742)
of New York City
=Heyltje Jans KUNST
Guleyn VIGNE of New York City
=Ariaentje CUVILJE
(2) Abraham VER PLANCK = Maria VIGNE = (1) Jan ROOS
d.c. 1670
James (Jacobus) ROOSEVELT
=Catharina HARDENBROECK
Johannes ROOSEVELT
=Heyltje SIOERTS
Catalyntie (Catalina) VER PLANCK
=David SCHUYLER
Gerrit ROOS
=(1) Aeltje LAMBERTS
Maria SCHUYLER
=Hendrick VAN DYCK
Johannes ROOS
=Cornelia —
Jacobus ROOSEVELT
=Annetje BOGERT
Lydia VAN DYCK
=Cornelius VAN SCHAACK
Cornelia ROOS
=Robert BENSON
Cornelius VAN SCHAACK Jr.
=Angeltje (Angelica) YATES
Tryntje BENSON
=Martin HOFFMAN
James J. (Jacobus) ROOSEVELT = Maria VAN SCHAACK
Cornelius Van Schaack ROOSEVELT
=Margaret BARNHILL
Theodore ROOSEVELT
=Martha BULLOCH
Theodore ROOSEVELT Jr.
1858-1919
26th U.S. President
=(1) Alice Hathaway LEE
(2) Edith Kermit CAROW
Isaac ROOSEVELT = Cornelia HOFFMAN
James ROOSEVELT = Maria Eliza WALTON
Isaac ROOSEVELT = Mary Rebecca ASPINWALL
James ROOSEVELT = Sara DELANO
Franklin Delano ROOSEVELT
1882-1945
32nd U.S. President
=(Anna) Eleanor ROOSEVELT, daughter (by Anna Livingston HALL) of Elliott ROOSEVELT, younger brother of Theodore ROOSEVELT Jr., above.

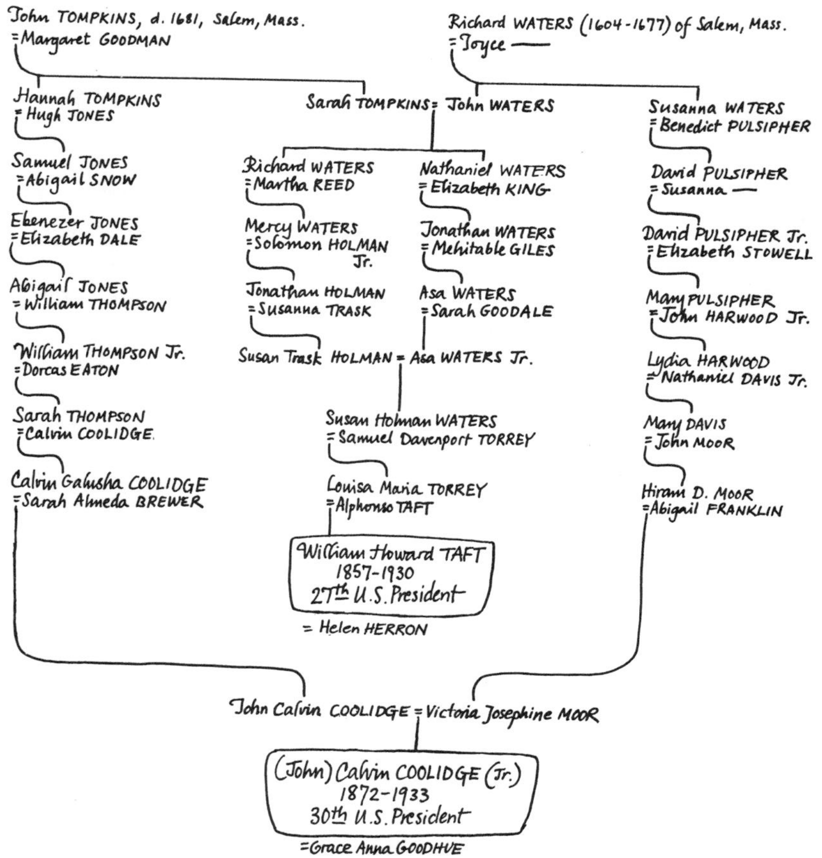
John TOMPKINS, d. 1681, Salem, Mass.
=Margaret GOODMAN
Richard WATERS (1604-1677) of Salem, Mass.
=Joyce —
Hannah TOMPKINS
=Hugh JONES
Sarah TOMPKINS = John WATERS
Susanna WATERS
=Benedict PULSIPHER
Samuel JONES
=Abigail SNOW
Richard WATERS
=Martha REED
Nathaniel WATERS
=Elizabeth KING
David PULSIPHER
=Susanna —
Ebenezer JONES
=Elizabeth DALE
Mercy WATERS
=Solomon HOLMAN Jr.
Jonathan WATERS
=Mehitable GILES
David PULSIPHER Jr.
=Elizabeth STOWELL
Abigail JONES
=William THOMPSON
Jonathan HOLMAN
=Susanna TRASK
Asa WATERS
=Sarah GOODALE
Mary PULSIPHER
=John HARWOOD Jr.
William THOMPSON Jr.
=Dorcas EATON
Susan Trask HOLMAN = Asa WATERS Jr.
Lydia HARWOOD
=Nathaniel DAVIS Jr.
Sarah THOMPSON
=Calvin COOLIDGE
Susan Holman WATERS
=Samuel Davenport TORREY
Mary DAVIS
=John MOOR
Calvin Galusha COOLIDGE
=Sarah Almeda BREWER
Louisa Maria TORREY
=Alphonso TAFT
Hiram D. MOOR
=Abigail FRANKLIN
William Howard TAFT
1857-1930
27th U.S. President
= Helen HERRON
John Calvin COOLIDGE = Victoria Josephine MOOR
(John) Calvin COOLIDGE (Jr.)
1872-1933
30th U.S. President
=Grace Anna GOODHUE

William TRASK, d. 1666, Salem, Mass. = Sarah —

William TRASK Jr.
= Anna —

John TRASK
= Hannah OSBORN

Samuel TRASK
= Anna BOND

Susanna TRASK
= Jonathan HOLMAN

Susan Trask HOLMAN
= Asa WATERS Jr.

Susan Holman WATERS
= Samuel Davenport TORREY

Louisa Maria TORREY
= Alphonso TAFT

William Howard TAFT
1857-1930
27th U.S. President
= Helen HERRON

Sarah TRASK
= Elias PARKMAN Jr.

William PARKMAN
= Elizabeth ADAMS

John PARKMAN
= Abigail FAIRFIELD

Esther PARKMAN
= Adam BROWN

Adam BROWN Jr.
= Priscilla PUTNAM

Israel Putnam BROWN
= Sally BRIGGS

Sally BROWN
= Israel C. BREWER

Sarah Almeda BREWER
= Calvin Galusha COOLIDGE

John Calvin COOLIDGE
= Victoria Josephine MOOR

(John) Calvin COOLIDGE (Jr.)
1872-1933
30th U.S. President
= Grace Anna GOODHUE

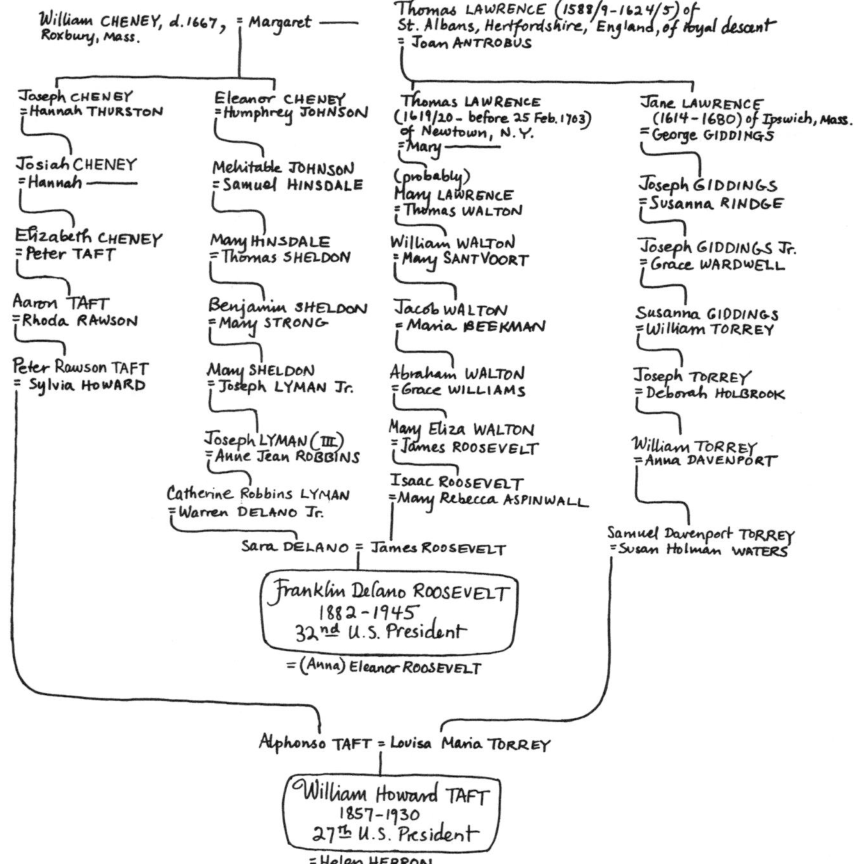
William CHENEY, d. 1667, Roxbury, Mass. = Margaret ——
Thomas LAWRENCE (1588/9-1624/5) of St. Albans, Hertfordshire, England, of royal descent = Joan ANTROBUS
Joseph CHENEY = Hannah THURSTON
Eleanor CHENEY = Humphrey JOHNSON
Thomas LAWRENCE (1619/20 - before 25 Feb. 1703) of Newtown, N.Y. = Mary ——
Jane LAWRENCE (1614-1680) of Ipswich, Mass. = George GIDDINGS
Josiah CHENEY = Hannah ——
Mehitable JOHNSON = Samuel HINSDALE
(probably) Mary LAWRENCE = Thomas WALTON
Joseph GIDDINGS = Susanna RINDGE
Elizabeth CHENEY = Peter TAFT
Mary HINSDALE = Thomas SHELDON
William WALTON = Mary SANTVOORT
Joseph GIDDINGS Jr. = Grace WARDWELL
Aaron TAFT = Rhoda RAWSON
Benjamin SHELDON = Mary STRONG
Jacob WALTON = Maria BEEKMAN
Susanna GIDDINGS = William TORREY
Peter Rawson TAFT = Sylvia HOWARD
Mary SHELDON = Joseph LYMAN Jr.
Abraham WALTON = Grace WILLIAMS
Joseph TORREY = Deborah HOLBROOK
Joseph LYMAN (III) = Anne Jean ROBBINS
Mary Eliza WALTON = James ROOSEVELT
William TORREY = Anna DAVENPORT
Catherine Robbins LYMAN = Warren DELANO Jr.
Isaac ROOSEVELT = Mary Rebecca ASPINWALL
Samuel Davenport TORREY = Susan Holman WATERS
Sara DELANO = James ROOSEVELT
Franklin Delano ROOSEVELT 1882-1945 32nd U.S. President
= (Anna) Eleanor ROOSEVELT
Alphonso TAFT = Louisa Maria TORREY
William Howard TAFT 1857-1930 27th U.S. President
= Helen HERRON

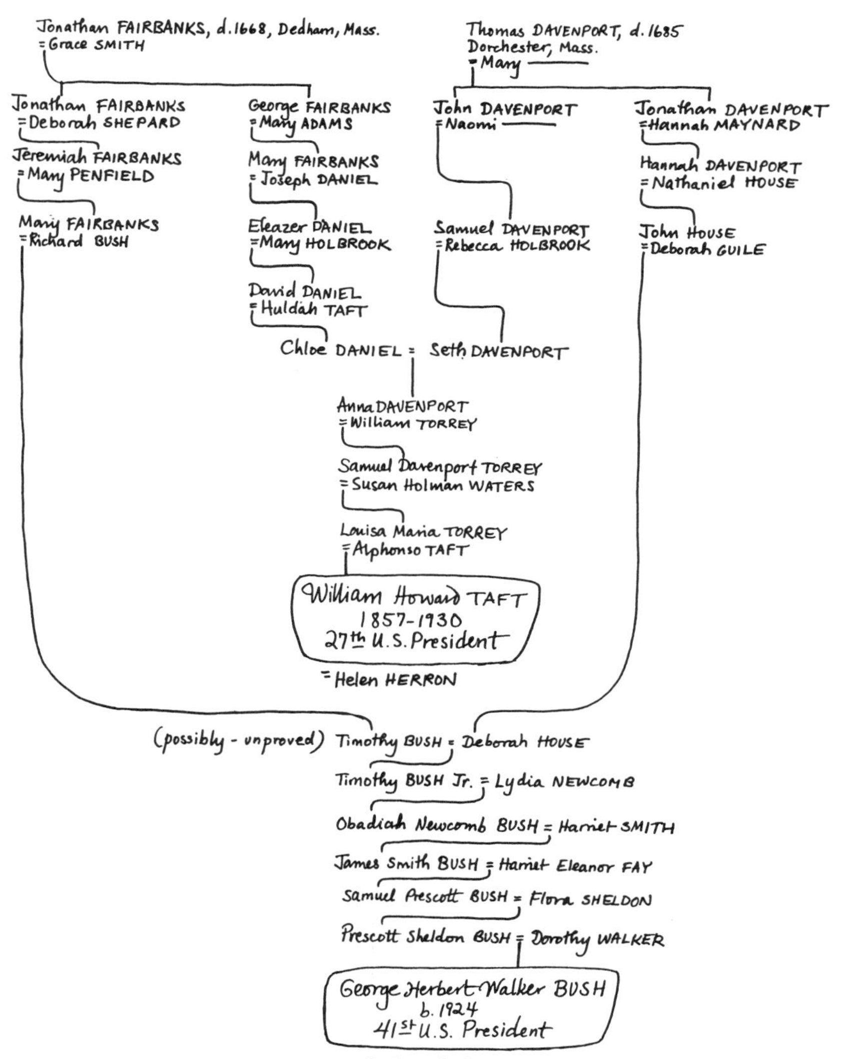
Jonathan FAIRBANKS, d. 1668, Dedham, Mass.
= Grace SMITH
Thomas DAVENPORT, d. 1685
Dorchester, Mass.
= Mary ——
Jonathan FAIRBANKS
= Deborah SHEPARD
George FAIRBANKS
= Mary ADAMS
John DAVENPORT
= Naomi ——
Jonathan DAVENPORT
= Hannah MAYNARD
Jeremiah FAIRBANKS
= Mary PENFIELD
Mary FAIRBANKS
= Joseph DANIEL
Hannah DAVENPORT
= Nathaniel HOUSE
Mary FAIRBANKS
= Richard BUSH
Eleazer DANIEL
= Mary HOLBROOK
Samuel DAVENPORT
= Rebecca HOLBROOK
John HOUSE
= Deborah GUILE
David DANIEL
= Huldah TAFT
Chloe DANIEL = Seth DAVENPORT
Anna DAVENPORT
= William TORREY
Samuel Davenport TORREY
= Susan Holman WATERS
Louisa Maria TORREY
= Alphonso TAFT
William Howard TAFT
1857-1930
27th U.S. President
= Helen HERRON
(possibly - unproved) Timothy BUSH = Deborah HOUSE
Timothy BUSH Jr. = Lydia NEWCOMB
Obadiah Newcomb BUSH = Harriet SMITH
James Smith BUSH = Harriet Eleanor FAY
Samuel Prescott BUSH = Flora SHELDON
Prescott Sheldon BUSH = Dorothy WALKER
George Herbert Walker BUSH
b. 1924
41st U.S. President
= Barbara PIERCE

Mary —— (2) = Experience MITCHELL, d. 1689 = (1) Jane COOKE, daughter of Mayflower passenger Francis COOKE
Bridgewater, Mass.

By (2) Mary:

Sarah MITCHELL
= John HAYWARD

Elizabeth HAYWARD
= Edmund RAWSON

Abner RAWSON
= Mary ALLEN

Rhoda RAWSON
= Aaron TAFT

Peter Rawson TAFT
= Sylvia HOWARD

Alphonso TAFT
= Louisa Maria TORREY

William Howard TAFT
1857-1930
27th U.S. President

= Helen HERRON

By (1) Jane COOKE:

Elizabeth MITCHELL
= John WASHBURN Jr.

Mary WASHBURN
= Samuel KINGSLEY Jr.

Samuel KINGSLEY (III)
= Mary ——

Silence KINGSLEY
= Samuel HERRICK

(alleged & likely, but further proof required)

Sarah HERRICK
= Nathaniel BUTLER

Samuel Herrick BUTLER
= Judith LIVINGSTON

Courtland Philip Livingston BUTLER
= Elizabeth Slade PIERCE

Mary Elizabeth BUTLER
= Robert Emmet SHELDON

Flora SHELDON
= Samuel Prescott BUSH

Prescott Sheldon BUSH
= Dorothy WALKER

George Herbert Walker BUSH
b. 1924
41st U.S. President

= Barbara PIERCE

Michael PIERCE, d. 1676, Scituate, Mass. =(1) (Persis?) EAMES

Mary PIERCE
=Samuel HOLBROOK

Mary HOLBROOK
=Eleazer DANIEL

David DANIEL
=Huldah TAFT

Chloe DANIEL
=Seth DAVENPORT

Anna DAVENPORT
=William TORREY

Samuel Davenport TORREY
=Susan Holman WATERS

Louisa Maria TORREY
=Alphonso TAFT

William Howard TAFT
1857-1930
27th U.S. President
=Helen HERRON

Ephraim PIERCE = Hannah HOLBROOK

Ephraim PIERCE Jr. = Mary LOW

Mial PIERCE = Judith ROUND

Nathan PIERCE = Lydia MARTIN

Isaac PIERCE = Anna FITCH

Levi PIERCE = Betsey S. WHEELER

Elizabeth Slade PIERCE
=Courtland Philip Livingston BUTLER

Mary Elizabeth BUTLER
=Robert Emmet SHELDON

Flora SHELDON = Samuel Prescott BUSH

Prescott Sheldon BUSH = Dorothy WALKER

George Herbert Walker BUSH
b. 1924
41st U.S. President
=Barbara PIERCE

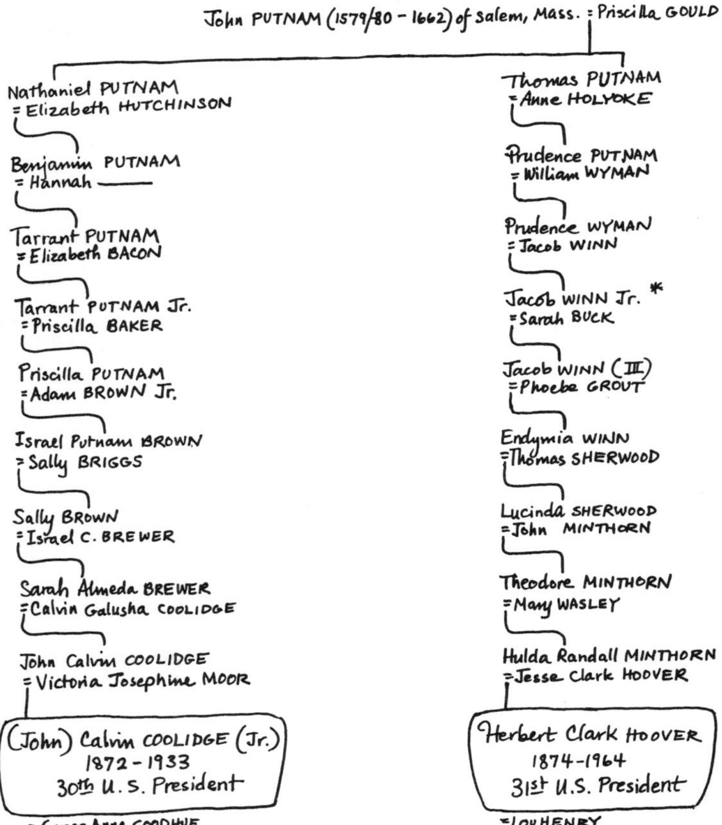

John PUTNAM (1579/80 - 1662) of Salem, Mass. = Priscilla GOULD
Nathaniel PUTNAM
= Elizabeth HUTCHINSON
Benjamin PUTNAM
= Hannah ———
Tarrant PUTNAM
= Elizabeth BACON
Tarrant PUTNAM Jr.
= Priscilla BAKER
Priscilla PUTNAM
= Adam BROWN Jr.
Israel Putnam BROWN
= Sally BRIGGS
Sally BROWN
= Israel C. BREWER
Sarah Almeda BREWER
= Calvin Galusha COOLIDGE
John Calvin COOLIDGE
= Victoria Josephine MOOR
(John) Calvin COOLIDGE (Jr.)
1872 - 1933
30th U.S. President
= Grace Anna GOODHUE
Thomas PUTNAM
= Anne HOLYOKE
Prudence PUTNAM
= William WYMAN
Prudence WYMAN
= Jacob WINN
Jacob WINN Jr. *
= Sarah BUCK
Jacob WINN (III)
= Phoebe GROUT
Endymia WINN
= Thomas SHERWOOD
Lucinda SHERWOOD
= John MINTHORN
Theodore MINTHORN
= Mary WASLEY
Hulda Randall MINTHORN
= Jesse Clark HOOVER
Herbert Clark HOOVER
1874-1964
31st U.S. President
= Lou HENRY

* The parentage of Jacob WINN (Jr.?), husband of Sarah BUCK, is subject to doubt.

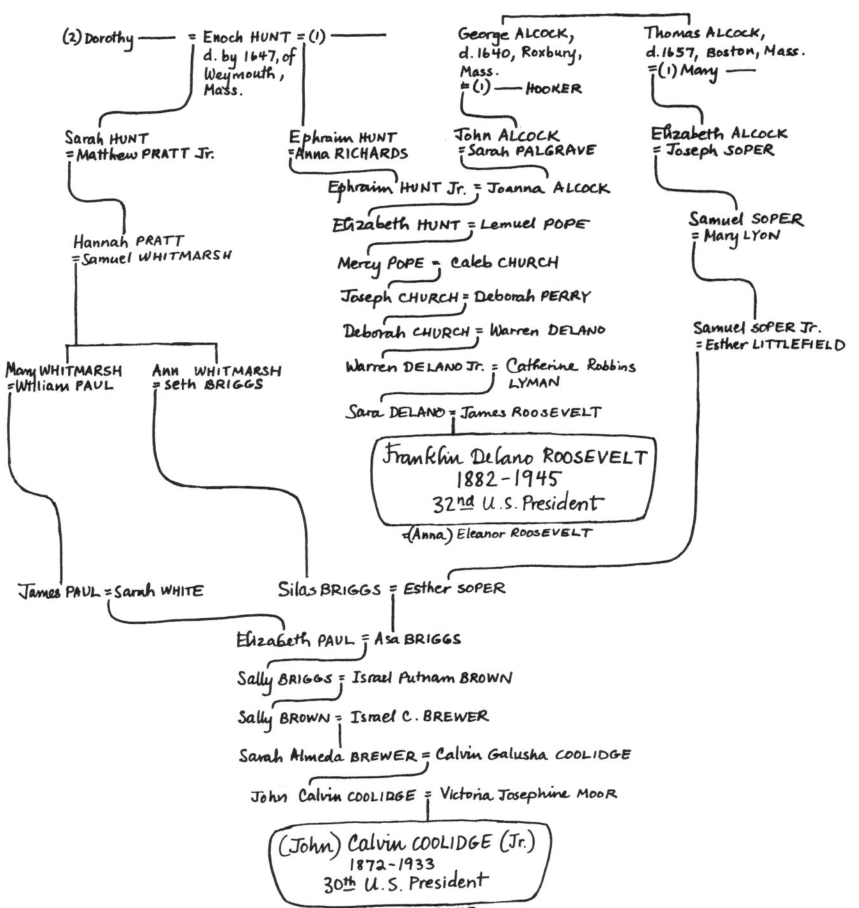
(2) Dorothy — = Enoch HUNT = (1) —
d. by 1647, of Weymouth, Mass.
George ALCOCK, d. 1640, Roxbury, Mass. = (1) — HOOKER
Thomas ALCOCK, d. 1657, Boston, Mass. = (1) Mary —
Sarah HUNT = Matthew PRATT Jr.
Ephraim HUNT = Anna RICHARDS
John ALCOCK = Sarah PALGRAVE
Elizabeth ALCOCK = Joseph SOPER
Ephraim HUNT Jr. = Joanna ALCOCK
Elizabeth HUNT = Lemuel POPE
Samuel SOPER = Mary LYON
Hannah PRATT = Samuel WHITMARSH
Mercy POPE = Caleb CHURCH
Joseph CHURCH = Deborah PERRY
Deborah CHURCH = Warren DELANO
Samuel SOPER Jr. = Esther LITTLEFIELD
Mary WHITMARSH = William PAUL
Ann WHITMARSH = Seth BRIGGS
Warren DELANO Jr. = Catherine Robbins LYMAN
Sara DELANO = James ROOSEVELT
Franklin Delano ROOSEVELT
1882-1945
32nd U.S. President
= (Anna) Eleanor ROOSEVELT
James PAUL = Sarah WHITE
Silas BRIGGS = Esther SOPER
Elizabeth PAUL = Asa BRIGGS
Sally BRIGGS = Israel Putnam BROWN
Sally BROWN = Israel C. BREWER
Sarah Almeda BREWER = Calvin Galusha COOLIDGE
John Calvin COOLIDGE = Victoria Josephine MOOR
(John) Calvin COOLIDGE (Jr.)
1872-1933
30th U.S. President
= Grace Anna GOODHUE

Peter COFFIN of Brixton, Devon, England = Joan KEMBER

Mary COFFIN
= Alexander ADAMS, d. 1677, Boston, Mass.

Elizabeth ADAMS
= William PARKMAN

John PARKMAN
= Abigail FAIRFIELD

Esther PARKMAN
= Adam BROWN

Adam BROWN Jr.
= Priscilla PUTNAM

Israel Putnam BROWN
= Sally BRIGGS

Sally BROWN
= Israel C. BREWER

Sarah Almeda BREWER
= Calvin Galusha COOLIDGE

John Calvin COOLIDGE
= Victoria Josephine MOOR

(John) Calvin COOLIDGE (Jr.)
1872-1933
30th U.S. President

= Grace Anna GOODHUE

Tristram COFFIN (1609/10-1681)
of Haverhill & Nantucket, Mass.
= Dionis STEVENS

Tristram COFFIN Jr. = Judith GREENLEAF

Mary COFFIN
= Joseph LITTLE

Daniel LITTLE
= Abiah CLEMENT

Sarah LITTLE
= William AYER

Daniel AYER
= Sarah ADAMS

Judith COFFIN
= John SANBORN Jr.

Judith SANBORN
= Ebenezer GOVE

Edward GOVE
= Bethiah CLARK

Nathaniel GOVE
= Susanna STICKNEY

Abigail GOVE
= William CHASE

Samuel AYER = Polly CHASE

John Varnum AYER
= Elida Vandeburgh MANNEY

George Manney AYER
= Amy Gridley BUTLER

Adele Augusta AYER
= Levi Addison GARDNER

Dorothy Ayer GARDNER
= (1) Leslie Lynch KING
(2) Gerald Rudolf FORD

Leslie Lynch KING, Jr.,
whose name was changed to
Gerald Rudolph FORD, Jr.
b. 1913
38th U.S. President

= Mrs. Elizabeth Ann (Betty) BLOOMER Warren

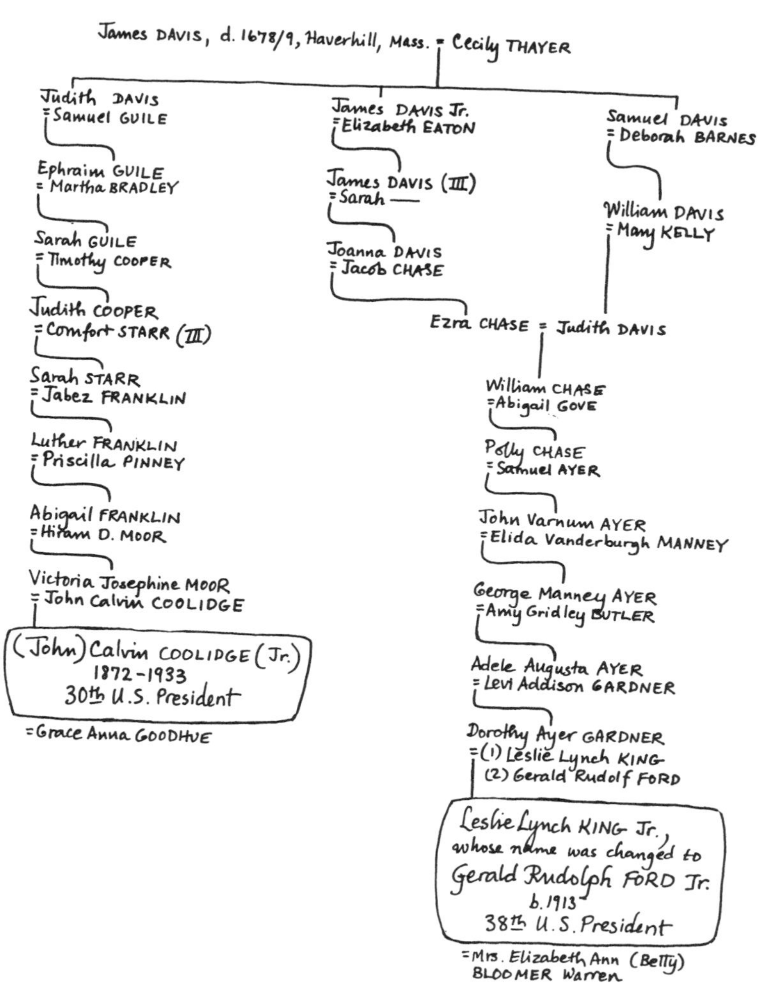
James DAVIS, d. 1678/9, Haverhill, Mass. = Cecily THAYER
Judith DAVIS
= Samuel GUILE
Ephraim GUILE
= Martha BRADLEY
Sarah GUILE
= Timothy COOPER
Judith COOPER
= Comfort STARR (III)
Sarah STARR
= Jabez FRANKLIN
Luther FRANKLIN
= Priscilla PINNEY
Abigail FRANKLIN
= Hiram D. MOOR
Victoria Josephine MOOR
= John Calvin COOLIDGE
(John) Calvin COOLIDGE (Jr.)
1872-1933
30th U.S. President
= Grace Anna GOODHUE
James DAVIS Jr.
= Elizabeth EATON
James DAVIS (III)
= Sarah —
Joanna DAVIS
= Jacob CHASE
Samuel DAVIS
= Deborah BARNES
William DAVIS
= Mary KELLY
Ezra CHASE = Judith DAVIS
William CHASE
= Abigail GOVE
Polly CHASE
= Samuel AYER
John Varnum AYER
= Elida Vanderburgh MANNEY
George Manney AYER
= Amy Gridley BUTLER
Adele Augusta AYER
= Levi Addison GARDNER
Dorothy Ayer GARDNER
= (1) Leslie Lynch KING
(2) Gerald Rudolf FORD
Leslie Lynch KING Jr.,
whose name was changed to
Gerald Rudolph FORD Jr.
b. 1913
38th U.S. President
= Mrs. Elizabeth Ann (Betty)
BLOOMER Warren

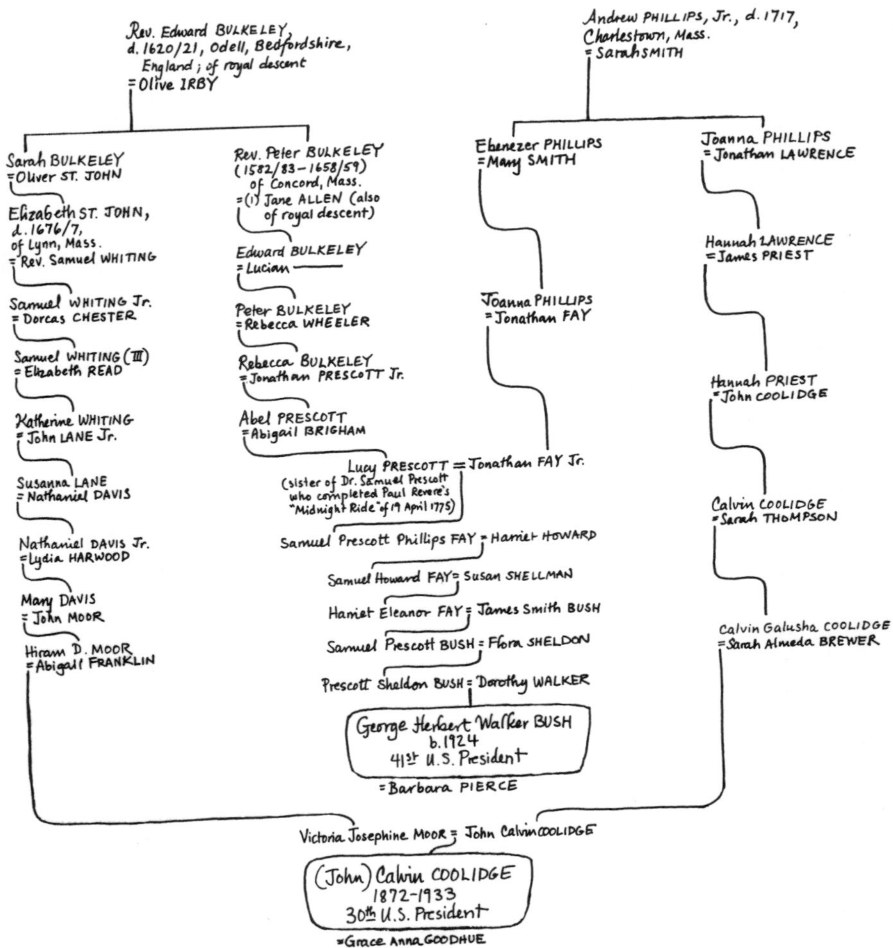
Rev. Edward BULKELEY, d. 1620/21, Odell, Bedfordshire, England; of royal descent
= Olive IRBY
Andrew PHILLIPS, Jr., d. 1717, Charlestown, Mass.
= Sarah SMITH
Sarah BULKELEY
= Oliver ST. JOHN
Rev. Peter BULKELEY (1582/83–1658/59) of Concord, Mass.
= (1) Jane ALLEN (also of royal descent)
Ebenezer PHILLIPS
= Mary SMITH
Joanna PHILLIPS
= Jonathan LAWRENCE
Elizabeth ST. JOHN, d. 1676/7, of Lynn, Mass.
= Rev. Samuel WHITING
Edward BULKELEY
= Lucian ——
Hannah LAWRENCE
= James PRIEST
Samuel WHITING Jr.
= Dorcas CHESTER
Peter BULKELEY
= Rebecca WHEELER
Joanna PHILLIPS
= Jonathan FAY
Samuel WHITING (III)
= Elizabeth READ
Rebecca BULKELEY
= Jonathan PRESCOTT Jr.
Hannah PRIEST
= John COOLIDGE
Katherine WHITING
= John LANE Jr.
Abel PRESCOTT
= Abigail BRIGHAM
Lucy PRESCOTT = Jonathan FAY Jr.
(sister of Dr. Samuel Prescott who completed Paul Revere's "Midnight Ride" of 19 April 1775)
Susanna LANE
= Nathaniel DAVIS
Calvin COOLIDGE
= Sarah THOMPSON
Nathaniel DAVIS Jr.
= Lydia HARWOOD
Samuel Prescott Phillips FAY = Harriet HOWARD
Samuel Howard FAY = Susan SHELLMAN
Mary DAVIS
= John MOOR
Harriet Eleanor FAY = James Smith BUSH
Calvin Galusha COOLIDGE
= Sarah Almeda BREWER
Hiram D. MOOR
= Abigail FRANKLIN
Samuel Prescott BUSH = Flora SHELDON
Prescott Sheldon BUSH = Dorothy WALKER
George Herbert Walker BUSH b. 1924 41st U.S. President
= Barbara PIERCE
Victoria Josephine MOOR = John Calvin COOLIDGE
(John) Calvin COOLIDGE 1872–1933 30th U.S. President
= Grace Anna GOODHUE

Thomas HORTON, d. ante 1715/6
Rehoboth, Mass.
= (1) Sarah (HARMON?)

John GARNSEY (c.1648-1722)
of Dorchester & Rehoboth, Mass.
= Elizabeth ——

Thomas HORTON Jr. = Hannah GARNSEY

Rachel HORTON = Philip FRANKLIN

Aaron FRANKLIN = Margaret ——

Jabez FRANKLIN = Sarah STARR

Luther FRANKLIN = Priscilla PINNEY

Abigail FRANKLIN = Hiram D. MOOR

Victoria Josephine MOOR = John Calvin COOLIDGE

(John) Calvin COOLIDGE (Jr.)
1872-1933, 30th U.S. President
= Grace Anna GOODHUE

John HORTON = Mehitable GARNSEY

Thomas HORTON = Keziah CARPENTER

Submit HORTON = Jeremiah WHEELER

Jonathan HORTON = Ann MILLARD

Comfort HORTON = Joanna WOOD

Jarvis WHEELER = Sarah HORTON

Betsey S. WHEELER = Levi PIERCE

Elizabeth Slade PIERCE = Courtland Philip Livingston BUTLER

Mary Elizabeth BUTLER = Robert Emmet SHELDON

Flora SHELDON = Samuel Prescott BUSH

Prescott Sheldon BUSH = Dorothy WALKER

George Herbert Walker BUSH
b. 1924
41st U.S. President
= Barbara PIERCE

Thomas LORD, d. 1667, of Hartford, Conn. = Dorothy BIRD

Amy LORD
= John GILBERT

Joseph GILBERT
= Elizabeth SMITH

Mary GILBERT
= William MINTHORN Jr.

William MINTHORN (III)
= Hannah ELDRIDGE

John MINTHORN
= Lucinda SHERWOOD

Theodore MINTHORN
= Mary WASLEY

Hulda Randall MINTHORN
= Jesse Clark HOOVER

Herbert Clark HOOVER
1874-1964
31st U.S. President

= Lou HENRY

William LORD
= ______

Richard LORD
= Elizabeth HYDE

Deborah LORD
= Nathan JEWETT

David JEWETT
= Sarah SELDEN

Elizabeth JEWETT
= Anselm COMSTOCK

Betsey COMSTOCK
= Daniel BUTLER

George Selden BUTLER
= Elizabeth Ely GRIDLEY

Amy Gridley BUTLER
= George Manney AYER

Adele Augusta AYER
= Levi Addison GARDNER

Dorothy Ayer GARDNER
= (1) Leslie Lynch KING
(2) Gerald Rudolf FORD

Leslie Lynch KING Jr.,
whose name was changed to
Gerald Rudolph FORD Jr.,
b. 1913
38th U.S. President

= Mrs. Elizabeth Ann (Betty) BLOOMER Warren

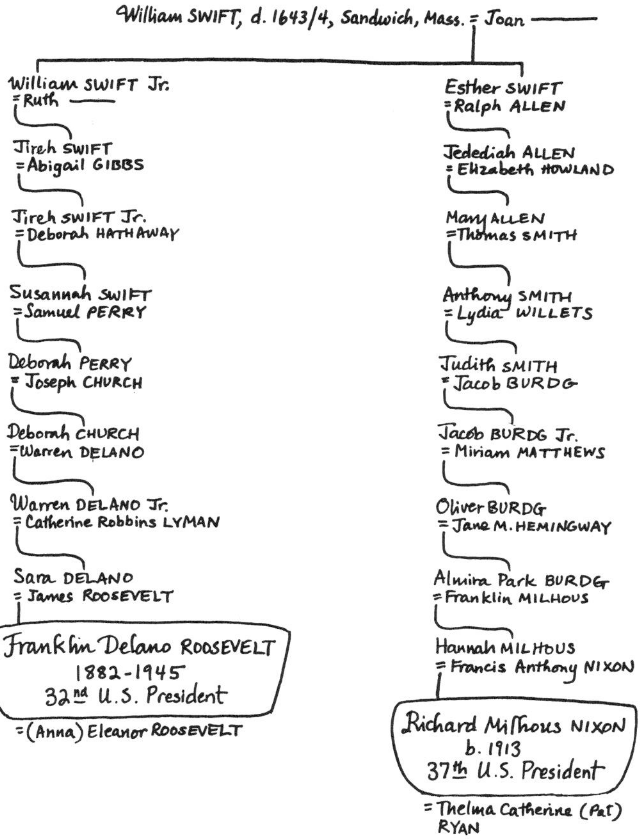
William SWIFT, d. 1643/4, Sandwich, Mass. = Joan ——
William SWIFT Jr.
= Ruth ——
Jireh SWIFT
= Abigail GIBBS
Jireh SWIFT Jr.
= Deborah HATHAWAY
Susannah SWIFT
= Samuel PERRY
Deborah PERRY
= Joseph CHURCH
Deborah CHURCH
= Warren DELANO
Warren DELANO Jr.
= Catherine Robbins LYMAN
Sara DELANO
= James ROOSEVELT
Franklin Delano ROOSEVELT
1882-1945
32nd U.S. President
= (Anna) Eleanor ROOSEVELT
Esther SWIFT
= Ralph ALLEN
Jedediah ALLEN
= Elizabeth HOWLAND
Mary ALLEN
= Thomas SMITH
Anthony SMITH
= Lydia WILLETS
Judith SMITH
= Jacob BURDG
Jacob BURDG Jr.
= Miriam MATTHEWS
Oliver BURDG
= Jane M. HEMINGWAY
Almira Park BURDG
= Franklin MILHOUS
Hannah MILHOUS
= Francis Anthony NIXON
Richard Milhous NIXON
b. 1913
37th U.S. President
= Thelma Catherine (Pat) RYAN

Henry HEAD, d. 1716, Little Compton, R.I. = Elizabeth ——

Innocent HEAD
= Nathaniel CHURCH

Caleb CHURCH
= Mercy POPE

Joseph CHURCH
= Deborah PERRY

Deborah CHURCH
= Warren DELANO

Warren DELANO Jr.
= Catherine Robbins LYMAN

Sara DELANO
= James ROOSEVELT

Franklin Delano ROOSEVELT
1882-1945
32nd U.S. President

= (Anna) Eleanor ROOSEVELT

Elizabeth HEAD
= Benjamin WILBUR

Meribah WILBUR
= Jonathan RICKETSON Jr.

Rhoda RICKETSON
= Hezekiah COLLINS Jr.

Elizabeth COLLINS
= John MANNEY

Elida Vanderburgh MANNEY
= John Varnum AYER

George Manney AYER
= Amy Gridley BUTLER

Adele Augusta AYER
= Levi Addison GARDNER

Dorothy Ayer GARDNER
= (1) Leslie Lynch KING
= (2) Gerald Rudolf FORD

Leslie Lynch KING Jr., whose name was changed to Gerald Rudolph FORD Jr.,
b. 1913
38th U.S. President

= Mrs. Elizabeth Ann (Betty) BLOOMER Warren

William HUTCHINSON = Anne MARBURY, of royal descent, killed 1643 by Indians
The noted religious reformer, "heretic" and a founder of Rhode Island

Edward HUTCHINSON = Catherine HAMBY, also of royal descent

Elizabeth CLARK (2nd wife) = Elisha HUTCHINSON = (1st wife) Hannah HAWKINS
(1641 – 1717) of
Boston, Mass.

Edward HUTCHINSON = Lydia FOSTER

Elizabeth HUTCHINSON = Nathaniel ROBBINS

Edward Hutchinson ROBBINS
= Elizabeth MURRAY

Anne Jean ROBBINS = Joseph LYMAN (III)

Catherine Robbins LYMAN = Warren DELANO Jr.

Sara DELANO = James ROOSEVELT

Franklin Delano ROOSEVELT
1882–1945
32nd U.S. President

=(Anna) Eleanor ROOSEVELT

Hannah HUTCHINSON = John RUCK

Hannah RUCK = Theophilus LILLIE

John LILLIE = Abigail BRECK

Anna LILLIE = Samuel HOWARD

Harriet HOWARD = Samuel Prescott Phillips FAY

Samuel Howard FAY = Susan SHELLMAN

Harriet Eleanor FAY = James Smith BUSH

Samuel Prescott BUSH = Flora SHELDON

Prescott Sheldon BUSH = Dorothy WALKER

George Herbert Walker BUSH
b. 1924
41st U.S. President

=Barbara PIERCE

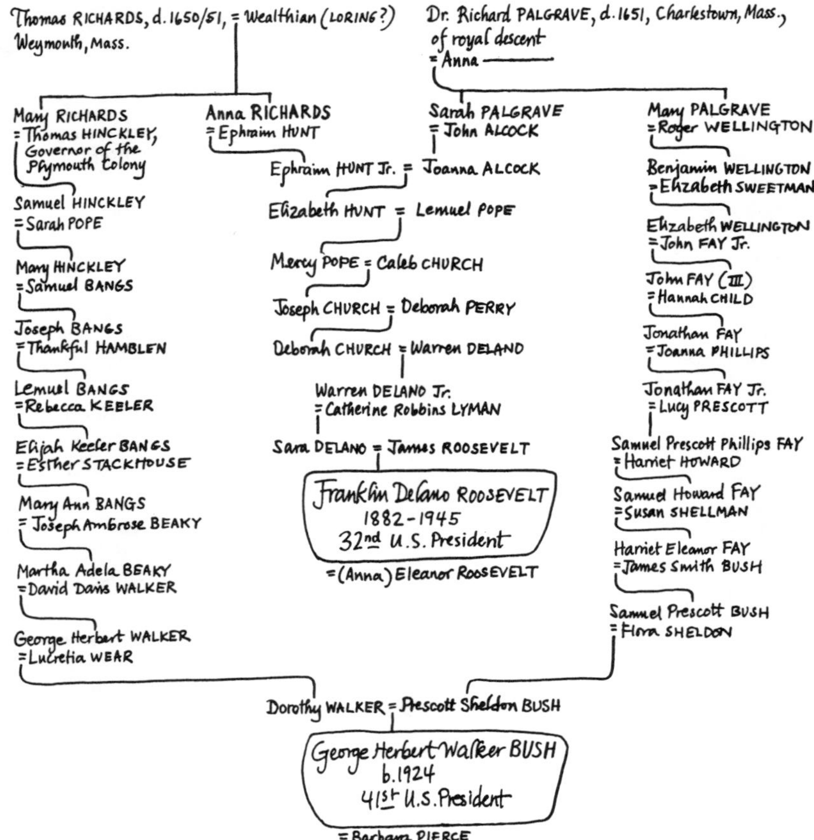

Thomas RICHARDS, d. 1650/51, = Wealthian (LORING?) Weymouth, Mass.
Dr. Richard PALGRAVE, d. 1651, Charlestown, Mass., of royal descent
= Anna ———
Mary RICHARDS
= Thomas HINCKLEY, Governor of the Plymouth Colony
Anna RICHARDS
= Ephraim HUNT
Sarah PALGRAVE
= John ALCOCK
Mary PALGRAVE
= Roger WELLINGTON
Ephraim HUNT Jr. = Joanna ALCOCK
Benjamin WELLINGTON
= Elizabeth SWEETMAN
Samuel HINCKLEY
= Sarah POPE
Elizabeth HUNT = Lemuel POPE
Elizabeth WELLINGTON
= John FAY Jr.
Mary HINCKLEY
= Samuel BANGS
Mercy POPE = Caleb CHURCH
John FAY (III)
= Hannah CHILD
Joseph BANGS
= Thankful HAMBLEN
Joseph CHURCH = Deborah PERRY
Jonathan FAY
= Joanna PHILLIPS
Deborah CHURCH = Warren DELAND
Lemuel BANGS
= Rebecca KEELER
Warren DELANO Jr.
= Catherine Robbins LYMAN
Jonathan FAY Jr.
= Lucy PRESCOTT
Elijah Keeler BANGS
= Esther STACKHOUSE
Sara DELANO = James ROOSEVELT
Samuel Prescott Phillips FAY
= Harriet HOWARD
Mary Ann BANGS
= Joseph Ambrose BEAKY
Franklin Delano ROOSEVELT
1882-1945
32nd U.S. President
= (Anna) Eleanor ROOSEVELT
Samuel Howard FAY
= Susan SHELLMAN
Martha Adela BEAKY
= David Davis WALKER
Harriet Eleanor FAY
= James Smith BUSH
George Herbert WALKER
= Lucretia WEAR
Samuel Prescott BUSH
= Flora SHELDON
Dorothy WALKER = Prescott Sheldon BUSH
George Herbert Walker BUSH
b. 1924
41st U.S. President
= Barbara PIERCE

Wilhelmus Hendrickse BEEKMAN (1623-1707) of New Amsterdam
= Catalina (Catharine) DE BOOGH of Albany

Gerardus BEEKMAN
= Magdalena ABEEL

Maria BEEKMAN
= Jacob WALTON

Abraham WALTON
= Grace WILLIAMS

Mary Eliza WALTON
= James ROOSEVELT

Isaac ROOSEVELT
= Mary Rebecca ASPINWALL

James ROOSEVELT
= Sara DELANO

Franklin Delano ROOSEVELT
1882 - 1945
32nd U.S. President
= (Anna) Eleanor ROOSEVELT

Hendrick (Henry) BEEKMAN
= Johanna LOPERS

Cornelia BEEKMAN
= Gilbert LIVINGSTON

James LIVINGSTON
= Judith NEWCOMB

Gilbert James LIVINGSTON
= Susanna LEWIS

Judith LIVINGSTON
= Samuel Herrick BUTLER

Courtland Philip Livingston BUTLER
= Elizabeth Slade PIERCE

Mary Elizabeth BUTLER
= Robert Emmet SHELDON

Flora SHELDON
= Samuel Prescott BUSH

Prescott Sheldon BUSH
= Dorothy WALKER

George Herbert Walker BUSH
b. 1924
41st U.S. President
= Barbara PIERCE

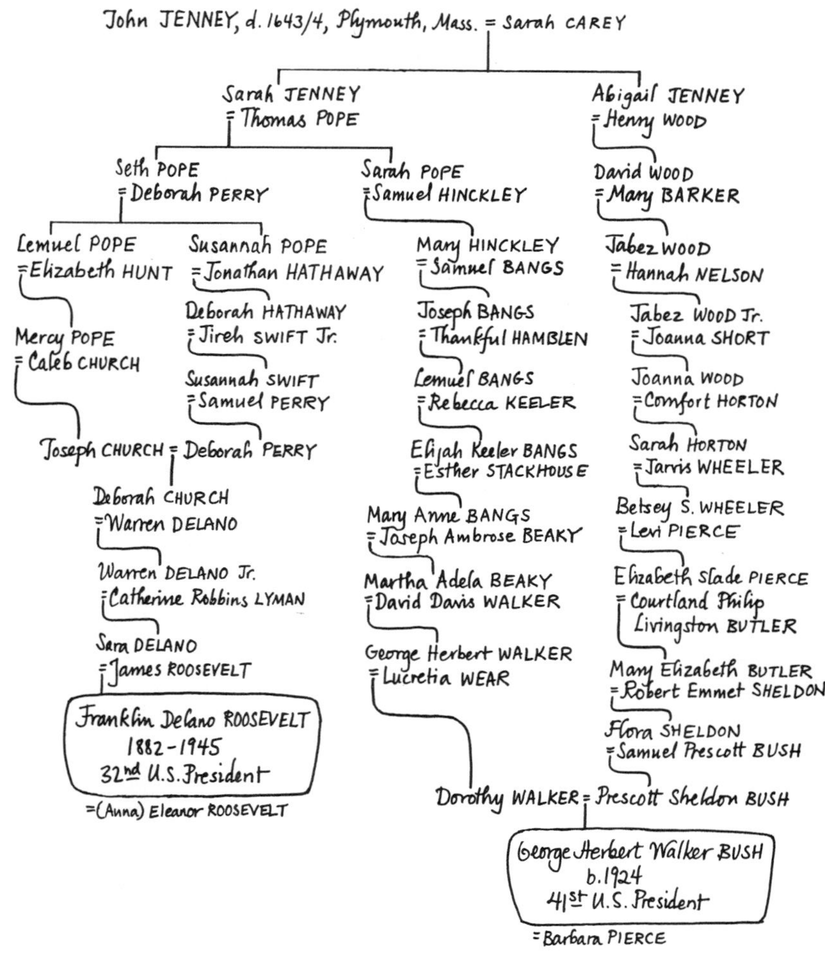
John JENNEY, d. 1643/4, Plymouth, Mass. = Sarah CAREY
Sarah JENNEY
= Thomas POPE
Abigail JENNEY
= Henry WOOD
Seth POPE
= Deborah PERRY
Sarah POPE
= Samuel HINCKLEY
David WOOD
= Mary BARKER
Lemuel POPE
= Elizabeth HUNT
Susannah POPE
= Jonathan HATHAWAY
Mary HINCKLEY
= Samuel BANGS
Jabez WOOD
= Hannah NELSON
Deborah HATHAWAY
= Jireh SWIFT Jr.
Joseph BANGS
= Thankful HAMBLEN
Jabez WOOD Jr.
= Joanna SHORT
Mercy POPE
= Caleb CHURCH
Susannah SWIFT
= Samuel PERRY
Lemuel BANGS
= Rebecca KEELER
Joanna WOOD
= Comfort HORTON
Joseph CHURCH = Deborah PERRY
Elijah Keeler BANGS
= Esther STACKHOUSE
Sarah HORTON
= Jarvis WHEELER
Deborah CHURCH
= Warren DELANO
Mary Anne BANGS
= Joseph Ambrose BEAKY
Betsey S. WHEELER
= Levi PIERCE
Warren DELANO Jr.
= Catherine Robbins LYMAN
Martha Adela BEAKY
= David Davis WALKER
Elizabeth Slade PIERCE
= Courtland Philip
Livingston BUTLER
Sara DELANO
= James ROOSEVELT
George Herbert WALKER
= Lucretia WEAR
Mary Elizabeth BUTLER
= Robert Emmet SHELDON
Franklin Delano ROOSEVELT
1882-1945
32nd U.S. President
= (Anna) Eleanor ROOSEVELT
Flora SHELDON
= Samuel Prescott BUSH
Dorothy WALKER = Prescott Sheldon BUSH
George Herbert Walker BUSH
b. 1924
41st U.S. President
= Barbara PIERCE

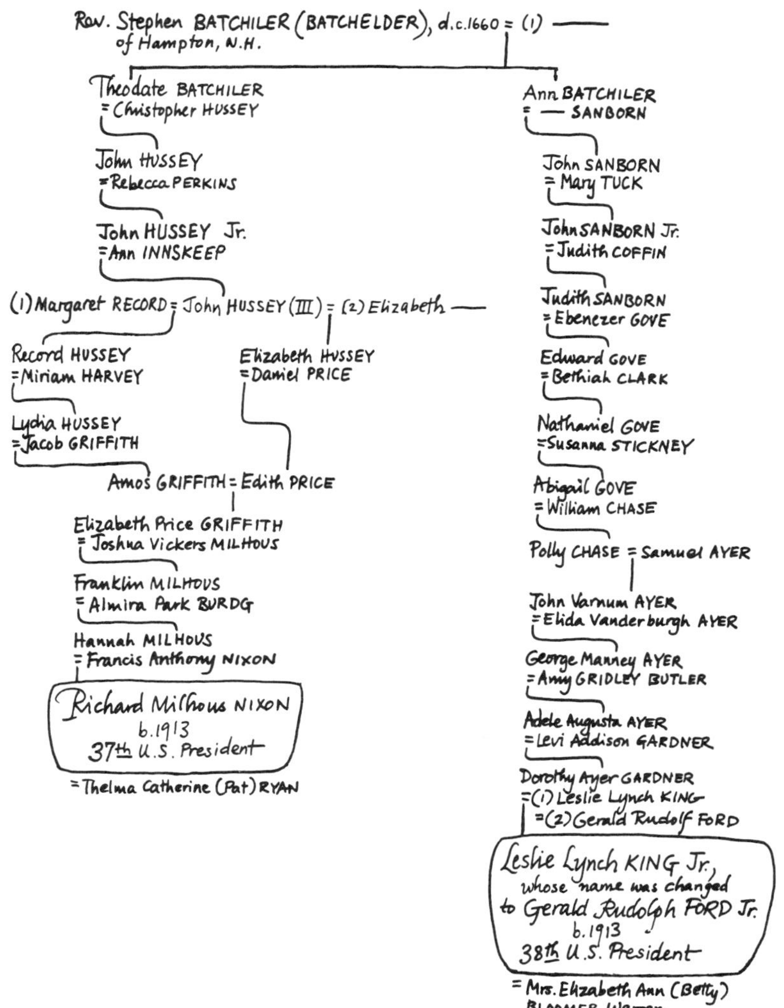
Rev. Stephen BATCHILER (BATCHELDER), d.c.1660 = (1) —
of Hampton, N.H.
Theodate BATCHILER
= Christopher HUSSEY
Ann BATCHILER
= — SANBORN
John HUSSEY
= Rebecca PERKINS
John HUSSEY Jr.
= Ann INNSKEEP
(1) Margaret RECORD = John HUSSEY (III) = (2) Elizabeth —
Record HUSSEY
= Miriam HARVEY
Elizabeth HUSSEY
= Daniel PRICE
Lydia HUSSEY
= Jacob GRIFFITH
Amos GRIFFITH = Edith PRICE
Elizabeth Price GRIFFITH
= Joshua Vickers MILHOUS
Franklin MILHOUS
= Almira Park BURDG
Hannah MILHOUS
= Francis Anthony NIXON
Richard Milhous NIXON
b. 1913
37th U.S. President
= Thelma Catherine (Pat) RYAN
John SANBORN
= Mary TUCK
John SANBORN Jr.
= Judith COFFIN
Judith SANBORN
= Ebenezer GOVE
Edward GOVE
= Bethiah CLARK
Nathaniel GOVE
= Susanna STICKNEY
Abigail GOVE
= William CHASE
Polly CHASE = Samuel AYER
John Varnum AYER
= Elida Vanderburgh AYER
George Manney AYER
= Amy GRIDLEY BUTLER
Adele Augusta AYER
= Levi Addison GARDNER
Dorothy Ayer GARDNER
= (1) Leslie Lynch KING
= (2) Gerald Rudolf FORD
Leslie Lynch KING Jr.,
whose name was changed
to Gerald Rudolph FORD Jr.
b. 1913
38th U.S. President
= Mrs. Elizabeth Ann (Betty)
BLOOMER Warren

Henry VANDERBURGH (c.1685-c.1750) of Poughkeepsie, N.Y. = Magdalena KNIGHT

Henry VANDERBURGH, Jr., Loyalist, lived in New Brunswick, c. 1783-87
= Sarah VAN KLEECK

Aeltje (Alida) VANDERBURGH
= Wines MANNEY

John MANNEY
= Elizabeth COLLINS

Elida Vanderburgh MANNEY
= John Varnum AYER

George Manney AYER
= Amy Gridley BUTLER

Adele Augusta AYER
= Levi Addison GARDNER

Dorothy Ayer GARDNER
= (1) Leslie Lynch KING
(2) Gerald Rudolf FORD

Leslie Lynch KING, Jr., whose name was changed to Gerald Rudolph FORD, Jr., b. 1913
38th U.S. President

= Mrs. Elizabeth Ann (Betty) BLOOMER Warren

Susanna VANDERBURGH
= Richard LEWIS

Susanna LEWIS
= Gilbert James LIVINGSTON

Judith LIVINGSTON
= Samuel Herrick BUTLER

Courtland Philip Livingston BUTLER
= Elizabeth Slade PIERCE

Mary Elizabeth BUTLER
= Robert Emmet SHELDON

Flora SHELDON
= Samuel Prescott BUSH

Prescott Sheldon BUSH
= Dorothy WALKER

George Herbert Walker BUSH
b. 1924
41st U.S. President

= Barbara PIERCE

Teuwis (Matheeus or Matthew) Abrahamse VAN DEU(R)SEN,
b.c. 1631, of Albany, N.Y.
= Helena ROBBERTS

Marritje VAN DEU(R)SEN
= Abraham Janse VAN ALSTYNE

Dirkje VAN ALSTYNE
= Martin VAN BUREN

Abraham VAN BUREN
= Maria HOES

Martin VAN BUREN
1782-1862
8th U.S. President

= Hannah HOES

Tryntje VAN DEU(R)SEN
= Samson BENSON

Robert BENSON
= Cornelia ROOS

Tryntje BENSON
= Martin HOFFMAN

Cornelia HOFFMAN
= Isaac ROOSEVELT

James ROOSEVELT
= Mary Eliza WALTON

Isaac ROOSEVELT
= Mary Rebecca ASPINWALL

James ROOSEVELT
= Sara DELANO

Franklin Delano ROOSEVELT
1882-1945
32nd U.S. President

= (Anna) Eleanor ROOSEVELT

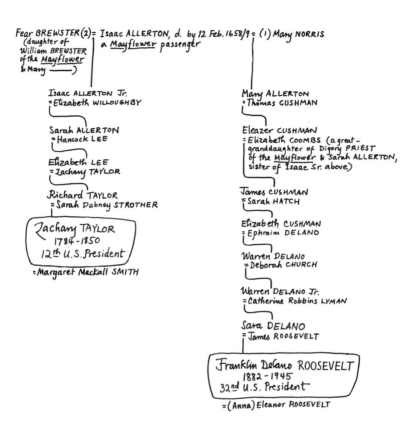

Fear BREWSTER (2) = Isaac ALLERTON, d. by 12 Feb. 1658/9 = (1) Mary NORRIS
(daughter of William BREWSTER of the *Mayflower* & Mary ——) — a *Mayflower* passenger

Isaac ALLERTON Jr.
= Elizabeth WILLOUGHBY

Sarah ALLERTON
= Hancock LEE

Elizabeth LEE
= Zachary TAYLOR

Richard TAYLOR
= Sarah Dabney STROTHER

Zachary TAYLOR
1784-1850
12th U.S. President

= Margaret Mackall SMITH

Mary ALLERTON
= Thomas CUSHMAN

Eleazer CUSHMAN
= Elizabeth COOMBS (a great-granddaughter of Digory PRIEST of the *Mayflower* & Sarah ALLERTON, sister of Isaac Sr. above)

James CUSHMAN
= Sarah HATCH

Elizabeth CUSHMAN
= Ephraim DELANO

Warren DELANO
= Deborah CHURCH

Warren DELANO Jr.
= Catherine Robbins LYMAN

Sara DELANO
= James ROOSEVELT

Franklin Delano ROOSEVELT
1882-1945
32nd U.S. President

= (Anna) Eleanor ROOSEVELT

Thomas EMERSON (1584-1666) of Ipswich, Mass. = Elizabeth BREWSTER, of no known kinship to William BREWSTER of the *Mayflower*

Nathaniel EMERSON
= Sarah ———

Thomas EMERSON
= Philippa PERKINS

Mary EMERSON
= Stephen STORY

Philippa STORY
= Ebenezer WOOD Jr.

Hepzibah WOOD
= Nathaniel FILLMORE

Nathaniel FILLMORE Jr.
= Phoebe MILLARD

Millard FILLMORE
1800-1874
13th U.S. President
= (1) Abigail POWERS
(2) Mrs. Caroline CARMICHAEL McIntosh

Joseph EMERSON
= Elizabeth WOODMANSEY

James EMERSON
= Sarah ———

Elizabeth EMERSON
= Joseph TAFT

Peter TAFT
= Elizabeth CHENEY

Aaron TAFT
= Rhoda RAWSON

Peter Rawson TAFT
= Sylvia HOWARD

Alphonso TAFT
= Louisa Maria TORREY

William Howard TAFT
1857-1930
27th U.S. President
= Helen HERRON

Robert MILLARD, d. 1699, Rehoboth, Mass. = Elizabeth SABIN

Nehemiah MILLARD
= Phoebe SHORE

Robert MILLARD
= Hannah EDDY

Abiathar MILLARD
= Tabitha HOPKINS

Phoebe MILLARD
= Nathaniel FILLMORE Jr.

Millard FILLMORE
1800-1874
13th U.S. President

= (1) Abigail POWERS
(2) Mrs. Caroline CARMICHAEL McIntosh

Nathaniel MILLARD
= Susanna GLADDING

Ann MILLARD
= Jonathan HORTON

Comfort HORTON
= Joanna WOOD

Sarah HORTON
= Jarvis WHEELER

Betsey S. WHEELER
= Levi PIERCE

Elizabeth Slade PIERCE
= Courtland Philip Livingston BUTLER

Mary Elizabeth BUTLER
= Robert Emmet SHELDON

Flora SHELDON
= Samuel Prescott BUSH

Prescott Sheldon BUSH
= Dorothy WALKER

George Herbert Walker BUSH
b. 1924
41st U.S. President

= Barbara PIERCE

John JOHNSON, d. 1659, Roxbury, Mass. = (1) Margery ——

Isaac JOHNSON
= Elizabeth PORTER

Elizabeth JOHNSON
= Henry BOWEN

John BOWEN
= Hannah BREWER

Abigail BOWEN
= Caleb KENDRICK

Benjamin KENDRICK
= Sarah HARRIS

Anna KENDRICK
= Benjamin PIERCE Jr.

Franklin PIERCE
1804-1869
14th U.S. President
= Jane Means APPLETON

Humphrey JOHNSON
= Eleanor CHENEY

Mehitable JOHNSON
= Samuel HINSDALE

Mary HINSDALE
= Thomas SHELDON

Benjamin SHELDON
= Mary STRONG

Mary SHELDON
= Joseph LYMAN Jr.

Joseph LYMAN (III)
= Anne Jean ROBBINS

Catherine Robbins LYMAN
= Warren DELANO, Jr.

Sara DELANO = James ROOSEVELT

Franklin Delano ROOSEVELT
1882-1945
32nd U.S. President
= (Anna) Eleanor ROOSEVELT

Bernard CAPEN, d. 1638, Dorchester, Mass. = Joan PURCHASE

Susanna CAPEN
= William ROCKWELL

Ruth ROCKWELL
= Christopher HUNTINGTON

John HUNTINGTON
= Abigail LATHROP

Martha HUNTINGTON
= Noah GRANT

Noah GRANT Jr.
= Susanna DELANO

Noah GRANT (III)
= Rachel KELLEY

Jesse Root GRANT
= Hannah SIMPSON

Ulysses Simpson GRANT
1822-1885
18th U.S. President

= Julia Boggs DENT

John CAPEN
= Mary BASS

Joseph CAPEN
= Priscilla APPLETON

Mary CAPEN
= Thomas BAKER Jr.

Priscilla BAKER
= Tarrant PUTNAM Jr.

Priscilla PUTNAM
= Adam BROWN Jr.

Israel Putnam BROWN
= Sally BRIGGS

Sally BROWN
= Israel C. BREWER

Sarah Almeda BREWER
= Calvin Galusha COOLIDGE

John Calvin COOLIDGE
= Victoria Josephine MOOR

(John) Calvin COOLIDGE (Jr.)
1872-1933
30th U.S. President

= Grace Anna GOODHUE

Richard MARTIN (1609-1694/5) of Rehoboth, Mass. = Elizabeth SALTER

John MARTIN
= Mercy BILLINGTON

Desire MARTIN
= Jotham CARPENTER

Jotham CARPENTER Jr.
= Mehitable THOMPSON

Sybil CARPENTER
= Henry INGALLS

Mehitable INGALLS
= James BALLOU (IV)

Eliza BALLOU
= Abram GARFIELD

James Abram GARFIELD
1831-1881
20th U.S. President

= Lucretia RUDOLPH

Grace MARTIN
= John ORMSBY

Martha ORMSBY
= James FRANKLIN Jr.

Philip FRANKLIN
= Rachel HORTON

Aaron FRANKLIN
= Margaret ——

Jabez FRANKLIN
= Sarah STARR

Luther FRANKLIN
= Priscilla PINNEY

Abigail FRANKLIN
= Hiram D. MOOR

Victoria Josephine MOOR
= John Calvin COOLIDGE

(John) Calvin COOLIDGE (Jr.)
1872-1933
30th U.S. President

= Grace Anna GOODHUE

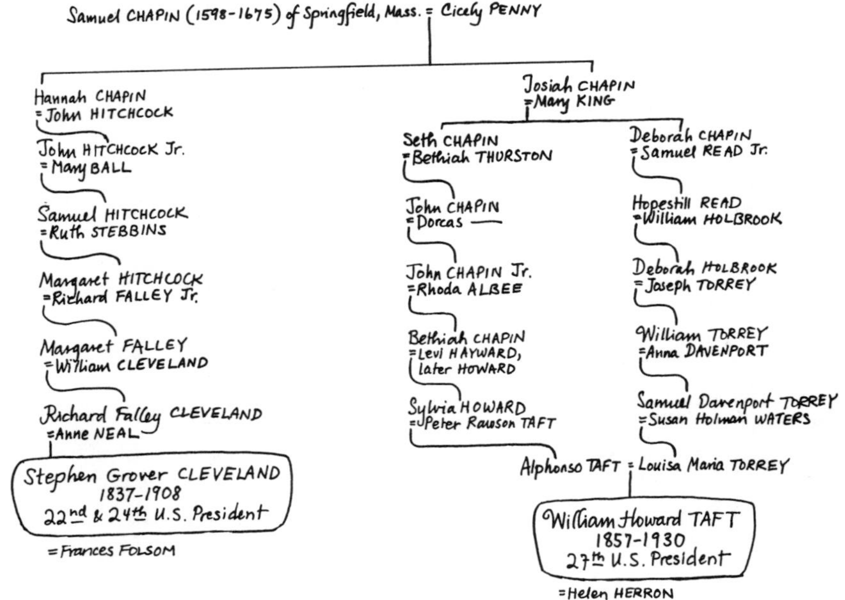
Samuel CHAPIN (1598-1675) of Springfield, Mass. = Cicely PENNY
Hannah CHAPIN
=John HITCHCOCK
John HITCHCOCK Jr.
=Mary BALL
Samuel HITCHCOCK
=Ruth STEBBINS
Margaret HITCHCOCK
=Richard FALLEY Jr.
Margaret FALLEY
=William CLEVELAND
Richard Falley CLEVELAND
=Anne NEAL
Stephen Grover CLEVELAND
1837-1908
22nd & 24th U.S. President
=Frances FOLSOM
Josiah CHAPIN
=Mary KING
Seth CHAPIN
=Bethiah THURSTON
John CHAPIN
=Dorcas —
John CHAPIN Jr.
=Rhoda ALBEE
Bethiah CHAPIN
=Levi HAYWARD,
later HOWARD
Sylvia HOWARD
=Peter Rawson TAFT
Deborah CHAPIN
=Samuel READ Jr.
Hopestill READ
=William HOLBROOK
Deborah HOLBROOK
=Joseph TORREY
William TORREY
=Anna DAVENPORT
Samuel Davenport TORREY
=Susan Holman WATERS
Alphonso TAFT = Louisa Maria TORREY
William Howard TAFT
1857-1930
27th U.S. President
=Helen HERRON

Edward WINN, d. 1682, Woburn, Mass. = Joanna ———

- Ann WINN = Moses CLEVELAND
  - Aaron CLEVELAND = Dorcas WILSON
  - Aaron CLEVELAND Jr. = Abigail WATERS
  - Aaron CLEVELAND (III) = Susanna PORTER
  - Aaron CLEVELAND (IV) = Abiah HYDE
  - William CLEVELAND = Margaret FALLEY
  - Richard Falley CLEVELAND = Anne NEAL
  - **Stephen Grover CLEVELAND, 1837-1908, 22nd & 24th U.S. President** = Frances FOLSOM

- Increase WINN = Hannah SAWTELLE
  - Jacob WINN = Prudence WYMAN
  - Jacob WINN Jr. * = Sarah BUCK
  - Jacob WINN (III) = Phoebe GROUT
  - Endymia WINN = Thomas SHERWOOD
  - Lucinda SHERWOOD = John MINTHORN
  - Theodore MINTHORN = Mary WASLEY
  - Hulda Randall MINTHORN = Jesse Clark HOOVER
  - **Herbert Clark HOOVER, 1874-1964, 31st U.S. President** = Lou HENRY

*The parentage of Jacob WINN (Jr.?), husband of Sarah BUCK, is subject to doubt.

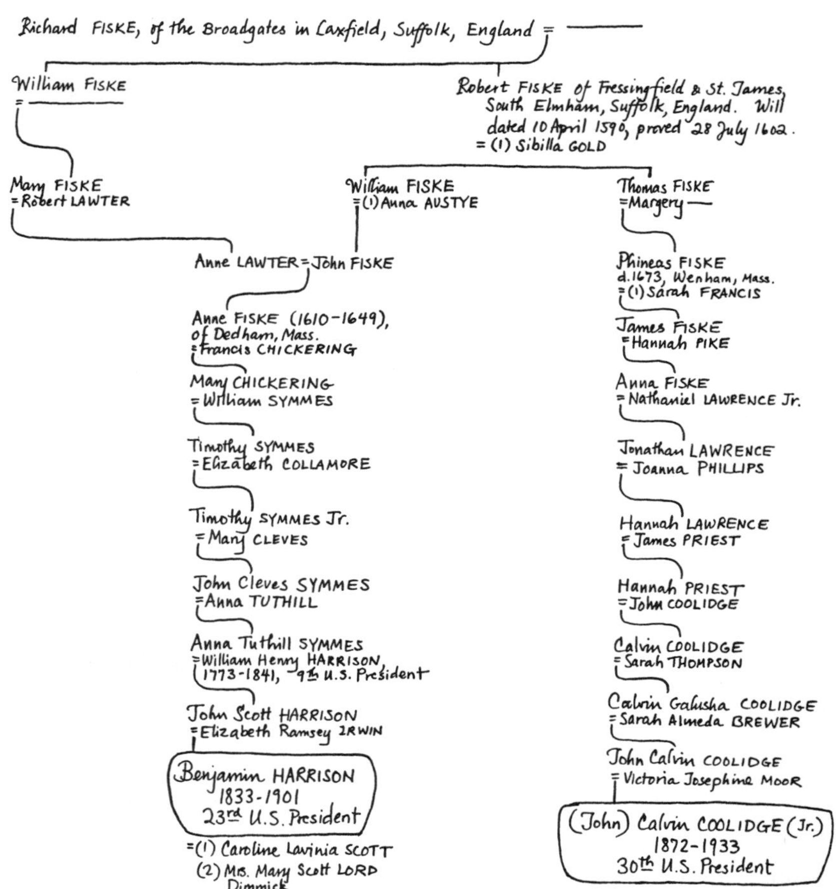

Richard FISKE, of the Broadgates in Laxfield, Suffolk, England = ———
William FISKE
= ———
Robert FISKE of Fressingfield & St. James, South Elmham, Suffolk, England. Will dated 10 April 1590, proved 28 July 1602.
= (1) Sibilla GOLD
Mary FISKE
= Robert LAWTER
William FISKE
= (1) Anna AUSTYE
Thomas FISKE
= Margery —
Anne LAWTER = John FISKE
Phineas FISKE
d. 1673, Wenham, Mass.
= (1) Sarah FRANCIS
Anne FISKE (1610-1649), of Dedham, Mass.
= Francis CHICKERING
James FISKE
= Hannah PIKE
Mary CHICKERING
= William SYMMES
Anna FISKE
= Nathaniel LAWRENCE Jr.
Timothy SYMMES
= Elizabeth COLLAMORE
Jonathan LAWRENCE
= Joanna PHILLIPS
Timothy SYMMES Jr.
= Mary CLEVES
Hannah LAWRENCE
= James PRIEST
John Cleves SYMMES
= Anna TUTHILL
Hannah PRIEST
= John COOLIDGE
Anna Tuthill SYMMES
= William Henry HARRISON, 1773-1841, 9th U.S. President
Calvin COOLIDGE
= Sarah THOMPSON
John Scott HARRISON
= Elizabeth Ramsey IRWIN
Calvin Galusha COOLIDGE
= Sarah Almeda BREWER
Benjamin HARRISON
1833-1901
23rd U.S. President
= (1) Caroline Lavinia SCOTT
(2) Mrs. Mary Scott LORD Dimmick
John Calvin COOLIDGE
= Victoria Josephine MOOR
(John) Calvin COOLIDGE (Jr.)
1872-1933
30th U.S. President
= Grace Anna GOODHUE

Pieter TJERCKS of Emden & Amsterdam, The Netherlands
= (1627) Geertruyt Philips VAN SCHUYLDER

David Pieterse SCHUYLER
(1636-1690) of Albany, N.Y.
= Catalyntie (Catalina) VER PLANCK

Maria SCHUYLER
= Hendrick VAN DYCK

Lydia VAN DYCK
= Cornelius VAN SCHAACK

Cornelius VAN SCHAACK Jr.
= Angeltje (Angelica) YATES

Maria VAN SCHAACK
= James J. (Jacobus) ROOSEVELT

Cornelius Van Schaack ROOSEVELT
= Margaret BARNHILL

Theodore ROOSEVELT
= Martha BULLOCH

Theodore ROOSEVELT, Jr.
1858-1919
26th U.S. President

= (1) Alice Hathaway LEE
(2) Edith Kermit CAROW

Philip Pieterse SCHUYLER
(1628-1683) of Albany, N.Y.
= Margareta VAN SLICHTENHORST

Alida SCHUYLER
= Robert LIVINGSTON the Elder,
New York colonial official,
1st Lord of Livingston Manor

Gilbert LIVINGSTON
= Cornelia BEEKMAN

James LIVINGSTON
= Judith NEWCOMB

Gilbert James LIVINGSTON
= Susanna LEWIS

Judith LIVINGSTON
= Samuel Herrick BUTLER

Courtland Philip Livingston BUTLER
= Elizabeth Slade PIERCE

Mary Elizabeth BUTLER
= Robert Emmet SHELDON

Flora SHELDON
= Samuel Prescott BUSH

Prescott Sheldon BUSH
= Dorothy WALKER

George Herbert Walker BUSH
b. 1924
41st U.S. President

= Barbara PIERCE

Richard GREENE of Bowridge Hill, Gillingham, Dorset, England; will proved 1608
= Mary HOOKER

Rachel GREENE
= Richard PERNE

Rachel PERNE
= Edward RAWSON (1615-1693)
Secretary of the
Massachusetts Bay Colony

Grindall RAWSON
= Susanna WILSON

Edmund RAWSON
= Elizabeth HAYWARD

Abner RAWSON
= Mary ALLEN

Rhoda RAWSON
= Aaron TAFT

Peter Rawson TAFT
= Sylvia HOWARD

Alphonso TAFT
= Louisa Maria TORREY

William Howard TAFT
1857-1930
27th U.S. President

= Helen HERRON

John GREENE (1597-1659)
of Providence, R.I.
= Joan TATTERSALL

John GREENE Jr.
= Anne ALMY

Phillip(pa) GREENE
= Caleb CARR

Caleb CARR Jr.
= Joanna SLOCUM

Patience CARR
= Joseph SLOCUM

Sarah SLOCUM
= William TRIPP

Phoebe TRIPP
= Amos HARDING

George Tryon HARDING
= Elizabeth MADISON

Charles Alexander HARDING
= Mary Ann CRAWFORD

George Tryon HARDING
= Phoebe Elizabeth DICKERSON

Warren Gamaliel HARDING
1865-1923
29th U.S. President

= Mrs. Florence Mabel KLING De Wolfe

Rev. Edward HOLYOKE, d. 1660, Rumney Marsh (Chelsea), Mass. = Prudence STOCKTON

Sarah HOLYOKE = John ANDREWS	Anne HOLYOKE = Thomas PUTNAM
John ANDREWS Jr. = Ann JACOBS	Prudence PUTNAM = William WYMAN
Anne ANDREWS = John GILES	Prudence WYMAN = Jacob WINN
Mehitable GILES = Jonathan WATERS	Jacob WINN Jr.* = Sarah BUCK
Asa WATERS = Sarah GOODALE	Jacob WINN (III) = Phoebe GROUT
Asa WATERS Jr. = Susan Trask HOLMAN	Endymia WINN = Thomas SHERWOOD
Susan Holman WATERS = Samuel Davenport TORREY	Lucinda SHERWOOD = John MINTHORN
Louisa Maria TORREY = Alphonso TAFT	Theodore MINTHORN = Mary WASLEY
William Howard TAFT **1857-1930** **27th U.S. President** = Helen HERRON	Hulda Randall MINTHORN = Jesse Clark HOOVER
	Herbert Clark HOOVER **1874-1964** **31st U.S. President** = Lou HENRY

*The parentage of Jacob WINN (Jr.?), husband of Sarah BUCK, is subject to doubt.

William WARDWELL, d. 1670, Boston, Mass. = (1) Alice ——

Uzal WARDWELL
= Grace ——

Grace WARDWELL
= Joseph GIDDINGS, Jr.

Susanna GIDDINGS
= William TORREY

Joseph TORREY
= Deborah HOLBROOK

William TORREY
= Anna DAVENPORT

Samuel Davenport TORREY
= Susan Holman WATERS

Louisa Maria TORREY
= Alphonso TAFT

William Howard TAFT
1857-1930
27th U.S. President

= Helen HERRON

Elihu WARDWELL
= Elizabeth WADE

Sarah WARDWELL
= Moses STICKNEY

Susanna STICKNEY
= Nathaniel GOVE

Abigail GOVE
= William CHASE

Polly CHASE
= Samuel AYER

John Varnum AYER
= Elida Vanderburgh MANNEY

George Manney AYER
= Amy Gridley BUTLER

Adele Augusta AYER
= Levi Addison GARDNER

Dorothy Ayer GARDNER
= (1) Leslie Lynch KING
= (2) Gerald Rudolf FORD

Leslie Lynch KING Jr.,
whose name was changed to
Gerald Rudolph FORD Jr.,
b. 1913
38th U.S. President

= Mrs. Elizabeth Ann (Betty) BLOOMER Warren

Adam MOTT (1596-1661) of Portsmouth, R.I. = (1) Elizabeth CREEL

Elizabeth MOTT
= Edward THURSTON

Mary THURSTON
= Ebenezer SLOCUM

Joanna SLOCUM
= Caleb CARR, Jr.

Patience CARR
= Joseph SLOCUM

Sarah SLOCUM
= William TRIPP

Phoebe TRIPP
= Amos HARDING

George Tryon HARDING
= Elizabeth MADISON

Charles Alexander HARDING
= Mary Ann CRAWFORD

George Tryon HARDING
= Phoebe Elizabeth DICKERSON

Warren Gamaliel HARDING
1865-1923
29th U.S. President

= Mrs. Florence Mabel KLING De Wolfe

Adam MOTT Jr.
= Mary LOTT

Elizabeth MOTT
= William RICKETSON

Jonathan RICKETSON
= Abigail HOWLAND

Jonathan RICKETSON, Jr.
= Meribah WILBUR

Rhoda RICKETSON
= Hezekiah COLLINS Jr.

Elizabeth COLLINS
= John MANNEY

Elida Vanderburgh MANNEY
= John Varnum AYER

George Manney AYER
= Amy Gridley BUTLER

Adele Augusta AYER
= Levi Addison GARDNER

Dorothy Ayer GARDNER
= (1) Leslie Lynch KING
= (2) Gerald Rudolf FORD

Leslie Lynch KING Jr.,
whose name was changed to
Gerald Rudolph FORD Jr.,
b. 1913
38th U.S. President

= Mrs. Elizabeth Ann (Betty) BLOOMER Warren

Richard SAWTELLE, d.1694, Watertown, Mass. = Elizabeth ———

Hannah SAWTELLE
= Increase WINN

Jacob WINN
= Prudence WYMAN

Jacob WINN Jr.*
= Sarah BUCK

Jacob WINN (III)
= Phoebe GROUT

Endymia WINN
= Thomas SHERWOOD

Lucinda SHERWOOD
= John MINTHORN

Theodore MINTHORN
= Mary WASLEY

Hulda Randall MINTHORN
= Jesse Clark HOOVER

Herbert Clark HOOVER
1874-1964
31st U.S. President

= Lou HENRY

Zachariah SAWTELLE
= Elizabeth HARRIS

Elizabeth SAWTELLE
= Joseph MORSE

Abigail MORSE
= Joshua HEMINGWAY (III)

Isaac HEMINGWAY
= Elizabeth HAVEN

James HEMINGWAY
= Elizabeth ARMSTRONG

James HEMINGWAY Jr.
= Hope MALMSBURY

Jane M. HEMINGWAY
= Oliver BURDG

Almira Park BURDG
= Franklin MILHOUS

Hannah MILHOUS
= Francis Anthony NIXON

Richard Milhous NIXON
b.1913
37th U.S. President

= Thelma Catherine (Pat) RYAN

*The parentage of Jacob WINN (Jr.?), husband of Sarah BUCK, is subject to doubt.

SUMMARY OF PRESIDENTIAL KINSHIPS

	President	Number of	Kinsmen among other presidents
1	Washington	3	Coolidge, FDR, Bush (Eng.)
2	J. Adams	4	J. Q. Adams, Fillmore, Taft, Coolidge
3	Jefferson	0	none
4	Madison	1	Taylor
5	Monroe	0	none
6	J. Q. Adams	7	J. Adams, 2 Harrisons (Eng.), Fillmore, Taft, Coolidge, FDR
7	Jackson	0	none
8	Van Buren	2	T. Roosevelt, FDR
9	W. H. Harrison	4	J. Q. Adams (Eng.), Tyler, B. Harrison, Carter
10	Tyler	2	2 Harrisons
11	Polk	0	none
12	Taylor	2	Madison, FDR
13	Fillmore	10	2 Adamses, Grant, Cleveland, Taft, Coolidge, Hoover, FDR, Ford, Bush
14	Pierce	5	Hayes, Coolidge, Hoover, FDR, Bush
15	Buchanan	0	none
16	Lincoln	2	Ford, Bush
17	A. Johnson	0	none
18	Grant	6	Fillmore, Cleveland, Coolidge, FDR, Ford, Bush
19	Hayes	7	Pierce, Cleveland, Taft, FDR, Nixon, Ford, Bush
20	Garfield	4	Taft, Hoover, Ford, Bush
21	Arthur	0	none
22	Cleveland	8	Fillmore, Grant, Hayes, Taft, Hoover, FDR, Ford, Bush
23	B. Harrison	8	J. Q. Adams (Eng.), W. H. Harrison, Tyler, Taft, Harding, Coolidge, Carter, Ford
24	Cleveland	8	as above
25	McKinley	0	none
26	T. Roosevelt	3	Van Buren, FDR, Bush
27	Taft	14	2 Adamses, Fillmore, Hayes, Garfield, B. Harrison, Cleveland, Harding, Coolidge, Hoover, FDR, Nixon, Ford, Bush
28	Wilson	0	none
29	Harding	5	B. Harrison, Taft, Nixon, Ford, Carter
30	Coolidge	13	Washington (Eng.), 2 Adamses, Fillmore, Pierce, Grant, B. Harrison, Taft, Hoover, FDR, Nixon, Ford, Bush
31	Hoover	9	Fillmore, Pierce, Garfield, Cleveland, Taft, Coolidge, Nixon, Ford, Bush
32	FDR	15	Washington (Eng.), J. Q. Adams, Van Buren, Taylor, Fillmore, Pierce, Grant, Hayes, Cleveland, T. Roosevelt, Taft, Coolidge, Nixon, Ford, Bush
33	Truman	0	none
34	Eisenhower	0	none
35	Kennedy	0	none
36	LBJ	0	none
37	Nixon	9	Hayes, Taft, Harding, Coolidge, Hoover, FDR, Ford, Carter, Bush
38	Ford	14	Fillmore, Lincoln, Grant, Hayes, Garfield, Cleveland, B. Harrison, Taft, Harding, Coolidge, Hoover, FDR, Nixon, Bush
39	Carter	4	2 Harrisons, Harding, Nixon

40	Reagan	0	none
41	Bush	15	Washington (Eng.), Fillmore, Pierce, Lincoln, Grant, Hayes, Garfield, Cleveland, T. Roosevelt, Taft, Coolidge, Hoover, FDR, Nixon, Ford

15 - FDR, Bush; 14 - Taft, Ford; 13 - Coolidge; 10 - Fillmore
9 - Nixon, Hoover*; 8 - Cleveland, B. Harrison
7 - J. Q. Adams, Hayes; 6 - Grant; 5 - Pierce, Harding;
4 - J. Adams, W. H. Harrison, Garfield, Carter
3 - Washington, T. Roosevelt
2 - Van Buren, Tyler, Taylor, Lincoln; 1 - Madison
0 - Jefferson, Monroe, Jackson, Polk, Buchanan, A. Johnson, Arthur, McKinley, Wilson, Truman, Eisenhower, Kennedy, LBJ, Reagan

"(Eng.)" indicates that the kinship between the two or more presidents in question was through English ancestors several generations behind American immigrants. With the sole exception of Washington's kinships to Coolidge and Bush via Spencers, the English ancestors through whom these kinships derive are among the ninth or tenth generation forebears of at least one of the presidents in question.

*If the kinships for H. C. Hoover through Jacob Winn (Jr.?) are disallowed, and Hoover is not considered a kinsman of Cleveland (via Winns), Coolidge (via Richardsons and Putnams) or Nixon (via Sawtelles) these totals are 15 - FDR, Bush; 14 - Taft; 13 - Ford; 12 - Coolidge; 10 - Fillmore; 8 - Nixon; 7 - J. Q. Adams, Hayes, Cleveland, B. Harrison; and 6 - Grant, Hoover

FAMILIES ANCESTRAL TO TWO OR MORE AMERICAN PRESIDENTS
(the Adamses and Harrisons are each treated as one)

*Problematic - includes descents for H. C. Hoover through Jacob Winn (Jr.?) or for G. H. W. Bush through Timothy Bush or Samuel Herrick Butler.

Appendix 1

Kin and "Kin of Kin" to Pocahontas (Mrs. Edith Bolling Galt Wilson and George Herbert Walker Bush respectively)

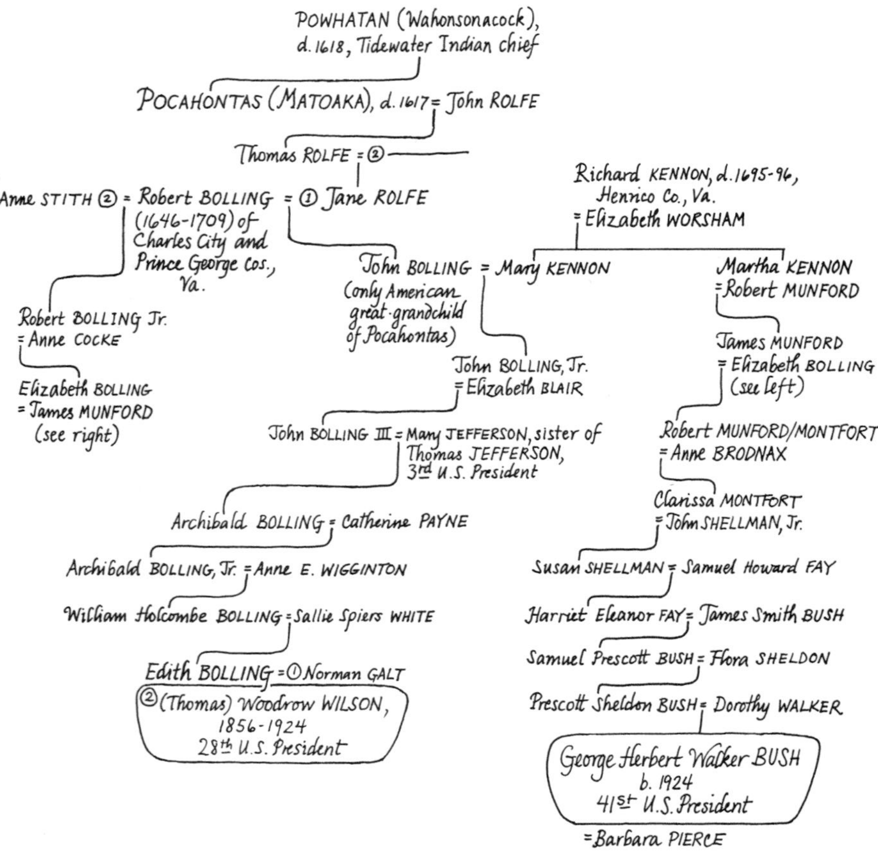
POWHATAN (Wahonsonacock),
d. 1618, Tidewater Indian chief
POCAHONTAS (MATOAKA), d. 1617 = John ROLFE
Thomas ROLFE = ②
Anne STITH ② = Robert BOLLING = ① Jane ROLFE
(1646-1709) of
Charles City and
Prince George Cos.,
Va.
Richard KENNON, d. 1695-96,
Henrico Co., Va.
= Elizabeth WORSHAM
John BOLLING = Mary KENNON
(only American
great-grandchild
of Pocahontas)
Martha KENNON
= Robert MUNFORD
Robert BOLLING Jr.
= Anne COCKE
Elizabeth BOLLING
= James MUNFORD
(see right)
James MUNFORD
= Elizabeth BOLLING
(see left)
John BOLLING, Jr.
= Elizabeth BLAIR
John BOLLING III = Mary JEFFERSON, sister of
Thomas JEFFERSON,
3rd U.S. President
Robert MUNFORD/MONTFORT
= Anne BRODNAX
Clarissa MONTFORT
= John SHELLMAN, Jr.
Archibald BOLLING = Catherine PAYNE
Archibald BOLLING, Jr. = Anne E. WIGGINTON
Susan SHELLMAN = Samuel Howard FAY
William Holcombe BOLLING = Sallie Spiers WHITE
Harriet Eleanor FAY = James Smith BUSH
Samuel Prescott BUSH = Flora SHELDON
Edith BOLLING = ① Norman GALT
② (Thomas) Woodrow WILSON,
1856-1924
28th U.S. President
Prescott Sheldon BUSH = Dorothy WALKER
George Herbert Walker BUSH
b. 1924
41st U.S. President
= Barbara PIERCE

See NEHGS NEXUS 3 (1986): 74-76, and sources cited therein, and APP 507-13.

Appendix 2

Presential Mayflower Descents or Connections (for the two Adamses, Taylor, Grant, Garfield, F. D. Roosevelt, Nixon, Ford, and Bush)

I, II: The ADAMSes

1 William MULLINS = Alice ———

2 Priscilla MULLINS = John ALDEN

3 Ruth ALDEN = John BASS

4 Hannah BASS = Joseph ADAMS, Jr.

5 John ADAMS = Susanna BOYLSTON

6 John ADAMS, Jr. 1735-1826, 2nd U.S. President = Abigail SMITH

7 John Quincy ADAMS, 1767-1848, 6th U.S. President
= Louisa Catherine JOHNSON

III : Zachary TAYLOR

1 William BREWSTER = Mary —

2 Fear BREWSTER = Isaac ALLERTON

3 Isaac ALLERTON, Jr. = Elizabeth WILLOUGHBY

4 Sarah ALLERTON = Hancock LEE

5 Elizabeth LEE = Zachary TAYLOR

6 Richard TAYLOR = Sarah Dabney STROTHER

7 Zachary TAYLOR, 1784-1850, 12th U.S. President
= Margaret Mackall SMITH

IV. Ulysses Simpson GRANT

1 Richard WARREN = Elizabeth ——

2 Nathaniel WARREN = Sarah WALKER

3 Mercy WARREN = Jonathan DELANO

4 Jonathan DELANO, Jr. = Amy HATCH

5 Susanna DELANO = Noah GRANT, Jr.

6 Noah GRANT (III) = Rachel KELLEY

7 Jesse Root GRANT = Hannah SIMPSON

8 Ulysses Simpson GRANT, 1822-1885, 18th U.S. President = Julia Boggs DENT

V. James Abram GARFIELD

1 John BILLINGTON = Elinor ——

2 Francis BILLINGTON = Christian PENN, widow of Francis Eaton

3 Mercy BILLINGTON = John MARTIN

4 Desire MARTIN = Jotham CARPENTER

5 Jotham CARPENTER, Jr. = Mehitable THOMPSON

6 Sybil CARPENTER = Henry INGALLS

7 Mehitable INGALLS = James BALLOU (IV)

8 Eliza BALLOU = Abram GARFIELD

9 James Abram GARFIELD, 1831-1881, 20th U.S. President
= Lucretia RUDOLPH

VI. Franklin Delano ROOSEVELT

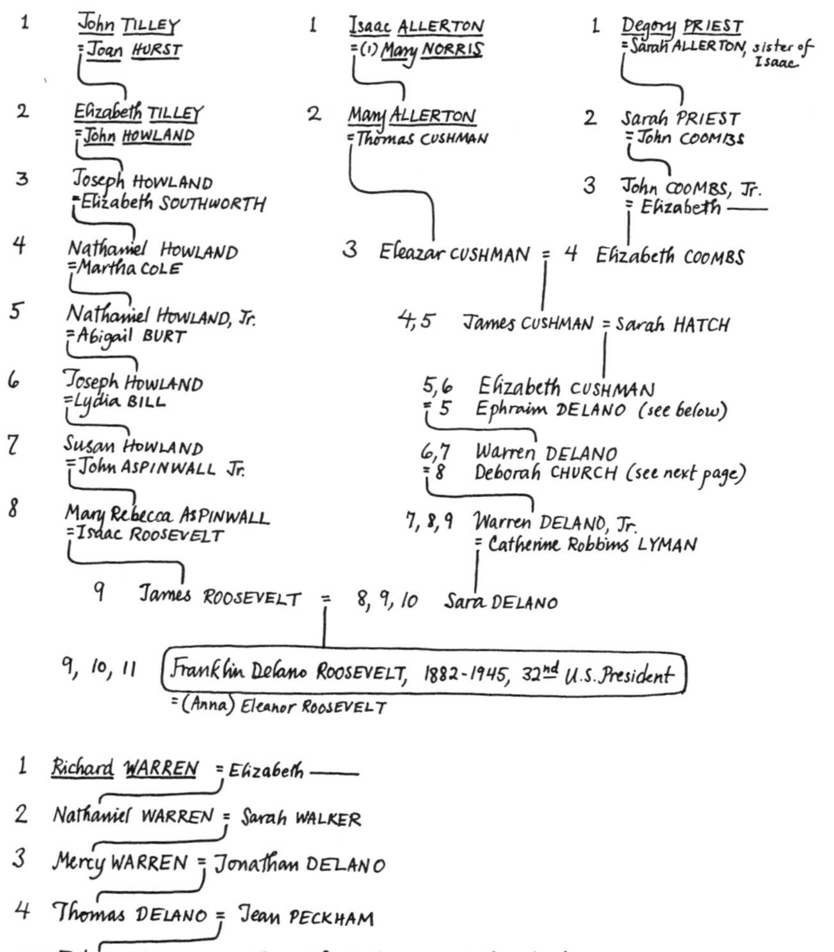

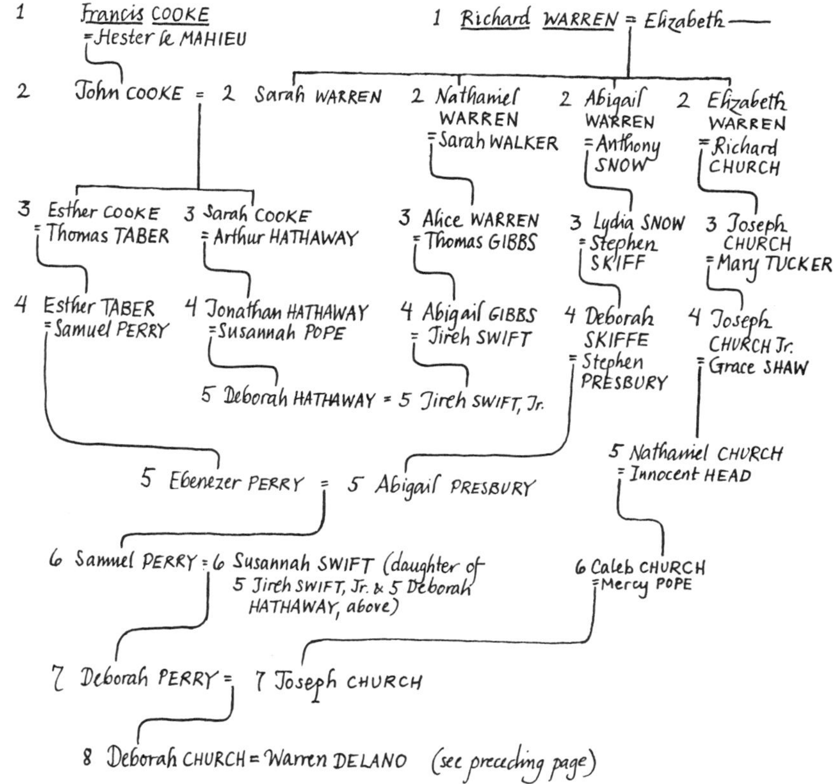

VII, VIII. Richard Milhous NIXON & Gerald Rudolph FORD, Jr.

For the descents of Presidents NIXON & FORD from Henry HOWLAND of Duxbury, Mass., brother of *Mayflower* passenger John HOWLAND, see the Howland presidential kinsmen chart elsewhere in this volume.

IX. George Herbert Walker BUSH

1 Francis COOKE
= Hester le MAHIEU

2 Jane COOKE
= Experience MITCHELL

3 Elizabeth MITCHELL
= John WASHBURN Jr.

4 Mary WASHBURN
= Samuel KINGSLEY Jr.

5 Samuel KINGSLEY (III) = Mary —

6 Silence KINGSLEY = Samuel HERRICK

7 (alleged & likely, but further proof required)
Sarah HERRICK = Nathaniel BUTLER

8 Samuel Herrick BUTLER
= Judith LIVINGSTON

1 John TILLEY = Joan HURST

2 Elizabeth TILLEY = John HOWLAND

3 Hope HOWLAND = John CHIPMAN

4 Hope CHIPMAN = John HUCKINS

5 Hope HUCKINS = Thomas NELSON

6 Hannah NELSON = Jabez WOOD

7 Jabez WOOD Jr. = Joanna SHORT

8 Joanna WOOD = Comfort HORTON

9 Sarah HORTON = Jarvis WHEELER

10 Betsey S. WHEELER
= Levi PIERCE

9 Courtland Philip Livingston BUTLER = 11 Elizabeth Slade PIERCE

10, 12 Mary Elizabeth BUTLER = Robert Emmet SHELDON

11, 13 Flora SHELDON = Samuel Prescott BUSH

12, 14 Prescott Sheldon BUSH = Dorothy WALKER

13, 15 George Herbert Walker BUSH
b. 1924
41st U.S. President
= Barbara PIERCE

Appendix 3

Kinships Through American Forebears Between Eleven U. S. Presidents (Washington, the two Adamses, Fillmore, Hayes, Cleveland, Taft, Coolidge, F. D. Roosevelt, probably Nixon, and possibly Bush, plus First Ladies Frances Cleveland, Edith Roosevelt, Ellen Wilson, Grace Coolidge, Bess Truman, and Nancy Reagan) and the Present British Royal Family - via H. M. Queen Elizabeth the Queen Mother and H. R. H. The Princess of Wales

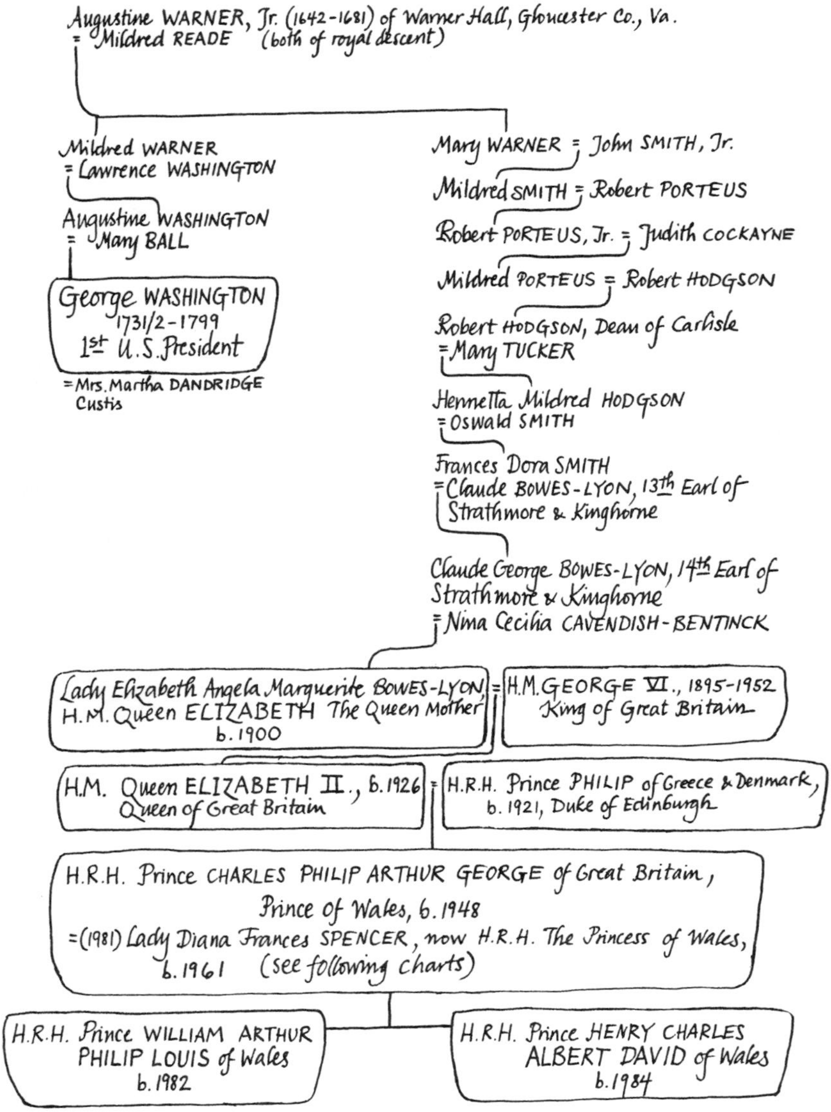

Augustine WARNER, Jr. (1642-1681) of Warner Hall, Gloucester Co., Va.
= Mildred READE (both of royal descent)

Mildred WARNER
= Lawrence WASHINGTON

Augustine WASHINGTON
= Mary BALL

George WASHINGTON
1731/2-1799
1st U.S. President

= Mrs. Martha DANDRIDGE Custis

Mary WARNER = John SMITH, Jr.

Mildred SMITH = Robert PORTEUS

Robert PORTEUS, Jr. = Judith COCKAYNE

Mildred PORTEUS = Robert HODGSON

Robert HODGSON, Dean of Carlisle
= Mary TUCKER

Henrietta Mildred HODGSON
= Oswald SMITH

Frances Dora SMITH
= Claude BOWES-LYON, 13th Earl of Strathmore & Kinghorne

Claude George BOWES-LYON, 14th Earl of Strathmore & Kinghorne
= Nina Cecilia CAVENDISH-BENTINCK

Lady Elizabeth Angela Marguerite BOWES-LYON, H.M. Queen ELIZABETH The Queen Mother, b. 1900 = H.M. GEORGE VI., 1895-1952 King of Great Britain

H.M. Queen ELIZABETH II., b. 1926 Queen of Great Britain = H.R.H. Prince PHILIP of Greece & Denmark, b. 1921, Duke of Edinburgh

H.R.H. Prince CHARLES PHILIP ARTHUR GEORGE of Great Britain,
Prince of Wales, b. 1948
= (1981) Lady Diana Frances SPENCER, now H.R.H. The Princess of Wales,
b. 1961 (see following charts)

H.R.H. Prince WILLIAM ARTHUR PHILIP LOUIS of Wales
b. 1982

H.R.H. Prince HENRY CHARLES ALBERT DAVID of Wales
b. 1984

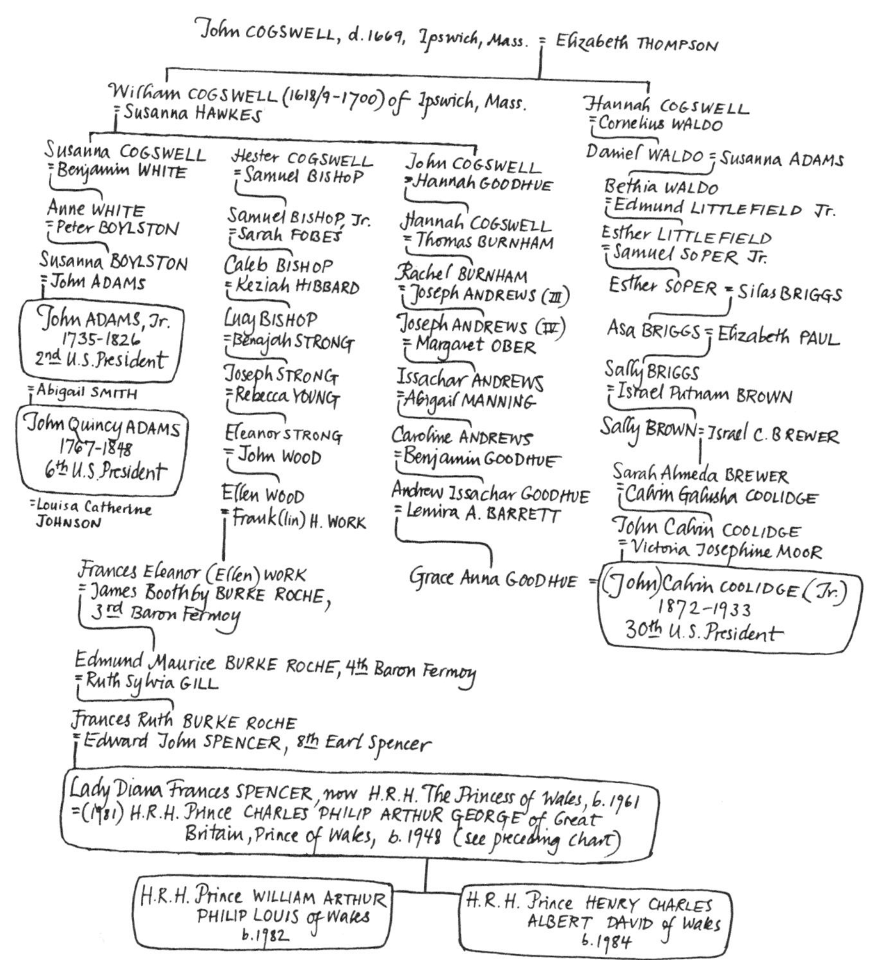
John COGSWELL, d.1669, Ipswich, Mass. = Elizabeth THOMPSON
William COGSWELL (1618/9-1700) of Ipswich, Mass.
= Susanna HAWKES
Hannah COGSWELL
= Cornelius WALDO
Susanna COGSWELL
= Benjamin WHITE
Hester COGSWELL
= Samuel BISHOP
John COGSWELL
= Hannah GOODHUE
Daniel WALDO = Susanna ADAMS
Anne WHITE
= Peter BOYLSTON
Samuel BISHOP, Jr.
= Sarah FOBES
Hannah COGSWELL
= Thomas BURNHAM
Bethia WALDO
= Edmund LITTLEFIELD Jr.
Susanna BOYLSTON
= John ADAMS
Caleb BISHOP
= Keziah HIBBARD
Rachel BURNHAM
= Joseph ANDREWS (III)
Esther LITTLEFIELD
= Samuel SOPER Jr.
John ADAMS, Jr.
1735-1826
2nd U.S. President
Lucy BISHOP
= Benajah STRONG
Joseph ANDREWS (IV)
= Margaret OBER
Esther SOPER = Silas BRIGGS
= Abigail SMITH
Joseph STRONG
= Rebecca YOUNG
Issachar ANDREWS
= Abigail MANNING
Asa BRIGGS = Elizabeth PAUL
John Quincy ADAMS
1767-1848
6th U.S. President
Eleanor STRONG
= John WOOD
Caroline ANDREWS
= Benjamin GOODHUE
Sally BRIGGS
= Israel Putnam BROWN
= Louisa Catherine JOHNSON
Ellen WOOD
= Frank(lin) H. WORK
Andrew Issachar GOODHUE
= Lemira A. BARRETT
Sally BROWN = Israel C. BREWER
Sarah Almeda BREWER
= Calvin Galusha COOLIDGE
John Calvin COOLIDGE
= Victoria Josephine MOOR
Frances Eleanor (Ellen) WORK
= James Boothby BURKE ROCHE, 3rd Baron Fermoy
Grace Anna GOODHUE = (John) Calvin COOLIDGE (Jr.)
1872-1933
30th U.S. President
Edmund Maurice BURKE ROCHE, 4th Baron Fermoy
= Ruth Sylvia GILL
Frances Ruth BURKE ROCHE
= Edward John SPENCER, 8th Earl Spencer
Lady Diana Frances SPENCER, now H.R.H. The Princess of Wales, b.1961
= (1981) H.R.H. Prince CHARLES PHILIP ARTHUR GEORGE of Great Britain, Prince of Wales, b.1948 (see preceding chart)
H.R.H. Prince WILLIAM ARTHUR PHILIP LOUIS of Wales
b.1982
H.R.H. Prince HENRY CHARLES ALBERT DAVID of Wales
b.1984

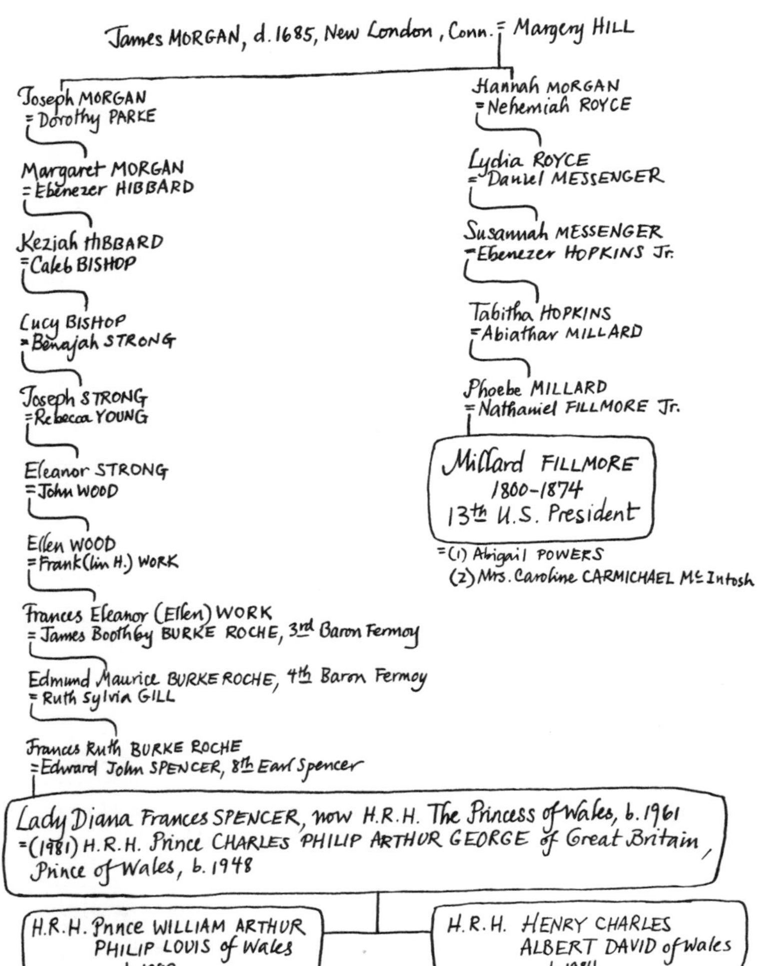

James MORGAN, d. 1685, New London, Conn. = Margery HILL
Joseph MORGAN
= Dorothy PARKE
Margaret MORGAN
= Ebenezer HIBBARD
Keziah HIBBARD
= Caleb BISHOP
Lucy BISHOP
= Benajah STRONG
Joseph STRONG
= Rebecca YOUNG
Eleanor STRONG
= John WOOD
Ellen WOOD
= Frank(lin H.) WORK
Frances Eleanor (Ellen) WORK
= James Boothby BURKE ROCHE, 3rd Baron Fermoy
Edmund Maurice BURKE ROCHE, 4th Baron Fermoy
= Ruth Sylvia GILL
Frances Ruth BURKE ROCHE
= Edward John SPENCER, 8th Earl Spencer
Lady Diana Frances SPENCER, now H.R.H. The Princess of Wales, b. 1961
= (1981) H.R.H. Prince CHARLES PHILIP ARTHUR GEORGE of Great Britain, Prince of Wales, b. 1948
H.R.H. Prince WILLIAM ARTHUR PHILIP LOUIS of Wales b. 1982
H.R.H. HENRY CHARLES ALBERT DAVID of Wales b. 1984
Hannah MORGAN
= Nehemiah ROYCE
Lydia ROYCE
= Daniel MESSENGER
Susannah MESSENGER
= Ebenezer HOPKINS Jr.
Tabitha HOPKINS
= Abiathar MILLARD
Phoebe MILLARD
= Nathaniel FILLMORE Jr.
Millard FILLMORE
1800-1874
13th U.S. President
= (1) Abigail POWERS
(2) Mrs. Caroline CARMICHAEL McIntosh

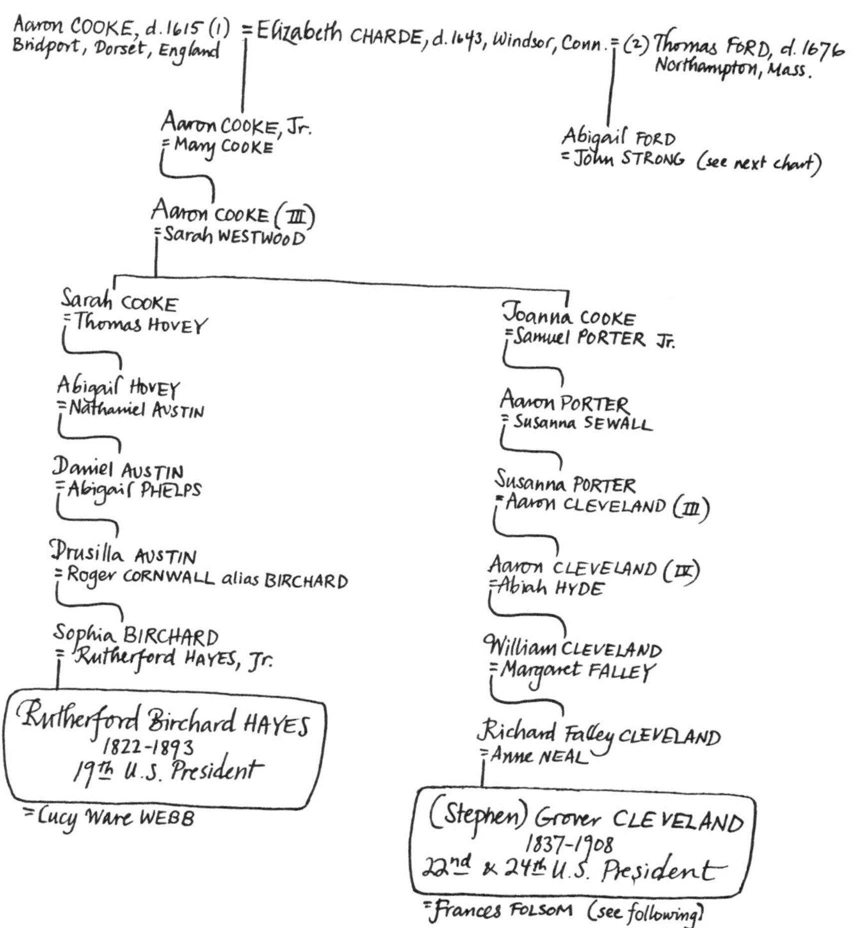
Aaron COOKE, d. 1615 (1) = Elizabeth CHARDE, d. 1643, Windsor, Conn. = (2) Thomas FORD, d. 1676
Bridport, Dorset, England
Northampton, Mass.
Aaron COOKE, Jr.
= Mary COOKE
Abigail FORD
= John STRONG (see next chart)
Aaron COOKE (III)
= Sarah WESTWOOD
Sarah COOKE
= Thomas HOVEY
Joanna COOKE
= Samuel PORTER Jr.
Abigail HOVEY
= Nathaniel AUSTIN
Aaron PORTER
= Susanna SEWALL
Daniel AUSTIN
= Abigail PHELPS
Susanna PORTER
= Aaron CLEVELAND (III)
Drusilla AUSTIN
= Roger CORNWALL alias BIRCHARD
Aaron CLEVELAND (IV)
= Abiah HYDE
Sophia BIRCHARD
= Rutherford HAYES, Jr.
William CLEVELAND
= Margaret FALLEY
Rutherford Birchard HAYES
1822-1893
19th U.S. President
Richard Falley CLEVELAND
= Anne NEAL
= Lucy Ware WEBB
(Stephen) Grover CLEVELAND
1837-1908
22nd & 24th U.S. President
= Frances FOLSOM (see following)

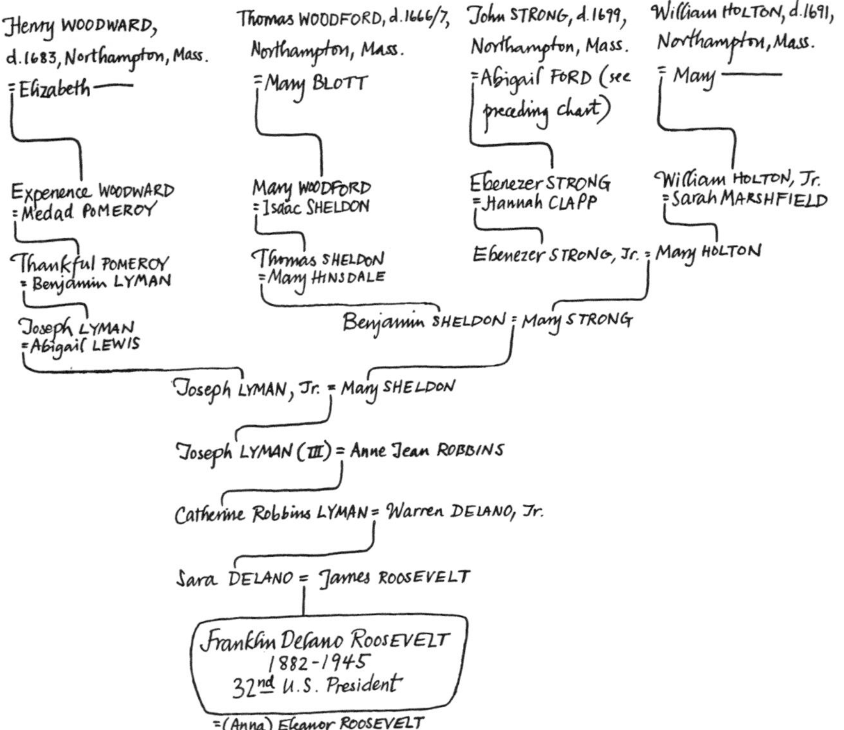
Henry WOODWARD, d. 1683, Northampton, Mass.
= Elizabeth ——
Thomas WOODFORD, d. 1666/7, Northampton, Mass.
= Mary BLOTT
John STRONG, d. 1699, Northampton, Mass.
= Abigail FORD (see preceding chart)
William HOLTON, d. 1691, Northampton, Mass.
= Mary ——
Experience WOODWARD
= Medad POMEROY
Mary WOODFORD
= Isaac SHELDON
Ebenezer STRONG
= Hannah CLAPP
William HOLTON, Jr.
= Sarah MARSHFIELD
Thankful POMEROY
= Benjamin LYMAN
Thomas SHELDON
= Mary HINSDALE
Ebenezer STRONG, Jr. = Mary HOLTON
Joseph LYMAN
= Abigail LEWIS
Benjamin SHELDON = Mary STRONG
Joseph LYMAN, Jr. = Mary SHELDON
Joseph LYMAN (III) = Anne Jean ROBBINS
Catherine Robbins LYMAN = Warren DELANO, Jr.
Sara DELANO = James ROOSEVELT
Franklin Delano ROOSEVELT
1882-1945
32nd U.S. President
=(Anna) Eleanor ROOSEVELT

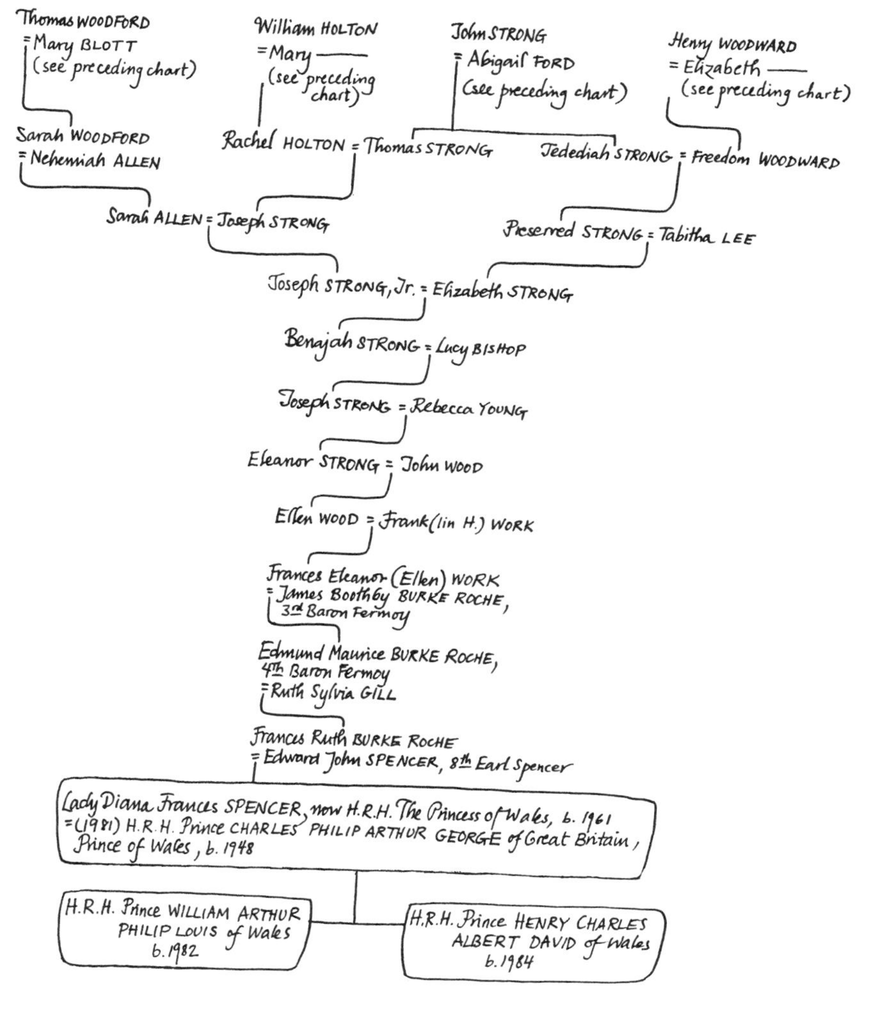
Thomas WOODFORD
= Mary BLOTT
(see preceding chart)
William HOLTON
= Mary ——
(see preceding chart)
John STRONG
= Abigail FORD
(see preceding chart)
Henry WOODWARD
= Elizabeth ——
(see preceding chart)
Sarah WOODFORD
= Nehemiah ALLEN
Rachel HOLTON = Thomas STRONG
Jedediah STRONG = Freedom WOODWARD
Sarah ALLEN = Joseph STRONG
Preserved STRONG = Tabitha LEE
Joseph STRONG, Jr. = Elizabeth STRONG
Benajah STRONG = Lucy BISHOP
Joseph STRONG = Rebecca YOUNG
Eleanor STRONG = John WOOD
Ellen WOOD = Frank (lin H.) WORK
Frances Eleanor (Ellen) WORK
= James Boothby BURKE ROCHE,
3rd Baron Fermoy
Edmund Maurice BURKE ROCHE,
4th Baron Fermoy
= Ruth Sylvia GILL
Frances Ruth BURKE ROCHE
= Edward John SPENCER, 8th Earl Spencer
Lady Diana Frances SPENCER, now H.R.H. The Princess of Wales, b. 1961
= (1981) H.R.H. Prince CHARLES PHILIP ARTHUR GEORGE of Great Britain,
Prince of Wales, b. 1948
H.R.H. Prince WILLIAM ARTHUR
PHILIP LOUIS of Wales
b. 1982
H.R.H. Prince HENRY CHARLES
ALBERT DAVID of Wales
b. 1984

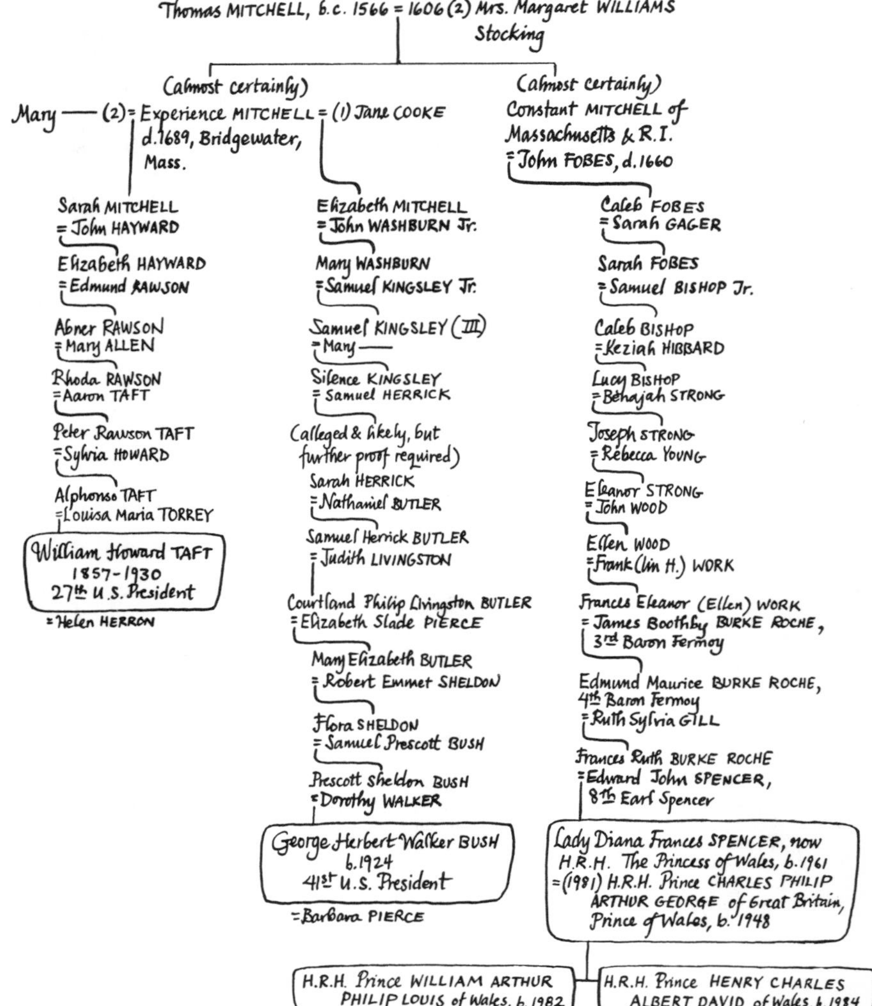
Thomas MITCHELL, b.c. 1566 = 1606 (2) Mrs. Margaret WILLIAMS Stocking
(almost certainly)
Mary —— (2) = Experience MITCHELL = (1) Jane COOKE
d. 1689, Bridgewater, Mass.
(almost certainly)
Constant MITCHELL of Massachusetts & R.I.
= John FOBES, d. 1660
Sarah MITCHELL
= John HAYWARD
Elizabeth HAYWARD
= Edmund RAWSON
Abner RAWSON
= Mary ALLEN
Rhoda RAWSON
= Aaron TAFT
Peter Rawson TAFT
= Sylvia HOWARD
Alphonso TAFT
= Louisa Maria TORREY
William Howard TAFT
1857-1930
27th U.S. President
= Helen HERRON
Elizabeth MITCHELL
= John WASHBURN Jr.
Mary WASHBURN
= Samuel KINGSLEY Jr.
Samuel KINGSLEY (III)
= Mary ——
Silence KINGSLEY
= Samuel HERRICK
(alleged & likely, but further proof required)
Sarah HERRICK
= Nathaniel BUTLER
Samuel Herrick BUTLER
= Judith LIVINGSTON
Courtland Philip Livingston BUTLER
= Elizabeth Slade PIERCE
Mary Elizabeth BUTLER
= Robert Emmet SHELDON
Flora SHELDON
= Samuel Prescott BUSH
Prescott Sheldon BUSH
= Dorothy WALKER
George Herbert Walker BUSH
b. 1924
41st U.S. President
= Barbara PIERCE
Caleb FOBES
= Sarah GAGER
Sarah FOBES
= Samuel BISHOP Jr.
Caleb BISHOP
= Keziah HIBBARD
Lucy BISHOP
= Behajah STRONG
Joseph STRONG
= Rebecca YOUNG
Eleanor STRONG
= John WOOD
Ellen WOOD
= Frank (Jim H.) WORK
Frances Eleanor (Ellen) WORK
= James Boothby BURKE ROCHE, 3rd Baron Fermoy
Edmund Maurice BURKE ROCHE, 4th Baron Fermoy
= Ruth Sylvia GILL
Frances Ruth BURKE ROCHE
= Edward John SPENCER, 8th Earl Spencer
Lady Diana Frances SPENCER, now H.R.H. The Princess of Wales, b. 1961
= (1981) H.R.H. Prince CHARLES PHILIP ARTHUR GEORGE of Great Britain, Prince of Wales, b. 1948
H.R.H. Prince WILLIAM ARTHUR PHILIP LOUIS of Wales, b. 1982
H.R.H. Prince HENRY CHARLES ALBERT DAVID of Wales, b. 1984

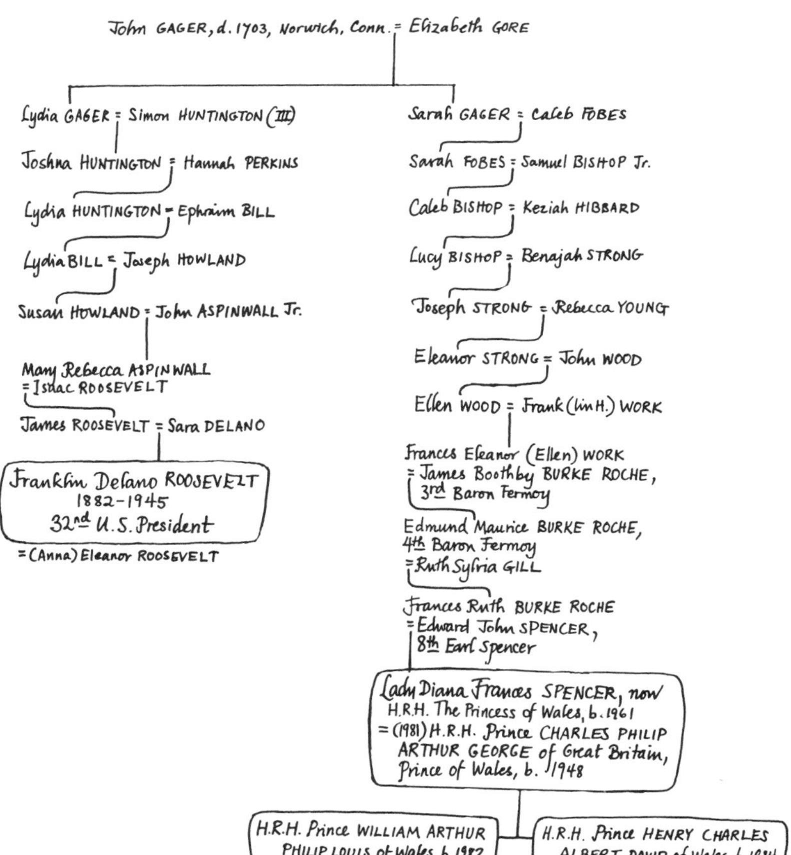
John GAGER, d. 1703, Norwich, Conn. = Elizabeth GORE
Lydia GAGER = Simon HUNTINGTON (III)
Joshua HUNTINGTON = Hannah PERKINS
Lydia HUNTINGTON = Ephraim BILL
Lydia BILL = Joseph HOWLAND
Susan HOWLAND = John ASPINWALL Jr.
Mary Rebecca ASPINWALL
= Isaac ROOSEVELT
James ROOSEVELT = Sara DELANO
Franklin Delano ROOSEVELT
1882-1945
32nd U.S. President
= (Anna) Eleanor ROOSEVELT
Sarah GAGER = Caleb FOBES
Sarah FOBES = Samuel BISHOP Jr.
Caleb BISHOP = Keziah HIBBARD
Lucy BISHOP = Benajah STRONG
Joseph STRONG = Rebecca YOUNG
Eleanor STRONG = John WOOD
Ellen WOOD = Frank (kin H.) WORK
Frances Eleanor (Ellen) WORK
= James Boothby BURKE ROCHE,
3rd Baron Fermoy
Edmund Maurice BURKE ROCHE,
4th Baron Fermoy
= Ruth Sylvia GILL
Frances Ruth BURKE ROCHE
= Edward John SPENCER,
8th Earl Spencer
Lady Diana Frances SPENCER, now
H.R.H. The Princess of Wales, b. 1961
= (1981) H.R.H. Prince CHARLES PHILIP
ARTHUR GEORGE of Great Britain,
Prince of Wales, b. 1948
H.R.H. Prince WILLIAM ARTHUR
PHILIP LOUIS of Wales, b. 1982
H.R.H. Prince HENRY CHARLES
ALBERT DAVID of Wales, b. 1984

John CLAYTON, d. 1704, of Shrewsbury & Chesterfield, N.J. = Alice MYRES

Zebulon CLAYTON = Mary HARTSHORNE

Thomas CLAYTON = Hannah ———

(probably) Thomas CLAYTON (Jr.) = Mary (WALKER?)

Mary CLAYTON = Isaac BROWN

Jane BROWN = Joseph Dickinson MOORE

Mary Louise MOORE = Thomas Wiley WADSWORTH

Sarah Ann WADSWORTH = Samuel Brady NIXON

Francis Anthony NIXON = Hannah MILHOUS

Richard Milhous NIXON
b. 1913
37th U.S. President

= Thelma Catherine (Pat) RYAN

Rachel CLAYTON = Michael NEWBOLD, Jr.

Sarah NEWBOLD = Thomas BOUDE

Joseph BOUDE = Barbara BLACK

Sarah Duncan BOUDE = John WORK

Frank(lin H.) WORK = Ellen WOOD

Frances Eleanor (Ellen) WORK = James Boothby BURKE ROCHE, 3rd Baron Fermoy

Edmund Maurice BURKE ROCHE, 4th Baron Fermoy = Ruth Sylvia GILL

Frances Ruth BURKE ROCHE = Edward John SPENCER, 8th Earl Spencer

Lady Diana Frances SPENCER,
now H.R.H. The Princess of Wales, b. 1961
= (1981) H.R.H. Prince CHARLES PHILIP ARTHUR GEORGE of Great Britain, Prince of Wales, b. 1948

H.R.H. Prince WILLIAM ARTHUR PHILIP LOUIS of WALES, b. 1982

H.R.H. Prince HENRY CHARLES ALBERT DAVID of Wales, b. 1984

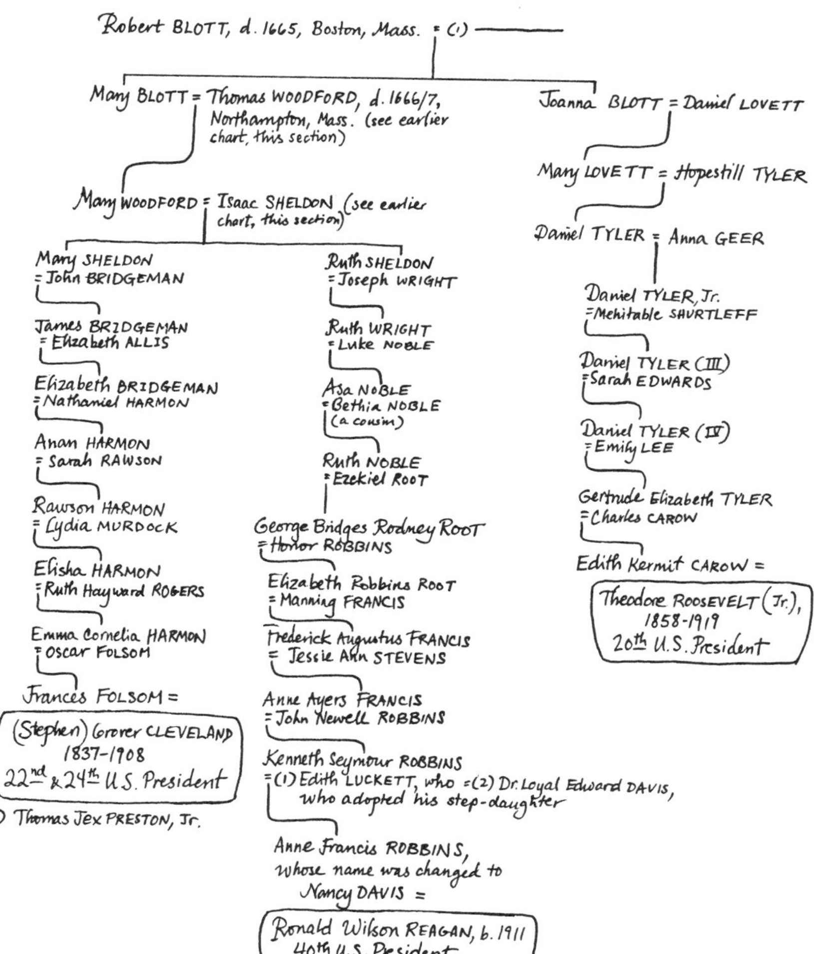
Robert BLOTT, d. 1665, Boston, Mass. = (1) ———
Mary BLOTT = Thomas WOODFORD, d. 1666/7, Northampton, Mass. (see earlier chart, this section)
Joanna BLOTT = Daniel LOVETT
Mary LOVETT = Hopestill TYLER
Mary WOODFORD = Isaac SHELDON (see earlier chart, this section)
Daniel TYLER = Anna GEER
Mary SHELDON = John BRIDGEMAN
Ruth SHELDON = Joseph WRIGHT
Daniel TYLER, Jr. = Mehitable SHURTLEFF
James BRIDGEMAN = Elizabeth ALLIS
Ruth WRIGHT = Luke NOBLE
Daniel TYLER (III) = Sarah EDWARDS
Elizabeth BRIDGEMAN = Nathaniel HARMON
Asa NOBLE = Bethia NOBLE (a cousin)
Daniel TYLER (IV) = Emily LEE
Anan HARMON = Sarah RAWSON
Ruth NOBLE = Ezekiel ROOT
Gertrude Elizabeth TYLER = Charles CAROW
Rawson HARMON = Lydia MURDOCK
George Bridges Rodney ROOT = Honor ROBBINS
Edith Kermit CAROW =
Theodore ROOSEVELT (Jr.), 1858-1919 20th U.S. President
Elisha HARMON = Ruth Hayward ROGERS
Elizabeth Robbins ROOT = Manning FRANCIS
Emma Cornelia HARMON = Oscar FOLSOM
Frederick Augustus FRANCIS = Jessie Ann STEVENS
Frances FOLSOM =
(1) (Stephen) Grover CLEVELAND 1837-1908 22nd & 24th U.S. President
(2) Thomas Jex PRESTON, Jr.
Anne Ayers FRANCIS = John Newell ROBBINS
Kenneth Seymour ROBBINS = (1) Edith LUCKETT, who = (2) Dr. Loyal Edward DAVIS, who adopted his step-daughter
Anne Francis ROBBINS, whose name was changed to Nancy DAVIS =
Ronald Wilson REAGAN, b. 1911 40th U.S. President

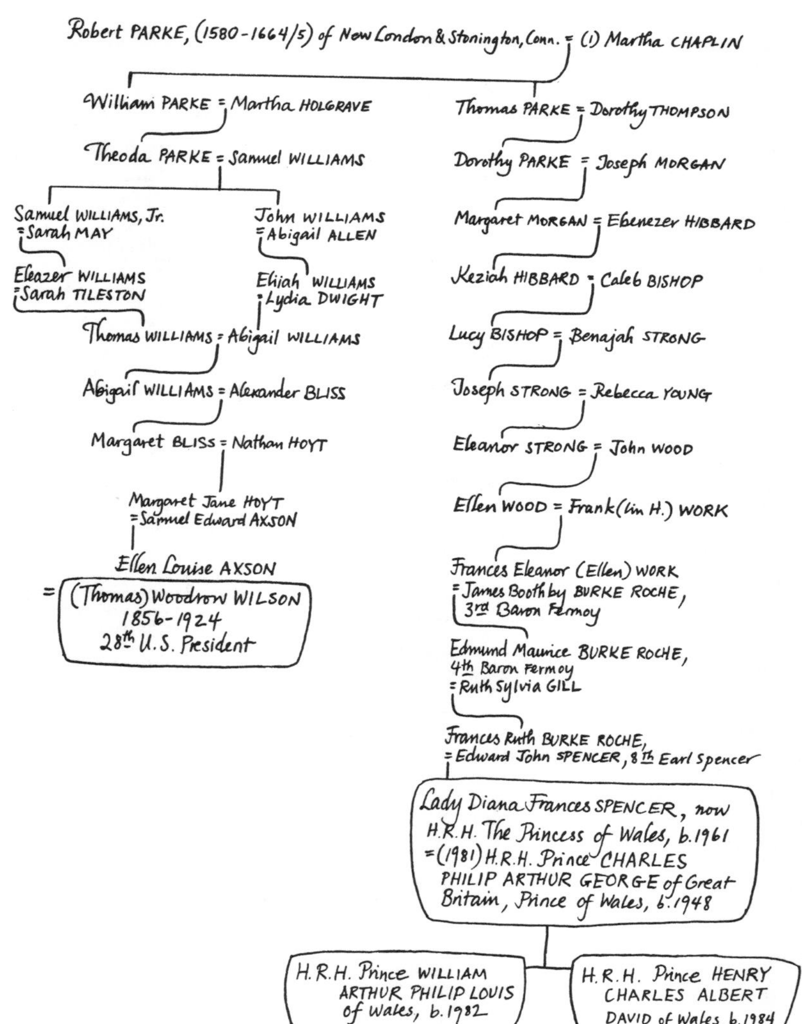
Robert PARKE, (1580-1664/5) of New London & Stonington, Conn. = (1) Martha CHAPLIN
William PARKE = Martha HOLGRAVE
Theoda PARKE = Samuel WILLIAMS
Samuel WILLIAMS, Jr. = Sarah MAY
John WILLIAMS = Abigail ALLEN
Eleazer WILLIAMS = Sarah TILESTON
Elijah WILLIAMS = Lydia DWIGHT
Thomas WILLIAMS = Abigail WILLIAMS
Abigail WILLIAMS = Alexander BLISS
Margaret BLISS = Nathan HOYT
Margaret Jane HOYT = Samuel Edward AXSON
Ellen Louise AXSON
= (Thomas) Woodrow WILSON 1856-1924 28th U.S. President
Thomas PARKE = Dorothy THOMPSON
Dorothy PARKE = Joseph MORGAN
Margaret MORGAN = Ebenezer HIBBARD
Keziah HIBBARD = Caleb BISHOP
Lucy BISHOP = Benajah STRONG
Joseph STRONG = Rebecca YOUNG
Eleanor STRONG = John WOOD
Ellen WOOD = Frank(lin H.) WORK
Frances Eleanor (Ellen) WORK = James Boothby BURKE ROCHE, 3rd Baron Fermoy
Edmund Maurice BURKE ROCHE, 4th Baron Fermoy = Ruth Sylvia GILL
Frances Ruth BURKE ROCHE, = Edward John SPENCER, 8th Earl Spencer
Lady Diana Frances SPENCER, now H.R.H. The Princess of Wales, b. 1961 = (1981) H.R.H. Prince CHARLES PHILIP ARTHUR GEORGE of Great Britain, Prince of Wales, b. 1948
H.R.H. Prince WILLIAM ARTHUR PHILIP LOUIS of Wales, b. 1982
H.R.H. Prince HENRY CHARLES ALBERT DAVID of Wales, b. 1984

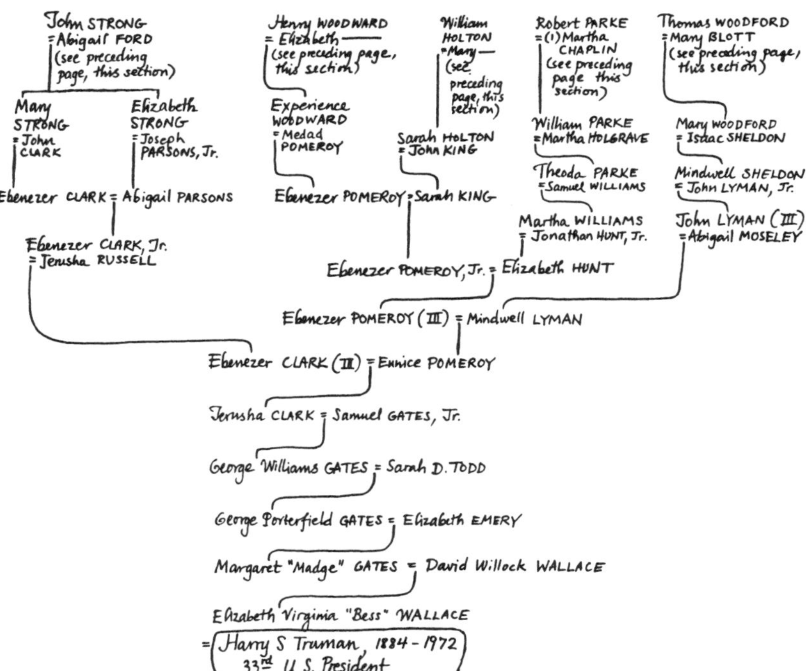
John STRONG
= Abigail FORD
(see preceding page, this section)
Mary STRONG
= John CLARK
Elizabeth STRONG
= Joseph PARSONS, Jr.
Ebenezer CLARK = Abigail PARSONS
Ebenezer CLARK, Jr.
= Jerusha RUSSELL
Henry WOODWARD
= Elizabeth ——
(see preceding page, this section)
Experience WOODWARD
= Medad POMEROY
William HOLTON
= Mary ——
(see preceding page, this section)
Sarah HOLTON
= John KING
Ebenezer POMEROY = Sarah KING
Robert PARKE
= (1) Martha CHAPLIN
(see preceding page this section)
William PARKE
= Martha HOLGRAVE
Theoda PARKE
= Samuel WILLIAMS
Martha WILLIAMS
= Jonathan HUNT, Jr.
Thomas WOODFORD
= Mary BLOTT
(see preceding page, this section)
Mary WOODFORD
= Isaac SHELDON
Mindwell SHELDON
= John LYMAN, Jr.
John LYMAN (III)
= Abigail MOSELEY
Ebenezer POMEROY, Jr. = Elizabeth HUNT
Ebenezer POMEROY (III) = Mindwell LYMAN
Ebenezer CLARK (III) = Eunice POMEROY
Jerusha CLARK = Samuel GATES, Jr.
George Williams GATES = Sarah D. TODD
George Porterfield GATES = Elizabeth EMERY
Margaret "Madge" GATES = David Willock WALLACE
Elizabeth Virginia "Bess" WALLACE
= Harry S Truman, 1884-1972
33rd U.S. President

Appendix 4

Charts Outlining the Nearest Kinships Between Twelve U. S. Presidents (Washington, Jefferson, J. Q. Adams, the two Harrisons, Cleveland, the two Roosevelts, Ford, Bush, and probably Taylor and Hoover) and Modern Royalty Generally - Through John of Gaunt, Duke of Lancaster (1340-1399), Sancha de Ayala (d. 1418, wife of Sir Walter Blount), and the Descendants of Henry VII (Tudor), King of England, and Elizabeth Plantagenet, and of Ferdinand and Isabella, the First Rulers of a United Spain

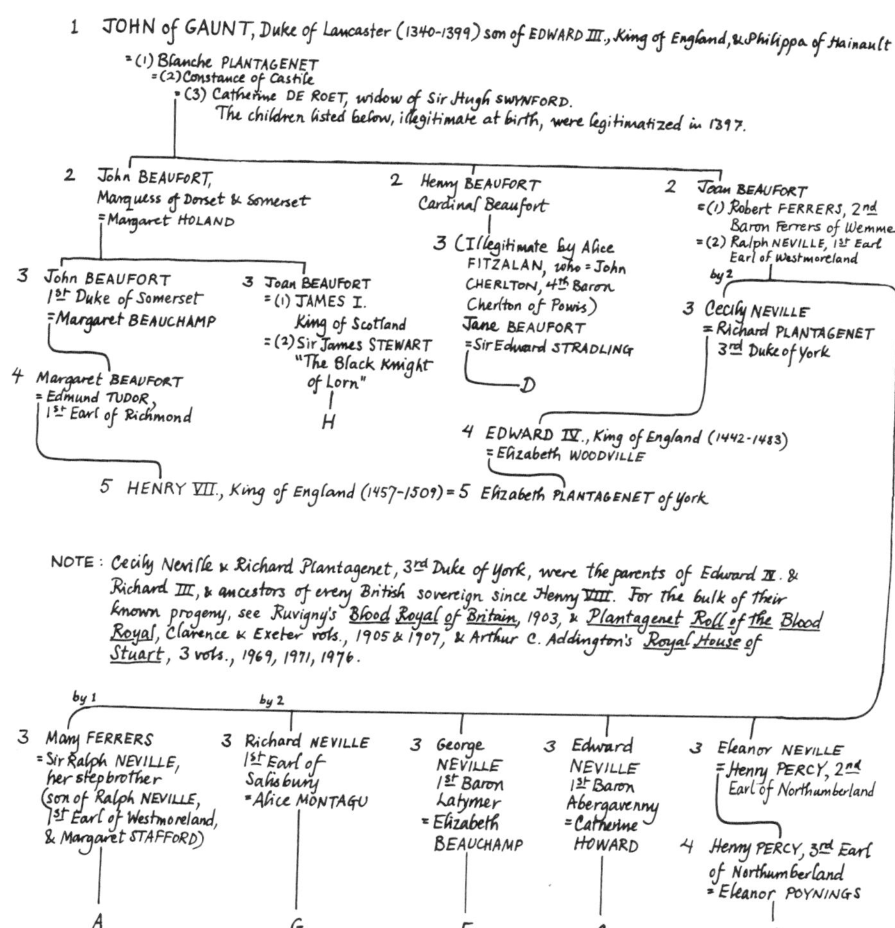
1 JOHN of GAUNT, Duke of Lancaster (1340-1399) son of EDWARD III., King of England, & Philippa of Hainault
= (1) Blanche PLANTAGENET
= (2) Constance of Castile
= (3) Catherine DE ROET, widow of Sir Hugh SWYNFORD.
The children listed below, illegitimate at birth, were legitimatized in 1397.
2 John BEAUFORT, Marquess of Dorset & Somerset = Margaret HOLAND
2 Henry BEAUFORT Cardinal Beaufort
2 Joan BEAUFORT =(1) Robert FERRERS, 2nd Baron Ferrers of Wemme =(2) Ralph NEVILLE, 1st Earl Earl of Westmoreland
3 John BEAUFORT 1st Duke of Somerset = Margaret BEAUCHAMP
3 Joan BEAUFORT =(1) JAMES I. King of Scotland =(2) Sir James STEWART "The Black Knight of Lorn"
H
3 (Illegitimate by Alice FITZALAN, who = John CHERLTON, 4th Baron Cherlton of Powis) Jane BEAUFORT = Sir Edward STRADLING
D
by 2
3 Cecily NEVILLE = Richard PLANTAGENET 3rd Duke of York
4 Margaret BEAUFORT = Edmund TUDOR, 1st Earl of Richmond
4 EDWARD IV., King of England (1442-1483) = Elizabeth WOODVILLE
5 HENRY VII., King of England (1457-1509) = 5 Elizabeth PLANTAGENET of York
NOTE: Cecily Neville & Richard Plantagenet, 3rd Duke of York, were the parents of Edward IV. & Richard III, & ancestors of every British sovereign since Henry VIII. For the bulk of their known progeny, see Ruvigny's Blood Royal of Britain, 1903, & Plantagenet Roll of the Blood Royal, Clarence & Exeter vols., 1905 & 1907, & Arthur C. Addington's Royal House of Stuart, 3 vols., 1969, 1971, 1976.
by 1
by 2
3 Mary FERRERS = Sir Ralph NEVILLE, her stepbrother (son of Ralph NEVILLE, 1st Earl of Westmoreland, & Margaret STAFFORD)
A
3 Richard NEVILLE 1st Earl of Salisbury = Alice MONTAGU
G
3 George NEVILLE 1st Baron Latymer = Elizabeth BEAUCHAMP
E
3 Edward NEVILLE 1st Baron Abergavenny = Catherine HOWARD
C
3 Eleanor NEVILLE = Henry PERCY, 2nd Earl of Northumberland
4 Henry PERCY, 3rd Earl of Northumberland = Eleanor POYNINGS
B

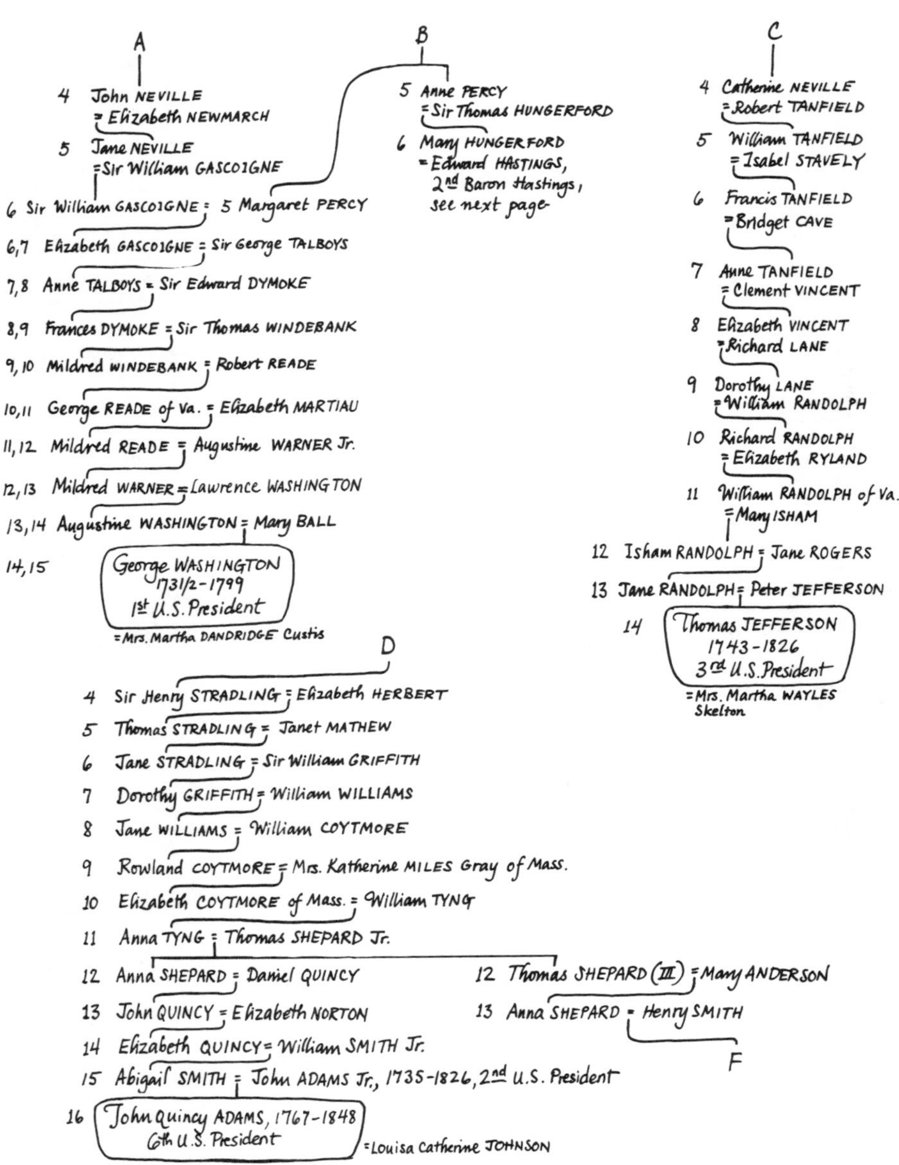
A
4 John NEVILLE
= Elizabeth NEWMARCH
5 Jane NEVILLE
= Sir William GASCOIGNE
6 Sir William GASCOIGNE = 5 Margaret PERCY
6,7 Elizabeth GASCOIGNE = Sir George TALBOYS
7,8 Anne TALBOYS = Sir Edward DYMOKE
8,9 Frances DYMOKE = Sir Thomas WINDEBANK
9,10 Mildred WINDEBANK = Robert READE
10,11 George READE of Va. = Elizabeth MARTIAU
11,12 Mildred READE = Augustine WARNER Jr.
12,13 Mildred WARNER = Lawrence WASHINGTON
13,14 Augustine WASHINGTON = Mary BALL
14,15 George WASHINGTON 1731/2-1799 1st U.S. President
= Mrs. Martha DANDRIDGE Custis
B
5 Anne PERCY
= Sir Thomas HUNGERFORD
6 Mary HUNGERFORD
= Edward HASTINGS, 2nd Baron Hastings, see next page
C
4 Catherine NEVILLE
= Robert TANFIELD
5 William TANFIELD
= Isabel STAVELY
6 Francis TANFIELD
= Bridget CAVE
7 Anne TANFIELD
= Clement VINCENT
8 Elizabeth VINCENT
= Richard LANE
9 Dorothy LANE
= William RANDOLPH
10 Richard RANDOLPH
= Elizabeth RYLAND
11 William RANDOLPH of Va.
= Mary ISHAM
12 Isham RANDOLPH = Jane ROGERS
13 Jane RANDOLPH = Peter JEFFERSON
14 Thomas JEFFERSON 1743-1826 3rd U.S. President
= Mrs. Martha WAYLES Skelton
D
4 Sir Henry STRADLING = Elizabeth HERBERT
5 Thomas STRADLING = Janet MATHEW
6 Jane STRADLING = Sir William GRIFFITH
7 Dorothy GRIFFITH = William WILLIAMS
8 Jane WILLIAMS = William COYTMORE
9 Rowland COYTMORE = Mrs. Katherine MILES Gray of Mass.
10 Elizabeth COYTMORE of Mass. = William TYNG
11 Anna TYNG = Thomas SHEPARD Jr.
12 Anna SHEPARD = Daniel QUINCY
13 John QUINCY = Elizabeth NORTON
14 Elizabeth QUINCY = William SMITH Jr.
15 Abigail SMITH = John ADAMS Jr., 1735-1826, 2nd U.S. President
16 John Quincy ADAMS, 1767-1848 6th U.S. President
= Louisa Catherine JOHNSON
12 Thomas SHEPARD (III) = Mary ANDERSON
13 Anna SHEPARD = Henry SMITH
F

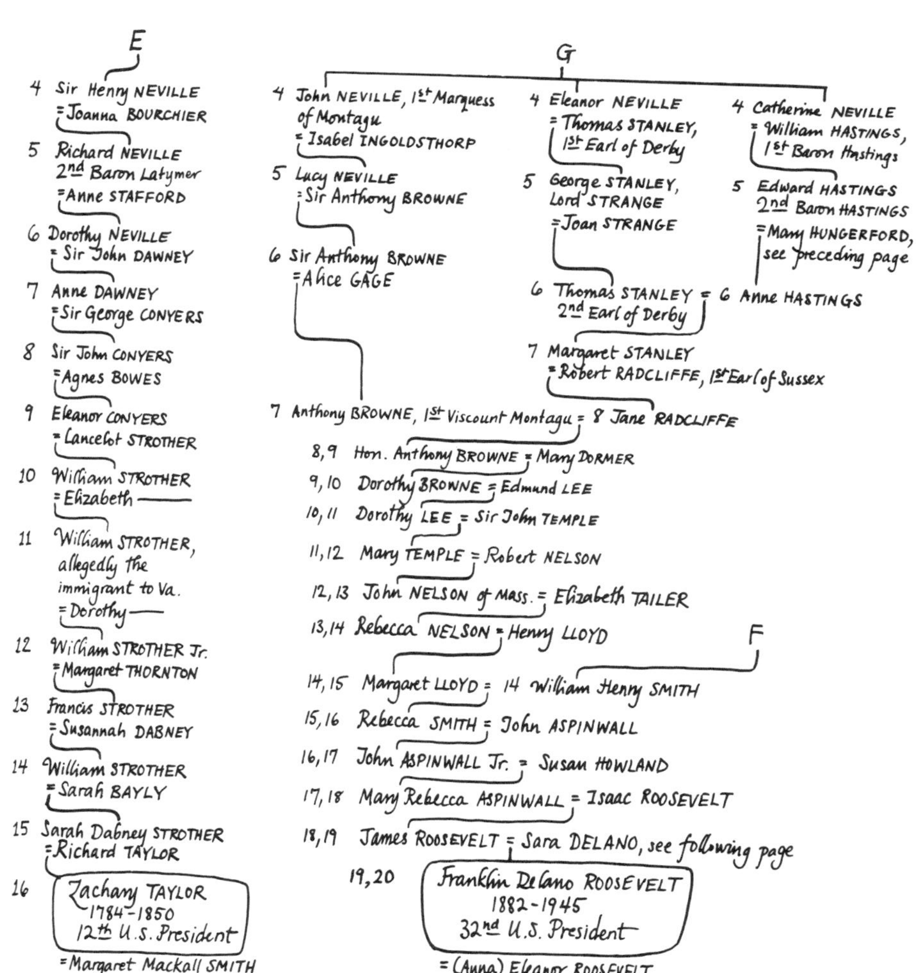
E
4 Sir Henry NEVILLE
= Joanna BOURCHIER
5 Richard NEVILLE
2nd Baron Latymer
= Anne STAFFORD
6 Dorothy NEVILLE
= Sir John DAWNEY
7 Anne DAWNEY
= Sir George CONYERS
8 Sir John CONYERS
= Agnes BOWES
9 Eleanor CONYERS
= Lancelot STROTHER
10 William STROTHER
= Elizabeth ———
11 William STROTHER,
allegedly the
immigrant to Va.
= Dorothy ———
12 William STROTHER Jr.
= Margaret THORNTON
13 Francis STROTHER
= Susannah DABNEY
14 William STROTHER
= Sarah BAYLY
15 Sarah Dabney STROTHER
= Richard TAYLOR
16 Zachary TAYLOR
1784-1850
12th U.S. President
= Margaret Mackall SMITH
G
4 John NEVILLE, 1st Marquess
of Montagu
= Isabel INGOLDSTHORP
5 Lucy NEVILLE
= Sir Anthony BROWNE
6 Sir Anthony BROWNE
= Alice GAGE
4 Eleanor NEVILLE
= Thomas STANLEY,
1st Earl of Derby
5 George STANLEY,
Lord STRANGE
= Joan STRANGE
4 Catherine NEVILLE
= William HASTINGS,
1st Baron Hastings
5 Edward HASTINGS
2nd Baron HASTINGS
= Mary HUNGERFORD,
see preceding page
6 Thomas STANLEY = 6 Anne HASTINGS
2nd Earl of Derby
7 Margaret STANLEY
= Robert RADCLIFFE, 1st Earl of Sussex
7 Anthony BROWNE, 1st Viscount Montagu = 8 Jane RADCLIFFE
8,9 Hon. Anthony BROWNE = Mary DORMER
9,10 Dorothy BROWNE = Edmund LEE
10,11 Dorothy LEE = Sir John TEMPLE
11,12 Mary TEMPLE = Robert NELSON
12,13 John NELSON of Mass. = Elizabeth TAILER
13,14 Rebecca NELSON = Henry LLOYD
F
14,15 Margaret LLOYD = 14 William Henry SMITH
15,16 Rebecca SMITH = John ASPINWALL
16,17 John ASPINWALL Jr. = Susan HOWLAND
17,18 Mary Rebecca ASPINWALL = Isaac ROOSEVELT
18,19 James ROOSEVELT = Sara DELANO, see following page
19,20 Franklin Delano ROOSEVELT
1882-1945
32nd U.S. President
= (Anna) Eleanor ROOSEVELT

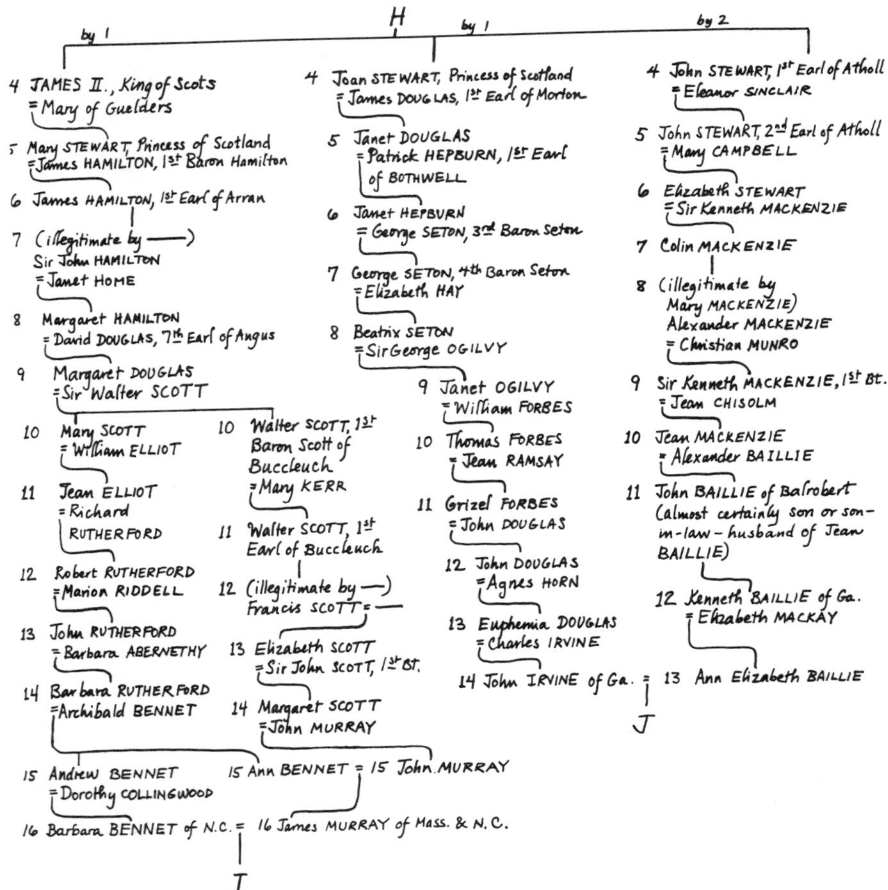
H
by 1
by 1
by 2
4 JAMES II., King of Scots
= Mary of Guelders
5 Mary STEWART, Princess of Scotland
= James HAMILTON, 1st Baron Hamilton
6 James HAMILTON, 1st Earl of Arran
7 (illegitimate by —)
Sir John HAMILTON
= Janet HOME
8 Margaret HAMILTON
= David DOUGLAS, 7th Earl of Angus
9 Margaret DOUGLAS
= Sir Walter SCOTT
10 Mary SCOTT
= William ELLIOT
11 Jean ELLIOT
= Richard RUTHERFORD
12 Robert RUTHERFORD
= Marion RIDDELL
13 John RUTHERFORD
= Barbara ABERNETHY
14 Barbara RUTHERFORD
= Archibald BENNET
15 Andrew BENNET
= Dorothy COLLINGWOOD
16 Barbara BENNET of N.C. = 16 James MURRAY of Mass. & N.C.
I
10 Walter SCOTT, 1st Baron Scott of Buccleuch
= Mary KERR
11 Walter SCOTT, 1st Earl of Buccleuch
12 (illegitimate by —)
Francis SCOTT = —
13 Elizabeth SCOTT
= Sir John SCOTT, 1st Bt.
14 Margaret SCOTT
= John MURRAY
15 Ann BENNET = 15 John MURRAY
4 Joan STEWART, Princess of Scotland
= James DOUGLAS, 1st Earl of Morton
5 Janet DOUGLAS
= Patrick HEPBURN, 1st Earl of BOTHWELL
6 Janet HEPBURN
= George SETON, 3rd Baron Seton
7 George SETON, 4th Baron Seton
= Elizabeth HAY
8 Beatrix SETON
= Sir George OGILVY
9 Janet OGILVY
= William FORBES
10 Thomas FORBES
= Jean RAMSAY
11 Grizel FORBES
= John DOUGLAS
12 John DOUGLAS
= Agnes HORN
13 Euphemia DOUGLAS
= Charles IRVINE
14 John IRVINE of Ga. = 13 Ann Elizabeth BAILLIE
J
4 John STEWART, 1st Earl of Atholl
= Eleanor SINCLAIR
5 John STEWART, 2nd Earl of Atholl
= Mary CAMPBELL
6 Elizabeth STEWART
= Sir Kenneth MACKENZIE
7 Colin MACKENZIE
8 (illegitimate by Mary MACKENZIE)
Alexander MACKENZIE
= Christian MUNRO
9 Sir Kenneth MACKENZIE, 1st Bt.
= Jean CHISOLM
10 Jean MACKENZIE
= Alexander BAILLIE
11 John BAILLIE of Balrobert
(almost certainly son or son-in-law-husband of Jean BAILLIE)
12 Kenneth BAILLIE of Ga.
= Elizabeth MACKAY

I

17 Elizabeth MURRAY = Edward Hutchinson ROBBINS

18 Anne Jean ROBBINS = Joseph LYMAN (III)

19 Catherine Robbins LYMAN = Warren DELANO Jr.

20 Sara DELANO = James ROOSEVELT, see preceding Chart

21 Franklin Delano ROOSEVELT
1882-1945
32nd U.S. President

=(Anna) Eleanor ROOSEVELT, daughter (by Anna Livingston HALL) of Elliot ROOSEVELT, brother of Theodore ROOSEVELT, Jr., see right

J

14,15 Anne IRVINE = James BULLOCH

15,16 James Stephens BULLOCH
= Martha STEWART

16,17 Martha BULLOCH = Theodore ROOSEVELT

17,18 Theodore ROOSEVELT, Jr.
1858-1919
26th U.S. President

= (1) Alice Hathaway LEE
= (2) Edith Kermit CAROW

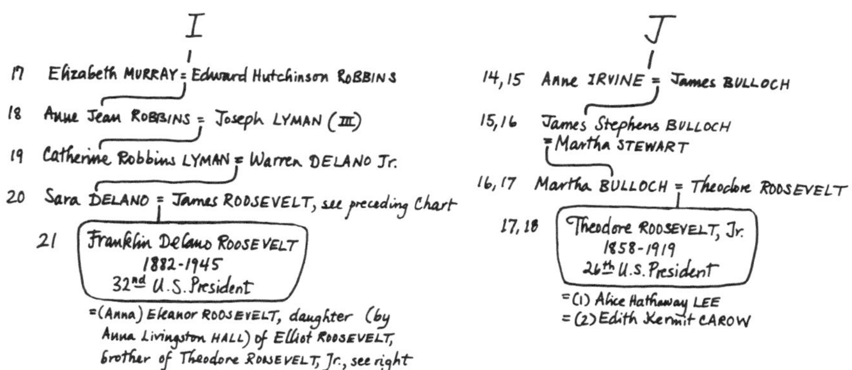

NOTE: Philippa PLANTAGENET, daughter of John of Gaunt & Blanche PLANTAGENET, married JOÃO I., King of Portugal, & was an ancestress of all later kings of that country; and Catherine PLANTAGENET, daughter of John of Gaunt & Constance of Castile, married ENRIQUE III., King of Castile, & was an ancestress of all later sovereigns of Castile & Spain. Philippa was a great-grandmother, & Catherine a grandmother, of ISABELLA of Castile, 1st Queen of United Spain, as follows:

1 John of Gaunt, Duke of Lancaster
= (1) Blanche PLANTAGENET
= (2) Constance of Castile

2 Philippa PLANTAGENET
= JOÃO I., King of Portugal (1358-1433)

3 João, Prince of Portugal
= Isabella of Braganza

2 Catherine PLANTAGENET
= ENRIQUE III., King of Castile (1379-1406)

4 Isabella of Portugal = 3 JUAN II., King of Castile (1405-1454)

4,5 ISABELLA of Castile (1451-1504)
= FERDINAND I., 1st King of United Spain (1452-1516); see the next chart for his English connections via Sancha de Ayala & a brief note concerning his & Isabella's royal progeny.

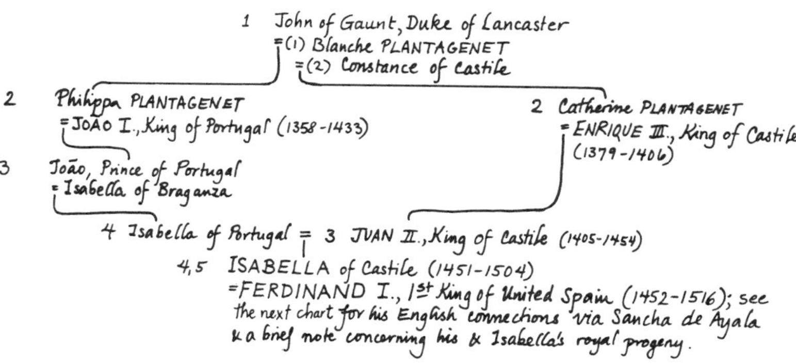

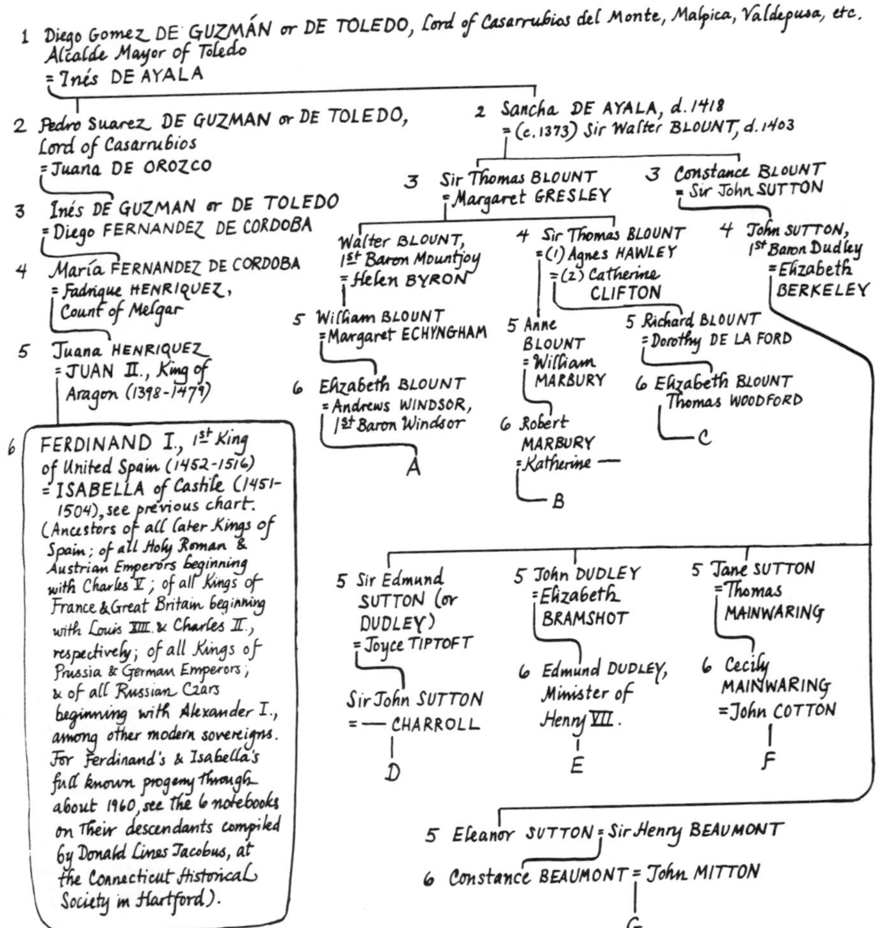
1 Diego Gomez DE GUZMÁN or DE TOLEDO, Lord of Casarrubios del Monte, Malpica, Valdepusa, etc. Alcalde Mayor of Toledo
= Inés DE AYALA
2 Pedro Suarez DE GUZMAN or DE TOLEDO, Lord of Casarrubios
= Juana DE OROZCO
3 Inés DE GUZMAN or DE TOLEDO
= Diego FERNANDEZ DE CORDOBA
4 María FERNANDEZ DE CORDOBA
= Fadrique HENRIQUEZ, Count of Melgar
5 Juana HENRIQUEZ
= JUAN II., King of Aragon (1398-1479)
6 FERDINAND I., 1st King of United Spain (1452-1516)
= ISABELLA of Castile (1451-1504), see previous chart. (Ancestors of all later Kings of Spain; of all Holy Roman & Austrian Emperors beginning with Charles V; of all Kings of France & Great Britain beginning with Louis XIII. & Charles II., respectively; of all Kings of Prussia & German Emperors; & of all Russian Czars beginning with Alexander I., among other modern sovereigns. For Ferdinand's & Isabella's full known progeny through about 1960, see the 6 notebooks on their descendants compiled by Donald Lines Jacobus, at the Connecticut Historical Society in Hartford).
2 Sancha DE AYALA, d. 1418
= (c. 1373) Sir Walter BLOUNT, d. 1403
3 Sir Thomas BLOUNT
= Margaret GRESLEY
3 Constance BLOUNT
= Sir John SUTTON
Walter BLOUNT, 1st Baron Mountjoy
= Helen BYRON
4 Sir Thomas BLOUNT
= (1) Agnes HAWLEY
= (2) Catherine CLIFTON
4 John SUTTON, 1st Baron Dudley
= Elizabeth BERKELEY
5 William BLOUNT
= Margaret ECHYNGHAM
5 Anne BLOUNT
= William MARBURY
5 Richard BLOUNT
= Dorothy DE LA FORD
6 Elizabeth BLOUNT
= Andrews WINDSOR, 1st Baron Windsor
A
6 Robert MARBURY
= Katherine —
B
6 Elizabeth BLOUNT
Thomas WOODFORD
C
5 Sir Edmund SUTTON (or DUDLEY)
= Joyce TIPTOFT
Sir John SUTTON
= — CHARROLL
D
5 John DUDLEY
= Elizabeth BRAMSHOT
6 Edmund DUDLEY, Minister of Henry VII.
E
5 Jane SUTTON
= Thomas MAINWARING
6 Cecily MAINWARING
= John COTTON
F
5 Eleanor SUTTON = Sir Henry BEAUMONT
6 Constance BEAUMONT = John MITTON
G

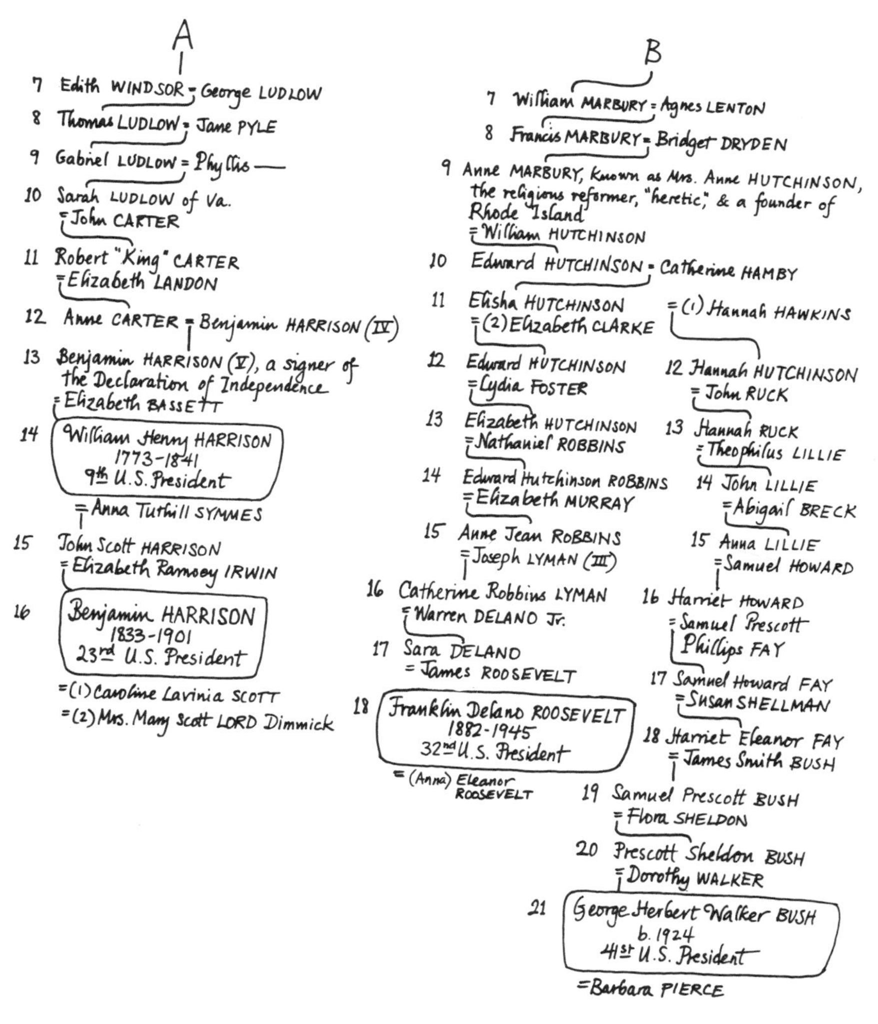
A
7 Edith WINDSOR = George LUDLOW
8 Thomas LUDLOW = Jane PYLE
9 Gabriel LUDLOW = Phyllis —
10 Sarah LUDLOW of Va.
= John CARTER
11 Robert "King" CARTER
= Elizabeth LANDON
12 Anne CARTER = Benjamin HARRISON (IV)
13 Benjamin HARRISON (V), a signer of the Declaration of Independence
= Elizabeth BASSETT
14 William Henry HARRISON
1773-1841
9th U.S. President
= Anna Tuthill SYMMES
15 John Scott HARRISON
= Elizabeth Ramsey IRWIN
16 Benjamin HARRISON
1833-1901
23rd U.S. President
= (1) Caroline Lavinia SCOTT
= (2) Mrs. Mary Scott LORD Dimmick
B
7 William MARBURY = Agnes LENTON
8 Francis MARBURY = Bridget DRYDEN
9 Anne MARBURY, known as Mrs. Anne HUTCHINSON, the religious reformer, "heretic," & a founder of Rhode Island
= William HUTCHINSON
10 Edward HUTCHINSON = Catherine HAMBY
11 Elisha HUTCHINSON
= (2) Elizabeth CLARKE
= (1) Hannah HAWKINS
12 Edward HUTCHINSON
= Lydia FOSTER
12 Hannah HUTCHINSON
= John RUCK
13 Elizabeth HUTCHINSON
= Nathaniel ROBBINS
13 Hannah RUCK
= Theophilus LILLIE
14 Edward Hutchinson ROBBINS
= Elizabeth MURRAY
14 John LILLIE
= Abigail BRECK
15 Anne Jean ROBBINS
= Joseph LYMAN (III)
15 Anna LILLIE
= Samuel HOWARD
16 Catherine Robbins LYMAN
= Warren DELANO Jr.
16 Harriet HOWARD
= Samuel Prescott Phillips FAY
17 Sara DELANO
= James ROOSEVELT
17 Samuel Howard FAY
= Susan SHELLMAN
18 Franklin Delano ROOSEVELT
1882-1945
32nd U.S. President
= (Anna) Eleanor ROOSEVELT
18 Harriet Eleanor FAY
= James Smith BUSH
19 Samuel Prescott BUSH
= Flora SHELDON
20 Prescott Sheldon BUSH
= Dorothy WALKER
21 George Herbert Walker BUSH
b. 1924
41st U.S. President
= Barbara PIERCE

C

Ursula WOODFORD
= Walter LIGHT

Elizabeth LIGHT
= Robert WASHINGTON

9 Lawrence WASHINGTON = 9 Margaret BUTLER

10 Lawrence WASHINGTON = Amphyllis TWIGDEN

11 John WASHINGTON of Westmoreland Co., Va.
= Anne POPE

12 Lawrence WASHINGTON = Mildred WARNER

13 Augustine WASHINGTON = Mary BALL

14 George WASHINGTON
1731/2 - 1799
1st U.S. President
= Mrs. Martha DANDRIDGE Custis

D

7 Margaret SUTTON
= John BUTLER

8 William BUTLER
= Margaret GREEKE

9 Margaret BUTLER

E

7 (illegitimate) Simon DUDLEY
= Emma SAUNDERS

8 John DUDLEY = (1) Elizabeth LEIGHTON

9 (probably by (1) or illegitimate)
Roger DUDLEY
= Susanna THORNE

NOTE: Roger Dudley's immediate patrilineal descent is much disputed & may NOT be as given above; <u>some</u> descent from John Sutton & Constance Blount, however, is quite probable.

10 Thomas DUDLEY, Governor of Massachusetts
= Dorothy YORKE

11 Anne DUDLEY, known as Mrs. Anne BRADSTREET, the poet
= Simon BRADSTREET, Governor of Massachusetts

12 Dudley BRADSTREET = Anne WOOD

13 Margaret BRADSTREET = Job TYLER

14 Hannah TYLER = John SPOFFORD (IV)

15 Phoebe SPOFFORD = John GROUT Jr.

16 Phoebe GROUT = Jacob WINN (III)

17 Endymia WINN = Thomas SHERWOOD

18 Lucinda SHERWOOD = John MINTHORN

19 Theodore MINTHORN = Mary WASLEY

20 Hulda Randall MINTHORN
= Jesse Clark HOOVER

21 Herbert Clark HOOVER
1874-1964
31st U.S. President
= Lou HENRY

F

7 Sir George COTTON = Mary ONLEY

8 Richard COTTON = Mary MAINWARING

9 Frances COTTON = George ABELL

10 Robert ABELL of Mass. = Joanna ——

11 Caleb ABELL = Margaret POST

12 Experience ABELL = John HYDE

13 James HYDE = Sarah MARSHALL

14 Abiah HYDE = Aaron CLEVELAND (IV)

15 William CLEVELAND = Margaret FALLEY

16 Richard Falley CLEVELAND
= Anne NEAL

17 (Stephen) Grover CLEVELAND
1837-1908
22nd & 24th U.S. President
= Frances FOLSOM

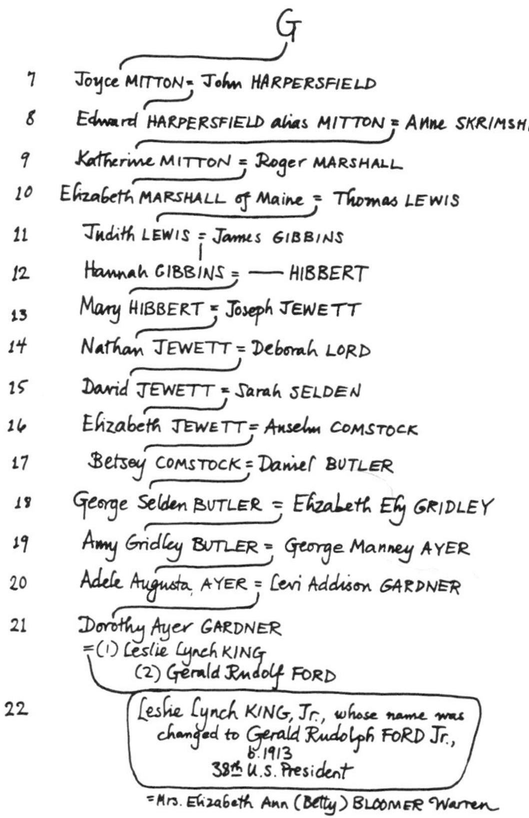

For the immediate family of Sancha de Ayala, see *National Genealogical Society Quarterly* 51 (1963): 235-38.

PLACE INDEX OF ANCESTOR TABLES

A number in the index below, such as 32:124, should be read as referring to Ancestor Table (president) number 32, ancestor #124.

AMERICA / UNITED STATES OF AMERICA

# # #

Foreign Nations

# # #

NAME INDEX OF ANCESTOR TABLES

A number in the index below, such as 32:124, should be read as referring to Ancestor Table (president) number 32, ancestor #124.

# # #